HIDDEN POWER

JAMES COCKAYNE

Hidden Power

The Strategic Logic of Organized Crime

OXFORD
UNIVERSITY PRESS

OXFORD

UNIVERSITY PRESS

Oxford University Press is a department of the
University of Oxford. It furthers the University's objective
of excellence in research, scholarship, and education
by publishing worldwide.

Oxford   New York

Auckland   Cape Town   Dar es Salaam   Hong Kong   Karachi
Kuala Lumpur   Madrid   Melbourne   Mexico City   Nairobi
New Delhi   Shanghai   Taipei   Toronto

With offices in

Argentina   Austria   Brazil   Chile   Czech Republic   France   Greece
Guatemala   Hungary   Italy   Japan   Poland   Portugal   Singapore
South Korea   Switzerland   Thailand   Turkey   Ukraine   Vietnam

Oxford is a registered trade mark of Oxford University Press
in the UK and certain other countries.

Published in the United States of America by
Oxford University Press
198 Madison Avenue, New York, NY 10016

Library of Congress Cataloging-in-Publication Data is available
James Cockayne.
Hidden Power: The Strategic Logic of Organized Crime.
ISBN: 9780190627331

Printed in India on acid-free paper

For the two hidden powers behind this book, JMC and RAD

CONTENTS

CONTENTS

CONTENTS

CONTENTS

CONTENTS

'In this episode ... the pressure of a hidden power was felt...'

Michele Pantaleone*

* Michele Pantaleone, *The Mafia and Politics* (London: Chatto & Windus, 1966), p. 190.

ACKNOWLEDGMENTS

This little expedition would not have found its way 'there and back' without a diverse set of supporters. I owe them all great thanks. The navigational guidance from two advisers at King's College London, Professor Mats Berdal and Professor Sir Lawrence Freedman, was central to my safe passage. Several bosses indulged and even encouraged my curiosity: at United Nations University, David Malone and Max Bond; at the Global Center for Cooperative Security, Alistair Millar. Comments on drafts from Louise Bosetti, Christopher Coker, Rachel Davis, John de Boer, Sebastian von Einsiedel, Antonio Giustozzi and Sonja Litz all helped send me in productive new directions. At Hurst, Michael Dwyer and Jon de Peyer provided invaluable support.

Staff at the New York Public Library, National Archives and Records Administration in College Park, Maryland, and the British National Archives, Kew, provided considerable assistance. Lori Birrell and Melinda Wallington at the University of Rochester deserve particular thanks. The entire undertaking depended upon the financial support of the Faculty of Social Science and Public Policy at King's College London.

A solo sailor also needs occasional visitors to his humble bark to provide moral support and an intellectual puff in his sails. I am grateful for such impetus to the following, some of whom may not fully appreciate the stimulation they provided: Enrique Desmond Arias, Sara Batmanglich, Ivan Briscoe, Mike Dziedzic, Vanda Felbab-Brown, Stefan Feller, Mervyn Frost, Peter Gastrow, Jean-Marie Guéhenno, Alison Hawks, Camino Kavanagh, Walter Kemp, David Kennedy, David Kilcullen, Michael Miklaucic, Rachel Locke, Francesco Mancini, Zoe

ACKNOWLEDGMENTS

Mentel, Rob Muggah, Tuesday Reitano, Mark Shaw and Kimana Zulueta-Fülscher. Were it not for two people in particular, however, I would long ago have given up on the whole expedition. My chief investor, JMC, gave me the means to set out in the first place, and the keel of faith that allowed me to hold my course. There was room for only one observer in the dinghy with me: RAD's utter reliability, good humour, moral encouragement, helpful commentary and grace, throughout the voyage, provided the wind in my sails. It is to those two hidden powers behind this enterprise that the result is dedicated.

ABBREVIATIONS

AFHQ	Allied Forces Headquarters
AMG or AMGOT	Allied Military Government of the Occupied Territories (Italy)
AQIM	Al Qaeda in the Islamic Maghreb
BANDES	Banco de Desarrollo Económico y Social, Cuba
CFRB	Comando Forze Repressione Banditismo (Command Force for the Repression of Banditry)
Church Committee	US Senate Select Committee to Study Governmental Operations with Respect to Intelligence Activities (94th Congress, 1975–76)
CIA	US Central Intelligence Agency
DC	Democrazia Cristiana (Christian Democrats, Italian political party)
DCI	US Director of Central Intelligence
DEA	US federal Drug Enforcement Administration
EVIS	Esercito Volontario per l'Indipendenza della Sicilia (Voluntary Army for the Independence of Sicily)
FNLA	Front national pour la libération de l'Azawad (Mali)
FRD	Frente Revolucionario Democrático (Democratic Revolutionary Front, Cuban counter-revolutionary organization)

FRUS	Foreign Relations of the United States. (See under US Department of State in 'Published official documents and government memoranda', in the References section)
G-3	Experimental Detachment G-3, cover name for Office of Strategic Services
GIA	Groupe Islamique Armé (Algeria)
GSPC	Groupe Salafiste pour la Prédication et le Combat (the Maghreb and the Sahel)
Islamic State	al-Dawla al-Islamiya al-Iraq al-Sham (a.k.a. the Islamic State of Iraq and the Levant (ISIL) or Islamic State of Iraq and al-Sham (ISIS))
JICA	US Joint Intelligence Collecting Agency
Kefauver Committee	US Senate Special Committee to Investigate Organized Crime in Interstate Commerce (81st Congress, 1950–51)
MAA	Mouvement arabe de l'Azawad (Mali)
McClellan Committee	US Senate Select Committee on Improper Activities in Labor and Management (85th and 86th Congress, 1957–60)
MIS	Movimento per l'Indipendenza della Sicilia (Movement for the Independence of Sicily)
MNLA	Mouvement National de Libération de l'Azawad (Mali)
MUJAO	Mouvement pour l'Unicité et le Jihad en Afrique de l'Ouest (West Africa and the Sahel)
ONI	US Office of Naval Intelligence
OSS	Office of Strategic Services
PLP	Progressive Liberal Party (The Bahamas)
PRG	Provisional Revolutionary Government (Cuba, 1933–34)
PRI	Partido Revolucionario Institucional (Mexico)
UBP	United Bahamian Party

LIST OF TABLES

PART ONE

A STRATEGIC APPROACH
TO ORGANIZED CRIME

1

INTRODUCTION

'We have become a mafiya power on a world scale.'

Boris Yeltsin, President of the Russian Federation, 1993[1]

In 1999 a former CIA director, Jim Woolsey, appeared before the Committee on Banking of the United States House of Representatives. 'If you should chance,' explained Woolsey:

> to strike up a conversation with an articulate, English-speaking Russian in, say, the restaurant of one of the luxury hotels along Lake Geneva, and he is wearing a $3,000 suit and a pair of Gucci loafers, and he tells you that he is an executive of a Russian trading company and wants to talk to you about a joint venture, then there are four possibilities. He may be what he says he is. He may be a Russian intelligence officer working under commercial cover. He may be part of a Russian organized crime group. But the really interesting possibility is that he may be all three—and that none of those three institutions have any problem with the arrangement.[2]

Woolsey was warning that mafias, business and states were becoming difficult to tell apart.

According to Spanish prosecutors, over the ensuing decade several other former Soviet regimes likewise evolved into 'mafia states' in which organized crime groups worked 'as a complement to state structures', doing 'whatever the government ... cannot acceptably do as a government', including trafficking arms, carrying out domestic assassinations, extortion, money-laundering, drug trafficking and controlling offshore investments in strategic industries (including aluminium and energy).[3] By 2012, a leading observer of transnational organized crime, Moisés Naím, was warning of the risk of 'mafia states' emerging worldwide.[4] Other leading analysts including Misha Glenny, Douglas Farah and John T. Picarelli all raised similar concerns, highlighting the convergence of criminal, political and business power in Latin America, Africa and Asia.[5]

It is not hard to find other signs of an apparent worldwide 'convergence' of organized criminal activity and armed political and military activity. The North Korean government stands accused of participation in global counterfeiting and drug-running activities.[6] In the Middle East, organizations such as Hezbollah in Lebanon and Islamic State in Syria and Iraq combine social service provision, localized governance and participation in a range of offshore illicit activities with militant activity.[7] Armed groups in Afghanistan, Colombia, Mali and Myanmar have engaged in drug trafficking, sometimes with the connivance or even participation of state actors. In Central Africa, the traffic in minerals and wildlife seems to fuel conflict.[8] In Somalia, organized piracy emerged a decade ago as a central factor in the country's political economy—and its complex politics and long-running civil war.[9] In the Sahel and North Africa, militant, terrorist and militia fortunes have been tied to dynamics in organized hostage markets and in drug, oil and cigarette smuggling.[10] In the Balkans, cigarette smuggling, organ trafficking, human trafficking and the trade in stolen cars have all been factors in the sub-region's recent bloody past and post-war politics.[11] And in Central America, skyrocketing homicide rates, the result of local actors' struggles to control the drug trade, human trafficking and extortion markets, have topped those of active war zones such as Afghanistan, Syria and South Sudan.

Global governance institutions such as the World Bank and United Nations Security Council increasingly recognize that organized crime and political instability have become entwined.[12] Global powers such as the United States have also begun to warn that this 'convergence' threatens their core interests. The 2011 White House *Strategy to Combat Transnational Organized Crime* asserted that criminal networks:

> threaten US interests by forging alliances with corrupt elements of national governments and using the power and influence of those elements to further their criminal activities... to the detriment of the United States.[13]

INTRODUCTION

What are the strategic implications of this apparent 'convergence' of political, military, business and criminal power? Some authors such as Naím and Farah argue that criminal power is now so ubiquitous and significant in the international system that it threatens to disrupt states' established ways of doing business. We may be entering, they imply, a dangerous new 'era' of mafia states. How are strategic decision-makers to tell if the executive in his $3,000 suit and his Gucci loafers is a government spy, a businessman, a crook—or all three? And if we cannot tell them apart, how are we to prevent mafias, or other criminal groups, from infiltrating global politics and abusing the privileges and powers of statehood? How do we prevent states from working with, or acting like, mafias? And how can states deal strategically with groups whose whole strategic approach is intended to keep their power—over governments, markets and civil society—hidden?

Making sense of criminal power

Popular jokes about 'crooked politicians' aside, we tend to think of 'criminals' and 'government officials' as having distinct roles. Indeed, the humour in those jokes derives from upending that normal distinction, because it reveals how hard it can be to differentiate politics from crime. The result of this blurring is, however, no joke, but rather an important blind-spot—both in our theoretical understanding of the political power of organized crime, and our practical responses to it.

Academics and policy-makers need to operate from clear categories. So starting out with a clear definition of organized crime is important. One respected academic definition suggests that criminal organizations are associations of people whose 'major occupational role is a criminal one'.[14] But if we cannot tell whether a politician's major occupational role is politics or crime, how can we tell criminal organizations and political associations apart? The answer, in much of the academy, has, perhaps surprisingly, largely been to ignore this blurring of roles. With some important exceptions we explore in Chapter 2, criminologists have studied organized crime, not politics, just as political scientists have studied politics, not crime. Yet the same wilful blindness is clear in policy-making: in the polite debating forums of the United Nations, it is rare for the ties between politics and organized crime to be explicitly named, lest the representatives of the country in question take offence and cease cooperating.

As a result, many of the responses that states and international organizations use to tackle organized crime overlook the central, uncomfortable truth laid out by Jim Woolsey in 1999—politics and crime are much harder to tell apart in practice than they are in theory. The White House *Strategy*, mentioned above, talks about organized criminals 'forging alliances' with state actors 'to further their criminal activities' to the detriment of the United States, but has little to say about how criminals forge and use these alliance—that is, their strategies.[15] This lack of attention to criminal strategy is not uncommon: one review of the academic literature on organized crime found that most studies focus on 'the structural dimensions and their determinants without attending to theory of organizational behavior'.[16] But by overlooking the power of criminal groups to shape their own strategic—including political—environments, our responses to criminal groups tend not to anticipate criminal spoiling behaviour.[17] They are, in other words, a-strategic.

This is dangerous. By ignoring the political power and strategies of criminal groups, we risk overlooking a major force shaping contemporary global affairs. Scholars have argued since the early 1990s that criminal actors were gaining power and influence within the international system,[18] and some have even suggested that organized crime is corroding state capacity and the state system itself.[19] The dangers are manifold: that we are forced to respond to threats from organized crime without a clear understanding of what strategies will be effective against it;[20] that security becomes a private service sold by criminal actors in a global market, rather than a public good provided by states;[21] and that states lose the ability to trust each other, undermining international cooperation.[22]

Our failure to understand the political strategies of criminal groups also makes it difficult to make sense of the large-scale criminal violence we see today in Central America, Afghanistan and parts of West Africa. Some of this rivals—or even outstrips—the violence of contemporary wars. Between 2007 and 2014, some 103,000 people were killed in Iraq and Afghanistan. In comparison, there were 164,000 homicides in Mexico in the same period.[23] For those caught within it, this organized criminal violence is just as devastating, and just as totalizing, as war was when it was explained by Clausewitz two hundred years ago.[24] As Roberto Saviano, an Italian public intellectual who grew up among the Camorra organized crime group in Naples, put it:

> When the armies take to the streets, it is impossible to move according to any other dynamic than their strategy; it is they who decide meaning, motives, causes.[25]

An insider of the Sicilian mafia (*Cosa Nostra*) is even more explicit about the similarity between large-scale organized criminal violence and war:

> It was as if I was a soldier for a state, my state *Cosa Nostra* ... I was only interested in the opinion of my people, the people of *Cosa Nostra*, I wasn't interested in anybody else's opinion, just as an Italian soldier wouldn't be interested in the opinion of [enemies such as] the Yugoslavs or Germans.[26]

As things stand, however, we struggle to explain this criminal violence and power, central to many people's lives today. We cannot foresee how and when criminal groups will develop the kinds of governmental power—the power to set norms, resolve disputes, and allocate resources—that can lead to this all-defining, all-consuming violence. We struggle to make sense of criminal strategy.

Entering a gallery of mirrors

This blindspot is in some ways surprising, given that criminologists have long recognized that, like some legal businesses, some criminal organizations maximize their profits through regulatory capture.[27] Some even suggest that access to and control of political power are the essential ingredients of criminal prosperity and longevity.[28] As we explore further in Chapter 2, some pioneering scholars are beginning to focus on the dynamics of this political-criminal interaction. But we still know relatively little about how criminal groups make the strategic choices that shape these collaborations with political actors. Why?

The label 'organized crime' is itself part of the problem. Like the term 'terrorism', by labelling the conduct in question as inherently illegitimate, it tends to create a knee-jerk preference for coercive response and to push states towards a-strategic responses.[29] A more effective approach would require policy-makers to develop an improved understanding of how criminal organizations develop and wield political and economic power.[30] The celebrated Sicilian anti-mafia magistrate, Giovanni Falcone, who was assassinated by *Cosa Nostra* in 1992, recognized this. Falcone argued that 'different strategies' were needed 'according to the type of Mafia one is dealing with', and that to determine that, we must not 'transform it into a monster … We must recognize that it resembles us.'[31]

But Falcone's own demise at the hands of the mafia reveals another reason for this gap in our knowledge: studying organized crime is both difficult and dangerous.[32] Criminals are a secretive bunch, and it can be risky to stick your nose into their business. Rumour abounds, making much existing data unreliable and corroboration challenging. The mystery, violence and power of organized crime makes it a subject that tends to attract gossip.[33] Government sources have reasons to distort criminal activity, whether to demonize it or to hide corruption and complicity.[34] One noted mafia historian describes over-reliance on state sources as entering a 'gallery of mirrors'.[35] The alternative—reliance on criminal sources—is no obvious or easy solution. It has been likened to listening to 'whispers in a labyrinth'.[36] Criminal organizations deliberately fragment information, making it hard to see the full picture.[37] And professional criminals are not exactly known for their honesty: rather, their stories tend to be self-serving, even fantastical.[38]

Yet the challenges facing the organized crime historian differ more in degree than kind from those facing 'regular' historians. Which historical source is not, in some way, partial and self-serving? This book seeks to address these serious investigative challenges by using multiple independent sources to develop an understanding of actors' strategic choices to resort to criminal methods and activity. This requires understanding how these actors defined their goals, the resources available to them and the constraints they faced in mobilizing and deploying those resources to achieve their goals. The book looks at the iterative process of adjustment between means and ends undertaken by specific actors in particular historical episodes. The aim of this case-study approach is not development of 'general theory' *per se*, but rather to add to our understanding of: a) the cases in question; and b) how strategic choices present themselves to policy-makers (in this case criminal and political leaders) and why and how strategic choices are made.[39] At most, the ambition is to identify recurring patterns in organized criminals' strategic decision-making—to identify their 'strategic logic'.

Insider accounts provide unique insights.[40] A full list of the sources relied upon is provided in the References section at the end of the book. The chapters in Part Two also begin with brief notes on the provenance, strengths and limitations of major sources relied upon. The most important insider accounts are memoirs by mafia leaders such as Joseph Bonanno and Nicola Gentile, both particularly useful in understanding the relationship between the Sicilian mafia and the New York Mob, and the 'Castellammarese War' within the New York underworld explored in Chapter 5.[41] Other significant insider accounts are found in reported interviews with leadership figures such as Lucky Luciano,[42] Meyer Lansky,[43] the gangster lawyer Dixie Davis[44] and the Mob soldier Joe Valachi.[45]

These insider accounts are corroborated through a variety of police, judicial and parliamentary proceedings. This includes US State and federal investigations into governmental corruption,[46] organized crime,[47] the waterfront,[48] racketeering[49] and the assassination of John F. Kennedy.[50] Chapter 6, examining the collaboration between the Mob and the US Navy during World War Two, draws on material contained in the Thomas E. Dewey archive at the University of Rochester Library in upstate New York, relating to a 1954 judicial investigation led by William B. Herlands, some of which has never previously been publicly referenced.[51]

Declassified intelligence analysis and diplomatic correspondence has also proven invaluable. One such source is the FBI's 'Mafia Monograph', written in 1958 after J. Edgar Hoover was forced—by the arrest of over sixty Mob figures at once in Apalachin, New York—to acknowledge the existence of the Mob. This unique monograph draws not only on extensive US government sources but also on detailed Italian government sources (now believed lost) and US informant testimony.[52] Other key government sources drawn on in Part Two include unpublished US, British and Italian government correspondence relating to Sicily and Cuba, found in the British National Archives in Kew and the US National Archives and Records Administration (primarily in College Park, Maryland).

About this book

This book considers the strategic logic by which criminal groups—especially, but not only, the Sicilian and American mafias—have competed, cooperated and collaborated with sovereign states and other political organizations, and moved from one state to another. Part One explores how we can think about organized crime as a strategic actor. The focus throughout this book is on the understudied question of what drives and shapes the choices and behaviour of criminal groups—rather than the more commonly studied question of the strategic actions of states and other political actors towards criminal groups. Chapter 2 sets out a framework for thinking about criminal organizations as strategic actors. The traditional view has been that criminal activity is either not logical—but rather irrational or at least disorganized—or, if logical, then not strategic in the sense relevant to politics, war and international affairs, since organized crime pursues profit, not power. Chapter 2 breaks with this traditional view, arguing that in some cases criminal organizations are shaped by the pursuit of governmental power. This power yields, and seeks to maximize, criminal rents—the value beyond the costs of production that can be extracted from a good or service the supply of which has been criminalized by one or more states, or that can be extracted from legal goods and services by criminal means.[53] But it is, in nature, form and impact, governmental. What distinguishes all criminal strategy from more conventional 'political' strategy, however, is that criminal strategy seeks to maximize governmental power without taking on the formal responsibilities of political rule. Criminal power is a hidden power.

Part Two of the book tests this analytical framework against historical evidence relating to political and criminal groups in New York, Sicily and the Caribbean between 1859 and 1983. It looks at the rise of Tammany Hall, the ascendancy and demise of Boss Tweed and Tammany's subsequent oscillation between political and criminal strategy. We consider the Sicilian origins and Atlantic migration of the mafia. We follow the dynamics of war-making and peace-making in the New York mafia's 'Castellammarese War', and see the Mob emerge from its ashes under the guidance of Lucky Luciano, taking advantage of the power networks vacated by Tammany. We explore how Luciano fell at the hands of Thomas Dewey, and discover the close collaboration between the Mob and the US government during World War Two, both in New York and in Sicily. We see what effects this had in Sicily, and find parallels in the Mob's collaboration with the government in Cuba. Finally, we watch as the Mob, thrown out of Cuba by Fidel Castro, tries desperately to claw its way back, through transnational attacks, attempted assassinations and failed regime change—intertwined with the Bay of Pigs, the Cuban Missile Crisis and possibly the assassination of John F. Kennedy—before finding new markets in The Bahamas and Atlantic City.

This discussion takes a strategic perspective, analysing how criminal groups perceive their strategic environment and seek to shape it.[54] While many of these episodes have previously been studied, this book breaks new ground in three ways. First, it draws on primary material—declassified government files and rare insider accounts by criminal and political actors—that has to date been entirely or largely overlooked. Second, rather than just recounting the history of each episode, the analysis focuses on understanding and tracking the strategic thinking of actors involved in organized crime. And third, by juxtaposing these episodes, the study identifies long-term developments in the strategic thinking of the groups involved.[55]

The episodes include periods of mafia 'war', peace-making and constitutional reform. We see shifts from accommodation to confrontation with a state, resorting to domestic insurgency, transnational terrorism and even attempts at regime change, deposing foreign governments. We see mafias 'migrating' from one country to another.[56] We watch political organizations becoming criminal cliques and criminal groups spawning political fronts, and we discover 'joint venture' government at both the municipal and national level. Perhaps most astonishingly, given the US government's recent warnings about the dangers posed by political-criminal collaboration, the study also reveals multiple episodes of extended collaboration between the American Mob and the US government, for the purposes of domestic espionage, management of the labour movement and assassination, invasion, occupation and transnational 'terror' attacks in foreign countries.

Two startling and unorthodox conclusions emerge from the evidence. First, some organized criminal groups—and not only states—make war. Recognition of this fact will have major implications for how we understand and seek to manage conflict worldwide. Second, the 'convergence' between political and criminal actors that we see around us may not be so new as we think—but rather an acceleration or intensification of long-standing patterns of interaction between states and organized crime. Although we may have forgotten it, this book reveals that states have a long, complex history of competition—and collaboration—with strategic criminal actors. Remembering that history may better equip us to deal with the intermingling of politics, war and crime that we see around the world today.

The final Part Three of the book offers a third set of insights by setting out, and explaining, six recurring patterns of political-criminal interaction that seem to emerge from the episodes studied in Part Two.[57] Chapter 10 identifies six distinct positioning strategies that criminal organizations adopt when competing with states in a 'market for government': 1) intermediation (used by mafias); 2) autonomy (used by warlords and gang rulers); 3) mergers (joint ventures with states); 4) strategic alliances in competitions against other political and/or criminal actors; 5) terrorism as a criminal strategy; and 6) relocation or blue ocean strategy.

The first three involve the kinds of accommodation between state and criminal groups that are sometimes described through the catch-all term 'mafia state'—but this analysis provides a more nuanced and analytically powerful framework for understanding the power configurations involved. The first—intermediation strategy—involves criminal groups brokering between the state and enclave markets or communities in which the criminal group enjoys governmental power. This is the classical strategy of the mafia, based on jurisdictional sharing of the market for government with the state. The second, based on a posture of criminal autonomy, requires limited territorial separation sustained by military force, and offers local control of criminal markets. This is classically the strategy of warlords, like those in Afghanistan, and local gang rulers, like those in Jamaica. The third, the merger strategy, sees criminal and political actors collaborating to develop and use governmental power through vertical integration of capabilities. It generates 'joint ventures' like those we have seen recently in Guinea-Bissau.

The three final positioning strategies arise in the context of confrontation between states (or other political organizations) and criminal rivals. One involves strategic political-criminal alliances against other political and/or criminal actors. The next involves the criminal group coercing the public, indirectly, to induce a change in state policy. This is terrorism as criminal strategy. And finally, a criminal group may seek to relocate within the market for government by changing the market's formal political structure—altering a state's constitution, or sponsoring state secession—in order to maximize its own governmental power. As this involves moving from a part of the market for government crowded with rivals and running red with their blood to a new arrangement with no governmental competition, this is termed 'blue ocean' strategy, following the management literature.

Finally, Chapter 11 briefly considers how these positioning strategies may be playing out in two contemporary, highly violent 'markets for government': Mexico and the Sahel. This leads to the conclusion that entrepreneurial armed groups are using illicit transnational flows to innovate new business-models—such as the cartel, the caliphate and *maras*—in the market for government. Statehood is increasingly challenged as the preferred organizational model for government around the world. In turn, hybrid approaches to government are emerging, including some combining elements of criminal governmentality with terrorist methods, others combining organized crime with traditional loyalties to tribe or clan, and yet others, such as the Islamic State, combining the trappings of statehood with terrorism and crime. And in some countries, as Jim Woolsey warned us, we see statecraft combining with methods similar to those of organized crime. The book closes with reflections on what an improved understanding of the strategic logic of organized crime may mean for understanding these new forms of governmental power, for managing their role in transitions from war to peace and for practical efforts to combat organized crime more generally.

2

THE STRATEGIC ORGANIZATION OF CRIME

'The logic of the Mafia ... is nothing more than the logic of power...'

Giovanni Falcone[1]

What is 'organized crime'? Argument over how to understand the concept is both semantic and empirical.[2] The respected criminologist Klaus von Lampe argues there is no single phenomenon of 'organized crime'.[3] Others argue that organized crime is simply whatever powerful states say it is.[4] A term originally coined during Prohibition in the US,[5] it has been explained through a variety of analytical frameworks—political, economic, social and cultural.[6] Yet to date there has been limited consideration of whether crime is organized 'strategically'.

Strategy is about how actors relate means to ends. As Lawrence Freedman succinctly explains, 'strategy is the art of creating power', where power is understood as the 'capacity to produce effects that are more advantageous than would otherwise have been the case'.[7] To understand an actor's strategy we must understand both the sources of its power, its advantage in relationships and the choices it makes to realize that power.[8] This chapter provides an analytical framework for considering whether crime is ever organized strategically. It begins with a brief review of what existing scholarship has to say about criminal strategy in collaborating with political actors (a section casual readers can safely skip). The chapter then considers four questions: first, do criminal

15

groups have strategic goals? Second, is crime rationally organized to achieve them? Third, where does strategic decision-making occur? And fourth, how are the means to achieve these ends organized?

What do we know about political-criminal interaction?

The fields of political science and strategic studies have traditionally ruled out criminal groups being considered strategic actors because they treat strategy as a question of pursuing power—and especially political power—rather than profit. War is seen as the paradigmatic form of strategic competition for power. As the eminent strategic theorist Colin Gray has put it, taking his cues from Clausewitz, 'War is about politics, and politics is about relative power.'[9] Violent competition between criminal groups, on the other hand, 'is not war', argues Gray, because criminal groups pursue economic, not political, goals.[10] Security scholars such as Mats Berdal and Mónica Serrano summarize this orthodox position as suggesting that crime is overridingly organized according to 'the logic of profitability and economic gain' rather than a political or strategic logic.[11] As recently as December 2015, in a major Special Issue of the eminent *Journal of Conflict Resolution* exploring Mexico's drug violence, the introductory article, summarizing the contribution to the issue by the renowned civil war scholar Stathis Kalyvas, stated simply that 'political violence is driven by ideology, or at least a mix of ideological and acquisitive motives. The same cannot be said of criminal violence.'[12]

These positions seem at odds with the mounting evidence of criminal-political collaboration, some of which was mentioned in Chapter 1. There is, as a former president of the International Association for the Study of Organized Crime noted, a 'lack of strong coherent explanatory scientific traditions that make sense of' the political power that organized crime does evidently wield at times.[13] There is an important—and more extensive—literature on Italian organized crime groups' influence in Italian politics, which we explore later in this chapter and in Part Two. But outside the Italian context, for many years the most important attempts have taken the form of case studies: Alan Block's study of the political-criminal collusion in New York between 1930 and 1950, Solnick's *Stealing the State* and Handelman's *Comrade*

Criminal on the recent history of Russia, or more recently, Michela Wrong's *It's Our Turn to Eat* on Kenya.[14] Peter Andreas' highly readable *Smuggler Nation* shows how this kind of analysis can be expanded to historical cases, explaining that 'smuggling was an essential ingredient in the very birth and development of America' as a country 'and its transformation into a global power'.[15]

A seminal multi-author volume in 2003 on the 'political-criminal nexus' suggested that these concerns could be found in a variety of contexts.[16] Yet comparative works, looking beyond single country or time-contexts are rarer. Those that do exist—like those of Bayart, Ellis and Hibou, and William Reno, on Africa, and Enrique Desmond Arias on Latin America—show how organized crime factors into governance arrangements on a broader regional scale, even as they highlight the importance of understanding local political dynamics.[17] In the last five years at the Global Initiative against Transnational Organized Crime, important work by Mark Shaw and Tuesday Reitano has begun to show how states and political elites, particularly in the Sahel, work with local figures involved in organized crime to build 'protection economies' and extract resources.[18] Ivan Briscoe at the Clingendael Institute in the Netherlands has also shed light on the recurring role of criminal actors in contemporary crisis, conflict and fragile contexts.[19]

Perhaps the most sustained academic inquiry into criminal-political collaboration is in the area of 'parapolitics' and the 'deep state', which explores 'criminals behaving as sovereigns and sovereigns behaving as criminals', focusing on relationships between intelligence services, clandestine far-right or conservative groupings (so-called 'occult powers') and transnational organized crime.[20] But much of this 'parapolitics' literature is descriptive, focusing on individual state settings and, to a lesser extent, comparative analysis, rather than exploring inter-state dynamics and risks—as the leading survey of the genre acknowledges—tipping over into 'grand conspiracy theory'.[21]

So the dynamics and logic of political-criminal interaction remain weakly understood. There have been attempts to remedy this gap. Robert Mandel's *Dark Logic: Transnational Criminal Tactics and Global Security* considers the relationship between violence, corruption and security, but does not explain how or why criminal groups choose different tactics at different times.[22] Alfredo Schulte-Bockholt's 2006 neo-

Marxist monograph *The Politics of Organized Crime and the Organized Crime of Politics* offers a similarly static explanation, treating criminal groups as agents of elite political interests.[23] These theories struggle to explain how or why criminal groups will turn against elite interests, as they clearly do at times—the assassination of the mafia prosecutor Giovanni Falcone, mentioned in Chapter 1, being a paradigmatic example.

One area of interaction between politics and crime that has received more attention, however, is the question of the role of crime in conflict. When, a decade ago, economist Paul Collier argued explicitly that all civil war could be understood as organized crime,[24] critics quickly emphasized that the diversity of motivations and organizational forms among contemporary armed groups defies such a generalized analysis.[25] The resulting debate helped to reveal, however, that even as some contemporary organized violence functions as 'the continuation of economics by other means' it does not lack political motives and effects.[26] R. Thomas Naylor added much to our understanding of the role of criminal activity during insurgency through his analysis of the 'insurgent economy'.[27] His insights into insurgency were extended by scholars such as Steven Metz[28] and Phil Williams and John Picarelli, who illuminated how criminal activity can serve political groups' interests and even underpin strategic alliances between criminal and insurgent organizations.[29] Nils Gilman, Jesse Goldhammer and Steven Weber went further, explicitly recognizing that 'deviant entrepreneurs wield political power' in the form of money and violence and through the provision of public goods and services.[30]

This debate has started to chip away at the hard and fast distinction between conflict and violent organized crime, creating space for reflection on whether some criminal groups may, actually, be strategic actors. Adam Elkus and John Sullivan have applied Clausewitzian strategic concepts to understand Mexican cartel military operations.[31] And General Sir Rupert Smith, in his seminal work *The Utility of Force*, highlights the importance of clandestine social networks and criminal activity as a basis for social action and 'protection' of populations by contemporary armed groups conducting 'war amongst the people'.[32] Recently, there has also been considerable debate over whether drug violence in Mexico can usefully be understood through the hybrid conceptual lens of 'criminal insurgency'.[33]

Perhaps the most important take-away from these debates is one that was crystallized in the work of Mary Kaldor, David Keen and other 'New Wars' scholars: even profit-oriented activity during war generates competition for control over normative order, dispute resolution and resource allocation—in other words over governmental power.[34] This point has perhaps been most powerfully explored to date by Vanda Felbab-Brown, who highlights how insurgent organizations use organized crime to achieve political effects, and has pointed to the significant role that criminal power plays in contemporary war-to-peace transitions, state building and development.[35]

What is lacking, however, is a broader framework for understanding the dynamics—and logic—of criminal-political interaction. When will political and criminal actors collaborate? When will they compete? When will one become the other? Michael Miklaucic and Moisés Naím have helpfully described a spectrum of criminal influence in politics ranging from 'criminal penetration' to 'criminal infiltration' to 'criminal capture', ending with a state of affairs they describe as the 'criminal sovereign', in which 'the apparatus of the state itself [is] engaged directly in criminal activity as a matter of policy'.[36] But this taxonomy describes the results of the interaction between criminal organizations and political actors, rather than the dynamics of that interaction. (Indeed, a range of authors have criticized the general concept of 'convergence' introduced in Chapter 1 on these and related grounds).[37] Doug Farah perhaps comes closest to offering such a dynamic model with his concept of 'criminalized states', which he defines as those where the senior leadership is involved in organized crime, 'levers of state power' are 'incorporated into the operational structure' of organized crime, and organized crime is 'used as an instrument of statecraft'.[38] Yet even this framework begs the question: what drives the development of such an arrangement in the first place?

The danger is, as the thoughtful American scholar-practitioner Robert J. Bunker has put it, that '[t]he creation of governmental policy [on organized crime] ... exists in a "strategic vacuum"'.[39] We lack understanding of what drives the strategic interaction between governments and criminal groups—especially on the international level. If there is a 'strategic logic' to organized crime, as there is to suicide terrorism, it has to date largely been overlooked, or even denied.[40]

Criminal strategy and governmental power

A large portion of existing criminological and sociological scholarship simply brackets off the political aspect of organized crime, treating organized crime instead as business or 'enterprise' operating under the special conditions of illegality.[41] This economic analysis of organized crime has offered powerful insights,[42] particularly into internal organization of criminal groups and the strategies of criminal groups towards each other.[43] But it has proven less adept in explaining criminal groups' relations with political and governmental entities.

This is in some ways surprising, given that one of the central insights of economic analysis of organized crime is that some criminal organizations take on governance roles within criminal markets—and under certain conditions can even tend towards a governmental monopoly, as do states. Illicit market actors face many challenges that those in legal markets do not, as a result of the absence of the state: uncertainties in property and possession; higher capital investment and borrowing costs; limited remedies for poor quality goods and services; limited information about counterparties; unclear rules; short business planning horizons; and limited asset disposal opportunities.[44] This creates a demand for protection from violent rivals, generating a market for protection services.[45] Diego Gambetta's seminal 1993 work *The Sicilian Mafia: The Business of Private Protection* showed how features of the Sicilian mafia sometimes ascribed to culture or norms may in fact serve organizational, branding or marketing logics.[46] Federico Varese has also successfully extended the model to post-Soviet Russia.[47]

To understand the nature of criminal power, however, we must recognize that the 'protection' that some criminal groups offer is not purely transactional, but also has a normative aspect. The absence of the state also creates a demand for governance functions within criminal markets—setting market and social norms, allocating resources and resolving disputes.[48] As the sociologist Charles Tilly pointed out, organized crime and statehood thus have much in common, providing complex protection and regulatory systems.[49] It is in this sense that, in the phrase made famous by the American analyst Donald Cressey, some organized criminal groups are 'both a business and a government'.[50] Those who can enforce the rules of the underworld accrue the power to set them. In different contexts, criminal organizations have thus variously been described as operating as 'governance structures',[51] 'de facto' or 'private governments',[52] 'primitive states'[53] or competitors in state-making[54] and the provision of governance.[55]

Even when this criminal governmental power has been recognized, however, it has largely been assumed that it operates in an underworld sphere entirely separated from that of formal or state politics—the so-called 'upperworld'. Eric Hobsbawm, for example, described criminal groups as pre-political or apolitical.[56] Criminal organizations, it seems true, usually do not seek to replace the state, as do insurgent and rebel groups. Rather, groups adopting criminal strategies seem largely to eschew the 'responsibilities of rule like a state'.[57]

A preference for dodging formal political authority in the upperworld does not however necessarily signify a lack of desire for political power over that upperworld. That is precisely the genius of criminal strategy: it involves the development of clandestine advantage in political relations with and in the upperworld, even if the rents and power accrued lie primarily in the underworld. Criminal strategy in fact requires leaving the state in power—at least formally.[58] Supplant the state, or some other higher political authority capable of declaring the market you operate in 'criminal', and you remove the criminal tariff (the rent you can charge because a good or service is illegal). A criminal strategy cannot seek to replace or eliminate the state entirely, but only to manipulate, constrain and exploit it, in the process shaping it to its strategic ends. The objective of criminal strategy is to build one's own power including through constraint of state policy, rather than to conquer and eliminate the state.[59] As Peter Andreas puts it in his review of the role that smuggling has played in shaping the United States, recalling Charles Tilly's reference to the relationship between the state and war, 'the state makes smuggling (through laws and their enforcement), and … smuggling in turn remakes the state'.[60]

Criminal power is consequently hidden and informal, and criminal strategy clandestine. But it is nonetheless political, in the sense that it involves an effort to shape the 'general arrangements' (Oakeshott)[61] or the 'normative order' (Weber)[62] of a defined community—not only the underworld itself, but the whole community, both upperworld and underworld understood together. After all, without the upperworld defining itself as an upperworld, rather than just 'the world', the underworld does not exist. As Mittelman and Johnston note:

> criminal elements do not seek to take over the state; they are … not revolutionary movements seeking to take over its apparatus… [But they] are alternative social organizations that … challenge the power and authority of the state to impose its standards, codified as law.[63]

They can come to operate, in other words, as covert political organizations, or, as some analysts put it, parapolitical associations.[64]

If criminal organizations eschew formal political authority, then, perhaps their interest in politics is not so different from the interest of legitimate business entities, who use lobbying and 'government affairs' to shape political choices and government regulation to minimize risk and maximize profit. Phil Williams has demonstrated that criminal organizations often cooperate for similar reasons that legitimate businesses do—so perhaps criminal groups' logic of cooperation with states will in turn mirror the logic of such cooperation by legitimate business?[65] The economic theory of organized crime would suggest precisely that criminal interest in politics is, fundamentally, a hedging strategy, intended to protect economic profit.

The problem with this investment theory-based explanation is that it fails to account for the experience of the individuals who make up these organizations.[66] It cannot account for the first-hand accounts from criminal actors that what drove them—what governed their decision-making—was not always the pursuit of profit, pure and simple, but the pursuit of power. Here is an explanation by Francisco Marino Mannoia, a major *pentito* who helped to reveal the inner workings of life in the Sicilian mafia:

> It is often believed that people work with the Cosa Nostra for the money. But that is only partly true. Do you know why I became a *uomo d'onore* [man of honour, *mafioso*]? Because before I had been a nobody in Palermo and then afterwards, where I went, heads bowed. You can't value that in money.[67]

Power operates within these criminal settings not only through impersonal market forces that Gambetta and the economists within the 'protection' literature have described so well, but also through choices made by individuals, regulating their own conduct in accordance with both formal and informal norms. And those norms relate not only, or purely, to profit-maximization, but also respond to a range of other values, such as power, honour, loyalty, family and even, as we see further below, religion. As Tuesday Reitano and Mark Shaw of the Global Initiative against Transnational Organized Crime recently put it:

> Competing groups will use the pillars of the legitimacy that they can draw upon (ethnic or clan based and/or religious) to secure their zone of protection, and will supplement these with violence, the delivery of services and corruption (which is the co-opting of political/electoral authority). In doing so they endeavor to create a zone of protection, or protection economy, in which they have full control.[68]

Criminal power, it seems, operates not only through exploitation and risk-minimizing manipulation of overt political 'institutions', but as a specific, hidden form of what Michel Foucault called 'governmentality': a normative system by which subjects regulate themselves.[69] Foucault described the state as just one specific 'episode in governmentality'.[70] This 'governmentality' is not just a governmental apparatus that disciplines and controls passive objects, but a normative system within which subjects take on a political identity and regulate themselves, self-governing mentally.[71] Foucault recognized that, until government became associated with states, all sorts of other actors were 'governed': children (hence, 'governess'); souls; families; the sick. 'Government':

> did not only cover the legitimately constituted forms of political or economic subjection, but also modes of action … which were destined to act upon the possibilities of action of other people. To govern, in this sense, is to structure the possible field of action of others.[72]

A 'governmentality' is a specific mode of government, a normative and practical system for structuring 'the possible field of action of others'. 'Government' is thus a strategic concept since, as we saw earlier, 'strategy is the art of creating power', where power is understood as the 'capacity to produce effects that are more advantageous than would otherwise have been the case'.[73] A 'governmentality' provides the language through which actors engage with the world, conditioning their understanding and expression of their own identities, interests, choices and preferences. It provides the mental framework or operating system through which they understand their world and seek to create advantage within it. Each specific governmentality thus provides, as Foucault neatly formulated it, a system for 'the conduct of conduct'.[74]

Some—but not all—criminal organizations come to operate according to their own common, hidden operating systems—their own specific governmentalities. This is why we speak not just of a criminal 'under-sector', but a criminal 'under-world'. That this criminal 'governmentality' is real and powerful in the life of organized criminals, and not merely a theoretical postulate, is made clear in an anecdote told by Nicola Gentile, a Sicilian-American mafia leader. We will meet Gentile again in Part Two, as he was called in to attempt to mediate a peace deal during a civil war within the New York Mob in the early 1930s. In 1949, after returning to Italy where he became involved in the strategic reorganization of the Sicilian mafia (discussed in Chapter 7), Gentile spent an afternoon talking to a young researcher. He explained the 'governmental' nature of a true *mafioso*'s power:

> *Duttureddu* ['little professor'], if I come in here unarmed, and you pick up a pistol, point it at me and say: 'Cola Gentile, down on your knees', what do I do? I kneel. That does not mean that you are a *mafioso* because you have forced Cola Gentile to get down on his knees. It means you are a cretin with a pistol in your hand.
>
> Now if I, Nicola Gentile, come in unarmed, and you are unarmed too, and I say to you: '*Duttureddu*, look, I'm in a bit of a situation. I have to ask you to get on your knees.' You ask me: 'Why?' I say: '*Duttureddu*, let me explain.' And I manage to convince you that you have to get on your knees. When you kneel down, that makes me a *mafioso*.
>
> If you refuse to get on your knees, then I have to shoot you. But that doesn't mean I have won: I have lost, *Duttureddu*.[75]

The true, hidden power of organized crime, Gentile was explaining, lies in its normativity, its governmentality. It is not just a negative agenda—reducing the risk of interference by the formal (state) government; but a positive agenda, aimed at shaping and governing its subjects' own, free choices. What distinguishes effective, strategic criminal power from mere coercion is that it makes its victims complicit in this criminal system. They view their choices to cooperate as at least partly voluntary. Even without the formal trappings of government institutions looming over them, criminal power comes to govern human actions, through the power it exercises over human minds.

A targeted carrot-and-stick 'threat-offer'—or, as it is sometimes called, 'throffer'—usually lies at the heart of criminal strategy.[76] It is reflected in the famous phrase *¿O plata, o plomo?*—'Silver, or lead?' In popular crime literature, this is known as the offer you cannot refuse. Such offers go beyond mere extortion by offering a genuine payoff to the target for complying, and not only a threat of something bad happening if they do not. Repeated a sufficient number of times, transactions structured in this way create an expectation of complicity, a clandestine relationship between the person making the threat-offer and the victim. This relationship is the foundation of the protection racket, whose legitimacy and authority may eventually be internalized by those within it. This is why criminal organizations frequently speak of those in their networks of influence not as their business associates or clients, but as their 'friends'. The exchange relationship is not merely transactional, but is also associative. Criminal power is not just economic; it is social and political.

The hidden web of organized criminal influence operates below, alongside and even within the formal state and other political structures. The covert, criminal order is sustained not simply through criminal coercion, but through the complicity of actors—including government officials—who act in line with what they believe are its demands, norms and discipline. It is this covert governmentality that underpins some criminal organizations' strategic success in generating and controlling criminal rents.[77]

The competition between organized crime groups and the state is thus totalizing, and political, in a way that business competition in the legitimate market is not. Businesses compete for an individual's customer loyalty vis-à-vis other providers of their goods and services, but rely on the state to govern the market and do not compete with it for that power. Strategic criminal organizations and the state compete not just to be the individual's protector, but to be the source of the rules and discretion by which that individual is ultimately governed. As it is for legal businesses, the key to long-term profit maximization for criminal groups may be to reduce competition, whether through collusion or the creation of a monopoly.[78] But for criminal groups the state is itself one such source of competition—because it is a supplier of governmentality. Contemporary legitimate businesses do not, usually, take on that role. Conversely, criminal groups use certain means to compete—violence and corruption—which are ruled out for legitimate firms. At least in theory; in fact, legitimate businesses often turn to organized crime groups to provide just these capabilities in order to achieve strategic advantage through corruption and regulatory capture, or to enforce cartel, racketeering and other illegal market arrangements.[79]

It should be no surprise, therefore, that some criminal organizations deliberately develop collusive and even collaborative arrangements with upperworld political actors, maximizing each organization's governmental power within their own territorial, social or commercial sphere of influence. A 1967 Task Force on Organized Crime established by US President Lyndon Johnson found that 'organized crime flourishes only where it has corrupted local officials'.[80] A 1976 Task Force on Organized Crime established by US Congress drew similar conclusions.[81] Respected Italian mafia scholar Letizia Paoli has explicitly argued that 'the most durable and powerful Italian mafia associations … are those that have been able to infiltrate state institutions most deeply'.[82] Other leading mafia scholars such as Sciarrone, Allum and Siebert have all similarly concluded that organized crime's success relies heavily on the development of political capital.[83] Likewise, recent analysis of violence in Mexico suggests a direct correlation between the disruption of criminal access to political channels (through which to enforce corruption arrangements) and upticks in violence.[84]

Some of this is, no doubt, a simple question of risk minimization; but the unorthodox hypothesis that follows is that *some* criminal organizations may, additionally, be seeking political power (and not simply seeking to limit others' influence over their economic power), and should be treated as legitimate objects of strategic analysis. Such a hypothesis is not entirely unprecedented. The sociologist Alan Block found that 'pursuit of power in one guise or another was the cement holding together under- and upperworlds' in New York in the mid-twentieth century.[85] Adam Elkus, an expert on Mexican drug cartels, describes their goal as 'power over people'.[86] Roberto Saviano describes the maxim of the Neapolitan Camorra as 'Power before all else.'[87]

The next question, however, is whether this pursuit of power is a collective and organizational activity, or simply one pursued individually.

Individual, network or organizational strategy?

To say that some crime is strategically organized is not to succumb to the populist fantasy of criminal masterminds operating according to some 'master plan'. For a criminal group to be 'strategic' does not require total control, but only the attempt to deliberately shape its environment, rather than simply reacting to it.[88] The argument here is that organizational choices matter: that the historical development and trajectory of some criminal activities is the result not just of underlying structural factors or opportunity structures, but also specific choices by human agents. The suggestion is that some such choices are 'strategic': they involve an effort to use available resources to shape the environment in which the actor operates, to achieve defined ends. Necessarily, such 'strategic' choices are dynamic and iterative, emerging out of experience and experimentation. This is just what researchers have begun to identify in the organization of rebellion.[89] Here, we extend the analysis to criminal organization.

Understanding strategic choice requires, as Thomas Schelling argued, understanding how actors perceive opportunities and incentives.[90] This generates two related threshold questions that must precede identification of strategically organized crime. First, does organized criminal behaviour involve planned, rational efforts to shape the strategic environment? Or is crime in fact better considered the disorganized response of individual actors reacting to recurring opportunity structures? And second, if crime is sometimes strategically organized rather than just a structural epiphenomenon, where is the strategic decision-making capacity located? Is it decentralized across criminal networks, or more centrally organized?

The first question concerns criminal motivations. As with terrorism, the label 'organized crime' can be a pejorative one applied by states to delegitimize conduct and demonize actors, hampering objective analysis. The application of the label can trigger a presumption that the conduct in question is irrational, anarchic or even atavistic. This tendency crops up repeatedly in more popular accounts of the convergence of war and crime, with terms such as 'anarchic' and 'irrational' being used interchangeably with 'criminal'.[91] Much criminal violence is indeed reactive—a product of brutalization, anomie and emotional impulse.[92] Indeed, gang violence prevention efforts have found great success in recent years through a model that empowers cool-headed, locally legitimate 'interruptors' to intervene in spiralling gang disputes, talking at-risk youth off emotional cliffs and walking them back from violent angry impulses.[93] But this does not mean that all violence associated with crime is unplanned or non-instrumental. Just as it is for military commanders, the challenge for criminal organizers is to channel and harness these violent impulses effectively. As Adam Elkus notes of Mexico:

> Much of the violence associated with the drug war is … vicious gang warfare, mutilation and beheadings, and bizarre pseudo-religious sects known as *narcocultos*. Such behaviors were once common in Europe—the Thirty Years' War being the most prominent example—and do not change the fact that deliberate policy and strategy guides the violence, not mass brutality. We would do well to pay heed to Clausewitz and note the constant tension between passion, chance, and reason.[94]

A recent review of available evidence concluded that most 'violence in illicit markets is typically selective and instrumental rather than random and gratuitous'.[95] Still, it is one thing to say that crime—and associated violence—is rationally planned by individuals, and another to say that it is systematically, collectively organized. This brings us to the second question: is violence an aspect of criminal activity, or of criminal association?[96]

Beginning in the 1960s economic analysts argued that organized crime is often centralized and hierarchical, like a business firm.[97] Subsequent empirical investigation called this orthodoxy into question, revealing illegal markets populated by small entrepreneurs, fluid 'action sets' and crews and complex family and commercial networks. This resulted in a shift away from firm-level to industry-level analysis.[98] Some scholars also began suggesting that much crime is in fact un-organized, and better thought of as opportunist.[99] This has in turn fuelled suggestions that even organized crime is better thought of not as a closed, directed enterprise, but as an open activity or method, culture, system or form of power into which a range of actors can tap. Henner Hess, a leading mafia scholar with extensive field experience, famously argued for many years that the Sicilian mafia did not exist as an organization, but was rather just a conceptual shorthand by which we sought to reify and explain illicit market forces.[100] Anton Blok, an anthropologist whose longitudinal study of mafia activity in a western Sicilian village is seen as something of a watershed,[101] argued that '[p]resenting mafia as a single unified structure neglects its structural flexibility and fluidity manifest in open-ended networks and action sets'.[102]

A particular vogue has emerged in recent years, perhaps amplified by the dominance of counter-terrorism discourse and research funding, to treat organized criminal activity as the product of network interactions, rather than either atomized market transactions or, at the opposite end of the spectrum, hierarchical enterprise behaviour.[103] Yet network analysis and organizational analysis are not mutually exclusive.[104] As Scott Helfstein of the US Military Academy's Combating Terrorism Center has noted, clandestine networks are 'subject to the same institutional and bureaucratic forces that influence any other purposeful organization'.[105] Karl von Lampe's recognition that criminal organizations are 'the results of action, being continuously shaped and re-shaped in exchanges between various stakeholders'[106] recalls the recognition in management theory in the 1980s that organizational behaviour is in part a product of contractual negotiation 'among self-interested individuals with divergent interests'.[107] Criminal enterprises emerge as institutionalized patterns of exchange within networks, just as networks emerge from recurring patterns of exchange within a market.[108] As Southerland and Potter note:

> viewed from a distance, criminal enterprises might give the impression of producing a very high volume of illicit activity, which because of its prevalence seems highly organized, and ... appears to be a single organization or several very large organizations. But ... the same structure viewed from the inside would look like a series of partnerships organized around specific criminal projects.[109]

This all suggests that actors within criminal networks can exercise different kinds of influence and power, depending on their position within the network.[110] As different actors are exposed to different risks, they develop different strategic perspectives and preferences.[111] The strategy of a criminal organization is thus best understood as the result of complex interplay between strategic choices made by individuals, operating in a variety of network and hierarchical forms. Depending on the shifting distribution of power and activity within these forms, the resulting strategy may be deliberate or 'directed' from the top down, or 'emergent' from internal transactions.[112] Criminal groups can be understood as providing a 'context of action', a governmental system of shared resources and common rules that constrain participating actors—who may have very diverging objectives and strategies, and may compete internally for power even as the group competes with external rivals.[113] Understanding the strategic behaviour of criminal networks thus requires looking inside those networks to understand shifts in internal power and influence, and their complex interaction with shifts in the strategic environment in which the network operates.

Social bandits and primitive criminal strategy

The difference between a-strategic and strategic criminal organization is illuminated by the special case of social bandits such as Robin Hood, Rob Roy, Jesse James and Pancho Villa. These are, as the British historian Eric Hobsbawm explained:

> outlaws whom the lord and state regard as criminals, but who remain within … society, and are considered by their people as heroes, as champions, avengers, fighters for justice, perhaps even leaders of liberation, and in any case as men to be admired, helped and supported.[114]

Bandits are of course organized criminals, in the sense that they organize bands that use violence to extract criminal rents, through robbery and plunder. Mancur Olson has famously suggested that bandits choose whether to rove, or, if it looks like it offers better returns, to become stationary autocrats, turning theft into 'taxation'.[115] But are these choices strategic?

As defined by Hobsbawm, social bandits are typically unmarried male youths who emerge as peasant rebels after some brush with the state or ruling class for an infraction considered socially legitimate but formally illegal.[116] Their 'ambitions are modest: a traditional world in which men are justly dealt with, not a new and perfect world'.[117] The term remains germane, with contemporary criminal leaders such as Joaquín 'El Chapo' Guzmán Loera, the former head of the Sinaloa Cartel in Mexico, still being described and regarded by some rural poor as a social bandit, despite appearing on the *Forbes* Rich List.[118] Hobsbawm explained that the poor would:

> protect the bandit, regard him as their champion, idealize him and turn him into a myth... In return, the bandit himself tries to live up to his role even when he is not himself a conscious social rebel.[119]

The social bandit is the product of emergent social protest, rather than the agent of strategic change, emerging in conditions of rural pauperization and economic crisis or, in some cases, slower-moving politico-economic transformation.[120] Social bandits usually struggle to establish a coherent social programme and typically do not emerge as governmental rivals to states, remaining vehicles for social protest. They are, in Hobsbawm's terms, 'primitive rebels'. As we shall see in the brief study in Chapter 7 of Salvatore Giuliano, the famous Sicilian bandit with ties to the mafia, bandit strategy is also rather primitive. As Hobsbawm has decisively shown, bandits tend to be men of action, not deep thinkers. They are 'activists and not ideologists or prophets from whom novel visions or plans of social and political organization are to be expected', tough leaders who 'hack out the way' rather than 'discover it'. Their social role is not one they choose, but one they are typically thrust into by popular acclaim: 'Bandits, except for their willingness or capacity to refuse individual submission, have no ideas other than those of the peasantry ... of which they form part.'[121] Indeed, once bandits start to select targets not because they are 'organic', well-known local sources of oppression, but rather on the basis of sophisticated 'political calculations', they are removed 'far from the sphere in which social banditry ... operates'.[122] In the figure of Salvatore Giuliano in Chapter 7 we see just how hard the transition from social bandit to strategic organized criminal can be.

Criminal capabilities

Existing scholarship has examined the resources—the means—used by specific criminal groups, and the operational tactics used to harness those resources.[123] Southerland and Potter demonstrated that criminal groups can develop competitive advantage within illicit markets through innovation to develop new capabilities.[124] Scholars have also explored how criminal groups compete to develop new, lower-cost methods for manufacturing, delivery, logistics, weaponry, marketing and money-laundering.[125] But to date there has been limited inquiry into how criminal groups combine these resources (their means) into strategic capabilities (organizational processes or ways).[126] Building on existing scholarship, this section explores how strategically organized crime involves the development of three capabilities—coercion, corruption, and communications—and combines them through a control system. This provides a basic framework for understanding the strategic organization of criminal capabilities, which is then applied in Part Two to decipher the strategic choices of real criminal organizations in the historical record.

Coercion

The absence of state enforcement power from criminal markets makes strategic coercion—the use of overt threats or actual force to influence another's choices[127]—central to criminal organization. As Paoli neatly summarizes, '[u]ltimately violence constitutes the backbone of [criminal] power'.[128] The simplest use of coercion is to capture the resources—the means—needed to extract criminal rents. This is simple predation and robbery—whether of the highway variety, or, as in the Somali piracy case, the high seas variety. Coercion is used to control both material and intangible resources, such as supply routes. In Mexico, for example, cartel violence is often focused on control of the *plazas*, strategic nodes in trafficking route networks.[129] Coercion is also used to enforce criminal deals and employment contracts.[130] The normalization of coercion as a sanction turns a criminal network into a more institutionalized organization, separating it from the broader environment. As Falcone stressed, the mafia:

> is a society, an organization which to all intents and purposes has its own legal system... Given that within the Mafia structure there are no courts and no police force either, it is essential that each of its 'citizens' knows that punishment is inevitable and that the sentence will be carried out immediately. Whoever breaks the rules knows he will pay with his life.[131]

This internal violence is legitimized through the logic of protection.[132] Protection from what? The criminal groups' rivals—both other criminal groups, and other governmental actors such as the state. Coercion is also used to directly attack those rivals, setting up the potential for arms races and security dilemmas. World Bank economist Stergios Skaperdas describes the resulting market structure in terms that sound very similar to descriptions of the inter-state system:

> a curious sort of monopolistic competition, whereby each gang has the local monopoly of protection within a certain area and this local monopoly is maintained by the gang's capability of mobilizing and using force against other gangs.[133]

Just as it is for states, for criminal groups coercion is closely tied to a strategy of deterrence. Building a reputation for violence can be as important as building the actual capacity for violence.[134] Criminal groups frequently engage in atrocity to deter potential rivals and reduce their own enforcement costs.[135] Saviano, the Camorra-watcher, explains that '[i]n Naples cruelty is the most complete and affordable strategy for becoming a successful businessman'.[136] Conversely, signs of weakness can be self-fulfilling. Alan Block notes that in the underworld:

> Displays of personal power are constantly necessary for both personal and financial security... Weakness undermines not only an individual's position but reverberates through the entire associational network...[137]

Strategic criminal coercion is consequently intimately tied to strategic communications. In Mexico, for example, the posting of videos of beheadings and torture has become normalized. Drug cartels routinely dump bodies with long and complex public messages—*narcomantas*—attached. A typical *narcomanta* from Monterrey in March 2007 read:

> Prosecutor: don't be an idiot, this will continue until you stop protecting Hector Huerta's people, 'Shorty' Guzman, and that queer 'La Barby.' Especially you, Rogelio Cerda [a local official], until all your children are dead... P.S. This is only the beginning.[138]

As with many arms races, it can be hard to prevent a race to the bottom, with increasing levels of barbarity becoming normalized.[139] The flipside of this use of coercion for external deterrence is what the renowned strategist Michael Howard described as the generation of 'reassurance' to those within one's protection.[140] Displays of violence help to remind participants in the criminal network of the potential harm they face from rivals, and the importance of the organization in protecting them from it.

Notwithstanding this tendency towards brutality when violence is deployed, organized crime groups tend to be selective about when to deploy it. Wide-scale confrontation between criminal groups, and between those groups and the state, is exceptional—just as, on the international plane, war is exceptional, while deterrence and coercion are ubiquitous. As John Bailey and Matthew Taylor have explained, this is because a campaign of violence requires capabilities—such as intelligence gathering, secrecy, coordination and weaponry—that depend on substantial organizational sophistication; and also because the costs of wide-scale confrontation are high, ranging from personal insecurity, internal defection and decreased business, to increased government repression. [141]

Criminal organizations are therefore more likely to resort to widespread violence when the predicted costs are low—because the military or enforcement capacity of the state or criminal rival is weakened. Once such a calculation becomes widespread, a chain reaction may set in, as we have seen in Mexico in recent years. When one cartel is wounded, others move in to prey on its resources, absorbing its personnel, taking over its trafficking routes, capturing its weapons, stepping into its relationships with businesses and government. [142] The competition for these resources hurts some actors, and the chain continues. This is why Mexico (and arguably Syria) at times seems to resemble the meltdown of the Thirty Years War. They are brutal mêlées fuelled by a dangerous domino effect.

Corruption

Corruption is the single most distinctive strategic capability of criminal organizations. Its importance is made clear by a recent analysis of the business model of the Sinaloa Cartel, one of the most powerful drug trafficking organizations in the world, which found that corruption payments constituted the single largest line-item expenditure in its budget. [143] So what is corruption?

'Corruption' is frequently defined as 'the abuse of a public position of trust for private gain'. [144] But this description overlooks the transactional nature of corruption, which exchanges an illegal or illicit exercise of governmental discretion (whether in a position of public office or private authority) for a criminal rent. Corruption subverts the exercise of governmental power through threats and/or payments, giving privileged access to public contracts, protecting criminals from law enforcement or targeting a criminal group's rivals. In some cases, criminal groups use corruption to influence the way that the state defines and regulates criminal activity, to their advantage.

As we shall see in Part Two, at this 'highest' level corruption often involves political campaign finance and support. This is intended to create broad systemic leverage, through what Frank Madsen aptly terms a 'futures market'.[145] A US Senate Committee in 1951 used the popular term 'the fix':

> The fix may ... come about through the acquisition of political power by contributions to political organizations or otherwise, by creating economic ties with apparently respectable and reputable businessmen and lawyers, and by buying public good will through charitable contributions and press relations.[146]

Strategic corruption thus involves the deliberate 'acquisition' of future 'political power' through investments in candidates, causes and parties.[147] In some cases, there is even evidence of such investments leading to criminal organizations vetting shortlists of candidates put forward by politicians (Italy, Mexico), dictating party programmes (Colombia), or even presenting their own candidates for office.[148]

The real utility of strategic corruption is not, however, its instrumental value in delivering material resources, or even human resources in the form of government officials. It is its creation of legitimacy. The corrupted bystander or rival suddenly becomes a 'friend'. This is what makes corruption unique from a strategic theory perspective: it presents as a voluntary exchange of governmental discretion in return for a reward or the non-execution of a threat.[149] It rests on the target's fear of future punishment being outweighed by the promise of current rewards. As early as 1901 an observer of the Sicilian mafia noted the way in which corrupt mafia exchanges allowed the *mafioso*'s 'friend' to 'flatter himself' that his 'tribute' was 'actually a gracious gift or the price paid for a service rendered'.[150] Almost a century later, the mafia *pentito* Tommaso Buscetta stressed to Italian prosecutors that the Sicilian mafia's influence:

> cannot be explained [solely] as the result of coercion. Those who cooper-ate expect certain advantages. True, one cannot expect these relationships to be on an equal footing, as it is always clear that one of the parties is [a *mafioso*]; yet the other party makes himself available.[151]

Strategic corruption is thus distinct from strategic coercion. As Lawrence Freedman has explained, the latter seeks to create a situation of:

> *force majeure*, a choice dictated by overwhelming circumstances. The target has a choice, but one that is skewed if he accepts that the consequences of non-compliance will be a denial of future choice.[152]

In contrast, strategic corruption aims not simply at one-off control, but at retaining the structure of ongoing bargaining and even amicable association. It creates a pretence of equality and reciprocity, disguising the power relations within an amicable relationship.

Why do criminal groups bother to keep up this fiction? Why not just threaten officials into submission? The traditional answer, drawn from economic analysis, is that corruption is cheaper over the long term. As the economic historian of Venice, Frederic Lane, explained, commer-cial enterprises are likely to pay tribute (bribes) to a higher political authority, rather than pay for their own armed protection, where the cost of tribute is lower than the rent they accrue from the resulting protection thus afforded. (That rent can be measured in terms of the change in production and distribution costs as a result of prevented violence).[153] Structuring the exchange as a voluntary one helps to reduce the criminal actor's enforcement costs, which would otherwise depend on ongoing monitoring and retention of a credible threat, until the corruption target exercised his or her discretion in the preferred manner. Seen from an industrial perspective, corruption thus repre-sents an attempt to purchase the loyalty of upstream suppliers of pro-tection, bringing them within the criminal group's supply chain and lowering its overall business costs.[154]

But corrupt exchanges have political effects that other commercial exchanges do not. They make the parties rely on each other to keep the exchange hidden. The result is a special kind of clandestine allegiance.[155]

Robert and Pamela Bunker have astutely described this as a Faustian bargain, from which there is no turning back.[156] As the Kefauver Committee put it in 1951, 'It is axiomatic in the underworld that once a public official' has corruptly exercised his discretion on one occasion, 'thereafter the underworld owns him'.[157] As Joe Valachi, the first major mafia informant in the US, said, 'once you are in, you can't get out'.[158] Or as an Italian convicted of corruption put it, 'I found myself in a mechanism that had a life of its own.'[159] Corruption does not generate control of territory, but rather complicity, the basis of criminal loyalty.[160] It is a kind of subversion.[161] As a strategic capability, corruption is thus neither 'hard power' (coercion) nor what Joe Nye calls 'soft power', which relies on affinity and persuasion.[162] It is better thought of as a source of 'hidden power', creating clandestine norms and expectations against which the subject self-regulates. It is, in other words, the foundation of criminal governmentality, through which individuals secretly 'conduct their own conduct', to recall Foucault's term.

Corruption works by aligning the victim's own incentives with the criminal organization's success; by remaking the individual as a subject within the hidden criminal system, a participant in an 'underworld'. This is not just a question of psychological and ideational incentives, but also extends to a variety of behavioural techniques and practices intended to bind the target into the criminal system. Criminal organizations have developed a surprising array of financial mechanisms binding supporters and collaborators together. Neapolitan Camorra drug traffickers have, for example, developed sophisticated pricing and subsidy mechanisms designed to force legal producers to become suppliers to criminal supply chains.[163] Michael Ross describes the use of what he calls 'booty futures'—a stake in the control of future criminal rents looted through war—as a capital-raising technique to attract illicit investment in aggressive resource capture schemes in Africa.[164] Somali pirates 'offer' coastal communities the opportunity to crowd-fund piracy operations, receiving a share of the pirate booty in return.[165] The Nuvoletta clan created a retail shareholder scheme for distributors in the cocaine market around Naples; and the Di Lauro clan adopted an Amway style 'circle' distribution arrangement, giving distributors (and not just suppliers) a commercial stake in promoting the criminal order.[166]

Communications

A review of the existing literature also hints that effective criminal organizations will develop processes for communicating with target audiences in ways that change the circumstances of other strategic actors (including the state), and give the criminal group competitive advantage over them.[167] Strategic communications involve shaping the normative order through efforts designed to legitimize and normalize criminal conduct and criminal influence within the upperworld. They aim, in other words, at enlarging the sphere of criminal governmentality.

To date this aspect of criminal organization has received limited attention. Many authors treat criminal groups' interest in public relations and self-promotion as a response to a psychological, rather than a strategic, need. Robert Lacey, the biographer of the mobster Meyer Lansky, whom we will get to know in Part Two, suggested for example that 'Gangsters revel in the folklore that popular culture has constructed around them' because it 'provides glamour and importance all too often lacking in their personal lives'.[168] Some analysts have explored the role that strategic communications play in positioning criminal actors against their commercial rivals.[169] Vanda Felbab-Brown, Steven Metz, Adam Elkus and Phil Williams have all also considered the role of criminal communications during insurgency.[170] But there has been limited attention to the role of criminal communications in developing political influence or governmental power in other contexts.

The strategic function of a communications capability is the same in a criminal organization as in other power-maximizing entities. As Lawrence Freedman put it: 'The trick of the powerful is to rule by encouraging the ruled to internalize the ruler's own values and interests.'[171] A communications capability is thus critical for a criminal organization to develop what Colin Gray has called the 'social dimension of strategy'.[172] Effective strategic criminal organizations go beyond a mere strategy of social influence and public relations, to one of governmentality. Criminal leaders often become legitimized as all-knowing father-figures dispensing unknowable, yet forceful, justice.[173] They create alternative—though secretive—social narratives, framed around justice claims, operationalized in specific behavioural codes such as the Sicilian mafia's code of *omertà* (silent non-cooperation with the state) which govern their members' and supporters' behaviour. As Falcone put it, through these narratives and codes, these groups function as hidden 'societies'.[174]

In many cases, criminal organizations seem to achieve this goal by becoming socially 'embedded', adapting and manipulating existing social narratives and structures.[175] In Italy and Russia, for example, mafias have co-opted Christian authority symbols.[176] Criminal narratives and media outreach also help to normalize illegality and violence. Saviano offers an account of the Camorra's deliberate use of the media during the 'Secondigliano War' in Naples to normalize the ongoing violence.[177] And as we explore further in Chapter 11, Mexican drug cartels likewise devote considerable attention to promoting a social culture of death and criminal power, in particular through the popularization of 'narcoballads', and through targeted attacks on traditional and social media outlets that dare to question cartel conduct or power.[178]

By stoking fear, strategic communications can also prime demand for protection. Criminal groups seek to generate legitimacy by providing livelihoods, social mobility, physical security and protection of property, or even social services such as disaster relief (the *yakuza*), welfare payments (criminal groups in Colombia) or medical services (Haitian gangs). Once criminal groups are seen as providers of livelihoods and public goods and services, the state is confronting a true rival for its population's allegiance.[179] And once that rival is seen as an alternative source of norms, the state is in deep trouble: when a government loses its power to secure support for the norms it promotes, then it is 'on the road to having to rely on brute force'.[180]

Strategic communications may also be shaped by the nature of the rents sought. Rents that require broad-based labour inputs—such as agricultural drug production or illicit alluvial mining—may require a criminal group to wield broad-based social control over the labour force.[181] Broader, public communications capabilities may be required. In contrast, rents that require control only of limited trafficking sites, or decision-making by a small number of highly placed state officials—for example to prevent law enforcement interference with trafficking activities—may not require such broad communications capabilities, but rather ones more narrowly targeted towards high-level state officials. These may focus on campaign support and efforts to create private influence and hidden social capital.[182] It may be that different criminal groups operating in the same space develop different approaches to communications, since they focus on different rents. And as different criminal rents become available, the same criminal group may need to alter its communications strategy. Dennis Rodgers describes, for example, a shift in *mara* strategic communications in Nicaragua, as gangs have shifted away from taxing local protection rackets, towards taxing transnational drug flows.[183]

Command and control

Effective strategy requires not only the development of capabilities, but also their combination and control. The inherently risky and clandestine nature of criminal organization poses special challenges for command and control.[184] In the absence of the dispute-resolution functions of the state, and because of the strongly corrosive presence of greed, criminal organizations are constantly susceptible to betrayal, defection and fragmentation.[185] They face an uphill battle recruiting members and maintaining loyalty.[186] The profit motive can radically undermine discipline and internal cohesion. Even ideologically inspired political insurgencies seem to have a tendency to devolve into criminal organizations over time, as financial incentives displace political goals.[187] As Samuel Huntington noted forty years ago: 'The criminalization of political violence is more prevalent than the politicization of criminal violence.'[188]

Many criminal organizations accordingly develop highly personalized command and control systems, closely tied to their leaders.[189] Yet the need for secrecy can also encourage the dispersal of risk away from the leadership. Flatter, cellular network structures may be less easily disrupted by competitors (including law enforcement)—but they may also facilitate defection. The tension between these two imperatives—towards centralization for control, and towards decentralization for resilience—seems to give rise to a recurring strategic solution among criminal organizations: decentralized decision-making guided by a common culture—or governmentality—and centralized sanctioning power.[190] Strategic criminal groups often adopt two-tier network structures, with an insulated 'core' providing general guidance and sanctioning misconduct, while a much larger network engages in semi-autonomous business.[191] In periods of stability, lower-level commercial and military activity may be conducted throughout the network, with the 'core' engaged in more consequential strategic direction setting—such as internal governance and handling external relations with higher-level state actors. When the organization is under attack, temporary centralization and creation of a more responsive command and control chain may, however, be necessary.[192] In Central America, for example, gang warfare between MS-13 and the Eighteenth Street Gang, together with the adoption of *mano dura* (heavy hand) policies by state actors, forced the diffuse *mara* networks to develop more cohesive command and control systems.[193] Similarly, in Naples, competitive pressures forced the centralization of the Di Lauro clan, moving from a liberal management system of autonomous cells to a wage-based hierarchy.[194]

When not operating in this more centralized mode, however, criminal networks often depend on their shared governmentality, sometimes codified into explicit but secret norms, to guide their members' decentralized decision-making. This clandestine governmentality depends on trust—the scarcest of commodities in the underworld.[195] Trust supplements violence as the basis for criminal command and control.[196] The sinews of criminal organizations typically follow the contours of trust networks born in common family, clan, childhood or prison experiences.[197] For example, Sicilian mafia slang for prison is *cunvittu*—convent, or boarding school—reflecting the perception that time served in prison works not only to isolate its boarders from broader society, but to provide a common socialization or education.

Criminal organizations institutionalize trust through initiation rituals designed to inculcate a sense of in-group and out-group identity, and create an 'imagined community' beyond the state.[198] To express the resulting obligations of loyalty, these initiation processes are often framed in terms of kinship rituals—for example induction into a mafia 'brotherhood' and adoption by a 'godfather'. In the Japanese *yakuza*, each criminal group is called a family (*ikka*) and hierarchical relationships are expressed in familial terms of protection and obedience.[199]

In most cases, these families—and criminal power—are utterly patriarchal. Many criminal structures idealize women as embodiments of traditional values such as family, honour, purity and respect; but this typically serves to objectify and subjugate women, denying them agency within criminal power structures, instead treating them as passive bystanders to men's choices. Women are routinely and ritually instrumentalized in men's often violent pursuit of criminal power. Some criminal organizations even use inter-marriage to build bonds of trust in conditions of anarchy—just as do tribes, royal families and terrorist networks such as Al Qaeda.[200] Marrying women off to other criminal actors serves as a hedge against distrust by increasing the time horizon over which potential rivals will assess returns. It follows a similar logic to free market actors' decisions to join a firm: as Ronald Coase explained, firms institutionalize and reduce transaction costs and free up resources that can then be used for external action. So do marriage alliances.

But this logic can also work in reverse: as Williams has shown in Mexico, strategic competition between drug cartels is overlaid at times by 'blood feud' logic, like the two decade-long feud between Chapo Guzmán and the Arellano Felix organization.[201] The creation of in- and out-groups can develop an irreversible momentum, reducing criminal organizations' flexibility in positioning themselves relative to the external environment. And the treatment of women as passive bystanders also carries significant risks because it overlooks the power that women do in fact enjoy, both in their own right and as shapers of male choices through their embodiment of governmental values such as family loyalty. In Chapter 6 we will see how costly this can be, when a male criminal leader—Lucky Luciano—fails to account for the possibility that female sex workers might betray him to the state. Interestingly, male criminals' obliviousness to female agency within their own lives also seems to open up the possibility of women helping to change their strategic outlooks, helping to woo them away from a life of violence— as has been used successfully in counter-terrorism efforts. We explore this possibility briefly in Chapter 11.

The framing of criminal organization in terms of fictive kinship also, sadly, facilitates the integration of children. Children cost less to feed, do not necessarily expect payment and are generally more impressionable and less demanding on organizational monitoring and disciplinary systems.[202] And the incorporation of children also strengthens a group's ties to the broader community through their (biological) families.[203]

The transformation of an individual's identity through entry into a criminal organization also resembles entry into a new family in other ways. Whereas legitimate business firms are built on 'purposive contracts' of limited effect, organized crime enterprises are built on 'status contracts' which, in Max Weber's terms, 'involve a change in what may be called the total legal situation (the universal position) and the social status of the persons involved'.[204] As Letizia Paoli puts it:

> with the entrance into the [criminal] group, the novice is required to assume a new identity permanently and to subordinate all his previous allegiances to the [criminal group] membership. It is a life-long pact.

Initiation magically transforms the individual, changing them from being subjects of one governmental system into subjects of another. It is, in Giovanni Falcone's terms, a 'religious conversion', a permanent Faustian bargain, a permanent submission to the governmentality of the criminal group. As the *pentito* Antonino Calderone was told when he was initiated into the Sicilian mafia:

> One cannot leave, one cannot resign from the Cosa Nostra. You'll see for yourselves, in a little while, how one enters with blood [a ritual pricking of the finger]. And if you leave, you'll leave with blood because you'll be killed. One cannot abandon, cannot betray, the Cosa Nostra, because it's above everything.[205]

The indelible nature of the transformation is sometimes represented through external marking: Russian and Japanese organized crime, outlaw motorcycle gangs and the *maras* all use tattoos to this effect. They publicly (and thus undeniably) brand the individual as the permanent subject of an alternative governmental (even cosmic) order. Of course, this also impedes operational secrecy; for that reason, some Central American *maras* now appear to be dispensing with the use of publicly visible tattoos.

Criminal corporate cultures are not just familial or religious, however; they are governmental in the sense that they rely heavily on the subject's self-regulation to ensure their behaviour accords with shared norms. The obligations of a member of the group are frequently informal and learned through participation and osmosis. But they may also be made explicit, through codes and constitutions.[206] Criminal governmentality provides a common operating system that can sustain even quite decentralized operational activity.[207] As R.T. Naylor has explained, financial ties within criminal groups are frequently the loose ties of an association or society, rather than the tighter ties of a firm—more Rotary Club than Standard Oil.[208] Once the subject has bought into the criminal system, they may in fact enjoy quite a large degree of autonomy, with the core leadership operating more like a clan head or market regulator than the commander of an army.[209]

Recognizing the strategic function of governmentality in criminal organization may also suggest certain limits to criminal power. Offshore ventures may be constrained by the group's ability to transnationalize a trust network or export a specific governmentality. Diaspora and immigrant networks are, for this reason, a recurring path of criminal internationalization; the development of criminal offshoots in entirely foreign environments from overseas appear to be less common—though as we shall see in Part Two, not entirely unfeasible.[210]

Conclusion

This chapter has developed a simple framework for understanding the development and decision-making of criminal groups in strategic terms. Based on an extensive review of existing scholarship, it suggests that some criminal groups—though by no means all—may pursue governmental power through the strategic development and combination of the capabilities of coercion, corruption and communications. Strategic decisions may emerge through the complex interaction of individuals within criminal networks, coalescing in some circumstances into more hierarchical criminal organizations.

The question is whether this analytical framework can help to explain the decision-making and development of specific groups found in the historical record. Part Two seeks to answer this question through a careful analysis of a series of episodes in the activities of political and criminal groups, particularly Tammany Hall and the Sicilian and American mafias, in New York, Sicily and the Caribbean in the nineteenth and twentieth centuries. Part Three returns to the question of how these criminal groups positioned themselves in relation to other governmental rivals such as states, and what this may imply for how theorists and practitioners approach strategy, efforts to combat organized crime and the management of spoilers in peace and transition processes.

PART TWO

EPISODES IN CRIMINAL STRATEGY

3

TAMMANY

'HOW NEW YORK IS GOVERNED', 1859–1920

'This population is too hopelessly split up into races and factions to govern it under universal suffrage, except by the bribery of patronage or purchase.'

Boss Tweed[1]

12 July 1863, a Sunday, found Manhattan quietly digesting the tragedy of the Battle of Gettysburg. Ten days earlier, Union and Confederate armies had fought the bloodiest engagement of the American Civil War. Though Union forces emerged victorious, the huge casualties inflicted on each side had brought the campaign to a political turning point. Public patience with Union generals was ebbing fast. Military volunteers had become so few over preceding months that President Lincoln had been forced to introduce conscription. In New York, it was to start the next day.

It was poorly timed. 12 July held special significance for Irish New Yorkers, whose mass immigration since the onset of famine in Ireland in 1845 had helped to triple Manhattan's population: it was the date on which the Loyal Order of Orangemen marked the Battle of the Boyne in 1690, in which Protestant King William of Orange defeated Catholic King James II of England. It was an anniversary traditionally marked by sectarian violence, and a terrible occasion on which to introduce the first federal draft in America—not least because of a $300 'commutation' loophole that allowed draftees to buy their way out. That was a sum easily within the reach of rich Anglo-Protestants, but far beyond poor Irish Catholics.

Irish-born volunteer fire crews—in those days a focus for neighbourhood organization and muscular volunteerism similar to football clubs in many parts of the world today—led the rioting that started on Manhattan the next morning. It continued for three days. African Americans were a major target. Irish workingmen feared Union war victory would draw large numbers of ex-slaves into north-eastern labour markets; indeed, African American labour had recently been used to break an Irish dockworkers' strike in New York. The Colored Orphans Asylum on 43rd Street was attacked. Two men were lynched. Uptown emptied. The state governor intervened, unsuccessfully urging rioters to desist while he attempted to convince the federal government to drop the draft. A mob ransacked the Second Avenue Armory, burned several police stations and started a looting spree, pillaging the downtown clothing store of Brooks Brothers, notorious for providing the Union army with 12,000 uniforms that fell apart in days. Local businessmen, largely Protestant, began to urge the imposition of martial law. If order was not brought to the richest, largest city in the Union, the results could be dire.

Five regiments of regular Union army troops rushed back from Gettysburg. Working with police, West Point cadets, 1,200 volunteers and a group of street workers organized by a young Tammany Society politician, Bill Tweed, restored order on the streets, though 105 bodies remained behind. But the larger political question of the draft remained. The governor pushed again for it to be dropped; President Lincoln stood firm. If he suspended the draft in New York, how could it be enforced elsewhere in the Union? Without it, his military advisers warned, Union forces would soon be overwhelmed and the Civil War lost.

William Magear Tweed saw his moment. Tall, broad, just thirty-nine years old, the Scots-Irishman was already chairman of Tammany Hall, the local Democratic Party outfit. The violence around him did not disturb him. He had come up, in fact, through the fire crews, as a violent, charismatic leader of the Lower East Side Engine No. 6, known as the 'Tigers'. In that role he commanded seventy-five toughs who regularly engaged in running street battles with rival fire crews and used their muscle and neighbourhood clout to run protection rackets. They also stuffed ballot-boxes and intimidated voters, giving him a fast-track into Tammany Hall, the wing of the Democratic Party that controlled Manhattan's municipal governance. In 1851 he and his crew were invited to meet President Millard Fillmore at the White House. In 1852, at just twenty-nine, he was elected on a Tammany ticket as a city alderman.

By 1863, Tammany Hall had emerged as a central intermediary between the state and the new Irish immigrant underclass in New York. Tammany's pro-Union stand during the war, breaking with many other Democrats, gave it crucial credibility with the Republican administration in Washington DC at this moment of crisis. And its legitimacy within the underclass, based on a culture of patronage and service-provision, gave Tammany crucial influence over the rioters. Tweed was perfectly positioned to broker a solution to the draft crisis.

Tweed used his dominance within the city's Board of Supervisors to engineer a solution. The Board would sell bonds to Wall Street and use the proceeds both to buy exemptions for draftees and to pay a market-rate bonus to volunteer substitutes. Draftees who chose to fight would keep the $300 that would otherwise have been spent on buying their commutation. Everyone would win: the state would get its soldiers, the Protestant commercial class would have order restored, Tammany's constituents would get relief from the draft and Tammany would use its control of the state's financial apparatus to protect its own political position. In Washington, Tweed met with the Secretary of War, Edward Stanton, and received his approval for Tammany to execute the scheme. By the end of September, of 1,034 draftees seeking Tweed's help, 983 had been substituted, forty-nine excused, and two chose to go to war. By the end of the war, Tweed's 'exemption' committee had supplied 116,382 recruits to Lincoln's army. But perhaps the biggest winner was Tweed. By becoming a mediator between the state and the street, a regulator of violence, he had built immense personal political capital.[2]

To what end? A political one, or the amassing of criminal profit? 'Boss Tweed', as he came to be known, is of course today remembered as a paragon of greed and corruption, not as an effective political mediator. Between 1859 and being turfed out of office in 1872, Tweed and his cronies used the state's financial and governmental apparatus to loot New York's treasuries of at least $45 million, worth $2 billion in today's terms. This was more than the US federal government's annual budget at the time.[3] Likewise, Tammany Hall, which dominated New York politics between the 1850s and 1930s, has become a byword for political corruption and 'machine' politics. Understanding Tammany power—how it was developed, amassed and used—offers unique insights into the complex relationship between criminal strategy and governmental power within a party political organization. It is an unusually well-documented case, in part because of the press, municipal and criminal investigations that led to the confessions of Tweed and several of his co-conspirators in the 'Tweed Ring'.[4] An understanding of Tammany power is also crucial for understanding the emergence of the New York Mob addressed in later chapters. Tammany shaped New York government, making organized crime and criminality 'inextricable parts of the political history of New York.'[5]

This chapter begins by exploring how Tammany Hall emerged as a political broker in New York, following the American War of Independence, through Irish immigration, culminating in Tweed's emergence as a strategic leader of the organization in the 1860s. The second section explores how Boss Tweed harnessed Tammany power to a criminal strategy, by the late 1860s developing a crude joint venture between politics and crime, in which a small clique within Tammany's leadership circle merged the state's and Tammany's capabilities to create a system of criminalized governance from which they skimmed massive criminal rents. By the early 1870s, Tweed was rewriting New York's constitutional arrangements in an effort to entrench this system and his own power. But a failure to control Orange Day rioting undermined his own popular legitimacy, and set the stage for his downfall after an effective press campaign and financial boycott. A third section briefly explores how Tammany survived this crisis and evolved, its strategic orientation morphing as different factions took control and positioned it differently in response to external rivals for governmental power. A concluding section reflects on theoretical insights from this case.

New York's government: machine made

Guardians of the Revolution

Tammany Hall was a product of competing visions of government in an independent United States. On 30 April 1789 George Washington stood on the balcony of Federal Hall on Wall Street and took the oath of office as the first president of the United States of America. For some in the new republic, the ascendancy of Washington and the patrician clique around him threatened the emergence of an American aristocracy and the death of their own dreams of democracy. Across Nassau Street from Federal Hall, just two weeks later, the former Continental Army soldier—now upholsterer—William Mooney established the New York chapter of the Society of St Tammany, or Columbian Order, an avowedly 'nativist' fraternal organization.[6]

The creation of Tammany was a direct response to Washington's ties to the Society of the Cincinnati, an exclusive fraternal organization created during the Revolution by a group of senior officers in the Continental Army including Lt Alexander Hamilton, then *aide-de-camp* to the Commander-in-Chief General George Washington. From its inception, the Society of Cincinnati attracted controversy.[7] It had the makings of a political organization, claiming the mantle of the protector of 'the ideals of the Revolution in an independent United States' and cloaking itself in the republican imagery of the famous patrician farmer-general, Cincinnatus, who twice in the sixth century BC resigned dictatorial commissions from the Roman Senate after discharging his mandated military missions, returning to a farmer's life. Membership was strictly limited to senior Continental Army officers (including some of the French aristocrats in those ranks) and their first-born sons, suggesting the makings of a paramilitary elite with dangerously unassailable post-revolutionary legitimacy and patrician or even aristocratic tendencies. The Cincinnati's first president general, from 1783 until his death in 1799, was George Washington; he wore a bejewelled Cincinnati lapel pin as his badge of presidential office. Hamilton, Washington's Secretary of the Treasury in his first cabinet, succeeded him as leader of the Cincinnati. Washington's Secretary of War, Henry Knox, was also a member—as were twenty-three signers of the US Constitution. Benjamin Franklin began to warn against an 'order of hereditary knights' taking power in the nascent democracy.[8]

The first Tammany Society, established in Philadelphia in 1772, in fact predated the Cincinnati. It, too, was created as a fraternal organization—but exclusively for American-born men, similar to the better-known Sons of Liberty who staged the Boston Tea Party in 1773. As a sign of their 'nativism', its founders misappropriated many indigenous American symbols, calling their halls 'wigwams', their rank and file 'braves' and their leaders 'sachems'. The group's name was adapted from Tamanend, a Lenape chief from the Delaware with whom William Penn appears to have treated for land in June 1683. The Indian chief was notionally 'sainted' to ridicule Loyalist (pro-British) societies that had sprung up at the time, which styled themselves the societies of St George, St Andrew and St David, depending on whether their founders' ties were to England, Scotland or Wales.

The creation of the New York chapter of the Tammany Society in 1789 was a direct response to the instalment of a Cincinnati-led executive in Federal Hall. The Cincinnati had become associated with federalist policies advocating a strong, centralized executive government. The Tammany Society emerged as a vehicle for promoting a rival vision of nativist, decentralized governance championed by the Democratic-Republican Party then emerging around Thomas Jefferson. The Tammany charter described these as 'the true and genuine principles of republicanism'.[9]

Political parties were emerging as mobilizers of political capital connecting the new federal government and electors at the state and sub-state level. In 1800 the New York Tammany Society played an important organizational role in the US presidential election for Aaron Burr—a founding, but lapsed, member of the Cincinnati who had emerged after Independence, together with Jefferson, as a key opponent of Hamilton and the federalists. Burr was a close friend of Tammany's founding grand sachem in New York, William Mooney, and used the Tammany Society to manoeuvre the city assembly to select a slate of Democratic-Republican presidential electors for the Federal Electoral College. This allowed him to strike a bargain with Jefferson, promising that New York would support him in the presidential vote, in return for Burr becoming his running mate and, ultimately, his vice-president.[10]

This was Tammany's first taste of how power at the city level could influence presidential elections, but by no means its last. Jefferson's presidential patronage accelerated Tammany's rise to power in New York, and Tammany proved adroit in enlarging Democratic-Republican influence by combining political and economic power. In an era when access to the franchise depended on property ownership, Tammany funded joint property purchases, enfranchising a range of supporters who would go on to become political leaders in New York and Washington, and whose names city landmarks still bear—Tompkins, Riker, Van Ness. But the city's access to patronage remained limited; most administrative offices were controlled by the state governor, George Clinton, a Tammany rival who used appointments to build his own factional power within the Democratic-Republican Party, outside Tammany influence.

In 1804, while still vice-president, Burr shot and killed Hamilton in a duel across the Hudson River from Manhattan. His second and third at the duel were both Tammany leaders. Burr was charged but never tried for murder; yet because of his close association with Tammany and the ignominy brought on by the episode, Tammany's political legitimacy collapsed.[11] Tammany's response to this crisis had long-term implications. It adopted a new constitution codifying what Gustavus Myers, the leading historian of nineteenth-century Tammany, described as its 'dual power'. It split in two. One face, a formal, chartered benevolent organization with a political orientation—the General Committee of the Democratic-Republican Party—came to be known as Tammany Hall. This stood notionally separate from the Tammany Society proper, a mass-membership social network. However, hidden from the outside, the strategic leadership of the Society and Hall were fused. As Myers explains, 'the Sachems knew that to continue appearing as a political club' without bringing greater transparency to their internal decision-making processes 'would be most impolitic', given the opprobrium around the hidden links between Burr and Tammany.[12] But instead of giving up their political aspirations, they hid them. Because of their control of votes, money and muscle through the mass membership of the Tammany Society, the most influential sachems within the Society controlled decisions by Tammany Hall's leadership group. These powerful figures came to be known as 'Bosses', a hidden

Society power behind the Tammany Hall throne. When Tammany Hall won electoral office, the Boss became the prime actor in the 'invisible government' with which Tammany became synonymous.[13]

Gangs of New York

Manhattan in the early nineteenth century was much like many rapidly urbanizing, fragile cities in the contemporary developing world. Formal governmental capacity was limited but in high demand, so those who could control it, or develop alternatives, stood to profit hugely. There was no municipal sewerage system. Cholera and yellow fever were recurring menaces. Fire safety in a largely wooden city depended on local volunteer fire crews. Credit was available through a small number of banks controlled by different social cliques tied to political parties—or otherwise through informal loan-sharks. The police force was routinely turned upside down when a new political faction came into office, usually working more to manage than to eradicate crime. The lines between faction, party and state were often blurred. For a period, a Federal District Court even operated out of the Tammany Hall building, paying rent to the political organization.[14] Petty corruption and graft in government institutions led to repeated scandals and electoral convulsions, with Tammany and anti-Tammany Democratic-Republicans alternating in office.[15]

As Manhattan's immigrant population grew in the 1820s, Tammany's electoral strategy shifted away from anti-immigrant nativism to support for new arrivals. Struggles between Democratic-Republican factions supporting John Quincy Adams (a native-born American) and Andrew Jackson (the son of Scots-Irish immigrants) were one spur, and electoral arithmetic the other.[16] Through the 1830s and 1840s Tammany influence grew steadily in Irish immigrant communities as it focused on providing patronage (especially in the form of livelihoods) and access to services. The terrible 'Potato Famine' in Ireland between 1845 and 1852 accelerated Irish emigration to the United States. By 1850, a quarter of New York City's population had been born in Ireland, much of that number packed in together on the Lower East Side of Manhattan. Most of these were unskilled farm labourers, many not speaking English. They were in need of assistance and critical of the *laissez-faire* economic policies with which the British government had responded to the Irish famine.[17]

Tammany tapped into the collective memory of the famine and positioned itself as the protector of the oppressed Irishman against the inhumanity of the (Anglo-dominated) market, advocating the use of governmental power to correct market predation.[18] Anxiety about the basic necessities of life—food, shelter, a steady income, dignity—made the new immigrant communities susceptible to the dull security offered by Tammany welfare. Even if private enterprise offered larger rewards in theory, it was deeply risky in practice. Lifelong loyalty to Tammany seemed a small price to pay for the security of a low-paid public sector job—with the police or a fire company or as a school teacher or contractor for the municipality.[19]

The resulting 'machine' politics provided cover for corruption and abuses of power. The memory of famine cast financial irregularities during public service as relatively unimportant, forgivable transgressions. Powerlessness and hunger were the greater enemies. 'I will vote for the devil incarnate if nominated by Tammany Hall,' said Irish Tammany leader John Cochrane in the 1850s.[20] This logic could produce strange outcomes. Tammany politicians were routinely bribed by private banks and insurance companies to weaken financial regulation, through secret gifts of bank stock, helping to contribute to the frequent bank collapses that undermined the savings of the working class that had elected the Tammany politicians in the first place. Despite the working poor's vulnerability to New York's boom and bust cycles, Tammany even lent President Jackson crucial political muscle in New York as he fought successfully to shut down the Second Bank of the United States in the 1830s (the precursor to the Federal Reserve system), returning control of money supply to the market. In turn Jackson supported the election of a Tammany grand sachem, Martin van Buren, as first vice-president, then president of the United States.[21]

The focus on the immigrant vote in the drive for political power also had significant unexpected influence on internal Tammany organization and strategy. It shifted power into the hands of violent entrepreneurs who could control electoral activity at the local level—the gangs of New York. These were drawn from the ranks of petty criminals and volunteer fire engine companies. Lower Manhattan then was somewhat like Port-au-Prince in Haiti or Kingston, Jamaica, or Nairobi or Karachi today. The weakness of law enforcement left space for violent entrepreneurs to emerge as providers of protection and regulators of both vice and voting markets. On election day gangs smashed, stole or stuffed ballot boxes, intimidated voters into supporting their political patrons and ensured that polling officials permitted some voters to 'repeat'.[22]

The saloon became the locus of power in lower Manhattan.[23] This was where gang leaders and Tammany politicians socialized and strategized, and where constituents would gather to seek informal welfare.[24] Soon, the ranks of Tammany leadership were filling with men who had been prize-fighters, gang leaders and saloon keepers, like John Morrissey. After emigrating from Tipperary at the age of two in 1833, Morrissey grew up as a petty criminal and loan collector for Irish gang leaders on the Lower East Side, then moved on to gambling and prize-fighting. In 1853 he acquired instant fame by beating the American heavyweight champion, Yankee Sullivan, in an illegal fight. The next year Tammany hired him to prevent another gang, the Bowery Boys, from seizing ballot boxes and rigging elections. In return, Morrissey's gang, the Dead Rabbits—later featured in Martin Scorsese's *Gangs of New York*—were permitted to operate illegal gambling facilities under police protection. One affray between the Rabbits and Bowery Boys killed ten people. By 1859 Morrissey had established illegal casinos and a (legal) race course in Saratoga Springs, New York, not far from the state capital Albany, serving the bored legislators stuck far upstate away from New York's bright lights. In 1866, with Tammany support, he was elected to Federal Congress, and later to the New York State Senate.[25]

The ghost in the machine

By the 1850s Tammany was functioning as a broker between formal political parties and a hard-to-reach immigrant population, providing one with votes and the other with access to governmental services and protection. Tammany's transactional approach, exchanging votes for patronage, remained essentially intact for the next eighty years. We know a great deal about it due to the candid revelations of Tammany leaders such as George Washington Plunkitt and close study by the reform-minded political scientist Joseph McGoldrick.[26]

Tammany's success depended on dedicated retail politics—getting to know, and being seen to serve, voters at the local level. The Tammany social (Society) and political (Hall) organizations operated in tandem at the local level, unified in the personage of the district or ward 'heeler'—so named because he was always out beating a path to constituents. Plunkitt—one such heeler—recorded a typical day: it involved assisting the victims of a house fire; securing the release of six drunks by speaking to a judge; paying the rent of a poor family to prevent their eviction and giving them money for food; securing jobs for four people; attending the funerals of two constituents (one Italian, one Jewish), a Bar Mitzvah and a wedding.[27] Such dedicated retail attention provided Tammany a steady flow of political capital.

The key to that capital was the ability to provide social support, which often required influence in governmental institutions. Over time, Tammany extended its networks of influence throughout the city bureaucracy. As McGoldrick explained, the heeler became the 'anode and cathode' of Tammany power, the conveyor of money and votes into the machine, and the conduit for its governmental power 'into the remotest corner of the city'. He was 'the chief point of contact … with the government itself', the arranger of licences, excuses from jury duty, transfers, reinstatements, promotions, sewer connections, passports, exemptions from tax.[28] Tammany control of elected offices gave heelers influence over civil service hiring and firing, and allowed them to turn some departments into what McGoldrick would call a 'soviet of political job-holders'.[29] Elective offices—which in New York included the district attorney (prosecutor) and judicial roles—were at times 'practically put up at auction'. Tammany membership or support became a necessary condition for access to many of these jobs, and once appointed, Tammany demanded financial tribute, often through ruses such as the purchase of tickets to social events or 'insurance'.[30] In fact, this is the source of the term 'racketeering': Tammany's practice of using gangs to force constituents to buy tickets to raucous parties ('rackets') at Tammany Hall.[31]

Control of judicial and policing power proved particularly valuable. By the early 1900s, each administrative district in New York had an elected civil court judge and a criminal magistrate appointed by the mayor. Typically, however, Tammany controlled both processes, and it was the Tammany district leader who presented the judge with his gavel, which as McGoldrick noted in 1929, 'unconsciously, reveals the true source of the new jurist's honor'.[32] Control of judicial power encouraged closer relations between Tammany actors and criminal entrepreneurs. In return for protecting criminal actors from the law, Tammany taxed them.[33] In 1894 State Senator Clarence Lexow revealed that the city's gambling-houses paid Tammany-appointed police $300 per month, with brothels paying even more. As late as 1932, only around 4 per cent of those being arraigned for illegal book-making were brought to trial.[34] The remainder paid bribes to escape prosecution. Gambling operators became crucial sources of political finance, operatives and candidates. Mark Haller, a Temple University historian, later told Congress that '[b]y the early 20th century, it would not be possible to understand the structure of local politics without a knowledge of the structure of gambling syndicates'.[35]

As the collector of these rents from criminal markets, the Tammany district leader united the acceptable political face of the organization with its hidden criminal methods. He paid part of the assessed funds in tribute to the political organization, used part for local activities—and was free to pocket the balance. Smart heelers spent a healthy amount on local strategic communications. 'A certain amount of benevolent work is necessary, particularly in the Winter,' noted McGoldrick.

> In Summer, there are children's picnics. A wealthy West Side leader main-tains a camp where all the poor children of the district are sent for two weeks. At all seasons of the year there are tickets to buy, flowers to send and dinners to attend. One leader estimates that he spends $1,500 a year on tickets, memberships and donations.[36]

Yet '[g]reat and constant as a leader's expenditures are, there is gen-erally a bountiful surplus. And this is his own.' Much of this was laun-dered through legitimate business—real estate, warehousing, on the docks, in the law—which benefited, of course, from corrupted gov-ernmental discretion. As it is in many contemporary cities such as Dakar, Nairobi or Macau that boom with laundered proceeds of crime, real estate speculation was particularly common: 'Their knowledge of prospective improvements and their contact with assessing and zoning authorities give them obvious advantages over other speculators.'[37]

Tammany rule had turned New York municipal government into a rackets machine. Tammany had 'proved itself the cleverest organization at exploiting the spoils of power in a city where everything was for sale'.[38] 'Tammany is for the spoils system,' proclaimed Plunkitt straightforwardly and publicly. Without this system, its leaders argued, normal citizens would have no incentive to invest time and energy in politics, and the republican system would collapse as lobbyists and corporate interests took over.[39]

Unlike the contemporaneous Sicilian mafia considered in the next chapter, however, Tammany had not developed a distinct alternative governmentality standing outside the state. Tammany's collective strategy was focused on achieving political power for its own end, rather than as a means to maximizing criminal rents. But it was susceptible to manipulation by Tammany members with more strategic criminal designs. Until the Draft Riots of 1863, no such clique had assumed leadership of the organization. Enter Boss Tweed.

Boss Tweed: Lord of the Rings

A quest for influence

Bill Tweed does not appear to have pursued power within Tammany with a vision of turning it into a looting machine. Instead, he appears to have arrived gropingly at the system for which he became famous, in which a gluttonous, hidden 'Ring' used New York's municipal apparatus to line its own bellies and pockets.

Tweed was a man of famous appetites. 'He seems always to have wanted more,' notes Pete Hamill. 'More food. More money. More power.'[40] At the height of his power Tweed was grand sachem of Tammany, the third-largest landowner in New York, director of the Erie Railroad, of two New York City railroad companies, two major banks and one insurance company, controller of a printing company with a monopoly on New York city government printing, controller of the New York Gas Light Company and proprietor of the Metropolitan Hotel.

Tweed's method was not, however, to enlarge himself by belittling others or creating a culture of fear. He was a gregarious leader who by his own characterization sought to enlarge his 'social influence among men'. He was a communicator who used corruption to make others around him complicit, not a coercive dictator. His court was held at Delmonico's in lower Manhattan, where he gorged his huge 300-pound frame on duck, oysters and tenderloin while surrounded by petitioners and sycophants. From as early as 1857 he was involved in selling his vote in the city and state institutions on which he sat, and 'collected heavy tribute' for the passage of legislation. At the time, this was common. Lobbyists described specific prices for different actions: $5,000 per member for a committee to issue a favourable report on a draft bill; and up to $25,000 more for a supporting vote.[41]

From 1859 Tweed began to organize. He began to work with a small 'ring' of other officials—from both Tammany and the Republican Party—in the New York Board of Supervisors (a financial oversight body) to rig the selection of inspectors of elections, to overbill the city by 15 per cent on municipal contracts (pocketing the profits) and to extract tribute from heads of department who desired political support. By the early 1860s, the members of a 'lunch club'—Tweed; the Irish Tammany strategist Peter Sweeny; the mayor, Andrew Oakey Hall; and later the city comptroller, Richard Connolly—emerged as the key players in this 'Supervisors' Ring'. By 1861 Tweed was chair of Tammany Hall's General Committee, and later was also elected grand sachem of the Tammany Society, fusing control of Tammany's social and political arms.[42] After his heroics in the Draft Riot, his star rose further. Tweed's ability to buy peace in the Union's most powerful city, together with the service of many Tammany men in the Union army (which many other Democrats had avoided), left Tammany in a powerful position in the Democratic Party after the war ended. By 1867 the Supervisors' Ring had raised the informal 'tax' rate on municipal contracts to 35 per cent, 60 per cent of which went to Tweed.[43]

By Tweed's own account, through the 1860s the Supervisors' Ring steadily evolved from a kick-back scheme into something much more ambitious, a broader criminal scheme that reached into all aspects of the city's governmental apparatus—executive, legislative and judicial, and even electoral—facilitating the systematic 'sacking' of the city's treasuries.[44] Tweed's control over Tammany appointments to the executive was almost absolute, giving him unrivalled influence.[45] He used it to champion a massive fiscal expansion. Huge new public works were begun: the chartering of the Metropolitan Museum of Art and the New York Stock Exchange, the extension of Lexington Avenue and the widening of Broadway, the commissioning of a tax-exempt elevated railway. The Brooklyn Bridge was started. City spending on orphanages and almshouses grew rapidly. All of this was farmed out to private contractors who created jobs for Tammany's electoral base and, in turn, provided kickbacks to Tweed and his ring in the form of stock, dividends and direct commissions.[46] In one notorious case, the city was found to have paid Tammany Hall for the use of the top floor of its own headquarters as an armoury. Not only was there no arsenal there, but the rent paid was also ten times the market rate.[47] Tweed and his cronies routinely bought up land marked for development, selling it to the city or at a huge premium in the market after the city paid for connection to sewerage, gas or roads. Insider trading allowed the extraction of massive rents.[48]

Many of these schemes depended not only on Tweed's control of executive power, but also his placing of allies in key judicial positions. In the late 1860s, while serving as a state senator, Tweed formed an alliance with two Wall Street buccaneers, James Fisk and Jay Gould. Gould later died as the ninth-richest American of all time. At Tweed's instigation, two key Tammany-backed senior judges, Barnard and Cardozo (father of the later Supreme Court justice), granted a series of orders that, together with legislative manoeuvres led by Tweed in Albany, wrested control of the Erie Railroad from Cornelius Vanderbilt and handed it to Fisk and Gould. Tweed was rewarded with a directorship and stock providing income of around $2.5 million a year (around $40 million today). Through similar schemes he gained interests in gas companies, real estate, iron mines and other schemes. By 1869 he was reputed to be worth $12 million ($210 million today).[49]

Despite its lock on New York City government, Tammany frequently did not control the New York State legislature in Albany because it was dominated by rural seats over which it (and the Democrats) had little control. Once again, however, Tweed successfully organized the fragmented market. He relied heavily on corruption to achieve legislative results, and his steady supply of largesse in Albany transformed legislators' behaviour. A bipartisan vote-sellers' cartel emerged, called the 'Black Horse Cavalry', incorporating thirty legislators who would secretly trade their votes as a (controlling) bloc, for the right price.[50] Its activities were common knowledge in Albany, but Tweed paid the newspapers to keep quiet.[51] Over time, others—especially corporations—got in on the act, steadily driving up legislators' prices.

Albany was becoming a true political marketplace, with Tweed as one of the most regular purchasers of legislative outcomes. But Tweed maintained an advantage over others competing for this governmental influence—both corporations and political rivals. He could offer legislators something these strategic competitors could not: sinecures for their constituents on a city payroll, providing untold electoral support.[52] (This practice, too, persists today in many weakly governed, fragile cities, for example in Haiti.)[53] Tweed and his inner circle were prepared to sacrifice seats in the state legislature in order to keep looting New York City. At the same time, as the scheme grew, it became both more normalized and, potentially, more vulnerable, resting on the complicity of an ever-expanding circle of politicians, judges, civil servants—and, crucially, the media.[54]

Tweed was careful to take care of his electoral base, boasting to a reporter that 'what I don't know' about how to buy 'political capital … isn't worth knowing'.[55] His looted wealth underwrote ostentatious benevolence. In 1869 he welcomed 260 pauper boys to his Connecticut estate. In the winter of 1870–71 he distributed $1,000 to each Tammany alderman to buy coal for the poor, eliciting comparisons with Robin Hood.[56] He organized Tammany judges to rubber-stamp the (probably improper) naturalization of hundreds of thousands of immigrants. Tammany-affiliated city employees filed the paperwork (printed on contract by Tweed's New-York Printing Company), provided witnesses and stumped up application fees. In 1868 alone, 41,112 new citizens were created this way; almost one-third the number of people who voted in that year's election.[57] Tammany-naturalized voters made loyal supporters: 'Tammany took the immigrant in charge, cared for him, made him feel that he was a human being with distinct political rights, and converted him into a citizen,' explained Myers.[58]

Tweed took other steps, too, to ease Tammany's way at the polls. At his instigation, restrictions on voter registration were weakened and election dates were consolidated, facilitating electoral fraud.[59] Speaking under oath near the end of his life, Tweed explained that '[t]hese elections really were no elections at all'. 'The ballots were made to bring about any result that was determined upon beforehand,' it was put to him. Yes, he replied. 'The ballots made no result; the counters made the result.' Tweed had found a way, he perhaps thought, to entrench his *de facto* political power. The next logical step would be to entrench it as a matter of law.[60]

Monarch of Manhattan

Around 1868 Tweed's strategic objectives seem to have enlarged, and a clique with a clear criminal strategy crystallized within the Tammany leadership. Tweed's power within Tammany and New York politics was already immense. He was chairman of the General Committee (the political arm) and grand sachem of the Society (the membership organization). His allies John Hoffman and Oakey Hall were the elected governor and mayor, respectively. He oversaw the construction of a new, opulent Tammany Hall building on 14th Street, which hosted the 1868 National Convention of the Democratic Party.

The convention seems to have given him a dangerous taste for national politics. He rented New York's Metropolitan Hotel, installing his son as manager. 'My design was to make it the national democratic headquarters,' he later explained, with 'all the appurtenances of a splendid political club there. It would then have been profitable as a lease and an auxiliary to power.'[61] He began an attack on August Belmont, long-time chairman of the Democratic National Committee (and namesake of the Belmont Stakes, the third leg of the famous Triple Crown horse racing series). Through the autumn of 1869 Tweed engineered denunciations by leading Tammany Democrats of Belmont's handling of the 1868 presidential election (which the Democrats had lost). But he had overreached. Belmont was a German immigrant, the North American agent of the Rothschild bank, and a founding member of the American Jockey Club. He called on his significant German immigrant backing across the mid-West, and his connections to rich Democrats around the country, using both to shore up support with Democratic leaders nationwide. Seeing that his campaign was not gaining traction, Tweed abandoned it, forced to recognize that his power was limited to New York.[62]

If it could not be broader, it must be deeper. Tweed turned his sights on deepening and entrenching his power in New York. He had built a strong command and control system inside Tammany: by enlarging the General Committee from twenty-one to 150 members he had made it too large to be operational, opening the door for the informal centralization of power in a core group—himself, Hall, city comptroller Richard Connolly and Tammany strategist Peter Sweeny. The enlarged membership of the Committee extended this group's patronage within the organization, creating an informal network that controlled local wards.[63] Next, he set about leveraging his position as a state senator in Albany.[64] In his first year as senator, he engineered the appointment of an ally as assembly speaker, giving him enlarged influence.[65] Using this influence, Tweed oversaw the adoption of a new state law that gave the New York City comptroller—Tweed's ally, Richard Connolly—the power to adjust and pay existing claims against the city. This looked like a straightforward piece of good civic housekeeping. But Tweed, Connolly and the contractors who had been working with them in the Supervisors' Ring repeated that earlier fraud, using the new, and supposedly temporary, Board of Audit to mark up past claims, with mark-ups kicked back to this new, smaller 'Tweed Ring' within the Board—Tweed, Hall, Connolly and Sweeny.[66]

Given how many claims were outstanding against the city, this opened the floodgates to a river of cash for Tweed and his allies. But the power of this core group of four, replacing the broader participation in the Supervisors' Ring, was causing tension within Tammany. In the winter of 1870 a group of younger Tammany members who had been cut out of the scheme, led by Jimmy O'Brien, the New York sheriff and a Tweed protégé, formed a new faction, 'Young Democracy'. With the Democrats for once controlling both legislative houses in Albany, Young Democracy introduced bills to repatriate powers from Albany to New York and reorganize the city's administration. Ostensibly, this was a response to a prior Republican programme that had given Albany control of New York's police force, school board, fire department and docks. But Tweed recognized the reform effort as a threat to his own control over New York's municipal apparatus, and responded with a stunning counterattack—a counter-proposal for constitutional reform that looked like a democracy, but in fact entrenched the hidden power of Tweed's Ring.

Sweeny drafted an alternative City Charter. Tweed raised funds from 'friends'—the contractors who had benefited from the Ring's kickback schemes, and others complicit in his earlier fraud schemes, such as Fisk and Gould. Using the resulting war chest, Tweed directed a campaign of bipartisan bribery costing almost $1 million (today around $20 million) to generate support for his proposals within the legislature. With Tweed wielding his position as chairman of the New York State Senate's Committee on Municipal Affairs, the Charter was approved almost unanimously.[67]

One legal scholar of the time called the new Charter 'an almost perfect document ... under which to administer the affairs of a municipality'. The only danger, he noted presciently, would be in the event that a 'band of thieves would place at each checking point one of the members of their own clique'.[68] Of course that was exactly the plan. The Charter institutionalized a new Board of Apportionment, which would control all city spending and even judicial appointments. It consisted of the mayor, the comptroller and the commissioner of public works—appointed by the mayor and unsackable for six to eight years. Tweed's ally Mayor Hall knew exactly who should be the commissioner, and appointed him promptly: Bill Tweed. As icing on the cake, the Charter package abolished the Board of Supervisors on which many of the Young Democracy rebels had depended. Tweed's victory was complete.[69]

Samuel Tilden, a lawyer who had long been a non-Tammany Democratic rival to Tweed, quickly identified the dangers of the new constitutional system. Under the Charter, he argued, 'you have a Mayor without any executive power', since it had been delegated to departmental commissioners; 'you have a legislature without legislative power; you have elections without any power in the people to affect the Government for the period during which these officers are appointed'.[70] Instead, power was vested opaquely in any clique that controlled the key appointments. But Tilden failed to press his case with the public, and the Charter went into effect. Tweed's kickback scheme was now transformed from a temporary arrangement for dealing with a set of old bills to a permanent constitutional arrangement. He had succeeded in incorporating the city's governmental apparatus into his criminal scheme. New York City's government had become a joint venture between actors with political, criminal and commercial strategies, operating through Tammany Hall.

Under cover of this new arrangement, the Ring members agreed to mark up new bills against the city by 50 per cent. Ten per cent would go to each of the four principals (Tweed, Hall, Connolly, Sweeny), 5 per cent to the two corrupt city clerks who actually administered the contracts and 5 per cent into a strategic corruption reserve earmarked for 'purchasing legislation'. But within six months, the pretence of equality within the Ring was dropped. Connolly and Tweed secretly negotiated a new split at Hall and Sweeny's expense. The markup on bills was raised to a staggering 65 per cent, with Tweed taking 25 per cent and Connolly 20 per cent. Sweeny kept 10 per cent, but Mayor Hall was forced to accept just 5 per cent. The two clerks seem to have been cut out of the picture, but the 5 per cent reserve for strategic corruption was maintained.[71]

This grand criminal scheme well hidden, Tweed's star continued to rise. In 1872, Republican President Grant ordered the USS *Guerrière* and USS *Narragansett* to drop anchor off Manhattan and the Eighth US Infantry to occupy the city's forts, as a deterrent to Tammany-led violence on election day. If the Republicans thought this sabre-rattling would change the election result, they badly misunderstood the source of Tammany's electoral support. Street muscle and coercion had its place, but Tammany's patronage system was also central to its popularity. At a rally at Tammany Hall, Tweed demanded a peaceful campaign, and on election day Tammany's stars Hoffman and Oakey Hall were re-elected in landslides. Senior Democrats came out in favour of Hoffman standing for president in 1872, and for Tweed moving to the US Senate.[72]

Yet around this time Tweed's aura of power also began to be mocked by the cartoons of Thomas Nast, creator of the famous images of the Democrat donkey, Republican elephant and our modern Santa Claus. Nast's cartoons in *Harper's Weekly* were becoming national talking-points, demonstrating the power of mass-produced imagery to convey political ideas to a largely illiterate (but often voting) population.[73] In October 1870 he portrayed Tweed as a shadowy courtier lurking behind Governor John Hoffman, wielding a sword of 'power', with cartoon captions reading 'The Tammany Ring-dom' and 'He [Hoffman]

Cannot Call His Soul His Own.' By January 1871, Tweed's power was even more overt in Nast's satirical imagery and others copying it: *The Evening Telegram* dubbed him the 'Monarch of Manhattan'. In April, taking his cues from the *Telegram*, Nast made him 'Emperor Tweed', a Napoleonic figure leading his troops through bursts of opposition fire.[74] All of this drove home the point: Tweed's power was becoming increasingly vast and unassailable.

Downfall

Yet within six months, the Ring had collapsed. Within two years, its members were under criminal indictment, or had fled New York. Tweed ended up spending much of the 1870s in gaol or on the run, dying in Ludlow Street Jail in 1878. What went wrong?

Tammany's political support amongst the lower classes rested on visible influence. But this led to recklessness. Tweed increasingly signalled his power and influence by flaunting his wealth: in his two steam-powered yachts, his Fifth Avenue mansion, in the immense 10.5-carat diamond he wore in his shirtfront, worth around $300,000 in today's terms.[75] Later, Tweed would recognize that in his pursuit of political power he had broken the cardinal rule of criminal strategy—remain hidden. His visibility made him a target. Asked what he thought his greatest mistake had been, Tweed replied:

> In pressing forward for leadership. I was always ambitious to be influential and to control... Liking busy occupation and social influence among men, I think I pressed on too confidently. I oughtn't to have tried to be the leader.[76]

'I should have remained hidden,' he was saying. His arrogant displays of wealth produced resentment and, from the middle of 1870, press criticism. Stoked by a campaign in the Republican-leaning *New York Times*, a group of civic leaders began to question the source of Tweed's wealth. As a counter, in early 1871 the Ring opened the comptroller's books to a group of six eminent citizens, including the millionaire J.J. Astor—who promptly gave the accounts a clean bill of health. It was later alleged that this pass was secured by threat of an inordinate rise in property taxes; the auditors had spent only six hours with the accounts supplied by Connolly.[77] But for the most part the city's business leaders went along to get along. In June 1871 they sent copious tribute to Tweed in the form of wedding gifts to his daughter: forty complete suites of household silver and fifteen diamond sets, one of which was worth $45,000.[78]

Tweed recognized that press complicity required assiduous courtship. Several newspapers in New York City were awarded over-priced advertising contracts. One Albany paper was awarded a legislative appropriation twenty times what it had previously been paid in order to secure a favourable editorial line. Another paper, associated with the Republicans, would for $5,000 allow Tweed to personally vet and edit critical articles before they were published. Reporters received $200 'Christmas presents', and stars received $2,500 annual retainers. Between 1869 and 1871, city spending on the press rose several hundred per cent to $2.7 million.[79]

In the end, however, even this was not enough. The turning point came on 12 July 1871, exactly eight years after the Draft Riots that had helped make Tweed's name. In July 1870, Orange Day violence between rival Orangemen and Catholic marchers led to five deaths. Many of the city's Protestant newspapers blamed Tammany and Irish Catholics for the violence, even pointing the finger at Tweed (despite his Protestant heritage).[80] As the 1871 marches approached, everyone expected a repeat of the violence—or worse. Between March and May, press accounts of the oppression of the Paris Commune heightened class consciousness and stoked an incipient security dilemma between Anglo-Protestants and Irish Catholics.[81] Orangemen factions circulated a broadside bellowing that the 'claims of Roman Catholicism' to ban the Orange Day marches 'are incompatible with civil and religious liberty', and many of the city's Protestant newspapers called for the forceful suppression of Catholic opposition to Orange Day parades. The Catholics, in turn, broadcast their willingness to fight to defend 'American freedom of expression' and, perhaps not entirely consistently, to suppress the 'English' Orangemen's marches.[82]

Stuck on the horns of this sectarian dilemma, in the early days of July 1871, Tweed, Hall and Connolly consulted. At Mayor Hall's direction the city's police commissioner Kelso revoked the permit of the Orangemen planning to march down the West Side from Protestant neighbourhoods into the Irish Catholic-majority Hell's Kitchen and Greenwich Village.

On 10 July Kelso went further, authorizing his officers to use force to prevent public processions on 12 July. There was an instant backlash in the Anglo-Protestant media. *The New York Times* complained that the city 'is absolutely in the hands of Irish Catholics' and the *New-York Tribune* contended that Kelso, the mayor and Tammany Hall had surrendered to 'the mob'.[83] This posed a major political conundrum for John Hoffman, the Tammany man who, with Tweed's support, had ascended to the state governor's office. If he failed to intervene, he risked being painted as anti-Protestant—a death knell to his presidential ambitions. So in the early hours of 12 July, breaking with his Tammany patrons, he issued a contrary order, permitting the march under the protection of the state militia—not controlled by Tammany.[84]

The next day, 200 marchers assembled at the Orange Lodge headquarters on the West Side at Eighth Avenue and 29th Street, protected by 500 state militiamen and police. As the march proceeded south it was showered with curses, brickbats, shoes, bottles and crockery. Soon this turned to sporadic pistol shots from shops and rooftops lining the route. At 25th Street a dense crowd blocked the route south. Mounted militiamen charged, clearing a path. At 23rd Street, where the route turned east, marchers came under more intense attack. State militiamen fired repeatedly without warning into the surrounding crowds and buildings, and mounted police charged, cracking skulls. When the smoke cleared, at least sixty-two civilians lay dead and a hundred wounded. Three militiamen and two police officers were also killed. Somehow the march continued several miles through mid-Manhattan and Greenwich Village to Cooper Union without further major incident.[85]

But the damage was done. Both Democratic- and Republican-leaning newspapers placed the blame squarely at the feet of the city's authorities. 'The blood of the innocent slaughtered yesterday rests upon the head of the men who ... not only tolerated but encouraged the murderous preparations of the aggressors,' thundered *The New York Times*, calling for 'a bitter reckoning' with Tammany Hall. '[T]he days of the Tammany gang are numbered,' it crowed. The *New-York Tribune* called the event 'the Tammany riot' and asserted that violence would continue as long as Tammany 'depends for its existence upon the votes of the ignorant and vicious'. Tweed tried to brush the events off, seeking to maintain power while avoiding responsibility. 'It was an unfortunate business from beginning to end,' he told one reporter, 'one of those remarkable fiascos for which it was impossible to tell who was to blame'.[86] But he was wounded. The credibility he had won eight years earlier as broker between the street and the state was in tatters.

Press attacks mounted. Nast's cartoons poured out, with 'every stroke of his pencil cut[ting] like a scimitar'.[87] In late July, *The New York Times* unleashed a new weapon: detailed figures from Connolly's own secret accounts, provided to the paper by Tweed's Young Democracy enemy, Jimmy O'Brien.[88] On Saturday 22 July 1871, under the first banner headline in its history, the *Times* began publishing detailed accounts of the Tweed Ring's corruption. It led with a story detailing work for 'repairs' and the supply of furniture to the lavish Italianate courthouse (just behind City Hall in downtown Manhattan, still known as the 'Tweed Courthouse') costing more than $5.6 million (around $106 million today), spent in just two months. One plasterer received $133,187 for two days' work. The courthouse had cost three to four times the expected amount—and twice the cost of purchasing the whole territory of Alaska in 1867. The amount paid for chairs would have purchased enough of them at market rates to stretch seventeen miles, claimed the newspaper. The carpet bill could have covered a route stretching half way to Albany. For cabinetry, 300 homes could have been furnished. A week of similar revelations ensued, with the *Times* detailing the sums involved and the circuitous financial paths which always, somehow, ended at the bank accounts of three contractors known as good friends of Tammany. In culmination, on Saturday 29 July, the *Times* published a special supplement entitled 'How New York is Governed: Frauds of the Tammany Democrats', with a full set of the 'secret accounts'. The initial print run of 220,000—the *Times'* largest to date—sold out in hours. More than 500,000 copies were ultimately sold, including a special German-language edition.[89]

It was not only Tweed's reputation that was gravely imperilled: it was also the city's creditworthiness. Tammany's municipal spending spree of the 1860s had been debt-financed. New York's debt rose from $36 million in 1869 to $97 million by the summer of 1871.[90] Most of this was in the form of municipal bonds issued by Connolly and sold to European investors. New York debt had looked like a safe investment, compared to volatile alternatives such as railroad stocks. Now these bonds looked suddenly risky, given the scale of the frauds that appeared to have been perpetrated. A new city bond issue failed to receive a single bid. The Berlin Stock Exchange banned New York city and county bonds from its trading list. The spectre of financial panic loomed. If the city could not raise funds by the end of October, it would default on an interest payment, ruining the city's creditworthiness—and likely that of all the banks in the city, and the financiers in Europe who were heavily exposed to its bonds. Given how significant Wall Street was for the American and European economies, this represented a major threat to international financial stability. Suddenly, Tweed's continuing power was a serious international problem. As Ackerman put it, '[p]olitics was one thing, but trifling with the flow of international money could not be tolerated'. The financial houses made it clear that New York government's leadership would have to change, and a group of leading New York businessmen formed a Committee of Seventy to achieve just that, looking to break Tweed's lock on the city's governing institutions.[91]

Tweed and his Ring looked for a way out. Multi-million dollar offers were secretly made to buy both the *Times'* and Nast's silence. Neither was swayed. Attacking Tweed was suddenly good business: *Harper's Weekly's* circulation had tripled since Nast's pictorial attacks began, while the *Times'* had jumped by 40 per cent.[92] Tweed went to ground at his country estate in Connecticut and began quietly transferring his extensive real estate holdings into the names of family members. Hall and Connolly, tied by their jobs to New York and facing daily press attacks, were forced to react. They offered to open the city's books, but with the Astor review of the previous year now viewed as a whitewash, no one would bite. Hall privately threatened to close down the *Times*— but that just led the paper to run more stories of fraud.[93]

As the establishment returned from its summer vacations an 'insurrection of capitalists' kicked into gear—effectively, a financial boycott. Reformers filed a lawsuit seeking to enjoin Connolly from spending any city money. To much astonishment, it was granted—by a Supreme Court judge, George Barnard, who owed his entire career to that point to Tweed's patronage. This was a sign of Tweed's vulnerability. 'We owe to Barnard all our troubles,' Tweed would later reminisce. The freeze on city spending drew workers into the streets, protesting, further undermining Tweed's credibility as a peace-broker. Tweed began to show the strain, threatening to kill George Jones, the *Times* editor.[94]

Sweeny and Hall pushed Connolly to resign as comptroller. Fearing he would be scapegoated, Connolly defected. Working with Samuel Tilden, he agreed to the appointment of an outside deputy who would have real spending power, while he stayed in place so that—under Tweed's own Charter—Mayor Hall could not replace him. Wall Street quickly stumped up $500,000 in an unsecured loan to allow the new deputy comptroller, Andrew Green, a close Tilden ally, to keep the city solvent and keep city workers off the streets. In return, Green imposed a range of governance controls: purging phantom workers from pay-rolls, barring political campaign finance collections within civil service ranks, and forbidding kickbacks. (All would be circumvented and rolled back by Tammany in the years ahead.)

With this manoeuvre, Samuel Tilden, a brilliant but introverted and stiff corporate lawyer, emerged as Tweed's chief rival within New York Democratic politics. Working with allies in the business community, Tilden mounted a forensically detailed audit into the Ring's financial dealings, using the results to demonstrate unequivocally Tweed's per-sonal receipt of over $1 million looted from the city Treasury. Building on that success, Tilden led a group of anti-Tammany Democrats to an almost clean sweep at municipal and state elections in early November 1871. Tweed himself was not so easy to dislodge. In late September 20,000 people gathered to support him at a rally at East Broadway and Canal Street, his home neighbourhood. Despite being arrested a week before election day, Tweed won re-election as a state legislator.[95]

It was a hollow victory: every other Tammany candidate was defeated. Tweed was now alone, surrounded by enemies such as Jimmy O'Brien, also elected to the State Senate. Tweed paid $22,359 from his own pocket to cover unpaid salaries of municipal workers, but this only attracted public opprobrium for his looseness with what appeared to be stolen public funds. He started burning his personal records. The main contractors in the kickback scheme fled. Sweeny ran to Paris. Connolly fled to Europe and Egypt, never to return to America. By the end of 1871, Tweed had been forced out as Tammany grand sachem and expelled from the Society. In 1873 he was found guilty of corruption. In 1875 he hatched a complex plot costing $60,000, escaped prison in

New York and fled to Cuba and Spain, but was extradited back to New York. He died in the Ludlow Street Jail in 1878, at just fifty-five.[96]

Tweed's criminal strategy had been highly effective while he controlled Tammany's political power and through it New York's governmental institutions, spreading benefits widely enough to buy complicity and silence. One of those benefits was that Tweed seemed, through Tammany, to be able to maintain public order on Manhattan. Once that capability came into question in the Orange Day riots of July 1871, the city's civic leaders and press proved only too willing to question Tweed's ostentatious displays of wealth, and the long-term implications of debt-funded municipal spending. Tweed's criminal power thus rested ultimately not only on corruption, but on the control of coercion and effective strategic communications that generated complicity in his criminal schemes. Once he lost control of coercion, his legitimacy proved vulnerable to the new power of the visual mass media developed through Nast's cartoons, and his downfall followed.

Honest graft

Tammany survived—and learned—from Tweed's downfall. One lesson was not to allow patronage and corruption—the means to power—to be seen to substitute for political ends. But in the subsequent decades, this strategic lesson was interpreted in two quite different ways by different factions within Tammany.

Tweed's successor as the leader of Tammany was 'Honest' John Kelly, a former congressman and alderman who had amassed a fortune as a Tammany city sheriff collecting taxes. Kelly came up through Tammany's political wing, and sought to recast the organization as a more singularly political outfit, disciplining freelancing by Tammany ward heelers in the city's vice markets.[97] Kelly tied the patronage given to heelers by Tammany's Executive Committee to the district's electoral performance. This encouraged heelers to focus on organizing votes, rather than organizing crime. But it also risked creating dissidents, so Kelly also centralized financial controls, reducing the prospects of internal rivals drawing on local revenue sources to challenge him. Within several years Tammany had been transformed from 'a mob' into 'an army', from a flatter network into a more hierarchical organization.[98]

Tammany's reorganization seemed to pay quick political dividends. Following corruption scandals around federal Republicans (the Crédit Mobilier scandal, the Whiskey Ring fraud and the Indian land-sale scandal), by 1874 a Tammany Democrat was back as mayor in City Hall. And Samuel Tilden—now a sachem in the 'reformed' Tammany—was governor of New York State.[99] Kelly's internal reforms had allowed Tammany to become more responsive to changes in the political marketplace. Heelers had less power to meet patronage demands through innovation at the local level; instead, electoral success was restored as the primary fountainhead of patronage. While the realities of retail politics remained similar, an influx of Jewish and Italian immigrants onto Manhattan was forcing a shift away from the focus on Irish identity and causes to a more inclusive stance. A Jewish Tammany operative, Louis Eisenstein, recalled that '[t]housands of new citizens [emigrating from Russia, Eastern Europe and Italy] found an impersonal government translated and interpreted here by personal touch'.[100] This, in turn, required a reframing of Tammany rhetoric, away from sectarian politics, into class terms.[101]

The resulting balance of retail, class-based politics and machine-based patronage seemed to work. As Eisenstein put it, the Republicans were too 'stiff' and 'aloof' to offer aid; the socialists 'were too busy preparing for the brave new world of the future to bother with the immediate needs of the present'.[102] Tammany seemed to find the sweet spot in the middle. But it was not the only political organization in that place: the rise in labour unions' political potential as mediators between the state and voters continued to force change inside Tammany. In 1882 New York had roughly a dozen labour unions. Four years later, that number was closer to two hundred. Tammany responded by casting itself increasingly in anti-monopolist terms, even opposing the Democratic presidential nomination of New York governor Grover Cleveland on the grounds that he was a friend of monopolists.[103] The electoral success of the United Labor Party also forced Tammany to present a more professional political profile. Kelly moved Tammany out of the saloons and gaming houses, developing 'clubhouses' in each district. In time this was to have profound unanticipated consequences, since it opened up strategic space for local-level entrepreneurs to govern New York's drinking, gambling and prostitution markets—space that gangsters would step into during Prohibition.

But for now, it achieved Kelly's desired effect, recasting Tammany in the public eye as a political, not a criminal, organization.[104]

Kelly retired in 1884, making way for Richard 'Dixie' Croker. He had a different vision of Tammany's future and its role in governing New York's political and informal economic markets. Whereas Kelly had come up through Tammany's political ranks, Croker had come up from the street, like Tweed. As an infant he lived in a shantytown in what is now Central Park. In his teens he emerged as a gang leader and prizefighter, and from there found his way into Tammany ranks as an entrepreneur and manager of street violence. By the age of forty he was a city alderman.[105] For Croker, politics was a strategic, zero-sum struggle for total victory, indistinguishable from war or business. And as in war and business, he argued in an 1892 journal article, effective internal organization, not external positioning in the market of ideas, was the key to success:

> Between the aggressive forces of two similar groups of ideas, one enter-tained by a knot of theorists, the other enunciated by a well-compacted organization, there is such a difference as exists between a mob and a mili-tary battalion.[106]

Accordingly, 'no political party can with reason expect to obtain power, or to maintain itself in power, unless it be efficiently organized,' he wrote. In the French Revolution, for example:

> we cannot fail to admire the success, the influence, the resistless power of the Jacobin Club, not because the club was praiseworthy, since its actions were abhorrent, but because it was skilfully organized and handled... They acted upon the principle that obedience to orders is the first duty of the soldier, and that 'politics is war.' ... Everything is war in which men strive for mastery and power as against other men... A well-organized political club is made for the purpose of aggressive war.[107]

His was a specifically managerialist outlook. Effective political orga-nization and city management, Croker wrote, required a 'combination of skill, enterprise, knowledge, resolution, and what is known as "executive ability"'. Maintaining those capabilities within an organiza-tion required providing adequate compensation; and compensation meant patronage appointments to civil service positions:

> The affairs of a vast community are to be administered. Skilful men must administer them. These men must be compensated... [T]here must be

officials, and since these officials must be paid, and well paid, in order to insure able and constant service, why should they not be selected from the membership of the society that organizes the victories of the dominant party?[108]

Croker's philosophy treated government as business, 'precisely the same as that which governs the workings of a railway, or a bank, or a factory',[109] or, as Plunkitt, a Croker protégé, put it, 'as much a regular business as the grocery or dry-goods or the drug business'. This was an argument for treating government as a market, parties as firms, and for creating professional political operatives: 'You've got to be trained up to it or you're sure to fall.'[110]

It was a short step to treating crime and politics as interchangeable strategies in a governmental marketplace, and governmental power as a means to profit. But whereas Kelly saw the Tweed episode as indicating a need to promote Tammany as a political organization, Croker saw the lesson of the episode as being the need to argue for the patronage system on its own merits, rather than hide it. In 1900, a legislative committee grilled Croker on links between Tammany support for judicial appointments and judicial approval of municipal contracts for Croker's own real estate firm. Croker was unapologetic about his transactional approach to government: 'We at least expect they [those we help to get elected] will be friendly to us,' he told his interrogator. 'Then you are working for your own pocket, are you not?' he was asked. 'All the time,' replied Croker. 'Same as you.' Nor did he stop there: 'We want the whole business, if we can get it,' he said. 'To the party belong the spoils.'[111]

Plunkitt, likewise, argued that profiting from public office was not just to be expected, but was what made the system work. The lesson from the Tweed episode, as he saw it, was that '[t]he politician who steals is worse than a thief. He is a fool.'[112] A distinction thus had to be drawn. 'Honest graft' consisted of using political power to harvest rents through political opportunism: 'I seen my opportunities and I took 'em,' Plunkitt famously stated. Insider trading, rigging of competitive tenders, exploitation of legislative power for personal gain were all perfectly acceptable, so long as the underlying activity was legal and '[t]he politician looks after his own interests, the organization's interests, and the city's interests all at the same time'. 'Dishonest graft', on the other hand, consisted of rent-seeking from outlawed activities: 'blackmailin' gamblers, saloon-keepers,

disorderly people', or simple 'political looting'—'robbing the treasury'.[113] Honest graft kept your supporters happy and yourself in power;
dishonest graft was plain stupid: 'Why should the Tammany leaders go
into such dirty business, when there is so much honest graft lyin' around
when they are in power?'[114]

Croker turned Kelly's centralized command and control structure in
this direction. Whereas previously Tammany heelers had carved out their
own social networks for influencing different parts of the city apparatus,
Kelly's centralization programme had given the leadership group control
of most of the municipal workforce. This turned the leadership into
middlemen with the ability to extract rents from a vast range of businesses dealing with myriad parts of the city bureaucracy.[115]

Huge population growth also meant a return to deficit spending. In
the first decade of the twentieth century New York's population grew
by 40 per cent, many of the newcomers immigrants from Italy. The
city's budget grew by 123 per cent in the same period.[116] This was
driven by huge new public service awards, which in turn fuelled land
speculation by Tammany leaders. Much of the Upper East Side was
developed this way.[117] Rapid population growth also led to a resurgence of the informal economy and vice industries—which entrepreneurial heelers, having seen patronage centralized in Tammany Hall,
saw as an alternative revenue source. Tammany men started privately
taxing informal gambling houses and thieves and fences, protecting
illegal saloons and bars and centralizing control of brothels.[118] In
Plunkitt's typology, this was 'dishonest graft'. But Croker justified
Tammany's involvement in starkly pragmatic terms: 'If we go down in
the gutter,' he claimed, 'it is because there are men in the gutter, and
you have to go down where they are if you are going to do anything
with them.'[119]

The re-emergence of Tammany's ties to the underworld did not go
unremarked. In the mid-1890s a Presbyterian minister, Charles
Parkhurst, documented connections between Tammany, corrupt police
and the vices of Lower Manhattan. Parkhurst quickly drummed up
support from the middle classes and in the press for an anti-Tammany
campaign, and threw his weight behind a reform candidate for mayor,
announcing, 'this is not a political campaign. It is simply a warfare
between that which is right and that which is wrong.'[120] Under attack,

Croker moved for a few years to Europe, ruling through a 'vice-regent'. But when the moral panic burned out in 1897 he quietly moved back to New York and resumed power. Tammany saw off several of these short-lived reform movements. Plunkitt described them as 'mornin' glories' which 'looked lovely in the mornin' and withered up in a short time, while the regular machines 'went on flourishin' forever, like fine old oaks'.[121] Against the professionals of Tammany, amateur civil society activists struggled.

During the second decade of the twentieth century, however, Tammany strategy took another turn—back towards a more reformist political agenda. The cloud of corruption that hung over Croker had led to his being forced out in 1902, replaced by the teetotaller 'Silent Charlie' Murphy. After a decade in power in Tammany, Murphy moved definitively towards a progressive political stance after the Triangle Shirtwaist Factory fire on 25 March 1911 killed 146 workers (123 women), near Washington Square, deep in Tammany's heartland. The fire proved a milestone in the rise of the labour movement, and forced Tammany to respond to a new rival in the political marketplace. Tammany began to take its legislative power more seriously, championing a series of workplace safety, child labour, minimum wage, insurance and compensation schemes, and even came out in favour of public higher education funding. Over the next two decades, under the leadership of Murphy and New York governor Al Smith, Tammany politicians developed much of the infrastructure of the welfare state in New York.[122]

In the late 1920s, Al Smith seemed poised to make a serious bid for the White House, and it looked like Tammany's progressive ideas—and direct influence—might graduate to the national level. Earlier Tammany-backed figures in Washington, such as President Van Buren, had hidden their Tammany links. Smith did not. But as with Honest John Kelly, Silent Charlie Murphy's repositioning of Tammany as a cleaner political force had left space for new organizations to emerge as governors of criminal markets. As we shall see in Chapter 5, it was Italian and Jewish criminal entrepreneurs who emerged in that space, and by the time Smith was ready to run for the White House, a professional criminal organization had colonized Tammany's networks of influence. To get to the White House, Smith would first have to go around the New York Mob.

Conclusion

Tammany was never, in Walter Lippmann's memorable phrase, 'wholly predatory nor wholly philanthropic'.[123] Both tendencies were present, sometimes one more dominant, sometimes the other. What remained consistent, however, was Tammany's governmental role, brokering across the gap between the state and the street, between Manhattan's municipal institutions on the one hand, and the poorer, more marginalized communities of the city—and the informal and illicit markets that flourished within them—on the other. That brokering role, in turn, depended on Tammany's control of coercion and corruption, and effective communication. The political roots of the organization, as first a nativist, and then an immigrant-protecting fraternal association, positioned it well to develop legitimacy as a communal protector. This in turn provided a framework within which some leaders could deploy Tammany's strategic capabilities to maximize criminal rents. Of these, Boss Tweed emerged as both the most successful—and the most disastrous. By adaptive innovation, he turned Tammany's capabilities towards a scheme in which New York City's governmental institutions became assets deployed to maximize his own criminal rents. With the Charter scheme, this reached extraordinary heights: New York City's political constitution was literally rewritten to entrench the Ring's joint venture within municipal government.

Tweed's Ring, like other criminal-political joint ventures we will see in later chapters, was a pyramid scheme, a confidence bubble built on society's willingness to pretend that the Emperor wore clothes. At first, as everyone seemed to benefit from the city's dynamism and growth, Tweed could purchase loyalty downtown through welfare, and uptown through patronage.[124] The city seemed physically to bloom: Tweed laid the groundwork for the Brooklyn Bridge and the Metropolitan Museum of Art, and the Upper East Side. But as the ring of complicity grew, so did the difficulty of maintaining control—and thus Tweed's vulnerability. The system was 'based on lies'.[125] At some point the bubble had to burst: the creditors would call in their debts, the system's governmentality would evaporate and the house of cards would collapse.

Near death, Tweed himself concluded: 'Our power was always precariously held... We broke ourselves down and injured this city by extending our patronage in the reach for influence and power.'[126] The events that triggered the loss of confidence in his system hold many lessons for similar contemporary 'joint ventures' between political and criminal cliques, especially in the developing world. One argument sometimes heard is that if poorer countries grow wealthier by indulging vices in richer countries such as drug consumption or irresponsible bank lending, that must be accepted as a fair capital-transfer mechanism that balances the inequalities inherent in contemporary global capitalism, notably the global north's refusal to liberalize those legitimate markets (agriculture) in which developing countries enjoy competitive advantage.[127] Tweed's downfall shows the danger of accepting such an argument. Once the press brought his corruption out into the open and the markets were forced to acknowledge that New York's accounts were riddled with financial impropriety, it was only a matter of time before a financial crisis. His regime came close to destroying New York's creditworthiness, jeopardizing the entire city's livelihoods. It was only the availability of an unprecedented bridging loan from Wall Street that kept New York solvent, and allowed the city to avoid massive budget cuts. New York City was simply too important to the world economy to be allowed to go bankrupt, too big to fail. What if it had not been? How much human damage would have ensued? These are the questions that poor countries, from Greece to Guinea-Bissau and Afghanistan to Angola, must consider before accepting a growth strategy based on systemic corruption and political protection of organized crime.

Tammany's evolving strategic approach also highlights the significance of investigative journalism as a check on criminal strategy. Without the free press, the markets, the political class and electors might all have continued happily to pretend that the Emperor was indeed wearing beautiful clothes, even as the size of the underlying problem grew. The ermine spots on Emperor Tweed's cloak of power were inkspots: he systematically and strategically corrupted the press, purchasing their complicity. It was his failure to corrupt *Harper's Weekly* and *The New York Times* that proved the chink in his armour. Tweed himself recognized this: 'If I could have bought newspapermen as easily as I did members of the Legislature, I wouldn't be in the fix I am now,' he told the *Brooklyn Eagle*.[128] It was not the state that brought Tweed down, but society—both local and international. It was not his loss of control of governmental institutions, but his loss of control over governmentality—or the weakness of his own influence in the face of the governmentality of global credit markets—that ultimately undermined his social legitimacy, and his power.

Tweed's demise was also an early signal of the fact that social legitimacy is the central terrain of competition between criminal and political actors. And it also pointed to the fundamental threat to Tammany's brokering role between politics and the people that the mass media posed. Tammany's retail politics—tending to the needs of individual Tammany clients—had been outmatched by the power of the press, which could transform the strategic environment with one piercing, unforgettable image. Here was an early sign that the strategic centre of gravity of organized crime is not, as we might think, its coercive capabilities, but its legitimacy. The press reflected, amplified—and then detonated—Tweed's power. In early 1870, he was the 'Monarch of Manhattan'. On election day 1871, Tom Nast transformed him into a Roman emperor watching heartlessly as the Tammany tiger ripped Lady Columbia apart on the coliseum floor. Tweed became 'a vulgar image, a scoundrel, an object of disgust, fat, evil, far removed from a human being'. He never recovered.[129]

The Tweed episode also showed the emerging populist potential in the political marketplace of an anti-crime narrative, broadcast through the media. Tilden and other Democrats who placed themselves at the vanguard of the popular and criminal prosecution of the Tweed Ring emerged as heroic protectors of civil morality. Jimmy O'Brien rode his new popularity to the US Congress. The judge who convicted Tweed became chief justice of the New York State Supreme Court. Tilden became a crime-fighting governor and won the popular vote in the 1876 presidential election, losing the White House only as a result of complicated manoeuvres in the Electoral College where he was defeated by one Supreme Court judge's vote for Rutherford Hayes.[130]

Finally, this analysis of Tammany strategy highlights the key role that coercion plays in differentiating criminal strategy from other strategies in the competition for governmental power. The regulation of coercion was central to Tammany's brokering power. It was Tweed's ability to broker peace during the Draft Riots of 1863 that marked him out from the Tammany pack; it was his inability to prevent the Orange Riot in 1871 that triggered the loss of uptown confidence and the unravelling of his legitimacy. But Tammany could only broker between the state and the street. It never developed sophisticated military or coercive capabilities within its own ranks. Tammany did provide operating space, funding and strategic advice to foreign militant organizations including the Fenians, the Irish Republican Brotherhood and Cuban independence fighters.[131] But its own route to power lay through the ballot box and downtown bars, not through bullets and the battlefield. People loved and feared Tammany because of its power over their lives—not for the risk that it might kill them. Tweed's threat to kill George Jones, *The New York Times*' editor, was an act of desperation, an idle bluff that Jones called. Tammany was a political organization whose leaders sometimes dabbled in criminal strategy, not a criminal organization dabbling in politics.

This begs a question: what if Tammany had indeed developed such independent coercive capabilities and turned them towards harvesting criminal rents through governmental power? What would an organization with such a strategy look like? On the other side of the Atlantic, at the same time that Tweed held power in New York, answers to these questions were emerging.

4

MAFIA ORIGINS, 1859–1929

'*The King of Italy might rule the island but men of my tradition govern it.*'

Sicilian mafia saying[1]

Gangi, a Sicilian village on a steep hilltop half way between Palermo and Mount Etna, is largely unremarkable. In January 1926, however, it was the venue for a remarkable scene: the Italian state besieging its own citizens. Paramilitary units of the ruling National Fascist Party surrounded the village, cut off its water supply and took women and children hostage, refusing to release them until their male relatives, hiding in the town, surrendered. Within two weeks, 450 arrests had been made; 149 people were detained for trial—many of them for up to two years. Two committed suicide. Seven men received life sentences with hard labour; eight received thirty years' imprisonment. Two women received twenty-five-year sentences, and most of the rest five to ten years' imprisonment. International reaction was swift—and approving. This was, *The New York Times* proclaimed, 'one of Premier Mussolini's great achievements'—an apparently decisive blow against the 'mafia'.[2] What was this 'mafia', and why was it perceived as such a grave threat?

In late 1925, the Italian state was undergoing a constitutional transformation. Benito Mussolini's evolution from Italy's prime minister to Fascist dictator was well advanced. A law adopted on Christmas Eve

1925 made him responsible only to the king, not to Parliament, and replaced locally elected mayors with *podestàs* appointed by the Senate, which he controlled. By late 1926 political parties had been banned. It seemed that little impeded *Il Duce*'s drive for total power.

Except in the south, in the poor, agrarian Mezzogiorno provinces of Campania, Apulia, Calabria—and above all in Sicily. A 1924 visit to Palermo had convinced Mussolini that Sicilians, in particular, did not adequately respect the state, and instead offered allegiance to a shadowy, alternative local power: the clandestine fraternal organization known as the 'mafia'. Such a concentrated source of power outside the state was anathema to the Fascist vision of totalitarian governmental power. It could not be tolerated. 'Your Excellency has carte blanche,' Mussolini telegraphed to Cesare Mori, his new prefect in Palermo, on his appointment in October 1925:

> The authority of the State must absolutely, repeat absolutely, be re-established in Sicily. If the laws still in force hinder you, this will be no problem, as we will draw up new laws.[3]

This was the go signal for Mori's iron-fisted crackdown. Over four years, some 11,000 people were imprisoned on suspicion of mafia ties.[4] Twenty major trials were held. One sentenced 244 people to a total of 1,200 years in prison. Mori came to be known as the 'Iron Prefect', making liberal use of torture and the *confine*—exile without charge on islands off Sicily.[5]

The siege of Gangi seems all the more remarkable now that we know from first-hand accounts that a notable landowner had, a month earlier, negotiated a mass surrender of the local mafia leadership.[6] The siege of Gangi was not an operational necessity: it was an exercise in strategic communication. As the Sicilian mafia historian Salvatore Lupo has explained, Mussolini and Mori considered that:

> In order to win on the terrain of folk values, the state had to gain itself a degree of 'respect' by behaving in a more *mafioso* fashion than the *mafiosi* themselves.[7]

Mori had understood that the mafia's power stemmed from its social influence and the normalization of *mafioso* culture. If the state wanted to beat the mafia in the competition for loyalty, it had to win back the hearts and minds of the Sicilian people. It had to win in the terrain of governmentality.

This chapter explores the origins of the Sicilian mafia's governmental power in Italy's post-unification political and economic transitions, and explains how mafia emigration reproduced mafia governmentality, organization and power in New York. It draws on a mixture of secondary sources, Italian and US governmental inquiries—and the first-hand accounts of *mafiosi* in both Sicily and New York, notably those of mafia leaders Joseph Bonanno and Nicola Gentile, the reliability of which has previously been tested and demonstrated.[8] Both accounts are particularly useful to our inquiry because both men were initiated into the Sicilian mafia before moving to the US and taking on leadership roles there. They both later moved back to Sicily to warm mafia welcomes. Both represented, in other words, authoritative voices within the mainstream mafia tradition on both sides of the Atlantic. As mafiologist John Dickie has pointed out, Gentile's often overlooked autobiography in particular offers an unparalleled understanding of 'the laws of motion of the mafia ... because his survival and success depended on that understanding'.[9]

Accounts provided by the lower-level mafia soldier Joe Valachi are also used in this chapter, but treated more cautiously.[10] As a *soldato* rather than a *capo*, Valachi was not privy to higher strategic decision-making processes within the mafia—only their results. Yet Valachi's account, the accounts of Sicilian *pentiti* such as Antonino Calderone and Francisco Marino Mannoia, and those of American mafia informants such as Mikey Franzese and Joe Cantalupo all provide rich, highly corroborative detail on matters of organization, culture and outlook.[11] Finally, there is the special case of *The Last Testament of Lucky Luciano*, purportedly based on unrecorded interviews the New York mafia leader Salvatore Lucania (a.k.a. Charles 'Lucky' Luciano) allegedly gave the screenwriter Martin Gosch shortly before both died.[12] The book represents the interpretation of Gosch's interview notes by Richard Hammer, a journalist Gosch had brought in on the project.[13] While the main timelines established by the book seem sound, Richard Warner has established that numerous small details and several longer passages in *The Last Testament* do not stack up against independent evidence.[14] Accordingly, this book does not rely solely on *The Last Testament*, or indeed on other sources based only upon *The Last Testament*, for any point of analytical significance.

Origins

Profiting from transition

On 11 May 1860 a former resident of New York's Staten Island landed on the westernmost tip of Sicily with a thousand red-shirted revolutionaries. Giuseppe Garibaldi had come to assist an uprising against the Kingdom of the Two Sicilies. As his rebel army marched across Sicily, it was joined by several *Squadri della Mafia*—'squads of mafia', a term which, at the time, meant something like 'braves'. By September 1860 Garibaldi's army had conquered Sicily and southern Italy, including Naples. In October, Garibaldi turned it all over to the Sardinian King Vittorio Emmanuele II who, in March 1861, became the King of Italy. It was the first time in thirteen centuries that Italy had been politically unified.

Unification upended both the political and social orders of southern Italy. Though legislative initiatives over the preceding half-century had aimed to unwind the feudal structure of the Kingdom of the Two Sicilies' economy, its wealth and markets remained tied to huge rural landholdings, the *latifundias*, owned by absentee aristocratic landlords. Post-unification governments, dominated by forces from Italy's industrializing north, quickly set about the liberalization of landholdings and markets in the south. But legislative decrees from Rome were not matched by state power or presence on the ground in the south. The reform initiatives ran up against the realities of how Sicily and the other Mezzogiorno provinces were governed. As Sicilian *mafiosi* still say today, *La presenza è potenza*: presence is power.[15]

Absentee landlords, including the Church, had long relied on local strongmen to manage their estates and to protect them from others' violence. These strongmen were organized first as local *guardiani* (guard militias) and after the formal abolition of feudalism in 1812 as tenants (*gabellotti*—'rentpayers') and stewards.[16] These leaseholders had relatively free rein to use violence against local peasants, and an incentive to maximize their own rents. This they did by driving down the rent their formal overlords demanded of them—through threatening reduced output or outright revolt—and by maximizing the rent they could extract from their own subtenants, often small landholding peasants.[17] Much of the countryside was consequently ruled by protection rackets, in which violent entrepreneurs aspiring to be appointed as *gabellotti* (or already colluding with them) manufactured threats through vandalism, robbery or kidnapping, and then, having hidden their involvement, encouraged the absent landlord to pay them for protection.[18] The pattern became ritualized.

The result was the emergence of a class of local strongmen brokers: men whose control of coercion turned them into problem-solvers, dispensers of patronage and informal local political authorities. The mafia *pentito* Nino Calderone recounted, a century later, how he and his brother, a local mafia boss, would joke about setting up a sign outside their office, where they received streams of visitors seeking their support and backing, labelled 'Welfare Office'.[19] Despite post-unification efforts to establish public institutions in Sicily's interior, these *mafiosi*, as they had become known, maintained their role as informal local governors, extracting tribute in return for the provision of rough justice and access to the state and its services.

Disputes between local *mafiosi* could resemble low-level armed conflict. A feud between two mafia groups in Monreale and Bagheria lasted from 1872 to 1878, killing dozens and displacing hundreds.[20] Post-unification governments adopted a strategy that presages the approach we now see adopted in contemporary conflict-affected contexts such as Afghanistan: they commissioned some of these groups to take on formal policing functions, enlisting the most violent bands as paramilitary auxiliaries of the state. Yet this proved as counterproductive in Sicily as it arguably has in Afghanistan.[21] As the nineteenth-century Tuscan researcher Leopoldo Franchetti concluded after a visit to southern Italy, by failing effectively to monopolize violence, the state had allowed others into the market—and allowed violence to enter the broader political economy.[22] What emerged in response was not, initially, a hierarchical organization, but rather myriad entrepreneurial groups who slowly coalesced around a common mafia strategy and repertoire.[23]

The *mafioso*'s power lay not, as is sometimes suggested, in isolated territorial control of *latifundia* separated off from state power, but rather in the control of a territory and population connected to external markets. Some post-unification bandits and brigands did control and tax local economies like warlords. What differentiated those that survived as mafia was their adaptation of coercion from this focus on local autonomy to a role more concentrated on brokering the flow of goods from those rural landholdings to consumption markets in the littoral cities and overseas. Mafia power emerged in the established wheat and olive supply-chains that, with new capital investments by northern industrialists, were being repurposed to sell citrus and sulphur—crucial in the galvanization of rubber—into export markets. Mafia networks also developed hidden inside the family-based commercial networks connecting rural *gabellotti* to urban fruit-sellers and bankers and lawyers.[24] Middle- and upper-class actors were drawn into mafia webs both through direct coercion and extortion, and through the weakness of their control over their estates, which gave mafia actors space to make them complicit in criminal activity such as trading in stolen goods.[25] As the British historian Eric Hobsbawm has explained, the mafia emerged out of a '*modus vivendi* with northern capitalism'. It was a product of Sicily's integration into a modernizing Italian political economy dominated by northern Italian capital.[26]

This economic transformation—and the mafia's brokering role—was, from the outset, nested within the newly unified political structures of the Italian state. As James Fentress has shown, early *mafiosi* used political patronage strategies, clandestine organizational techniques and social networks acquired during cooperation with Garibaldi and other revolutionary forces between 1848 and the early 1860s. Indeed, in Fentress' account, many of the early *mafiosi* were revolutionaries who, after unification, turned away from politics to organized crime.[27] By the 1870s, Fentress has shown, an established pattern of corrupt exchange between *mafiosi*, politicians and officials, especially police, had emerged. Politicians ensured that officials did favours for *mafiosi* and their economic allies; the *mafiosi*, in turn, used their coercive power to deliver electoral outcomes. Michele Pantaleone, a noted anti-mafia activist, remembered that in the first part of the twentieth century:

> election campaigns were ushered in with threatening letters, robberies, cattle-killing, crop, hay-loft and rick firing, the felling of trees, the cutting down of vines and the pollution of water in wells and cisterns.[28]

Democratic politicians in unified Italy quickly became dependent on mafia intermediaries for access to local votes. Mafia gangs' operational areas soon coincided with electoral districts, as the mafia-backed *gabel-*

lotto became the 'chief elector' for his political 'friends'.[29] One hundred years later, the mafia *pentito* Nino Calderone explained that a similar electoral logic was still in place, using Palermo as an example: with 1,500 to 2,000 operational *mafiosi* in the city, and each mustering forty to fifty votes through family and friends, the mafia controlled a package of 75,000 to 100,000 votes, even before intimidation of the broader public was considered.[30] Of course, in the nineteenth century, when suffrage was limited to propertied men, the social network needed to develop political capital was even smaller. Failure to cooperate with the mafias could spell electoral suicide.

Post-unification politicians generally did not become members of the violent organizations they were patronizing, but rather their 'friends' and 'associates', partners in a system of corrupt exchanges.[31] So unassailable was the *mafioso*'s legitimacy that he could be quite open about his political contribution. This brashness ensnared the mafia's friends in a web of complicity, encouraging them to buy into the silence around the mafia's criminal conduct. It was not the power of the criminal actor, but his criminality, which had to be hidden. The politician 'had good reasons for' being silent, explains Pantaleone:

> he was not only defending his votes but also safeguarding himself against the scandal which would result if the man known to be his 'chief elector' had to be tried in a court of law.[32]

Criminal power hid in plain sight, becoming embedded within an informal clientelist protection system inside the new Italian state, protected by a culture of silence—*omertà*.[33] The director of the district police for Palermo, writing in the early twentieth century, stated simply that the mafia were:

> under the protection of senators, members of parliament, and other influential figures who protect them and defend them, only to be protected and defended by them in return.[34]

This system gave a 'virtual licence' to the mafia.[35] For northern Italian politicians, concluded Hobsbawm, the south:

> could provide safe majorities for whatever government gave sufficient bribes or concessions to the local bosses who could guarantee electoral victory. This was child's play for Mafia... But the concessions and bribes which were small, from the point of view of northerners (for the south was poor) made

all the difference to local power... Politics made the power of the local boss; politics increased it, and turned it into big business.[36]

The mafia did not so much move into politics as emerge out of it. Said Pantaleone: 'The history of the Mafia is essentially one of political collusion.'[37] It was embedded in the electoral and administrative systems of the unified state, serving as an instrument of political and social control—a partner in the governmental marketplace, operating not on the basis of a strict territorial but rather a jurisdictional segmentation. Even peasant rebellions in the 1890s did not dislodge it. 'The tacit partnership between Rome with its troops and martial law and *mafia* was too much for them,' concluded Hobsbawm.

> The true 'kingdom of Mafia' had been established. It was now a great power. Its members sat as deputies in Rome and their spoons reached into the thickest part of the gravy of government: large banks, national scandals.[38]

Writing in December 1899 under the pseudonym 'Rastignac' in *La Tribuna*, a Milanese broadsheet, an anonymous political commentator described recent events in Sicily:

> Here was a mysterious and subtle poison... under the façade of the Mafia the power of politics was at work, and under the façade of politics the power of the Mafia was at work.[39]

Organizing the Sicilian mafia

As Franchetti explained, the democratization of violence that resulted in southern Italy from unification spawned an entire 'industry of violence'. The *mafioso* was an entrepreneur in that industry, an entrant into a market for illicit government with few barriers to entry. The *Mafioso*:

> acts as capitalist, impresario and manager. He unifies the management of the crimes committed ... he regulates the division of functions and labour, and he controls discipline amongst the workers... To him falls the judgement from circumstances as to whether violence should be suspended for a while, or multiplied and made more ferocious. He has to adjust to market conditions to choose which operations to carry out, which people to exploit, which form of violence to use best to achieve the desired objective.[40]

Mafiosi were, in other words, strategic organizers of crime. They were building governmental power out of crime, developing internal norms, resolving disputes, allocating resources. Steadily, a specific governmentality emerged in which autonomous mafia groups organized using common forms, ranks, codes, rituals and tactics.[41] Each mafia unit was known as a *cosca*, or 'tuft', pointing to the fact that, like tufts of grass connected by subterranean rhizomatic roots, they were both autonomous and connected to a deeper, hidden network, a 'fractional form' of a larger whole, as the FBI later put it.[42]

The roots of the *cosca* being in violence, its structure was quasi-military. The leader was the *capo* (head or chief), usually above several *sottocapi* (underbosses or deputy chiefs). Each *sottocapo* oversaw several *regimi* (regiments or units, also called *decina*), each of which was led by a *caporegime* (lieutenant), and was made up of *soldati* (soldiers, also *picciotti*). Additionally, the *capo* was also usually advised by a senior *consigliere* (counsellor), a staff officer adjacent to the formal, linear command structure.[43] This militaristic terminology has misled many observers to misunderstand the system as highly centralized, hierarchical and bureaucratic—like an army. Because the system's organization was clandestine, it in fact operated more as a network or 'context of action'. Mafia 'ranks' are best understood not as fixed steps within a homogenous command structure, but rather as indicators of power differentials in a network. As an official Quebec investigation into the mafia explained in the 1970s, 'not all members of the same ranks are necessarily equal'.[44] Even within a given *cosca*, authority could be fluid and contested.

The clandestine nature of mafia criminal activities such as extortion and election rigging placed a premium on trust. Unsurprisingly, mafia *cosche* emerged out of established trust and kinship networks. Because these groups were often found in one town or village, *cosche* were sometimes known as *borgati* (townships or boroughs).[45] Joseph Bonanno, who rose ultimately to be a senior *capo* in the New York mafia, stated simply that it is impossible to understand events—whether they are marriages, political alliances or killings—unless there is some understanding—literally—of just who was related to whom.[46]

As the Sicilian economy integrated first with that of northern Italy, and then with European and trans-Atlantic markets, family networks steadily became dispersed. Recruitment morphed from actual to fictive kinship arrangements, giving rise to the *compare* or *padrino* (godfather) system in which an initiated *mafioso* would sponsor the membership of an outsider (often a talented prospect who had been observed for some time) under his surrogate fatherly patronage and guidance.[47] Kinship structures were also central to the secret initiation ceremony and internal disciplinary code. The initiation process appears to have been reasonably uniform across the mafia and over time—a good indicator that *cosche* arrived at their common organizational approach not by accident but as a result of organizational choice and mimicking. Initiation involved the symbolic spilling of blood through the pricking of a finger and the swearing of a ritual oath to abide by the mafia's code—which emphasized loyalty to the group, including through silence, on pain of death and, by many accounts, a commitment not to interfere with female members of other *mafiosi*'s families.[48]

As in many criminal organizations, women were never admitted into the mafia. They were treated as passive vehicles for traditionalist values rather than seen as social agents in their own right. Even as the mafias urbanized and became more commercialized, the territorial and familial roots of their origins remained as referents of a shared heritage and identity, useful in the mobilization of loyalty and internal organization.[49] In America, *cosche* later became formally known as 'Families'. By the 1950s, through interaction between deported American mobsters and Sicilian *mafiosi* (discussed in Chapter 7), that term (*famiglia*) had gained currency back in Sicily.

Mafia *cosche*, though separately run, shared a common strategic alignment vis-à-vis the state. The *capo* acquired his position through the development of a reputation for effectively resolving disputes— whether through violence or arbitration.[50] This required the acquisition of a group of followers through personal charisma, family loyalty (including marriage) or wealth.[51] And it required a reputation for toughness and independence, an unwillingness to kowtow to the state. The esteem in which such individuals were held was demonstrated by the connotation *uomo di rispetto* ('man of respect') or *uomo d'onore* ('man of honour').[52] Yet there was a paradox here: the more effective a *mafioso*'s capacity to organize and threaten violence became, the more invisible was that violence. A reputation for being capable of effective violence became socially institutionalized as 'respect' or 'honour'.[53] The *mafioso*'s power was hidden—but its source well understood. As the *pentito* Calderone put it plainly: 'Every mafioso knows perfectly well, when all is said and done, where his power comes from.'[54] Nicola Gentile put it even more bluntly: *Se non si è feroci non si diventa capi*: 'Those who are not ferocious do not become mafia leaders.'[55]

Mafia culture justified violence as the way to remain independent of an untrustworthy and unjust state, even as Sicilian politicians frequently tried to co-opt mafia values and social legitimacy. Campaigning in Palermo in 1925, former Prime Minister Vittorio Emmanuele Orlando, who had led the Italian delegation to the Versailles Peace Conference, could with a straight face proclaim:

> If by 'Mafia' we mean an exaggerated sense of honour, a passionate refusal to succumb to the overbearing and arrogant, a nobility of spirit that stands up to the strong and indulges the weak, a loyalty to friends that is more steadfast and enduring even than death—if these characteristics, albeit with their excesses, are what we mean by 'Mafia', we are dealing with ineradicable traits of the Sicilian character, and I declare myself to be Mafioso, and I am happy to be such.[56]

Mafiosi cloaked themselves in the trappings of conservative resistance to imposed, foreign and unjust change, giving them the 'romantic aura of popular heroes'.[57] They were, in a sense, descendants of social bandits, though where the social bandit rebelled openly against the established order, the *mafioso* covertly colluded with it.[58] The *mafioso* played a double game. The mafia mentality stood for Sicilian parochialism and rejection of foreign rule. But the *mafioso* also profited from keeping order as the agents of absent foreign rulers and as intermediaries in economic and political exchange between Sicily and outside markets.[59]

Raab describes mafia *cosche* as constituting a 'substitute, extra-legal government'.[60] But it is more accurate to say that the mafia supplemented, rather than substituted for, the state.[61] The mafia's governmental power differed from that of the state in two crucial ways. First, in its invisibility. Mafia power was, from the outset, a hidden power, organized to be not just private but secret. Its social effectiveness depended in part on society being enlisted into keeping the fact of mafia organization and influence secret, even as *mafioso* culture was celebrated. From the outset, the practice of *omertà*—the mafia's 'code of silence', notionally enforced on pain of death—was critical to its success.[62] Formally, *omertà* applied only to 'made' or initiated members. But in practice, its shadow lay heavily across those communities within which *cosche* operated. It encouraged communal complicity with the mafia and a secret subversion of communal allegiance to the state, 'insubordination to the rules of the state'.[63] State power, by contrast, is intrinsically public. But so long as that division of labour—between the state as the public face of power, and the mafia as its hidden intermediary in society—could be sustained, there was an apparent complementarity between these two forms of power. It was only when the state sought to displace the mafia as even a private form of governmentality on the island, as Mussolini's totalitarian project aimed to; or when the mafia seemed to seek to substitute its own decisions for public governmental discretion, as it did with its bombing campaigns in the 1980s and 1990s, that the two powers were bound to collide.

The second key difference between the mafia and the state's governmental power lay in its structure. Within Sicily, the Italian state purported to monopolize coercion and legal authority. The same could not be said of the mafia, even within its underworld. The mafia was not a governmental monopoly, but more of an oligopoly: a system of criminal power organized via multiple *cosche*. In that sense, the organizational structure within the mafia was similar to the inter-state arena, with individual organizations monopolizing control over certain territories and, in some places, intermingling and competing for influence. Without a system of public justice, the *cosche* relied on clandestine violence—often through *vendetta*—and negotiation to maintain orderly relations across *cosche* lines.[64] At times, diplomatic relations between *capi* were even institutionalized through temporary commissions or a 'general assembly'.[65] In some cases, this 'general assembly' even took on the role of a ritual tribunal, collectively ratifying death sentences proposed by the *capi*.[66] But until the creation of a permanent Commission in the American mafia (Chapter 5) and a 'Cupola' system in Sicily (Chapter 7), these structures remained more inter-governmental than governmental, and temporary rather than standing bodies.

Mafia migration

When Salvatore Lucania arrived on the Lower East Side of Manhattan from central Sicily at the age of nine in the spring of 1907, the conditions he encountered were in some ways more like those we would today expect to find in a refugee camp or a 'fragile state' than a thriving, modern city. Lucania's family lived on East 13th Street near Second Avenue. The overcrowded tenements in that part of Manhattan typically had twelve rooms housing four immigrant families, with one toilet per floor. Most apartments doubled as garment piecework factories. The streets were cobbled or sometimes unpaved, and filthy. And the neighbourhood was extremely crowded: 20,000 new inhabitants arrived on Manhattan in May 1907—in just one day. Some 237,000 Italians had immigrated to America the previous year.[67]

Italian unification had not brought prosperity to southern Italy. The New World promised a new life. Around 2.1 million Italians moved to the US between 1900 and 1910 alone, 80 per cent from the Mezzogiorno including Sicily.[68] In the first fifteen years of the twentieth century roughly a quarter of Sicily's population migrated to America, usually entering through, and often staying in, New York.[69] The city was home to more Italians than Florence, Venice and Genoa combined.[70] The East Village tenements around 'Mulberry Bend' (Mulberry, Mott, Hester, Prince and Elizabeth Streets) where many Italian immigrants pitched up had long been the stronghold of Tammany Hall, the local Democratic political organization that served as an intermediary between the city's municipal institutions and the city's immigrant communities, providing access to governmental services in return for votes (see Chapter 3). Other notable Italian immigrant clusters were found in East Harlem and Williamsburg. Yet in addition to massive Italian immigration, between 1870 and 1900 New York's Jewish population also grew from 60,000 to 300,000.[71] At the same time, the Irish-born population was dropping steadily, and moving off Manhattan to New York's outer boroughs. Tammany's power within the Lower East Side was loosening, and along with it Tammany's traditional role in governing lower Manhattan's vice markets.

When Lucania arrived in 1907, the Lower East Side was threatening to become ungovernable. In the months after his arrival, a series of strikes paralysed large parts of lower Manhattan. One was led by Italian street cleaners, with rotting garbage piling up in the streets, and the risks of epidemic spiralling. Police escorting strike-breakers were pelted with refuse and bricks. Soon after, the meatpackers went on strike, with butcher shops closing down across the city. Given the very limited access to fresh produce and refrigeration, riots and disease threatened. Again, the police were called in.

In some ways this political economy resembled the one in Sicily that Lucania and his fellow immigrants had left.[72] 'Access to the labor market' in both places, argues John Dickie, was 'similarly controlled by tough-guys and local bosses'. Sicilians fully appreciated, Dickie writes:

> how important it could be, in terms of their livelihoods, to be loyal to the right faction in town… Many had no illusions about what it took to get on in politics and business… Like Sicily, the world of the new immigrant in North America was one where power was invested not in institutions, but in tough, well-networked individuals.[73]

It was an environment potentially ripe for the reproduction of mafia-type power. Yet there is a longstanding dispute within the research literature about how the Italian-American mafia emerged in New York and other US cities. The economist Donald Cressey and various US government investigations in the mid-twentieth century treated the American mafia as a 'branch' or 'offshoot' of its Sicilian forebear, the result of a kind of criminal colonization or offshore strategy. A critical perspective has suggested, on the contrary, that the American mafia is better understood as the result of local responses to local conditions, modelled on but not directly established by its Italian cousins. Diego Gambetta has argued, for example, that:

> Mafia families were not exported to America but emerged spontaneously, as it were, when the supply of protection and the demand for protection met: when, in other words, a sufficient number of emigrants moved there for independent reasons, some bringing along the necessary skills for organizing a protection market, and when certain events, notably the Great Depression and Prohibition, opened up a vast and lucrative market for this commodity.[74]

This structuralist analysis, which treats the mafia as vehicles for impersonal market forces, is somewhat ahistorical. And, as it turns out, a little inaccurate. The reality is that the protection market in New York already existed, well before the Depression and Prohibition—but was effectively governed by the Tammany organization, which operated primarily as a patronage organization, describing its style of politics as based on 'honest graft'.[75] Italian immigrants to New York, and other cities such as New Orleans, began developing their own schemes in the shadow of these established protection providers.[76]

The Black Hand

As Lucania arrived, however, Tammany grip on local-level criminal activity was weakening, both as the result of its Irish clientele moving off Manhattan, and as a result of Tammany reforms in response to the emergence of another rival for the role of intermediary in the political marketplace—the labour movement.[77] As a result, space for violent and criminal entrepreneurialism in New York's immigrant neighbourhoods was beginning to open up. Local youth gangs controlled the pickpocket and illegal craps rackets.[78] Lucania fell in with this crowd, before being packed off to a 'secure school' in Brooklyn—where he mingled with other similarly delinquent youth, gaining a valuable education in petty crime at the state's expense.[79] Some of these gangs also began to take the place of earlier Irish gangs as election day enforcers for the Tammany organization, forging exploitable ties that would later provide invaluable political protection.[80]

From August 1903, an epidemic of extortion gripped the Italian American community across the country. Victims would usually receive several letters making extortionate demands, signed by the *Mano Nera* (Black Hand). If the victim did not comply, a 'friend' of the victim would often step forward as a 'conciliator'. But payment could often lead to further demands. Non-payment, however, frequently led to bombing. Seventy such attacks were recorded in 1911 in New York City alone.[81] A 1909 report by Giuseppe ('Joe') Petrosino—a pioneering New York police officer who was assassinated by the Sicilian mafia in Palermo just a couple of months later—identified structural factors in New York that facilitated Black Hand extortion. They could be lifted straight from a contemporary United Nations report considering the possibilities for criminal activity in a 'fragile state':

> Here there is practically no police surveillance. Here it is easy to buy arms and dynamite. Here there is no penalty for using a fake name. Here it is easy to hide, thanks to our enormous territory and overcrowded cities.[82]

With such low costs and risks, anyone could get involved in Black Hand extortion. Such tactics—though not the Black Hand symbol, specifically—were well-known in southern Italy,[83] especially among the Neapolitan Camorra.[84] Insider accounts suggest that there was no centralized 'Black Hand Society', as the contemporary press theorized. Indeed, Italian *mafiosi* who had emigrated to the US were not, apparently, major Black Hand proponents.[85] Instead, Black Hand extortion was an open-source criminal methodology that spread through mimicry not only by thugs but also by businessmen seeking an edge over their rivals.

This was disorganized, not organized, crime. There was a collective incentive for all Black Hand copy-catters to have their activities perceived as the product of a vast, powerful conspiracy, since this raised the perceived risks of non-compliance.[86] Some small extortion rings did emerge, but they tended to endure not on the basis of their income from extortion, but through developing other criminal rents, notably from counterfeiting and narcotics. The terrorizing nature of Black Hand extortion offered no basis for such rings to develop sustainable support within the Italian-American community, nor to develop political protection. Tammany could not protect those involved in terrorist bombings, and as early as 1904 backed the formation of a special 'Italian squad' in the New York Police Department to deal with Black Hand bombings.[87]

Modern Family

Black Hand extortion thus created a new opportunity for *mafiosi* in the US: to provide protection. Early American *mafiosi* presented themselves precisely as protectors of the Italian-American community, stepping in to settle Black Hand disputes, as well as to protect Italian-American interests from police brutality and extortion. But with Black Hand activities conducted so furtively and in such a disorganized way, the only way to prevent and control them was not through direct physical pressure, but through social influence.

Sicilian mafia *capi* and leaders of other southern Italian criminal organizations such as the Neapolitan Camorra and the Calabrian 'Ndrangheta who had emigrated from Italy brought their reputations, and their wealth of respect, with them.[88] They were well-positioned to play a local public order role. As the leading historian of the early

Italian-American mafia David Critchley concludes, the '[o]riginal American Mafia chieftains were frequently pillars of the Italian community, involving themselves in politics, and earning a living from self-employment.'[89] Their power stemmed particularly from their ability to govern these kinds of illicit markets and transactions. As Joe Bonanno put it: 'By performing such favors [such as resolving extortion disputes], large and small, the "man of honor" made himself indispensable.'[90] As in Sicily, the new American *mafioso's* power rested on what one Mob leader's son described as 'a thousand friendships'—the power of his social network.[91] Mafia leaders' dispute resolution efforts placed people in their debt, both figuratively and often literally: mafia mediators would often take a cut of the settlement negotiated with Black Hand extorters, and also lend the victim the money needed to pay the settlement (often at extortionate rates).[92]

These pioneers were not envoys of Italian criminal organizations, sent strategically to build new branches in New York, but rather unwitting vessels for the transplantation of mafia strategy and techniques. The initiation rituals for these early American mafia *cosche*, for example, seem to have been directly copied from those in southern Italy.[93] The connections they developed back to Italian criminal groups were not hierarchical, but fraternal. There was no unified command structure; there was a shared operational culture and system of governmentality. In these early days, *mafiosi* emigrating to the US could hold dual membership of both the Italian and US organizations. American organizations would accept a 'letter of consent' from a Sicilian *capo* as a basis for admission to an American *cosca*, and 'made' members moved back and forth between the organizations.[94]

The most important leader to emerge in this way was Giuseppe Morello, whose *cosca* wielded influence from New York to Chicago and Louisiana in the 1910s. The Morello *cosca* is sometimes described as the 'First Family' of the American mafia. Morello was born in Corleone in western Sicily in 1867. By the time he migrated to New York in 1894 to escape imprisonment for counterfeiting, he was a powerful member of the Corleone *cosca*. By 1900, he had become a leader in the manufacture and distribution of counterfeit notes in New York, and his seniority in the mafia in Sicily gave him high standing in the US, with some insider accounts describing him as the first *capo di tutti capi* (boss of all bosses).[95] Dickie describes Morello's gang as an early transplant of the Sicilian *mafioso* culture to New York, using the same techniques of protection, patronage and police corruption.[96]

Morello's operation, however, demonstrated several strategic vulnerabilities. First, it lacked strategic depth. Critchley's research into primary records suggests that it was organized like a rural Sicilian *cosca*, with only ten or twenty members, leaving Morello without 'buffers' between him and the rank and file, 'creating an obvious risk of exposure of the leadership to prosecution'.[97] In Sicily, the Corleone *cosca* could rely on the powerful normative hold of *omertà* over the broader population to provide cover. In New York, the influence of *omertà* was notably less extensive. Second, Morello built his organization around a core *Corleonesi* kinship network involving overlapping marriages between the Morello and Terranova families. As his operation grew and required more personnel, he relied on members of this group to vouch for new members from outside the network, expanding into a broader Sicilian network, but with only very limited reach into the Calabrian and Neapolitan communities.[98] This fostered operational security, but again at the expense of social reach. No charismatic communicator, Morello lacked the social connections in New York (or beyond) that would have allowed him to broker resolutions to larger disputes. He was not, in other words, able to develop broader governmental power within the emerging Italian-American underworld, or political power beyond it.[99] Morello consequently failed to develop effective protection from the state. While he did corrupt numerous judges and police officers, it proved inadequate.[100] Counterfeiting was a federal crime, and federal officials lived in places, both literal and figurative, that Morello could not reach. Later, for exactly this reason, the American mafia would formalize a ban on engagement in counterfeiting, and mafia members were specifically warned not to harm federal agents.[101] In 1910, he was jailed for twenty-five years on counterfeiting charges.

Around the same time, two other distinct mafia-style groups began to consolidate in Brooklyn, both descendants of the Neapolitan Camorra. One was based around the Brooklyn Navy Yard and one around Coney Island. For a period they were bloody competitors, but eventually banded together to wipe out the (Sicilian) Morellos.[102] Yet they also suffered from a lack of strategic depth due to their failure to move beyond their

own specific immigrant communities, and their long bloodletting significantly diminished their own coercive capabilities.[103]

The question of whether these criminal groups should replicate the
provincialism of their Italian forebears or move beyond it, overlooking
ethnic identity, became a central political and strategic question within
the organizations. It was a question of trust. Sicilians were not used to
trusting Calabrians or Neapolitans. Joe Bonanno, a 'traditionalist',
argued throughout his life that non-Sicilians could not fully understand
the Sicilian 'Tradition'.[104] FBI records from as late as the 1960s point
to formal vertical and horizontal separations between *mafiosi* of different (Italian) geographic heredity in the St Louis, Philadelphia and
Cleveland mafia *cosche*.[105] Yet by the late 1910s, Neapolitans and
Calabrians were increasingly being recruited into the more cosmopolitan, Sicilian-led mafia *cosche* that were emerging on the Lower East
Side and in East Harlem. Some Sicilians were also beginning to collaborate with Irish, Jewish or other gangs. On the Lower East Side,
Salvatore Lucania was beginning to make a name for himself (as Lucky
Luciano) through collaboration with a Neapolitan kid, Vito Genovese,
a Calabrian immigrant, Francesco Castiglia (Frank Costello) and even
a Russian Jewish immigrant, Maier Suchowljansky (Meyer Lansky).
Luciano was adapting the Sicilian tradition, with its emphasis on real or
fictive kinship, to create a 'modern family', stretching beyond traditional *cosche* lines. 'I used to tell Lansky,' he would later say, 'that he may
have been Jewish, but someplace he must have been wet nursed by a
Sicilian mother.'[106]

Illicit government

The *cosche* or 'Families' that were emerging in America were, just like
their Sicilian *cosche* forerunners, governmental.[107] Members became
embedded in a secret normative order. The:

> family embraced an individual's whole life and demanded his total loyalty.
> Within its confines family members learned a common set of roles,
> norms, and values, which not only regulated their behavior within the
> family but structured their relationships with the outside world as well. In
> his relations with outsiders, a man never acts simply as an individual, but
> rather as a representative of his clan.[108]

This was the sense in which even *mafiosi* from different American *cosche* would refer to their shared world as 'Our Thing', *Cosa Nostra*. It conveyed the impression of a shared, secret outlook, a shared way of being or way of life; this secret order gave them more in common with each other than what they shared with others.[109] It set them secretly apart.

The *cosca* had immense power over its members' lives. Nothing controversial, not even a marriage, could be undertaken without considering its impact on other *mafiosi*, and in many cases without seeking approval from mafia superiors.[110] Initiates specifically swore loyalty to the *cosca* 'family' over their own biological families.[111] And the word of a mafia's superior was law, even in matters of life and death, as Joe Valachi, an American *mafioso* who famously turned state's witness in the early 1960s explained to a US congressional committee:

> Mr. VALACHI. . . . If he wants to get rid of anybody, he has such a way that he finds a way of legalizing it. In other words, for instance, he will make up stories and there is no one there to dispute him.
>
> The CHAIRMAN. You mean legalize–
>
> Mr. VALACHI. Legalize it amongst ourselves.
>
> The CHAIRMAN. You mean your own crowd? In other words, his word becomes law, that makes it legal?
>
> Mr. VALACHI. Right.
>
> The CHAIRMAN. Can he and does he pass out death sentences?
>
> Mr. VALACHI. He passes them out. They tell you he was a rat, he is this. They tell you anything they want to.[112]

Secrecy was crucial. Members did not all know each other. More junior members relied on coded introductions to get to know the network. A member was introduced as 'a friend of ours', a non-member as 'a friend of mine'.[113] Yet membership of an American *cosca* (later, 'Family') was not like becoming a salaried bureaucrat. In return for participation in mafia violence, *soldati* and other members received a licence to pursue their own criminal rents, including through the use of violence, within a system regulated by the mafia hierarchy. Michael Franzese, a made member of the Colombo Family, explained: 'we weren't given a salary or put on somebody's payroll. It was up to each man to make his way.'[114] Another Colombo Family member, Joe

Cantalupo, similarly recalled that 'the rules of the game were simple. Make money any way you can.'[115] As Edelhertz and Overcast, two criminologists, put it: 'To be "made" one has to be a producer, not a mouth to feed.'[116] Again, Valachi explained:

> Senator MUNDT. ...I am trying to determine what your income was as a soldier working for Genovese.
>
> Mr. VALACHI. You don't get any salary, Senator.
>
> Senator MUNDT. Well, you get a cut, then.
>
> Mr. VALACHI. You get nothing, only what you earn yourself. ...
>
> Senator MUNDT. In other words ... all you got out of your membership of this family was protection from somebody cutting in on your racket?
>
> Mr. VALACHI. That would be a good way to put it.[117]

Such 'protection' included that from the state. In his testimony, Valachi also clarified that the Family would provide a range of support services to members and their families, including legal assistance—providing bail, a lawyer and often pulling strings in the judiciary. A member's biological family would also be looked after while he was serving time in prison, drawing on a centralized welfare fund financed through the dues and tributes paid by lower-ranking members. Other evidence makes clear the same system pertained in Sicily.[118]

The then-director of the New York State Organized Crime Task Force explained the resulting pattern of innovation and control in an interview with *New York Magazine* in 1992. The mafia, he explained, has:

> always been looked at as a corporation... But it's not... In a corporation, people at the bottom carry out the policies and perform the tasks assigned to them by executives at the top. In the Mob, the people at the bottom are the entrepreneurs. They pass a percentage of their income upward as taxes in return for governmental-type services: resolution of disputes, allocation of territories, enforcement and corruption services.[119]

The distinction between a corporate and governmental model is also borne out in the different allocations of authority within the system. To become a 'made' or initiated member in the mafia was less about ascending in the bureaucracy than entering the aristocracy. Joe Pistone, who spent six years undercover in the mafia as an FBI informant using the name 'Donnie Brasco', explained:

A made guy has protection and respect… You are elevated to a status above the outside world of 'citizens'. You are like royalty… A made guy may not be liked, may even be hated, but he is always respected.[120]

Nick Caramandi, a former *capo* in the Philadelphia-based Scarfo Family, saw the distinction in even more extreme terms. Once made, he said, 'You become like a god. Your whole life changes. You have powers that are unlimited.'[121]

The mafia's governmental power depended, however, on keeping the state at bay. As Henry Hill, a famous mafia informer, explained, what the mafia itself provided to its members to achieve this was protection and connections.[122] Connections stood for trust, and reduced transaction costs—protection from interference, cheating, prison. An individual's power in the mafia was thus linked to his ability to mobilize and deploy coercion and—above all—to his ability, through corruption and communications, to make and keep useful connections. As Pantaleone explained, 'Above all', a *Mafioso*:

> must have connections in all levels of society. If he is isolated he cannot be strong; even if he is the most feared and violent man in the 'family' or the 'cosca', and the most experienced 'killer' amongst them, he will never become a chief.[123]

Politics, it seemed, were at the root of mafia power from the outset.

The Iron Prefect

Back in Sicily, by the late 1910s the mafia was playing an important role as a broker within the island's political order, particularly by controlling the communal violence that might otherwise have arisen from Sicily's slow-motion economic modernization.

Don Calogero Vizzini, a leading mafia *capo* from Villalba in central Sicily, provides an example of how this worked. In the wake of World War One, socialists, labourers, peasants and activists from the Popular Party (the ideological precursor to the Christian Democrats) agitated for land reform. In 1920 they forcibly occupied the holdings of a major *latifundia* around Villalba, where Don Calò was based. Twelve years earlier he had brokered a solution to a similar dispute between a Paris-based absentee landlord, a Palermo-based administrator, local peasants and the Catholic Rural Fund, which granted him a lease with a local cooperative as tenants. Now he repeated the scheme, with variations. In 1921 he brokered the sale of the land by its owner, Cavaliere Matteo Guccione, to a Cooperative of War Veterans of Villalba, put together by Vizzini, presided over by Vizzini's brother and financed by an agricultural bank Vizzini had founded. The sale provided for the distribution of the land to small landowners—but only after six years, during which they had to continue to pay rent to Vizzini, and surrender the proceeds of the harvest to him. After the arrangement ended in 1926, both Vizzini and his sister had somehow acquired titles over significant tracts of the land.[124] Both the landowner and the local land-workers had avoided their least-preferred outcomes—violence for the landowner, the status quo for the workers—but Vizzini proved to be the real winner.

Through such manoeuvring the mafia had emerged as a conservative force in the politico-economic transition, slowing down the process of land reform and wealth redistribution that might otherwise have led to the emergence of a middle class.[125] This served the interests of conservative political forces, as did the role that the mafia played as strike-breakers and labour market brokers in Sicily's agricultural sector, unhampered by the unionization that had arisen in more urbanized economies. As Mussolini rose to power in the mid-1920s, it was this very mediating power of the mafia that seemed to represent an obstacle to the realization of the Fascist programme in Sicily. This became clear in the 1924 general election. While the Fascists won a landslide victory nationally, in Sicily mafia mobilizers secured victories for the opposition Popular Party and Liberal Party. Mussolini toured the island, hoping to drum up support, but received a cold reception in mafia areas. His response was the appointment of Mori and his anti-mafia campaign.

Mori's attack on the mafia was both an effort to break its power and a cover for the Fascists to 'destroy the freedom of political organization' more broadly on the island, asserting their totalizing vision of unitary power.[126] It was an effort to remove the mafia as an alternative source of governmental or political power, all of which, under its ideology, was to run through the National Fascist Party. In 1925 the Fascists abolished parliamentary elections, depriving the mafia of 'its main currency for purchasing concessions from Rome'.[127] Mori himself characterized the subsequent anti-mafia campaign as not simply 'a police campaign on a more or less grand scale, but instead an insurrection of the conscience, a revolt of the spirit, the action of a people'.[128] He recognized that the mafia 'obtains exceptional strength from a logic which is all its own', and that *omertà*, based in fear, was key to this logic.[129] His response was an explicitly moral appeal to Sicilians' sense of self and identity:

> [W]e must turn ... to pride as an instrument with which to react to arrogance and bullying; courage to react to violence; strength to react to strength; and rifles to react to rifles.[130]

The siege of Gangi in 1926 was thus intended to show that he could be more *mafioso* than the *mafiosi*. It was an attempt to show that the Fascists, not the mafia, were the viable brokers between the state and the population, the embodiment of cherished values of fortitude and self-reliance, and the most powerful governmental actors. These were themes Mori would emphasize in speeches in the towns and villages where his crackdown took place, and in interviews with the press.

Yet Mori recognized that his battle with the mafia required attacks along a material front as well as a conceptual front. He took several steps to undermine the rackets on which the mafia thrived, creating a tighter registration and branding system to undermine cattle-rustling and investing state resources in more regularly assessing land rents against yields, to prevent the mafia from forcing landowners to rent land to them at unrealistic prices.[131] Yet under his rule, agricultural wages fell by 28 per cent. The Fascists had 'not so much ... eliminated the *Mafiosi*,' as the historian Alexander Stille later put it, but rather 'replaced them by acting as the new enforcers for the Sicilian landowning class'.[132] With his campaign of intimidation, the abolition of party politics and the state's increased role in the economy, the mafia's brokering power was steadily corroded, and increasingly higher-level mafia actors moved into the Fascist Party.[133]

Mori's apparent success against the mafia appears to have come by splitting the 'upper' mafia—the parts of the mafia network that connected into the landowning classes, the urban professionals, the politicians—from the 'lower' mafia. As Lupo explains, most of those punished by Mori's campaign were *campieri* (field guards on the large estates) and *gabellotti* (estate managers, often foisted on landowners by the mafia). The campaign specifically left the traditional landowners themselves— many of whom had collaborated with, if not joined the mafia— untouched. The few landowners who were entangled in the campaign escaped punishment by successfully pleading 'necessity' at trial. And when Mori seemed set to begin to go after this 'upper' mafia, including some with open ties to the Fascist Party, he was suddenly recalled to Rome.[134] The Fascists declared victory over the mafia. It was premature. The preservation of the latifundist system left in place the bottlenecks in the Sicilian economy that the mafia was able to exploit, and much of the mafia network remained in place. Unsurprisingly, once Mussolini had moved on, the mafia quietly clawed back its power, laying the seeds of its resurgence after World War Two, described in Chapter 7.[135]

The Iron Prefect's crackdown did, however, have one other profound impact. Scores of young *mafiosi* fled to the US, including future leaders in the American mafia such as Joseph Bonanno, Carmine Galante and Joe Profaci.[136] The exodus helped to accelerate the transplantation of mafia expertise and techniques to the New World. This was particularly the case when those leaving were more senior *mafiosi*, at the *sottocapo* or *capo* level. Of these, one in particular stands out, a *capo* from the *cosca* in Castellammare del Golfo, a seaside town west of Palermo. His name was Salvatore Maranzano, and his arrival in New York would soon lead to upheaval in the American mafia.

Conclusion

The Sicilian mafia was born out of the limited governmental power in Sicily of the unified Italian state. *Mafiosi* emerged as entrepreneurial brokers during the Sicilian politico-economic transition, using their control of local coercion to develop governmental power. These entrepreneurs shared a common positioning strategy, interposing themselves between local communities and supply-chains, and the state. Over time, this loose group came to share an operational culture and organizational techniques, likely stimulated by interaction with the clandestine revolutionary networks of the 1850s and early 1860s. What emerged was not just a clandestine association, but a secret society, a private normative order with its own values, rules and repertoire structuring the possible actions of its members and associates. The Sicilian mafia represented, in other words, a specific, criminal governmentality.

The mafia's emergence in the United States followed a similar pattern: not through a deliberate colonization by Sicilian *cosche*, the Neapolitan Camorra or Calabrian 'Ndrangheta, but through the use of imported mafia techniques and strategies to govern an unruly underworld. The American mafia *cosche* coalesced among Italian immigrant communities who turned to the mafia system to govern the Black Hand extortion epidemic and petty crime more generally.[137] As Varese and Gambetta have argued, the American mafia families were the 'lineal descendants' of the Mezzogiorno mafias, rather than their colonial outposts.[138]

In Sicily, the mafia's governmental power was from almost the outset nested inside the formal political structure of the state. Mafia *cosche* were a powerful brokering force in keeping order and delivering votes. Mussolini's vision of a unified party-state left no room for the mafia to continue to play such a brokering role in Sicilian government. The campaign led by Cesare Mori to eradicate the mafia took place not only in the military or coercive domain through a sustained, large-scale show of force, but also in a political and normative, or as Mori saw it, moral dimension, through strategic communication. Through speeches, the press, military operations and trials designed for their signalling power as much as their operational necessity, Mori sought to portray himself and the Fascist Party, rather than the mafia, as the true protectors of traditional community values. He sought to position the Fascist Party as the monopoly provider of governmentality, driving the mafia out of the market.

In New York, the governmental brokering role that the mafia played in Sicily was instead played by gangs and the Tammany political organization, as described in Chapter 3. With an American mafia system emerging as a potential governmental actor, could these two brokering organizations, Tammany and the mafia, co-exist?

5

WAR AND PEACE IN THE AMERICAN MAFIA, 1920–1941

'He wanted something more terrible than money: he wanted power.'

Mafia *capo* Nicola Gentile[1]

'The real problem is to remove the influence of the racketeer from politics.'

Thomas E. Dewey[2]

On 10 September 1931 Salvatore Maranzano, the newly confirmed *capo di tutti capi* of the American mafia, was sitting in his office in the recently opened Helmsley Building that towered above Grand Central Station in midtown Manhattan. He was waiting for a visit by the federal Internal Revenue Service. When they arrived, the IRS agents flashed their identity cards and asked Maranzano to follow them into his interior office. One stayed outside in the waiting room, where, producing a gun, he bailed up the bystanders and forced them to face the wall. Inside Maranzano's office, the agents' guns jammed. So they stabbed Maranzano to death instead.

These were not IRS agents, but Jewish mobsters working for another mafia boss—Lucky Luciano. It was the second time in five months that Luciano had worked with non-Sicilians to assassinate a superior in the mafia. With these manoeuvres, and the organizational reforms he instituted after Maranzano's death, Luciano rose to preeminence within the American mafia, and a coalition of mafia Families and Jewish gangsters who came to be known as 'the Mob' emerged as the dominant power within the American underworld. By 1935 this coalition had not only gained control of rackets in most of New York's legitimate and illegitimate industries, but also developed innovative new gambling markets nationwide and—through ties between gambling and politics—leverage within New York and national-level Democratic politics. Yet in 1936 Luciano was convicted at trial and sentenced to fifty years' imprisonment in an upstate prison nicknamed 'Little Siberia'. What went wrong?

In this chapter we explore the rise and apparent fall of Lucky Luciano. Diego Gambetta has famously described the Sicilian mafia as a product of the business of private protection.[3] Here, we explore how Luciano's fate—and that of the American mafia—was shaped not just by the business of private protection but also by the politics of public protection. The first section considers the role of Prohibition as an accelerator of strategic competition in the American underworld, leading to civil war in the mafia between 1929 and 1931. After a period in which rival mafia leaders attempted to reach a mediated settlement, the conflict was finally concluded by Luciano's assassination of his mafia *capo* and Maranzano's rival, Giuseppe Masseria, at lunch in a restaurant in Coney Island. The second section considers the underworld political settlement that emerged from the civil war, the events at Maranzano's office and Luciano's subsequent constitutional reforms. A third section explores the political and economic effects of strategic reorganization within the underworld. The economies of scale opened up to the Mob allowed it to expand its governmental power, but also fostered rivalries. The fourth section considers how these rivalries for governmental power—including both underworld and upperworld actors—brought Luciano down.

Like other periods of violent strategic crisis and change, the history of the events treated in this chapter has been clouded through exaggeration and dramatization in popular journalism. This chapter relies not only on secondary sources but also a balanced array of primary accounts of these events. In the case of the 'Castellammarese War' within the American mafia, treated in the first and second sections, this includes the accounts of strategic decision-makers such as Joe Bonanno, chief of staff to

Maranzano, and Nicola Gentile, a mafia *capo* brought in to mediate a peace settlement between Maranzano and Masseria. Largely because his account remains difficult to come by, and perhaps because it is in Italian, many English-language researchers have to date overlooked this important source.[4] One notable exception is David Critchley. His detailed history of this period receives special attention.[5]

For the 'post-War' period, the 1939 series of *Collier's* magazine articles by Richard 'Dixie' Davis, formerly the lawyer of the Jewish gangster Dutch Schultz, helps to provide insight and context.[6] Tom Dewey's *Twenty Against the Underworld* affords a window into the approach of the prosecutor who brought down Luciano, but, as this chapter emphasizes, needs to be understood as an artefact of careful strategic communication by a very effective politician.[7] In some ways more useful is the popular journalist Hickman Powell's *Lucky Luciano*.[8] Powell's reporting of the speech of Mob figures, his own explanation of how he wrote the book, and triangulation against case files in New York municipal archives indicate that *Lucky Luciano* is based on access to Dewey's case-files during the Luciano trial, including transcripts of pre-trial testimony by over seventy Mob-linked witnesses. That makes it a uniquely valuable source of insight into the trial, and the Mob activities it explored.

War

Prohibition as a driver of innovation

When the Eighteenth Amendment to the United States Constitution came into effect on 16 January 1920, criminalizing the manufacture and sale of all alcoholic beverages, new rents were created, attached to a huge unmet demand. Strategic competition for control of these rents would transform the American underworld.

Prohibition resulted in part from a social backlash against the immigrant waves of the late nineteenth and early twentieth centuries. White, Protestant Middle America mobilized to defend its pastoral, family-oriented values against the perceived decadence, dissolution and corruption of America's booming cities, with their huge new alien populations.[9] Exactly for that reason, from the outset Prohibition did not take hold in New York City, the immigrant metropolis. By 1923 the New York State Legislature had terminated police cooperation with federal enforcement authorities. By 1925 the World League Against Alcoholism was reporting that 'To all intents and purposes anyone can now engage in the liquor traffic unmolested in the City of New York.'[10]

With barriers to entry low, the new market spurred innovation. Huge profits were available. The mark-up on locally produced beer was around 700 per cent, and on a case of imported Scotch whisky around 4,000 per cent—comparable to cocaine today.[11] Illicit stills sprang up in urban basements and country barns. Local street gangs that had focused on theft and extortion and illegal gambling quickly moved into production and distribution. Within a couple of years, Lucky Luciano's street gang on the Lower East Side had an annual payroll of about $1 million—about $14 million in current terms. Revenues, however, were roughly twelve times this size.[12]

Prohibition changed the strategic environment for criminal activity in New York in two fundamental ways. First, it created a huge new pool of resources which criminal groups not only had an incentive to capture, but also needed to prevent their rivals from capturing. Second, it provided social complicity, offering the strategic depth that the Sicilian mafia had enjoyed in Sicily, but which Morello's *cosca* had not been able to that point to generate. Overnight, Prohibition weakened the bonds of allegiance of the average citizen to the state, turning 'thousands of law-abiding Sicilians into bootleggers, alcohol cookers and vassals of warring mobs'.[13] To be enjoyed, alcohol needed to be consumed socially, in bars and clubs, with entertainment. That required a diverse labour force, space and a clandestine supply-chain. The result was a whole criminal ecosystem, a huge new market for illicit government, 'in which there were no courts to fix, no penalties to evade. The statutes were six-shooters, the constitution a machine-gun.'[14]

The result was a surge in organized crime. Established Irish and Jewish mobs with links to gambling syndicates were particularly well-placed at the outset to dominate high seas importation, since it required significant capital investment.[15] In contrast, moonshine and bootlegging operations—domestic production and overland distribution—offered higher risks and lower rewards, but also lower barriers to entry. As a result, the market remained fragmented. Some groups built distribution networks and production cooperatives. The Jewish syndicate led by Waxey Gordon, for example, soon controlled thirteen breweries in Pennsylvania, New York and New Jersey.[16] But most enterprises remained highly localized, opening up space for the Italian-American street gangs and the mafia to provide protection.[17]

The illicit alcohol market seemed to breed a particularly violent gangster because of the ease with which the bulky cargo could be hijacked during transit.[18] As a result, coercion became a key strategic capability for operators in the bootlegging market. The need to scale up their coercive capabilities forced the emerging Italian-American mafia *cosche* to expand and innovate, bringing in immigrants and street toughs who had grown up in America, such as Luciano.[19] Some even began to cooperate with non-Italians. It also encouraged the formation of cartel structures. In the larger urban centres the only way to achieve scale was through cooperation with other mobs.[20] Luciano cooperated from early on with a gang led by a young Russian Jewish immigrant, Meyer Lansky, by their own telling driven by the brute logic of economies of scale: 'We were in business like the Ford Motor Company,' Lansky would later explain. 'Shooting and killing was an inefficient way of doing business. Ford salesmen didn't shoot Chevrolet salesmen. They tried to outbid them.'[21]

This meant winning on cost, and one way to do that was to reduce the costs incurred from violent rivals and state interdiction—to buy protection. From the outset, the bootleggers' business model depended heavily on police corruption. The most important kerbside liquor exchange in downtown New York was at the junction of Kenmare and Mulberry Streets—just two blocks from the local police precinct house and a stone's throw from Manhattan's state and federal courthouses. As crime writer Tim Newark has succinctly put it, Prohibition unwittingly 'introduced a level of corruption into public affairs that enabled criminal gangs to get a firm grip on the American metropolis'.[22] Peter Andreas reports that between 1920 and 1926 one in twelve Prohibition enforcement agents was fired on corruption-related charges.[23] In the process of developing these corrupt ties, the mafia moved out of the Italian neighbourhoods, into the broader city—and then beyond.[24] The emergence of a national liquor market created 'the opportunity to organize on a national scale, and to gain internal discipline on a national scale'.[25] Smuggling and distribution networks emerged, with their leaders meeting frequently to sort out operational and organizational problems in leisure spots where demand for alcohol was high and protection from law enforcement could be assured: Miami, Havana, Hot Springs, Arkansas, or, most famously, Atlantic City in May 1929.[26]

The organization that emerged was not unitary or hierarchical; it was more like a world or ecosystem in which certain groups and networks dominated. These were predominantly based in New York because New York was the key node in the production and distribution networks— what is today in Mexico called a *plaza*. New York was the busiest port in the country, the starting point for rail distribution networks thoughout the country, a chokepoint in the smuggling network and a relatively safe operating environment.[27] There were other important entry and choke-points—such as Detroit[28]—but New York was also one of the biggest consumption markets, a major source of finance—and of political protection that transferred well to other parts of the country.

Civil war in the American mafia

For much of the first half of the 1920s, the landscape of bootleggers and enforcers was highly fluid, with alliances and rivalries shifting kaleidoscopically. These entrepreneurial criminal networks were not consolidated into regular organizations, but tended to operate as highly flexible 'crews' (known to criminologists as 'action sets'), coming together for a particular job, disassembling and then forming new patterns for another job.[29] The central strategic challenge for these mobs was one of internal organization.[30]

The southern Italians had one crucial competitive advantage over other local mobs and crews: their access to the codes and repertories of pre-existing secret criminal societies: the mafia, Camorra and 'Ndrangheta. These provided the scarcest of resources in the under-world—trust—and offered ready-made criminal organizations with normative and social reach into immigrant communities. Jewish mobsters such as Meyer Lansky, Bugsy Siegel and Louis 'Lepke' Buchalter could and did develop power through violence, but they had no such ready-made governmental systems on which to draw. It was to prove a decisive difference.

By the second half of the 1920s, two rival mafia networks had emerged as major players in the US liquor markets, one led by Joseph Masseria, and the other by Salvatore Maranzano. Maranzano was born on 31 July 1886 in Castellammare del Golfo in Sicily, and married into a powerful *Castellammarese* family with deep mafia ties. He quickly rose to influence in the Trapani region, developing close ties to leading politicians.[31] In the 1920s, fleeing Mori's crackdown, Maranzano migrated to the US, pitching up in Williamsburg and bringing a small fortune with him.[32] His familial ties to the Schiro *cosca*, dominant in western New York State, provided a route into the New York mafia. Within just a couple of years, he had become a major moonshiner and bootlegger, with several large distilleries upstate in Dutchess County. He had charisma and a gift for oratory. Joe Bonanno, who became his chief of staff, said that 'When Maranzano used his voice assertively, to give a command, he was the bell-knocker and you were the bell.'[33] By the late 1920s, Maranzano was *consigliere* of the Schiro *cosca*, operating primarily in Williamsburg. A second *cosca*, led by Salvatore D'Aquila, was active primarily in Harlem; and a third, including the remnants of the Morello *cosca*, continued to operate in lower Manhattan and Harlem, under the leadership of Giuseppe Masseria.

Masseria was a year younger than Maranzano, born in 1887 outside Marsala, Sicily—not a known mafia stronghold. He moved much earlier than Maranzano to New York, and while Maranzano was rising through the mafia ranks in Sicily, Masseria was involved in Black Hand activities, kidnapping and robbery on the Lower East Side of Manhattan.[34] He was close to Giuseppe Morello.[35] His fortunes were transformed by Prohibition, since his gang was based in the neighbourhood that hosted the most important wholesale curb exchange at Kenmare Street. Masseria had a particularly bloody reputation, having killed more than thirty rival bootleggers and gambling organizers.[36] Unlike the Schiro and D'Aquila *cosche*, however, Masseria's outfit was not built on a biological kinship network.[37] By the mid-1920s he had taken another young Sicilian street tough, Luciano, under his wing. Like Masseria, Luciano was born (as Salvatore Lucania) in a Sicilian town (Lercara Friddi) that was not a noted mafia base. Luciano's gang reflected his upbringing in cosmopolitan New York, incorporating individuals from outside the Sicilian tradition such as Vito Genovese and Joe Adonis (Neapolitan), Frank Costello and Albert Anastasia (Calabrian) and, later, close relations with Meyer Lansky (Jewish).[38]

As Masseria's power over moonshine and bootleg operations expanded in lower Manhattan, he confronted hostility from the D'Aquila *cosca* based in Harlem.[39] After a series of hits on each other's criminal networks, Masseria began sponsoring challenges to mafia leaders backed by D'Aquila around the country, most successfully in Cleveland in 1927.[40] In October 1928, D'Aquila himself was gunned down on Avenue A in the East Village. Insider sources suggested Masseria was responsible.[41] This left Maranzano as Masseria's major rival within the American mafia.

Maranzano's network was more narrowly 'Sicilian'. His *sottocapi* and *capiregime* included Joe Bonanno (from Castellammare, Sicily) and Joe Profaci (from Palermo), and Maranzano had placed 'traditionalist' protégés in key locations throughout New York State.[42] When a *Castellammarese capo* in Detroit, Gaspar Milazzo, was gunned down on 31 May 1930, Maranzano blamed Masseria, and called on other *Castellammarese* across the country to revolt against Masseria's increasingly overbearing power.[43] A later interview with Nicola Gentile, a mafia elder statesman called in to negotiate an end to the violence that resulted from the Maranzano-Masseria rivalry, threw light on what had been at stake:

> *Chilanti* [*the interviewer*]: I don't understand what Maranzano wanted. Was it a question of money, of whiskey…?
>
> *Gentile*: Not at all. In that period money was not needed. There were mountains of dollars available to everyone…
>
> *Chilanti*: But then what was Maranzano after?
>
> *Gentile*: He wanted something more terrible than money: he wanted power.[44]

The violence within the mafia was intensely political. Masseria's ascendancy in the late 1920s had generated resentment and resistance. He antagonized Sicilian traditionalists through his willingness to empower non-Sicilians.[45] Going over the heads of local Sicilian *capi* he initiated Al Capone (a Neapolitan) into the mafia and appointed him as his deputy in Chicago.[46] The assassination in Detroit suggested that Masseria would not stop until he controlled American *cosche* nationwide.[47] His adversaries, such as Joe Bonanno in Brooklyn, saw Masseria pursuing power 'through a combination of intimidation, strong-arm tactics, bullying and tenacity'.[48] Gentile concluded that:

> The actions of the Masseria government were imposed through a dictator-ship, through exasperating commands which did not allow reply… They ruled by force of terror.[49]

Maranzano mobilized a coalition to contest Masseria's centralization of power.[50] Active resistance appears to have begun in late 1929. The Masseria *capo* installed to run the *cosca* in Cleveland was assassinated.[51] In the Bronx, a *sottocapo*, Tommaso Gagliano, prepared a revolt against another Masseria-installed *capo*, and reached out to Maranzano for support.[52] Maranzano used the killing in Detroit as a pretext to stoke dissent, describing it as 'tantamount to a declaration of war against all Castellammarese'.[53]

The violence that followed, now known as the 'Castellammarese War', was not a pitched battle between the established regime and a united opposition. It was, like many civil wars, a series of opportunistic engagements between shifting alliances organized around two poles of power. Both poles were based in New York, and this was the primary operational theatre of the war. Recalling Stathis Kalyvas' explanation of the way that local disputes come to be recast in the context of civil war violence,[54] Critchley explains that, during the Castellammarese War, murders outside New York were the outcome of chiefly localized dynamics exploding or simmering just below the surface before the war began, while being influenced by personalities and events as they emerged in New York.[55]

Concerned for his safety, Schiro, still the nominal *capo* in the Brooklyn-based *cosca* despite Maranzano's growing personal influence, went into hiding. In July 1930, after a major financial backer for the Schiro *cosca* was assassinated, Maranzano was formally designated 'war commander'.[56] *Soldati* sent their families away for safety. A centralized chain of command was created stretching across both the Schiro and Bronx-based Gagliano *cosche*, with Joe Bonanno as chief of staff to Maranzano. Centralized intelligence and communications apparatus were created, and the group began importing guns. Similar arrange-ments were also put in place on Masseria's side.[57]

Both sides began raising substantial funds. The mafia leaders Magaddino and Aiello provided perhaps as much as $5,000 per week to the *Castellammarese*. Gagliano put up $150,000, and Maranzano made a similar contribution.[58] These funds were used both for materiel, and to pay the frontline soldiers, many of whom were holed up in safe houses awaiting orders, or undertaking surveillance—and thus unable to run their normal rackets.[59] Human smuggling from Europe also appears to have played an important financing role for Maranzano.[60] Masseria (and Luciano) may have turned to drug trafficking from Europe.[61] These financing and logistical networks quickly generated an arms race. Both Masseria and Maranzano took to riding in armour-plated cars, and Maranzano had a swivel-mounted machine gun installed in the back seat.[62]

Maranzano went on the offensive, hitting several targets before Masseria could retaliate. On 15 August 1930, Maranzano's forces killed Masseria's mentor, Morello, and two others at 352 East 116th Street. On 5 September 1930, Gagliano's men killed a Masseria-allied *capo* in the Bronx, with that *cosca* then formally defecting to Maranzano's cause.[63] This was a major strategic development. The new *capo* in the Bronx, Gagliano, was not a *Castellammarese*: he was born in Corleone, Sicily. Masseria now found himself confronted not just by a *Castellammarese* kinship network, but by a broader alliance of Sicilians claiming to protect the Sicilian 'tradition'. In November 1930, a joint operation by Schiro and Gagliano *soldati* penetrated a secret Masseria conclave in the Alhambra apartments at 760 Pelham Parkway in the Bronx, killing two and almost killing Masseria himself.[64] Masseria's vulnerability was now obvious to all.

Mediation and betrayal

Maranzano sought to press home his advantage. Despite his gains, he was running out of time. For much of 1930, the police had stood by.[65] Gentile claims that the police commissioner told the mafia *capi* that 'so long as they killed amongst themselves, it did not concern him'. But as press alarm grew (magnified by leaks from the belligerents, using the press as a bullhorn to stoke fear and intimidate their rivals) the commissioner indicated to the *capi* that they must either resolve the matter themselves—without resorting to gunfire—or they could expect a police crackdown.[66]

Maranzano switched from a military to a political track. Demonizing Masseria as a despot, he sold himself to the mafia rank and file as a bridge-building alternative leader.[67] Drawing on Sicilian practice, he instigated the convening of the first 'General Assembly' of the American mafia in Boston on 1 December 1930. The Assembly elected a neutral Boston *capo*, Gaspare Messina, as provisional *capo di tutti capi* and created an impartial five-man commission (including Nicola Gentile) charged with negotiating a peace settlement.[68] The commissioners met with Maranzano for four days and offered to organize new elections for a permanent *capo di capi*. But Maranzano insisted Masseria must go, and tried to convince the commissioners to approve his replacement by his *sottocapo*, Vincent Mangano. Desperate, Masseria disappeared from view while telling his supporters to unilaterally disarm and offering himself to become a 'plain soldier'.[69] Once they felt they had amassed adequate political support, Maranzano's supporters circulated a letter calling a new General Assembly, this time in Maranzano-supporting New York.[70] There, in front of some 300 *mafiosi*, Maranzano gave a rousing speech that increased pressure for Masseria's assassination.[71] The commissioners proposed a two-month truce, but Maranzano rejected the idea, and soon after another key Masseria financier, Joseph Catania, was assassinated.[72]

Critchley's description of the role of this General Assembly paints a picture of peace-making between mafia Families that could easily describe a contemporary civil war peace process overseen by the United Nations:

> Parties in dispute were 'encouraged' to discuss solutions to problems, but it was ultimately left to Family heads to accept or to reject them. The system left the general assembly during the War in the difficult position of aiming to restore peace but without the means to enforce it.[73]

Just as successful international conflict resolution often depends on underlying military factors, so Maranzano's political ascendancy in the American mafia flowed from his forging of an unassailable military coalition. Yet he had not delivered the *coup de grâce*. Masseria, though humiliated, lived. Maranzano turned to Masseria's own war commander, Lucky

Luciano, to settle the matter.[74] On 15 April 1931, Luciano, Vito Genovese and Joe Adonis met Masseria at the Nuovo Villa Tammaro restaurant in Coney Island, and assassinated him at the lunch table.[75]

Luciano's decision to betray Masseria and throw his weight behind Maranzano decided matters in Maranzano's favour. But this begs a question. Why did the other *capi*, many of whom were older and of higher standing than Luciano, go along with this move? Luciano was not, after all, *capo* of his own *cosca* at this point; ordinarily, his assassination of his own *capo* would risk harsh punishment by other *capi*. Luciano's move was justified by his peers in classic *realpolitik* terms, as a necessary evil to protect the integrity of the mafia from the twin threat of internal collapse and external invasion (by the state). Gentile summarized this thinking neatly: 'It was a just decision because the Masseria government was already in crisis, no longer exercised power, and was thus a danger to us all.'[76]

Peace

Five Families

Maranzano quickly instituted a series of organizational reforms designed to entrench his power. A third General Assembly was held in May 1931 in Chicago, reorganizing New York's *cosche* into the 'Five Families'.[77] These later came to be known by the names of the *capi* who succeeded the leaders in place at this point. Maranzano's *Castellammarese*-based group ultimately became the Bonanno Family, after Joe Bonanno. Luciano's group went on to become known as the Genovese Family, after Vito Genovese. Tommy Gagliano's Bronx-based group was known as the Lucchese Family, and the remnants of the Aquila *cosca* became the Gambino Family. Joe Profaci, who had managed to stay largely neutral through the war, led the fifth group, later known as the Colombo Family.[78]

The creation of these 'Five Families' was about more than leadership appointments and names, however. It was a post-war political settlement within the American mafia. It provides the constitutional foundation for the American mafia to this day. Because of the political and economic dominance of the New York *cosche* within the Italian-

American underworld, their reorganization triggered realignment across the country. The way in which this settlement was carefully hammered out and publicized suggests a deliberate and strategic organization of the American mafia, belying the contention of sociologist Francis Ianni that American mafia Families were 'not consciously constructed formal organizations'.[79]

Joe Bonanno, Maranzano's right-hand man, records a series of conclaves between Maranzano and other mafia leaders in Chicago and upstate New York that allowed each leader to 'identify and place himself within the new political constellation'.[80] The settlement was then publicized to New York *soldati* at a meeting in the Bronx. Maranzano was to be *capo di tutti capi*.[81] New, clearer, rules were introduced to deal with disputes between the Families.[82] The old rules forbidding *mafiosi* from using force against each other were also emphasized.[83] While the war had forced changes in command and control structures to respond to operational tempo, the Bronx meeting made clear that old command hierarchies were reinstated.[84] The new settlement was not a wholesale change: it represented a codification and formalization of old approaches, adapting them to new realities. The governmentality was old, but the governmental institutions were new.[85]

Coup d'état

In early August 1931 a three-day testimonial 'banquet' was held to mark the end of the Castellammarese War and to ratify Maranzano's new regime. A total of $115,000 in tributes was raised through $6 tickets and contributions in cash envelopes. Maranzano's supporters were dancing, almost literally, on Masseria's grave: the banquet was held at the Coney Island restaurant where he had been murdered.[86]

Such an ostentatious show of power suggested a tin ear on the part of a leader who had earlier promoted rebellion precisely on the basis that his predecessor had grown too big for his boots. In short order, Maranzano's political coalition began to fray. While he was a natural military commander, even his chief of staff, Bonanno, conceded that Maranzano 'became somewhat of a misfit' in the peacetime environment.[87] He seemed to be stuck in war mode, unable to make the transition to the diplomacy required for peacetime coalition government.

Instead of distributing the Coney Island funds as a peace dividend, he pocketed them, arguing that he needed them to maintain his regime's security.[88] He warned Magaddino and Capone that he sensed 'very strongly the possibility of the outbreak of a [new] war'.[89] Outwardly conciliatory, he secretly prepared a target-list of sixty underworld opponents to be purged.[90] These were senior and mid-level leaders 'he could not get along with'—all originally in opposition during the war, or slow to join Maranzano's winning team.[91] Lucky Luciano was at the top of the list. He had recent form when it came to double-crossing a *capo di tutti capi*.[92] Maranzano hired an Irish hit-man, Vincent 'Mad Dog' Coll, to kill Luciano.[93] But one of Maranzano's supporters spilled the beans to Luciano, Capone and Mangano.[94] Luciano went to ground and turned to his Jewish gangster friends for help.

In the middle of 1931, Maranzano had taken a protection contract—which Luciano had already turned down—in the garment industry, setting the mafia at odds with Louis 'Lepke' Buchalter, a Jewish gangster whom Luciano had worked with during Prohibition. Buchalter was working for the other side in the garment dispute.[95] Maranzano's intervention worked against Luciano's interests, both at a financial level (he had interests in Buchalter's racketeering venture) and politically (by signalling to the Jewish gangsters that he could not protect them from Italian-American interference). But it also gave him an advantage: an interest amongst the Jewish gangsters to get rid of Maranzano. Luciano and his *consigliere* Costello appear to have met with Lepke Buchalter, Meyer Lansky and Ben 'Bugsy' Siegel and hatched the plan to assassinate Maranzano.[96]

Maranzano had overreached, creating a whole new set of enemies. Luciano and his supporters carefully consulted with a range of Italian and Jewish supporters around the country.[97] As stated, the hit was carried out in Maranzano's office not by Luciano's own men, but by Jewish gangsters under Meyer Lansky's control, masquerading as federal tax officials. Maranzano's men would probably have recognized Luciano's men; they did not recognize Lansky's.[98] In the days that followed, several other Maranzano supporters were also killed.[99] In return for their help, Luciano and Gagliano in turn appear to have helped Lansky and his associates in their 1933 'Jewish War' against Irving 'Waxey Gordon' Wexler, scoping, planning and carrying out the assassination of Murray Marks.[100]

A new governmental approach

Luciano's *coup* against Maranzano left him in a strong position to assume individual leadership of the American mafia. But he recognized that both Masseria and Maranzano had become vulnerable precisely because they had sought to install themselves as *capi di tutti capi*. Luciano took a different tack, creating a new governmental approach within the mafia. Under his leadership, a coordinated, national, multi-ethnic 'Mob' emerged for the first time.

Luciano's signature institutional reform was the creation of a permanent 'Committee of Peace', later called 'The Commission'. This brought together the heads of the Five Families, Capone from Chicago and Ciccio Milano of Cleveland.[101] (This was later expanded to ten to twelve *capi*.) The Commission would exercise key aspects of the Families' governmental power collectively, to resolve disputes and maintain peace.[102] Unsurprisingly, this was welcomed by the other Family *capi*. 'He was not trying to impose himself ... as had' his forebears, concluded Bonanno.[103] Still, the Commission, like any committee, was not a level playing field. Though all members were formally equal, there were subtle informal power factors in play, including tenure and proximity to New York's Five Families.[104] Luciano served as *de facto* 'chairman' from its establishment until his imprisonment in 1936.

The Commission idea seems to have been put to, but rejected by, Maranzano.[105] Luciano made it a priority. It was this body, not he acting alone, that would now have the power to 'decide policy, establish jurisdiction, and make agreements'[106]—in other words, to govern mafia affairs. Dixie Davis, lawyer to the Jewish gangster Dutch Schultz, described the impacts of Luciano's regime:

> ...the organization was no longer a loose, fraternal order of Sicilian black-handers [*mano nero*] and alcohol cookers, but rather the framework for a system of alliances which were to govern the underworld.[107]

Members looked to the Commission as 'the ultimate authority on organizational disputes'.[108] When in the 1960s Joe Bonanno pushed to take over territory in California and Canada without prior Commission authorization, two *sottocapi* from the Genovese Family were caught discussing it on tape. One opined:

If one member can dispute a Commission order you can say good-bye to Cosa Nostra, because the Commission is the backbone of Cosa Nostra. It will be like the Irish mobs who fight among themselves and they [the mafia] will be having gang wars like they had years ago.[109]

The Commission system was seen, in other words, as the foundation of effective collective government within the American mafia. The Commission could even place a Family under temporary collective trusteeship.[110] 'The organization would be supreme; its parts, replaceable,' as Raab put it.[111]

The Commission's collective control of mafia capabilities was reflected in several further organizational innovations. First, though in practice it rarely happened, *soldati* were in theory allowed to appeal to the Commission not through their *capo* but through their Family's *consigliere*. This gave the sense that the system was more of a 'constitutional government' than the previous feudal arrangement, since the *soldato*'s rights seemed no longer to depend, at least formally, entirely on the discretion of his *capo*. As Gentile remarked, 'The government, so composed, gave assurance of trust, because everyone could turn to it without being coerced in their ideas.'[112]

Second, during the 1930s, the Commission established a collective coercive capability ('Murder, Inc.'), a squad of a dozen specialist assassins, disconnected from any particular Family, which it used as a collective enforcement arm.[113] This squad was notable both for the sheer number of contract murders it appears to have carried out—at least sixty, but perhaps as high as 400—and because it had a mixed membership, including significant numbers of Jewish gangsters, helping to bind them into the 'Mob' orbit of the Commission. Murder, Inc. was, in fact, initially led by Louis 'Lepke' Buchalter, who had assassinated Maranzano.[114]

Third, the Commission established collective corruption capabilities, including a consolidated 'Buy-Money Bank'—a strategic fund used for bribing politicians and bureaucrats.[115] And fourth, under the leadership of the Commission, the mafia began developing joint business ventures, with Families taking equity positions in syndicates bringing together not only mafia Families but also non-mafia criminal groups (notably Jewish gangsters such as Meyer Lansky and Bugsy Siegel) to develop and manage new operations.

Just as important as these formal institutional changes, however, was the shift in the mafia's broader concept of itself and the rules that governed mafia conduct—its governmentality. All Five Family *capi* approved by Maranzano had been born in Sicily. Luciano, however, appointed a Neapolitan, Vito Genovese, as his *sottocapo*, and a Calabrian, Frank Costello, as *consigliere*. What was more, he made clear his intent to continue to collaborate closely with Jewish mobsters, even inviting Lansky to sit in on some Commission meetings as an observer.[116] The Commission formally governed only the mafia Families, but in practice it set the course for the broader Mob, including Lansky, Siegel and their criminal associates.

Because these reforms made the mafia 'more businesslike' (as Joe Bonanno and Joe Valachi separately put it),[117] they are sometimes styled a 'managerial revolution'.[118] The reforms were indeed revolutionary, in the sense that they escaped the path-dependency of the Sicilian mafia tradition. As Gutiérrez Sanín and Giustozzi have noted, 'organizational solutions' adopted by clandestine militant leaders 'weigh heavily over the solutions that will be adopted tomorrow, because they create know-how and social interactions that are organization-specific'.[119] Luciano's genius was in finding a way to adapt the mafia's approach without any apparent normative revolution. He did this by developing a strategic approach that repositioned mafia governmentality in the context of American capitalist culture.

Luciano himself described his approach in business terms. He encouraged managerial reforms within Families' operations, fostering specialization of labour.[120] He referred to the Commission as the 'board of directors'.[121] 'The Mafia's like any other organization except we don't go in for advertising,' he told an undercover cop. 'We're big business, is all.'[122] Luciano saw himself and other leaders as strategic managers, breaking down situations into solvable problems: 'We was like analysers; we didn't hustle ourselves into a decision before we had a chance to think it out.'[123] His respect for Lansky was based on his recognition of Lansky's strategic nous: he 'was a guy who could always look around corners,' he reportedly told Martin Gosch.[124] Luciano and Lansky were, in their own perception, different from the mafia traditionalists: 'We was tryin' to build a business that'd move with the times and they was still livin' a hundred years ago.'[125]

As Eric Hobsbawm observed, under Luciano the mafia 'embodied ... the values of "Americanism"'. What 'could be more American than the success stories of penniless immigrant boys clawing their way to wealth and respectability by private enterprise?'[126] Luciano's success lay in connecting the Sicilian tradition and the American mentality. He was seen by his peers as a man of 'two worlds': 'He lived among us, the men of the old Tradition,' said Joe Bonanno, the *Castellammarese* traditionalist; 'but he also lived in a world apart from us', in a 'coterie whose views of life and of moneymaking were alien to ours'.[127]

Perhaps the most significant impact of Luciano's adoption of a more 'managerial' strategy has, however, been overlooked: the external impact. Both the other heads of the Five Families and criminal actors outside the mafia saw that Maranzano's rule spelled ongoing violence within the mafia, threatening intervention by the state across the underworld. Luciano, in contrast, knew how to do business across Family and ethnic lines. Throughout Prohibition he had worked closely with Jewish—and even Irish—criminal organizations. As Dickie has pointed out, these contacts were a 'key resource that he brought to bear *within* the mafia'.[128] The internal and external strategic environments were intertwined.

His emergence as a consensus candidate to replace Maranzano, and the resulting Jewish participation in the *coup*, were based on the prospect of a period of stability and potential growth for all. His reforms sought to make good on that promise. Success would depend not only on maintaining political stability within the mafia—the purpose of the Commission—but also on effective dealings with non-Italian groups, and, ultimately, political organizations and state officials. Maranzano was defeated by a strategic adversary who had understood that the dispute within the mafia was not just over who would rule the mafia and how it should be internally organized, but also over how the mafia should relate to its broader strategic environment, including how it should position itself relative to broader social norms and other sources of governmental power. Both Masseria and Maranzano proved incapable of the kind of 'influence peddling' necessary for effective coalition government.[129] Luciano proved much more adept.

Consolidating power

Racketeering and union power

The creation of the Commission opened up new economies of scale for its members. By forming investment and management 'syndicates' or 'combinations' Commission members could mobilize large volumes of capital and expertise to sink into new markets, dwarfing their strategic rivals. This was to prove of particular importance as the imminent repeal of Prohibition became obvious in 1932 and criminal groups jockeyed for control of alternative revenue streams from illegal gambling, prostitution and racketeering.

Mobsters moved heavily in the early 1930s into racketeering—collusion, often forced, between employers and/or labour, to artificially control demand and supply and extract oligopoly prices.[130] Racketeering often emerges where certain structural conditions pertain: where inelastic demand or consumers' inability to differentiate products facilitates over-pricing, or where barriers to a firm's entry or exit are high.[131] Under such circumstances, suppliers have an incentive to collude to fix prices. Coercion and corruption can become important, though secret, commercial capabilities. The Mob stood ready to supply those capabilities—and to force legitimate businesses that were not colluding to do so. One commentator noted 'open declarations … by some of the country's most notorious criminals' that they were getting out of bootlegging and into racketeering.[132] The Mob could draw on a formidable pool of coercive capabilities experienced in extortion,[133] and it also enjoyed access to capital and other scarce resources such as liquor. As Luciano explained, the spread of Mob influence was steady and insidious:

> We gave the companies that worked with us the money to help them buyin' goods and all the stuff they needed to operate with. Then, if one of our manufacturers got into us for dough that he could not pay back, and the guy had what looked like a good business, then we would become his partner.[134]

Whether, that is, he wanted a Mob partner or not. As Gambetta summarizes, 'protectors, once enlisted, invariably overstay their welcome'.[135] Just as it had for the Sicilian mafia, dominance in the market

127

for private coercion was turning the Mob into a dominant provider of private protection. Unlike the Sicilian mafia, however, the Mob was a multi-ethnic system operating within a mafia culture. The Families collaborated with Lansky, Siegel and Buchalter on a range of initiatives, notably Murder, Inc., racketeering in the garment industry and Lansky's struggle with Irving Wexler.[136]

Truckers ('teamsters') and stevedores were also major targets for Mob racketeering.[137] Both handled bottlenecks in supply-chains where employers were vulnerable to extortion, especially in an era when refrigeration remained limited and the loss of perishable goods during transit could inflict severe commercial damage. A 1932 New York State investigation led by Samuel Seabury found racketeering in a staggering list of industries from floristry to the fish market, from millinery to window cleaners.[138] Mob Families quickly penetrated the fish, poultry, greengrocery and dairy distribution chains. Working together with allied Jewish gangs, Mob Families took over the $50-million-a-year kosher chicken racket—extracting rents from producers, wholesalers and retailers.[139] Sanitation disposal followed.[140]

Union power was the next target. The Mob used its street muscle to funnel recruits and dues to allied unions, then graduated to strike-breaking and enforcement of union discipline. It was a short step for the Mob to stack a local union chapter with its affiliates. In time, specific union locals came to be considered the 'property' of particular Families. A prominent example was Local 1814 of the International Longshoremen's Association (ILA), operating in the Brooklyn waterfront neighbourhoods. The ILA controlled the assembly of stevedoring crews, giving it significant power to create bottlenecks in the waterfront economy and to extort both employers and employees, as famously represented in Elia Kazan's *On the Waterfront*. The neighbourhood mafia *capo*, Vincent Mangano, stacked Local 1814 with Mangano Family associates, with the brother of *sottocapo* Albert 'The Executioner' Anastasia, a key figure in Murder, Inc., installed as leader of Local 1814.[141] Through the local, the Anastasias developed significant waterfront loan-sharking, illegal gambling and marine hijacking activities. The Mangano (later Gambino) Family emerged as the broker of the corrupt exchanges that kept Brooklyn waterfront traffic flowing.[142] It was exactly this control that would make it necessary for the US Navy to turn to the Mob during World War Two, as we explore in the next chapter.

The power that the Mob was accruing through union infiltration was not limited to the underworld. It stretched into upperworld politics and institutions.[143] The Anastasias filled other union branches with their own supporters and began placing them into formal governmental roles.[144] In the mid-1930s Albert Anastasia's son-in-law Anthony Scotto controlled the appointment of the commissioner of the city's Department of Ports and Terminals, giving him influence over maritime traffic, waterfront contracts and real estate. Scotto's personal attorney sat on a government commission appointed to investigate corruption on the waterfront. At a later trial, two former New York mayors, a New York state senator and the president of the AFL-CIO (the peak union body in the US) all testified as character witnesses for Scotto—a sign of how far the Anastasias' influence reached.[145]

One important 'friend' of the Anastasias was Brooklyn district attorney William O'Dwyer.[146] O'Dwyer was famous for convicting members of Murder, Inc. It was only later, when he was New York City mayor, that evidence surfaced suggesting he may have protected the Anastasias during that case, possibly procuring the death of a star witness.[147] A US congressional investigation found that '[n]o matter what the motivation of his choice, action or inaction, it often seemed to result favorably for men suspected of being high up in the rackets'.[148]

Gambling innovation and political finance

As Prohibition ended, the gambling sector was one of the few that seemed to offer revenues approaching those from bootlegging. The onset of the Great Depression had increased desperation and participation in gambling. The sector quickly became a Mob 'mainstay', with the Commission increasingly asserting its power over everything from local 'numbers' and 'policy' games (informal lotteries) to backroom craps games and casinos.[149]

As in other industries, the Mob's route to control lay not through direct confrontation, but through iterative development of leverage over established operators: rendering coercive services and offering (or often imposing) protection; leveraging that into equity investments and debt; and then steadily taking over beneficial ownership, and sometimes also management.[150] 'By 1936,' claimed Dixie Davis, 'nobody could run a gambling joint … unless he stood in with the Italian mob.'[151] In cities where the Mob had not previously been dominant, it would take a coordinated syndicate approach and 'split up the gambling rights among the mob barons from various cities'. This was the approach taken in Miami, Las Vegas and—later—Havana.[152]

The gambling expansion owed much to the innovative leadership of two non-Sicilians close to Luciano. The first was Meyer Lansky. Lansky learned from Arnold Rothstein, the entrepreneurial criminal financier who backed many of the Jewish bootlegging outfits during Prohibition, probably rigged baseball's 1919 World Series and was close to Tammany bosses such as 'Big Tim' Sullivan and Mayor Jimmy Walker.[153] Under Lansky's supervision, the Mob adapted the 'wire' then being used to allow nationwide betting on horse races into a sophisticated risk-hedging system for 'lay-offs' among local 'policy' and 'numbers' games (lotteries). The Mob forced local lottery operators to pool risk; if one of them suffered large losses, they were insured and protected, and would not collapse.[154] This helped to maintain stability, a steady flow of rents—and minimize violence. The Mob was acting as a prudential regulator for the American underworld, and in the process keeping the state off its back.

The second innovator was Frank Costello. Beginning in 1931 he led a Mob takeover and expansion of the slot machine industry. The Mob created a national distribution network, forcing the machines on small business owners operating under Families' 'protection' all over the north-east, using a candy-vending outfit (True Mint Novelty Co.) as a front.[155] In 1933 the Mob had 25,000 one-armed bandits grossing about $500,000 per day. By 1940, there were 140,000 slot machines operating nationwide, generating $540 million in annual revenues.[156] Strategic coordination among the Families and their close non-Italian allies was crucial to this explosive growth. So, too, was political protection. Costello hired politicians as distribution agents and partners, buying off local law enforcement and opening up new markets.[157] During the 1932 Democratic National Convention in Chicago, for example, Costello negotiated a deal with Senator Huey Long of Louisiana, who was desperate for campaign finance.[158] New Orleans was soon flooded with slot machines, with Long taking 10 per cent of the proceeds.[159]

Such rapid growth risked fostering violent competition within the Mob and undoing the political settlement that Luciano had cobbled together with such success after the Castellammarese War. Yet Luciano and Lansky proved spectacularly successful in managing political coalitions within the Mob, using the syndication model to carefully distribute the benefits of growth. When necessary, however, they would also resort to violence. A good example was provided by the Las Vegas venture in the 1940s. Las Vegas already served as a kind of onshore 'offshore' centre for the US, a normative enclave that provided a range of services such as boxing and divorce that had been prohibited elsewhere.[160] Its growth into a gambling powerhouse in the 1940s was financed by a Mob consortium initially managed by Bugsy Siegel. Siegel had grown up with Lansky and Luciano on the Lower East Side, and worked successfully for the Mob on the West Coast, running gambling operations in Los Angeles and infiltrating the stagehands' union in Hollywood. But his management of the Mob's venture in Las Vegas, notably the Flamingo hotel and casino, was disastrous. At a meeting in Havana at Christmas 1946 (discussed in Chapter 8), the Commission, together with Lansky, ruthlessly agreed to jettison him. He was murdered in June 1947. The Flamingo—and the Las Vegas venture—rolled on without him.

Effective management of internal and external politics were, however, intertwined. In the 1950s, when Miami emerged as an important gambling market under Meyer Lansky's leadership, a Chicago mafia Family muscled in by underwriting (with over $300,000 in donations) the Democratic gubernatorial campaign of Fuller Warren. Once elected, Warren appointed special investigators to look into the Mob syndicate that controlled gambling in Miami, forcing Lansky and others to give the Chicago Family a larger cut in order to buy protection from Warren.[161] The investigation came to nought.

The connection between gambling and political fundraising was highly significant. 'Losing' a hand at cards or dice is an age-old way to pass a bribe. And the Depression had made gambling an even more important source of political finance than it had been in the past as other sources dried up. The intertwining of gambling and political fundraising could be found in a wide range of American cities controlled by political 'machines' of both Democratic and Republican stripes.[162] Because it required both careful internal coalition management and protection by external governmental actors, the Mob's expansion into gambling both increased risk for the circle immediately around Luciano, notably Frank Costello and Meyer Lansky, and also made them more powerful nodes in the Mob network. In time Costello came to be known as the 'Prime Minister' of the underworld, reflecting his emergence as the first among equals in the pseudo-parliamentary Commission and for his growing influence over the political networks within Tammany Hall. (Lansky, in turn, was nicknamed the 'Henry Kissinger' of the underworld, referring to his central role in the Mob's overseas operations—discussed further below).[163]

Costello was born 'Castiglia' in Calabria, but changed his name after falling in with the Irish gangster William Dwyer in East Harlem during Prohibition.[164] Through Dwyer he forged strong ties with Tammany's then largely Irish power networks.[165] When Costello aligned with Luciano and Lansky during Prohibition, they used the 'Buy-Money Bank' to spread influence through corruption of these networks.[166] Politicians still needed the same things they had in the nineteenth century, when Tammany rose to prominence—a way to discipline voters on election day and money to campaign.[167] An article in *The Forum* in 1931 noted that gangs still played a 'considerable part in elections … the tricks of colonizing districts, of repeating, of stuffing ballot boxes, and of terrorizing voters often require the assistance of gangs'.[168] Control of vice and gambling thus served for the Mob as a doorway to the corridors of upperworld power. As Tammany Mayor O'Dwyer (no relation to the gangster William Dwyer, but the same O'Dwyer tied to the Anastasias in Brooklyn), who was elected with Costello's help, told the Kefauver Committee: 'It doesn't matter whether it is a banker, a businessman, or a gangster, his pocketbook is always attractive.'[169]

Tammany links proved vital in extending Mob power.[170] By 1942 Costello had 'major influence' within Tammany, determining the succession at the top of Tammany Hall, and proving able to summon Tammany leaders at will.[171] Tammany links with the judiciary also proved important. A 1930 New York Supreme Court inquiry found that court officers at every level were beholden to Tammany, routinely exercising their powers not with reference to their legal or administrative duties, but in an 'entrepreneurial' fashion.[172] Police would routinely set up vulnerable innocents—especially poor women who would be charged with prostitution—in order to extort legal fees, bribes and other rents.[173] And this influence also extended into the upper judicial echelons. In 1943 a wire-tap picked up Thomas Aurelio, Tammany's new nominee for a position on the state Supreme Court, thanking Costello for pulling the strings to get him nominated, and assuring him of his 'undying loyalty'.[174]

Costello insisted to the Kefauver Committee that he was 'not a politician, only a friend of politicians'.[175] It was an unconvincing distinction: by 1934 the Mob controlled the district attorneys of both Manhattan and Brooklyn, the major contracting and financial offices of municipal institutions, police officials and major port controllers.[176] Paradoxically, when the reform-minded Republican, Fiorello La Guardia captured City Hall that year, it increased the Mob's sway over Tammany. The loss of access to revenues from state patronage and public procurement made Tammany more dependent on private financing. The Mob, with its growing control of racketeering, gambling and other criminal markets, offered it.

Fall of a czar

Playing kingmaker

For Mob leaders, influence over upperworld politicians and government officials was not just instrumentally desirable to protect profits, but also intrinsically desirable in itself. It made them feel powerful. Luciano later recalled a night in 1923 when he had distributed a huge block of tickets to a heavyweight world title fight *gratis* to the police commissioner, Tammany politicians, the press and celebrities.[177] That was, he said, the night he first 'had the feelin' of real power'.[178] By 1932 Luciano was setting his sights even higher: influence over the White House.

The 1932 Democratic presidential nomination had come down to a contest between two New York politicians: Al Smith, a reform-minded Tammany former governor; and Franklin Delano Roosevelt, the sitting governor, not aligned with Tammany. If he was to win the nomination at the Chicago Democratic Convention, Roosevelt needed to neutralize the Tammany threat. As a growing power in Tammany affairs, the Mob leadership saw a huge strategic opportunity. Luciano, Costello and Lansky all accompanied the Tammany Hall delegation to the Convention in Chicago, where Al Capone provided much of the (still illegal) alcohol and entertainment. Costello shared a hotel suite with Jimmy Hines, the Tammany grand sachem, who announced Tammany support for Roosevelt.[179] But another Tammany politician, Albert Marinelli, announced that he and a small bloc were defecting and would not support Roosevelt.

Marinelli was Tammany's leader in the Second Assembly District, its heartland below Manhattan's 14th Street. During Prohibition he had owned a trucking company—run by Lucky Luciano.[180] Luciano had helped him to become the first Italian-American district leader in Tammany, and in 1931 forced the resignation of the city clerk, who was replaced by Marinelli, giving Luciano and Marinelli control over selection of grand jurors and the tabulation of votes during city elections.[181] Now, Luciano was sharing Marinelli's Chicago hotel suite. The Mob and Tammany appear to have been playing both sides, looking either to hedge their bets or, more likely, to place themselves as brokers in the Democratic nomination process in order to extract maximum influence over the winner.[182]

Roosevelt needed his state delegation's full support—and thus Tammany's—if he was going to win the floor vote at the Convention. But he also needed to avoid being tainted by the whiff of scandal that hung stubbornly around Tammany. Roosevelt responded to the split in Tammany by issuing a statement denouncing civic corruption, while carefully noting that he had not seen adequate evidence to date to warrant prosecution of sitting Tammany leaders, despite an ongoing investigation run by an independent-minded prosecutor, Sam Seabury. Marinelli, in turn, dropped his opposition, giving Roosevelt Tammany's full support and the momentum needed to claim the two-thirds majority required for nomination. Tammany's role was not determinative; Roosevelt's nomination had numerous fathers, not least John Garner, a rival candidate to whom Roosevelt offered the vice-presidency in return for the votes of the Texas and California delegations.[183] But it was a factor. If the Mob leaders were not quite kingmakers as they had hoped, they were certainly players. As Luciano reportedly put it, 'I don't say we elected Roosevelt, but we gave him a pretty good push.'[184]

Luciano was nonetheless a newcomer to upperworld politics, and seems to have been quickly outsmarted by FDR. Having secured the presidential nomination, FDR loosened the reins on Seabury's investigation of corruption in New York, making clear that if it developed new evidence, he might be prepared to back prosecutions after all. Seabury quickly exposed significant Tammany graft in the New York administration. The city sheriff had amassed $400,000 in savings from a job that paid $12,000 a year. The mayor had awarded a bus contract to a company that owned no buses but was happy to give him a personal line of credit. A judge with half a million dollars in savings had been granted a loan to support thirty-four 'relatives' found to be in his care. Against the backdrop of Depression New York, with a collapsing private sector, 25 per cent unemployment and imploding tax revenues, this was shocking profligacy and nepotism. By September 1932 the mayor had resigned and fled to Paris with his showgirl girlfriend.[185]

In early 1933 FDR moved into the White House, and broke off the formal connection between Tammany Hall and the national Democratic Party for the first time in 105 years. He even tacitly supported the election of the reformist Republican La Guardia as New York mayor. Luciano was pragmatic:

> ...he done exactly what I would've done in the same position, and he was no different than me ... we was both shitass doublecrossers, no matter how you look at it.[186]

Mobbing up

Luciano's pragmatism suggests a failure to understand the danger that FDR's ascendancy posed to Tammany and thus to his own political protection. Luciano presumed that Tammany would still protect him in New York, whoever was in power in the White House. Luciano did not understand that the Mob's ability to penetrate Tammany in the early 1930s was a sign not only of his and the Mob's increasing power, but also Tammany's decline as a broker of governmental services for underserviced populations in New York such the African American and West

Indian populations in Harlem, and women.[187] The arrival of radio (and later television) presented a further problem for Tammany, as it allowed politicians to communicate directly with voters without the aid of an intermediary organization. And finally the movement of social welfare from the city and state level to the federal level under the New Deal would also corrode Tammany's brokering power.[188]

Tammany leaders realized by the early 1930s that they were in deep trouble, and that they needed to find new income and sources of power. Jimmy Hines recognized that Al Marinelli's alliance with the Mob offered Marinelli new revenue sources and muscle, and thus posed a powerful threat to his own position within Tammany. Looking for a counterweight, he set up a meeting with one of the few major New York gangsters who had remained independent of the Mob: Dutch Schultz.

Schultz was a Harlem-based gangster who had risen to power through a violent takeover of Irish beer distribution organizations during Prohibition.[189] By 1932 he had control of the city's restaurant rackets and was a major player in the city courts' 'bonding' racket, particularly around Harlem.[190] The bonding racket turned law enforcement into a money making exercise for both the cops and the robbers: police officers could be bribed to present evidence in a manner that would tilt towards or against warranting bail, and gangsters used their control over this discretion to extract fees from those charged with crimes.[191] Schultz's outfit remained 'one of the last strong independent organizations to stand up against a consolidation of underworld power [in] a nationwide fabric of interlocking mobs,' as his lawyer, Dixie Davis, later put it.[192] He was 'one of the last independent barons' as the Mob coalesced around Luciano.[193] And his strategic approach was quite different: Luciano was a coalition-builder; Schultz focused on coercion. He deliberately adopted a divide-and-conquer approach to internal discipline, telling Davis: 'That's the way Napoleon did, kept his generals fighting among themselves. Then none of 'em got too big.'[194] He had delusions of grandeur, telling his lawyer that the Bolshevik revolutionaries in Russia were 'just like me… They're just a mob. If I'd been there with my mob, I could have taken over, just like they did.'[195] He was personally violent and deliberately unpredictable. Davis describes life with Schultz as 'palace politics around a dictator'.[196]

In 1932 Schultz was attempting to expand his power even further, through a violent takeover of the informal 'policy' lottery in Harlem—so named because of its similarity to the sale of penny insurance policies. For as little as a nickel or dime a consumer could place a bet on a three-digit number. If his number came up—as determined by some random event, such as the last three digits of the New York Stock Exchange at closing, for example—he was paid off at odds of around 600:1. With the odds of a win at 998:1, even with a 'fair' system the house almost always won. The Harlem policy market was the most lucrative in the city, taking in as much as $80,000 per week.[197] Schultz began a violent attempt to take it over. But his stand-over tactics made him vulnerable to law enforcement. He needed police protection. As Schultz's lawyer and counsellor, Dixie Davis, later put it, he realized that 'to run an organized mob you've got to have a politician'.[198]

Jimmy Hines, who needed campaign finance, had large influence over police appointments and assignments, and the district attorney's office.[199] He, in turn, understood that 'In politics, the thing to do is to build yourself an army.'[200] And he had already showed his willingness to amass an army through crooked deals and corrupt dealings.[201] An alliance between Hines and Schultz made sense to them both. They quickly reached agreement. Schultz would provide $500 (later raised to $1,000) per week, plus separate election campaign contributions in the tens of thousands of dollars, physical protection and support during elections. Hines would use Tammany connections to protect Schultz from law enforcement. Both sides made good on their promises, Hines ensuring that cases against Schultz were allocated to Tammany-linked magistrates who threw them out. In return, he received both finance and votes, using Schultz's gangsters as repeat voters.[202]

As time passed, Hines and Schultz appear to have become increasingly close, moving from a transactional relationship to something closer to a genuine partnership. Davis describes sitting with Hines and Schultz:

> as we plotted ways by which, with the Dutchman's mob and money, Hines might extend his power over still other districts and seize ... control of Tammany.[203]

They had become strategic allies in a conflict being fought in two different worlds: Schultz was using Tammany's protection to control the Harlem policy rackets and maintain his independence within the underworld from the Mob, while Hines was using Schultz's muscle and finance to enlarge his power within Tammany and upperworld politics.

The Boy Scout

For a year or so the scheme paid off. But then the strategic environment began to shift. In 1933, an ambitious young federal prosecutor, Thomas Dewey, had Schultz indicted on tax evasion charges. For the best part of two years, Schultz operated from hiding, relying on his 'minister of foreign affairs', Abraham 'Bo' Weinberg, to represent him. Hines' reach did not extend into the federal office where Dewey worked, so the investigation could not be terminated. But once the case came to trial, Hines' influence told. A Tammany-linked judge agreed to move the case to the tiny town of Malone near the Canadian border. Schultz used some canny spending and strategic communications (including showering a local children's hospital with flowers and cards) to win local sympathy with the jury. He was quickly acquitted.[204] The acquittal went to his head. 'Any guy who can lick the government can lick anybody,' he told Davis.[205] Emerging from hiding, he became concerned that Weinberg had been plotting with the Mob to double-cross him. In early September 1935 Weinberg's feet were set in concrete and he was dumped in the Hudson River.[206] Now, without consulting Luciano, the Commission or other Mob leaders, Schultz signalled his intent to assassinate Dewey.[207]

Luciano was alarmed by Schultz's recklessness. The Commission 'decided we wouldn't hit newspaper guys or cops and D.A.'s,' he reportedly said. 'We don't want the kind of trouble everybody'd get if we hit Dewey.'[208] He wanted to avoid direct confrontation with the state and was prepared to kill Schultz if that was necessary. Yet this was also an important strategic test for Luciano's organizational reforms: under the Commission's collective security system, it was not just his views that mattered. This was the first time the Commission had been asked to take a collective decision of such consequence—to kill someone not just outside the mafia, but clearly outside the broader Mob.[209] The Commission was being asked to take on a role governing the broader relationship between the underworld and the upperworld. As

Luciano supposedly put it, the Commission 'was either gonna work or the whole thing could fall apart right then and there'.[210] The Commission agreed to have Murder, Inc. kill Schultz.[211] The hit took place at the Palace Chop House in New Jersey on 23 October 1935, killing five others in the process.[212]

With Schultz out of the way, the Mob's wealth and power seemed even less vulnerable, and Luciano even more to have the air of a 'czar'. That was the term used for him when, within just a year, he was on trial, facing off directly with the prosecutor Tom Dewey.[213] Though only thirty-three, Dewey had already made a mark through his earlier pursuit of Dutch Schultz (and Waxey Gordon). But Luciano and the Mob were not too concerned. 'What do they think of me?' Dewey asked a knowledgeable journalist. 'They regard you as a Boy Scout,' came the reply, 'hopelessly mismatched against their terrorist tactics and political connections.'[214]

It was to prove a dangerous underestimation of this highly effective politician. When Schultz was killed, Dewey set his sights instead on Luciano after stumbling across evidence of Mob control of New York's prostitution industry.[215] The Mob had moved into the prostitution market during the autumn of 1933, filling the protect-and-tax role that Tammany had once occupied.[216] The Mob syndicated the industry, with the revenues from specific brothels providing dividends to different groups of Families and other Mob players.[217] This was good Mob politics. But it did not leave everyone a winner. The Mob had followed its playbook from its imposition of rackets on other industries, muscling in first on the madams who controlled the brothels, and then imposing taxes also on the male 'bookers' who operated like 'theatrical agents', booking sex-workers into brothels 'after the manner of vaudeville circuits, with a change of entertainers every week'.[218] Over time, the fees imposed by the Mobs were raised. The madams complained that the tax burden was too high and would make the brothels commercially unviable. The Mob did not seem particularly to care: a heavily indebted brothel was an easy target for Mob loan-sharks and, ultimately, hostile takeover.[219] Luciano's stated objective, as a witness during his trial would famously claim, was to turn the system into a modern business: 'We can take the joints away from madams, put them on salary or commission, and run them like a syndicate, like large A&P stores,' he reportedly said, referring to a new Canadian supermarket chain.[220] But in this industry the strategy generated 'widespread tax dodging' by madams and bookers, looking to avoid the Mob's charges.[221] The Mob's coercive response helped to create a pool of resentful underworld players, not used to Mob rule, not deeply socialized in mafia governmentality and not governed by values of *omertà*. Luciano seemed oblivious to the danger: after all, in the highly violent, male-dominated underworld that he ruled over, what did he have to fear from a group of women?

When Dewey's investigation gathered steam, first madams, then female sex-workers, then male booking agents began to roll over, turning state's witness in return not just for immunity from state prosecution, but also protection from the Mob.[222] The testimonies of the sex industry labour force—especially the women—ultimately proved crucial at Luciano's trial. Not one of the witnesses against him, notably, was Italian-American. Their prior silence was the result of fear, not a positive affinity with the Mob.[223] For them, the Mob was frightening, even terrifying; but not ultimately a source of binding governmentality. If the state could credibly promise protection, they would defect.

By mid-1936 Luciano had been tried and convicted, on a sentence of thirty to fifty years, after coming off second best in a courtroom contest with Dewey. Dewey used the female sex-workers who testified against Luciano as props in stoking a moral panic: he portrayed them as powerless victims of a terrifying criminal organization, bent on corrupting them and threatening all New York's traditional family values. It was a story the middle class, and the jury, were happy to hear, notwithstanding New York's long traditions of vice and prostitution.

Luciano and his henchmen struggled to make sense of their adversary's approach. Unable to fathom that they had been rendered vulnerable by women, they claimed that the conviction must have been stitched up. Luciano, they pointed out, had never been directly involved in the prostitution racket. But this was something Dewey conceded. That was not his case. His case was instead that Luciano governed the prostitution industry, as his opening statement at trial made clear:

> Luciano will be proved not to have placed any women in any house, not to have directly taken any money from any women, but [rather] to have sat way up at the top in his apartment at the Waldorf as the czar of organized

crime in this city where his word, and his word alone, was sufficient to terminate all competitive enterprises of any kind.[224]

Once they realized the danger posed by the female witnesses, the mafia turned to their normal approach: threats of violence. Several witnesses recanted their testimony after the trial. But it was too late. Luciano's appeal was unsuccessful.[225] It seemed he would die in prison.

For Dewey, though, this was just the beginning. Over the next decade, he wrapped himself in the mantle of the community's chief protector against (immigrant-born) corruption and crime and the champion of civic virtue and traditional (white, Protestant) morality. He rocketed to fame. Newsreel coverage of the Luciano trial nationalized his image. After Luciano's conviction, national polling showed Dewey, almost unknown outside New York a year earlier, with a huge lead over even FDR as preferred president.[226] In August 1937 he accepted the Republican nomination for Manhattan district attorney, and cruised to victory after a radio campaign 'blasting away at Tammany Hall by telling true detective stories on the radio, hair-raisers about the power of the underworld,' as Dixie Davis put it.[227] Dewey found a politically astute formula linking his anti-mafia efforts with Republican values of small government and protection of the family:

> There is today scarcely a business in New York which does not somehow pay its tribute to the underworld, a tribute levied by force and collected by fear. There is certainly not a family in the City of New York which does not pay its share of tribute to the underworld every day it lives, and with every meal it eats.[228]

It was a breathtaking piece of rhetoric. In Sicily, the mafia had presented itself as the protector of the community and its traditional values from an overbearing governmental force, the state. Here, Dewey, the state official, was using the same argument to claim the role of community protector, with the mafia itself treated as the overbearing governmental force.

Half a year after being elected Manhattan district attorney, Dewey secured the Republican nomination for governor of New York. Though he narrowly lost the election, eight months later he declared for the presidency, riding a further wave of popularity resulting from his successful prosecution of Jimmy Hines.[229] By 1941, at thirty-nine, he was governor of New York, and in 1944 and 1948 he was the Republican nominee for the presidency. While he never quite made it to the White House, the springboard that his attacks on the Mob had provided, shooting an unknown prosecutor to national political prominence, did not go unnoticed by other politicians. Fighting organized crime, it was clear, was a great way to build a brand in the political marketplace.

Conclusion

The story of Luciano's rise and fall is, at its heart, a story about the development and management of governmental power, and the politics of protection. The Commission system instituted by Luciano in 1931 provided a platform for Mob collaboration that saw its governmental power rapidly spread across a range of rackets and industries. The system offered an underworld social contract, institutionalizing trust and releasing mobsters from their nasty, brutish and short Hobbesian existences during Prohibition. It released them from having always to rely on coercion as the way to resolve disputes. Without that governmental system, it is entirely conceivable that competition for new revenue streams after Prohibition would have led to further underworld violence. Through the Commission the mafia became, as the Kefauver Committee would later put it, the 'cement' that increasingly bound a nationwide underworld together.[230] By creating a flexible and enduring system of pseudo-parliamentary governance for the mafia, the Commission reduced transaction and capital acquisition costs and provided Mob actors access to economies of scale. The Mob exploited these opportunities smartly through the development of shared strategic capabilities such as Murder, Inc. and the Buy-Money Bank, through joint investments and innovation and through collective external positioning, particularly in relation to upperworld political actors.

But the Commission system did not turn the American underworld into a unitary firm or single organization. The Commission itself was a purely Italian-American mafia structure, not formally encompassing Jewish gangs. Some orbited it in informal alliances, and the resulting coalition acted increasingly coherently as a collective Mob, through strategic coordination at the leadership level. But independent criminal organizations could and did continue to exist outside the Mob's orbit, as Dutch Schultz's operations made clear. And the Commission system always left individual criminal groups, even mafia Families, room to develop their own political connections and power networks in the upperworld. This was made clear by the Mangano Family's ties into Brooklyn Democratic Party and union politics, which did not run through Luciano's clique, nor Tammany. Upperworld and underworld power networks could, and did, connect through multiple nodes. The Mob was not an armada with a single commander-in-chief; it was a flotilla, with multiple *capi* sailing their own vessels, their moral compasses responding to a shared criminal governmentality.

Luciano proved at first highly effective at leading this network. What brought him down was not a mismanagement of coalitions among mafia *capi*, but rather an over-extension of the Mob's reach into groups not sufficiently disciplined by its governmentality. He failed to understand the political risks the Mob faced from an alliance between underworld (largely female) dissidents and a crusading prosecutor looking to portray himself as a community protector. The clash between Luciano and Dewey was a competition between two normative systems vying to impose their own governmentality over a community. It was a competition to govern. The political nature of this competition is, for obvious reasons, written out of most official analyses: the official 'big-man' or 'kingpin' theory of organized crime treats it all as a personal enterprise, downplaying the broader normative power of organized crime. Dewey spun political capital by peddling the narrative that his convictions of the kingpins Luciano and later Hines had 'smashed whole mobs'.[231]

It was this kind of approach that misled the FBI to conclude that American mafia strategy was highly centralized and hierarchically directed, with a narrow group of leaders who 'define the criminal objectives, give the orders, and provide the means for reaching the objectives'.[232] The historical record shows a more complex, negotiated and collective decision-making process, the kind of mixture of directed and emergent strategy that often results from complex coalition arrangements. Luciano's imprisonment did not lead to a sudden, violent battle for power in the underworld. As Raab has noted, a mafia Family 'did not disintegrate at the sudden absence of its head man'.[233] On the contrary, the Commission structure functioned effectively for sixty more years. Such nuances tend to spoil a good political narrative.

More electoral credit can be reaped from portraying the fight against organized crime in Manichean and highly personalized terms, claiming the mantle of community protector.

Yet the astonishing speed with which Dewey's political star rose points to an important change in the market for government: the incredible amplifying power of film, radio and television. These media offered a way to bypass traditional intermediary and brokering political organizations such as Tammany and speak directly to electors, building a national profile. The 1951 television broadcasts of congressional hearings on organized crime led by Senator Kefauver had a similar effect, paving the way for his vice-presidential nomination.[234] This was one of the first modern major television 'events', drawing unprecedented audiences of thirty million viewers.[235] Attacks on corruption and organized crime have ever since remained an important route into American politics: Republican New York mayor Rudy Giuliani and New Jersey governor Chris Christie both started out as crusading prosecutors in the Dewey mould. Democrat senator, later secretary of state, John Kerry, even wrote a book on the topic.[236]

Some Mob figures recognized upperworld actors' political interest in developing governmental power through occasional public attacks, notwithstanding hidden cooperation. In notes for a memoir, Meyer Lansky argued that Kefauver and Dewey both used attacks on organized crime 'as a political hammer'.[237] But others were slower to this realization, to their detriment. Frank Costello, for example, chose to appear before the Kefauver Committee on one condition: that his face remained hidden. Perhaps he felt this would somehow keep his power hidden, too. It did not. The cameras focused instead on his hands, which, with his gravelly, disembodied voice, became 'the symbol of an otherwise unseen criminal empire'.[238] Costello spent fifteen months in prison for contempt of Congress for his evasive answers to the Kefauver Committee, and when he returned, he was forced out of power by the younger Vito Genovese. Lansky, who had avoided the glare of the TV spotlight, remained comparatively untroubled.

Luciano allegedly concluded near the end of his life that 'It was my publicity that really cost me the best ten years of my life.'[239] 'You gotta stay out of the papers,' he said. 'You gotta pay people good to stick their necks out while you stay in the background... all the smart ones stayed out of the papers.'[240] Once organized crime was in the public eye, its mere existence represented a disruption of the state's narrative of providing order and justice, its claim to a monopoly in the market for government. Confrontation became inevitable. Only by remaining in the shadows could the gangster expect to remain unmolested, and retain his hidden power over people's private behaviour.

6

THE UNDERWORLD PROJECT, 1941–1943

'I'll talk to anybody, a priest, a bank manager, a gangster, the devil himself.
This is a war.'

Lt Commander Charles Haffenden[1]

It was chilly by President Grant's Tomb in Riverside Park at midnight on 26 March 1942. Joe 'Socks' Lanza could probably recall that detail, twelve years later, because of what an unusual night it turned out to be. Lanza, forty-one, was the brother-in-law of a Tammany leader, elected head of United Seafood Workers Local 16975 and boss of the Fulton Fish Market—the primary seafood market for New York and the American north-east, and one of the largest in the world at the time. Lanza was also a former federal prisoner, a mafia *caporegime* and a close associate of Lucky Luciano. Frank Costello was best man at his wedding in 1941.

In March 1942 Lanza was under indictment by the Manhattan district attorney's office—until a few months earlier still run by Tom Dewey— for racketeering. He had negotiated pay rises for his union members while taking payoffs from employers to keep those rises within secretly agreed limits. So why, at midnight on 26 March, could he be found sitting on a bench on Manhattan's Upper West Side—far from his usual stomping ground on the Lower East Side—with Murray Gurfein, the head of the Rackets Division of the Manhattan district attorney's office?[2]

What were Lanza, so close to Luciano, and Gurfein, a Dewey protégé, doing there together? The venue had been carefully chosen to shield them both from prying eyes and suspicions that they were collaborating. It was just as well, because that was exactly what Gurfein was now proposing: collaboration. Not, however, to help the DA's office prosecute the Mob. No: a collaboration to 'assist the war effort'. [3]

Thus began what would come to be known in the US Navy as the 'Underworld Project': secret wartime collaboration between the US Navy, the Manhattan district attorney's office and the Mob. [4] Today the US government may express concern about the convergence of foreign state and criminal actors threatening US interests; but during World War Two it actively engineered such a convergence. Over several years, the Mob helped the US government police the New York waterfront and defend America's littoral approaches from German U-boat attacks. Mob help allowed US authorities to quickly track down four Nazi saboteurs who landed by U-boat in the Hamptons at the eastern end of Long Island. And the collaboration also drew the Mob into a range of domestic security roles of highly questionable legality: attacking union activists, infiltrating alleged Falangist organizations in Harlem and breaking into foreign consulates. In 1942 and 1943, the collaboration took a new turn, with mafia Families providing detailed operational intelligence that helped the Allies plan and execute the amphibious invasion of Sicily. As a reward for facilitating all of this collaboration in 1946 Lucky Luciano was released from prison and deported to Italy.

Luciano's release caused great controversy and criticism for the governor who ordered it: Thomas E. Dewey. Why would the very same man who had sent him to prison in the first place, ten years before, now order his release? With the US military unwilling to reveal the Underworld Project to the public, speculation filled the void. The entire Underworld Project had been, by agreement between the Navy and the Mob, 'off the record'. At the end of the war, the records that did exist were destroyed. [5] In 1953, Governor Dewey—by then a national figure, having picked up the Republican presidential nomination in 1944 and again in 1948—was forced to counter rumours that he had been bribed by the Mob to release Luciano. He tasked the New York State commissioner of investigation, the unimpeachable William B. Herlands, to conduct a secret judicial inquiry. He hoped that the resulting analysis, once published, would put the controversy to bed.

Herlands' investigation obtained sworn testimony from fifty-seven witnesses—mobsters such as Joe Lanza and Meyer Lansky, Navy and other intelligence officials, and law officers—stretching to 2,883 pages. The resulting 101-page report, sent to Dewey in 1954, was never published. Though its findings did indeed clear Dewey entirely, the underlying facts were too potentially damaging to the Navy for it to be released. The Navy convinced Dewey to put the report in a drawer and leave it there.

At the end of his life, the contents of Dewey's files—including the Herlands investigation materials—were archived in the library of the University of Rochester in upstate New York. Only two major prior publications, Rodney Campbell's 1977 *The Luciano Project*, and Tim Newark's *Mafia Allies*, have previously drawn on these materials. Campbell's 1977 book does not place the episode in the broader context of the Mob's development—our understanding of which has developed significantly in the intervening four decades. Newark's volume is much more successful in this regard, but his coverage of the Herlands investigation materials is far from comprehensive.

This chapter pieces together the story of the Underworld Project from the original Herlands investigation materials, other original FBI records and relevant secondary sources. The Mob's wartime alliance with the US government helps to explain how the Mob's strategic horizons enlarged from the national to the international level, and lays the groundwork for understanding the events in occupied Italy explored in the next chapter. The first section of this chapter explores how and why the US government enlisted the Mob in its war effort, and the evolution of the Mob's role from an intelligence focus to a domestic auxiliary enforcement role. The second section considers the Mob's provision of local knowledge and access to its Sicilian mafia cousins during the Allied invasion of Italy, and explains how this led to Luciano's release. The chapter concludes with some reflections on what this episode tells us about the evolution of the Mob's power and strategy, and the dangers of seeing the crime-politics 'convergence' as an entirely novel phenomenon.

'This is a war'

Enlisting the underworld

Lanza and Gurfein's cloak-and-dagger meeting in March 1942 was the result of a significant but shocking realization by US authorities: the Mob might offer strategic capabilities that the US government lacked and was now desperate to acquire, specifically governmental reach into New York's docks and the fishing fleet that operated in the Atlantic approaches to the eastern seaboard.

The US was reeling from several strategic setbacks. On 7 December 1941, Japanese forces attacked Pearl Harbor, killing over 2,000 US personnel and gravely damaging its Pacific fleet. Germany and Italy declared war on the US a few days later. The combined chiefs of staff of the Allied nations agreed that the basic war strategy would be 'Victory First in Europe'. But in March 1942 that was looking like an increasingly tall order, as control of the North Atlantic also seemed to be slipping away, and with it Britain's prospects of holding out against the Nazis. Britain needed more than one million tonnes of supplies per week. Between December 1941 and March 1942 German U-boats wreaked havoc on Allied shipping in the North Atlantic, with seventy-one vessels lost.[6] In January, a Norwegian oil tanker was sunk just sixty miles off Montauk (Long Island, NY), and Latvian and US vessels were sunk off North Carolina.[7] The outcome of the war seemed, as Commissioner Herlands would recall, to 'hang in the balance ... extremely grave'.[8]

How could the German submarines be operating so far from home? After survivors of U-boat attacks who had been taken aboard those U-boats reported observing American supplies on board, commercial fishing fleets came under suspicion as a possible source of refuelling and re-supply.[9] Suspicion fell on the Italian-American and German-American communities, both deeply involved in commercial fishing—and in particular 'criminal elements' within those communities. By early February 1942, US naval intelligence was hypothesizing that (a) information as to convoy movements and (b) assistance in refuelling of submarines might be traced to criminal elements of Italian or German origin on the waterfront in the metropolitan area. The theory was that such persons might sell information, or give information to the enemy out of alien sympathies; or even that some among them who had been rum-runners during the days of Prohibition might be finding a new source of revenue from running oil supplies to the enemy submarine fleet.[10]

The true source of logistical support was quite different: the Germans were running new, long-range U-boats, supported by *Milchkühe* ('milk-cow') refuelling U-boats. If this was known from decoded German signals intelligence, it was not knowledge that had reached the operational level of the Third Naval District, charged with controlling New York Harbor and its approaches.[11] There, U-boat refuelling was not the only concern. Sabotage was also feared. In late 1941, New York had witnessed a high-profile trial and conviction of thirty-three German sympathizers, twenty-five of them American citizens, on espionage and sabotage charges. Now, concerns about a potential 'fifth column' amongst the German and Italian-American communities began to reach fever pitch.[12]

On 9 January 1942 fire destroyed a pier and several buildings on the west side of Manhattan. A month later, the largest and one of the fastest luxury liners in the world, the SS *Normandie*, burned and capsized as she sat at Pier 88 at 48th Street on Manhattan's west side, wounding 128 servicemen and killing one. The largest vessel destroyed in the war to that date, she had been seized by the US government after France fell to German forces, and was being retrofitted as a troop carrier, the *Lafayette*. Worth $56 million, she was to be the US Navy's largest troop transport, expected to carry 10,000 personnel. She was due to set sail to Europe three weeks later.[13] Had she been sabotaged?

History suggests not. Mob sources would later try to claim responsibility for the fire, suggesting they had set it in order to push the Navy into their waiting arms.[14] But there are no corroborating sources. The fire appears to have been caused by sparks from welding and poor safety controls caused by a rush to get the vessel's refit finished.[15] At the time, however, the sinking of the *Normandie* fanned concerns that enemy agents might be operating in and around New York Harbor. US Office of Naval Intelligence (ONI) personnel swarmed the docks, looking for spies and saboteurs. They were quickly rebuffed by the Mob-controlled labour force, resistant to all government penetration and control. No-one was talking.[16]

The head of ONI in the Third Naval District was Lieutenant Commander Charles Haffenden, a World War One veteran, former private investigator and hotel association executive. His previous work appears to have brought him into contact with the Mob, and he now conceived and sponsored a plan to use, among others, persons with underworld associations, their underworld associates and their contacts as instrumentalities of naval intelligence.[17]

'I'll talk to anybody, a priest, a bank manager, a gangster, the devil himself,' Haffenden would later recall himself thinking. As he saw it:

> This is a war. American lives are at stake. It's not a college game where we have to look up the rule book every minute, and we're not running a headquarters office where regulations must be followed to the letter. I have a job to do.[18]

'He did not care from what source we got information as long as it was for the war effort,' explained one of his underlings later.[19] Haffenden told his team that they had 'several sore spots that we could not get to unless [with] the assistance of the underworld'.[20] He concluded that effective counter-intelligence might require 'enlisting the "underworld"'.[21] He decided to 'set up a flow of information from the underworld to combat the possibility' of enemy operations.[22] His plan was known at the highest level of naval intelligence in Washington DC, with no opposition being voiced.[23]

Mob cooperation was now deemed crucial to securing effective US surveillance of its own waterfront in its richest port. But Haffenden also saw the effort as a necessary defensive manoeuvre in a balancing game. If the US government did not form a tactical alliance with the Mob, he told his team, there was a danger that the Fascist powers would—and use it to attack New York directly. By working with the Mob, ONI would both augment its own human intelligence capabilities, and 'neutralize the possible use of the underworld by the enemy'.[24] It was a clear recognition of the strategic significance the Mob now possessed—not just in the underworld, but in broader geostrategic terms.

Regular guys

On 7 March 1942, ONI approached the district attorney, Frank Hogan, who had been the main interrogator of sex industry workers during Dewey's prosecution of Lucky Luciano, and who was also deeply involved in the prosecution of Jimmy Hines. Hogan threw his weight behind the plan for intelligence cooperation with the Mob, telling his office to open their files to the Navy and help them identify waterfront informants.[25]

Why? Why would the newly-elected Manhattan district attorney, who had made his name battling organized crime, put his reputation, political future (and livelihood) at risk by working directly with these same adversaries? Why would he increase the Mob's leverage over current and future prosecutions? To date, this has been put down to simple patriotism or expediency. Another possible explanation presents itself, however: politics. Though Dewey had become a major Republican figure, Hogan, his aide, was elected to succeed him with Tammany (in other words, Democratic) support.[26] Hogan's willingness and ability to connect ONI to the Mob may have had something to do with his electoral debt to Tammany, which by this point was firmly under Costello's Mob influence.

Whatever the motivation, ONI and Hogan's office realized that if intelligence was to flow from the docks and fishing fleets, they would first need the Mob leadership's cooperation. Hogan suggested working through Lanza, the head of the United Seafood Workers Union that controlled the Fulton Fish Market—whose brother was the local district leader for Tammany. The outstanding indictment against Lanza, they argued, would give the district attorney leverage.[27] With Hogan's approval, Gurfein and Lanza met on 26 March near Grant's Tomb.

A week later, Lanza met again with Gurfein, Haffenden and Dominick Saco—a former private investigator, now working as an undercover naval intelligence agent. The venue this time was Haffenden's inconspicuous civilian office in the Executive Members' Association suite, on the mezzanine floor of the Astor Hotel in New York's Times Square. Lanza agreed to cooperate 'one hundred percent', and Saco was appointed as a go-between. Within days, Lanza was helping ONI to place naval intelligence agents in the fishing industry along the whole length of the eastern seaboard. Lanza agreed to 'get union books and put them in as regular guys', inserting naval agents into the union books of the Building Service Employees' International Union (Local 32B), and the International Brotherhood of Teamsters, Chauffeurs, Warehousemen and Helpers (Local 202).[28]

Liaising frequently with Haffenden, over the following weeks Lanza and Ben Espy—a former rum-runner—worked their contacts on the docks. They encouraged suppliers to inform them if there were unexpectedly large purchases of fuel or other supplies by fishing smacks heading out to sea. Crews were instructed to report anything suspicious they saw on the docks or at sea. Lanza and Espy checked up on specific boats and personnel who had attracted ONI's suspicion, such as Edward Fiedler, a fishing captain of German descent who operated out of Easthampton, and Lanza's associates began passing on names of possible 'fifth columnists' to ONI.[29]

Naval intelligence agents were soon installed in the ports of Long Island, in fishing industry trucks and on fishing boats operating out of ports up and down the coast, from Maine down to North Carolina.[30] ONI also installed short-wave radio communications equipment on Mob-controlled fishing boats to create an offshore submarine lookout network. This reported relevant sightings, such as wreckage, aeroplane parts, and even human remains.[31] Soon, the major oil and gasoline suppliers to the fishing fleet were brought in on the project. This not only allowed monitoring of gasoline purchases but also, since most gasoline was sold on spec, close monitoring of the financial situation of much of the fleet—which could facilitate detection of a sudden improvement of operators' position, perhaps due to sales to enemy boats.[32]

The stream of intelligence opened to the US government flowed from both Lanza's union authority and his Mob ties. When an attempt to get the naval agent Dominick Saco a job on one of the local trucks 'created a little bit of controversy', it was Lanza's union contacts who produced a union card for Saco that smoothed things over.[33] Lanza also drew on his Mob connections, introducing some agents into Mob networks as 'our friend', a mafia code word that allowed them to 'conduct their operations or surveillance' without interference.[34]

Lucky's break

What was in this collaboration for Lanza? The DA's office repeatedly insisted that his cooperation would have no bearing on his prosecution, that it would not buy him any immunity or reduction of sentence. But since he was already under indictment, what did Lanza have to lose? Potentially quite a lot: if he were seen by his Mob superiors to have committed *infamità*, breaking *omertà*, his life would be in danger.[35]

Lanza's enthusiastic and rather unhesitating cooperation with ONI and the DA's office thus leads to the strong suspicion that he must have sought and won approval from Mob superiors from the outset.

That meant getting Lucky Luciano involved. Despite having been in prison for five years, Luciano remained an active and highly influential Mob leader, operating remotely through Frank Costello and Meyer Lansky. For Lanza to have cooperated without Luciano's approval with Frank Hogan, who helped to put Luciano away, would have been highly risky, to say the least. The US government's approach offered Luciano a huge break. But if Luciano knew about Lanza's cooperation from the outset—as seems highly likely—he was careful not to rush. Had the Mob immediately pushed the DA's office and ONI to get Luciano involved, they might have balked. At the outset, Luciano's power was best kept hidden.

Within six weeks, however, ONI was discovering the limits of Lanza's underworld authority. Though he could get naval agents on boats in North Carolina and Maine he professed impotence in securing access to the West Side or Brooklyn waterfronts, controlled by different mafia groups. And his influence seemed 'largely confined to the fishing industry'.[36] Meanwhile, the strategic situation in the North Atlantic continued to deteriorate. Between March and May, forty-seven Allied ships were sunk by U-boats. This made 272 since the start of the war—the most serious threat to US naval strength in the Atlantic since the War of 1812.[37]

In late April 1942 Lanza told Haffenden that in order to be of further assistance he 'needed contacts that he could not make himself and for which he required the "O.K." of Charles "Lucky" Luciano'. Other witnesses recalled that Luciano had to give 'clearance' as he had 'overall control', and his 'illegal operations along the waterfront had as much influence with conditions on the docks as the shipping people themselves, and in many cases, more'. A 'higher echelon of the underworld' needed to be engaged, ONI concluded, if the 'field for possible help [was to] be greatly enlarged'.[38] Luciano's involvement was, they quickly appreciated, unavoidable. He was the one player who 'could snap the whip in the underworld in the entire USA'.[39] He was the ally they needed to exert true power within that underworld.

With the DA office's support, ONI approached one of Luciano's defence lawyers, Moses Polakoff. He had previously been head of the criminal division of the district attorney's office and oversaw the administration of elections in New York—before becoming Luciano's attorney.[40] Polakoff recommended working through another of his clients: Meyer Lansky. He was 'the man who could serve most effectively as the chief intermediary between Luciano in prison and his outside contacts and associates'. As Polakoff explained, 'if Lansky said he was acting for Luciano, that statement would not be questioned'.[41]

The bargaining began. Haffenden and Gurfein met with Lansky to sound out the prospects of approaching Luciano, making clear that nothing was being offered in return.[42] Wary that Luciano, who had never been naturalized, might end up helping the Italians, Gurfein asked Lansky if Luciano could be trusted. Lansky's reply was affirmative: 'His whole family was here, his mother and father and two brothers and sister with children.' But it was not clear whether, in Lansky's mind, this was a sign of where Luciano's allegiance lay—or whether he was simply pointing out that the US government had leverage over Luciano.[43] Lansky asked for a sign of the government's good faith to help convince Luciano of the seriousness of the approach. ONI and the DA's office leaned on the state commissioner of corrections, John A. Lyons, and convinced him to move Luciano on 12 May 1942 from a prison at Dannemora near the Canadian border (from which two inmates notoriously escaped in 2015) to Great Meadow Prison just north of Albany.[44]

The first of almost two years of secret, government-sponsored meetings between Luciano and his Mob associates occurred in early June 1942. Lanza, Lansky and Polakoff travelled upstate to visit Luciano in prison and he approved the collaboration subject to it remaining secret from the broader public. Ostensibly, he was concerned that if he fell into the hands of Fascist powers—either because they won the war, or because he was released but deported to Italy (as in fact later occurred)— 'he might get lynched' for supporting the Allied war effort. But he recognized that if his name was behind the project, 'everything will go smoother'.[45] Haffenden agreed. It was not in his interest, either, for the Underworld Project to become public. Henceforth all the top mobsters involved were referred to in government documents by codename. The whole project was to be kept hidden.[46]

Soon, all the leading Mob figures were involved. Lansky was the main go-between, ferrying instructions to and from Luciano. Costello and Adonis supported. Other mobsters from outside Luciano's Family who were known enforcers on the docks, including Johnny Dunn and the Camarda brothers, were roped in. Bugsy Siegel and Willie Moretti went to visit Luciano in prison to obtain 'instructions with respect to the use of his name in certain quarters and reporting back to him'. More than twenty visits took place, sometimes with seven or eight mobsters together at once.[47] Alive to the possibility that these meetings—most of which lasted several hours—might provide cover for Luciano to reinsert himself into Mob life, Hogan ordered wiretaps on Joe Lanza's phone. These failed, however, to reveal anything which would require termination of the project.[48] And the authorities conspicuously refrained from bugging the meetings themselves, held in a room next to the prison warden's office.

With Luciano's name now being openly invoked on the docks and throughout Mob networks, the collaboration took off. As Lansky put it, the visits to Luciano allowed him 'to instruct' mobsters that Luciano 'was personally interested', that 'it was also their duty and to stress to go allout [sic] to give this assistance'. Instead of the Mob brokering access, but then largely standing passively by as US agents operated on their territory, Mob members now went out of their way to support the achievement of US government strategic objectives. Lt Commander Kelly—one of the ONI team, with twenty-five years of experience as a police investigator in civilian life—summed up the change: prior to getting Luciano involved, ONI 'ran into great difficulty in obtaining reliable informants along the waterfront … they just refused to talk to anybody, war effort or no war effort.' Once Luciano was brought in, there was no longer any 'hedging', but rather 'full and whole-hearted cooperation', 'a decided and definite cooperative approach'. Investigations proceeded far faster, and the information gathered was more reliable. The Mob became an active source of operational advice to the Navy, suggesting ways that ships could be packed and unpacked more safely and quickly, speeding the sending of wartime aid to Europe and the Soviet Union. And interventions by Lansky, Costello, Adonis, Mangano and Willie McCabe soon extended the collaboration to the West Side, Brooklyn, Harlem, Jersey and beyond—even other eastern seaboard cities. McCabe, a Mob leader in Harlem, stated simply, 'Anything the boss wants; we'll do anything for him.'[49] In these places it was Luciano, not the US, whose edicts governed. The US was pig-gybacking on Mob authority, 'starting with Lanza and Luciano,' as Commissioner Herlands put it, and 'fanning out through known inter-mediaries and informants' into the Mob's trust network.[50]

From watchdog to attack dog

That network quickly generated spectacular results: the spotting and capture of four Nazi saboteurs. On 13 June 1942 four Germans famil-iar with the US came ashore under cover of darkness at Amagansett Beach on Long Island, carrying four trunks of explosive equipment and $80,000 cash. They had been trained in Nazi Germany as saboteurs and were under instructions from the German High Command to target military and industrial sites. The operation was named 'Pastorius', after the leader of the first group of German colonists to move to America in 1683. It was a spectacular failure. Coming ashore, the saboteurs encountered a US Coast Guard patrolman. They were able to talk their way past him, but not before his suspicions had been awakened and the alarm raised. Rattled, the novices' operational discipline quickly evapo-rated. They were all captured within two weeks, tried by a military commission, and most were executed.[51]

The process by which the saboteurs were spotted and captured has long been opaque, with the FBI publicly taking the credit. But over-looked testimony before the Herlands investigation by ONI agents who worked closely with the Mob—one of whom was awarded an official commendation for helping to catch the saboteurs—strongly suggests that the Mob was integral to the counter-intelligence efforts. It appears to have been a boat in the Mob-backed coastal surveillance network that spotted the saboteurs landing, and reported it to the US Coast Guard, who then investigated. Once the saboteurs had been spotted, Haffenden's agents appear to have worked directly with Lanza's Mob contacts on Long Island to track down the first saboteurs, who then led authorities to the others.[52] The role of the Mob was rapidly airbrushed out of the official story.

With this demonstration of their strategic utility, Mob figures appear to have begun ratcheting up the scope of their collaboration in ways that reinforced their own power. Past accounts have characterized the Underworld Project in terms of the intelligence role played by the

Mob for the government. But a close reading of overlooked material in the original Herlands investigation file reveals the Mob playing a larger role from mid-1942, working as an auxiliary coercive asset for Haffenden—not just a watchdog, but a domestic attack dog. Much of this activity seems to have been illegal. As we saw earlier, Haffenden did not feel constrained to follow regulations 'to the letter', nor did his superiors complain.[53]

The first area of enlarged collaboration related to controlling union activity. Lanza specifically assured Haffenden that there would 'not be any trouble on the waterfront during the crucial time' and that the unions would not be allowed to jeopardize the war effort through strikes or wage demands. The Mob worked actively to ensure that incipient workplace disruptions were 'rectified' in order 'that there be a free and uninterrupted flow of supplies out of this Port of New York to the war theatre—and to England'. After ONI raised concerns about the impending visit to New York by an Australian-born labour activist, Harry Bridges, Lanza himself beat up Bridges to prevent him headlining a rally at Webster Hall.[54] Mob lawyer Moses Polakoff reported Haffenden to be very appreciative.[55]

The site of collaboration was moving away from the waterfront to other targets around the city. Using his power as a union official, Lanza organized for undercover government agents to be installed in buildings and business of particular strategic concern, including factories supplying the Navy, and hotels, bars, restaurants and nightclubs on Manhattan. One even appears to have been installed in a Mob operation overseeing the 'Italian lottery'.[56] Soon ONI agents and Mob figures were collaborating on some fifty 'surreptitious entries' into buildings for broader espionage purposes, including inside (notionally immune) foreign consulates. The Mob surveilled the buildings, helped ONI agents gain access through placement in Mob-controlled unionized janitorial and cleaning crews—and even trained ONI agents in specialized burglary skills such as lock-picking.[57] Some of these agents later used these skills for the Office of Strategic Services, the precursor to the Central Intelligence Agency that was established in June 1942 to unite the intelligence arms of the different military services.[58] One ONI agent told Herlands that this 'surreptitious entry' operation provided 'conclusive evidence of a German espionage ring using a dozen agents in six large American cities', which was consequently broken up within a month.[59]

Nor was it only foreign states that were targeted. The ONI-Mob collaboration also led to actions to disrupt local political and press activity that was arguably protected by the US Constitution. First, the Mob helped ONI to infiltrate and disrupt foreign subversive organizations in Harlem. Willie McCabe, who had taken over the Harlem policy racket after Dutch Schultz's death, used his lottery 'runners'—who couriered instructions and revenues between the retail outlets and headquarters— as surveillance assets. At the Mob's suggestion, the same role was extended to the Mob's installers and servicemen handling 'vending machines' (slot machines) in Harlem.[60] This collaboration led to the identification of alleged Spanish Falangist and Japanese propagandist groups operating in Harlem and Greenwich Village, which were soon broken up.[61] Next, when a US Senator and former governor of Massachusetts, David I. Walsh, was caught in a homosexual brothel in Brooklyn with ties to both the Navy Yard and alleged Nazi sympathizers, ONI turned to the Mob to help suppress the story, 'encouraging' the press to accept that it was a case of mistaken identity.[62]

It was a short step to Mob personnel taking orders directly from ONI. Meyer Lansky organized 'contracts' under which waterfront enforcers, such as cross-eyed Johnny 'Cockeye' Dunn (executed in 1949 for first degree murder), worked directly under the 'specific instructions' of Haffenden.[63] Dunn was, at the time, on bail on racketeering and extortion charges.[64] His job, as Lansky later explained, was not just to be a Navy 'watchdog', but to instil 'discipline' on the waterfront.[65] Dunn seems to have taken his new duties seriously—perhaps too seriously. After two characters ONI suspected of being German agents disappeared, ONI asked the Mob in future to clear any such hits with them.[66] It became routine for ONI to directly task Mob enforcers with jobs. 'Usually,' Meyer Lansky later testified, 'I would introduce them and then they would follow up in their own way.'[67]

Invading Italy

Local knowledge

In early 1943, President Franklin D. Roosevelt and Prime Minister Winston Churchill agreed to create a second front in Europe by invading Sicily. But the Americans soon discovered a problem. As Rear

Admiral W.S. Pye, the head of the Naval War College, would put it just a year later, US naval intelligence had been 'sadly neglected' before the war, because there had been a failure to recognize 'the importance of the intelligence function in the conduct of war'. The problem was acute, 'especially … in Italy' where the Navy 'found that we lacked much information required for effective planning'.[68] The US Navy's attention had long been focused on the Pacific and Atlantic. Planning for war in the Mediterranean had not been a priority. They needed all the help they could get, particularly regarding the maritime approaches to Sicily and potential landing spots.

Once again, evolutions at the strategic level in World War Two gifted the Mob a source of strategic advantage, which they exploited adroitly. ONI tried approaching Sicilian, Neapolitan and Calabrian Americans directly for information about geography, highways, water supplies and power structures, trying to collect old photographs, illustrated postcards, school textbooks and private diaries. But they met resistance and hostility, just as they had when they tried to gather intelligence in New York's docks.[69] Once again, the Mob seemed to hold the key to access.

Haffenden's Underworld Project team was now charged by Navy superiors with gathering intelligence for the Allies' amphibious assault on Sicily. At his request, Lanza assembled the 'bosses of the gangs' and Haffenden asked them for help in gathering intelligence from the Italian-American community.[70] Haffenden later testified that 'the greater part of the intelligence developed in the Sicilian campaign was directly responsible to the number of Sicilians that emanated from the Charles "Lucky" contact'.[71] Shepherded by Adonis and other mafia leaders, Sicilian and Mezzogiorno immigrants began showing up in large numbers at Haffenden's Manhattan office, providing detailed descriptions of their hometowns and villages.[72] Some Mob leaders such as Vincent Mangano, who was heavily involved in smuggling from Sicily, proved reluctant, and had to be leaned on heavily by Adonis before they would cooperate.[73] The information thus solicited:

> gave detailed knowledge of beach conditions … details of mountain trails, good roads, short cuts and locations of fresh water springs… Photographs, snapshots, picture post cards and similar objects dealing with the country-side of Sicily and Italy were shown to the informants and when a specific area was recognized, a native of that particular place was found and sent in to report to the Naval Authorities.[74]

All this information was synthesized through a large purpose-built map on Commander Haffenden's wall. It had a cellophane overlay on which intelligence information was marked up, summarized and cross-referenced to specific coded human sources.[75] Luciano and the Mob leadership also passed on the names of 'trustworthy' contacts in Sicily, which the Navy later found to be '40% correct'.[76] A 1945 inquiry initiated by Governor Dewey before he agreed to release Luciano found that through these contacts, 'much valuable information was obtained relative to the position of mine fields, enemy forces and strong points.'[77]

Creating a fifth column

Emboldened, Luciano began to offer operational advice. Was it a sense of historical irony, or perhaps revenge, that led Luciano to recommend an amphibious landing supported by aerial bombardment in the small Golfo di Castellammare to the west of Palermo, whence hailed the *Castellammarese*?[78] He even suggested that he himself be 'dropped in by parachute' and use his personal clout 'to win these natives over to support the United States' War Effort'—leading a fifth column against Mussolini from within Italy. Haffenden, remarkably, supported the suggestion, and presented the proposal in Washington, where it was refused.[79]

Yet the idea of Italian criminal groups serving as a fifth column began to find some traction. The British Secret Intelligence Service's 1943 *Handbook on Politics and Intelligence Services* for Sicily had already identified a figure, Vito La Mantia, as a mafia boss and a possible source of 'valuable information: uneducated but influential'.[80] But the Americans went further. The *Special Military Plan for Psychological Warfare in Sicily*, issued by the joint chiefs of staff in April 1943, suggested using Sicilian-American *mafiosi* to establish 'contact and communications with the leaders of separatist nuclei, disaffected workers, and clandestine radical groups, e.g. the Mafia, and giving them every possible aid'. Allied forces would supply weapons and explosives for use against strategic targets including bridges and railways.[81] This plan, though not executed, was approved in principle by the operational theatre commander—Dwight D. Eisenhower.[82] As we shall see in Chapter 9, two decades later, as president, Eisenhower authorized a remarkably similar collaboration between the CIA and the Mob to remove Fidel Castro from power in Cuba.

Members of Haffenden's intelligence team who had worked closely with the Mob in New York, including during the Long Island search for Nazi saboteurs, went ashore with the first wave of the invasion of Sicily, Operation Husky, on 9–10 July 1943.[83] One of the agents, Anthony J. Marsloe, later secretly testified that the intelligence gathered via Mob connections in New York helped those landing understand the role of the mafia in Sicily: Sicilian 'customs and mores … the political ideology and its mechanics on lower echelons … the chains of command'. All of this 'enabled us to carry out the findings and purpose of our mission'.[84]

A story has long circulated suggesting that a golden handkerchief with the letter 'L' (for Luciano) was dropped from a plane to signal to the Sicilian mafia that they should cooperate with the Allies. This, it was said, explained the rapid advance of the Allies through western Sicily.[85] Tim Newark has conclusively shown the story to be apocryphal.[86] But overlooked material in the Herlands file shows that the concept underlying the story—that Allied cooperation with the mafia provided specific military advantages facilitating the advance—is in fact true. Once ashore, operating to a specific plan, Haffenden's agents actively sought out and contacted mobsters who had been deported from the US, using them as both literal and figurative translators, brokering access to local Sicilian mafia *capi*.[87]

Unpublished Herlands investigation testimony and an unpublished manuscript by one of the agents, Anthony J. Marsloe, explain just how useful this access proved. Lt Paul A. Alfieri, who went ashore at Licata, in Sicily's south-east, made contact with a *mafioso* 'cousin' of Luciano, whom Luciano had earlier helped to flee the electric chair in New York after he had killed a policeman on the Lower East Side. Gunmen from his *cosca* led Alfieri to the local naval headquarters, which they attacked. Alfieri then used lock-picking skills learned from the Mob during the 'surreptitious entry' operations in New York to open a safe, where he discovered priceless operational intelligence: the order of battle and location of Italian and German naval forces for the Mediterranean; a radio codebook; and minefield maps. These were used both to aid the American advance in western Sicily and 'to accelerate the Italian surrender'.[88]

Alfieri, then a mere lieutenant, junior grade, was awarded the Legion of Merit.[89] Joe Titolo, another member of this team, explained how he repeated this approach as he was deployed steadily north in Italy. He repeatedly 'sought out members of the criminal element' to provide intelligence and other forms of cooperation.[90] And in Sardinia, Titolo used underworld contacts to capture nineteen escaping high-ranking Italian officers, and prevent three different sabotage operations.[91]

Release and exile

By 1942 Luciano had been in prison for six years, and would not be eligible for parole for another twenty-four. If he did not press his advantage now, it might evaporate. While the district attorney's office had made clear to Lanza that any Mob cooperation with ONI was not going to lead to any deals, it had also told Luciano's lawyer that 'if Luciano made an honest effort to be of service in the future, they would bear that in mind'.[92] Luciano's lawyers moved for a reduction of sentence. The motion was considered by the same judge, Supreme Court Justice Philip J. McCook, who had sentenced him. He privately interviewed both Commander Haffenden and Murray Gurfein, and while denying the motion for release indicated opaquely that '[i]f the defendant is assisting the authorities and he continues to do so, and remains a model prisoner, executive clemency may become appropriate at some future time'.[93] By mid-1944 the maritime threat to the eastern seaboard had largely been seen off, and Italy was under Allied control. The Mob's utility to the US government's war effort was waning. Haffenden was reassigned to active service in the Pacific (where he was badly injured on Iwo Jima), and the Underworld Project came to an end.[94] It seemed like Luciano's chance at release had slipped through his fingers.

On the day the war ended in Europe, 8 May 1945, Lucky tried his luck once more. His lawyers wrote to Governor Dewey, seeking clemency. This posed a political conundrum for Dewey. If he denied Luciano clemency, he risked the Mob and its Tammany allies leaking the fact of the government's cooperation with the Mob during the war, causing him serious political headaches. The government seemed unlikely to agree to the release of details of the cooperation. But if he released

Luciano without explanation, that could also cause public consterna-tion. So Dewey kicked the question to the Parole Board, who mounted a limited investigation of Luciano's claim to have assisted the war effort. On 3 December 1945 the Parole Board recommended that while Luciano's sentence should be commuted, since Luciano had never been formally naturalized, he should be deported. It was a neat compromise. The governor granted the commutation on 3 January 1946.[95] His public statement explained straightforwardly that:

> Upon the entry of the United States into the war, Luciano's aid was sought by the armed services in inducing others to provide information concern-ing possible enemy attack. It appears that he cooperated in such effort...

Dewey further specified that if Luciano ever re-entered the US, he should be treated as an escaped convict.[96] After a final round of visits with Costello, Lansky and other Mob associates, Luciano was released—and deported to Italy on 10 February 1946.

Conclusion

In 2011 the White House released a *Strategy to Combat Transnational Organized Crime* that warned that criminal networks:

> threaten US interests by forging alliances with corrupt elements of national governments and using the power and influence of those elements to further their criminal activities ... to the detriment of the United States.[97]

Yet seventy years earlier, it was the US government that was forging alliances with criminal networks in an effort to thwart the perceived designs of its own adversaries. World War Two proved to be a strategic gift for the Mob, transforming its positioning options and its field of vision. Before the war, the Mob understood its relationship with the US government in domestic, binary terms: they competed and collabo-rated largely within the confines of the American political economy. The war transformed the field from a domestic to a transatlantic one, bringing in new players: the US' enemies. This transformed the Mob's positioning options, opening up the possibility of balance-of-power alliance strategies. The Mob could exploit the old logic of 'My enemy's enemy is my friend' to ally itself with the US government, buying strategic space at home and piggybacking on the war effort to extend its reach overseas.

Both sides explicitly recognized the defensive logic underpinning the alliance within the Underworld Project. Meyer Lansky described the state's participation as a 'great precaution' against the creation of a fifth column.[98] Lt Marsloe, a central figure in Haffenden's team, similarly describe the project as intended to provide a 'system ... which will prevent the enemy from securing aid and comfort from others ... [including] the so-called underworld.'[99] The US Navy's defensive logic behind allying with the Mob against the Fascist powers was similar to the logic that Jimmy Hines had in allying with Dutch Schultz against political rivals such as Al Marinelli (in turn backed by the Mob). Both episodes involved strategic alliance between upperworld and underworld actors in a larger competition for power. The only structural difference was the strategic setting: one played out within the confines of New York politics, while the other played out in the transatlantic theatre of World War Two.

The prospect of the Mob actually allying itself with Hitler and Mussolini was probably never very high. Meyer Lansky, for example, had been active in forcibly breaking up rallies of the German American Bund (a Nazi-aligned organization) in New York in the 1930s, so he was probably an unlikely candidate to become a Fascist agent.[100] But the prospect of some American *mafiosi* collaborating with the Fascists was also not zero. Vito Genovese, one of Luciano's main lieutenants who had fled New York to escape a murder charge in 1937, spent the Italian war cooperating closely with senior Fascists in Naples. Some suspect him of organizing for Mussolini the assassination of an anti-Fascist labour activist in New York, Carlo Tresca. During the war Genovese was, indeed, presented Italy's highest civilian award by the Fascist government.[101]

Even if the probability of Mob elements developing into a fifth column was low, the fear that it might was very real in intelligence circles in 1941. Commissioner Herlands, in his report, argued that the authorities had been forced by their sense of 'grave emergency and national crisis' to adopt an 'essentially pragmatic' approach, moving to a form of 'total mobilization' that induced them to use 'the entire community and every useful element in it'.[102] The state of war, in other words, represented a normative rupture: pure strategic considerations forced the state to ignore the very norms that, during peacetime, would prevent it cooperating with organized crime. The sense of crisis altered the strategic landscape, creating fears that the Mob exploited cannily, ratcheting up its role from one of waterfront intelligence cooperation, to waterfront enforcement, to broader intelligence and enforcement cooperation—and ultimately assisting the US in the intercontinental projection of force. It gave the Navy real results: improved access to maritime intelligence, assistance tracking down Nazi saboteurs and suspected Falangist agitators, access to auxiliary enforcement capabilities including specialized break-and-enter skills and valuable operational intelligence and contacts in Italy. Commissioner Herlands concluded that there could 'be no question about the usefulness of the project'.[103]

The problem with such collaboration, whether the Mob took the role of watchdog or attack dog, was summed up by one of Haffenden's agents, Lt Harold MacDowell: 'When you go to sleep with dogs, you get up with fleas.'[104] The US government may have gained much from the Mob, but the Mob received at least as much in return. The integration of the Mob and ONI's coercive apparatus—with naval agents operating in Mob-controlled workplaces, and Mob enforcers taking direct orders from naval officers—amplified both parties' power. It extended the Navy's power in the underworld and zones it could not reach, such as the unionized waterfront, fishing fleet and hotels. But it also amplified the Mob's power by making the state complicit in some of its activities. Several aspects of the collaboration—notably those involving domestic espionage and interference with the free press—were of questionable legality. The Mob's collaboration with ONI not only protected it from other state actors, but also sent a signal to potential rivals of the Mob—whether underworld rivals or legitimate rivals for its political mediation role, such as Communist-leaning union factions—that it had enlarged room to manoeuvre, possibly even impunity.

Mob leaders were fully aware what a 'break' they had caught from the Underworld Project.[105] If nothing else, Luciano, sentenced to thirty to fifty years in prison, was now out—in less than ten. Four outstanding indictments against him had been quietly dropped.[106] Yet Lucky had also been exiled to Italy—a poor, ruined, post-conflict state.

That was a grim prospect. Had their strategic decision to cooperate with the Navy backfired?

If the Mob's ambitions were limited to the US, then indeed the permanent exile of their uncontested leader was perhaps a steep price to pay. But this exile also seems to have encouraged Luciano and the Mob leadership to conceive the Mob's potential in larger geographic terms. The Mob had helped the US government project power across the Atlantic, and in the process acquired new, transnational strategic options. The first of these lay exactly where Luciano was now headed: occupied Italy.

7

GOVERNING SICILY, 1942–1968

'The "roaring twenties" in America were nothing compared with Sicily of today.'
Brigadier-General George S. Smith, 1945[1]

'Politicians, governments and men in power change, while the Mafia stays the same.'
Don Calogero 'Calò' Vizzini[2]

At 5 pm one day in early January 1944, the British minister resident in the Mediterranean and future prime minister, Harold Macmillan, called at an office in the centre of Palermo. Macmillan was serving as Churchill's liaison in the Mediterranean theatre. The office in question belonged to the most senior American in the Allied Military Government for Occupied Territories (AMG or AMGOT), which governed Sicily and southern Italy. This was Colonel Charles Poletti, the first Italian-American to become a state governor in the US (of New York), and as Macmillan later put it, 'Tammany personified'. Poletti, Macmillan reported back to London, had 'clearly run Sicily with enthusiasm and gusto'. But he seemed to consider himself the '"boss" of Sicily'. '[T]he shadow of ... Tammany Hall,' Macmillan concluded, had 'been thrown ... across the Island.'[3]

Macmillan's analysis was trenchant. For much of his time in Italy, Poletti employed an 'interpreter': Vito Genovese, the Luciano Family lieutenant, collaborator with the Italian Fascists and later top New York

169

Mob boss. Genovese's job, it appears, was to 'interpret' between the upperworld and the underworld, organizing and governing the booming, volatile black market that seemed to pose a major threat to Allied control. With the AMG's connivance, the governmental power of organized crime in southern Italy was being revived. Even prior to the invasion, Allied planners recognized that 'there were two enemies to be faced in Sicily'—the openly hostile Fascist forces, and the hidden power of organized crime.[4] The Allied invasion and occupation of Sicily defeated the Fascists, but arguably left organized crime welded into Italy's post-war system of government.

Drawing extensively on unpublished British and American wartime correspondence, intelligence analyses and published secondary sources, this chapter explores the underappreciated strategic impact of organized crime during the Allied Military Government for Occupied Territories, the Sicilian separatist movement of 1943–1945 and Sicily's post-war transition. The interactions between the AMG, Italian political organizations and the American and Sicilian mafia hold numerous insights for contemporary military interventions, peace operations and post-conflict transition processes, touched on here and further explored in Chapter 11.

The first section explores the hidden history of AMG officials' handling of the mafia during the initial occupation. The second section explores the role of the Sicilian mafia in the emergence of a Sicilian separatist movement in the immediate post-occupation transition, and the Italian government's efforts to avoid a separatist insurgency through secret accommodation and negotiation efforts. The third section explores different approaches to criminal strategy during Sicily's post-war transition, focusing briefly on the unsuccessful efforts of Salvatore Giuliano, the notorious 'Prince of Bandits', which contrast with the much more successful efforts of Salvatore Lima, Mayor of Palermo. The final section briefly reflects on lessons from these episodes, particularly for contemporary post-conflict transitions.

'A bargain has been struck'

Black market rents

Prime Minister Churchill and President Roosevelt had agreed prior to the invasion of Sicily that it would serve their strategic interests to give the AMG a largely American face, because of the ties between Sicily and America built up by immigration over the previous decades. Despite America's supposed familiarity with Sicily, Allied occupation planning failed to appreciate how local criminal actors would exploit the vacuum of political authority and absence of effective law enforcement capabilities during the occupation. The US War Department's directive for Allied administration of Sicily proposed a dismantling of the Fascist Party, removal of all Fascist personnel from authority and the insertion of the Allies' own nominees. As Tim Newark has pointed out, this approach created 'a rush to fill the political vacuum left behind by the Fascists—a process that would attract the Mafia'.[5] In this, the British and American occupation of Sicily uncannily foreshadowed the course of events in Afghanistan, Iraq and Libya six decades later.

When the occupation forces arrived, southern Italy was a failing state. In Sicily, a month after the occupation, all railways remained cut, most large towns had no bread and less than twenty-four hours' food on hand at any time, and large numbers of dead were still being buried.[6] By late October AMG officials were reporting that mafia groups were hoarding wheat, stealing it in attacks on AMG-controlled reserves and selling it at up to four times its true market value.[7] By December, food shortages were critical and posed '[t]he main threat to security… This lack of food leads to general unrest and is exploited by criminal and political factions'.[8] By early 1944, food prices were higher even than during the last year of Fascist wartime rule.[9]

The war reduced the costs of organizing crime. Some gangs looted weapons from battlefields and poorly defended state arsenals.[10] Others used the proceeds of the black market to purchase leftover materiel—machine guns, trench mortars, land mines, field radios, even light field artillery—and hid it away in caves and secret stores.[11] In Naples—which, like Sicily, was under AMG control—Norman Lewis, a British intelligence officer and later a celebrated travel writer, described seeing '[e]very single item of Allied equipment' on open sale.[12] By the spring of 1944, the US Psychological Warfare Bureau was estimating that one-third of Allied supplies were disappearing into the black market—which was the source of almost two-thirds of Neapolitan households' income.[13] Mass prison break-outs as the Fascist powers fled ahead of advancing Allied forces, abandoning their guard posts, sent hardened criminals and desperate men into a labour market with no jobs.[14] Armed gangs of bandits and hardened war veterans began to roam the countryside of Sicily and parts of southern Italy, pillaging and looting.[15]

War and deprivation broke down normative barriers to participation in criminal activity, making people increasingly 'illegality-minded'. 'An entire generation of young people addicted to legal abuses and criminal violence began to grow up,' argued Michele Pantaleone, a leftist politician who lived through the period.[16] The post-conflict black market was playing a similar role to Prohibition in New York: breaking down mental barriers to participation in organized crime, and stoking a Darwinian competition between criminal groups for control of resources that weeded out the weak and consolidated the strong. The US War Department directive had promised to manage such problems through price controls and direct assault on racketeers. But there were only limited law enforcement assets available to undertake that assault. Just sixty-five British policemen were deployed to AMG operations.[17] In early September, a joint British-American operation planned by Scotland Yard and the New York Police Department arrested two mafia leaders and seventeen of their associates. But the operation was apparently based on tips from other *mafiosi*, pointing dangerously towards manipulation of the Allies by mafia factions.[18] And this operation seemed to be the exception, not the rule.

AMG officers at the tactical level were forced to innovate. In Corleone, the British administrator attempted—with apparently limited success—to simply cut black market racketeers out of the picture, buying the harvest straight from producers. No doubt due to mafia pressure, he found the sellers reluctant, and the *caribinieri* uncooperative.[19] Other AMG officers took the opposite course, turning to local 'persons of influence' to 'act as mediators with the local communities'.[20] AMG officials discovered how helpful the mafia could be. Haffenden's ONI team, now inserted into the civilian administration in Sicily, worked to identify local criminal leaders, whom they found to be 'extremely cooperative'.[21] One former Underworld Project operator, Lt Paul Alfieri, worked with local *mafiosi* to use the Sicilian fishing fleet as an intelligence apparatus, specifically 'patterned after the fishing fleet project under Commander Haffenden' in New York.[22]

The Office of Strategic Services (OSS) claimed to have gone even further. Precursor to the CIA, the OSS' presence in Sicily was led by

Joseph Russo, whose father had been born in the Sicilian mafia strong-hold of Corleone. Russo sought out mafia leaders as collaborators.[23] In a secret internal report archived in the US National Archives, filed under the OSS codename 'Experimental Department G-3', Russo made a pragmatic case for engaging the mafia: 'Only the Mafia is able to bring about suppression of black market practices and influence the ... majority of the population.' Russo claimed with striking bravado to have turned the mafia into a strategic asset:

> We at the present time can claim ... the Mafia. We have had conferences with their leaders and a bargain has been struck that they will be doing as we direct or suggest. A bargain once made here is not easily broken...[24]

Where would this supposed bargain lead?

'Wine and women and champagne'

The AMG's improvisational and apparently uncoordinated approach to dealing with the mafia at the tactical level might suggest a lack of awareness of the problem at the strategic level. This was not so. As with many contemporary peacekeeping and military operations that grapple with criminal spoilers, the issue was not so much a lack of awareness of the problem as an absence of a clear, coordinated strategic response.

The man in charge of AMG's administration of Sicily was Major-General Francis Baron Rennell of Rodd. A former diplomat and banker, Lord Rennell had won the Royal Geographical Society's Founder's Medal in 1929 for a study of the Touareg nomads of the Sahel, suggesting an anthropologist's eye for social complexity. He was not blind to the danger posed by the mafia. In fact, he specifically warned his superiors that '[t]he aftermath of war and the breakdown of central and provincial authority provide a good culture ground for the [mafia] virus',[25] and that the 'Mafia is far from dead'. Only the 'intimate local knowledge' of local police could combat it.[26] The AMG insisted on exercising indirect control over the Sicilian population, with 'the Sicilians doing' the actual 'governmental work'.[27] But after a decade of Fascism, there were few alternative authorities capable of assisting the Allies to restore order and welfare on the island.[28]

Rennell concluded that the interventionist approach favoured by the Americans—removing all Fascist institutions—was unwittingly playing into mafia hands:

Unfortunately owing to the zeal which Allied Military Government Officers have shown in the removal of Fascist [mayors] they have fallen into the trap of appointing the most pushing and obvious person, who in certain cases are now suspected as being the local Mafia leaders. In certain parts of Sicily there is no doubt that the election of [mayors] will result in virtually unanimous voting for local MAFIA leaders.[29]

Mafiosi found that the AMG's door pushed open very easily. Many of the AMG's initial mayoral selections resulted from AMG officers 'following the advice of their self-appointed interpreters who had learned some English in the course of a stay in the USA'. Many were American mobsters who had fled the US or been deported back to southern Italy. Under their influence, concluded Rennell, AMG officials 'invariably chose a local Mafia "boss", or his shadow, who in one or two cases had [themselves] graduated in an American gangster environment.'[30] AMG officers' 'ignorance of local personalities' led them to appoint 'a number of mafia "bosses"'.[31] In Villalba, Don Calogero Vizzini, a major mafia leader in western Sicily, was appointed mayor.[32] And in Naples, Lewis recorded how Genovese and local associates had quickly 'manoeuvred into a position of unassailable power in the military government... In so far as anyone rules here, it is the Camorra.'[33]

American officers seem to have taken longer than their British counterparts to accept that the mafia posed a problem. There were deep cultural and organizational divisions between the two Allies, and AMG organization was frequently chaotic.[34] (Again, the parallel with the experience in occupied Iraq sixty years later is striking.) American officers denied there was a problem, some arguing there was no formal mafia organization in Sicily, just a system of hereditary chieftainship.[35] British officers kept calling for an AMG-wide policy.[36] But the basic problem was in identifying who exactly was a *mafioso*. The British government historian later noted that all foreign occupiers face difficulty in weighing up 'the value or danger of local characters'.[37] But in Sicily, as Rennell pointed out, there was an additional problem:

> Here my difficulty resides in the Sicilian Omerta code of honour. I cannot get much information even from the local Caribinieri who in outstations inevitably feel that they had better keep their mouths shut and their skins whole if the local AMGOT representative chooses to appoint a Mafioso, lest they be accused by AMGOT of being Pro-Fascist. The local Mafiosi

who of course had no love for the [Fascist] regime, which persecuted the Mafia, are naturally not slow in levelling accusations of Fascist sympathies against their own pet enemies.[38]

The AMG was, in a sense, flying blind. By October 1943 the Americans were forced to admit that there might be a problem, and commissioned a military intelligence officer, Captain W.E. Scotten, who had served three years as American vice-consul in Palermo, to develop ideas to address the 'grave and urgent' problem of the mafia. After consulting with Allied military and political intelligence officers and local Sicilian informants, Scotten produced a remarkable six-page confidential memorandum entitled 'The Problem of Mafia in Sicily' which was circulated not only amongst AMG leaders but also in Allied HQ in Algiers and London.[39]

Scotten demonstrated a nuanced appreciation of mafia power. He explained the mafia as the product of 'a system of private safeguards' that had emerged in the absence of effective state capabilities in the centre of Sicily, degenerating from a 'feudal system' of rackets into 'a criminal system' aimed at committing 'extortion and theft with impunity'. It was both an 'association of criminals', disciplined through a code of silence, and, because of the imposition of that code on the public, 'more than an association; it is also a social system'.[40] It nurtured its own power through deliberately cultivating governmental power, showing:

> the desire to entangle in its meshes persons in high places who could serve to protect its own members when need arose, even to the extent of intervention in Rome on their behalf. As a matter of fact, Mafia, before the advent of Fascism, had reached the position of holding the balance of political power in Sicily. It could control elections, and it was courted by political personages and parties...[41]

It was wrong, Scotten argued, to think that the Fascists had wiped out the mafia. Mori was ordered back to Rome, he explained:

> when it became apparent that a complete housecleaning would involve too many high-ranking professional and business people and even influential members of the [Fascist] Party...[42]

The mafia had, Scotten asserted, quickly regenerated its power in Sicily during the brief Allied occupation by using these links and its own social networks to assert control over the black market. Now, he argued, the 'grave implications' of resurgent mafia power not only for Sicily's political future but also 'on the mainland of Italy' must be recognized in AMG headquarters.[43]

Yet the AMG's strategic leadership did not seem too concerned. Though British officers on the ground were increasingly worried, their leaders seemed resigned to the fact that the mafia would inveigle itself into the post-war political system. Macmillan wrote almost flippantly to the Foreign Secretary Anthony Eden in September 1943:

> Whatever Fascism may have been in theory or on the mainland of Italy, in Sicily it was obviously just a legalized 'racket'. It is worth remembering that Al Capone was a Sicilian. Of course, in due course AMGOT and Control Commissions will pass away, the 'racket' will return, 'democracy will then resume its reign/and with it, wine and women and champagne'.[44]

Macmillan was adapting a satirical ditty by Hilaire Belloc from 1923, 'On a General Election', which had skewered the British political parties for being more similar than different:

> The accursed power which stands on Privilege
> (And goes with Women, and Champagne and Bridge)
> Broke—and Democracy resumed her reign
> (Which goes with Bridge, and Women and Champagne).[45]

An election that brought a change of government in truth simply changed the ordering of priorities, not their underlying content, he was implying. Macmillan was picking up this theme, suggesting that the war, and Allied occupation, would have a similar effect in Sicily—that is, not much. Ultimately, he suggested, the mafia and the Fascists were not so different.

'Our good friends'

The Allies did not plan to put the mafia back in power. Nor, however, was it simply, as Tim Newark has argued, 'a mistake', in which the AMG allowed the mafia to 'put themselves back in positions of power'.[46] Rather, it was an approach based on an implicit recognition of the convergence of mafia and AMG interests. It was not blindness, but wilful blindness; not ignorance, but acquiescence. And in some individual cases, it went even further: connivance and collusion.

As early as October 1943 Captain Scotten was reporting 'numerous cases' of both local Sicilian mafia figures and American mobsters operating inside AMG ranks.[47] The unpublished draft official history of the AMG concluded that its 'interpreters', many of whom had acquired their knowledge of English 'while members of some of the most unscrupulous racketeering gangs in the United States', used AMG armbands, motor-car labels and other official markings to facilitate their criminal activities.[48] Allied military supplies were imported tax-free; they could be diverted and sold into the Italian black market at huge mark-ups, while still sold at a steep discount on official prices. Genovese's system, as one example, drew in the Neapolitan Camorra, Neapolitan judges, the Mayor of Nola and the president of the Bank of Naples, as well as Don Calò and the Sicilian mafia.[49]

As a result, Scotten asserted as early as October 1943, the local population was beginning to see the AMG as 'the unwitting tools of Mafia'.[50] But as evidence of active collusion mounted, it became clearer that some AMG officers were actually the witting tools of the mafia. Genovese's extensive operations clearly benefited from some level of protection within AMG. Suspicion fell on his boss, Charles Poletti, the Tammany man who had briefly been governor of New York. During the 1930s and 1940s, when Frank Costello's influence over Tammany and judicial appointments was clear, Poletti became counsel to the Democratic National Committee, then justice of the New York State Supreme Court, then lieutenant-governor of New York and then, for just twenty-nine days, governor of New York. It was precisely this experience in the senior levels of government that was seen as qualifying him for the post of senior civil affairs officer in the AMG, the highest American post. But the model of government he brought to Sicily, as Macmillan had noted, was drawn straight from the Tammany tradition—which, as we have seen, had long included friendly relations with organized crime. Lucky Luciano described Poletti as 'one of our good friends', often mafia code for signalling that someone was an initiated *mafioso* himself.[51] There is a trail of annotations and asides in archived British government wartime memoranda noting concern about Poletti. Lewis, a military intelligence officer, concluded simply that Poletti provided Genovese with 'high-placed protection'. The Herlands investigation materials in the University of Rochester archives also seem to corroborate the idea that Poletti worked with Genovese to 'operate the black market'.[52]

Genovese's run was ultimately interrupted by a fearless twenty-four-year-old military investigator, Orange Dickey, who bravely ignored his superiors' active obstructions and single-handedly returned Genovese to face outstanding murder charges in Brooklyn—charges he had somehow been evading the whole time he served as the official interpreter to a former justice of the New York State Supreme Court and governor, Poletti. During his investigation, Dickey turned up other Tammany figures in Italy, notably Bill O'Dwyer, the district attorney in Brooklyn who appears to have deliberately bungled the investigations into Murder, Inc. By the time Dickey got Genovese back to New York, the main witness against Genovese in the murder case had himself been murdered in prison. Genovese walked free. He was now one of the most senior mobsters in New York, with a new, lucrative transatlantic network connecting the Mob even more directly than before to Italy. And, best of all, the Allied Military Government seemed disinclined to interfere with his activities.[53]

Mafia separatism

Confrontation, accommodation or withdrawal?

Scotten set out three strategic options open to the AMG for dealing with the mafia. The first was confrontation: a quick and direct action to bring the mafia under control, through the arrest of 500 or 600 top mafia leaders and their detention or deportation without trial. But for this option, Scotten noted:

> time ... is of the essence. Mafia has not yet regained its old strength ... its organisation is still to a considerable degree disrupted and localised, and the public at large is not yet under the incubus of fear and silence which mafia knows how to impose. But this fear is rapidly returning, and once it has set in, the problem for the police will be multiplied many times over.[54]

Scotten himself favoured this approach, seeing it as 'the only one consistent with the expressed objectives of military government'. Yet he also recognized what a strategic challenge it posed: it 'requires a careful appraisal of the ways and means available at the present juncture'. He was doubtful that the AMG could ensure the secrecy required for such an operation to be effective, or the political willingness to arrest and deport five or six hundred leaders, some of considerable social standing.

A second option was accommodation: the deliberate negotiation of a truce with mafia leaders, trading an agreement by the mafia to liberalize the trade in foodstuffs and staples, and not to interfere with AMG personnel and operations, for a commitment by the AMG to not come after the mafia. Scotten considered this impracticable because such an agreement could not be kept secret. And were any such agreement to leak, it would irreparably damage the political credibility of the AMG in the eyes of the populace.[55]

A third option was withdrawal: 'abandonment of any attempt to control Mafia throughout the island', with the AMG withdrawing into enclaves where military government could function properly—ceding the rest of the island to the mafia. Scotten described this third option as 'the course of least resistance'. But it would also be interpreted as 'weakness':

> by the enemy, by the rest of Italy, by other enemy-occupied countries who are watching the experiment of AMG, and by the home populations. It may well mean the abandonment of the island to criminal rule for a long time to come.

'On the other hand,' he noted wryly, 'its chance of success is certain.'[56]

Though Scotten's analysis was circulated throughout the AMG leadership and in Allied HQ, there is no evidence that it received much active discussion or debate. Instead, the AMG's mafia strategy emerged more by accident than active design. Scotten had made clear that the third option—withdrawal in the face of the mafia into AMG enclaves—was a political non-starter. The first option—confrontation—also seemed unlikely, given the absence of attention to the issue in the AMG leadership, and the forces' limited policing capabilities. Allied military and intelligence personnel were likely to be seen as needed elsewhere to fight the war, rather than investigating and arresting mafia-linked businessmen and agriculturalists in southern Italy. Nor was local law enforcement up to the task. An American field intelligence report from 3 December 1943 described how the *carib-*

inieri were forced into crime to feed their families because their weekly salary could barely cover the cost of three loaves of bread. As the report noted, '[n]aturally this leads to lack of respect for law and order, and plays in to the hands of the political parties which might wish to foster disturbances for their own ends'.[57]

That left, by default, the second option—accommodation. Scotten had discounted this option on the grounds that a negotiation could not be kept secret. But perhaps there was some other, more indirect, way to reach accommodation, other than through the AMG negotiating directly with the mafia—through more acceptable, notionally political intermediaries, such as the emerging Sicilian political parties.

The logic of mafia separatism

By the end of 1943 the central question for the Mob, the Sicilian mafia and other potential players in Italy's post-war transition was what form the new, post-occupation political settlement in Italy would take. The AMG's policy on this question was difficult to discern. In February 1944 a group of Allied intelligence officers concluded in exasperation that 'Nothing is known about the kind and form of civilian government for Sicily that will be supported, or at least encouraged, by the Allies.'[58]

Captain Scotten argued that the absence of policy was creating a drift towards separatism, in part because the mafia had surrounded the AMG with 'separatist friends and advisors'. The AMG, he noted, had 'consistently appointed to public office either outright separatists or persons of separatist sympathy'.[59] As a result, he concluded, 'the AMG has not only placed itself at a disadvantage to deal with Mafia, it has even gone so far as to play into its hands'.[60] The mafia's dealings with political parties should not, Scotten argued, be surprising, since it had always operated as 'a system of political racketeering on the higher levels and criminal racketeering on the lower levels'.[61] While the mafia was dealing with a wide range of parties, including leftists, both Scotten and the Foreign Office predicted that they would ally with the emerging clandestine 'Separatist movement'.[62]

An alliance appears in fact to have been agreed in a series of meetings around that time.[63] The separatists were now, as Monte Finkelstein, the preeminent English-language historian of the separatist movement put it, under the mafia's protection.[64] There was significant, though hidden, overlap between the leadership groups of the two organizations. A noted later *pentito*, Tommaso Buscetta, would later claim that the primary separatist leader, Finocchiaro Aprile, was a member of his mafia *cosca*.[65] The British vice-consul in Palermo at the time, Manley, felt that 'in many cases' the mafia and the separatists 'are the same individuals'.[66] More broadly, the strategic interests of the two groups seemed to be aligning. The large landowners who formed the backbone of the emerging separatist movement had traditionally relied on the mafia to coerce the population. Now, lacking a social base of their own through which to win governmental power, an alliance with the mafia, bandits or some other 'counterpower to the state' became necessary.[67] A January 1944 analysis by the US military concluded that the mafia's control over the Sicilian population made it the natural ally of the Separatist movement.[68]

Alliance with the separatists also served mafia interests. When the occupation ended and the black market it fuelled disappeared, the mafia's ability to extract criminal rents would depend on its traditional source: economic supply chains originating in the countryside areas that remained, despite Fascist efforts, under the influence of the landowners at the heart of the separatist movement. The break-up of the *latifundia* had never been truly completed; 1947 figures showed that more than a quarter of Sicilian territory was still held in that form.[69] This was the economic logic, but it also mapped onto a separatist political logic. The US military intelligence apparatus concluded that:

> the Mafia members want an autonomous Sicily because in order to accomplish their criminal aims, they can easier intimidate the Civil public servants, then [*sic*] they could those residing in far-away Rome.[70]

The mafia alliance with the separatists was thus both radical and conservative. It was radical because for the first time, 'instead of inserting itself into an existing power structure' the mafia 'seemed bent on contributing directly to a political hypothesis'—formal Sicilian separation from the Italian state, the creation of a new political entity within which to maximize the mafia's hidden power.[71] But it was also conservative, since it aimed at conserving an existing political economy.[72] Political radicalism—separatism—was necessary in the service of economic conservatism. The mafia would, as Pantaleone saw it, pick as a political ally whichever party was 'as "governmental" as possible'—in other words, whichever party offered it the greatest prospect of exercising governmental power in Sicily.[73] While that appeared to be the separatists, mafia support would continue. Should that change, the mafia's criminal strategy could dictate a change in political alliances.

The strategy seemed to be working. As the Allies handed formal administrative control over Sicily back to the Italian state on 11 February 1944, they left behind a native Sicilian as governor. It was Poletti's pick; he nominated Francesco Musotto, a former mafia defence lawyer. The OSS reported simply that the mafia had 'won out'.[74]

Seeking Great Power protection

But the game was not over. By early 1944 it was apparent that Sicily's strategic location in the Mediterranean could make it an important theatre in the emerging competition for influence in post-war Europe. The separatist-mafia alliance moved to exploit these shifts in the geostrategic environment by acquiring the protection of a Great Power.

The traditional *latifundisti* and mafia posture had been one of clientelism to patrons in Rome. Mafia power had been built on brokering between rural Sicily and political and economic power in northern Italy. Replacing Rome and Milan with Washington and London was not a giant strategic leap. Separatist leaders began a quiet communications campaign, assuring Allied intelligence officers of their 'conviction that either American or British domination would result in economic benefits'.[75] These leaders first floated the idea that Sicily should adopt a constitution modelled on Malta's, placing it not only within the British Commonwealth but ceding external relations power to the UK.[76] In July 1944 the separatist leader Finocchiaro Aprile wrote directly to Prime Minister Churchill to appeal to him to back Sicilian independence,[77] telling *The Times* that an independent Sicily 'would gladly accept British protection'.[78] When this did not produce results, separatist and mafia leaders switched their attention to the US. Don Calò, the preeminent Sicilian mafia *capo*, emerged as the leader of a separate, pro-American political party—the Partito Democratico d'Ordine, later rebranded the Fronte Democratico d'Ordine Siciliano—which argued not for Sicilian independence, but rather for Sicily to join the United States of America as a state or overseas territory. Its propaganda material and party branding adopted the stars and stripes.[79]

The likelihood of either the US or UK supporting Sicilian independence was always slim to non-existent. It declined further as the separatist movement became increasingly violent. As early as 9 December 1943 the mafia had made clear, in a meeting with the separatist leadership, its willingness to use violence to promote the separatist agenda amongst the Sicilian population.[80] Mafia-sponsored agitation ensured that Communist and nationalist politicians received a rough welcome when they campaigned in mafia-controlled areas.[81] Allied intelligence quickly became concerned that the separatist movement might be turning into a 'revolutionary movement'.[82] Through the first six months of 1944, this nascent revolutionary movement indeed seemed to be gaining considerable traction. In February, the movement held its first formal meetings, and established a Youth League. Provincial committees were formed, and separatist mouthpieces established in the press. By April the movement had become formalized as the Movimento per l'Indipendenza della Sicilia (MIS).[83]

But between April and June public order deteriorated sharply. In Palermo, criminal homicide tripled and robbery more than quadrupled in the first half of 1944.[84] Kidnapping exploded. Rival political rallies turned into running battles between gangs supporting different political factions.[85] With the economic situation still dire and public safety in free fall, *anomie* and lawlessness rose, and the *intralazzo* (racket) took hold. It became impossible to escape corruption. Free market norms had been replaced by racketeering. 'Straightforward commercial transactions … are no longer possible,' wrote a US intelligence analyst. And public administration had lost its legitimacy: 'to be an official personage is synonymous with having a "racket" on the side… officials are assumed to be dishonest until proven otherwise.'[86] Scotten's prediction—that a failure to confront or otherwise address the mafia early on would lead to a resurgence of organized crime—seemed to be playing out.

It was not until mid-1944 that the Allies began to muster the political will to tackle the problem—and even then, only through cracking down on the mafia's upperworld avatars, the separatists. In June 1944 dire food shortages provoked civil disorder. The Allies suspected the *latifundisti* and mafia of stoking the crisis to reap windfall black market profits. Their patience wearing thin, Allied officials recommended to the Italian authorities the 'removal from Sicily (with the help, if necessary, of the Security Branch) of the heads of the Separatist Movement'.[87] The separatist efforts to attract Great Power protection seemed to have failed.

Negotiating peace with the mafia

The new Italian government was not yet sufficiently strong, however, to confront the mafia and *latifundisti* by detaining the separatist leadership. Instead, it replaced Musotto, the separatist-leaning high commissioner, with Salvatore Aldisio, a more moderate Christian Democrat (Democrazia Cristiana, or DC), and charged him with pursuing Scotten's second strategic option: accommodation. Scotten had suggested that the AMG could offer the mafia more liberal market policies in return for peace. Aldisio recognized that the Sicilian mafia in fact sought something more enduring: the preservation of their position as governmental powerbrokers. He could neutralize separatism by making clear the DC's willingness to accommodate the mafia's governmental power on the island.[88] Aldisio began secretly wooing the mafia away from the MIS, convening meetings of mafia leaders and DC party members, and working with Don Calò to end the grain crisis.[89]

The *latifundisti* and MIS leadership faced a choice: abandon their support for separatism and throw their lot in with the DC; or encourage continued mafia support by accelerating the separation process. They chose the latter. Over the summer of 1944 MIS leaders began seriously to plan an insurgency, while stepping up outreach to foreign powers to prepare the ground for a possible declaration of independence later in the year.[90] At a congress in August 1944, the MIS formally adopted a platform contemplating military action. The party's slogan switched from 'Plebiscite and Independence' (*Plebiscito e Indipendenza*) to 'Independence or Death' (*Indipendenza o Morte*).[91] On 13 September, a large crowd of separatists disrupted a meeting between a minister visiting from Rome and the (unitarian) Democratic Party of Labour, then marched to MIS headquarters in Palermo. There they held a rally without government permission and chanted threats of a 'new Sicilian Vespers'—the successful but bloody rebellion against

French-Capetian rule in 1282.[92] On 16 September, a leading Sicilian Communist figure, Girolamo Li Causi, was shot in the leg, and fourteen of his supporters badly injured, during a speech in Villalba, Don Calò's home turf.[93] A separatist congress in Taormina on Sicily's east coast began laying out detailed plans of revolution covering military strategy, political coordination and diplomatic outreach.[94]

Rumours of the planned uprising soon leaked out. American officials advised Aldisio to exercise restraint, arguing that nothing would happen unless there was a clear trigger for mass revolt.[95] Aldisio, however, prepared to arrest the plotters and exile them to the same outlying islands on which Mori had imprisoned mafia leaders almost twenty years earlier. The police raided MIS headquarters and confiscated membership lists, shutting down the office. Separatist leaders threatened 'war'.[96]

Even as it pressed the MIS leadership, the Italian state continued its efforts to peel away mafia support. Aldisio reached out again to Don Calò, encouraging him to throw mafia support behind the Christian Democrats.[97] While Vizzini apparently declined a formal alliance, the party that he controlled—the Fronte—altered its platform to favour autonomy, not separatism, splitting with the MIS.[98] Responding to this promising signal from a key mafia leader, Rome sent a senior military commander to Sicily to open talks aimed at resolving the separatist question. This envoy, Giuseppe Castellano, was quickly 'convinced that the strongest political and social force to be reckoned with is the Maffia', and redoubled negotiation efforts.[99] Castellano told the Allies point blank that a political settlement was possible, if 'the system formerly employed by the old and respected Maffia should return'.[100]

Within five weeks he had presented a detailed political reform proposal to Rome. It included support for regional autonomy—'which will deflate the program of the separatists'—and 'extraordinary measures in the administrative-judicial department' to deal with 'banditry and criminal elements'. What were these extraordinary measures? 'The Maffia in Sicily,' Castellano wrote, 'is not a negligible force. It will be necessary to select the most influential leaders (who are also capable) and confer responsible posts upon them.' Castellano was proposing directly enlisting the mafia as an instrument to enforce the legal and political order of the state.[101]

Castellano called together top MIS, Fronte and mafia leaders. Around twenty mafia leaders attended. Castellano explicitly framed the talks as an effort to find common ground around autonomy proposals, made urgent by rising Sicilian support for Communism and the increasingly obvious split between the Atlantic powers and the Soviets. Out of these talks emerged a specific proposal. Virgilio Nasi, the mafia *capo* in Trapani province, would lead a new mafia-backed movement for autonomy (not independence), take over from Aldisio as high commissioner and serve as the groups' envoy to the Italian government in Rome. In return, Don Calò promised Castellano that he would ensure that the landowners and their conservative allies in Palermo would get behind this new arrangement, and that the mafia would work against Communism. The proposal was put to Nasi by Castellano, Don Calò and other *mafiosi* at a meeting on 18 November 1944 in Castellammare del Golfo.[102]

Castellano worked to enlarge the momentum of the autonomy proposal through bilateral meetings in December 1944 and January 1945 with an expanding circle of political party leaders, including Li Causi for the Communists and Aldisio for the Christian Democrats. He proposed formal roundtable talks to back autonomy and to choose a representative to negotiate with the Italian government, but the factions were unable to agree on the question of the inclusion of the MIS leadership in the talks.[103] Castellano pushed on, attempting to mediate a solution through shuttle diplomacy, without a formal roundtable discussion. Under pressure, the MIS leadership contemplated a federal political settlement—but only if Sicily became a sovereign republic 'be it only for a day' before joining with Italy.[104] The idea did not take hold. An agreement remained elusive, and the risk of civil war loomed.

A bandit army

As these secret negotiations proceeded, the state became increasingly alarmed at the separatists' rising popularity. In late 1944 the Italian government estimated that the MIS could count 400,000 to 500,000 supporters. Other parties could boast less than 10 per cent as much support.[105] A Sicilian revolution seemed a real possibility.

In mid-December 1944 a call by the Italian government for recruits to fight alongside the Allies met with a hostile public response. Sicilians were tired of war and reluctant to fight for a far-off Roman power that was in the midst of an island-wide crackdown on the black market in grain and flour—the Sicilian staple. Whipped up by separatist agitators, violence broke out targeting government buildings, telecommunications facilities, banks and food stores in Catania and Palermo. In the south, a rebel band in Palma di Montechiaro occupied strategic approaches, cut communication, set fire to municipal offices and destroyed documents inside (including property registers and tax records), seized stored weapons and held the town for four days.[106] Attacks on government military and police barracks continued into January.[107] Some sources saw the hand of the mafia.[108]

The Allies realized that the weak Italian government now faced a nascent 'rebellion' or 'insurgency', and that they might be forced to intervene militarily.[109] But the Italian government's announcement of support for an autonomy package seemed to buy some time. The MIS leadership vacillated. It came close to calling for an uprising, but ultimately decided not to—at least not yet.[110] For some of their supporters, however, Rome's embrace of autonomy was cause for desperation. At Comiso in Ragusa Province in early January 1945, a breakaway group of former Fascists within MIS ranks declared a republic and established a 'provisional government'. Heavy fighting left fifteen Italian personnel dead. It took the arrival of an artillery regiment with a tank and armoured car escort to bring the situation under control.[111]

Despite significant popular support for Sicilian independence in late 1944, by the end of 1945 the MIS was spent as a political force. Finkelstein explains that the MIS' leadership, drawn from the ranks of traditional landowners, urban merchants and service professionals, failed to develop an effective organization beyond the island's northern urban centres, in the poorer southern towns and the rural interior. In those areas support shifted rapidly through 1945 towards the better organized Partito Comunista Italiana (Italian Communist Party), whose programme of socio-economic reform seemed more attuned to a post-war agenda, and offered more concrete deliverables than the abstract, and rather utopian, notion of 'separatism'.[112] The rapid collapse in separatist support became clear when the security services began to outnumber the crowd at MIS rallies. Increasingly desperate and all too late, the MIS leadership began to issue shrill calls for revolution and even Allied military intervention.[113]

As early as late April 1945, the separatist headquarters in Palermo was ransacked by an angry mob, possibly with the connivance of the authorities.[114] Attacks on separatist supporters and offices followed in other cities, and the MIS quickly shut down those that remained operational. With the political currency and utility of the MIS collapsing, mafia leaders with separatist links began looking for other potential conservative allies, including monarchists.[115] There is some evidence that both Poletti and Nicola Gentile—the mediator in the Castellammarese War—may have been involved in these negotiations.[116]

As the MIS' political strategy fell apart, it turned in desperation to the military option. Its leadership had been quietly building a clandestine paramilitary wing, the Esercito Volontario per l'Indipendenza della Sicilia (EVIS) since 1943, under the guise of the separatist Youth League.[117] EVIS was led by Antonio Canepa, a wartime partisan leader. Canepa managed to build a network of informants within Italian state structures, develop a staff structure and detailed military planning, but the MIS could provide no support base from which to recruit.[118] Aldisio told the Allies:

> If I were to say EVIS does not exist I would be guilty of exaggeration, but I should not be far from the truth. There is certainly a central headquarters and a general staff of EVIS, but it is a general staff whose army is more on paper than in the field.

By late 1945 the movement had 'six or seven thousand deluded supporters', but no real fighting force.[119] So Canepa was forced to try to co-opt coercive capabilities from other sources: mafia bands, former partisans and prisoners of war, unemployed rural workers and common criminals.[120] By mid-1945 the power vacuum in the Sicilian hinterland had led a variety of war veterans, unemployed labourers and toughs to form '[a]rmed bands, in full "war" equipment, with arms, ammunition, supplies, logistic and medical services' roaming Sicily's interior, staging train robberies and shooting at police.[121] Reprising its role from the 1860s, the mafia emerged as a mechanism for governing this private violence. EVIS now looked to the mafia to help it recruit some of these violent enterprises into its ranks.

A typical example was the mafia's approach to Salvatore Giuliano, a charismatic young bandit born in Montelepre, a hill town between Palermo and Castellammare del Golfo. He was twenty-one when the Allies invaded. Despite no prior criminal history, the deprivations of the era drew him into the black market as a survival strategy. Arrested, he shot a *caribiniero*, made his escape, then killed another to escape a dragnet in Montelepre. After breaking some friends out of prison, he formed a bandit gang in the hills above his hometown. Through extortion and kidnapping of wealthy landowners, rural companies and urban businessmen, Giuliano was able to build a small force of twenty to thirty committed bandits, supplemented by part-timers who would participate in specific operations for a commission. Farmers, shepherds and peasants were paid handsomely for information, supplies and transport from the proceeds of robberies outside the area.[122] Giuliano had became a celebrity, partly out of a reputation for violence—his band killed some 430 people in seven years—but partly because he had taken on the air of a social bandit, directing much of his violence at traditional objects of hostility of the peasantry, notably landowners, loan-sharks and, later, urban industrialists.[123]

Sometime in late 1943 or early 1944 the mafia recruited Giuliano.[124] Canepa also tried to recruit Giuliano into EVIS' ranks, without luck. However, after Canepa was killed in June 1945, his successor, Concerto Gallo, was more successful. This was perhaps unsurprising: Gallo was not just EVIS' leader, but also apparently a made member of the Catania mafia *cosca*. In September 1945 Giuliano issued a declaration of support for EVIS, apparently in return for promises of future immunity from prosecution for his band, the rank of colonel in a future Sicilian army and 1 million lire with which to recruit, train and equip forty to sixty more men.[125]

EVIS' acquisition of Giuliano's coercive capabilities seemed promising. Giuliano's band was by then operating almost at will in the areas around Palermo, raiding, attacking police and military sites and convoys and kidnapping wealthy figures for ransom. But EVIS was dependent on the mafia for its access to these capabilities. It was the mafia that was, in Eric Hobsbawm's words, using bandits as the 'nucleus of effective political rebellion';[126] it was not the rebels who were using the mafia to their own ends. The pattern was demonstrated in early

1945 when a captured EVIS rebel informed the authorities that he had been personally recruited to EVIS by Don Calò. His captors, unaware of the state's efforts to reach an accommodation with the mafia, rashly threatened to arrest Don Calò. US military intelligence reported that as a result:

> the Maffia has threatened to order active participation by the Sicilian Maffia on the side of EVIS and the outlaw bands. Because of their known power, this would mean real civil war in Sicily.[127]

Alarmed, High Commissioner Aldisio intervened, negotiating a 'compromise' whereby Vizzini left Palermo without being arrested.[128] The mafia, it seemed, was calling the shots.

Settlement and betrayal

In October 1945 the Christian Democrats came out firmly in favour of Sicilian regional autonomy. Confident of mafia support, the Italian authorities now moved decisively against the MIS, exiling its leaders to administrative detention on an offshore island and shutting down the party's offices across Sicily.[129] The MIS had failed to find a sustainable source of political support, whether from popular legitimacy, protection by a Great Power—or protection by the mafia. When the MIS leadership was arrested, the mafia did not intervene.

Instead, at a meeting in Palermo on 21 November 1945, mafia leaders from Palermo, Trapani and Agrigento met to chart a new way forward. Henceforth the mafia would aim to influence or control a variety of political parties, most notably the Christian Democrats. Having secured Sicilian autonomy within the Italian political system, and with influence over the emerging leaders of an autonomous Sicily, the mafia was abandoning its strategy of constitutional separatism, and returning to its traditional strategy, interposing itself between the state and the local population. The decision was ratified a week later by a larger group of forty-seven mafia leaders from across the island. The American consul, informed of these developments, suggested this new mafia group with its ties to the Christian Democrats might provide 'the foundation of the strongest political force which has yet existed in Sicily'.[130]

Mafia leaders told the OSS that they were abandoning EVIS, and would 'work and cooperate with the authorities to maintain tranquillity throughout the island'.[131] At the same time, however, they lobbied the Italian authorities to 'allow these misdirected EVISsts to disband and return to their homes'. They added a guarantee: should remnants of EVIS remain active, 'the Mafia themselves would quickly liquidate' them.[132] Soon the police began to find bandit leaders dead, cause unknown; and tip-offs from the population increased dramatically.[133]

In late December 1945, EVIS' leader, Concerto Gallo, was captured. Other separatist bands such as the one led by Salvatore Giuliano fought on. Concerned about the state's possible use of air power, Giuliano attacked Bocca di Falco airfield, just outside the Palermo city centre, as well as several *carabinieri* bases.[134] In early 1946 the Italian government sent nearly 1,000 battle-hardened Garibaldi Regiment troops, equipped with armoured cars, to try to finish off the remnants of EVIS. The force included reconnaissance aircraft and four bombers, and had the power to declare martial law in specified operational theatres, such as around Montelepre, Giuliano's home base. Within two weeks, 600 suspected bandits had been captured, along with two anti-tank guns, machine guns, rifles, grenades and other battlefield weaponry.[135]

EVIS had been broken as a military force, and the separatist threat had been seen off. In March 1946 the Italian government released the separatist political leaders it had detained. In May, it devolved significant additional power to the high commissioner and established a new twenty-four-member regional assembly for Sicily. Outmanoeuvred, the separatists fared poorly in the 2 June parliamentary elections, collecting just 8.7 per cent of the vote and taking only four of forty-nine Sicilian seats in the new parliament in Rome.[136] They were a spent force. The mafia was not.

Nor was Salvatore Giuliano. In 1949 the British representative in Rome, Sir Victor Mallet, assessed Giuliano as an expert in 'estimating the amount which he can reasonably demand as a ransom and gauging the strength of his terror'.[137] He was, in other words, tactically astute in the use of force. But he could not marry that tactical nous to an effective political strategy. He had cultivated an image of himself as protector of the underdog, carrying a photo of himself inscribed 'Robin Hood'.[138] By rebranding his band as a part of EVIS' apparatus he seemed to be positioning himself in the political marketplace. But this manoeuvring also made him dependent on mafia and separatist protection. His failure to develop an effective strategy that would give himself an independent source of governmental power beyond his own immediate theatre of operations left him highly vulnerable, should the mafia or EVIS disappear or, worse, betray him.

Through the course of 1946 and 1947, while continuing his notionally separatist guerrilla operations, Giuliano put out feelers to both monarchists and Christian Democrats, announcing himself as a potential ally in the looming struggle with Communism.[139] Unsuccessful there, Giuliano turned to foreign state sponsors for protection, writing directly to President Truman, indicating his intention to 'annihilate' Communism in Sicily and offering his services as a military asset, even suggesting the admission of Sicily as the forty-ninth state of the American Union.[140]

Giuliano's big blunder came on May Day 1947, when he attacked a peaceful Communist rally at Portella della Ginestra. Eleven people died, four of them children. Thirty-three others were wounded. And that was just the beginning. Attempting to position himself as a political enforcer for the right, over the next two months he attacked numerous leftist rallies, peasant unions and collectivist headquarters. Several times he tried to assassinate the leader of the Communist Party in Sicily, Girolamo Li Causi. A press release on 24 June 1947 made his intentions clear, calling on Sicilians to 'fight' the 'Red gangsters'.[141]

Giuliano's sudden turn to terrorism alienated the population beyond his home district, destroyed his prospects of building a post-war political career at the regional or national level, and undermined his foreign public support. Both the British and Americans concluded that Giuliano had been duped by right-wing political patrons, probably including the mafia, who had promised him 'immunity' and perhaps some kind of formal political role.[142] He was being used as a vanguard force in a domestic political battle with the Communists.[143]

When Giuliano's patrons did not deliver on their promises, and the realization that he was being used dawned upon him, he apparently turned on them, renewing his attacks on the state. In 1948, several senior Sicilian Christian Democrats were assassinated. In July 1949, Giuliano's men ambushed a police patrol, killing five officers. For some in the mafia, Giuliano was now becoming more than a nuisance: he was endangering their own relationship with the DC in Palermo and Rome, and the settlement they had brokered. On a tour to Sicily in 1948, the British ambassador found the Sicilian elite 'shamefaced and reticent' about the 'renewal of brigandage'.[144] The mafia decided to deal with the problem.

Mafiosi began collaborating with a new 1,500-strong paramilitary force established by Rome, the Comando Forze Repressione Banditismo (CFRB, Command Force for the Repression of Banditry). The CFRB occupied Montelepre, imposed a curfew and rounded up anyone suspected of harbouring Giuliano's men. It stayed for almost a year, conducting counter-insurgency-style operations against Giuliano.[145] With the mafia's help, the CFRB slowly unravelled Giuliano's network. One of his units disappeared; eight charred corpses were found soon after. Giuliano supporters across western Sicily turned up dead, reported as killed in clashes with police, but with signs that they had been killed elsewhere and their bodies dumped. Some disappeared completely.[146] Giuliano fled eighty kilometres south into the protection of a mafia *cosca* around Castelvetrano. He may have had hopes of being smuggled to Tunis and then on, perhaps to America.[147] His body was found in a courtyard in Castelvetrano in July 1950, apparently betrayed by his right-hand man, Gaspare Pisciotta, on orders from the mafia. Pisciotta himself was murdered by strychnine poisoning in a Palermo prison in 1954—apparently by the mafia.[148]

Negotiating Sicily's transition

A Sicilian political machine

As the open hostilities of World War Two transitioned in 1947 to the Cold War with the Soviet Union, Sicily emerged as an important proxy battleground. An October 1947 report from the CIA (successor to the OSS) stated:

> It is of vital strategic importance to prevent Italy from falling under Communist control… Militarily, the availability to the USSR of bases in Sicily and southern Italy would pose a direct threat to the security of communications throughout the Mediterranean.[149]

In the Italian national elections of April 1948, the Christian Democrats emerged as the dominant political force in northern Italy, and garnered 48.5 per cent of the vote nationwide. But the Communists, with their programme of land reform and economic transformation, continued to do well in impoverished Sicily. For both the mafia and the Christian Democrats, cooperation against the Communists made sense.[150] The mafia gave the DC instant social reach and electoral power where it most needed it. An April 1948 conclave of mafia bosses threw its weight behind the DC, and it was in mafia-controlled districts that the DC's Sicilian vote was highest in that month's national elections.[151]

The mafia was not, however, content to cooperate with the DC through an arm's length alliance. Instead, it turned to the same 'branch-stacking' techniques that the Anastasia brothers had used in Brooklyn.[152] Giuseppe Alessi, one of the founders of the Christian Democrat Party in Sicily, recalled the leadership's acquiescence in this mafia colonization:

> The Communists use similar kinds of violence against us, preventing us from carrying out public rallies. We need the protection of strong men to stop the violence of the Communists … [so] the 'group' [the mafia] entered *en masse* and took over the party.[153]

The hyper-local nature of the DC's political organization, similar to the model used by Tammany in New York, worked well for the mafia. As John Dickie has explained, DC faction leaders:

> could offer exactly the kind of personal relationships that *mafiosi* preferred. The exchanges between politicians and criminals that had become so difficult under Fascism could at last be restored: one hand washes the other, as the Sicilian saying goes.[154]

The DC's political networks and structures offered the Sicilian mafia a formalized patronage apparatus within which the mafia could hide its informal power and system of corrupt exchange, much as the American Mob had hidden within Tammany structures in New York. Better still, that apparatus connected directly to the corridors of power in Rome. This was crucial, not so much for enlarging the mafia's power over criminal rents as for simply keeping it. The Sicilian political economy was changing. Sicily was becoming ever more integrated into the Italian, European and global markets. The DC-dominated government in Rome favoured liberal internationalism, and Italy's post-war recovery was to be tied, through exports, to the recovery of broader

Western consumption. The primary industry supply-chains out of which the mafia's power traditionally grew were being forced to contend with external competition. If the mafia wanted to maintain power it needed to control the institutions in Palermo and Rome that would regulate these supply-chains and allocate the new public spending directed to Sicily in compensation for the disruption caused by this economic transition.[155]

The post-war structural transformation of the Sicilian economy generated rapid movement of labour from the countryside to the cities, where the state became a source of economic subsidy and welfare. At the same time, this labour market transformation created significant pressure for the finalization of the century-long process of land reform, transforming the agricultural labour force from objects of patronage into active political subjects. The pre-war system of rule—in which Rome had relied on the landowning class to control the rural population, through collaboration with the mafia—was no longer viable, and no longer offered the mafia a reliable political power-base. Instead, the mafia looked to the mass party organization of the DC as a means to control public patronage and continued governmental power.[156]

Having penetrated the DC, the mafia targeted Sicily's land reform process. In 1950 a leftist-dominated Sicilian Regional Assembly initiated the sale of 500,000 hectares of land.[157] Oversight of land redistribution was handed to local land 'boards', parastatal organizations that became patronage engines for local DC politicians—with *mafiosi* right behind them.[158] The land redistribution scheme expanded mafia capital, giving *mafiosi* formal titles and hidden beneficial ownership over significant land tracts. But it also amplified the mafia's power in a range of civil society institutions with traditional ties to the land, such as the Coldiretti (Farmers' Association), banks and the Church.[159] Each expansion of the circle of mafia influence also helped to move mafia power beyond the DC to other political parties; at election time, like many modern corporations, the mafia would provide some support to several parties, often of quite different ideological hues, as a hedging strategy.[160] By the early 1950s, mafia networks fanned out beyond the DC, so that 'direct participation in the mafia' by the 'elite corps of postwar Sicilian politicians' was probably 'widespread'.[161]

Structural transformation in Sicily's economy also changed the geography of mafia power, shifting its centre of gravity from the countryside to the urban centres, especially Palermo. Mafia power followed the money: the portion of the Sicilian workforce involved in agriculture dropped by roughly 20 per cent in the 1950s, while the portion involved in construction grew by around 25 per cent. Sicily was becoming increasingly reliant on public spending; it reached 70 per cent of Sicilian GDP by the 1990s. The portion of the workforce employed by the state grew dramatically, in turn fuelling political patronage—not just in formal municipal institutions, but also in those civil society institutions dependent on state funding: hospitals, educational institutions, cultural bodies and, increasingly, development finance institutions. '*Mafioso* practices' were spreading throughout the Sicilian political economy.[162]

Wisdom of the Mob

Sicily's economic transition stimulated innovation. The transformation of established markets and the emergence of new ones—particularly in its rapidly growing urban centres—provided the opportunity to capture new rents. This quickly exposed differences between mafia *cosche*. One major division that emerged was between the more traditionalist, rural *cosche* and the port-based *cosche* who had worked more closely with American mobsters during the AMG occupation to control the import-export sector. A surprising number of Mob figures from the American east coast were active in southern Italy at the time, including both fugitives from justice (such as Genovese and Gentile) and deportees (including Luciano and, later, Adonis).[163]

The American policy of deporting aliens with US criminal records served to export American organizational know-how and social networks to Sicily, just as it has in Central America in the last two decades, turning Californian Hispanic prison gangs into the transnational criminal systems called *maras*. The deported mobsters appear to have worked with their host—in many cases, ancestral—*cosche* in Sicily to develop smuggling activities, first in tobacco, and then in heroin. In conflict-affected southern Italy, cigarettes had become a second currency. Sicilian *mafiosi* and American mobsters developed an increasingly governmental role in the black market in cigarettes, financing inventory purchases, offering security during transit and resolving disputes.[164]

The American mobsters convinced the Sicilians to adopt the syndication system they had developed during Prohibition: instead of organizing their own supply lines, the *cosche* collaborated, allocating equity in co-shipments, pooling risk and increasing volume. Steadily these smuggling networks consolidated and diversified into Turkish, Syrian and Lebanese heroin. Through the course of the 1950s, the Sicilian mafia's ties to the Mob, and the steady stream of Sicilian agricultural exports to the US—olive oil, oranges, pasta—gave it a cost advantage over the other major global drug smuggling entrepôt, Marseille.[165] The risks involved, the potential profit and the need for organizational unity in order to deal with foreign partners (notably the Mob) all slowly pushed the mafia towards organizational consolidation.[166]

The growth of the smuggling industry also, however, created tensions between the different *cosche*, which intersected with those arising from the physical transformation of Sicily's urban centres. Two types of sites emerged as key rent-extraction and governance nodes, or what Mexican cartels call *plazas*: urban markets and harbour ports. When the Palermo food market was transferred in 1956 from its established site, controlled by traditionalist hinterland *cosche*, to a new site closer to the harbour—where it was likely to be controlled by the export-oriented urban *cosche*—open violence broke out within the mafia.[167]

In mid-October 1957, an extraordinary summit was called at the Grand Hotel et Des Palmes, an opulent *Belle Époque* hotel near the Palermo waterfront. Twenty-seven top American Mob and Sicilian mafia leaders met over several days in the Sala Wagner, named because the composer had orchestrated his last opera, *Parsifal*, there.[168] The summit, chaired by Lucky Luciano, aimed to sort out the mess created by the shifting balance of power within the Sicilian mafia. Whatever else was agreed at that meeting, it is clear from the testimony of one of the Sicilian leaders present that one major piece of strategic advice was taken on board from Joe Bonanno, an American Mob Commission member born in Castellammare del Golfo. Many of the Sicilian *mafiosi* at the summit also hailed from Castellammare. Bonanno advised the Sicilians to copy Luciano's organizational innovations of a quarter-century earlier and adopt a 'commission' structure to govern the Sicilian mafia. It was a clear message: if you want to continue to do business with us in America, and grow the profits of transatlantic drug trafficking, you need to get your house in order. Soon afterwards, the Sicilian *Cupola* system was born.[169]

Like the Commission, the *Cupola* was not a system of unitary control, but rather a committee system for regulating relations between 'sovereign' *cosche* that had previously operated as 'a mosaic of small republics with topographical borders marked by tradition'.[170] Also like the Commission, the *Cupola* was not intended to centralize power, but rather to regularize it: the aim 'was to apply overall rules that gave more freedom to individual mafiosi'.[171] As one Cosa Nostra *pentito* involved with leadership decisions at the time, Tommaso Buscetta, put it, the Commission was 'an instrument of moderation and internal peace … a good way of reducing the fear and risks that all mafiosi run'.[172] And like the Commission, the *Cupola* became the central political forum for the Sicilian mafia, with collective enforcement powers: it placed several *cosche* under trusteeship, removed and replaced *capi* for misconduct, and even disbanded troublesome *cosche*.[173] Dickie concludes that it was not 'a board of directors'; it was more 'a creature of politics … than business'.[174]

The sack of Palermo

As with New York's mafia Commission, the creation of the Sicilian *Cupola* seems also to have served to facilitate coordinated interaction between the mafia and upperworld political actors, particularly in Palermo.[175] Starting around 1958, the DC and mafia worked together to organize and deliver a decades-long construction boom that obliterated the city's *Conca d'Oro* green belt, replaced its historical belle époque villas with shoddy and frequently unsafe apartment buildings and condemned hundreds of thousands to live in poorly planned and serviced housing commissions. This was the *scempio*, or 'sack', of Palermo.[176]

The years between 1957 and 1963 were the high-point of the housing boom, with the focus in the 1970s and 1980s shifting to infrastructure. The pattern was similar to the system used by Boss Tweed at the high-point (or low-point) of Tammany rule in New York in the 1860s: a municipal council passing zoning regulations and granting development contracts, and compliant legislative and executive officials giving mafia figures inside information to allow them to capture windfall profits.[177] Historic buildings were torn down the night before new zoning laws would come into effect. Parks were cemented over. Historic and beautiful central Palermo was ravaged. By the 1990s Sicily had the highest per capita cement consumption rate in the world.[178]

The central DC figures were Salvatore Lima, Mayor of Palermo (1958–1963 and 1965–1968), and Vito Ciancimino, assessor of public works. Both worked closely with mafia construction entrepreneurs such as Francesco Vassallo, Angelo La Barbera and Tommaso Buscetta. As Judith Chubb has explained, by centralizing licensing authority, Lima changed episodic favouritism:

> undertaken without any broader strategic vision and limited to a restricted social elite, into a comprehensive strategy of urban expansion and DC power, managed directly from key posts of power within the city administration.[179]

This new system tied together DC operators, legitimate business actors, mafia figures (as brokers of capital and labour) and legitimate banks into corporate networks designed to hide the beneficial ownership of politicians and the involvement of mafia figures.[180] In Lima's first five years in power, over 4,000 building licences were granted—60 per cent to three pensioners who had no background in construction but made convenient fronts for hidden beneficiaries. Both the mafia and DC, like Tweed and Tammany, were able to use the resulting jobs and spending as a source of patronage underwriting continuing popular support.[181]

This was a strategic departure for the Sicilian mafia. Its traditional relationship to political power had been based on arm's-length exchange, the essence of a mafia strategy. Now, its brokering power was increasingly entwined with a political organization—the DC—in the collaborative management of the state to extract private rents from public spending. This moved it away from a traditional mafia strategy towards something closer to a joint venture in which state capabilities were turned to the maximization of criminal rents, and criminal capabilities were used by the state to govern. For decades, Palermitans, Sicilians and other Italians endured this system. The state's economic investment in southern Italy helped to create a consumer market for internal exports from the north. The outsize and negative influence of the mafia, Camorra and 'Ndrangheta within the DC was clear, but the alternative—ceding electoral ground to the political left—was not palatable, either to Italy's establishment or her Western friends and patrons.[182] Only with the fall of the Soviet Union, and the removal of the Communist threat, would that strategic logic change.

Conclusion

The mafia's return to a governmental role in Sicily after World War Two was not inevitable. It was the result of deliberate neglect by the Allies and active accommodation by the Italian Christian Democrats, each of which appears to have identified interests converging with those of the mafia. But it was also the result of canny strategic manoeuvring by mafia leaders, finding and creating leverage through the shifting circumstances of the end-of-war black market, the post-war political settlement process and Sicily's subsequent economic transformation. The mafia proved capable of coordinated adjustment both to its internal organization—as demonstrated by the adoption of the *Cupola* system—and to its external positioning relative to governmental rivals— working with the AMG, threatening separatism, drawing back to a more traditional brokering role, and then developing a joint venture with Lima and the Sicilian DC to use the institutions of Palermo's municipal governance to expand criminal rents.

The Sicilian mafia's strategic trajectory during this period has something in common with the evolution of American mafia power during and after Prohibition. World War Two and Prohibition both broke down the mental barriers to mass participation in criminal activity, enlarging the ranks of an underworld governed by local gangs and mafia entrepreneurs. In the 1930s, the American Mob leveraged this power into influence over Tammany upperworld power networks; in post-war Sicily, the mafia leveraged its governmental power in the black market into influence over the AMG and post-war political parties, notably the Christian Democrats. These similarities may be more than an accident: the chapter points to the involvement of some key American Mob actors in both processes—Genovese, Adonis, Profaci, Bonanno, Luciano.

Yet there was also one profound difference in the strategic environments involved in these episodes. In New York, the political settlement within the upperworld was never in question as the Mob was emerging (only later, when the Fascist powers declared war). In Sicily, it was in flux just as the mafia was seeking to re-emerge; monarchists, republicans, Communists, separatists and unitarians all vied to shape the post-war political settlement. The Sicilian mafia proved adept at using this uncertainty to augment its own governmental power, first allying with separatists, then switching to a more traditional brokering role once Sicilian autonomy had been assured. This shift might be mistaken for evidence that the Sicilian mafia did not have a political strategy. In fact it did; what it lacked was a rigid political ideology. The mafia's political objective remained constant throughout: the maximization of its governmental power in order to control criminal rents. What changed, as the strategic environment altered, was its preferred way to achieve this goal.

The mafia's return to power was also, however, the result of mafia choices—and not just its opponents' failures or accommodation. This is made clear by the failure of Salvatore Giuliano, another leader who tried and failed to develop criminal activity into a governmental role. Giuliano met the social bandit's 'standard end' as identified by Hobsbawm: betrayal by more powerful actors, brought on by making 'too much of a nuisance of himself'.[183] (The other Salvatore—Lima, sometime Mayor of Palermo—ultimately met the same fate, assassinated by the mafia in 1992 for his failure to protect the mafia leadership from judicial investigation.) Giuliano proved too recklessly violent for mainstream politics, and far too visible for his band to take on a hidden role in Sicily's government. He might have found more success as a local politician in Montelepre. But he failed both to develop his roving paramilitary band into a stationary governing force, or to renounce violence and switch tracks to parliamentary politics. Instead, his strategy suggested an increasingly desperate search for political relevance and protection, zigzagging between seeking alliance with the mafia and EVIS, then seeking foreign sponsorship by the US, and finally moving desperately to terrorism.[184] By the end he was, as Hobsbawm concluded, 'the plaything of political forces he did not understand'.[185]

Giuliano learned the hard way what the mafia already knew: that '[a]bove all,' as Michele Pantaleone reflected, effective criminal strategy depends on 'connections in all levels of society'. As Dutch Schultz had failed to appreciate in New York, if a criminal leader is 'isolated he cannot be strong'.[186] Salvatore Lima's Palermo joint venture with the mafia showed that, on the contrary, by embedding itself in the governmental institutions not just of the state, but also the economy—and society more broadly—a criminal group could become almost unassailable. But that approach required remaining patiently hidden, and fostering a criminal governmentality—*omertà*—to achieve that goal—not appearing in photoshoots in international magazines, as did Giuliano. Unlike Giuliano, the Sicilian mafia and the DC were meticulous in keeping their violence hidden. When in 1947 the *L'Ora* newspaper ran a series of mafia exposés, two bombs exploded in its printing department, terrorist attacks designed to intimidate the press back into silence. When, eleven years later, the same newspaper ran another such series, further bombings ensued.[187]

The silence of the state, under DC influence, was at least as important as the silence of the press in reinforcing the governmentality of *omertà*.[188] Leftists continued to agitate against the mafia in Rome and, more riskily, in Sicily. But the official silence of state authorities spoke loudly. Ultimately, it was this silence, acquiesced in and perhaps actively supported by Italy's NATO partners, that institutionalized *omertà* and re-established the power of the mafia's criminal governmentality on the island.

8

THE CUBA JOINT VENTURE, 1933–1958

'There's no such thing as a lucky gambler. There are just the winners and the losers. The winners are those who control the game.'

Meyer Lansky, before the Cuban Revolution[1]

'I crapped out.'

Meyer Lansky, after the Cuban Revolution[2]

The 1957 Palermo summit was not the first such seaside gathering of mafia top brass. At Christmas in 1946 a similar get-together of American mafia leaders occurred at the Hotel Nacional in Havana, Cuba, famously featuring Frank Sinatra as chief entertainer. Like the Palermo summit, the Havana summit was presided over by Lucky Luciano. Less than a year after his release and deportation from New York to Italy, and following a brief stay in Allied-occupied Palermo, Luciano had found his way to Havana, just ninety miles from Florida. He had come to lay claim to continuing leadership of the Mob and to receive tribute from the other Mob bosses. If he could not rule the Mob from inside the US, Havana offered a good substitute, not least because of the strong partnership that the Mob had, by 1946, forged with Cuba's ruling class. The summit was facilitated by Cuba's governing Partido Auténtico, which provided heightened security and intervened to expeditiously resolve a hotel labour dispute that threatened to disrupt proceedings.[3]

The Havana summit did not have the results that Luciano was hoping for. Within months the US government had forced his deportation, again to Italy. But the Mob stayed on in Havana. Under the leadership of Meyer Lansky and a Floridian mafia *capo*, Santo Trafficante, Jr., its partnership with the Havana 'Palace Gang' led by the military strong-man Fulgencio Batista flourished into a fully-fledged governmental joint venture. By the mid-1950s Cuba's economic development had, through combined state and Mob action, been reoriented to focus on maximizing rents, both licit and illicit, from tourism, gambling and drug trafficking.

By 1958 the Mob and Batista thought themselves to be sitting pretty. But both had failed to recognize the corrosive impacts their scheme was having within their own organizations, and on their social legiti-macy in Cuba. By early 1959, the Cuban 'joint venture' was in tatters: Batista had fled to Florida, and a rebel military force was in power in Havana, its attitude to the Mob seemingly hostile. That was ironic, given that US intelligence had warned in the 1940s that the man who now led the rebels 'may soon become a fully fledged gangster'. His name was Fidel Castro.[4]

This chapter explores the rise and fall of Fulgencio Batista between 1933 and 1958. The episode in question reveals the pursuit of crimi-nal strategies by both local and foreign actors and provides new insight into both the triggers for, and the military course of, Castro's Cuban Revolution. Chapter 9 explores the Mob's reaction to the failure of its strategic partnership with Batista in Cuba. As in previous chapters, the analysis draws from a mixture of declassified govern-ment archival sources (mostly in the National Archives and Records Administration in College Park, Maryland), protagonists' memoirs and relevant secondary sources. While some of this material has been discussed by Jack Colhoun's excellent history, *Gangsterismo*, Colhoun's monograph focuses on Cuba's history rather than the questions of criminal strategy explored here.[5] Eduardo Sáenz Rovner unique study of rarely accessed Cuban archival material detailing criminal activities during the period, *The Cuban Connection*, has also proved uniquely valuable as a means to triangulate and corroborate US gov-ernment and Mob sources.[6]

Buying into Cuba

Rise of a strongman

The roots of the Mob's move into Cuba lie in the US invasion of 1898, which realigned Cuba's political economy away from Spain and towards America, while leaving it a separate political and legal entity. Cuba might have become a US state, but for American sugar beet farmers' insistence on maintaining tariff protections against Cuban sugar. US Congress nonetheless made its expectation of a free hand in Cuba clear by adopting the Platt Amendment in 1901, which authorized the executive to intervene unilaterally in Cuban affairs as and when it saw fit. For the next three decades, the US used force—and the threat of force—to protect its commercial interests in Cuba, staging a series of invasions and propping up a range of plutocratic governments. By 1958 Cuba was all but an American economic colony. Some 58 per cent of Cuba's primary export—sugar—and 67 per cent of all other exports were sold into the United States. A full three-quarters of Cuba's imports came back the other way.[7]

With US capital dominating Cuba's economy in the first half of the twentieth century, the free market offered only limited upward mobility to Cuban entrepreneurs. As in any imperial or colonial system, there were two roads to wealth and power: either through the patronage networks backed by the imperial power—in this case dominated by the so-called 'sugar barons' who owned the rural sugar plantations—or otherwise through informal and illicit markets not formally governed by the imperial power.[8] Starting in 1920, the United States' policy of Prohibition offered those who chose the second track huge new payoffs, and new ways to connect with sources of power inside America. Havana quickly emerged as an important Caribbean gambling, bootlegging and narcotics transportation centre, including for outfits linked to the Mob.[9]

Cuba nonetheless suffered terribly through the Great Depression. In the summer of 1933 protests by the *clases populares* calling for more inclusive governance culminated in a general strike that forced the president, General Machado, from power.[10] The response of the US government to such disorder in Cuba over the previous decades had been military intervention. But in his inaugural address on 4 March

1933, President Franklin D. Roosevelt had set a new tone by announcing a non-interventionist 'Good Neighbor' policy towards Latin America. Cuba's formal economy remained closely tied in to America's, but US political and military control was being relaxed. The short-term result in the summer of 1933 was a power vacuum in Havana. Two men, one American and one Cuban—both born poor outsiders, both charismatic leaders of armed groups, both adroit balancers of factional support—seized this opportunity. They would become lifelong friends, and their strategic decisions would significantly influence Cuba's political landscape—and the US' immediate strategic environment—for the next thirty years.

The first was Meyer Lansky, the young Jewish mobster whose alliance with Lucky Luciano had underpinned the formation of the American 'Mob' system. As a junior partner in the mafia-dominated Mob, Lansky seems to have avoided relying solely on violence to maintain his strategic position. Instead, he made himself indispensable as a business operator, and as something of an honest broker between different mafia factions. 'I listened and read about men in all kinds of endeavour,' he would later tell an interviewer. 'The men who mostly went to the top were men with integrity.'[11] Lansky recognized that his greatest strategic asset was that rare quality within the underworld: trust. Lansky's casinos were known, ultimately worldwide, for their honesty—at least in dealing cards. 'Everyone who came into my casino,' he later claimed, 'knew that if he lost his money it wouldn't be because he was cheated.'

Nor was this mere self-aggrandizement. A visitor to Havana in the 1950s asked the US ambassador why all the American mobsters were tolerated by the government. 'It's strange,' the diplomat responded, 'but it seems to be the only way to get honest casinos.'[12]

As we saw in Chapter 5, by 1933, Lansky and Luciano were working actively to replace the revenues that would be lost when Prohibition ended by expanding into new gambling markets. One such market beckoned in Havana. Lansky had spent time there during Prohibition and got to know some of Cuba's leading political and military figures.[13] Perhaps Havana could now be turned into a gambling enclave like those controlled by the Mob in Atlantic City, Saratoga Springs, Broward County in Miami and, later, Las Vegas. All offered handy and lucrative exceptions to the staid moral codes and legal order of much American life, sustained through the 'fix': corruption of local law enforcement and political figures.[14] Equally significantly, since gambling was legal in Cuba, it offered a potentially unique venue for money-laundering. In the spring of 1933 Lansky proposed to Luciano that they 'approach a contact in the Cuban government' to '"buy in" with the Cubans so that the Mob could begin to develop its own gambling infrastructure on the island'.[15]

Lansky and Luciano's next move was telling, and shows how deft they had become in marrying internal strategic organization and external strategic positioning. Rather than strike out on their own to exploit this new market and gain an edge over their internal Mob rivals, they chose to bring those rivals in on the exploitation of Cuba's gambling potential, spreading risk and costs, and further entrenching the collective governance system of the Commission. In the spring of 1933, Luciano and Lansky called a meeting of Mob bosses at Luciano's suite in New York's Waldorf Towers and presented a plan for the Mob to invest as a syndicate in the Cuban gambling sector. Each *capo* was asked to sink $500,000 for bribes and 'to buy goodwill'—'the fix'. In return, each would get a piece of the action, either through control of a particular establishment, or through equity ('points') in syndicate-run nightclubs and casinos.[16] In subsequent years, the Mob adopted a similar syndicated approach for joint gambling enterprises in Miami and Las Vegas.[17] Having secured the group's approval Lansky flew to Cuba, and spoke to his contact in the Cuban military—a young sergeant named Fulgencio Batista y Zaldívar. He promised Batista huge sums: allegedly $3 million up front and at least as much annually thereafter.[18]

Like Lansky (and Luciano), Batista was also born an outsider. Hailing from an impoverished family in eastern Cuba, his personal charisma and leadership qualities propelled him rapidly to prominence in the Cuban army. On 4 September 1933, claiming that ongoing civil unrest following the fall of the Machado government demanded a more forceful, if sympathetic, response than the military leadership was offering, Batista led a rebellion of young non-commissioned officers. Between September 1933 and January 1934 a loose coalition of radical activists, students, middle-class intellectuals and junior army officers formed a Provisional Revolutionary Government, nominally led by a popular intellectual, Dr Ramón Grau San Martín. The PRG's political authority, however, clearly rested on Batista's military support.[19]

The PRG steadily began to challenge the existing political settlement. First, it weakened ties with the US by unilaterally rejecting the Platt Amendment and dissolving Cuba's existing political parties. Next, it decreed a series of socio-economic and civil rights reforms: an eight-hour workday, female suffrage, improved labour regulation and a minimum wage for cane-cutters. When it promised land reform, the established sugar barons and their American patrons began to push back. In January 1934, under pressure from these interests, and with the backing of the US State Department, Batista pushed Grau San Martín from power, and installed a new president. The message was clear: Batista was the real power behind the throne in Cuba.[20]

The 'Batista Palace Gang'

Batista was not, however, content to be a puppet through whom the established sugar barons could ventriloquize. He wrote his own strategic script, seeing himself not as the guardian of an existing strategic environment, but as the developer of a new one:

> [M]any want to forget that I am the chief of a constructive social revolution, and see me as a mere watchdog of public order. My idea of order is that of an architect rather than that of a policeman.[21]

Batista's populist strategy rested on forging a direct relationship with the Cuban people—especially its labour force—slowly circumventing the control that Cuba's *caudillos* and sugar barons wielded at the sugar mill and plantation level. Batista in Cuba recognized what Giuliano in Sicily did not: that industrialization and urbanization were changing the geography of power, transforming labour relations from a policing issue to a political issue. This was at the heart of the social unrest of 1933. As a British Foreign Office dispatch of the time noted, if he was to retain power, Batista had to 'remove the political grounds for economic discontent'.[22] After consolidating his military control, he began quietly to reinstitute some of the social protections and market reforms proposed by the PRG that he had deposed in 1934. At the same time, he led a campaign to force out tens of thousands of foreign workers—mainly Jamaicans and Haitians—on the grounds that they were taking Cuban jobs, in the process stoking Cuban nationalism and establishing himself as a community protector.[23]

In 1937 Batista went further, presenting a Three Year Plan for social reform, including the redistribution of state land and more intrusive regulation of the sugar industry. This elicited significant resistance from the sugar barons. In response, Batista un-banned the Cuban Communist Party and entered a tactical populist alliance with it. Having demonstrated to the sugar barons his willingness to work directly with labour, he offered them a way out, creating a Sugar Stabilization Institute to set policy for the industry in which they would control 50 per cent of the vote.[24] It was an offer of partnership. At the same time, Batista was consolidating coercive power within the national military, working around the sugar barons' rural militias. To do this, however, he had to find new means to control the sugar barons and landowners. The solution was a highly personalized patronage system. But that required revenue. And this was where criminal rents—and collaboration with the Mob—became crucial: not just as a business scheme, but as a basis of patronage-based government.

From 1936 Batista set out to expand the role of legalized gambling and associated illicit activities in Cuba's economy. Lansky and the Mob provided the expertise and the start-up capital. In 1936, Batista legalized games of chance in select casinos and nightclubs, and gave the military control of their oversight. At the same time, he officially hired Lansky as a 'consultant' to reform the Cuban government-owned Gran Casino Nacional.[25] Lansky was soon owner and manager of three casinos, including one at the premier local racetrack.[26] The national lottery, something of an institution since its founding in 1812, was transformed from a weekly to a daily event. Favoured politicians and military leaders were given blocks of tickets to sell, and were commissioned to collect bets.[27] While the lottery was formally legal, the normalization of gambling also led to the expansion of illegal gambling, such as *bolita*, a Cuban game of chance very similar to the American 'numbers' rackets. A 1943 special investigation by the US Federal Bureau of Narcotics found that gambling-related corruption was 'one of the largest sources of revenue' in Cuba, much of it disappearing into politicians' pockets.[28]

Large-scale narcotics trafficking and prostitution ventures also contributed to the patronage system. A confidential US dispatch explained that 'the illicit narcotic racket in Cuba is "sponsored" and fully protected by the Cuban National Police and very high Cuban Government officials comprising the "Palace Gang"'. This 'Palace Gang' controlled narcotics trafficking through the Cuban director of sports and the chief of the National Police, both aides to President Batista.[29] Batista was remaking Cuban government from an agricultural oligarchy operating under American protection into a system of criminalized patronage operating in collaboration with transnational criminal networks. This was a precursor to the criminalized governance and rule through disorder we have seen more recently in Africa and Asia. As in those environments, Batista's emergence as the preeminent actor within that patronage system transformed notionally democratic politics into a modern 'court' system, with him at its centre.[30]

The system rested on three legs: widespread corruption; Batista's control of Cuba's coercive apparatus; and careful strategic communication representing Batista as the source of order amongst pervasive violence, a 'strongman' protector of the community. His 'constructive social revolution' was a key part of that communications strategy, building support from the *clases populares* independent of the established economic interests. Yet located so close to Florida, and with the US increasingly agitated by both Fascist and Communist ideologies, Batista could ill afford to appear either too leftist in his social policies, or too militaristic in his ways of achieving them.[31] In the late 1930s, Batista therefore attempted a subtle shift, casting himself as a constitutional democrat, moving his focus from economic reform to civil liberties, dressing in suits rather than military uniforms.

Events overtook him. After winning the Cuban presidency as a 'civilian' in 1940, he ushered in a liberal democratic constitution that contained numerous social protection and welfare provisions. These leftist positions, his inclusion in the cabinet of several figures with Communist links and an apparent further leftward drift during 1943–1944 alarmed the US. With the 1944 presidential election approaching, the US government sent word to him—possibly through Lansky, as an offshoot of the Underworld Project—that he would do better by retiring to Florida than by standing again for election.[32] The US government, it seemed, still held the whip hand over Cuban governance, despite Batista's efforts to develop an independent populist power-base. Batista moved into temporary exile in Daytona Beach, Florida, where Lansky was a highly influential figure. His Palace Gang had lost its captain.

Gangsterismo

Batista's move from military strongman to populist constitutionalist had been presented as placing 'the people' at the heart of Cuban government. In practice, however, his reforms served to personalize political power, as the protector of a range of criminal interests, both local and foreign. When he left for Florida in 1944 a vacuum of political power opened up behind him. Ten years of life under Batista had reconstituted the power of the established sugar barons, moving them away from their agricultural bases, incorporating them—and a range of new actors—into factionalized patronage networks running through the military and police and converging in the 'Palace Gang'. With Batista's removal, these networks began to compete—often violently—for governmental power. The Cuban term for the era tells the story: it is known as the period of *gangsterismo*.

Gangsterismo was characterized by these political networks and their organizational partners—political parties, labour unions and student groups—developing urban militias that competed for informal political and economic power. Competition was no longer conducted peacefully in political institutions and through jockeying within the presidential palace for patronage: it was conducted violently in the street.[33] Political factions' prospects depended on access to a steady supply of easily controlled militants, and the resources to arm, feed and reward them. In a pattern since replicated in other developing countries, such as Nigeria, student groups at universities became a major recruiting ground, and protection and other criminal rackets became their income source. The violence on campus was significant: assassinations of student leaders were common. Lectures were not infrequently interrupted by gun battles.[34] Political actors protected young gangsters from prosecution, paid for their arms and cars and put gangster thugs on official payrolls.[35]

Over time these 'gangsters' graduated from running local protection rackets to serving as enforcers for more lucrative, clandestine, politically sponsored criminal activity—trafficking, prostitution and high-stakes gambling. Leading politicians such as the Prío Socarrás brothers—one, the prime minister, later president; another a senator—amassed fortunes from trafficking heroin and cocaine into the US, using local gangsters as muscle and labour.[36] The Prío Socarrás brothers also moved to use the state's assets not only to protect criminal activity, but also as an asset in the production of criminal rents. In the mid-1940s, the Prío brothers and the Florida Mob boss Santo Trafficante Jr. established Aerovías Q: a commercial airline entitled to use Cuban Air Force gasoline, replacement parts, maintenance staff and pilots—and with exclusive rights to operate out of military airports, avoiding customs. Aerovías Q quickly became an important cog in the developing pan-American cocaine network, flying coca paste from Colombia to Camagüey in central Cuba where the paste was refined before shipment on to consumers in Havana nightclubs and the US.[37]

The Príos' entrepreneurialism made clear that there was untapped potential in Cuba. But no strongman emerged to replace Batista. Cuba's criminal markets were fractious and poorly governed, 'no more regulated than a fairground whose operator subcontracted the individual sideshows and stalls,' in the memorable terms of Robert Lacey.[38] The Mob saw an opportunity. Within six months of his deportation to Italy, Luciano had applied for an Italian passport and a Cuban visa. With help from Lansky and a Cuban congressman and senator he was in Havana by November 1946.[39] US government records indicate that he told the Cuban authorities that he had come 'to buy a piece of the gambling rackets', but his governmental authority within the Mob seemed to suggest something else: that the Mob could help the Cuban elite to develop Cuba's criminal markets.[40] Luciano was quickly spotted in Havana fraternizing with Cuban leaders, including both Prío Socarrás brothers. He rented a house from the chief of the Cuban general staff, and began laying the groundwork for a range of business projects in partnership with Cuban political figures.[41]

This was the context in which the summit at the Hotel Nacional described in the prologue to this chapter took place. A dozen Mob leaders, including Lansky, Bonanno, Genovese, Adonis, Joe Profaci and Albert Anastasia came to 'pay allegiance' from 22 to 26 December 1946.[42] They handed over cash tributes totalling almost $150,000, confirming

Luciano's supremacy and providing him seed capital for ventures in Cuba.[43] Cuban expansion plans were a central agenda item, as was Las Vegas.[44] Luciano and Lansky suggested working with local politicians to build a new casino resort outside Havana. Aerovías Q would provide a dedicated private air bridge to Florida so that high-rollers would not have to go through immigration and customs in Cuba.[45]

It was not to be. Luciano's presence in Havana was reported in the US press—possibly as a result of a leak by Vito Genovese, whose own Mob leadership ambitions, stoked by his success working with AMG figures in occupied Italy, were threatened by Luciano's return. The US government, which had been tracking Luciano in Havana, felt that it could not be seen as tolerating him sitting on America's doorstep, and promptly pressured the Cuban authorities to deport him back to Italy. Cuba's politicians resisted. The president, prime minister and minister of the interior met and decided to allow Luciano to stay. The interior minister and the national secret police chief were deputized to tell the US embassy that there was no legal reason to deport Luciano.[46] In response, the US government withheld all supplies of medical drugs to Cuba. Reluctantly, the Cuban government abandoned Luciano, forcing him back to Italy in early 1947.[47] A US official reported shortly thereafter seeing one of Luciano's Cuban political allies, Senator Chivas, walk up to President Prío on the floor of the Cuban Senate, slap him in the face, and say, 'From Luciano to you'.[48]

Luciano's gambit to take control of Cuba's criminal markets had failed, and it set back his power within the Mob irreparably. Stuck in Italy, he would remain an influential figure in Mob affairs, but never again return to its active leadership. This did not mean, however, that the Mob's ambitions in Havana were at an end. But the continuing political instability and absence of a strong governing force in Havana made investment highly risky.

In 1948 Lansky seemed to have smoothed the way with Cuba's political factions for Batista's return to Cuba from exile in Florida, and his prompt installation in the Senate.[49] When Lansky was married for the second time later that year in a senator's office in Havana, Batista was one of a handful of guests.[50] Over the next four years, while Batista served out a constitutionally mandated period outside the presidential office, Lansky patiently laid the groundwork for the expansion of Havana's gambling scene. He coordinated joint investments in Havana's nightclubs and casinos by a range of Cuban politicians and Mob figures.[51]

In 1952 Batista moved once again to take the reins of formal political power in Cuba. He was nominated as a presidential candidate for an election scheduled for June 1952, but polling suggested he was stuck in third place.[52] On 10 March 1952, working with army officers, he staged a second bloodless *coup d'état*. Having effectively co-opted the labour movement, there were no populist forces to oppose him.[53] The strongman was back in the palace, and his collaboration with the Mob was set to move to a whole new level.

A joint venture in government

The Havana Mob

Batista's unique, personal authority over the military and internal security agencies—not replicated by any of the civilian politicians who had ruled in his absence—allowed him to effectively monopolize force. With his return to power, the *gangsterismo* period of competition between local protection rackets looked set to end. Instead, against the ideological schisms of the Cold War, it mutated. The factional fighting between gangster squads of the 1940s morphed into the Cold War proxy conflict of the 1950s. *Gangsterismo* figures from the right, such as Rolando Masferrer, a student leader rival to Fidel Castro when they were both attending the University of Havana, became Batista's enforcers; *gangsterismo* figures from the left, including Castro himself, became Batista's political opponents.[54]

By 1950, declines in the sugar price and shifts in the terms of trade meant that Cuba was running a budget deficit.[55] The island needed to diversify its economy. But to do so, it needed capital investment, particularly in infrastructure and human resources. Where was Batista to find this capital? Cuba did have oil reserves, but these were largely controlled by US commercial interests. Without other natural resource endowments or increased foreign debt, Batista was unlikely to be able to develop the more centralized state he had long advocated.[56] Batista turned to three alternative sources of investment capital: his own people's savings—using gambling to channel them into state coffers, and encouraging union pension funds to invest in new capital projects, especially hotels; bringing in foreign private investment through tourism; and the proceeds of foreign crime looking for an effective money-laundering centre. For several years, the approach appeared highly successful, in pure economic terms. Legitimate American private sector investment in Cuba in the 1950s grew from $142 million to $952 million.[57]

State-controlled growth of the gambling industry was the key to mobilizing all three sources of capital. And Mob finance—and expertise—was essential to this reorientation of Cuba's economy. A few months after resuming his role as Cuba's strongman, Batista officially invited Lansky to resume his old position, bringing him back as Cuba's 'adviser on gambling reform' for an annual retainer of $25,000.[58] Soon the American Mob and Batista's clique had formed a new joint venture: a 'Havana Mob' which 'ran a network of untouchable businesses, in which semi-legal control merged with gang-style law'. This Havana Mob enjoyed governing power over domestic criminal operators. It used it not only to tax them, but also to regulate them: through inspections and raids, state law enforcement agencies forced a general improvement in customer service standards across Havana's gaming joints, improving Havana's positioning and reputation in the North American gambling market and attracting new visitors and revenues.[59] In the US, Lansky had used the Mob's governmental power to create a prudential regulatory system to grow the illicit gambling economy; here, he was using the formal governing power of the Cuban state to regulate and grow licit gambling markets, and all the ancillary illicit markets that came with gambling.

The *Batistianos* (Batista supporters, as the Havana Mob was also known) protected Lansky and other members of the American Mob in return for a 'skim' from the rackets and casinos they ran, the skim then underwriting political patronage.[60] Frequently, these rackets—from casinos to narcotics trafficking—involved joint operations and joint investment by both American mafia members and Cuban political and military leaders. One example was described by Mariano Faget y Diaz, the head of Batista's Bureau for the Repression of Communist Activities (BRAC)—an internal security agency—after he fled to the US in 1959:

> Prostitution and illegal gambling were taxed by the police, and the proceeds went directly to the Chief of Police. Smuggling was protected by

MANUEL PEREZ BENITOA, administrator of Customs in Havana. The illegal traffic in drugs was directed from the Bureau of Investigations and controlled by the Assistant Chief, Commander RICARDO MEDINA, behind the back of his immediate chief, Colonel ORLANDO PIEDRA.[61]

Batista's brother-in-law Roberto Fernández y Miranda controlled slot machines—which were supplied by the Mob—taking 50 per cent of revenues.[62] General Cantillo, head of the Cuban army headquarters, was tied up with Santo Trafficante in the Sevilla-Biltmore casino.[63] The head of the secret police owned a piece of Trafficante's Havana night-club, the Sans Souci, which was managed by Norman Rothman, a New York mobster. Rothman also appears to have been a player in the Cuban narcotics trade in the 1950s, while Trafficante worked with a local poli-tician to run the local *bolita* market. Topping it all off, the Mob's attor-ney in Cuba was Batista's son-in-law.[64]

Just as Lansky allowed a variety of Mob actors to enjoy the fruits of this collaboration, so Batista ensured that a wide range of his cohorts benefited. But Batista also recognized that the careful distribution of criminal rents was a way to develop and maintain his own social legiti-macy. By removing Cuba's national lottery from the national budget, he created a special revenue fund he could use as a means of political leverage and corruption. Decree Law 2185 (1954) gave him the right to make grants from lottery funds to educational, social welfare and cultural organizations. Batista himself has described how he doled out money to journalists ($1.3 million), the Catholic Church ($1.6 mil-lion), unions ($1.3 million) and pension funds ($3.6 million). Overall he claims to have *officially* distributed more than $63 million in six years, purchasing wide support for his continuing rule.[65]

The masterstroke in the new governmental joint venture between the American and Havana Mobs was, however, the creation of the Banco de Desarrollo Económico y Social—the Bank for Economic and Social Development or BANDES. The American Mob had established close connections to key private Cuban banks, controlled by senior political figures, including one established by President Batista himself. These were used for general banking, for raising capital and as money-laundering channels.[66] The BANDES was something else entirely: a state-backed development finance institution. It aimed for nothing less than the strategic reorientation of Cuba's economic growth through centrally controlled, debt-financed infrastructural development, particularly around tourism—especially gambling. Roads, an airline, the airport, the main Havana racetrack and especially hotels all became major BANDES investments.[67]

BANDES was placed within a policy regime that encouraged and facilitated foreign investment in Cuba—whatever its provenance. This included a ten-year tax holiday on new corporate investments; the waiver of import duties on construction materials (which helped to create a thriving black market in such materials); a guaranteed gambling licence to each and every approved $1 million hotel project—or any $200,000 nightclub casino—without background checks on the proprietors; and two-year work visas for workers with specialized gambling expertise, such as card dealers.[68] As T.J. English has put it, BANDES was intended to tie Mob interests 'into the economic and social development of Cuba itself, so that the fortunes of the Mob in Cuba were one and the same with the fortunes of the Cuban people'.[69]

BANDES also served as a mechanism for consolidating Batista's power within Cuba's factionalized political system, using rents extracted from foreign investors as a means of political patronage. BANDES-backed deals required foreign investors to take on local partners—*Batistianos*—as minority shareholders. Infrastructure project pricing was inflated to allow Cuban political sponsors a 'skim'. Allocation of these roles allowed Batista to buy off the private militias that lingered from the period of *gangsterismo*. BANDES subsidized the move of Cuban gangsters such as Barletta and Battisti into casinos and nightclubs in Havana. Rolando Masferrer received government resources and funds to fight Castro's rebel forces in the Sierra Maestra.[70] Batista himself did not walk away empty-handed: he received a $250,000 facilitation fee from each BANDES deal, plus monthly kickbacks totalling perhaps $10 million annually.[71] Moreover, BANDES consolidated his power within the domestic economy: Cuba's private banks were 'implicitly forced' to buy BANDES-issued bonds, giving Batista leverage over private capital-raising and consolidating his control over potential internal rivals.[72]

The result was a debt-financed construction boom and money-laundering bonanza. Twenty-eight new hotels were constructed in five years.[73] Five new major hotel casinos opened with Mob money and personnel between 1955 and 1958: the Capri, the Hilton, the Deauville and the Riviera in Havana, and the Comodoro in suburban Miramar. Havana's hotel rooms increased from 3,000 in 1952 to 5,500 in 1958.[74] Lansky's Riviera, the largest casino-hotel outside Las Vegas, cost $14 million, $6 million of which came from government financing institutions.[75] With the Cuban state formally legalizing activities that remained illegal in the US (such as gambling) and informally licensing others (prostitution, narcotics, pornography), Havana became an offshore vice capital and money-laundering centre.

The scheme made the Havana and American Mobs partners in a governmental joint venture in Cuba. Along with Cuba's security service leaders, they were bound 'together in defense of a repressive, but for them profitable, political status quo on the island'.[76] Yet as Batista's regime became increasingly inequitable Cubans became increasingly resentful. While the boom created jobs, Cubans were all too aware of how heavily indebted they were becoming as a result—and who ultimately stood to profit. A July 1957 article in the magazine *Bohemia* described Havana's new hotels as 'constructed with funds stolen from the people'.[77] A story in *Life* magazine ran:

> Standing outside the Riviera, one Cuban said, 'That cost *us* $6 million. It cost the owners $8 million. If it makes money, *all* the profits will be siphoned off to the US. If it loses money, we Cubans have a $6-million white elephant on our hands. What kind of deal is that for Cuba?'[78]

The same article reflected the political risk attached to the American Mob's investments in Cuba: if Batista 'fell from power, the gambling mob would have to make a whole new set of deals with a different bunch of politicians'.[79] But that was a day that the American Mob did not see coming, at least not soon. On the contrary, they were busy fighting over the joint venture's spoils.

Rebellion in the Mob

The Cuban gambling boom was a fountainhead of patronage not only for Batista, but also for Lansky and the Mob. But it also fuelled jockeying and internal rivalries, just as had the bootlegging boom in Prohibition New York (Chapter 5) and the cigarette and heroin smuggling boom in Palermo (Chapter 7). It was Lansky—not Batista—who first had to stare down a rebellion in his ranks.

As the US Federal Bureau of Narcotics recognized, the Mob served as the 'organizational medium' through which Batista's gambling boom was realized.[80] Yet even after Luciano's organizational reforms (Chapter 5), the Mob functioned more as a coalition or confederation of autonomous Families than as a unitary structure. Even on questions of external positioning and offshore activity, the Families were free to operate autonomously within strategic parameters coordinated by the Commission. In Havana, that translated into a variety of operational arrangements. While Lansky was the acknowledged coordinator of Mob interests, some nightclubs and casinos were owned and run by specific actors within the Mob, with Trafficante having the largest and most lucrative portfolio after Lansky. Others were operated on a syndicated basis, with different Mob figures allocated 'points'—stock—by the Commission.[81] With five major new casino hotels coming online in just a few short years, jockeying for control of the rents they would generate was inevitable. And as T.J. English has put it, 'decisions made on the island created a ripple effect' out through the ranks of the Mob.[82]

Rival camps coalesced around Lansky—with a strong base in New York—and the Trafficantes, who hailed from Florida. Like the New York mobsters, the Trafficantes had drawn on the southern Italian mafia tradition to amass control of Florida's bootlegging, narcotics and gambling rackets in the 1920s and 1930s. They had strong ties to Cuba, through the Cuban immigrant community in Florida and through running Cuban rum during Prohibition. Like Luciano, Santo Trafficante Sr. literally murdered his competition in these markets, assuming a dominant position before passing control to his son, Santo Trafficante Jr.[83] Trafficante Jr. himself apprenticed for a time in New York with the Gagliano Family.[84] And like the New York Families, the Trafficantes' power in both Florida and Cuba relied on careful cultivation of law enforcement officials and political actors.[85]

As a formal member of the Commission, Trafficante wielded significant power within the mafia. His Family's long-standing Cuban connections and Spanish language skills further amplified their importance to the Mob's operations in Cuba. In the mid-1950s Trafficante Jr. appears to have begun exploring ways to form alliances with some of the New York Families, to challenge the network around Lansky for a greater share of Havana's criminal rents.[86] One promising prospect was Albert Anastasia, the former leader of Murder, Inc., who by the mid-1950s had killed his way to power in the Mangano (later Gambino) Family in Brooklyn. Anastasia would normally have been subject to discipline by the mafia Commission for his unsanctioned violence. But he had sought protection within the Commission from Frank Costello, in turn promising to provide Costello with physical protection from Vito Genovese, who had attempted to have Costello assassinated in May 1957.

In mid-1957, at the height of the building boom in Havana, Anastasia, perhaps encouraged by Trafficante and emboldened by his apparent protection by Costello, appears to have demanded a larger piece of the action in Cuba. Lansky offered Anastasia a share in the new Hilton Hotel, due to open in 1958. It would be the largest hotel in Havana, and have a large casino. But when Anastasia visited Havana in September 1957 to conduct due diligence, he discovered that he would be sharing ownership and control with fifteen other investors, ranging from Cuba's hotel workers' union (a key source of political support for Batista) to the junior US senator from the state of Nevada (where the Mob had Las Vegas gambling interests to protect).[87] Lansky, in contrast, controlled the Nacional and Riviera outright; and Trafficante controlled three establishments—the Comodoro, Deauville and Capri. Anastasia returned to New York and met with Trafficante to discuss his concerns about the deal. Trafficante appears to have suggested that he could help Anastasia secure a deal with Batista to buy the Hilton concession outright. In effect, Trafficante was proposing to cut Lansky out of the process, while hiding his hand behind Anastasia.[88]

Lansky had attempted to avoid becoming involved in the power struggle that had emerged between Costello and Genovese, and a hit on Anastasia could leave his old ally Costello dangerously exposed. But Anastasia's push to outflank Lansky in Cuba threatened his own authority too seriously to remain unanswered. Two days after he had met with Trafficante, Anastasia was murdered, gunned down in a barber's chair at the New York Park Sheraton Hotel. The murder was never solved, but unpublished analysis by the Federal Bureau of Narcotics housed in the US National Archives suggests that Lansky cut a deal with Genovese: Genovese hired two Cuban-Americans who assassinated

Anastasia; and in return, Lansky sanctioned Genovese taking over from Costello as the leader of Luciano's own Family, which now became known as the 'Genovese Family'.[89]

Revolution in Cuba

In mid-1958 the Movimiento 26 de Julio (July 26 Movement) insurgency led by Fidel Castro numbered only a few hundred soldiers in mountains in the east of Cuba, far from the capital. Yet six months later it had taken power in Havana. Batista's regime collapsed with stunning speed, reminiscent of subsequent regime collapses such as that in Mali in 2013. What happened? Evidence suggests that in both countries—Cuba in the 1950s and Mali more recently—corruption was at the heart of the matter. The political class' reliance on criminal rents led not only to the collapse of the regime's popular legitimacy but also the hollowing out of its military effectiveness and the creation of political space into which a rival political and military organization then stepped.

By 1958, corruption had become normalized in Cuba. Questioned about graft, Batista would quote back the words of the former US ambassador to Cuba, Spruille Braden: 'Of course there was always corruption… but also on Manhattan … there are similar situations of … criminality.'[90] The US Treasury Representative in Havana reported back to Washington that amnesties were being routinely used to 'whitewash' corruption 'in all branches of the Cuban government', justified on grounds of rehabilitation and 'a new start in life'.[91]

This gave Castro a significant political opportunity to attack Batista's social base. He made criticism of Batista's cooperation with foreign corporate and criminal actors a central target of his communications strategy. Speaking in his own defence at his trial for an attack he led on the Moncado barracks on 26 July 1953, Castro argued that Batista's 1933 'revolution' had been nothing of the sort, but:

> merely brought with it a change of hands and a redistribution of the loot among a new group of friends, relatives, accomplices and parasitic hangers-on that constitute the political retinue of the Dictator.[92]

This recalled Macmillan's words about 'wine and women and champagne'.

By 1958 the July 26 Movement, named in remembrance of the date of the attack on the Moncado barracks, was focused on attacking economic targets in eastern Cuba to send a political message. Its fighters burned sugar mills and cane fields, set fire to jet fuel at an Esso oil refinery, took foreign workers hostage, attacked an American-owned mining plant and threatened Freeport mining interests. They also went to work on the morale of the Cuban military, dropping leaflets including photographs of Cuban army commanders indulging themselves in Havana's nightclubs and houses of prostitution. A September 1958 FBI report noted that even soldiers 'loyal' to Batista were 'disgusted' with the 'lack of leadership and graft on the part of commanding officers'.[93]

Through the course of 1958, Castro increasingly found that his military effort involved pushing at an open door. Since criminal rents were ultimately controlled and protected by the military and security apparatus, command appointments in Cuban national military ranks had increasingly been awarded on the basis of patronage logic rather than merit.[94] Over time this contributed considerably to demoralization and the degradation of operational effectiveness. Soon the maximization of criminal rents began to displace other strategic goals even in operational decision-making. One high-level Cuban security official later explained how Batista's brother-in-law, granted command of a regiment, turned it over to organizing seventeen gambling houses, staffing them with troops taken away from posts in 'important towns which were later occupied by the rebels without any resistance'.[95]

Military campaigning against Castro's forces became sporadic. Even when the armed forces had the insurgents on the back foot, they would fail to finish them off. The insurgents' persistence eroded Batista's credibility and the morale of his own supporters. As defections mounted Batista became legitimately more suspicious of rivals within his own ranks. In November 1958 he foiled two coup attempts, the first led by the chief of army operations, the second by the chief of the naval air corps. In December the chairman of Cuba's joint chiefs of staff sought US support for his own coup. Batista kept his most loyal troops in Havana, for his own protection. Those he sent east to fight Castro were those with more questionable loyalties—and thus less incentive to fight forcefully for him.

Batista also worried about the sugar barons deserting him. So he assigned troops to fixed positions for much of the dry harvest season to deter baronial rebellion, particularly in the west near Havana, allowing Castro to build up his strength. Only when the rains set in and plantation workforces (and baronial militias) dispersed could these troops be released to move east; and by then it was too wet for effective operational manoeuvre. From the middle of 1958, the Cuban army began to withdraw whenever Castro's forces attacked. The result was not so much a series of victories by the July 26 Movement, but rather a shrivelling back towards Havana of Batista's coercive capabilities. Eventually Batista's operational commander in the east, charged with prosecuting the campaign against Castro, instead opened direct talks with him.[96]

On New Year's Eve, recognizing he had a losing hand, Batista folded and fled Cuba with perhaps $300 million in looted state assets.[97] As Domínguez notes, his military 'had not been defeated in the battle of Havana—there never was any such battle, because Batista surrendered state power'. His coercive capability simply collapsed, the victim of cronyism, demoralization resulting from corruption and distrust. His strategy for governing Cuba had failed. Domínguez says simply: 'Batista's manner of rule, and the nature of the regime he designed, explains why and how he fell.'[98]

The Mob was largely blindsided. It had taken only minimal steps to mitigate the rising popular discontent. In a ham-fisted attempt to buy public support, in 1957 the Mob backed a mass-market bingo game in Cuba, giving away new-model American cars far beyond the purchasing power of ordinary Cubans.[99] Lansky purchased the services of one of Cuba's leading columnists and radio personalities, Diego González (known as Tendelera), and enlisted him to place pieces supportive of Batista and public investment in gambling and tourism.[100] But Lansky was largely unconcerned by Castro, telling his colleagues that he was confident he could pay off anyone who replaced Batista.[101] Trafficante and some New York financiers hatched a plan to offer Castro $1 million for assurances that he would allow gambling to continue in Havana. Indeed, bribes and guns were offered to several members of Castro's political support network in the US, including the president-to-be, Urrutia.[102]

The Mob badly underestimated the risk Castro posed. Trafficante told his lawyer that he thought the Mob 'would never stop making all that money in Cuba'. 'Who would have known that crazy guy, Castro, was going to take over and close the casinos?'[103] Even after he took power, the Mob remained in denial. Trafficante recalled thinking:

> He's not going to be in office or power for long... Batista will return or someone else will replace the guy because there's no way the economy can continue without tourists, and this guy is closing all the hotels and casinos. This is a temporary storm. It'll blow over.[104]

In fact, when Batista fled, the Mob's losses were significant. Lansky, Trafficante and other Mob figures were in Havana and witnessed the upheaval that followed. While Batista's departure did not lead to widespread violence, the casino resorts that BANDES had funded did become a target for vandalism and symbolic protest. Seven of the thirteen casinos in Havana suffered major damage.[105] The vandalism was an expression of the population's understanding and rejection of the joint venture with the Mob that Batista's governing regime had become.[106]

It was a major strategic defeat for the Mob. As Lansky put it, years later, 'I crapped out.'[107] The episode's seminal emotional impact on Mob leaders and organizational self-perception is made clear by a personal account of a Chicago Mob leader's daughter, Antoinette Giancana. Her father, Sam Giancana—who features prominently in the next chapter—would fly into a rage at the mention of Castro's name, once yelling: 'Don't ever mention that bastard's name in this house again ... ever... Do you have any idea of what he's done to me ... to our friends?' As she put it, the Havana casinos 'were the golden lode whence the profits flowed into the Chicago mob's treasury—and into the coffers of other crime families across the country'.[108] Castro had deprived the Mob of the goose that laid the golden eggs. Now, they wanted revenge.

Conclusion

Though the close relationship between military action and political power has long been understood within strategic theory, as we saw in Part One, there has long been an insistence that organized crime is something else entirely. Perhaps more clearly than any other single episode studied here, the period of Fulgencio Batista's political ascendancy in Cuba between 1933 and 1958 shows that this is not necessarily always so. Governmental power in Cuba in that period derived not just from military sources and political action, but also from the strategic organization of crime.

Batista's path to power did indeed start with the development of influence and authority in the Cuban military, but then ran through canny manipulation of corruption and patronage, buttressed by a sophisticated approach to communication. As Cuba's strongman he regulated and controlled competition between Cuba's relatively autonomous sugar barons, his presidential palace emerging as a court in which their networks competed for patronage and access to criminal rents. The Mob provided a significant, independent source of criminal expertise and capital that helped him develop this system in size, sophistication and reach, tying a broad range of interests into his governmental project.

When the US intervened to remove Batista from the Cuban political scene in 1944, the patronage networks that had grown in Batista's shadow were deprived of their protection. A period of strategic competition for governmental power, known as *gangsterismo*, followed. Only with Batista's reinsertion into Cuba's governmental marketplace in the 1950s was stability re-established, at which point Batista reinstated the system he had previously relied upon. This time, however, he supercharged it through aggressive pursuit of economic growth in sectors offering new and larger criminal rents. This was made possible by the use not only of state law enforcement and military institutions, but also the state's economic regulatory institutions, such as BANDES. The governmental joint venture of the 1950s between the American and Havana Mobs soon put the collaboration of the 1930s in the shade. Criminal capabilities were used to govern, and governmental assets in criminal enterprises.

Here was the prototype for an array of subsequent such 'joint ventures' between organized crime and the state. The demise of the Havana joint venture is, consequently, potentially highly instructive for contemporary policy-makers wrestling with 'mafia states' and other forms of criminal-political 'convergence'. Some commentators argue that structural inequalities in global markets push marginalized communities into illicit activity, since this is one of the few areas in which they enjoy competitive advantage. The Havana Mob episode makes clear that even if turning a blind eye to illicit activity generates substantial short-term economic growth, it comes at huge social costs likely to outweigh these short-term benefits. BANDES and the gambling economy promoted by Batista and the Mob infected Cuba with a hidden version of what economists call 'Dutch Disease'—skewing the allocation of capital and labour towards the extraction of criminal rents and hollowing out productive sectors of the economy. Everyday Cubans suffered the consequences: under-investment in the rest of the economy, systematic corruption, violence and inefficient labour and capital pricing. What was worse, most of the rents were not recycled in the economy, but rather looted and sent to safe offshore accounts. We arguably see this pattern repeated in many contemporary situations where local communities are stuck in a developmental 'crime trap', with kleptocratic ruling elites forming joint ventures with criminal organizations to extract wealth from local resources and illicit trafficking, passing the environmental, social and economic costs on to the community. We return to this phenomenon in Chapter 11.

The Cuban experience helps to explain why these joint ventures prove fragile over the long run: they undermine their own social legitimacy. The Cuban joint venture between Batista's cohorts and organized crime ultimately undermined the legitimacy of his regime. Once popular confidence failed, the regime was vulnerable to collapse, as the population looked for a new source of governmentality. In Havana, that came in the form of the July 26 movement, led by Castro. In today's Afghanistan, it may take the shape of the Taliban, or in Mali, the shape of Touareg-Islamist insurgency. In the next chapter we consider how the Mob reacted to this unexpected strategic failure in Cuba.

9

THE BLUE CARIBBEAN OCEAN, 1959–1983

'We've been operating a damned Murder Inc. in the Caribbean.'

President Lyndon Johnson[1]

September 1960, at the Fontainebleau Hotel in Miami. A senior US Central Intelligence Agency official meets with two men—'Sam Gold' and 'Joe'—contracted for what the official later calls 'a sensitive mission requiring gangster-type action'. The term 'gangster-style' was not accidental. The two men were Sam Giancana and Santo Trafficante Jr., both members of the mafia Commission, both at the time on the FBI's list of the ten most wanted criminals. Their sensitive mission? The assassination of Fidel Castro.[2]

Over the next three years, the CIA equipped the Mob with cash, radios, guns and even deadly botulinum pills with which to poison Castro. But the Mob also went further. It mounted full-scale transnational armed attacks into Cuba directed at both government and civilian targets. And it helped to organize and finance Cuban governments in exile with the hope that once they were installed in power they would return the Mob to its hidden role in Cuban government. The CIA-Mob collaboration to kill Castro and install an alternative government in Cuba ultimately failed, but not before seemingly impacting other US counter-revolutionary efforts such as the paramilitary invasion at the Bay of Pigs. And ultimately the costs of these failed collaborative schemes may have been even higher: Lyndon Johnson, Robert F. Kennedy and a US House of Representatives Select Committee all saw signs that the cooperation may have backfired, ultimately killing not the leader of Cuba, but rather the leader of the US—President John F. Kennedy.[3]

Why was the CIA cooperating with the Mob to begin with? And why would the Mob risk exposing its leadership, networks and organizations to penetration by the US government for such an operation? This chapter offers an explanation, and explores the potentially major strategic implications of that cooperation.

The first section explores the strategies developed by Mob actors between 1959 and 1963 to wrest back control of Cuba's criminal rents from Castro's revolutionaries, ranging from corrupting Castro's regime to the more coercive methods just described. The second section considers the unintended consequences of the US government's cooperation with the Mob during this period, looking at its connection to the failed American invasion at the Bay of Pigs, the Cuban Missile Crisis and the assassination of President John F. Kennedy. The third part of the chapter considers the Mob's reaction once its removal from Cuba sank in—including an attempt to use force to install itself in Haiti; and a much more effective and enduring scheme in The Bahamas. An epilogue briefly explores how the ripples from these events in the Caribbean found their way back to the shores of Atlantic City.

Drawing particularly on original archival research in declassified CIA files and congressional testimony in the US National Archives in College Park, Maryland, this chapter shows the Mob leadership learning from strategic failure. It also suggests the emergence of a new approach by the Mob to position itself in the governmental market, based not on jostling with rival organizations for advantage in a crowded market, but instead adopting what business management literature calls a 'blue ocean strategy' to find or create a new, uncrowded market.[4] As W. Chan Kim and Renée Mauborgne, the originators of blue ocean strategy theory explain, this involves reconstructing the value chain (and industrial space) rather than competing within existing parameters through product differentiation or over cost.[5] In this chapter, we see the Mob striking upon just such an approach: rather than compete with other criminal organizations or political parties for governmental power, it learned that it could create new governmental spaces to dominate. It could not only react to strategic opportunities as they arose, but carve them out for itself. As Kim and Mauborgne put it, 'strategy can shape structure'.[6]

'A gangland style killing'

Accommodation or confrontation?

When Fulgencio Batista fled Cuba on New Year's Eve of 1958, the damage that Mob leaders had sustained suddenly dawned on them. On 5 January 1959, even before Castro reached Havana, Lansky desperately began trying to cut a deal. 'All we know now is that there is a new government in power,' Lansky told the *Times of Havana*. 'We want to do everything possible to cooperate with it.'[7] Santo Trafficante Jr. provided Castro's officials with gifts and free sex at his Sans Souci nightclub, even offering to assist Cuban intelligence (G-2) operations in the US. An unpublished US intelligence report in the US National Archives suggested it was Castro himself who nixed the idea, punning, *O es demasiado santo, o demasiado traficante* (He is either too much of a saint, or too much of a trafficker).[8]

Arriving in Havana, Castro warned that he would 'clean out all the gamblers who used the influence of Dictator Batista's regime to build an empire here'. Most of the casinos in Havana suspended operations.[9] But when casino closings generated street demonstrations by laid-off workers, Castro proved more pragmatic. In mid-February 1959 he allowed casinos to reopen, serving foreigners only, and under tightened state controls.[10] By May, short on income, the new regime began heavily taxing casinos and seizing private assets.[11] In early June, under pressure from the US government, the Cuban authorities detained numerous Mob figures, including Meyer Lansky's brother, Jake, and Trafficante himself.[12] Negotiations between Castro and Trafficante continued, with Trafficante leaving immigration detention to attend his daughter's wedding at the Havana Hilton.[13] Several sources appear to corroborate that one visitor to Trafficante was a young hoodlum, Jack Ruby (about whom more later), trying to sell jeeps to Castro in return for Trafficante's release.[14] By early 1960, all of the mobsters had indeed been released. Trafficante's nightclub, the Sans Souci, struggled on, tending to the few tourists not scared off by the Revolution. But the heady days of the Mob's Cuban gambling empire were over.[15] While Castro remained in power, Mob leaders began to recognize, those golden days could not be revived. If corruption would not produce the sought accommodation, perhaps they would have to turn to other methods—such as coercion and confrontation.

Elements of the two Mobs—from America and Havana—began organizing a military counter-attack on Castro. The Havana Mob had reassembled in Florida, using looted Cuban funds to set up in Miami's hotel industry. A syndicate comprising Batista, his brother-in-law (General Fernández) and the former head of the Cuban national police bought Miami's Biltmore Terrace Hotel, installing Norman Rothman, a mobster close to both Trafficante and Lansky, as the new hotel manager.[16] Lansky—who had lost perhaps more, financially and politically, as a result of the Cuban Revolution than any other Mob leader—pushed for a Mob counter-attack. It was not entirely new territory for him. He had been intimately involved in the Mob's support to the US invasion of Sicily, and after the UN voted in 1948 to partition Palestine, he had quietly helped the Haganah (the Israeli paramilitary organization) with fundraising and arms-brokering in America.[17]

The Biltmore soon became an informal planning headquarters. Rothman and other mobsters arranged access to money, arms and explosives. Mob-hired pilots, including Rolando Masferrer—Castro's *gangsterismo* rival, later Batista's enforcer—began air raids into Cuba from the Yucatán Peninsula in Mexico. They burned sugarcane fields and attacked sugar mills in Cuba, hoping to destabilize the Cuban economy and swing public opinion against Castro.[18]

The US government was aware of these transnational military operations—and took no steps to stop them. By October 1959, Castro was openly condemning the US government for complicity in international 'terror' attacks.[19] Yet the attacks also failed to draw the hoped-for results. There were few signs of disorder or rebellion in Cuba. The Mob began to realize that a bigger push might be needed—and that this would require more active cooperation with the US government. Lansky met secretly with the FBI in Miami to try to motivate government action by warning of Castro's leftward turn. Lansky 'held himself out as a historian,' the FBI agents recalled, showing an 'excellent grasp of political science, current and past'. He warned that 'the time was ripe for communist factions to entrench themselves' in Castro's government, and, seeking to make common cause, suggested using Mob contacts within Cuba to assist the US government.[20] His entreaties had no immediate effect; and if anything the attacks in Cuba seemed to be helping Castro rally support for the Revolution. By the summer of 1960, the Mob and exiled Cuban leadership decided to take a more direct approach, striking at Castro directly, and began engaging in their own assassination plotting.[21] One plot involved using one of Castro's lovers to poison him.[22] Another plot involved using Juan Orta, the head of Castro's executive office, secretly on Trafficante's payroll, to bomb Castro's office.[23]

Who would replace Castro if the assassination efforts succeeded? Lansky pushed the leadership credentials of Manuel Antonio de Varona y Laredo ('Tony Varona'), a former Cuban prime minister and senate president under President Prío Socarrás. Lansky invited Varona to his house in Miami and offered him several million dollars to establish a government-in-exile and to pay for a public relations campaign. Varona appears to have accepted. Lansky hired the Edward Moss Agency, a respected Washington DC public relations firm with longstanding connections to both organized crime and the CIA. (Moss' secretary and mistress was the sister of the manager of gambling rooms at the Mob-controlled Casino Nacional, Tropicana and Sans Souci nightclubs in Havana.) The Moss agency became a conduit for between $2 and $4 million to be passed from the Mob to the anti-Castro forces over the next couple of years.[24] All Lansky asked in return was 'that if Varona or his allies should ever come to power in Cuba, the Mafia would be able to re-establish their gambling activities in Cuba'.[25]

Internationalizing Murder, Inc.

Castro was still, however, firmly in place. The Mob's attempts to dislodge him—first indirect, then more direct—had not succeeded. Nor had they attracted clear support from the US government. In fact it took some time for the Eisenhower Administration to reach the conclusion that it could not work with Castro. A National Security Council briefing on 6 January 1959 noted that 'Fidel Castro has often asserted his desire for friendship with the US'.[26] A consultative committee of US business interests recommended that the US government recognize Castro's July 26 government, as the US proceeded to do the next day.[27] President Eisenhower, personally sceptical of the Castro brothers' intentions and concerned that the US 'simply could not afford to appear the bully', at first adopted a studied coolness.[28] When Castro visited Washington in April 1959, Eisenhower went to play golf at Augusta National in Georgia. Yet as American public perceptions of Castro steadily darkened through 1959, official US reporting began to suggest growing Communist influence in Castro's regime. In May, agrarian reforms threatened to nationalize almost half of the $900 million of US private investment in Cuba. By July the American foreign policy establishment in Washington DC was actively considering how to overthrow Castro.[29]

On 5 November 1959 Eisenhower secretly authorized efforts to remove Castro from power. The 'Good Neighbor' era was over. By January 1960 the State Department and CIA were working jointly to encourage a change of government in Cuba.[30] Although President Eisenhower does not appear to have specifically authorized assassination *per se*, the CIA began to explore it as an option.[31] In late 1959 the CIA attempted to infiltrate two Cuban exiles with a sniper's rifle into Havana, but they were arrested.[32] Over the next six months, it worked to develop a more sophisticated assassination or disruption capability. Some of the options considered verged on the bizarre: lacing Castro's cigars with an LSD-like substance so that he would make a public spectacle of himself; or using thallium salts to make his beard fall out, undermining his macho persona.[33] By mid-March 1960, the intelligence community had concluded that it would be difficult to take Castro, his brother Raúl and the key adviser Che Guevara out in one 'package', as might be necessary to achieve regime change. High-level attention turned away from the assassination plotting to a broader paramilitary effort to topple the whole regime, authorized in January 1960 by the National Security Council's Special Group.[34]

On 17 March 1960 President Eisenhower approved a secret $4.4 million paramilitary programme on Cuba, expected to be operational later that year. This effort would ultimately conclude in disaster at the

Bay of Pigs in April 1961. The basis of the Eisenhower administration's confidence in the CIA's ability to sponsor a covert paramilitary invasion was its earlier success in similar enterprises in Iran in 1953 and Guatemala in 1954 (the failed attempt to displace Sukarno in Indonesia in 1958 conveniently forgotten).[35] Copying the Guatemala template, the US aimed in Cuba to mount a propaganda campaign via short-wave radio, then land 100–150 exile commandos who would connect with a clandestine 'intelligence and action organization' that would be set up inside Cuba. The organization would cut its teeth through acts of economic sabotage, which would combine with a US embargo of the island to disrupt Cuba's economy and undermine military and popular support for Castro, just as such policies had undermined support for Jacobo Árbenz in Guatemala. Once Castro was knocked out, a US-backed government-in-exile would be installed.[36]

By mid-1960, the US government was thus engaged in developing several different ways of removing Castro—assassination, sabotage and transnational paramilitary attack stoking popular unrest—each of which overlapped with the limited efforts already being rolled out by the American and Havana Mobs. Over the next few months it proved to be a short step for the CIA from adopting the same ways as the Mob to sponsoring the very means being offered by the Mob.

Having failed to develop an effective in-house assassination capability, the CIA began to consider its options to purchase one off the shelf.[37] The Agency recognized that it shared a strategic objective with the Mob: Castro's elimination.[38] And the Mob, it considered, might have the means it lacked—intelligence assets in Cuba, effective lines of communication into Cuba and potentially the capability to project force into secure locations within Cuba.[39] As a later US Senate Select Committee investigation—the Church Committee—put it, 'underworld figures were relied upon because it was believed that they had expertise and contacts that were not available to law-abiding citizens'.[40]

Of course, this raised sensitive questions of complicity with organized crime—sensitivities of which the CIA was well aware. As a CIA official told Congress in 1975, 'We weren't proud of this thing.'[41] Indeed, ever since, the CIA officials involved have insisted that 'only a small group' within the Agency, perhaps six people, were briefed. However, a 1967 internal CIA inspector-general's report, not shared with Congress until many years later, made clear that the true number of CIA officials briefed was probably closer to twenty.[42] This was likely to have included the Director of Central Intelligence (DCI), Allen Dulles.[43] But not others: senior government decision-makers, including those involved in planning the US' paramilitary efforts against Castro, were never explicitly briefed on the Mob collaboration.[44]

Close examination of the historical record suggests that collaboration was an idea developed by a group of CIA officials who had prior Mob contacts, well before the project was cleared by DCI Dulles—but after the Mob efforts were already under way.[45] Why would the Mob seek US government involvement? Was there not a risk of government penetration or prosecution for this, or other criminal activities? The short-term motivation was clearly not pecuniary. The US government did ultimately promise the mobsters involved at least $150,000 if Castro was eliminated—but the Mob refused the offer.[46] It was not interested in money (and this was, anyway, peanuts for the Mob). Instead the Mob appears to have seen two strategic benefits: access to the political and military resources not just to kill Castro but to install and protect a more favourable Cuban government; and CIA protection from US law enforcement for the Mob's other activities at home.[47] Mobsters involved in the plot to kill Castro successfully blackmailed their way out of US federal prosecution, deportation proceedings and possibly even congressional subpoena throughout the 1960s by threatening to publicly expose the story. The Mob even convinced the CIA to install a bug in a Las Vegas hotel room so that Sam Giancana, the Chicago mafia *capo* at the Fontainebleau Hotel, could spy on his girlfriend; in May 1962 Robert Kennedy ordered the Department of Justice to secretly drop cases against Giancana and other mobsters resulting from this episode, 'in the national interest'.[48]

In August 1960, once the idea for cooperation had been approved, the CIA Deputy Director for Plans—the CIA's clandestine service—Richard Bissell tasked an employee with determining if the Agency 'had assets that may assist in a sensitive mission requiring gangster-type action. The mission target was Fidel Castro.'[49] In mid-September 1960, while Castro was visiting New York for the annual gathering of heads of state and government at the United Nations General Assembly, the CIA met at the Plaza Hotel with Johnny Roselli, a Giancana lieutenant.[50]

Roselli 'agreed to connect' the CIA to 'Sam Gold'—Sam Giancana, his *capo*. Giancana, Roselli explained, could connect the CIA's frontman and his 'Wall Street backers' to Cuban exiles who would carry out the job.[51] The CIA met several times in September and October 1960 in Miami with Roselli, 'Sam Gold', Cuban exiles and an 'interpreter' named 'Joe'.[52] This was Santo Trafficante, Jr.—like Giancana, one of the US Department of Justice's top ten most wanted criminals at the time. Like Genovese in Sicily, his role was not just to interpret between English and Italian, but to connect the state with underworld governmental capabilities in the exiled Havana Mob.

The CIA proposed to the mobsters that Cuban exiles carry out 'a gangland style killing', in other words, a fusillade, killing Castro inside Cuba. The mobsters responded that it would be impossible to recruit someone to do the job, given the low chance of escape. Instead they proposed poison.[53] The CIA had been experimenting for several months with different delivery vehicles to poison Castro—cigars, tea, coffee, bouillon—and a variety of toxins.[54] Giancana indicated that if the CIA supplied pills, the Mob would pass them to a contact inside Cuba—in fact Juan Orta. As we have seen, the Mob was already working independently with Orta to kill Castro, even before the CIA became involved—though they did not mention this to the CIA.[55] A little-noticed secret 1967 CIA internal review concluded that the CIA

> found itself involved in providing additional resources for independent operations that the [mafia] syndicate already had under way... In a sense CIA may have been piggy-backing on the [mafia] syndicate ... supplying an aura of official sanction.[56]

Within weeks of meeting with the CIA, Sam Giancana was boasting to other mobsters that 'Fidel Castro was to be done away with ... in November', and that he 'had already met with the assassin-to-be on three occasions' at the Fontainebleau Hotel.[57] But technical glitches meant that the CIA did not deliver the poison pills to the Mob until February 1961.[58] Unbeknownst to the CIA, Orta meanwhile lost his prime minister's office position. This showed just how weak the command and control mechanism for this sensitive venture really was: 'while the Agency thought the gangsters had a man in Cuba with easy access to Castro, what they actually had was a man disgruntled at having lost access'.[59]

Seeking protection

By the time John F. Kennedy took power as president of the United States in early 1961, the prospect of confrontation between the US and Cuba had increased considerably, and taken on broader geostrategic implications. The Mob was becoming a chess piece—though perhaps not simply a passive pawn—in the larger Cold War game.

Matters had escalated through 1960, the year of the presidential election. Cuban exile commando attacks, backed in part by Mob money and arms, had provoked only a closing of ranks in Castro's regime, with leftists installed in important administrative positions and more liberal voices in the media being closed down. By mid-1960, President Eisenhower found the US without allies in Cuban politics, and moved steadily towards coercive policies. In turn, Castro began to seek Soviet protection from American belligerence. In February 1960 Cuba and the USSR agreed a five-year trade and investment deal. By May, Soviet crude oil was being delivered to Cuba.[60] The Eisenhower Administration leaned on Esso, Texaco and Anglo-Dutch Shell not to refine the Soviet oil, and blocked sales of Cuban sugar to the US.[61] In response, Cuba started receiving arms shipments from the Soviets. On 9 July, Soviet leader Khrushchev upped the ante, warning the US that the Soviets might provide military support to Cuba in the event of a US invasion. By September, with Soviet strategic backing becoming more certain, Castro moved against US commercial interests in Cuba, nationalizing cattle ranches, oil refineries, sugar mills and banks worth around $1 billion. On 19 October 1960—around the time the CIA was meeting with the Mob in Miami—the Eisenhower administration retaliated, imposing an embargo on US trade with Cuba in anything other than food and medicine. The embargo would endure for more than five decades.

Momentum towards confrontation increased with John F. Kennedy's election to the presidency in November 1960, taking office in late January 1961. Kennedy's position on Cuba had become more hawkish during the election campaign. His initial campaign book, *The Strategy of Peace*, criticized Eisenhower and Nixon for failing to embrace Castro when they had the chance.[62] But by October 1960, probably after a briefing by DCI Dulles that highlighted growing ties between Castro and Khrushchev, Kennedy was warning that the Iron Curtain now lay 'ninety miles off the coast of the United States', and asking of Richard Nixon, his Republican rival for the presidency: 'If you don't stand up to Castro, how can you be expected to stand up to Khrushchev?'[63] On 21 October he called publicly for US government support to Cuban exiles in an effort to overthrow Castro.[64] As American attitudes became more confrontational, Moscow and Havana quickly drew closer together. Khrushchev and Castro met publicly at the September 1960 UN General Assembly. Soon after, Che Guevara was fêted in Moscow. A strategic partnership that had started as a response to arm's-length US paramilitary pressure was now taking on the shape of Cold War confrontation, and in the process radicalizing Cuba's revolutionaries.[65] The involvement of the Mob, with its own designs and stratagems, was about to become either a major asset or a major liability for the United States.

Subversion and its unintended consequences

What went wrong at the Bay of Pigs?

By the time Kennedy entered office in late January 1961, the CIA's plans for paramilitary intervention in Cuba had evolved considerably. US government planning now called for a full-scale amphibious invasion by a US-trained brigade of Cuban exiles on the south coast, with US air cover. It was still intended to be dressed up as an internal revolt.[66] But against the backdrop of escalating US-Soviet tensions, the invasion plan now carried greater geopolitical risk. On taking office, Kennedy expressed concern at the high risk of Soviet escalation if the US' hand in the operation were clear.[67] At his request, the number of US airstrikes on the Cuban air force prior to the landing was reduced. Other mistakes were also made—such as moving the landing site away from the mountains, where the invasion force was expected to shelter. When the invasion began on 17 April 1961, the Cuban air force, which was supposed to have been disabled by airstrikes, was instead quickly able to assert control of the airspace over the Bay of Pigs where the landing was taking place, devastating the paramilitary ground forces and their naval supply lines.[68] By 19 April the invasion force had run out of ammunition and its remnants surrendered. Kennedy refused requests from the CIA and joint chiefs of staff to send in US forces to rescue the brigade, concerned that it would lead to all-out war.[69] Castro's victory was decisive. In all, 114 Cuban exile commandos died and 1,189 were captured. As both Che Guevara and US intelligence would later assess, the Bay of Pigs strengthened, rather than weakened, Castro's hold on power in Cuba.[70]

What went wrong at the Bay of Pigs? Lawrence Freedman has demonstrated that the US failure was in no small part the result of the absence of key elements present in the overthrow of Árbenz in Guatemala—US air-cover and local military defections.[71] It also seems possible, however, that one contributing factor was the failure of the CIA's assassination plotting with the Mob. Traditionally, the two efforts have been seen as entirely distinct and unrelated. But there was, it turns out, an overlap in personnel. An unpublished internal CIA analysis located in the US National Archives in Maryland concluded that some of these personnel viewed the assassination plots 'as being merely one aspect of the over-all active effort to overthrow the regime that culminated in the Bay of Pigs'.[72]

How closely connected were the two plans—and the two failures? There is reason to believe that they were, initially, intended to be complementary—but that the connection between the two was lost as each plan was developed. The invasion planning, in particular, was bent far away from a central initial premise: that the military invasion would coincide with a political shock inside Cuba, something triggering either an uprising or a failure of the Cuban military. Where would that come from? The CIA's assassination planning seems to provide the answer: as a later newspaper article based on CIA sources explained, the original 'intent was to eliminate the Cuban dictator before the motley invaders landed on the island'.[73] Bissell later told a retired Foreign Service officer that the assassination plan had been 'intended to parallel' the exiles' landing.[74] A secret CIA assessment of the mission found that 'Bissell probably believed that Castro would be dead at the hands of a CIA-sponsored assassin before the Brigade ever hit the beach.'[75] This helps to explain why the CIA failed to alert President Kennedy to the low likelihood that the landing of exiles at the Bay of Pigs would create 'a critical shift of popular opinion away from Castro,' as a December 1960 Special National Intelligence Estimate put it.[76] The CIA may have been expecting that strategic effect to come through other methods—

the Mob's assassination efforts. They may have suggested this to Kennedy: a few weeks before the Bay of Pigs landing, President Kennedy commented to his close friend Senator George Smathers that he had been 'given to believe' by the CIA that Castro would be dead by the time of the invasion.[77]

This also helps to explain the acceleration of the CIA's cooperation with the Mob in early 1961. In March, Roselli, Giancana and CIA officials met again in Miami—ostensibly for a world title boxing match, but in reality to hand over several botulinum pills.[78] Cuban exiles were to administer the pills via a contact at one of Castro's favourite Havana restaurants.[79] The CIA also provided $18,936.65 for expenses.[80] Roselli told his CIA handler soon afterwards that the pills had been placed in Cuba, but the attempt had failed. Various explanations have been offered as to why. One possibility is that the 'go signal' was never passed via Tony Varona to the agent in Cuba who would have delivered the pills,[81] possibly because uninformed US officials had isolated Varona for several days to prepare him to take governmental power after the invasion—a central breakdown in Bissell's coordination of the assassination and Bay of Pigs plans.[82] Alternatively, the message may have been passed, but the attempt simply failed. Ultimately, the failure of the CIA's cooperation with the Mob to kill Castro was not the only mistake that led to the disaster at the Bay of Pigs. But it may have played more of a role than has hitherto been recognized.

Learning from the Mob?

A week after the Bay of Pigs, President Kennedy explicitly acknowledged that Cold War confrontation would now move into the covert sphere, relying on 'infiltration instead of invasion, on subversion instead of elections, on intimidation instead of free choice, on guerrillas by night instead of armies by day'.[83] Suddenly, the methods of the Mob looked all the more important—and the failure of the CIA-Mob initiative to exploit those methods was not yet understood. Rejecting Cuban overtures to set up back channel negotiations, President Kennedy tasked his brother Robert, his attorney-general, with supervising the CIA's Cuba planning, and established an internal panel to come up with new policy options, looking not only at military and paramilitary options, but also other 'activities which fall short of outright war'.[84]

Covert activity was the focus of this new subversive effort. A report prepared for the joint chiefs of staff considered staging fake Cuban attacks on US naval bases on Guantánamo or those on other Latin American countries, or fake Cuban government terrorist attacks on Cuban exiles in the US, as a trigger for US intervention.[85] In November 1961, Kennedy established Operation Mongoose, a covert operation intended to stoke a Cuban popular uprising as a pretext for US intervention. At its peak in the summer of 1962, the Miami-based operation involved 600 CIA staff and some 4,000–5,000 contractors running sabotage, infiltration and arms positioning missions into Cuba.[86] Cuban exiles began calling the CIA the 'Cuban Invasion Authority'.[87]

Despite the scale of the effort, the CIA concluded that it needed new covert capabilities. Richard Bissell and another senior official, Richard Helms, tasked William Harvey—also charged with leading Operation Mongoose, and already in contact with Roselli—with overseeing a new project codenamed ZR/RIFLE, known informally as 'Executive Action'. This was not to be a specific operation targeted at a particular leader, but rather 'a general stand-by-capability to carry out assassinations' across the Agency's files.[88] Harvey sought advice from the British Security Service, MI5, on how to carry out arms-length assassination. They recommended recruiting hit-men from the Sicilian mafia.[89] Harvey recruited a European professional criminal as an assassin and tasked him with spotting other suitable 'individuals with criminal and underworld connections'.[90] One potential asset in the Middle East, for example, was 'the leader of a gambling syndicate' with 'an available pool of assassins'.[91] 'Executive Action' seemed to promise something every clandestine operator—whether state or non-state—sought: an on-call, plausibly deniable, surgical force-projection capability. It was the CIA's answer to Murder, Inc., a 'magic button', as Harvey put it, in the CIA's arsenal: one press and the CIA's enemies would magically drop dead.[92]

Like many magic tricks, though, it turned out to be a dangerous illusion. One of the hit-men hired through Executive Action was aptly codenamed WI/ROGUE.[93] 'Rogue' was unleashed in Congo in late 1960 to assassinate Patrice Lumumba, the independence leader who was proving hard to control. But 'Rogue' turned out to be, in the memorable words of the CIA station chief, 'an unguided missile' who 'seemed to act on his own without guidance or authority'.[94] He was removed from the project. In November 1961, however, despite this warning sign of how hard it would be to control Executive Action assets, Bissell and Helms instructed Harvey to apply Executive Action to Cuba.[95] Harvey began reactivating the CIA-Mob collaboration, which had been put on hold earlier in 1961. In April 1962 Harvey met again with Roselli, passed him four more 'poison pills' and provided explosives, sniper rifles, handguns and a boat radar, encouraging Roselli to work with Varona to infiltrate a team of hit-men into Cuba.[96] Roselli soon reported back that the plans were operational.[97] For the Mob, this may have been a charade. The CIA had no way to confirm what Roselli told them, and there are signs that Roselli was duping them.[98] By the summer of 1962 the Mob may in fact have lost interest in getting rid of Castro, and turned its attention to other ventures elsewhere in the Caribbean (discussed below). But the Mob had strong domestic incentives to keep stringing the CIA along, namely protection against prosecution, even as assassination of Castro ceased to be 'a viable option'.[99]

Many questions have been asked, including by US Congress, about what precisely the Kennedy brothers knew about all these efforts. The answers are highly revealing because they highlight the extent to which Mob and CIA methods converged—and the affinity between organized crime and covert state action more generally. Neither President Eisenhower nor President Kennedy ever gave a documented, explicit directive to assassinate Castro. Kennedy, on the contrary, took active steps to distance himself from the assassination option.[100] But both administrations recognized the importance of 'plausible deniability' in tackling Castro: achieving the result without the US' role being visible.[101] That was the nature of covert action—and hidden power.

Indeed, both Kennedys were intimately aware of the steps taken by Mob leaders to insulate themselves from knowledge of operational details once they had given a general order for a hit.[102] As a US senator, John F. Kennedy sat on the McClellan Committee, the Senate Select Committee that investigated the role of the Mob in US labour racketeering. Robert Kennedy served as chief counsel to that committee, driving its pursuit of Jimmy Hoffa and the Teamsters Union. He worked closely in this investigation with Frank Hogan, the Manhattan district attorney involved in the Underworld Project, and wrote a best-seller about the McClellan investigation, *The Enemy Within*.[103] Introducing the first televised congressional statement by a former mobster, Joe Valachi, Bobby Kennedy demonstrated a detailed understanding of how Mob leaders covered their tracks when ordering assassinations:

> [B]ecause the members of the [mafia] Commission, the top members, or even their chief lieutenants, have insulated themselves from the crime itself, if they want to have somebody knocked off, for instance, the top man will speak to somebody who will speak to somebody else who will speak to somebody else and order it. The man who actually does the gun work ... he does not know who ordered it. To trace that back is virtually impossible.[104]

The similarity with the 'inherently ambiguous' command and control system for the CIA's Executive Action programme is clear. CIA officials might have planned assassinations without an explicit authorization; but equally:

> this ambiguity and imprecision leaves open the possibility that there was a successful 'plausible denial' and that a Presidential authorization was issued but is now obscured.[105]

The Kennedy brothers could not have been clearer that the overall strategic objective was Castro's removal from power. After the Bay of Pigs, they both 'chewed out' Bissell, the CIA's official responsible for covert operations, in the White House cabinet room for 'sitting on his ass and not doing anything about getting rid of Castro and the Castro regime'.[106] Bobby made clear at a National Security Council subgroup meeting in January 1962 that 'a solution to the Cuban problem' remained the president's 'top priority'.[107] And they also seemed to be dropping hints that they would not be averse to assassination as a method to achieve this goal. In October 1961 the president expressed interest in planning for Castro's being 'unexpectedly removed'.[108] In March 1962 Bobby pushed for 'action' against Castro when he visited a 'shrine' to Ernest Hemingway near Havana.[109] By October 1962 the planning group Bobby led had decided 'to develop new and imaginative approaches with the possibility of getting rid of the Castro regime'.[110] At least some in the CIA took such hints to mean that assassination was implicitly authorized—even desired.[111] The situation was, one Church Committee member suggested, analogous to that in England in 1170

AD, when King Henry II complained of Thomas Becket, 'Who will rid me of this turbulent priest?'[112]

When he assumed office following President Kennedy's subsequent assassination, and was briefed about what had been going on in Cuba, President Lyndon Johnson exclaimed simply: 'We've been operating a damned Murder Inc. in the Caribbean.'[113] CIA officials did not seek specific clarification of the instruction to assassinate Castro because—like mafia *soldati* and members of the Mob's Murder, Inc.—they were accustomed to carrying out implicit orders without jeopardizing their superiors' security. Compartmentalization of information was as engrained in the CIA's organizational DNA as it was in the Mob's. CIA official Richard Helms explained:

> I don't know whether it was in training, experience, tradition or exactly what one points to, but I think to go up to a Cabinet officer and say, am I right in assuming you want me to assassinate Castro ... is a question it wouldn't have occurred to me to ask.[114]

Helms was just discharging his role, as he understood it; he was self-regulating in accordance with the prevailing clandestine operators' governmentality: 'I was just doing my best to do what I thought I was supposed to do.'[115]

CIA officials also appear to have interpreted their instructions as allowing direct collaboration with the Mob, notwithstanding the absence of explicit authorization to that effect.[116] CIA officials later explained to Congress that they were not surprised that they had not seen any such explicit authorization, since they assumed that in order to 'protect' the president, the CIA would inform the White House of only the minimum amount of operational detail. '[D]ue to its sensitive and unsavory character, it was not the type of program one would discuss in front of high officials.'[117]

Bobby Kennedy was certainly briefed that Operation Mongoose would attempt to work with Cuban gangsters, and the lead military planner, Lansdale, had previously cooperated with criminal groups in Vietnam.[118] Kennedy did not protest about the criminal aspect of Mongoose, nor when he was apparently informed by the FBI, on his first day in office, of the Mob's direct collaboration with the CIA (though not its assassination elements, it seems).[119] By May 1961 the attorney-general also knew that it was Sam Giancana—one of his primary domestic organized crime targets—with whom the CIA was working in this 'dirty business' against Castro.[120] He did not order the cooperation shut down: instead he simply insisted the FBI 'follow up vigorously'. That they did. But this only compounded the mess, since the resulting surveillance revealed that the president shared a mistress, Judith Campbell, with Giancana. Campbell had even called the president at the White House from Giancana's house.[121]

It was not until early May 1962 that the CIA told Robert Kennedy explicitly that their cooperation with the Mob had aimed at assassinating Castro; but CIA officials claim that they also indicated (wrongly) that these efforts had been terminated back in May 1961.[122] Again, Robert did not tell the CIA that he would resist such cooperation with the Mob in future. Rather he simply insisted that he must be 'the first to know'.[123] Yet CIA officials continued to work with the Mob to kill Castro—without specifically informing the attorney-general.[124]

The CIA leadership's decision-making logic was highlighted in an exchange between Richard Helms and a member of the Church Committee. A member asked: '[A]s I understand your position on the assassination of Castro, no one in essence told you to do it, no one in essence told you not to do it … is that correct?' 'Yes, sir,' Helms replied.[125] The culture was, in other words, one of 'Don't Ask, Don't Tell'.[126] The 'Don't Tell' aspect—with its overtones of the mafia's *omertà*—was highly significant. It was not just a policy of passive silence, but active silence engendering complicity. It helps to explain why CIA officials went out of their way to cover their tracks, lying not only to Robert Kennedy but apparently also to the Church Committee about their ongoing contacts with the Mob after May 1961.[127] They were conducting themselves in accordance with an internalized code; they were bound by the covert operator's governmentality. It was a governmentality that Mob actors would recognize, and easily integrate with.

Whether or not the Kennedys specifically set out to copy the Mob, what emerges from this episode is a recognition that the strategic organization and decision-making of the clandestine intelligence and security services of states may be more similar to those of criminal organizations than previously allowed. This is not to say that they have the same strategic goals, but rather similar ways and means. The similarity of the set-ups almost invites inter-operability. This extends to the role of secrecy, compartmentalization of information and the structure of strategic decision-making. In both the intelligence and organized crime contexts, trust is paramount, and top leaders must be isolated from some risky operational information. This is why family members are perfectly placed to serve as the trusted cut-out between political leadership and the covert world—because of the well of trust they bring to the role. In dealing with the CIA, Robert Kennedy seems to have taken on that role. Brothers and sons regularly play a similar role: Marko Milošević in Serbia, Ousmane Conté in Guinea (Conakry), Uday and Qusay Hussein in Iraq, Wali Karzai in Afghanistan.

Cold War wildcard: the Missile Crisis

If the extent of senior Kennedy administration approval for the CIA-Mob assassination plots is unclear to us fifty years later with the benefit of hindsight and access to declassified government records, it can only have been doubly unclear for Fidel Castro at the time. As the Church Committee recognized, 'it is unlikely that Castro would have distinguished the CIA plots with the underworld from those plots not backed by the CIA'.[128] And as the House Select Committee pointed out,

> when Castro erred in his assumptions, it was in the direction of attributing more, not less, responsibility for attempts to depose him to US government actions than might have been merited.[129]

The CIA-Mob efforts were, after all, consonant with the US' traditionally meddlesome strategic approach to Cuba. The US had not hesitated in the past to escalate arm's-length policies of subversion to direct military intervention. Nor, seen from Havana, was there necessarily a clear difference between the CIA collaborating with the Mob to reinstall American gamblers in Havana, and the CIA collaborating with the United Fruit Company to protect American capital in Guatemala. Seen from Havana, the boundary between the US government, business and criminal groups must have been beginning to blur, just as the distinction between Russian business, state and criminal interests blurred for Jim Woolsey decades later. Castro indeed began to describe American diplomats and officials as 'gangsters'.[130] The CIA's collaboration with the Mob had raised the risk that Castro would mistakenly perceive Mob freelancing as part of a broader US strategy. That made the Mob a potentially dangerous wildcard in the geopolitical confrontation now playing out in the Caribbean.

A major Cold War confrontation seemed increasingly likely as Castro moved rapidly towards the Communist camp in the wake of the Bay of Pigs. In December 1961 he proclaimed himself a Marxist-Leninist, and the Cuban state took control of 90 per cent of industrial output.[131] With the US rehearsing amphibious landings in the spring of 1962, the USSR and Cuba began to explore a formal defence treaty. Soviet personnel and arms began to arrive in numbers in July 1962. By late August 1962, US intelligence had identified that the Soviets were shipping surface-to-air missiles (SAMs) to Cuba. The Director of Central Intelligence, McCone, hypothesized that the Soviet leader Khrushchev was risking nuclear war in the belief that by secretly putting offensive missiles in Cuba, the Soviets could mitigate their huge lag behind the US in production and possession of inter-continental ballistic missiles, and potentially create strategic leverage for use in other global hotspots, including Berlin.[132] McCone's hypothesis took time to find support in Washington. Others saw the SAMs simply as a deterrent to US military intervention in Cuba, and refused to believe Khrushchev would place nuclear warheads in Cuba.[133] In fact, by mid-October 1962, forty-two medium-range ballistic missile launchers, sixty-six nuclear warheads, forty MiG jets, nine bombers and 42,000 Soviet troops had reached Cuba.[134]

Meanwhile, the Kennedy administration continued to search for a covert mechanism to dislodge Castro. But events were quickly overtaking the covert option, especially once US surveillance overflights discovered the Soviet-assisted development of medium-range missile sites in Cuba.[135] Soviet moves were forcing the confrontation into the open—though earlier than Khrushchev had hoped. The puzzle for the Kennedy administration—which it argued over furiously for days—was how to win the confrontation without it escalating into nuclear war.[136] Covert activity was starting to become not just irrelevant, but possibly dangerous: killing Castro was no solution to the larger strategic threat posed by the Soviets, and Castro's death would probably gravely inflame the situation and risk Soviet retaliation in Berlin, leading to nuclear war.[137] Freelance Mob-backed paramilitary or assassination activities now risked triggering a full-blown nuclear superpower confrontation.

When US intelligence indicated that some of the Soviet missiles in Cuba were becoming operational, Kennedy opted for a naval 'quarantine' of Cuba and called on Khrushchev to remove the missiles.[138] The blockade involved 150 vessels, 250 aircraft and 30,000 mobilized personnel, and the US' Strategic Air Command moved to Defense Condition 2 (DEFCON 2)—one level below nuclear war, the first time this level had been reached. The military prepared in case full-scale invasion of Cuba became necessary.[139] Amidst this tension, the CIA's Harvey decided to send commando teams to Cuba by submarine, without clearing it with the White House. When the Kennedys got wind of it, they realized the potential wildcard danger posed by the ongoing covert activities. On 26 October the administration formally suspended 'sabotage or militant operations during negotiations with the Soviets'.[140]

On 27 October, Khrushchev publicly proposed a trade: the Soviets would remove their missiles in Cuba if the Americans would remove theirs in Turkey—and leave Cuba to its own devices.[141] It took several more days—and near misses—before a deal was agreed.[142] Kennedy had to resist considerable pressure from his military advisers to launch an attack on Cuba, and Khrushchev had to overcome similar belligerence from Castro.[143] Even after the deal was done, Castro complained that while the US might formally guarantee Cuban sovereignty, it could continue to attack him through 'piratical', mercenary and criminal proxies.[144] In order to be seen to honour its promise of non-intervention, the US government moved towards a policy of supporting exile groups only where they operated from outside the US. Both Operation Mongoose, which had supported exile groups' operations from inside the US, and the cooperation with the Mob were finally shut down.[145]

This was not, however, the end of the Mob's attempts at transnational subversion. Instead, the withdrawal of American government sponsorship led some American *mafiosi* and Cuban exiles to create another government-in-exile which they would seek to install in Cuba through their own independent use of force.[146] The main Cuban partner was the Junta de Gobierno de Cuba en el Exilio (Junta for the

Government of Cuba in Exile—JGCE), an umbrella group that included Prío Socarrás, veterans of the Bay of Pigs and a network of Cuban exile groups coordinated by Paulino Sierra Martinez. A consortium of Las Vegas-linked mobsters offered Martinez up to $30 million to fund these groups, in return for the reestablishment of the mafia's 'gambling colony' in Cuba after Castro was removed.[147]

Sierra Martinez's networks, operating from Central America, made considerable operational progress in 1963, emerging as potential spoilers of the fragile truce. In mid-March 1963 the Alpha 66 group, a member of Sierra Martinez's coalition, mounted attacks on Soviet vessels and several Soviet installations in Cuba. The Kennedy administration immediately distanced itself from the attacks, but the Soviets protested loudly.[148] In August 1963, members of Sierra Martinez's network organized an aerial bombing of a sugar mill in Camagüey in central Cuba.[149] Yet Sierra Martinez proved unable to sustain support for these operations within the fractured Cuban exile community, and they slowly folded.

Santo Trafficante Jr. also returned to the fray, financing operations and brokering access to arms. A planned air raid on the Shell Oil refinery near Havana, planned by Trafficante associate Michael McLaney, was broken up by US authorities. The FBI also seized 2,400 pounds of dynamite and twenty bomb casings in a farmhouse owned by McLaney's brother.[150] The CIA was made aware of some of these plans—but told the Mob that, time around, 'it would not provide assistance'. Once again, however, no mention was made of preventing the Mob activities.[151]

This may have represented a deeper recognition within the Kennedy administration concerning the limited strategic utility of subversion. The US naval blockade against Cuba that had forced the resolution of the Missile Crisis had offered, said General Maxwell Taylor, a 'classic example of the use of military power for political purposes'.[152] As Deborah Shapley writes, 'The object [of the blockade] was not to shoot anybody but to communicate a political message to Khrushchev.'[153] The signal to the Mob that the government would no longer cooperate with it on Cuba may have reflected a realization that traditional military forces, with their finely honed command and control arrangements, were better calibrated for conveying such political messages than covert operations carried out through criminal proxies at arm's length. Criminal groups, it turned out, had their own political and military strategies—and their own, unpredictable, strategic effects.

Did the magic button backfire?

It may be the case that the most unpredictable of these effects was felt not in the Caribbean, but at home in the United States of America. Warnings to the US government about the costs of collaboration with the Mob were early and frequent. In January 1961, a US assistant secretary of defense warned the Eisenhower administration of a 'serious impact upon United States prestige throughout Latin America' if the Castro assassination efforts became known.[154] FBI director J. Edgar Hoover warned Bobby Kennedy of domestic political blowback from the CIA's collaboration with the Mob.[155] William Harvey warned his CIA superiors of the 'very real possibility' that the mafia would blackmail the CIA, as indeed it did.[156] No-one warned, however, about what would happen if Frankenstein's monster turned on its former master.

In *The Enemy Within*, Bobby Kennedy had called for a 'national scale attack' on organized crime.[157] When he became attorney-general, he mounted that attack. Department of Justice indictments of Mob figures rose from thirty-five in the last year of the Eisenhower administration to 121 in Bobby's first year as attorney-general, and 615 in 1963 (his last).[158] His campaign was conclusively establishing the existence, structure and activities of the mafia Commission, and the mafia's 'deep-rooted and extensive record of political activism'. It caused 'deep frustration' amongst Mob leaders at the disruption of 'their long-established connections with the political establishment'.[159] Federal investigations and prosecutions had broken through the wall of *omertà*. Six weeks before President Kennedy was killed in November 1963, Joe Valachi became the first Mob insider to testify before Congress, live on television, introduced by Bobby Kennedy himself. When Mob leaders discovered government bugs in their Las Vegas casino counting-houses, further suspicion and distrust was sown in Mob ranks.[160] Joe Bonanno was openly flouting mafia Commission authority by refusing to meet with other Commission members. Several other *capi* were known to be plotting each other's assassinations. Sam Giancana, known to the

CIA as 'Sam Gold', felt all this pressure acutely, with the FBI (under Kennedy's direction) disrupting his influence over the Chicago City Council, police and prosecutor's office in 1962 and 1963.[161] FBI wiretaps established that Giancana and other Mob leaders directly blamed the Kennedys for these disruptions, and that they had even off-handedly thrown around the idea of killing the Kennedy brothers.[162]

Speculation about the Mob's involvement began almost as soon as President Kennedy was assassinated in Dallas on 22 November 1963. Both Bobby Kennedy and President Johnson privately voiced suspicion about underworld involvement.[163] And a variety of theories have canvassed the possibility of the Mob carrying out the killing alone, or in cooperation with Castro. Castro had warned that 'United States leaders should think that if they are aiding in terrorist plans to eliminate Cuban leaders, they themselves will not be safe', and Kennedy had himself acknowledged that if the US should compete with its adversaries in 'tactics of terror, assassination, false promises, counterfeit mobs and crises … we would all be targets'.[164] If the US government could work together with the Mob to kill Castro, what was to stop Cuban officials plotting with disgruntled mobsters to kill Kennedy?[165] Was this not exactly the kind of 'fifth column' risk that the US Navy had warned about when justifying the Underworld Project?

There was a trail of breadcrumbs that seemed to implicate the Mob, somehow.[166] Key figures in Kennedy's assassination—including Lee Harvey Oswald and Jack Ruby—had connections to Mob leaders.[167] Ruby may have been a cash courier for the Trafficantes, and (as we saw in the previous chapter) appears to have been involved in the effort to extricate Santo Trafficante Jr. from immigration detention in Havana in 1959.[168] One witness later claimed that Trafficante had told him that President Kennedy would 'be hit'.[169] Trafficante—and other Mob figures, including Jimmy Hoffa—certainly seem to have welcomed the news that the Kennedys would be off their backs.[170]

Even if we cannot determine, as a matter of historical fact, whether the Mob was involved in President Kennedy's assassination, the fact is that key figures such as his own brother and the succeeding US president—Lyndon Johnson—thought that this might have been the case.[171] That mere possibility is significant, since it suggests that through its collaboration with the CIA (and perhaps, earlier, with the US Navy and the AMG), some Mob actors now saw themselves, in the words of a 1979 congressional report, as capable of 'using the resources at their disposal to increase their power … by assassinating the President'.[172] The Mob was not content to react to the strategic environment, but was now actively seeking to shape it. That approach was already playing out, elsewhere in the Caribbean.

The Bahamas and the birth of offshore capitalism

Invading Haiti

Even as signs emerged in 1958 that Batista's grip on power in Cuba was slipping, Lansky was considering duplicating the Havana joint venture elsewhere in the Caribbean. He led a series of exploratory trips by Mob leaders to Puerto Rico, Jamaica, Barbados, Trinidad and Tobago, Martinique and the Dominican Republic.[173] In some cases Mob leaders conducted extensive talks with political leaders, notably Johnny Abbes García and possibly President Trujillo in Dominican Republic.[174]

Haiti offered interesting possibilities. When an exiled Haitian army captain, Alix Pasquet, began selling futures in gambling concessions in a new, proposed post-Papa Doc Duvalier Haitian government, he found willing buyers in Lansky and Florida mobsters. A Florida police official with ties to Lansky's network flew to Port-au-Prince and tried to activate a revolutionary movement. He was deported, and his contacts rounded up and executed. Undeterred, the police official and Pasquet raised new funds and mounted a small 'invasion'. In late July 1958 they seized the Dessalines Barracks in Port-au-Prince, near the presidential palace. Eventually they were overrun by Duvalier's *Tonton Macoute* and annihilated.[175]

By 1961, however, Duvalier had recognized the attractiveness of Mob involvement in gambling. David Iacovetti, a member of the Gambino Family from Brooklyn, established a state-backed 'numbers' game: a 'Republic of Haiti Welfare Fund Sweepstakes', with tickets distributed and bought by the Haitian diaspora, and winners determined by the results of key horse races. In 1965, Duvalier sold a casino and slot machine concession to Joe Bonanno. Bonanno spent a year in Haiti.[176] Smarting from their failed joint venture with Batista, the Mob

251

this time took a more proactive approach to ensuring government protection against popular insurrection, actively equipping Duvalier with arms.[177] But whether because of linguistic barriers, because Duvalier was not the reliable partner that Batista had been or because Bonanno was not able to muster a broad coalition of Mob investors as Lansky had in Cuba, Port-au-Prince never became the tourist destination that Havana had been. The Mob had to look elsewhere.

Casino capitalism

The Bahamas was another obvious target: as close to Florida as was Cuba, and its official language was English. Better yet, it had long depended on rents generated by flouting the rules of international society: first as a base for large-scale piracy; then from a maritime racket involving first wrecking, then salvaging, ships; later, from busting the Union blockade on Confederate cotton during the American Civil War; and then, during Prohibition, from bootlegging.[178] The small, white establishment clique that ruled The Bahamas—known as the 'Bay Street Boys' after their main gathering point—were comfortable bending international society's rules to their advantage.

Lansky had contacts in The Bahamas from rum-running during Prohibition.[179] He may have been involved in an effort to develop a gambling industry in The Bahamas in 1945–6, after Batista first lost power in Cuba, and appears to have returned to the notion around 1958.[180] Lansky travelled to The Bahamas and offered $1 million to Sir Stafford Sands, then minister of finance, for exclusive control of gambling on the islands.[181] The idea dovetailed with Sands' efforts to turn one of The Bahamas' least promising islands, Grand Bahama, into a free industrial port. In 1956 Sands had negotiated an official government agreement with Wallace Groves, a convicted American fraudster who may have had ties to Meyer Lansky before he arrived in The Bahamas.[182] The agreement gave Groves, in the words of a contemporary account, 'the authority of a feudal baron' on the island.[183] While the Bahamian government abstained from taxing commercial activity in the zone for ninety-nine years, Groves was left free to impose fees, award and remove licences and control access to the territory.[184] This made him the perfect partner for the Mob in a joint venture.

In 1960 the Mob and the governing party in The Bahamas, the United Bahamian Party (UBP, controlled by the Bay Street Boys) met in Miami—at the Fontainebleau Hotel, where the CIA would, later that same year, also meet with the Mob. The UBP leadership agreed to turn over part of the free trade zone on Grand Bahama to a hotel and resort complex.[185] Groves' port authority formed a partnership with DevCo, a Mob front operated through several characters involved in the armed attacks in Cuba, notably Michael McLaney, and 'Trigger Mike' Coppola—a Luciano *sottocapo* who had driven the getaway car when Luciano's men hit Joe Masseria in Coney Island.[186]

DevCo built a new resort on Grand Bahama, the Lucayan Beach Hotel, which had a mysterious, giant 9,000-square-foot 'handball court' at the centre of its plans.[187] In September 1961, with the hotel already under construction, Groves and DevCo executives wined and dined the Bahamian premier, attorney-general, treasurer and colonial secretary and their wives at a series of get-togethers in The Bahamas and Miami Beach to convince them to legalize gambling at the resort. The strategic communications nature of these meetings was explicit: DevCo and Groves called it 'Operation Indoctrination'.[188] As a result of these meetings, DevCo soon counted among its paid 'consultants' the Bahamian premier and attorney-general, the premier's son (the speaker of the Legislative Assembly) and the editor of the main Bahamian newspaper.[189] DevCo also promised to pay the UBP itself $10,000 per month, disguised as Sands' legal retainer.[190] (In 2015, Sheldon Silver, who had been speaker of the New York State Assembly for twenty-one years, was accused of taking graft in the same form—a 'legal retainer').[191] The most influential independent voice in the Executive Council and editor of the Nassau *Tribune*, Eugene Dupuch, suddenly dropped his editorial opposition to the approval of a gambling licence.[192] Sands, himself a member of the Executive Council, received over $500,000 in fees for managing the process, and a continuing consultancy contract that promised $50,000 per year if the venture retained its gambling licence.[193]

The corruption campaign paid off handsomely, turning Grand Bahama—if not The Bahamas as a whole—into a joint venture between the Bay Street Boys and Lansky's faction of the Mob, repeating the pattern from Havana. The 'handball court' was now revealed for what it had always been intended to be: a gambling floor. By 1963, Sands was directly in business in the casino, through a new company, Bahama Amusements Limited, whose other hidden beneficiaries were Groves and Mob actors, notably Lansky.[194] Lansky and other Mob partners—probably including Costello and Santo Trafficante Jr.—lent the casino a $600,000 float and helped establish it within the North American high rollers' circuit. Their entire debt was paid off within a year.[195]

As Hank Messick has explained, control of the casino bankroll gave the Mob the 'trump cards' in the entire scheme. While others financed and owned the port, the hotel and surrounding businesses, they were all set up to operate—at a loss if necessary—to feed gamblers into the casino.[196] The casino was the central *plaza* in the system, the point at which the most lucrative criminal rents were extracted. The UBP provided political and physical protection, with the police commissioner also on the payroll.[197] The Mob fed 'high rollers'—many of them American organized criminals looking for a way to launder profits—into the system. To prevent them having to travel to The Bahamas with suitcases of cash, the casino advanced credit—making Mob knowledge of American underworld characters, and their creditworthiness, indispensable.[198]

Mob expertise was also crucial to structuring this money-laundering scheme, and set precedents for the later era of 'casino capitalism'.[199] Instead of 'skimming' the casino take by shovelling cash into suitcases before the authorities could count the day's winnings, the mobsters introduced a system where nothing was skimmed, and everything was counted. Casino managers simply received huge bonuses of several hundred thousand dollars at the end of the year, passing on significant amounts to their silent backers.[200] This was organized through Bahamian banks—and their correspondent banks in Miami—with The Bahamas soon becoming one of the leading hubs for offshore banking and the establishment of offshore shell companies.[201] Another method developed by the Mob in Havana, The Bahamas and Las Vegas—the 'junket skim'—is still in use today, notably for moving cash out of China through Macau.[202] Under this system, the Mob would underwrite an apparently independent travel agency that would organize high rollers' travel and give them a 'float'. When those high rollers lost to the casino, they paid not the casino, but the travel agent. The 'winnings' never ran through the casino books—but still found their way back to the Mob, through the travel agency.[203] Some two-thirds of The

Bahamas casinos' nominal profits derived from these junket tours in their early years.[204]

Ballots, not bullets

By 1966, the Lucayan Beach casino was taking in at least $8 million annually. Mobsters spread out from the Lucayan to new Bahamian casinos.[205] Side rackets in drugs and prostitution were also flourishing. The Bahamas became a pioneer in the use of offshore shell companies, international tax evasion and international securities fraud.[206] Steadily, it was also drawn into international narcotics and arms trafficking, and used for delivering offshore bribes to American judges and officials.[207]

Yet as successful as the Mob's joint venture with the Bay Street Boys was proving, it suffered from the same vulnerability as its joint venture with Batista in Cuba: its reliance on an elite minority for political protection. And just as the Havana Cuban joint venture reduced Batista's legitimacy through the stain of corruption, so was the Grand Bahama joint venture stoking popular discontent with the UBP. But this time the Mob adopted a radically different political strategy, to vastly superior effect, suggesting it had learned from its Cuban mistakes.

In the early 1960s the Progressive Liberal Party (PLP), a black empowerment party led by a Nassau-born lawyer trained at King's College London, Lynden Pindling, was pushing for Bahamian decolonization. Through gerrymandering, corruption and economic patronage, the Bay Street Boys' UBP had until the mid-1950s kept a lock on seats in the Legislative Assembly. But in 1956 the PLP managed to win six of twenty-nine seats; and in 1962 it won nine of thirty-three seats—but 65 per cent of the popular vote.[208] Emboldened, Pindling began pushing for political reform and even independence from Great Britain. He insisted that he 'did not wish violence ... [or for] the fate of Cuba ... to befall the Bahamas'.[209] But the UBP's responses to PLP gains—such as hiring South African and white Rhodesian officials, and playing South African government radio programmes—seemed designed to engineer confrontation.[210]

The Mob knew from Cuba what that heralded. This time, Lansky decided to side with the revolution. Lansky and his associates 'set out to capture Pindling'.[211] McLaney—involved in the aerial bombing in

Cuba and in DevCo—was put in charge. He provided the PLP around $60,000 of in-kind campaign support: office space, communications support and aerial transportation.[212] He also went into the blueberry farming business with Pindling, a somewhat odd venture in the tropical Bahamas, given that plant's preference for chilly winters.[213] In return, backing away from earlier anti-gambling rhetoric, the PLP agreed not to abolish gambling if it came to power, but to tax it and use the resulting revenues for social programming and public works.[214]

Growing in confidence that they had an alternative partner in Pindling, the Mob leaked documentary evidence of UBP corruption, under the watchful eye of a New York public relations firm, Hill & Knowlton, to the press.[215] Groves briefed the US *Saturday Evening Post*.[216] Speaking to the *Wall Street Journal*, Pindling railed that under the UBP The Bahamas were 'being sold out to "gangsterism"'.[217] Sands responded: 'As to the idea that I get a good share of the country's prosperity, of course I do... But it's worth remembering that I've been a part of making all the islands a lot more prosperous.'[218] Such statements, redolent of Tammany's 'honest graft' in New York, only served to underline the white minority's sense of entitlement, greatly bolstering electoral support for the PLP.

When the election results were returned in January 1967, the PLP squeaked into government with the support of two independent MPs. The Mob's hedging strategy seemed to have paid off. It had helped to organize, as one British newspaperman called it, 'a peaceful revolution'.[219] Yet the high-risk move of leaking details of UBP corruption to the press brought significant scrutiny in the form of a Royal Commission. In the wake of the investigation, a few mobsters were deported, but the underlying casino management structure was left largely intact.[220]

The reality was that the PLP picked up where the UBP left off. Seventeen years later, another official government investigation:

> revealed massive smuggling operations and political corruption. High Bahamian officials, and/or intimate associates of the prime minister [(Pindling) had become] the quintessential middlemen, selling protection and a resting place for contraband, permitting transporters for a fee to establish their headquarters on different islands and cays, tipping them off about D.E.A. raids and informants, and bringing together American pilots and Colombian [cocaine] producers.[221]

The criminologist Alan Block concludes: 'the Commission of Inquiry proved that The Bahamas [itself] was a racket'.[222] Between 1977 and 1984, Pindling and his wife spent eight times their reported earnings, probably receiving significant payoffs from Colombia's Medellín cartel in return for complete control over Norman's Cay, a Bahamian island used as a trans-shipment hub for moving cocaine into the United States.[223] In all, by the mid-1980s some fifteen islands and cays were either totally or partially controlled by drug-runners.[224]

Through this period, The Bahamas evolved into an exemplar of the offshore *plaza* in a globalizing illicit economy. Narcotics, arms and corruption deals were sealed at Bahamian resorts, with illicit merchandise stashed handily nearby, and money-laundering services offered via the casino or the local banks. Local banks' provision of eurodollar services—deposits denominated in US dollars, but not under US Federal Reserve jurisdiction, and thus not subject to US tax regulation—were particularly useful. By the mid-1980s, The Bahamas had become a major offshore banking centre, with more than $100 billion in eurodollar deposits.[225] By the 1980s, other mafia groups had recognized the power of this offshore banking model. The Cuntrera-Caruana *cosca* of the Sicilian mafia, the so-called 'bankers to the mafia', had developed a similar platform for cocaine trafficking and money-laundering through a joint venture with state officials on the Dutch island of Aruba, near Colombia and Venezuela.[226] The application of the blue ocean model in the Caribbean—striking out to find new markets that could be governed by organized crime—appeared to have succeeded.

Epilogue: a city by the Atlantic

By the time Meyer Lansky died in 1983, the Mob's blue ocean strategy had turned Grand Bahama into an offshore tax haven and money-laundering capital. Yet perhaps the most curious application of the blue ocean strategy was not offshore at all, but onshore, and not in the Caribbean, but beside another ocean, the Atlantic.

Atlantic City, just south of New York on the Atlantic coast of New Jersey, was, long before, the site of Lansky's first honeymoon in May 1929, timed to coincide with a bootleggers' coordination meeting. Like Grand Bahama, Atlantic City started out as an insect-infested, economically unproductive, scrubby island. In both cases, a visionary—perhaps somewhat reckless—developer recognized the potential for a new form of transport to turn the island into a leisure resort and vice centre for American consumers. In Atlantic City's case in the late nineteenth century, this meant bringing weekenders from Philadelphia's steel mills and New York's tenements by railway to New Jersey seaside amusements.[227] In the case of Grand Bahama, like Havana, it involved bringing the middle class and professional criminal class in by airliner.

In both cases, entrepreneurs realized that it was the very exceptionalism of the place that attracted American tourists. Going to Atlantic City or tripping to Havana or Grand Bahama meant taking a holiday— from work, from the rules—from responsibility. They were places where one could temporarily, and permissibly, loosen the codes that normally governed one's life. The same was true of that other Mob town, Las Vegas—whence 'What happens in Vegas, stays in Vegas.' In such places, founded on moral and governmental exceptionalism, purveyors of vice grew wealthy and powerful, collaborating with politicians to govern through a joint venture. In Atlantic City, it was Nucky Johnson's informal licensing of alcohol consumption throughout Prohibition that underpinned governmental power, as celebrated in the television series *Boardwalk Empire*.[228] In Grand Bahama, it was the formal licensing of gambling.

In the mid-twentieth century, however, Atlantic City had fallen on hard times. There were two connected reasons for this. First, the availability of plane travel had made mass tourism available to a wider array of more exotic locations—Las Vegas, Havana and Grand Bahama amongst them. Second, many of those destinations offered access to entertainments that Atlantic City could, or would, not provide. Most significant among these was gambling, which remained illegal in New Jersey. In the mid-1970s, however, politicians from Atlantic City pushed for a constitutional amendment to permit gambling in New Jersey as part of an effort to revive Atlantic City's fortunes. The first attempts were disastrous failures. In contrast, in 1976, they were successful. Why? The answer may be that the campaigners learned strategic lessons from the Mob's experience in The Bahamas—and from the Mob itself.

The 1976 constitutional referendum campaign was bankrolled—to the tune of $250,000—by a Bahamian company called Resorts International. Resorts was, in fact, the rebadged Mary Carter Paint Co., a company which had partnered with the Mob-backed Bahama Amusements to buy and run first the Bahamian Club, then the Paradise Island casino, in the Bahamas. With ties to the Mob, Resorts allegedly purchased protection from Pindling through corrupt payments made through an intermediary 'consultant'.[229] In New Jersey, Resorts bankrolled the creation of a bipartisan strategy group, which agreed to pursue a much narrower constitutional exception than that which had been defeated at a referendum in 1974. Instead of seeking the legalization of gambling state-wide, this time permission would be sought only for legalized gambling in Atlantic City. Resorts paid for a public campaign that focused on the revenue gains the state would enjoy from licensing gambling, and how these would be passed on to ordinary citizens.[230] The similarity to Batista's strategic distribution of lottery revenues to legitimize gambling in Cuba is notable.

As soon as the referendum passed, Resorts began lobbying for political influence in the institutions that would approve casino licences. It secretly hired the brother and uncle of leading state congressmen, and the legal counsel to both the sitting and a former governor as 'advisers'.[231] One business intelligence report also suggested that it began 'buying off' New Jersey's political parties by making significant contributions to local and county party machines and failing to declare these contributions, instead accounting for them as 'lobbying expenses'. When these financial contributions did not generate the expected support for approval of a Resorts-backed casino, Resorts apparently switched from corruption back to coercion. Using a private security subsidiary, Intertel, with deep connections into US law enforcement networks, a law enforcement network mobilized against Resorts' opponents, with 'the more recalcitrant local politicos ... sent to jail by US Attorneys and federal judges associated with ... Intertel'.[232]

Perhaps to Resorts' surprise, however, civil servants in New Jersey uncovered its links to organized crime, and recommended against Resorts being granted a gambling licence. With corruption and coercion having failed, Resorts turned back to strategic communications. Resorts went on the front foot in the media, buying large blocks of advertising to again stress the public benefits of the redevelopment of Atlantic City.[233] This helped to create the political buffer that the New Jersey Executive, notably Governor Byrne, needed. He soon signalled his intention to proceed with a redevelopment scheme with Resorts at its heart, despite the earlier adverse recommendation by the licensing body.[234] Before the final decision on a permanent licence could be made, the Legislative Assembly amended the controlling legislation to allow Resorts to receive a temporary licence after meeting a much lower propriety test. The investigative team that had uncovered Resorts' Mob ties resigned in disgust. The licence was granted.[235]

The new Resorts casino opened its doors in Atlantic City on 28 May 1978, just over forty-nine years after Meyer Lansky's honeymoon there, when both gambling and drinking had been illegal. Literally thousands of people were waiting in line. In its first year-and-a-half of operation, the casino took in more than $366 million. It was, at the time, the most profitable casino in the world.[236]

Conclusion

Castro's rise to power in Cuba created many losers, including the Havana Mob, the American Mob and the US government. Within twenty months of his arrival in Havana elements of all three groups were cooperating to assassinate him. The traditional account has suggested that this was a CIA-run conspiracy, with mafia guns and Cuban exiles simply brought in as 'plausibly deniable' covert assets. The closer examination of the historical record provided in this chapter suggests something quite different: that the American Mob formulated its own plans to kill Castro, which the CIA then decided to 'piggyback' upon and sponsor. This was exactly the kind of 'convergence', with criminal elements manufacturing state support for their own criminal designs, about which the White House would warn fifty years later in its *Strategy to Combat Transnational Organized Crime*.

The episode studied in this chapter suggests that the Mob enjoyed a much greater level of autonomous agency in international affairs than has previously been appreciated. When Cuba became a critical site of superpower confrontation during the Cold War, that autonomy turned out to have unexpected consequences for the US. The US failure at the Bay of

Pigs may have been in part a result of its manipulation by the Mob, and its expectation that the Mob would have removed Castro. And Mob autonomy also enlarged the risk of Soviet misunderstanding of US actions during and after the Cuban Missile Crisis. That the Mob did not accidentally trigger nuclear war or spoil the deal negotiated by Kennedy and Khrushchev may be in part because the Mob's interest in Cuba had waned in the early 1960s, as it found success with its 'joint venture' model of collaborative government elsewhere in the Caribbean.

Mob efforts to relocate the joint venture model from Cuba to a new Caribbean location also suggest a role for centrally directed strategy in criminal relocation that many contemporary theorists, such as Carlo Morselli, deny exists.[237] Mob adaptation to changing political circumstances in The Bahamas also suggests strategic learning amongst some Mob leaders, notably Meyer Lansky, as a result of the strategic failures in Cuba. In Cuba, the Mob had no real Plan B should Batista fall. In The Bahamas, in contrast, when the political winds shifted, the Mob proactively cultivated a relationship with the political opposition, helped it into power and successfully rode the wave of decolonization. As with its efforts to achieve regime change in Cuba, this suggested a Mob that not only responded to political developments, but also sought to shape them. It was a group that was not afraid to use force, but which had also come to understand the limited strategic utility of force.

This was in part because of the changing geography of power. The globalization of finance and trade was changing the role of territorial control in the extraction of rents—both licit and illicit—and thus changing the location at which criminal power could most effectively be organized. New transportation and communication technologies had rendered both capital and labour mobile. The utility of political and juridical sovereignty was changing. Instead of deriving power from territorial control and the extraction of rents from fixed assets, rulers were now confronted by a regulatory race to the bottom in an effort to attract fickle, private transnational flows of capital. A new economic strategy was open to state leaders who dared to adopt it: they could now derive wealth and power from arbitrage simply by legalizing or licensing—whether formally or informally—goods, services and activities that were illegal nearby, using casinos and financial institutions as money-laundering services. In Cuba, much of Havana was rented out to criminal interests in this way. In The Bahamas, it was most of Grand Bahama. In Atlantic City, the logic was taken one step further, formalizing a constitutional exception to legalize in Atlantic City what was otherwise illegal in New Jersey.

Where the CIA-Mob collaboration in Cuba had suggested a convergence between organized crime's coercive methods and state covert operations, the subsequent developments in the Caribbean and Atlantic City point to a convergence between the strategic logic of organized crime and economic statecraft. Like a mafia's power, for some state actors power in the international system seemed increasingly to lie in using their control of sovereignty and governmental institutions to broker between two levels: international capital flows and local jurisdiction.[238] The same rentier logic applied whether the underlying economic activity was legal or illegal—and that, too, was, ultimately, something that sovereignty allowed the state to control and instrumentalize. The weakness of global financial regulation left few checks on states' choices to use their own prerogatives and apparatus to organize—and even formally legalize—activities that broader international society might otherwise frown upon.

This was the gap into which the offshore tax and banking havens would step in subsequent decades. This new approach to 'casino capitalism' offered a powerful realization of the Mob's strategic vision: the creation of venues for the private accumulation of capital, without the loss of any of that capital to public governmental purposes through redistributive taxation, social welfare or the provision of public goods. As the criminologist Alan Block puts it:

> In the minds of those working in the subterranean economy, capital is always private, having no actual intrinsic or important relationship with the public order. This means that rules and regulations, which might in some fashion restrain capital accumulation, or even worse, recognize that some capital is surplus and that the public weal is better served when a portion of that surplus is distributed to aid those with comparatively little, are to be resolutely resisted.[239]

The strategic logic of organized crime and the economic logic of states seemed to be converging. The stage was set for the merger of criminal groups' political strategies with states' economic strategies, hinted at by the term 'mafia states'.

To understand how that convergence has played out in contemporary cases, we must first reflect on the different 'positioning' strategies adopted by criminal groups in relation to state power—positioning strategies illuminated through the episodes we have studied in the preceding chapters of Part Two. Not all collaboration between criminal and political actors involved the joint ventures of Tweed's New York, Lima's Palermo, Batista's Havana or the UBP's Grand Bahama. Some involved looser alliances, while others involved segmentation of governmental roles along territorial, jurisdictional or other lines. It is to the task of understanding these differences, and the implications for both theory and practice, that we now turn.

PART THREE

THE MARKET FOR GOVERNMENT

10

STRATEGIC CRIMINAL POSITIONING

> '...to reign is worth ambition, though in Hell:
> Better to reign in Hell, than serve in Heaven.'
>
> Satan, in Milton's *Paradise Lost*[1]

What can we learn about contemporary interactions between states and organized crime from the historical episodes of criminal strategizing considered in Part Two? The episodes explored in Part Two reveal criminal organizations using several approaches to compete—and cooperate—with states for governmental power. Irish, Jewish and Italian neighbourhood gangs in New York sometimes kept to themselves, avoiding the state, as did some Sicilian hinterland bandits, but also in some cases formed alliances with political actors such as Tammany Hall. Other groups, such as the Sicilian mafia and New York Mob, emerged as brokers in their own right between the state and local communities. In a third set of cases, collaborative joint ventures emerged between political actors and organized crime, as we saw in New York, Havana, Palermo and The Bahamas. In some cases, the same mafia actors who cooperated with some political actors confronted others—for example the Mob's differing approaches to the US Navy and some labour activists during World War Two. Some mafia groups cooperated with one state, but actively confronted another, mounting domestic insurgency (Sicily) or transnational armed attacks (Cuba,

267

Haiti). Some cases saw criminal groups relocate, whether as a result of migration (from Sicily to the US), deportation (the US to Sicily) or by design (to Cuba, Haiti and The Bahamas). Understanding what explains the differences may offer insights into contemporary interactions between states and organized crime, and into the deeper strategic logic of organized crime.

The traditional structuralist approach to explaining these variations suggests that criminals organize where the state is 'failed' or absent, or in 'ungoverned spaces'.[2] World Bank economist Stergios Skaperdas speaks of 'power vacuums'.[3] Criminologists such as Vincenzo Ruggiero and Nikos Passas write of a 'paradigm of deficit'[4] and 'criminogenic asymmetries'.[5] But the episodes in Part Two show that while criminal organization can develop where the state is absent or very weak (in post-war Sicily), it can also develop where it is abstinent (on Grand Bahama); where it is present but ineffective (in immigrant slums on Manhattan's Lower East Side, on New York's wharves during World War Two, or in occupied Palermo); and even where the state is present and effective but susceptible to corruption or coercion (for example in New York in the 1850s and 1860s, and Havana and Palermo in the 1950s). State presence, absence or abstinence are not the golden keys that unlock the riddle of criminal power.

As the discussion in Part One of this book suggests, scholars have explored the complexities of political-criminal interactions in contexts as diverse as Afghanistan, Bosnia-Herzegovina, Brazil, Colombia, Indonesia, Jamaica, Myanmar, Pakistan, the US and West Africa.[6] This chapter, drawing on Part Two, as well as on these authors' insights, identifies recurring patterns in criminal groups' positioning vis-à-vis states and other political organizations. It suggests that rather than treating criminal organizations as filling a governance vacuum or gap, we should treat them as competing with other actors, including states, in a market—a market for government.

The market for government

The market for government involves competition not only to control formal government decision-making and institutions, but also to supply governmentality, as that term was described in Part One. This is a very different prospect from competing to supply illegal drugs or illegal services—or, for that matter, legal products such as hamburgers or cars. The market for government involves competition for a specific type of social legitimacy—for the allegiance of individuals and groups as consumers and participants in a specific normative system by which they can regulate their own conduct—whether we think of that system as political, religious or in some other terms.[7] The market for government involves competition not simply to control legislatures, courts and police—institutions—but, more fundamentally, to become the source of the normative order that 'sets the possible field of action for others' (see Chapter 2). In the case of criminal power, the system—and one's allegiance to it—is secret and hidden, and the group peddling this criminal governmentality will deliberately avoid a formal governmental role. But, as we have seen, though clandestine, its role is governmental nonetheless.

Understanding the interaction and competition between states, criminal actors and other providers of government in these 'market' terms encourages us to think about how these rivals strategically position themselves in relation to each other, and the different capabilities—of coercion, corruption, communications—required. Business management theorists such as Michael Porter long ago pointed out that market structure is not a static artefact, but better understood in terms of its dynamic interaction with enterprise strategy; and Phil Williams has suggested that such analysis can usefully be extended to the dynamics of competition in markets for illicit goods and services, such as narcotics.[8] This chapter suggests extending this approach to understanding how criminal strategy reflects, and influences, competition in the market for government.

Understanding criminal strategy in terms of market competition helps explain the focus to date on how criminal power relates to state 'absence' and 'failure'. Where other governmental rivals are absent or weak, criminal organizations enjoy a sustainable pricing advantage because the costs of supplying governmentality are lowered—and, as the sole provider of governmentality, monopoly prices can be levied. Roberto Saviano, the astute observer of the Camorra whom we met in Part One, describes this organizational logic at play in Naples: 'Everything that is impossible to do elsewhere because of the inflexibility of contracts, laws, and copyright is feasible here.'[9] Here, criminal organization becomes both more attractive to participants—and more obvious to observers. For that reason, some commentators have speculated that there is a natural tendency on the part of organized crime towards monopoly and even the development of state-like characteristics, one of the reasons that Vanda Felbab-Brown speaks of organized crime and the state as 'competitors' in 'state-making'.[10] But in many cases, as we have seen in Part Two, criminal groups forego such a monopolistic role within the upperworld, eschewing formal political authority in favour of hidden political influence, or even collaboration with formal political actors to supply governmentality—a point that resonates with analysis of contemporary examples by authors such as Mark Shaw, Tuesday Reitano, Desmond Arias and Ivan Briscoe. How do we explain these criminal positioning strategies which take place not in the absence of the state, but alongside, underneath and even, at times, apparently from within the state? This book suggests that a key part of the answer lies in understanding how some criminal organizations understand their strategic opportunities and seek to exploit them. States' choices clearly matter, too: but they have been more closely studied to date. The new insights offered by this book relate to the criminal side of the equation, helping to explain the different patterns of interaction between criminal and other actors.

The episodes in Part Two suggest that criminal organizations' approach to political power depends in part on the capabilities available to a group—and the positioning strategy it adopts to exploit those capabilities. The two strategic aspects—internal capabilities and external positioning—are closely intertwined. Groups with more effective corruption and communications capabilities were often able to maintain stable relations with local formal political actors, whereas those groups that had to fall back on coercion—such as the Mob in Cuba after 1959—had to contend with higher levels of conflict with those political actors. That was not always, however, a bar to success: as the efforts of the mafia in Sicily in the post-war period demonstrated, the use of force could, if married to an effective political strategy, prove highly effective in repositioning a strategic criminal organization.

The same connection between internal capabilities and external strategy appears to be present today. Adam Elkus suggests, for example, that:

[Mexican drug] cartels are similar to medieval barons who engaged in constant struggles for power and alliance politics. Often times, inter-cartel battles are an outgrowth of internal cartel political intercourse, much as external wars are expressions of internal state politics. External shocks often have a destabilizing influence on internal group politics and dynamics.[11]

Certain patterns recur within this market as criminal organizations seek to combine internal capabilities in ways that deliver sustainable market positions. For example, criminal groups in the radically different contexts of Prohibition New York and post-war Sicily both adopted a 'syndication' or 'cartel' arrangement—as did criminal groups in Colombia in the 1980s. The strategic logic was the same in each situation: pooling risk, reducing costs and accessing economies of scale. And in each case this had both internal organizational and external political effects. In the New York Mob, the Commission became an instrument not only of internal governance and effective command and control but also for coordinated positioning in relation to state officials (in the creation of the 'Buy-Money Bank', and the attempt to influence the 1932 US presidential nomination process). In Sicily, syndication led to the *Cupola* system, facilitating the emergence of the Palermo joint venture. And in Colombia, cartelization was driven by economic considerations, but also produced coordinated strategy in dealing with the state on extradition and demobilization.[12]

What other such patterns can we find in how groups with criminal goals position themselves relative to states? Drawing on the episodes in Part Two, this chapter identifies six ideal-type positioning strategies adopted by criminal groups in the market for government, providing a new, more nuanced way of understanding the apparent 'convergence' between states, business and organized crime on the global stage. Key features of these strategies, and what they suggest about the shape of potentially effective state responses, are captured in Tables 1 and 2, below. Three of these ideal-type positioning strategies involve accommodation with the state: 1) *intermediation*, as pursued by mafias; 2) criminal *autonomy* as pursued by warlords and local gang leaders; and 3) *joint venture* strategy, in which criminal groups and states vertically integrate capabilities. Three other positioning strategies emerge out of situations of confrontation: 4) *strategic alliance* against third parties; 5) *terrorism* as a criminal strategy; and 6) criminal *blue ocean* strategy, a strategy of deliberate, directed relocation.

Table 1: Three Criminal Accommodation Strategies

	Intermediation	Autonomy	Merger
Actors associated with this positioning strategy	Mafias	Warlords and gang rule	Joint ventures
Underlying market logic	Jurisdictional sharing	Territorial segmentation	Vertical integration
Criminal rents available exceed internal costs plus...	Cost of corrupting governmental capabilities	Cost of excluding state and developing alternative governmental capabilities	Cost of integration of capabilities
Conditions for emergence	Rapid structural or normative change creates unmet demand for government Low costs of corruption	State enforcement capabilities ineffective Low cost of organizing alternative governmental capabilities (e.g. fragmenting military structures; or local protection groups)	Elite political or military group controls state assets with weak public oversight Poor rent extraction opportunities in local licit economy
Geography	Mafias locate at sites of formal legislative, spending and policing power	Communities where state capabilities are consistently weak—for warlords, peripheries; for gangs, slums	State-run security and economic operations—e.g. military airports and installations, development banks, financial regulators
Governmentality	Protection of traditional	Protection of local identity and	Court politics

	community values within formal political system	interests without secession	
Effective state responses	Remove unmet demand for government through regulatory reforms of markets (e.g. ending prohibition) Raise costs of corruption, inc. through higher-level enforcement (e.g. federal)	Physical extension of governmental capabilities Localization of governance, subject to centralized corruption monitoring	Promotion of democratic control of state institutions (armed forces, development banks, financial regulators, campaign finance reform) Inter-state accountability

This is not the first effort to develop an analytical framework for understanding how criminal groups are positioned vis-à-vis states. Peter Lupsha's tripartite typology of predation, parasitism and symbiosis has received considerable attention.[13] Third-generation gang warfare scholarship offers a related model, describing gangs as evolving from 'aggressive competitor' to 'subtle co-opter' and then 'criminal state successor'.[14] The problem with these models, however, is that they offer no theory of change. They cannot explain when, how or why a criminal organization will shift from one position to another. The analytical framework offered here may help us address this problem and, as we explore in the final chapter, provide useful avenues for further research and practical guidance.

Intermediation: mafia logic

The default positioning strategy adopted by the Sicilian and American mafias in most of the episodes studied in Part Two was one of jurisdictional segmentation of the market for government.[15] Mafias—such as the Sicilian mafia, the American mafia, the Jewish gangs considered in Chapter 5, the Havana Mob considered in Chapter 8 or, more recently, groups in Russia and Kenya[16]—are clandestine governmental intermediaries, operating not just in the underworld, but at the interface between the upperworld and underworld.[17] In this arrangement, a strategic actor exercises governmental power over a group or market operating beyond the state's social, rather than physical, reach, intermediating between the two. As Eric Hobsbawm explained, mafia power rests on the creation of 'a virtual parallel or subsidiary system of law and power to that of the official rulers'.[18]

Mafias broker corrupt exchanges, providing marginalized groups with access to the goods and services controlled by higher political powers, to protection and to social mobility, while providing upperworld governmental actors with access to assets in enclave populations and hidden markets: criminal finance, illicit labour and votes.[19] As the Italian organized crime expert Pino Arlacchi put it, mafias' power thus derives 'from the privileged access they enjoy to the levers of State power'.[20] As Anton Blok found, this can create a stable system in which mafias 'exercise jurisdiction … in conjunction with formal authority'.[21]

An actor's power within a mafia thus depends on his position as an intermediary between the internal and the external, his control of internal violence and his influence over outsiders, including state actors. While coercive capabilities are significant, corruption and communications capabilities are central to the maintenance of the mafia's governmental power. As we saw in Chapters 5 and 6, Luciano's power derived both from his effective use of force to see off internal rivals, and his influence over external rivals—whether Jewish gangsters or the state. He could change the Mob's culture to one based on a more collaborative, non-parochial outlook precisely because he was feared internally as the most ruthless and violent *capo*, having killed his two predecessors. Equally, once he was in power he could moderate his violence because he could offer *mafiosi* access to resources from outside their own ranks. He was what Henner Hess called the 'optimal strategic position' to be the 'provider of, and channel for' productive exchanges between these two strategic levels.[22]

The specific criminal governmentality promoted by mafias matches this secret intermediary role. Mafia governmentality is inherently clandestine, hidden inside and often drawing from prevailing mores and conventions. It is built on humans' insatiable desire to have it both ways: their 'desire to do so many things which they also desire to prohibit'.[23] Mafia strategic communications frequently straddle two quite distinct normative orders, balancing state-supporting political quietism with a claim to defend the values and security of marginalized populations.[24] The Sicilian mafia achieved this through emphasizing traditional values such as self-sufficiency, family, honour and, to some extent, Roman Catholicism. Luciano, in contrast, leading a mafia embedded in a modern American capitalist environment, oversaw the Mob's adoption of a more entrepreneurial and materialistic governmentality. Both used *omertà* as the framework for influence and control, but the governmentality within each organization differed appreciably—at least until the 1950s, when the encounter with American power and culture during the AMG occupation, and direct Mob interactions with and influence over the Sicilian mafia, may have begun to change the Sicilian mafia's external outlook and internal organization.

Treating mafias as products of intermediary positioning strategy also provides potentially powerful insights into where mafias are likely to emerge, a major topic of current criminological research.[25] Part Two suggests that mafias are likely to emerge where two conditions hold: 1) major structural changes have created new or poorly governed markets, or weakened norms against participation in illegal activity, creating an unmet demand for government; and 2) governmental capabilities are available at a corruption price that is lower than the payoff from available criminal rents. Such conditions seem likely to hold consequent to a variety of politico-economic shocks: war, revolution, rapid mass immigration, the formal prohibition of a market, or the creation of new forms of property. The Sicilian mafia emerged in the context of the expansion of private property rights and Sicily's sudden integration into the Italian political economy through political unification, without a concomitant extension of the state's governmental capabilities.[26] The American mafia Families emerged in marginalized immigrant communities as a protection against the threat posed by the Black Hand to private property, and their development was accelerated by the advent of Prohibition. More recently, the Russian *mafiya* emerged with the introduction of the norm of private property in the context of post-Communist transition in the late twentieth century.[27]

This lens also helps us read the geography of mafia power. Mafias are likely to corrupt those institutions, and emerge at those levels of government, where governmental discretion could extend power into these hidden markets and marginalized populations, through defining norms (legislatures), enforcing them (police and courts) and allocating resources (expenditure decisions). If government institutions do not have these powers, then the payoffs from corruption are unlikely to exceed the costs. Thus in the US, a federation that gives most of these powers in the first instance to cities and states, mafias emerged first at the municipal level before extending their power to states; the interest in national politics was limited and late. In Italy, the mafia emerged first within specific *latifundia* (policed and run by *gabellotti*), then over time developed influence in Palermo, Rome and Brussels, as each of those became centres of legislative, judicial or spending power relevant to their operations. Likewise, we see contemporary mafias emerging at the local and state level in federations (such as Mexico and Somalia), and in capitals in more centralized polities (such as Kenya). In federal jurisdictions, in particular, this points to a potential state policy response: creating federal-level enforcement mechanisms to target local mafias. In Part Two, we saw the Mob carefully avoiding federal crimes and jurisdiction because of its limited reach into federal institutions.

Understanding mafia logic in these terms thus helps us to analyse where mafias emerge, the nature of their governmentality and, potentially, to identify opportunities for effective state response. As hinted at in Table 1 above, these centre on addressing the opportunity structures that mafias exploit, by reducing the gap between the state and enclave markets or populations through regulatory reform; and raising the costs of systematic corruption, including through introducing enforcement mechanisms from higher levels to provide oversight of local governance arrangements. In Chapter 11 we explore in more detail what such policy responses might look like.

Autonomy: warlordism and gang rule

Some of the episodes considered in Part Two also point to a very different criminal strategy for segmenting the market for government: not through jurisdictional sharing, but through territorial segmentation. The result is what we might call 'criminal autonomy'.

Armed groups enjoying military control of territory have a short path to governmental power over both illicit and licit market exchanges within that territory. This can occur both where the state lacks effective territorial control—as we saw in post-conflict Sicily—or where a local organization such as a neighbourhood gang develops sufficient coercive and corruption capabilities to balance the state's military or policing capabilities, and can begin to operate autonomously—as we saw at a micro-scale with the local neighbourhood gangs of the Lower East Side, as we saw again with the *gabellotti* of post-Unification Sicily and, to a degree, with the sugar barons of Cuba. Where the state goes along with the arrangement, we see a territorial segmentation of the market for government, with local actors emerging as *de facto* rulers.

Coercive capabilities are thus a central component of criminal auton-omy, essential to the maintenance of effective control over a territory. In a rural context, we often call such actors 'warlords', in part because they tend to emerge out of the ashes of war and the military structures of collapsing state, imperial and insurgent armies.[28] In recent decades, this pattern has appeared particularly in Africa and Central Asia.[29] Warlords emerge where 'state institutions play little, if any, role in regu-lating political competition'.[30] Warlords take on basic governmental functions and authority themselves, setting norms, allocating resources and resolving disputes.[31] Warlords' governmental power usually strad-dles the grey area between the formal and illicit economies, and crimi-nal activity has, historically, been a major source of warlords' govern-mental power, from 1920s China to post-colonial Africa and Asia.[32] In fact, these criminal connections may help to explain why states turn a blind eye to warlords on their territory: it may enable the development of criminal rents from which the state can benefit through extortion (tribute) without the incursion of associated production costs, or the risk of threatened rivals banding together.[33] It can sometimes serve the interest of state powers to informally outsource the government of territories heavily dependent on organized crime, for example from illicit opium production (Afghanistan, Myanmar) or illicit mineral traf-ficking (Democratic Republic of the Congo).

The same strategic logic holds in urban contexts where particular neighbourhoods become *plazas* for illicit traffic, as has occurred with the *posses* in Kingston, Jamaica, and in some Brazilian *favelas*.[34] In this case, the groups exercising criminal autonomy tend to be self-starting protection groups rather than remnants of shrinking state military institutions. In the case of The Bahamas studied in Chapter 9, we saw a variation on this type, with the state deliberately carving out an autonomous zone through the creation of a 'baronial' free-trade zone on Grand Bahama. In all of these situations of autonomy, the local actor adopts a 'neofeudal' posture to the state, seeking neither to replace nor to secede from it, but rather to exploit coercive capabilities, control over economic activity and state forebearance to exercise a high degree of local political autonomy, while offering some level of fealty to the state.[35]

As with intermediation, the pursuit of criminal autonomy as an external positioning strategy seems to go hand in hand with a specific governmentality. Because, like mafias, they do not seek national power, warlords and gang leaders tend to advocate corrections of injustices within the existing normative order rather than its revolutionary over-throw.[36] But warlord politics is usually framed in much more 'local' and place-specific terms than mafia culture; and warlord and gang rule is also much more overt. Warlords frequently present as community protectors resisting excessive state centralization; urban gang leaders often emphasize highly localized quality-of-life issues. Like mafias, warlords and local bosses may threaten formal secession, but that usu-ally proves to be a temporary negotiating tactic designed to maximize local governmental power and balance between rival neighbouring states. In Myanmar, Khun Sa and other ethnic separatists relying on criminal markets (such as opium and jade trafficking) played this game for several decades, alternating between espousal of autonomy and advocacy of secession.[37]

The adoption of an autonomous posture in the market for govern-ment is also closely tied to internal organization. Depending upon coercive control of territory, warlords and gang rulers tend to adopt more centralized, hierarchical command structures than mafias and other criminal groups who are more dependent on clandestine opera-tions, corruption and subversion. But their focus is military; as Giustozzi notes, warlords frequently develop a 'neopatrimonialist atti-tude' towards the populations they govern, with 'institutionalization weak or absent'.[38] The governmental system often involves undifferen-tiated political, military and economic authority in the person of the warlord or gang leader. Unless, that is, the extraction of rents incentivizes the development of a more complex and differentiated governmental apparatus.[39]

If rents can be extracted from non-labour-intensive activity such as taxing transnational flows, the governmental apparatus is likely to be limited, as the warlord or gang leader can use his coercive capabilities to tax the trade, and piggyback on existing non-state authority structures to ensure local control.[40] This is the pattern in some parts of Afghanistan today.[41] It was also arguably the strategy adapted by Batista as Cuba's strongman during the 1930s, taxing transnational flows while relying on the local 'sugar barons' for political support. But if larger rents can be derived from local production, there may be incentives for developing a more elaborate governmental apparatus and welfare system in order to engage the local community in that production. This was arguably Batista's strategy in the 1950s, when he needed local labour to participate in the tourism economy he was promoting. It is arguably also the trajectory followed by Ismail Khan, a warlord in western Afghanistan.[42]

Cuba's experience also provides insight into what happens when a stable territorial segmentation of the market for government loses its guarantor, as occurred when Batista left for Florida in 1944: *gangsterismo*. Political networks connecting the sugar barons into Batista's Palace Gang began competing violently over market-share in the market for government. Politics became criminalized and paramilitarized. This may offer important lessons for countries today where a weak capital relies on local warlords and tribal militias for stability—Afghanistan, Libya, Somalia, Syria, Yemen—and, as discussed in Chapter 11, for contemporary peace operations' exit strategies.

Understanding the difference between mafias and warlords may also help us predict where each will emerge. Mafias, as we have seen, seem likely to emerge where there is a suddenly-created demand for government and corruptible governmental capabilities are at hand, together with local actors with the corruption and communications capabilities to exploit these opportunities. Warlords and gang rulers, by contrast, are likely to emerge where governmental authority is withdrawing or collapsing, and coercive capabilities are left behind. As highlighted in Table 1, this points us to several possible remedial opportunities to address the emergence of criminal autonomy, such as the physical extension of governmental authority (whether to border areas or through improved urban planning and design) and the localization of governance (subject to effective corruption monitoring). These matters are discussed further in Chapter 11.

Merger: joint ventures

Batista in 1950s Havana, Salvatore Lima in Palermo and the Bay Street Boys in The Bahamas all partnered with criminal groups in a third form of accommodation in the market for government: merging capabilities. Where autonomy requires an informal territorial segmentation of the market for government, and intermediation requires a jurisdictional segmentation, in the joint venture strategy the capabilities of criminal and political organizations are vertically integrated to operate simultaneously across the upperworld and underworld.[43] Government becomes a co-production.

If there were 'mafia states' on display in Part Two, these were they. In each of the joint venture episodes studied, criminal actors used political assets within their criminal enterprises, and political actors used criminal capabilities as instruments of political action and statecraft.[44] They adopted a strategy of 'mutuality, where the political and economic systems become dependent upon and subject to many of the services the criminal organizations have to offer', and crime is likewise organized—and not just protected—through political and state institutions.[45] Batista, Lima and the Bay Street Boys all used the state's legislative capabilities, financing capabilities and security institutions to develop and grow criminal markets, and all in turn used the financial and coercive capabilities of criminal organizations for patronage-based governance and, in the latter cases, political campaigning. Access to criminal organizations' clandestine force-projection capabilities and international corruption networks meant access to realms beyond day-to-day politics.[46] And governance of political factions' participation in organized crime ventures became a basis for domestic government.[47]

Understanding joint ventures in these terms also helps us to identify where they may emerge, and the developmental and geostrategic consequences. Post-conflict and post-transition states with weak local rent-extraction opportunities in the licit economy seem particularly vulnerable to joint venture strategies between local political elites and foreign criminal groups. And once a joint venture arrangement is in place, it skews economic development. As we saw in Batista's Havana, Lima's Palermo and on Grand Bahama, the development of a broad productive base and effective taxation system is displaced as the basis of government by criminal patronage.[48] Democratic politics gives way to, or hides, 'court politics', with rulers minimizing the provision of, or inclusive control over, public goods in order to maximize dependence on the ruler's favour.[49]

Maintaining such a joint venture depends on the maintenance of a system of social repression, though that system can become internalized and normalized, as the Sicilian experience with *omertà* makes clear. As Batista learned the hard way, if a ruler's grip on this system slips, the hollowing out of state institutions—particularly in the security sphere—can become counter-productive. The corrosive effects of corruption on the Cuban military opened the door to Castro's revolution, just as corruption in the British military contributed to the success of the American revolutionaries in the eighteenth century,[50] corruption in the Malian military contributed to the success of the Touareg insurgency in 2011 (see further below), and corruption in the Iraqi military opened the door to the military successes of Islamic State more recently.[51] (The pattern may not be a universal one, but the similarities do suggest, at the least, a need for further study.)

This also points us to remedial opportunities for addressing joint ventures, centred around promoting the democratic accountability of the state's governmental capabilities and institutions, such as armed forces, economic development organizations and financial regulators. Promoting such accountability weakens the ability of political and military elites to form clandestine joint ventures with local and foreign organized crime actors. The episodes in Part Two suggest that campaign finance reform will be particularly important for limiting opportunities for strategic corruption, a point further explored in Chapter 11.[52]

But as Jim Woolsey's discussion of the hypothetical Russian trading executive at the beginning of this book suggests, joint ventures also raise particularly acute concerns at the inter-state level. They make it hard to figure out whether a state's behaviour is guided towards classical political objectives and the long-term welfare of the state, or the short-term enrichment of state rulers. Will Reno warns of the criminal manipulation of 'the façade of the … State's globally recognized sovereignty for … commercial gain'.[53] As Moisés Naím has pointed out, this risks destabilizing systemic effects, corroding trust within international society and reciprocity as the basis for international order.[54] The guarantees afforded by the international system to sovereign states—territorial integrity, a large degree of immunity from external coercion, and eternal life—start to lose credibility. First, they risk being seen to promote free-riding on the privileges of sovereignty, a concern heightened by allegations that states such as North Korea are deeply engaged in drug trafficking and counterfeiting.[55] Second, sovereignty guarantees are at risk of being seen as ineffective if states can use criminal proxies to penetrate each other's borders, economies and governmental apparatus.

The danger is that the second dynamic becomes self-fulfilling: as trust corrodes within international society, states may increasingly look to strategies of subversion and to covert and 'hybrid' tactics to develop strategic advantage. For an idea of what this may entail, we can look to the Mob's role in post-revolution Cuba (Chapter 9) or to recent events in Ukraine. The head of Russia's general staff Valery Gerasimov describes 'hybrid conflict' as a strategy involving 'the broad use of political, economic, informational, humanitarian and other non-military measures', as well as 'concealed' armed forces.[56] This apparently includes organized crime.[57] In Crimea, sometimes known as 'Ukraine's Sicily', the Russian-backed premier was, at the time of writing, a local strongman nicknamed 'the Goblin'.[58] The Cuban cases studied in Part Two make clear the dangers in such an approach, even for the proxy's nominal puppet-masters: the loss of command and control, the introduction of autonomous 'wildcards' into inter-state rivalries and the muddying of strategic signalling processes.

Strategic alliances

The turn to criminal proxies in inter-state rivalries suggests a fourth positioning strategy that criminal groups can adopt in the market for government: strategic alliances, not with each other, but with states or other political organizations, against other rivals in the market. This moves us away from the question of how states and organized crime accommodate one another in the market for government to an exploration of the dynamics of confrontation. In this section and the two that follow we consider three positioning strategies in the context of confrontation: strategic alliance; terrorism; and 'blue ocean' strategy, which is, in a sense, a strategy of withdrawal. The essential features of each are captured in Table 2, below.

Table 2: Three Criminal Confrontation Strategies

	Strategic Alliance	Terrorism	Blue Ocean
Role of third party	Common adversary of both state and criminal group	Public—source of pressure on the state	Potential new state host
Underlying strategic approach	Balance of power	Indirect strategy	Structural transformation
Criminal vulnerability	Defection and betrayal	Alienation and popular resistance	Lack of local knowledge
Effective state responses	Defection/ wedge strategies	Strategic communication to delegitimize criminal violence	Inter-state responsibility and elite accountability

Phil Williams has explained that the formation of strategic alliances between criminal organizations follows the same logic guiding alliance formation between legitimate businesses: it represents an effort to create competitive advantage against their rivals by sharing risk, accessing new resources, customers and revenues, and creating new products, value and economies of scale.[59] How does this logic play out in alliances between criminal organizations, on the one hand, and states and other political organizations, on the other?

The Underworld Project (Chapter 6) and CIA-Mob alliance against Castro (Chapter 9) make clear that states and criminal groups sometimes form military alliances to compete with other states or other political actors. These cases are by no means unique: there is also evidence of long-term US government cooperation with the *yakuza* in occupied Japan,[60] and with drug traffickers in Central America[61] and Asia.[62] Nor is it a purely American phenomenon: there is evidence of state officials from all five permanent members of the Security Council—China, France, Russia, the UK and the US—cooperating with organized criminal groups, though in some of these cases this cooperation was targeted not at foreign states, but at defeating rivals in the domestic market for government.[63] The Mob's cooperation with the US Navy to combat union disruption to war efforts during World War Two (Chapter 6) offers another such example, as does the Italian state's cooperation with the mafia to defeat Giuliano and Genovese's possible collaboration with the Italian Fascist government to kill a labour activist in New York (Chapter 7). And we can also imagine two rival mixed alliances, each incorporating at least one state or political organization and at least one criminal group, facing off. This study includes no clear examples of such competition at the inter-state level, but it does at the domestic level: the competition between the Marinelli-Mob and Hines-Schultz alliances discussed in Chapter 5, and the Cuban *gangsterismo* discussed in Chapter 8.

Such political-criminal alliances differ from intermediation and criminal autonomy strategies because they do not involve a segmentation of the market between the allies, but rather collaboration in defeating a mutual rival. As the Underworld Project showed, however, such an alliance may depend upon tacit accommodation between the state and criminal groups. Nor are alliances the same as joint ventures: the latter involve the integration of capabilities, while the former leaves them separate. As the Underworld Project and subsequent events in post-war Sicily showed, however, alliances may provide fertile ground for the partners to develop such joint ventures. But joint ventures can also be created by independent design, as the Cuba (Chapter 8) and Bahamas (Chapter 9) episodes show.

Alliance with a political organization such as the state can, however, leave a criminal group vulnerable to defection and betrayal. In Chapter 9 we saw how the protection afforded to the Mob through its cooperation with the CIA against Castro ended when the US government reached an accommodation with Castro's own protector, the USSR, as a result of the Missile Crisis. The Missile Crisis also made clear that, just as Williams has discussed in the context of alliances between criminal groups, success in political-criminal alliances requires strong coordination mechanisms. Otherwise the activities of subordinate or peripheral actors can derail the alliance.[64] Freelancing attacks by Mob actors following the Missile Crisis risked spoiling the fragile truce negotiated by the US and USSR. This highlights the risks of unintended or misunderstood strategic signalling, and the difficulty of inter-state deterrence once public institutions turn to private instrumentalities to promote the state's strategic interests, as occurs through strategic alliances and joint ventures. Yet this appears to be the trend, particularly with the rise of 'state capitalism', explored briefly in Chapter 11 below.[65] An improved understanding of the strategic logic of political-criminal alliances may therefore be even more useful to states in the future than it was in the historical period on which this study has focused.

Terrorism as criminal positioning strategy

A fifth positioning pattern can emerge—often temporarily—when an organized criminal group responds to confrontation by a state with an indirect strategy intended to intimidate the state's citizens into forcing a change in state policy.[66] The logic of this approach is succinctly captured in the words of Salvatore 'Toto' Riina, the Sicilian mafia *capo di tutti capi* who ordered the assassination of politicians, judges and policemen as well as the bombing of a church and the Uffizi Gallery in the early 1990s: 'Wage war on the state first, so as to mould the peace afterwards.'[67] The mafia's attacks were intended to directly degrade the investigative and prosecutorial capabilities of the state—but even more so to degrade the morale of the state—and of society more broadly. This is terrorism as a criminal positioning strategy.

Where warlords and gang leaders confront the state directly in order to achieve a balance of military power and criminal autonomy, terrorism as a criminal strategy is the more obvious strategy of confrontation for clandestine criminal networks lacking standing military forces. The issues that generate acute confrontation between states and mafias—law enforcement policies, extradition, prohibition of certain commodities or services, prison conditions—tend to matter a great deal to those groups, but far less to the general public. Accordingly, if the criminal group can inflict significant costs on the public in a short time (and perhaps even attract sympathy to boot), the public may demand that the state sue for peace.

This was the logic behind the American and Havana Mobs' attacks on civilian installations in Cuba, especially sugar mills and oil refineries, intended to cause economic pain and foment civil disorder (Chapter 9). This was the logic of the attacks mounted by Pablo Escobar in Colombia in the 1980s and 1990s, which included the mid-air bombing of a civilian airliner, the assassination of several presidential candidates and an armed attack on the Supreme Court building, with a view to forcing the state to change its extradition policies. And it was likewise the logic of the Primeiro Comando da Capital, a powerful prison gang which carried out three waves of attacks in São Paulo, Brazil, in 2012 designed to force changes in prison policies. Over 100 buses were firebombed, and banks, police stations, a metro station and important government offices were bombed or hit with grenades. São Paulo ground to a halt.[68]

The worldwide proliferation of kidnapping as a tactic of non-state armed groups also owes something to this strategic logic, and can highlight divergences within an armed group over whether the maximization of criminal rents or ideological violence is the ultimate goal. Kidnapping for ransom is a highly effective form of predatory capital accumulation. Al Qaeda-affiliated groups are thought to have received at least $125 million in ransom payments from European governments in recent years.[69] But kidnapping as a tactic also responds to a deeper strategic communications logic: it serves as a blunt instrument for armed groups to communicate with a large audience, attacking symbols of external oppression and claiming the mantle of community protector, while also encouraging the group or public associated with the targets to bring pressure to bear for a change of policy.[70] Armed groups from Colombia to Nigeria, from Afghanistan to Syria, have used kidnapping as a terror tactic in this way.[71] But as we see in the following chapter, in some cases—such as AQIM in the Sahel, and the Taliban—these strategic uses of terror tactics can come into direct conflict around the question of how to deal with hostages: as commodities to be sold, or as instruments for strategic communication through symbolic violence.

Treating terrorism as a criminal positioning strategy also points to an important nuance in how we understand the relationship between terrorism and organized crime.[72] The strategic approach developed here suggests moving past treating 'terrorist' groups and 'criminal' groups as fixed identities, and instead looking at how armed factions strategically instrumentalize violence against civilians for a range of political, ideological and criminal purposes. This suggests that we recognize that a group's overall organizational strategy is the product of numerous internal and external forces, potentially including competition between different strategies promoted by different factions within the same group. Complex strategic actors such as Hezbollah and Islamic State cannot easily be pigeon-holed as 'terrorist', 'insurgent', 'criminal' or even 'governmental'; they are organizations whose strategic goals and methods shift over time, in part as different internal factions prove more or less successful in strategically exploiting the opportunities and capabilities available to them.[73] Only by carefully parsing these groups' use of terror tactics can we assess whether they are adopted in the pursuit of maximizing control over criminal rents, or in pursuit of more ideological goals.

Still, criminal groups turn to terrorism at their own peril. Terrorism significantly raises the profile of the group, which may reduce the chance of accommodation with the state. It can be difficult to calibrate terrorist violence to ensure that, rather than persuading the public to push for a change in state policy, it does not end up alienating the public and fostering popular resistance, as Giuliano's May Day attack, the Mob's attacks on Cuba, Escobar's terrorism in Colombia and Sicilian mafia terrorism in the early 1990s all seem to have done.[74] By making the coercive foundation of criminal power so brutally obvious, criminal groups that turn to terrorism risk undermining the notionally consensual basis of the corrupt exchanges that underpin their power over the long term. Terrorism involves moving from the 'throffer' of corruption (see Chapter 2) to a direct threat, from a mix of deterrence and inducement to a compellent strategy. That is likely to be perceived, by the target, as a loss of power: they are suddenly transformed from notionally autonomous partners in crime to obvious subordinates to the criminal group's will.

Even if a population is alienated by a criminal group's turn to terrorism, however, it may still succeed, if political actors and state agents feel the reputational or political costs of the campaign of terror are too high.

That, indeed, was the outcome for the Primeiro Comando da Capital in Brazil, where terrorism won the demanded relaxation of prison policies.[75] And current litigation is Italy is exploring whether, similarly, the result of Riina's assault in the early 1990s was, notwithstanding public horror at mafia violence, a secret pact between the Italian security services, leading political figures and the mafia leadership.[76]

Relocation and blue ocean strategy

The final ideal-type positioning strategy also emerges in response to confrontation, but involves relocation. Scholars and analysts have long argued that pressure by one state on a criminal group can lead that group to withdraw and relocate elsewhere—the so-called 'balloon effect'. But as Morselli and others have correctly pointed out, the journalistic representation of criminal relocation as 'effortless' ignores the constraints imposed by social, economic and regulatory context.[77] As Diego Gambetta has noted, the mafia 'is a difficult industry to export. Not unlike mining, it is heavily dependent on the local environment.'[78] Foreign mafias, simply put, lack local knowledge and connections because of the long-term relational nature of the corruption required to secure protection from the state.[79] Some of the episodes in Part Two bear this out. As Frederico Varese has indicated, foreign mafias usually face stiff competition from well-established local organizations with deeper social capital and access to trust networks, including state actors working illicitly.[80] In New York, Italian-origin mafias faced just such competition from Tammany Hall, Irish and Jewish gangsters.

Yet Part Two also reveals several cases where criminal organizations did relocate, despite these barriers to entry into foreign markets. In the case of the Sicilian mafia's transplantation to New York, and the Mob's post-war reconnection with Sicily, this happened through migration or displacement of a kinship network with knowledge of mafia techniques, just as Morselli and others have identified in other cases.[81] Here, as Varese predicts, mafia migration resulted not from a 'rational decision to open a branch in order to conquer a territory in a faraway land', but was 'more likely the outcome of unintended consequences'.[82] But Part Two also includes at least two other cases where mafia relocation was precisely the result of a 'rational decision to open a branch ... in a faraway land': the Mob's move to Havana in the 1930s and to The Bahamas in the 1950s. Its efforts to stand up governments-in-exile to install in Cuba in the early 1960s, and its attempt to force its way into Haiti, arguably represent two failed further attempts. Here are examples of precisely that 'directed' relocation for which Morselli and colleagues say there is no real evidence.[83]

As we saw in Chapter 9, this deliberate relocation was successful where it followed a criminal 'blue ocean' strategy. Rather than jostling with rivals for advantage in a crowded market, an ocean running red with the blood of competition, the Mob sailed off on its own into a 'blue ocean', finding a new, relatively uncontested market through vision and innovation.[84] This succeeded where mobsters convinced local strongmen and governing elites to form joint ventures and transform the local market for government—Batista in Cuba, the Bay Street Boys (and then Pindling) in The Bahamas. They failed—in Haiti, and with Castro—where they could not form such a joint venture. In each case, the Mob was doing exactly what Kim and Mauborgne suggest 'blue ocean' strategy requires: not competing with other rivals on product differentiation or on cost, but reconstructing the value chain through novel combinations of existing capabilities.[85] In the process, they restructured the market for government.

In Sicily, when the mafia took this approach through its sponsorship of separatism, it raised the prospect of a criminal group acting as midwife to the creation of a new sovereign state. Although this did not happen, it did lead to Sicily being granted significant governmental autonomy, changing the Italian constitutional system. As Kim and Mauborgne put it, 'strategy can shape structure'.[86]

11

INNOVATION, DISRUPTION
AND STRATEGY BEYOND THE STATE

'In a society where the concept of citizenship is disappearing whilst the desire for a sense of belonging is growing stronger, where the 'citizen' with his rights and duties is giving way to the clan, the following, the clientele, in such a society as this, the Mafia looks increasingly like the model for the future.'

Marcelle Padovani[1]

The episodes considered in Part Two suggest that—though we may have forgotten or deliberately overlooked it—there has long been a variety of forms of competition, cooperation and collaboration between states and organized crime in the pursuit of governmental power. The positioning strategies identified in Chapter 10 suggest that these may fall into certain ideal-type patterns. What can these patterns tell us about the strategic implications of organized crime today, and the apparent 'convergence' between statecraft, business and organized crime that former CIA director Jim Woolsey warned of two decades ago? Are 'mafia states' the result of new trends, or an old phenomenon repackaged?

In this final chapter, we consider two contemporary cases of protracted violence—Mexico and the Sahel—in which the strategic logic of organized crime has played an important role. These cases suggest that while criminal groups are still using the same positioning strategies that emerged in the historical episodes considered in Part Two, globalization may be intensifying the apparent 'convergence' between politics and crime by lowering barriers to entry into the market for government in ways that foster innovation by armed groups with new forms of governmentality. The result is the emergence of new, hybrid forms of governmentality and, increasingly, the disruption of state sovereignty's dominance as the model of government around the world.

The implication is clear: strategy and statecraft need to look beyond the state. The chapter and the book close with brief reflections on how understanding the strategic logic of organized crime may strengthen not only strategic theory, but also practical efforts to combat organized crime, and the management of criminal spoilers in peace and transition processes—in other words, contemporary statecraft.

Innovation and disruption

Mexico: from narcocartels to narcocults

Drug trafficking-related violence in Mexico between 2006 and 2012 officially led to at least 60,000 deaths.[2] The seventy-one-year rule of the Partido Revolucionario Institucional (PRI) at the federal level in Mexico during the twentieth century provided a framework for relatively peaceful competition between various governmental actors, including drug-trafficking mafias operating at the state and regional level in cooperation with corrupt local politicians and federal military actors.[3] Just as the 1944 removal of Cuba's strongman, Batista, triggered the violent competition known as *gangsterismo*, similarly the PRI's loss of political power in Mexico at the turn of the century set the stage for increasingly violent competition between 'cartels' in the Mexican underworld.[4] This violence was, however, also fuelled by changes in US border control (increasing the profits to be made from drug sales in the US); the expiry of a US ban on the sale of assault weapons in 2004, lowering barriers to entry into the competition for even small criminal groups; and vacancies in hemispheric drug trafficking supply-chains resulting from stepped-up law enforcement in Colombia and the Caribbean.[5] The result was a rapid escalation of violence as cartels developed different positioning strategies, and different governmentalities, in response to local conditions in the market for government and the capabilities to hand.

One of the first movers was the Sinaloa Cartel, amongst the wealthiest drug-trafficking organizations in the world. A classic trafficking mafia, it had long intermediated corrupt exchanges between Mexican underworld and upperworld actors to move illicit narcotics to the US.[6] Like other mafias, it developed out of a kinship network—this one around a pioneering trafficker in Sinaloa State in the 1960s, Pedro Avilés Pérez. His nephew, Joaquín 'El Chapo' Guzmán, emerged in the 1990s as Sinaloa's leader. After 2009 El Chapo appeared in *Forbes'* global Rich List, his net worth around $1 billion.[7] Notwithstanding Guzmán's notoriety, Sinaloa kept a generally low profile, claimed to eschew kidnapping and extortion, and may at times have worked with other cartels to minimize inter-cartel violence in an attempt to avoid confrontation with the state, just as the American mafia Commission sought to in the 1930s.[8]

It may have been Sinaloa's market revisionism after the PRI's fall that triggered a dangerous arms race amongst the cartels, with the rival Gulf Cartel hiring members of the Mexican Army's elite GAFE unit, joined by Guatemalan Kaibiles unit counterparts. The group, known as Los Zetas after their military call-signs ('Z-#') soon broke away as an independent and dangerously disciplined, well-trained criminal unit.[9] The group's martial culture quickly differentiated it from other cartels: rather than intermediating, the Zetas used military-style 'clear and hold' tactics, asserting monopolistic extortion powers over criminal and licit markets alike within their territory.[10] They were moving towards a posture of criminal autonomy. The Zetas quickly expanded from drug trafficking into extortion, racketeering, kidnapping, human smuggling and oil theft. But because their rents were extracted through predation, rather than production, they had little need for popular support; to achieve control of territory they terrorized the population into submission, notoriously massacring seventy-two migrants near the town of San Fernando (Tamaulipas), dumping forty-nine decapitated victims near Cadereyta (Nuevo León) and burning down a Monterrey casino.[11]

In the US, debate has raged as to whether the Zetas' military tactics justify their characterization as a 'criminal insurgency', or whether their reliance on terror tactics means they are better thought of in terms of 'narcoterrorism'. This is not merely a semantic debate; it could also have major legal and bureaucratic implications. Both analytic approaches stumbled, however, on whether the Zetas had political goals—as is expected of both insurgents and terrorists. In late 2011 a series of narcomantas in Nuevo Laredo seemed to suggest they did. One proclaimed: 'Let it be clear that we are in control here and although the federal government controls other cartels, they cannot take our plazas.' But a new set, weeks later, signalled a more oligopolistic goal:

> We do not govern this country, nor do we have a regime; we are not terrorists or guerrillas. We concentrate on our work and the last thing we want is to have problems with any government, neither Mexico nor much less with the US.[12]

What was going on? The 'positioning strategies' framework offered in the previous chapter provides an answer. The Zetas comprised neither a mafia, an insurgency, nor a terrorist group: they were pursuing a strategy of criminal autonomy, using force to develop a monopoly on illicit governmental power within specific territories, with a view to extracting criminal rents, yet with little interest in formal governmental responsibility. It was becoming more like a federation of warlords than a traditional mafia.

The Zetas' search for autonomy soon led them beyond Mexico's borders. As early as 2007 (though some contest this timeline) they may have formed a strategic alliance with Guatemala's Overdick mafia, sent 500 paramilitary operatives over the border into Guatemala's northern Petén province and consolidated the alliance by assassinating the scion of an Overdick rival, the Leone family.[13] The Zetas may thus have acquired a strategic reserve space in Guatemala where they could operate relatively unmolested by the Mexican or Guatemalan state, or their Mexican criminal rivals. This was akin to a multi-national corporation or a state outflanking a local rival by opening up a new foreign front with the aim of acquiring new resources or, if the local rival decided to compete on the foreign front, draining the rival's resources. Indeed, Sinaloa appears quickly to have taken the bait, forming its own alliances with local Guatemalan criminal groups, internationalizing Mexico's drug war.[14]

But the Zetas faced other strategic problems in Mexico. As the organization's core ex-military expertise was eroded by confrontation with the state and rival cartels it was forced to recruit increasingly from local gangs and Mara Salvatrucha 13 (MS-13), a transnational street gang formed in California and exported to Central America through US deportation policies in a manner similar to the transatlantic mafia migrations over the previous century.[15] The Zetas' military training and culture was steadily diluted. Increasingly its local outfits began forming links with local state actors and reverting to the intermediation approach of mafia *cosche*. The Zetas' governmental grip over their own units and, increasingly, over local populations, was weakening. By 2011 the group was facing populist revolts in some communities, sometimes organized through online social media. By 2012–13 the leadership structure was under sustained assault from the state. The organization became increasingly decentralized, and slowly began to fragment, also losing its influence in Guatemala.[16]

The Zetas' combination of criminal strategy and martial culture and organization was not the only such experiment in Mexico with hybrid governmentality. Two others emerged in the state of Michoacán, home to major marijuana production and the drug precursor importation hub of Lázaro Cárdenas. The first was La Familia Michoacana, part narcocartel, part narcocult.[17] In 2004, Nazario Moreno González (a.k.a. 'El Chayo'—'the Rosary' or 'El Mas Loco'—the 'Craziest One') spun off from a Michoacán criminal group La Empresa (literally, 'the company'). His new group adopted the terrorizing paramilitary tactics of the Zetas, and like them expanded from drug trafficking into extortion, human smuggling and kidnapping. But Moreno González's background was not in the military, like the Zetas' founders; he was a zealously evangelizing Jehovah's Witness. That religious sect's traditions became the source from which La Familia spun its new organizational culture and governmentality in a manner recalling, in some ways, the occult origins and rituals of Chinese triads.[18]

La Familia recruited from the ranks of drug addicts, alcoholics, and juvenile delinquents, promising rehabilitation, empowerment and self-renewal. Members were indoctrinated through compulsory bible study and the enforcement of codes requiring abstinence from alcohol, tobacco and drugs. This created a sense of in-group identity and superiority to the morally destitute external population. Both its internal and public rhetoric characterized La Familia members as self-liberated agents of 'divine justice' in a Manichean struggle.[19] All of this served to create a cult-like governmentality among the membership, framed in terms of fictive kinship. Just like child soldiers being indoctrinated into armed groups, Familia recruits were forced to disown their old family in favour of their new *familia*, or risk violent recriminations against both themselves and their biological kin.[20] Out of loyalty to this new family and its god, Familia members committed acts of astonishing savagery. The announcement of their arrival on the scene came attached to five severed heads lobbed onto a nightclub dance floor. Later victims were cooked.[21]

In the absence of strong leftist political parties during this period, cartel propaganda including the hugely popular *narcocorridos* (narcoballads)[22] developed into a quasi-political discourse framed around notions of personal and collective redemption and resistance to injustice.[23] This 'narcoculture' served to normalize crime, providing the social foundation of what George Grayson has described, in the case of Michoacán, as 'dual sovereignty':

> parallel to the elected government stands a narco-administration that generates employment (in growing and processing drugs), keeps order (repressing rival cartels), performs civic functions (repairing churches), and collects taxes (extorting businesspersons).[24]

This recalled the Italian Parliamentary Anti-Mafia Commission's description, a decade earlier, of the accommodation between the state and the Sicilian mafia as a non-aggression pact between 'two distinct sovereignties'.[25] By 2009, however, Mexico's federal state sovereignty was in direct confrontation with La Familia's criminal sovereignty. In 2009 the federal government revealed close, corrupt ties between La Familia and an array of municipal, state and federal politicians and officials in Michoacán.[26] La Familia responded with attacks on federal military and police sites in eight cities, leaving nineteen federal personnel dead in two days. The state escalated its own response, and when in 2010 Moreno González appeared to have been killed the remaining Familia leaders formally dissolved the organization.

One group, however, probably with Moreno González hidden amongst them (having faked his own death), set up their own spin-off organization: the Caballeros Templarios, or Knights Templar. The original Knights Templar was a medieval military order during the Crusades

(1129–1312 AD), charged with defending pilgrims in the Holy Land, known for its members' piety, military prowess—and wealth. The Mexican Knights Templar combined the religious fervour of La Familia and the martial culture of the Zetas. They were governed by a written code of ethics positioning Knights as temporal intermediaries between the community and their unjust oppressors (the state and other criminal rivals), and as spiritual intermediaries between the community and a divine upperworld. 'The members of the Order must fight against materialism, injustice and tyranny in the world,' this code thundered, even as the Knights fought for controlling shares in local criminal markets. The code described their mission as an 'ideological battle to defend the values of a society based on ethics', and even instructed the Knights to be 'noble' and 'chivalrous'.[27] Beyond their own walls, the Knights broadcast similar messages through the mass media, aiming to position themselves as protectors of traditional Michoacán values and culture.[28]

Some have described the Knights as representing a new form of 'spiritual insurgency'.[29] This suggests, misleadingly, that the Knights sought to overthrow the existing political system. That is not the case; like medieval knights, they were happy to wield violence selectively and instrumentally, dressing their violence up as corrections of injustice within the system. As with medieval knights, mass violence was not directed at the overthrow of the governmental system itself (feudalism then, the state now), but rather at rivals within the system, or those treated as enemies of the system. Spiritualism served as a framework for the Knights to develop a niche intermediary role in the market for government, as it does for local armed groups in other parts of Latin America.[30] In communities where the Knights held sway, shrines to 'Saint Nazario' ('El Chayo') sprang up, supplicants praying to him as the 'protector of the poorest' and a 'representative of God' to intercede on their behalf with the ultimate upperworld power.[31] Yet effective governmental intermediation also required more prosaic, temporal methods. The Knights are suspected of having donated millions of dollars to multiple political parties in Michoacán's 2011 gubernatorial campaign; having provided thugs to intimidate campaign staff and damage campaign premises; having blocked highways to reduce votes in some districts; and having corrupted vote-counting and polling station officials.[32] This was more a spiritualized mafia than a spiritual insurgency.

The shifting sands of the Sahel

Just as changes in the global strategic environment provoked innovation in Mexico's market for government, so they have stimulated innovation in the Sahel over the last decade and intensified the convergence of crime and politics in that region.

The interdiction efforts in the Caribbean that contributed to the growth in Mexican drug violence also created a balloon effect in West Africa and the Sahel as, starting around 2002, Colombian and Venezuelan drug traffickers pioneered new trans-shipment routes to European markets. Huge sums of money suddenly became available to local state authorities and tribal and militia leaders willing to accommodate these foreign traffickers, transforming the Sahelian market for government.[33] The increased access to cash led to purchases of vehicles and new navigation technologies which increased mobility across the Sahel, improving access to weapons and rivals' turf.[34] In the littoral and urban centres, narco-dollars fuelled political corruption and planted the seeds of several joint ventures between state rulers and foreign trafficking organizations, the most spectacular in Guinea-Bissau. Recalling Aerovías Q in Cuba, Bissau-Guinean military leaders put airports, ports and naval vessels at foreign traffickers' disposal, turning state assets into criminal resources, and using criminal rents as a basis for government patronage.[35] In ensuing years, cocaine trafficking seemed to become increasingly integral to formal politics along the West African coast from Mauritania to Benin, and to the more informal tribal politics of the Sahel.[36] Competition between rival political-criminal alliances sometimes played out through political assassinations (Guinea-Bissau), and sometimes through direct inter-cartel violence.

As in Cuba, the boom in the illicit economy eroded state capacity and upset existing power structures, especially in northern Mali.[37] Northern Mali, sparsely populated and weakly governed by the state after several decades of Touareg militancy, and long a venue for informal cross-border trade and illicit smuggling, became a key location for drug, arms and hostage exchanges.[38] Between $40 million and $65 million in ransoms appears to have been paid by European governments to actors in the region between 2008 and 2012, a huge windfall for non-state competitors in the market for government.[39] All of this 'empowered a new criminal class who mediated the distribution of profits' from these illicit markets.[40] Drug and ransom money was laundered through local 'development' and construction projects into local politicians and tribal leaders' pockets. A 2010 Malian state audit found that $224 million in rural development funds had gone missing. Across local Arab and Touareg communities, traditionally 'vassal' clans used criminal revenue to revise political settlements, defeating traditional 'noble' clans. An affluent area of Gao, a northern Malian city, became known as 'Cocainebougou' or 'Cocaine-ville'.[41]

Even as Western donors hailed Mali as a democratic and development success story, some state officials were quietly accommodating their criminal rivals. Echoing the mafia's sponsorship of Sicilian separatism half a century earlier, traffickers appear to have played an important role in convincing the state to back a policy of administrative decentralization adopted for northern Mali around 2006–7, ostensibly as a political resolution to long-standing conflict with Touareg separatists. Decentralization created many small, weak local councils over which traffickers could more easily develop power.[42] Organized crime became locally entrenched, manipulating the post-conflict settlement to its own benefit.[43]

When Muammar Gaddafi fell from power in Libya in 2011, thousands of Touareg soldiers serving in his armed forces returned to northern Mali with a considerable arsenal. This provided another external shock on the market for government in the Sahel, significantly lowering the costs of organizing coercion. Touareg Libya veterans and defectors from the Malian army quickly created several new separatist groups, most notably the Mouvement national de libération de l'Azawad (MNLA),[44] which indicated that it would use 'all means necessary' to end Mali's 'illegal occupation' of 'Azawad'—the Tamshek-language name for the western Sahel north of Timbuktu.

The MNLA made rapid military advances. As in Cuba under Batista or during the recent collapse of the Iraqi military in the face of Islamic State's onslaught, the Malian national military was revealed as a hollow shell, its morale and effectiveness fatally weakened as criminal patronage had replaced operational considerations in appointments, investment and planning.[45] As informal regulators of cross-border exchanges, military leaders had become influential brokers in drug trafficking and hostage markets, and the military had become more a criminal patronage system than a fighting force.[46] Competition within the drug market had also fuelled trafficking in arms from state arsenals, further weakening military readiness.[47]

In the face of Touareg insurgent gains, in March 2012 a group of despondent mid-level military officers in Bamako led a *coup d'état*. By April Touareg forces had taken control of most of Mali north of Mopti and declared the independence of a new secular state, Azawad.[48] At this point, however, tensions emerged between the MNLA and its Islamist allies in the Touareg insurgency. One of these was Ansar Dine ('Defenders of the Faith'), formed by Iyad Ag Ghaly.

Ag Ghaly was nicknamed 'the Strategist'. He had been an important Touareg rebel leader in the late 1980s, a Malian diplomat in Saudi Arabia in the early 2000s and then an influential broker in northern Mali's hostage market. When he failed to win leadership of his Touareg tribe and the MNLA he adopted a new positioning strategy, drawing on his familial connections to the leading regional Islamist militant group, Al Qaeda in the Islamic Maghreb (AQIM), to create a new Touareg Islamist organization—Ansar Dine.[49] Ag Ghaly was the cousin of the leader of AQIM, itself the successor to the Groupe Islamique Armé (GIA) and the Groupe Salafiste pour la Prédication et le Combat (GSPC) in Algeria, displaced from the Maghreb into the Sahara by Algerian military action in the 1990s. The GSPC had looked to the Sahara as a staging area for strategic action in northern Algeria's population centres. But over time its positioning strategy shifted from a transnational terrorist approach to something closer to criminal autonomy. The GSPC's Sahelian wing put down local roots as it forged commercial, political and marriage alliances with Arab tribes and trafficking networks. The leader of this Sahelian wing, Mokhtar Bel Mokhtar, became known as 'Mr Malboro' for his role in trafficking cigarettes to the Maghreb. The group's strategic communications increasingly emphasized issues not of Maghreb politics, but local Sahelian autonomy.[50] But this shift in the Sahelian group's strategic outlook led to significant inter-factional tensions within the GSPC after 2004, particularly over whether hostages should be treated as sources of criminal rent (ransoms, Bel Mokhtar's view) or instruments for symbolic political messaging through violence (the view of the GSPC's leadership in the Maghreb).[51] In 2007 the Arab leadership of the GSPC reasserted the group's terrorist identity, pledging allegiance to Osama bin Laden and turning the GSPC into an official Al Qaeda franchise, Al Qaeda in the Islamic Maghreb (AQIM). But by declaring the focus of the organization to be the Maghreb, and with its leadership entirely Arab, that left space in the Sahelian market for a group with more localized branding and communications. The Mouvement pour l'Unicité et le Jihad en Afrique de l'Ouest (MUJAO) was spun off in mid-2011, announcing itself with videos featuring sub-Saharan Africans speaking in both English and Hausa. Through engagement with the Sahel's illicit economy, it thrived 'as both a criminal enterprise and a jihadist organization'.[52]

MUJAO, AQIM and Ansar Dine all supported the MNLA during the Touareg insurgency of 2011–12. But when the MNLA declared Azawad's independence as a secular nation-state, the divergence in the groups' strategic goals became clear. AQIM, MUJAO and Ansar Dine all sought the imposition of Islamist rule. By mid-2012 the three Islamist groups had pushed the MNLA out of northern Mali's urban centres, imposing a harsh interpretation of *sharia* law, and absorbing many MNLA gunmen into their own ranks.[53] At this point, however, the Islamists' own strategic differences emerged. Ansar Dine sought to achieve Islamist rule within the framework of Malian sovereignty, while AQIM and MUJAO sought to replace the Malian state, and other Sahelian states, with a transnational Islamist governmental structure. While they all sought to create 'a stable Islamic state', the AQIM leadership in the Maghreb wrote to its lieutenants and to Ag Ghaly, 'it is too early for that, God knows. Instead, it is necessary to be cautious in the matter and we must be more realistic.' AQIM's leaders warned about the over-hasty imposition of Wahhabi interpretations of *sharia* and the destruction of local Sufi shrines, which risked alienating the local population. They pushed for AQIM and Ansar Dine militants to take a more incremental approach, continuing to work as allies with the Touareg separatists, to spread political risk and the costs of 'administration of the region' which, they assessed, 'exceed our military and financial and structural capability for the time being'.[54]

Apparently unpersuaded by their Maghreb-based colleagues, the Islamist militants in northern Mali remained hostile to the Touareg separatists. Governmental power in northern Mali was quickly territorially segmented amongst them: AQIM and Ansar Dine controlled Timbuktu, Ansar Dine controlled Kidal alone, and MUJAO controlled

Gao. In Gao and Kidal, MUJAO and Ansar Dine forged close relations with Touareg traffickers, and separatism (which the traffickers had previously backed) seemed to lose political ground.[55] In Timbuktu, however, when Berabiche Arab traffickers formed a local militia called the Front national pour la libération de l'Azawad (FNLA) and attempted to form an alliance with AQIM against the MNLA, AQIM rejected the proposal, and expelled the FNLA. It dissolved, only to re-emerge as the Mouvement arabe de l'Azawad (MAA).[56]

Despite this political instability, a French military intervention in early 2013 managed to limit violence largely to northern Mali. That intervention, which gave way to a United Nations stabilization force, in turn caused a reshuffling of alliances, as strategic competition shifted from overt military hostilities to political negotiations, with many Touareg nobles who had allied with Ag Ghaly and Ansar Dine breaking away to form a succession of political groups, such as the hybrid Mouvement islamique de l'Azawad and the Haut Conseil pour l'unité de l'Azawad. The MNLA in turn renounced its declaration of independence.

Militant and trafficking networks in northern Mali have thus generated a variety of separatist, Islamist and hybrid organizations over the last two decades. As Sahel-watcher Wolfram Lacher concludes, 'The lines between groups are often blurry, alliances are temporary, and networks overlap.'[57] 'In the last year alone,' one Touareg subject interviewed for a 2014 study claimed, 'there are people who have changed from Malian military, to separatist rebel, to jihadist, to French ally, all while being narco-traffickers.'[58] Market and organizational structures changed in kaleidoscopic fashion as governmental entrepreneurs innovated, attempting to match the coercive capabilities to hand with persuasive governmentalities, responding dynamically to changes in the strategic environment.[59]

Yet while there was organizational fluidity to the market for government, there was also a certain stability in the market for drug transshipment. A recent empirical study concluded that 'the collapse of the Malian state and subsequent Islamist takeover … had a negligible impact on illicit trafficking in northern Mali'.[60] External shocks to the market for government might force rebranding and repositioning, but they did not disrupt the underlying logic of organized crime.[61]

The disruption of sovereignty

In both Mexico and the Sahel, violent governmental entrepreneurs are innovating strategically, using the resources and capabilities at hand to respond to changing local conditions and opportunities. Innovation is not, in and of itself, new—but this innovation is leading to new governmental arrangements, and appears now to be happening at a particularly rapid pace, as the barriers to entry into the market for government are lowered by structural changes in the global (and local) economy.

In both Mexico and the Sahel, violent governmental entrepreneurs are mixing and matching different sources of trust and governmentality well beyond statehood and citizenship: martial loyalty, kinship, clan membership and tribal affiliation, and religion. The complexity of this innovation makes clear that there is no substitute for careful analysis of the capabilities and strategies of each organization, and even for the different strategic approaches of different factions within such organizations. Broad labels such as 'mafia states' and 'criminal insurgency' risk discouraging such nuanced analysis, without actually telling us much about a particular group's strategic outlook or how it will 'conduct its conduct', to use Foucault's term.

Why is the dominance of sovereignty as a business model in the market for government being similarly disrupted in theatres so geographically and socially far apart? The episodes studied in Part Two and the Mexico and Sahel cases just considered point to two basic reasons, each with major theoretical and practical implications.

First, all these cases suggest that rival governmental providers emerge where there is an unmet or under-served demand for government. As we saw in the preceding chapter, this is likely to be the case when populations are rapidly integrated into new markets, or old governmental arrangements withdraw or collapse, or new, weak political or regulatory structures are suddenly introduced. But it may also occur where populations lose faith in existing governmental arrangements, and look for new governmental solutions, as we may be seeing in Mexico and the Sahel. The result in each case is the same: space in the market for non-state providers of government. That space may, if anything, grow in the years ahead, as states struggle with the structural and social transformations that will be wrought by unprecedented urbanization, youth bulges, resource scarcity and climate change-induced natural disasters. Trust and other forms of social capital may be scarce, particularly where societies have been damaged by shocks such as conflict or mass population movements. The space for alternative providers of government such as gangs, warlords and mafias may expand.[62]

Second, as suggested in Chapter 10, alternative providers of government seem likely to emerge only where the costs of organization (whether through corruption of existing governmental capabilities, development of new ones or integration of criminal and state capabilities) are lower than the resulting rents. The episodes in Part Two and the cases earlier in this chapter suggest that globalization has steadily transformed the geography that solves this equation by changing cost structures and reorganizing value chains. Today, even local armed groups have much easier, cheaper access to the strategic capabilities that are needed to organize crime and provide governmentality—coercion, corruption and communications—significantly lowering the barriers to entry into the market for government. As Ivan Briscoe puts it, 'Access to circuits of transnational organized crime can provide greatly increased earnings for armed groups and a major material advantage over rival factions or social groups.'[63] Globalization has specifically lowered costs in three areas: transportation, finance and communications.

The globalization of transportation gives groups controlling local resources, territory or officials the opportunity to tap into globalized value chains. In Cuba, the Bahamas and the Sahel, the result was access to new gambling and trafficking revenues that transformed local political economies. Cheaper transportation also means easier access to foreign weapons sources, lowering the cost of organizing coercion; Mexico and the Sahel show the disruptive results.

The globalization of finance simultaneously improves access to offshore safe havens and investment opportunities once rents are captured, disembedding rents and rulers from local markets. As we saw in The Bahamas, criminal groups can become important brokers of laundering services for a range of political and governmental actors looking to move their profits into the global financial cloud. The same pattern has played out in Mexico.[64] The result is a weakening of the link between local economic activity and political power, as political and military actors' interests become more closely aligned with foreign financiers and corporate interests (both licit and illicit), and less dependent on local communities and labour.

Finally, the globalization of communications cheaply connects local groups to a highly dispersed and fragmented market of potential consumers of new forms of governmentality. This allows remote association. Clandestine organizations such as terrorist groups have traditionally recruited through pre-existing social networks, using the social capital and trust within those networks to develop a governmentality which can induce young men and women to abandon their families and move around the world to participate in a cause, or even to suicide for the perceived benefit of strangers.[65] But increasingly global social media offer non-state actors the prospect of bypassing these intermediating social networks, just as the advent of film, radio and television allowed Dewey, Kefauver and other American politicians to bypass the municipal political machines, forming a direct relationship with political consumers. Following this strategic logic, Al Qaeda in the Arabian Peninsula, Islamic State and Mexican drug cartels have all developed sophisticated social media capabilities, connecting directly with consumers of the governmentality they are offering, regardless of their location.[66]

These changes in market conditions are producing an intensification of the interaction and convergence between 'crime' and 'politics', as they make criminal positioning strategies more cost-effective and viable. This suggests that we can expect organized criminal groups to remain a factor in politics and conflict. But perhaps even more significantly, it suggests that we are seeing a disruption of sovereign statehood as the dominant business model for government. Entrepreneurial providers are experimenting with both external positioning strategy and internal organization to generate new governmental forms. They are drawing on a range of other sources to construct the methodologies, norms and practical repertoires needed to govern the conduct of dispersed networks. Some adopt fraternity-based models, organized around the social networks of tribes, clans and social cliques.[67] Some adopt faith-based models, drawing on religious sources ranging from Salafi neo-jihadism to the warped evangelism of La Familia.[68] And some adopt business-like franchise models, from the Sicilian mafia to the Central American *maras*, as well as outlaw motorcycle clubs. Speaking about the expansion of the Islamic State brand to Libya, Algeria and Egypt, the Libyan ambassador to the UAE recently warned: 'The Islamists … have learned the franchizing model from McDonald's.

They give you the methodology, standards and propaganda material.'[69] They provide, in other words, a common governmentality, replete with a how-to manual for conducting your conduct: it is up to local entrepreneurs to adapt these strictures to local conditions. This they do, as we saw in the case of AQIM considered earlier in this chapter, through combination with local governmental capabilities and forms.

Still, the strength of the governmental bonds developed through such innovation remains to be seen. Social media allows organizations such as Islamic State to lure teenagers thousands of miles to join their cause, and aids the spread of gangster and mafia culture. But the costs of monitoring and discipline are inevitably high in a virtual network, and it may prove difficult to maintain strategic discipline across such large distances, as Al Qaeda leaders have found in dealing with their various franchises. Strategic discipline may be easier to maintain in a co-located social group, or amongst state citizens—which is one of the reasons Islamic State, with its territorial control in Syria and Iraq, may be finding more coherence than Al Qaeda did. Hybridization and local-ization of governmental forms may not always produce effective results. On the contrary, as AQIM learned in the Sahel, it may lead to transnational political organizations losing control of their constituent parts as they become captured by local interests. Understanding what drives an individual embedded within multiple governmental net-works—such as Woolsey's putative Russian government official, or an Iyad Ag Ghaly or an El Chayo—may depend on understanding the rela-tive strength of these different bonds, and how they interact.

Implications

War and strategy beyond the state

The startling conclusion that emerges from the evidence in this book is that not only states, but also some organized criminal groups, make war. Despite its unorthodoxy, this conclusion can be seen not as a radical departure, but a return to Clausewitzian roots. Clausewitz thought of war as the pursuit of *politik* by other means—that is, violence. But this *politik* was not solely state policy, but rather 'the interests of the com-munity'.[70] He contemplated war-making by a range of non-state communities, including the 'semi-barbarous Tartars, the republics of antiquity, the feudal lords and trading cities of the Middle Ages'.[71] A Clausewitzian take on organized crime thus requires recognizing that some criminal groups form communities that may pursue *politik*—and not just simply greed—through the strategic use of violence. These groups may not be co-located in a particular territory, nor aspire to formal recognition or even political authority; but the cases studied in this book suggest that their power within and over politics is no less real.

Treating organized criminal groups as potential war-makers suggests a need to rethink our treatment of these groups in both strategic and international relations theory. Criminologists have recognized that criminal groups in illicit markets operate like states in the international system (strategically, under anarchy).[72] But international relations theory treats the two realms as mutually exclusive, on the presumption that 'the criminal does not threaten the effective control of the state; in fact it relies on the state for providing the hierarchical [Westphalian] system in which to exist'.[73] This study seriously challenges that assumption. It shows criminal organizations wielding substantial power directly on the international level, invading states, seeking to effect regime change, transforming political economies and political settlements, even threatening to create new states. There is a need for international relations theorists to re-examine the influence of private criminal organizations as strategic players in the international system in their own right.[74]

Moreover, the study suggests a need to revisit the very notion of state 'sovereignty'. It suggests not just that sovereignty may be being 'softened',[75] but that it now co-exists with a variety of other powerful allegiances and 'social sovereignties'.[76] In this sense, the future of the market for government may in some ways resemble the pre-Westphalian period, with individual and group strategies shaped by multiple overlapping identities, obligations and incentive-structures. Still, we should be cautious of proclaiming the Westphalian era dead, and the arrival of a 'New Middle Ages'.[77] The effects of globalization are not to displace the state entirely, but to disrupt its existing business model, forcing it to compete, co-opt and collaborate with other providers of government, such as organized crime. The role of organized crime as a competitor for governmental power is not, as Part Two makes clear, entirely new; but globalization does, it appears, facilitate the use of criminal strategy by lowering some of the costs of entry into and survival in the market for government. In the future, effective strategy may depend on understanding the incentives not only of states, their leaders and citizens, but also of complex transnational networks, some of them deliberately hiding their power from view.[78] Competing with organized crime will be a central part of this task.

Combating criminal governmentality

If states are successfully to combat the convergence of organized crime and politics, they will need to heed the lessons from their own past experiences dealing with—and even collaborating with—organized crime. One crucially important practical insight that emerges from the episodes considered in this study is that the competition to govern is ultimately won and lost in the mind. It is a battle for social legitimacy.

In New York, Sicily, Cuba, The Bahamas, Mexico and the Sahel, the hidden power of organized crime derived from people's choices to regulate their own conduct according to the secret rules and rulings of a private criminal system rather than the public rule of law. The less effective state government appeared, the more overt popular support for criminal governmentality became. Defeating organized crime means changing the calculus of these individual choices of allegiance, so that people choose to be governed by the state, and not by criminal governmentality.

The case of Mali is instructive. One Touareg leader interviewed for a 2014 study stated simply:

> We have become a mafia culture... Everyone wants to be a part of it. Every youth in our society now wants to be part of the black economy... It makes development impossible.[79]

Expert observers such as Wolfram Lacher argue that political power in northern Mali grows out of 'alliance with local criminal networks', and that any effective 'approach to the conflict must include strategies to break these alliances'.[80] Yet at the time of writing, the international community lacks a clear strategy for 'breaking these alliances' beyond strengthening law enforcement and interdiction capabilities—whether in Mali or in similar contexts such as Afghanistan. How can such alliances be defeated when these criminal networks draw their own governmental power from the 'mafia culture' described above? As in occupied Sicily, foreign military actors dealing with traffickers in Mali have chosen to favour stabilization over transformation, eschewing efforts to confront or delegitimize mafia culture. 'Our priority is counterterrorism,' one French diplomat told researchers. 'When we stop a car, we are looking for weapons and explosives. Other than that, we let them go,' even if there are suspicions of involvement in trafficking.[81] Unsurprisingly, there are signs of the re-emergence of systematic corruption in Mali's politics, with several suspected drug traffickers elected to parliament.

The cases considered in this book also suggest, though, that where the state confronts organized crime solely through law enforcement and military means, short-term success rarely endures. Mori gaoled thousands, but the mafia returned to power. Dewey felled Luciano, only to be forced to release him ten years later. In the memorable phrase of mafia historian John Dickie, this is the common pattern of state strategy: 'sleep-walking into repression and then recoiling towards tolerance'.[82] Strategic criminal groups figure this out. Research shows that states' all-too-predictable strategic reversals send a signal of competitive weakness that criminal adversaries learn to exploit.[83] All they have to do is out-last state confrontation, and one form or another of accommodation is likely to return. Yet the heavy focus on law enforcement and repression in contemporary efforts to combat organized crime at the global level suggests that states have not yet understood the implications of these historical experiences.

What would a more effective state approach look like? The lesson of Part Two seems to be that organized crime is weakened and its impacts on society greatly constrained when society rejects criminal governmentality—the 'mafia culture' described by the Touareg leader above. Criminal governmentality is organized crime's 'centre of gravity', a term Clausewitz used to symbolize an actor's 'hub of power', the central element of its forces or capabilities that keeps them all together, the source of its internal 'political connectivity'.[84] A criminal group that is unable to maintain criminal governmentality is vulnerable to its members defecting, as Luciano, Giuliano and Batista all learned. A group that can extend its governmentality to new players can, in contrast, ride out even major political changes and state hostility, as the Sicilian mafia did after World War Two, and the Mob did in The Bahamas. This study suggests that more effective state policies for combating organized crime would need to focus much more on strategic communication and related methods to uncover, contain and delegitimize criminal governmentality. Five avenues in particular stand out as potentially promising for research and policy development.

First, states would invest significantly more in effective anti-corruption mechanisms within government institutions. Randomized control trials indicate that the credible threat of sanction created by effective anti-corruption monitoring systems is the most effective way to deter organized corruption in developing countries.[85] Anti-corruption monitoring serves both as an effective preventive measure against criminal governmentality, and to expose actual corruption, which, once uncovered, can then be targeted for investigation, prosecution, or broader social delegitimization.

Second, states would focus more on harnessing the power of broadcast (and today, social) media when delegitimizing criminal governmentality. Dewey's radio addresses were crucial to Luciano's fall. Cracks in the dam of *omertà* in the US began to appear with the televising of the hearings of the Kefauver Committee and later Valachi's testimony. Criminal groups understand this vulnerability. The Sicilian mafia's attacks on the press were designed to safeguard *omertà*, and today Mexican cartels have made independent journalists and social media activists a recurring target for attack.[86] Long-term investment in investigative journalism, the protection of journalists and free media may be crucial to resisting the hidden power of organized crime.[87] Yet this is, at present, almost entirely absent from state and intergovernmental frameworks to combat organized crime. On the contrary, the increasing insistence in some quarters on secrecy on the grounds of counter-terrorism and 'national security' could hardly be better designed to create a more fertile environment for the development of ties between state intelligence institutions and criminal networks.

Third, state and intergovernmental policies would also work through other, context-specific strategic communications channels to combat criminal governmentality. One source of potential models is North American anti-gang programming, which has found particular success through an epidemiological approach designed to disrupt the normalization of violence,[88] and 'focused deterrence' efforts designed to ensure that state agencies are better coordinated and thus send more consistent deterrence signals to specific criminal groups.[89] Such models will need to be adapted to other contexts, for example by working with local tribal leaders, religious authorities and civil society organizations to counter criminal narratives and promote an alternative, more positive vision of statehood and citizenship.

In some contexts, women may have a particularly important role to play by encouraging men to be governed not by violent, macho criminal culture but by more socialized, family-oriented values. Some counterterrorism efforts encourage potential offenders to marry precisely because marriage seems negatively to correlate to participation in violent extremism. There is also evidence that women can be influential in antigang and community violence reduction initiatives for similar reasons, changing individuals' perceptions of their strategic outlook from one of violence leading to glory or death, to one of long-term family development and social respectability.[90] Of course, women are also sometimes violent actors in their own right: we must be cautious that, in adopting a 'gender' lens, we do not reproduce the reductionist gender stereotypes that often characterize criminal governmentalities.

Fourth, in some cases, states may need to harness the organizational capabilities of groups involved in organized crime, in order to develop more effective delivery of governmental services under the state's own patronage.[91] Careful further research is needed to identify the conditions under which such collaboration with local groups involved in organized crime will lead to the state co-opting them, and when it will lead to the opposite—accommodation and corruption. In El Salvador, a recent attempt by the state, working with the Catholic Church, to co-opt the *maras* through a truce process may have backfired, enlarging those groups' political capital and strategic sophistication.[92] In contrast, in Haiti, the UN and NGOs found success working with local gangs to develop local rain harvesting, water distribution, sanitation, youth education, women's health and recreational services.[93] As Robert Muggah puts it, '[i]nstead of marginalizing gangs' these programmes brought them 'into an iterative process of negotiation, dialogue, and ultimately self-regulation'.[94] The process transformed these groups from being organized within a criminal system to being organized within the framework of civil society protected by the state. But the limited evidence and analysis relating to the incentive structures, amnesty conditions and reintegration programmes needed for such transformation programmes to be successful requires further expansion.[95] As Table 1 in Chapter 10 suggests, in some cases folding the governmental capabilities of armed groups into the state system may also require extending state authority, whether in regulatory terms (for example, by moving from prohibitionist to licensing regimes for criminalized goods and services) or in physical terms (for example, through improved urban design, as has been effective in Medellín in recent years).

Fifth, states might invest in improvements in the metric systems used to measure the risks posed by organized crime, and the impacts of different interventions on those risks. To date, because we have lacked a clear framework for analysing the strategic risks posed by organized crime, many efforts to develop such metric systems have substituted measurements of violence or criminal market activity for measurement of strategic risk. Similarly, they have substituted measurement of interventions' outputs (numbers of police trained, number of criminals arrested) for measurement of outcomes (reduced risk). The shortcomings of such approaches is increasingly recognized by some donors such as USAID and the UK Home Office, both of whom are investing in efforts to measure the impacts of counter-organized crime interventions. But unless such efforts develop a clear framework explaining how and when criminal activity will pose different types of risks to different actors (such as states, different state agencies, civilians or legitimate business) they may struggle to maintain the diverse support they need. The framework offered in this book may offer new ways to conceive the risks posed by organized crime, and the effectiveness of interventions designed to combat it. This becomes particularly clear when we consider how we can better manage the impacts of criminal strategy on efforts to resolve conflict, build peace and manage constitutional transitions—matters to which we now briefly turn.

Managing criminal spoilers in peace and transition processes

Many of the episodes studied in this book lend support to the hypothesis that armed conflict is criminogenic: it facilitates the organization of crime. War often creates a gap in the market for government, by weakening the governmental capabilities of the state and loosening the ties of state governmentality that bind citizens to the state. At the same time, war lowers the costs of developing the strategic capabilities—coercion, corruption, communications and command and control—needed to provide alternative sources of governmentality.

In Italy and the Sahel, wars made the means of coercion more readily available (on the battlefields of Sicily, and in the outflows of arms from Libyan arsenals to northern Mali). War trained young men in violence, and lowered the cognitive barriers to the use of violence to resolve disputes. It lowered the price of corruption and forced populations into black markets as a survival and coping strategy. And wars also tend to harden in-group/out-group identity, allowing violent entrepreneurs and organized criminals to cloak themselves in the mantle of community protection—as mafia-backed separatists did in Sicily, and trafficker-backed separatists have in northern Mali. This pattern has also played out in Bosnia and Iraq.[96]

War also seems, however, to weaken commitment to political solutions to conflict, even among organizations with strong political or ideological identities. As we saw in Chapter 2, political insurgencies have a tendency to devolve into criminal organizations over time, as financial incentives displace political goals.[97] This pattern may now be playing out in Afghanistan where, according to a—rather controversial—UN investigation published in February 2015, some elements of the Taliban leadership are 'increasingly acting more like "godfathers" than a "government in waiting"'. Taliban wartime involvement with illicit mining, the hostage market and opium trafficking has, the report claims, rewarded factions pursuing a criminal strategy at the expense of those with more ideological goals.[98]

For these reasons, organized crime is often cited as a major potential 'spoiler' of peace processes. The 'spoiler' concept was elaborated by Stephen Stedman to describe actors who use violence to oppose, undermine or manipulate peace processes and post-conflict transitions.[99] In Part Two, we saw criminal groups doing just that: the Sicilian mafia stoked violence and ultimately separatist insurgency in an attempt to turn the post-war transition to their own advantage (as, less successfully, did Salvatore Giuliano). We saw the American Mob both participating in armed conflict (during World War Two) and seeking to instigate conflict (in Cuba and Haiti). But we also saw criminal groups actively avoiding conflict (the Mob in The Bahamas), or working to bring it to an end (the Sicilian mafia, once they had secured Sicilian autonomy). Some criminal actors also worked to end violent conflict between criminal groups: hence the creation of a peace-mediation commission during the Castellammarese War, and the Mob Commission's forestalling Schultz's attack on Dewey to avoid a war with the New York authorities. Organized criminal groups may be opponents of peace, but they may also welcome peace if they think they can turn it to their advantage, as traffickers in northern Mali appear to have done in 2006–7 (see above).

As with all spoiler management, what this points to is a need to understand the worldview, interests, capabilities—and strategy—of specific actors. How does actual or potential access to criminal rents affect that worldview and those interests, those capabilities and that strategy? Answering that question requires moving beyond an assumption that organized criminal actors will necessarily seek to oppose or exploit peace or transition processes; they might, under certain conditions, equally see the process as working in their favour. This leads to two further questions, which both require analysis in specific cases: 1) under what conditions will the group in question act as an ally to, not a spoiler of, the peace process?, and 2) what arrangements are needed to ensure that the short-term participation in peace processes of actors with criminal strategies does not lead to the longer-term undermining of that process or of democratic development?

This book has not set out to answer those questions. But it does offer some glimpses into what appear to be potentially promising research avenues for those who would attempt to answer them. In particular, it suggests a need to look more closely at how armed actors perceive the illicit political economy around them and their ability to extract criminal rents, and governmental power, from it. Careful value-chain analysis and mapping of the illicit political economy may provide insights into a range of risks associated with different criminal positioning strategies.

First, it may provide insights into the dynamics of violence during conflict, including risks of harm to civilians. This might be directly applicable both to conflict assessment, mediation planning, and protection of civilians. Each criminal positioning strategy seems likely to be associated with a different calculus. As explored in Chapter 10 (see Table 1), mafias seem likely to emerge where the value of criminal rents is predicted to outstrip the costs of corrupting available governmental capabilities. For warlords and gangs, the equation is different: they are more likely to emerge where the value of criminal rents is perceived as outstripping the costs of keeping the state at bay, plus the costs of developing the limited new governmental capabilities required to extract the rents. And joint ventures are more likely to emerge where the costs of integrating capabilities (including developing new capabilities to exploit criminal rents) are seen as lower than the resulting rents. In each case, this requires a careful analysis of both the rents available from the local political economy, and the costs of corrupting, integrating or developing governmental capabilities.[100]

In the eastern part of the Democratic Republic of the Congo, for example, recent research found that whether an armed group chose to incur the costs associated with establishing autonomous rule over a village, or instead took on an intermediary brokering role (more like a mafia), depended on the village's position in gold and coltan value chains. It was, in other words, a function of how the armed group perceived the rents that could be extracted from each strategic approach, reflecting Olson's analysis that bandits' approach to government depends on their expectations of the length of their tenure and the rents that can be extracted during it.[101] This may have implications for being able to predict which locations are likely to be seen as valuable strategic assets for which criminal spoilers will violently compete. Risks of violence may be higher at bottlenecks in illicit transnational value chains, or *plazas*, since they are always highly valuable assets. Indeed, Cockburn argues that military dynamics in the Syrian war are significantly shaped by just such competition for the choke-points in cross-border illicit flows.[102] Similarly, in Afghanistan, there is evidence of increasingly violent competition between the Taliban, the Haqqani network and warlords for control of specific resource-extraction sites that are likely to become increasingly important sites of economic and strategic power as Western forces draw down.[103]

Mapping illicit political economies in this way may also potentially offer insights into Protection of Civilians ('PoC') risks: other recent research suggests that the ability to extract rents from transnational flows, without local production, may increase the likelihood of attacks on civilians because an armed group has less need of local social support.[104] (On the other hand, if these flows derive from foreign donations, attacks on local civilians may place them in jeopardy—a pattern that may be at play in Syria).[105] Predicting risks for civilians also requires, however, understanding how a specific group is likely to react to state (or international) confrontation: whether, as explored in Chapter 10, it will seek to form a defensive strategic alliance, turn to terrorism or seek to relocate. Recent work by Melissa Dell suggests that the risk of violence in Mexico goes up in areas adjacent to districts where criminal groups anticipate state confrontation, for example because a political party promising confrontation has just been elected to office.[106] As the costs of corrupting government change, so does the risk–return calculus, encouraging drug cartels to withdraw from the district in question and relocate to their neighbours' turf, mounting a hostile takeover bid. But such cost structures cannot tell us everything: as the evidence in Part Two made clear, criminal actors' strategic choices are also determinative. So conflict assessments will need to provide not only criminal rent maps, but also actor-level analysis of outlooks, goals and strategic approaches.

Second, mapping the illicit political economy (and conflict actors' approaches to it) may improve our ability to chart a viable path out of conflict to peace, and our ability to protect transitional processes against exploitation by greedy criminal spoilers. The question for mediators and others managing political and economic transitions is how to develop what Stedman calls a strategy of 'inducement' and de Waal calls the 'buy-in scenario'.[107] Some point out that disputes over divisible resources—such as economic goods—may actually be more amenable to effective conflict resolution than disputes over less divisible goals, such as the realization of certain political ideologies.[108] But others, notably Benjamin Lessing, point out that criminal war may operate according to a different calculus to that of civil war, especially relating to potential payoffs (no prospect of international legitimacy) and post-settlement risks (subversion may continue even after an end to violence is agreed).[109] A related danger, however, is that in 'inducing' groups with (hidden) criminal agendas into the peace process, we risk trading off short-term stability and peace for the longer-term subversion of the process or, even more disturbingly, subversion of democratic development. Instead of these armed groups' governmental capabilities being folded into the state system, actors with hidden criminal strategies can emerge as mafias clandestinely brokering between the state and criminal markets, as appears to have happened in Kosovo, Afghanistan[110] and Myanmar.[111] Political cliques may use their power over transitional processes to capture criminal rents and even grow them through the use of state policy, legislative, financing and regulatory institutions, as we saw in post-war Palermo.[112]

Encouragingly, the episodes studied here point to several specific areas of risk in transition processes, offering starting points for developing practical approaches to reducing the risk of criminal spoiling. The first is in mediation planning and the design of post-conflict political settlements. These are arguably better thought of as 'political-economy settlements', since, where the rules set by the state are contested (as is the case in the underworld, and during armed conflict), competitions over wealth and governmental power are frequently linked. Planning mediation and peace processes, and post-conflict political settlements, without conducting a careful mapping of illicit political economies is thus inherently foolhardy: it is like trying to settle an argument between two sides, without knowing the core interests of the parties, which they will not name. It cannot be a surprise, therefore, that many mediations, peace processes and demobilization and disarmament processes become sidetracked by hidden criminal agendas.[113] Improved mapping of illicit political economies will give mediators and other actors better insights into the stakes in play—and thus an improved chance of finding workable settlements.

One related point that emerges from the preceding analysis is that different factions within an armed group may require different inducement strategies, and have different buy-in costs. Mediators and peace operations may need to provide different conflict-exit pathways for different factions, for example with specialized DDR (disarmament, demobilization and reintegration) programming tailored to address the factions of armed groups with specialist organized crime capabilities. Recent analysis of the subversion of international development assistance to Colombia and Afghanistan likewise suggests that it can best be explained by understanding the role of corruption in local political economies, with a particular focus on how local actors use organized crime to develop political power. Organized crime, the authors conclude, 'is dynamic, driven by multiple and just rational motives, and endogenous to the local politics of power across the conflict to post-conflict continuum'.[114] All of this points to a need to understand the very localized and plural logic of organized criminal networks and markets in conflict-affected areas. 'Above all,' the authors argue, 'the political aspirations of organized crime actors in conflict, which are key to how they relate to the state and military power, ought to be fully integrated in conceptual frameworks.'[115]

This points to a need for different strategies for dealing with different groups. As has been evident in Northern Ireland, and may now be emerging amongst the Taliban, those insurgent factions responsible for smuggling, weapons procurement and financing may be even more reluctant than their fellow insurgents to lay down arms, and may pose a particular threat to transitional processes. Tailored combinations of confrontation and legitimate accommodation (for example through judicially regulated amnesty or suspended prosecution arrangements), and specialized reintegration strategies, may be necessary to encourage these groups to re-enter society and abandon not only conflict, but also organized crime. This has immediate relevance in, for example, the peace processes in Myanmar and Colombia.

A second specific area where we might strengthen our ability to manage criminal spoilers is in the conduct of post-conflict and transitional elections. Elections serve to restore the political legitimacy of the post-crisis state. But a rush to elections risks pushing politicians into the arms of actors with hidden criminal strategies, since they are often flush with cash and may also offer the organizational capabilities (including street coercion) needed for effective political campaigning. In turn, elections offer those groups a chance to leverage their capabilities to entrench themselves as post-transition mafias.[116]

So much was already clear in Sicily. Six weeks after the Allies landed, the Foreign Office sent Lord Rennell a questionnaire about the strategic outlook in southern Italy. One of the questions asked explicitly whether locals had the capacity 'to put democracy into practice'. Rennell replied, cannily, 'beware of Mafia'.[117] But the Allied Military

Government (AMG) did nothing to act on this insight. Today's post-conflict electoral assistance programming should not make the same mistakes, but instead ensure that appropriate campaign finance transparency, lustration and vetting mechanisms are in place to protect against elections being used to launder illicit economic power into ongoing political influence.

The mistakes of Sicily point to another specific area where an improved understanding of criminal strategy might strengthen transitional processes. The AMG oversaw a devolution of power to the local level that helped the mafia back into power. Something similar occurred in northern Mali in 2006–7. As we saw earlier, there is empirical evidence suggesting that the credible threat of oversight for corruption can deter systematic corruption. Yet the current 'governance' orthodoxy in post-conflict transitions is to localize governance, without localizing anti-corruption efforts. We should not be surprised if the results are similar to Sicily. But equally, the findings on corruption suggest a cost-effective solution: combining randomized anti-corruption oversight measures with allocation of resources to those areas that an illicit political economy mapping suggests are most likely to be targeted for corruption.

A fourth area that might benefit from improved illicit political economy mapping is law enforcement and accountability. Conducting law enforcement interventions without first mapping actors' criminal strategies and the illicit political economy risks playing into those actors' hands. Law enforcement efforts risk attacking groups that some local actors may see as legitimate sources of governmental services, fostering hostility to the state, as the UN has learned in Haiti and Kosovo. Rushed efforts to build local law enforcement risk unwittingly strengthening local criminal actors by passing materiel or skills on to them, by knocking out their rivals, or, worse, generating a violent chain reaction of criminal rivals seeking to exploit each other's vulnerability.[118] And ill-timed interventions may even drive actors willing to cooperate with the state back into the arms of opposing forces, as appears to have happened in Afghanistan.[119]

Fifth, and closely related, improved analysis of illicit political economies should strengthen the effectiveness of targeted financial and travel sanctions. Well-targeted sanctions can raise the costs and risks of crime—though, as Peter Andreas points out, sanctions-busting is not a new feature of warfare, having played a major role in shaping the course of both the American War of Independence and the American Civil War.[120] As his analysis and others show, sanctions can also create a rally-around-the-flag effect: there is some evidence that sanctions have actually encouraged targets to draw closer to criminal networks, including in Bosnia, Iraq and Afghanistan.[121] Improved understanding of illicit political economies might provide greater insight into where leverage exists within these relationships, and how to ensure that targeted sanctions are achieving their deterrent and disruptive aims.

Yet coercive responses—such as law enforcement and sanctions—ultimately serve to exclude potential spoilers from the transitional process rather than transforming them into allies. The problem, as Ivan Briscoe trenchantly notes regarding sanctions targeted at Mali and Iraq, is that 'selectively fighting crime merely so as to starve the armed radicals in the desert will do nothing to undermine the systemic base that allows illicit activity to reproduce'.[122] To address the opportunity structures that criminal strategies exploit, mediators and those managing transitional processes may need to turn to other sources of leverage to induce participation, such as the 'focused deterrence' and epidemiological approaches discussed in the previous section.

Finally, even if criminal spoilers are effectively managed in the short term, there is a real danger that this is achieved only by international actors inserting themselves in the place of the local state as the guarantor of the local political settlement. This risks engendering dependence, lest the departure of the UN or international 'strongman' generates, as Batista's departure from Cuba did, an explosion of criminal violence as rival factions seek to destroy each other and gain power. De Waal sees this as a recurring outcome in Africa, explaining that large external military interventions 'become the monopsonistic purchaser of loyalty and the Leviathan that enforces' internationally negotiated peace agreements.[123] Kilcullen makes a similar point with respect to the NATO presence in Afghanistan.[124] This raises difficult questions about how actors such as the UN can broker peace accords in such situations without creating an open-ended commitment to stay. Those questions require careful further reflection and study—not least, because in this tendency to become an informal political magnet standing behind, and potentially retarding, the development of effective state capabilities, international interventions risk producing structural outcomes that seem similar to those produced by strategic criminal groups. Only with a deeper understanding of how the market for government operates in a particular society can the international community hope to develop sound intervention strategies.

Envoi: the rise of criminal statecraft

The idea that states can protect peace processes from criminal spoilers, and perhaps even defeat organized crime by attacking criminal governmentality, rests on an assumption that consumers of government can tell the two products—statehood and organized crime—apart. Perhaps the most troubling insight from this study is that this may be becoming more difficult. If a former director of the CIA like Jim Woolsey cannot tell a state official from a crook, why should the average consumer of governmentality—the average citizen—be able to do so?

The problem is not just that organized crime groups have started to act like states. It is also that some states have started to act like organized crime. As we saw in Chapter 9, there is a similarity in methods between state subversion and criminal organizations' covert actions. And as we saw in Cuba in Chapter 8 and The Bahamas in Chapter 9, as early as the 1950s and 1960s there were signs of convergence between some states' economic strategies—harvesting rents from private transnational capital flows through wholesale deregulation of trade and especially financial markets—and the strategic logic of organized crime. If anything, this strategic convergence has arguably grown further since then, as the Washington Consensus has promoted a reduction of social service provision by the state and the liberalization of trade and financial markets.[125] The result has been a disembedding of global markets from social community, and a winding back of the role of the state in either directly providing public goods and services, or managing markets to ensure they do so.[126] All of this risks generating an unmet demand for government, creating space for alternative providers.

The bottom-up growth of organized crime may be into this space; but it is also matched by other governmental actors moving up and out from the state level, into an elite, private offshore arena in which capital and power circulate hidden in plain sight, and free of the demands of socially responsible government. The Mob's innovations in Havana and The Bahamas helped to connect the underworld, and their corrupt political partners, to a globalized financial system deliberately disconnected from the real economy, liberated from the shackles of income and corporation tax and the chains of the social contract.

At the same time, 'state capitalism' has emerged as a combination of statecraft with corporate strategy, with global markets treated as a site for extending the state's geopolitical interests.[127] State capitalism can serve powerful public purposes, for example by finding productive investment opportunities for public savings; but it can also mask criminal joint venture, with elites using sovereignty to maximize private wealth creation and downright theft. Casino resorts, such as in Cyprus and Macao, remain an important gateway between the two systems— state capitalism and disembedded global finance—with corrupt state capitalists first siphoning off national wealth and then moving it through casino-based money-laundering gateways into private offshore bank accounts.[128] Grand corruption at the state level, and organized crime, begin to become hard to tell apart. Here are Olson's 'stationary bandits', sustained through the support of a global infrastructure that puts their ill-gotten wealth beyond reach. The bandits can remain stationary, because their loot has become mobile.[129]

The resulting appearance of convergence between organized crime and statecraft has deeply damaged some consumers' faith in statehood as an effective model of government. Those doubts have been amplified by globalized financial shocks that have revealed individual and corporate players in this system as 'too big to fail' and 'too big to gaol', highlighting states' relative impotence to govern them, and the externalization of the costs of government onto the '99 per cent'.[130] In the developing world, populations watch as unprecedented economic growth leads not to prudent preparation for the transformations that climate change, urbanization and youth bulges will bring, but instead to growing inequality. And the geopolitical backdrop is important, too, to global public perceptions: one decade after calling for a rules-based 'New World Order', the global superpower flouts the global rules to invade Iraq without the support of the UN Security Council. Its allies around the world, many notional proponents of the global rule of law, quietly aid and abet its construction of a global gulag archipelago of terrorist interrogation black-sites.

All of this feeds a growing popular perception that responsible statehood is a façade and that those who follow the rules do not get ahead.[131] The perception of a Russian businessman in the 1990s risks becoming globalized:

> The truth is, everything you see around you, all our success, is not thanks to our wonderful economic laws. It's thanks to the fact that we do not obey them.[132]

Globalized social media promotes a culture of affluence that seems increasingly out of reach—if you play by the rules.[133] Organized crime offers a powerful alternative, and a way to fulfil dreams of consumption promoted by globalization, but unmet by states.[134] The result is what President Yeltsin described (in the quote at the very beginning of Chapter 1) as becoming a 'mafiya power', and what the Touareg leader described above as succumbing to 'mafia culture'. Customer loyalty to statehood as the preferred model of government is waning.

For states to defeat criminal governmentality, therefore, they must not only change perceptions of organized crime, but also arrest the slide in the perception of statehood—and consumers' growing inability to tell the two apart. They must address statehood's brand problem. The system of global governance built for the inter-state era must be re-engineered, to re-embed the globalized economy—and the globalized market for government—within a socially responsible framework.[135]

This means strengthening the notion of 'sovereignty as responsibility',[136] and moving away from the 'negative sovereignty' model towards a conditionalization of sovereignty through specification of positive norms of expected state conduct.[137] In weak and conflict-affected states, it means rebuilding the brand of the state through long-term 'recreation of the link between governance and service provision', as Reitano and Shaw describe it.[138] At the international level, it means being more forthright in using the United Nations Security Council and the UN Human Rights Council to name and shame those states complicit in organized crime, and to unmask joint ventures. The willingness of the Security Council in December 2014 to take up the question of the human rights situation in North Korea, intimately bound up with slavery, forced labour, trafficking and other organized criminal activities, is a positive sign, and builds on other positive steps such as the international prosecution of Charles Taylor for the crimes associated with the joint venture he oversaw in Liberia. The Security Council has also found innovative means, in recent years, to mandate corporate due diligence to remove conflict minerals from specific supply chains.

The United Nations is, however, more a trade association for states than an independent regulator of the market for government. Like other trade associations, its ability to act as a referee is limited by its membership, especially their control of its finances and enforcement capabilities—and their willingness to hold each other to account. Ultimately, if states want to promote responsible statehood as the preferred model of government it is up to them to hold each other accountable for their performance. Only by doing so will statehood be perceived as a more effective, credible and rewarding system of government than the other options that are increasingly becoming available in the market, from the Islamist caliphate model of Islamic State to the transnational gang model of the *maras*. If states—and society more broadly—do not hold each other responsible, the attractiveness of other forms of governmentality will continue to grow. And with it, the hidden power of organized crime.

NOTES

1. INTRODUCTION

1. Quoted in Stephen Handelman, *Comrade Criminal: The Theft of the Second Russian Revolution* (London: Michael Joseph, 1994), p. 25.
2. Quoted in Misha Glenny, *McMafia: A Journey through the Global Criminal Underworld* (London: The Bodley Head, 2008), pp. 110–11.
3. 'US embassy cables: Russia is virtual "mafia state", says Spanish investigator', *The Guardian* (UK), 2 December 2010.
4. Moisés Naím, 'Mafia States: Organized Crime Takes Office', *Foreign Affairs*, vol. 91, no. 3 (2012).
5. Misha Glenny, *McMafia*; Douglas Farah, *Transnational Organized Crime, Terrorism, and Criminalized States in Latin America: An Emerging Tier-One National Security Priority* (Carlisle PA: US Army War College, April 2012); Michael Miklaucic and Jacqueline Brewer, eds, *Convergence: Illicit Networks and National Security in the Age of Globalization* (Washington DC: National Defense University Press, 2013); John T. Picarelli, 'Osama bin Corleone? Vito the Jackal? Framing Threat Convergence through an Examination of Transnational Organized Crime and International Terrorism', *Terrorism & Political Violence*, vol. 24 (2012), pp. 180–98. See also Naím, 'Mafia States', pp. 100–11.
6. Sheena Chestnut, 'Illicit Activity and Proliferation: North Korean Smuggling Networks', *International Security*, vol. 32, no. 1 (Summer 2007), pp. 80–111.
7. Matthew Levitt, *Hezbollah: The Global Footprint of Lebanon's Party of God* (London: Hurst, 2013).
8. Katherine Lawson and Alex Vines, *Global Impacts of the Illegal Wildlife Trade: The Costs of Crime, Insecurity and Institutional Erosion* (London: Chatham House, February 2014).
9. See David M. Anderson, 'The New Piracy: The Local Context', *Survival*, vol. 52, no. 1 (February–March 2010), pp. 44–51.

10. Wolfram Lacher, 'Organized Crime and Conflict in the Sahel-Sahara Region' (Washington DC: Carnegie Endowment for International Peace, September 2012); Global Initiative Against Transnational Organized Crime, 'Illicit Trafficking and Instability in Mali: Past, Present and Future' (Geneva: GITOC, 2014); Mark Shaw and Fiona Mangan, *Illicit Trafficking and Libya's Transition: Profits and Losses*, Peaceworks No. 96 (Washington DC: US Institute of Peace, 2014).

11. UNODC, *Crime and its Impact on the Balkans* (Vienna: UNODC, March 2008).

12. World Bank, *Conflict, Security and Development: 2011 World Development Report* (Washington DC: World Bank, 2011); UN Security Council, Resolution 2195, 19 December 2014.

13. President Barack Obama, *Strategy to Combat Transnational Organized Crime: Addressing Converging Threats to National Security* (Washington DC: The White House, 19 July 2011).

14. Alan Block, *East Side, West Side: Organizing Crime in New York 1930–1950* (New Brunswick NJ: Transaction Publishers, 1983), p. 10; Mary McIntosh, 'New Directions in the Study of Criminal Organizations', in Herman Bianchi, Mario Simondi and Ian Taylor, eds, *Deviance and Control in Europe: Papers from the European Group for the Study of Deviance and Social Control* (London: Wiley, 1975), p. 147.

15. Obama, *Strategy*.

16. M.D. Southerland and G.W. Potter, 'Applying Organization Theory to Organized Crime', *J. Contemporary Criminal Justice*, vol. 9, no. 3 (1993), p. 251.

17. Hew Strachan, 'The Lost Meaning of Strategy', *Survival*, vol. 47, no. 3 (2005), pp. 33–54.

18. See Phil Williams, 'Transnational Criminal Organizations and International Security', *Survival*, vol. 36, no. 1 (1994), pp. 96–113; Mats Berdal and Mónica Serrano, 'Introduction', in Mats Berdal and Mónica Serrano, eds, *Transnational Organized Crime and International Security: Business as Usual?* (Boulder CO: Lynne Rienner, 2002), pp. 1–9.

19. Roy Godson and Phil Williams, 'Strengthening Cooperation against Transnational Crime: A New Security Imperative', in Phil Williams and Dimitri Vlassis, eds, *Combating Transnational Crime: Concepts, Activities and Responses* (London/Portland OR: Frank Cass, 1998), p. 324; Susan Strange, *The Retreat of the State: The Diffusion of Power in the World Economy* (New York: Cambridge University Press, 1996), p. 121.

20. Lawrence Freedman, *Deterrence* (Cambridge: Polity Press, 2004), pp. 83, 110–11.

21. Martin van Creveld, *The Rise and Decline of the State* (Cambridge: Cambridge University Press, 1999), p. 407.

22. Naím, 'Mafia States', p. 101.

23. Jason M. Breslow, 'The Staggering Death Toll of Mexico's Drug War', *Frontline*, 27 July 2015.

24. Carl von Clausewitz, *On War*, eds/trans. Michael Howard and Peter Paret (Princeton NJ: Princeton University Press, 1976, revd ed. 1984).

25. Roberto Saviano, *Gomorrah* (New York: Picador, 2007), p. 87.

26. Quoted in Roberto Scarpinato, 'Il Dio dei mafiosio', *Micromega*, vol. 1 (1998), p. 48. Author's translation.

27. On regulatory capture see Samuel P. Huntington, 'The Marasmus of the ICC: The Commission, the Railroads, and the Public Interest', *Yale Law Journal*, vol. 614 (1952), pp. 467–509; for extension of the concept to transition processes, see Joel S. Hellman and Daniel Kaufmann, 'Confronting the Challenge of State Capture in Transition Economies', *Finance & Development*, vol. 38, no. 3 (2001), pp. 31–5.

28. Roy Godson, 'The Political-Criminal Nexus and Global Security', in Roy Godson, ed., *Menace to Society: Political-criminal Collaboration around the World* (New Brunswick/London: Transaction Publishers, 2003), p. 4; Michael Kenney, 'Turning to the "Dark Side": Coordination, Exchange, and Learning in Criminal Networks', in Miles Kahler, ed., *Networked Politics: Agency, Power, and Governance* (Ithaca NY: Cornell University Press, 2009), p. 82.

29. Compare Lawrence Freedman, 'Terrorism as a Strategy', *Government & Opposition*, vol. 42 (2007), p. 315.

30. Antonio Giustozzi, 'The Debate on Warlordism: The Importance of Military Legitimacy', Crisis States Discussion Paper 13 (London: Crisis States Research Centre, October 2005), p. 7.

31. Giovanni Falcone, *Men of Honour: The Truth about the Mafia* (London: Warner Books, 1992), pp. 70, 100.

32. Robert Mandel, *Dark Logic: Transnational Criminal Tactics and Global Security* (Stanford CA: Stanford Security Studies, 2011), pp. 7–9.

33. Eric Hobsbawm, *Primitive Rebels* (Manchester: The University Press, 1959), pp. 9–10.

34. Jean-Louis Briquet, 'Organized crime, politics and the judiciary in post-war Italy', in Felia Allum and Renate Siebert, eds, *Organized Crime and the Challenge to Democracy* (Abingdon: Routledge, 2003), pp. 188–201.

35. Salvatore Lupo, *History of the Mafia*, trans. Antony Shugaar (New York: Columbia University Press, 2009), pp. 18–19.

36. John Dickie, *Mafia Republic* (London: Sceptre, 2013), p. 133.

37. Pino Arlacchi, *Addio Cosa Nostra: La Vita di Tommaso Buscetta* (Milan: Rizzoli, 1994), pp. 84–5; compare Hickman Powell, *Lucky Luciano: The Man Who Organized Crime in America* (New York: Barnes & Noble, 1939/2006), p. xxiv.

38. Cesare Mattina, 'The transformations of the contemporary mafia: a perspective review of the literature on mafia phenomena in the context of the internationalisation of the capitalist economy', *International Social Science Journal*, vol. 62, issue 203–4 (2011), pp. 241–2; and see Robert Lacey, *Little Man: Meyer Lansky and the Gangster Life* (Boston MA: Little Brown & Co., 1991), p. 312.

39. Freedman, *Deterrence*, p. 45.

40. See generally Thomas A. Firestone, 'Mafia Memoirs: What They Tell Us About Organized Crime', *J. Contemporary Criminal Justice*, vol. 9, no. 3 (August 1993), pp. 197–220.

41. Joseph Bonanno, *A Man of Honour* (London: Andre Deutsch, 1983); Nick Gentile, *Vita di capomafia* (Rome: Editori Riuniti, 1963).

42. Martin Gosch and Richard Hammer, *The Last Testament of Lucky Luciano* (London: Macmillan London Limited, 1975).

43. Lacey, *Little Man*; Dennis Eisenberg, Uri Dan and Eli Lanau, *Meyer Lansky: Mogul of the Mob* (New York: Paddington Press, 1979); Gary Cohen, 'The Lost Journals of Meyer Lansky', in *American Mafia*, January 2006, at http://www.americanmafia.com/Feature_Articles_331.html, accessed 14 March 2015.

44. J. Richard Davis, 'Things I Couldn't Tell till Now', *Collier's*: Part I, 22 July 1939, pp. 9–10, 38, 40–2; Part II, 29 July 1939, pp. 21, 37–8, 40; Part III, 5 August 1939, pp. 12–13, 43–4; Part IV, 12 August 1939, pp. 16–17, 29–30; Part V, 19 August 1939, pp. 12–13, 34–8; Part VI, 26 August 1939, pp. 18–19, 35, 38.

45. Peter Maas, *The Valachi Papers* (New York: Perennial, 1968/2003).

46. Supreme Court of New York, Appellate Division, First Judicial Department, *In the Matter of the Investigation of the Magistrates' Court, Final Report of Samuel Seabury, Referee*, New York, 28 March 1932.

47. President's Commission on Law Enforcement and the Administration of Justice, *Task Force Report: Organized Crime. Annotations and Consultants' Papers* (Washington DC: Government Printing Office, 1967); US Senate, Committee on Government Operations, Permanent Subcommittee on Investigations, *Organized Crime and Illicit Traffic in Narcotics* ('McClellan Hearings') (Washington DC: US Government Printing Office, 1964); US Senate, Special Committee to Investigate Organized Crime in Interstate Commerce ('Kefauver Committee'), *The Kefauver Committee Report on Organized Crime* (New York: Didier, 1951); Kefauver Committee, Hearings, 81st Congress, 1st Session (Washington DC: US Government Printing Office, 1951).

48. New York State Crime Commission, 'Interim Report of Evidence Adduced by the State Crime Commission Relating to Six Brooklyn Locals of the

International Longshoremen's Association: Confidential', September 1952, in CURBML.

49. US Senate, Select Committee on Improper Activities in the Labor or Management Field ('McClellan Committee 1958'), *Investigation of Improper Activities in the Labor or Management Field* (Washington DC: Government Printing Office, 1958).

50. President's Commission on the Assassination of President John F. Kennedy, *Report* ('*President's Commission Report*') (Washington DC: US Government Printing Office, 1964); US House of Representatives, Select Committee on Assassinations, *Final Assassination Plots Report*, 95th Congress, 2nd Session (Washington DC: Government Printing Office, 1979) (henceforth '*Final Assassination Plots Report*', referring to Vol. V unless otherwise stated); US House of Representatives, Select Committee on Assassinations, *Hearings*, 95th Congress, 2nd Session (Washington DC: Government Printing Office, 1979).

51. Thomas E. Dewey archive, University of Rochester Library, New York, Series 13, Boxes 11–17. This includes the transcripts of testimony by fifty-seven witnesses, running to 2,883 pages of evidence, and a 101-page analytical report. On earlier treatments of this material, see the beginning of Chapter 6 of this book.

52. FBI, 'Mafia Monograph', July 1958, in FBI Vault.

53. See Thomas Schelling, 'What is the Business of Organized Crime?', *J. Pub. Law*, vol. 20, no. 1 (1970), pp. 71–84; Jean Cartier-Bresson, 'État, Marchés, Réseaux et Organisations Criminelles Entrepreneuriales', paper presented at the Colloquium on 'Criminalité Organisée et Ordre dans la Societé', Aix-en-Provence, 5–7 June 1996 (Aix-en-Provence: Aix-Marseille University Press, 1997); Gianluca Fiorentini and Sam Peltzman, 'Introduction', in Fiorentini and Peltzman, eds, *The Economics of Organized Crime* (Cambridge: Cambridge University Press, 1995/1997), pp. 1–30; and R.T. Naylor, *Wages of Crime: Black Markets, Illegal Finance, and the Underworld Economy* (Ithaca NY/London: Cornell University Press, 2004, revd ed.), p. 15.

54. Phil Williams, 'Organizing Transnational Crime: Networks, Markets and Hierarchies', in Phil Williams and Dimitri Vlassis, eds, *Combating Transnational Crime: Concepts, Activities and Responses* (London/Portland OR: Frank Cass), p. 84; compare Raymond Aron, 'The Evolution of Modern Strategic Thought', *Adelphi Papers*, vol. 9, issue 4, Special Issue: Problems of Modern Strategy: Part I (1969), p. 7.

55. One of the few other major texts that takes such a long-term perspective is Peter Andreas' excellent *Smuggler Nation: How Illicit Trade Made America* (New York: Oxford University Press, 2013), which 're-narrates

the story of America and its engagement with the world as a series of highly contentious and consequential battles over illicit trade' (p. xi).

56. Compare Federico Varese, *Mafias on the Move: How Organized Crime Conquers New Territories* (Princeton NJ: Princeton University Press, 2011).

57. Alexander B. George and Andrew Bennett, *Case Studies and Theory Development in the Social Sciences* (Cambridge MA: MIT Press, 2005), p. 45.

2. THE STRATEGIC ORGANIZATION OF CRIME

1. Giovanni Falcone, *Men of Honour: The Truth about the Mafia* (London: Warner Books, 1992), p. 57.

2. Alan Wright, *Organised Crime* (Cullompton: Willan, 2005), p. 203.

3. Klaus von Lampe, 'The Interdisciplinary Dimensions of the Study of Organized Crime', *Trends in Organized Crime*, vol. 9, no. 3 (2006), pp. 77–95.

4. See e.g. Peter Andreas and Ethan Nadelmann, 'The Internationalization of Crime Control', in H.R. Friman, ed., *Crime and the Global Political Economy* (Boulder CO: Lynne Rienner, 2009), pp. 21–33.

5. President's Commission, *Task Force Report: Organized Crime*; Donald Cressey, *Theft of the Nation: The Structure and Operations of Organized Crime in America* (New York: Harper and Row, 1969).

6. See Phil Williams and Roy Godson, 'Anticipating Organized and Transnational Crime', *Crime, Law & Social Change*, vol. 37 (2002), pp. 335–9.

7. Lawrence Freedman, 'Strategic Studies and the Problem of Power', in Lawrence Freedman, Paul Hayes and Robert O'Neill, eds, *War, Strategy, and International Politics: Essays in Honour of Sir Michael Howard* (Oxford: Clarendon Press, 1992), p. 294.

8. Lawrence Freedman, 'Terrorism as a Strategy', *Government & Opposition*, vol. 42 (2007), p. 318.

9. Colin Gray, *Another Bloody Century: Future Warfare* (London: Phoenix Press, 2005), p. 37.

10. Colin Gray, 'What is War? A View from Strategic Studies', in Colin Gray, *Strategy and History: Essays on Theory and Practice* (New York: Routledge, 2006), p. 185.

11. Mats Berdal and Mónica Serrano, 'Introduction', in Mats Berdal and Mónica Serrano, eds, *Transnational Organized Crime and International Security: Business as Usual?* (Boulder CO: Lynne Rienner, 2002), p. 7.

12. David Shirk and Joel Wallman, 'Understanding Mexico's Drug Violence', introducing a Special Issue on the topic, *Journal of Conflict Resolution*, vol. 59, no. 8 (December 2015), p. 1369; and see Stathis N. Kalyvas, 'How Civil Wars Help Explain Organized Crime—and How They Do

Not', *Journal of Conflict Resolution*, vol. 59, no. 8 (December 2015), pp. 1517–40.

13. Robert J. Kelly, 'An American Way of Crime and Corruption', in Roy Godson, ed., *Menace to Society: Political-criminal Collaboration around the World* (New Brunswick/London: Transaction Publishers, 2003), p. 99.

14. Alan Block, *East Side, West Side: Organizing Crime in New York 1930–1950* (New Brunswick NJ: Transaction Publishers, 1983); Steven Solnick, *Stealing the State. Control and Collapse in Soviet Institutions* (Cambridge MA: Harvard University Press, 1999); Stephen Handelman, *Comrade Criminal: The Theft of the Second Russian Revolution* (London: Michael Joseph, 1994); Michela Wrong, *It's Our Turn to Eat: The Story of a Kenyan Whistle-blower* (London: Fourth Estate, 2009).

15. Peter Andreas, *Smuggler Nation*, p. xi.

16. Roy Godson, 'The Political-Criminal Nexus and Global Security', in Roy Godson, ed., *Menace to Society*. The role of the CIA was explored by Alfred McCoy in his seminal *The Politics of Heroin in Southeast Asia* (New York: Harper Colophon Books, 1973).

17. Jean-François Bayart, Stephen Ellis and Béatrice Hibou, *The Criminalization of the State in Africa* (Bloomington IN: Indiana University Press, 1999); William Reno, *Warlord Politics and African States* (Boulder CO/London: Lynne Rienner, 1998); Enrique Desmond Arias, 'Understanding Criminal Networks, Political Order, and Politics in Latin America', in Anne L. Clunan and Harold A. Trinkunas, *Ungoverned Spaces: Alternatives to State Authority in an Era of Softened Sovereignty* (Stanford CA: Stanford Security Studies), pp. 115–35; Enrique Desmond Arias, *Criminal Politics: Illicit Activities and Governance in Latin American and the Caribbean*, forthcoming.

18. Tuesday Reitano and Mark Shaw, *Fixing a Fractured State? Breaking the Cycles of Crime, Conflict and Corruption in Mali and Sahel* (Geneva: Global Initiative against Transnational Organized Crime, April 2015).

19. Ivan Briscoe and Pamela Kalkman, 'The new criminal powers: the spread of illicit links to politics across the world and how it can be tackled', CRU Report, Clingendael Netherlands Institute of International Relations, The Hague, January 2016.

20. See Eric Wilson, ed., *Government of the Shadows: Parapolitics and Criminal Sovereignty* (London/New York: Pluto Press, 2009).

21. Robert Cribb, 'Introduction: Parapolitics, Shadow Governance and Criminal Sovereignty', in Wilson, *Government of the Shadows*, p. 3.

22. Robert Mandel, *Dark Logic: Transnational Criminal Tactics and Global Security* (Stanford CA: Stanford Security Studies, 2011).

23. Alfredo Schulte-Bockholt, *The Politics of Organized Crime and the Organized Crime of Politics* (Lanham MD/Oxford: Lexington Books, 2006), p. 22.

See also R.T. Naylor, 'The Insurgent Economy: Black Market Operations of Guerrilla Organizations', *Crime, Law & Social Change*, vol. 20 (1993), pp. 20–2.

24. Paul Collier, 'Economic Causes of Civil Conflict and Their Implications for Policy' (Washington DC: World Bank, 2000); Paul Collier, 'Rebellion as a Quasi-Criminal Activity', *Journal of Conflict Resolution*, vol. 44, no. 6 (December 2000), pp. 839–53.

25. See Karen Ballentine and Jake Sherman, eds, *The Political Economy of Armed Conflict: Beyond Greed and Grievance* (Boulder CO: Lynne Rienner, 2003).

26. David Keen, *The Economic Functions of Violence in Civil Wars* (Oxford: OUP, 1998), p. 11.

27. R.T. Naylor, 'The Insurgent Economy', pp. 13–51.

28. Steven Metz, *The Future of Insurgencies* (Carlisle PA: US Army War College, 1993); Steven Metz, *Rethinking Insurgency* (Carlisle PA: Strategic Studies Institute, 2007).

29. Phil Williams, 'Insurgencies and Organized Crime', in Phil Williams and Vanda Felbab-Brown, *Drug Trafficking, Violence, and Instability* (Carlisle PA: Strategic Studies Institute, 2012), pp. 27–72; Phil Williams and John T. Picarelli, 'Combating Organized Crime in Armed Conflict', in Karen Ballentine and Heiko Nitzschke, eds, *Profiting from Peace: Managing the Resource Dimensions of Civil War* (Boulder CO: Lynne Rienner, 2005), pp. 125–6.

30. Nils Gilman, Jesse Goldhammer and Steven Weber, 'Deviant Globalization', in Michael Miklaucic and Jacqueline Brewer, eds, *Convergence: Illicit Networks and National Security in the Age of Globalization* (Washington DC: National Defense University Press, 2013), p. 9.

31. Adam Elkus, 'Mexican Cartels: A Strategic Approach', *Infinity Journal*, IJ Exclusive, 28 June 2011; John P. Sullivan and Adam Elkus, 'Strategy and insurgency: an evolution in thinking?', 16 August 2010, at http://www.opendemocracy.net/john-p-sullivan-adam-elkus/strategy-and-insurgency-evolution-in-thinking, accessed 14 March 2015.

32. Rupert Smith, *The Utility of Force: The Art of War in the Modern World* (London: Allen Lane, 2005), pp. 328–30.

33. See Robert J. Bunker, 'The Mexican Cartel Debate: As Viewed Through Five Divergent Fields of Security Studies', *Small Wars Journal*, 11 February 2011; and John P. Sullivan and Robert J. Bunker, 'Rethinking insurgency: criminality, spirituality, and societal warfare in the Americas', *Small Wars & Insurgencies*, vol. 22, no. 5 (2011).

34. Mary Kaldor, *New and Old Wars. Organized Violence in a Global Era* (Stanford CA: Stanford University Press, 1999), esp. pp. 90–111; Mark Duffield, *Global Governance and the New Wars: The Merging of Development and Security* (London: Zed Books, 2001).

35. See especially Vanda Felbab-Brown, *Shooting Up: Counterinsurgency and the War on Drugs* (Washington DC: Brookings Institution Press, 2009); Vanda Felbab-Brown, 'Human Security and Crime in Latin America: The Political Capital and Political Impact of Criminal Groups and Belligerents Involved in Illicit Economies', Florida International Univeristy, Applied Research Center, September 2011; Vanda Felbab-Brown, *Aspiration and Ambivalence: Strategies and Realities of Counterinsurgency and Statebuilding in Afghanistan* (Washington DC: Brookings Institution, 2012); Vanda Felbab-Brown, 'Fighting the Nexus of Organized Crime and Violent Conflict while Enhancing Human Security', in *Drug Trafficking, Violence, and Instability* (Carlisle PA: Strategic Studies Institute, US Army War College, 2012; and Vanda Felbab-Brown, 'Crime, Low-Intensity Conflict and the Future of War in the Twenty-First Century', in Ingo Trauschweizer and Steven M. Miner, *Failed States and Fragile Societies: A New World Disorder?* (Athens OH: Ohio University Press, May 2014), pp. 89–118.

36. Michael Miklaucic and Moisés Naím, 'The Criminal State', in Miklaucic and Brewer, *Convergence*, p. 149.

37. Notable critiques include the essays in Anne L. Clunan and Harold A. Trinkunas, eds, *Ungoverned Spaces: Alternatives to State Authority in an Era of Softened Sovereignty* (Stanford CA: Stanford Security Studies, 2010); Andreas, *Smuggler Nation*, especially pp. 330–52; and the work of Vanda Felbab-Brown.

38. Douglas Farah, *Transnational Organized Crime, Terrorism, and Criminalized States in Latin America: An Emerging Tier-One National Security Priority* (Carlisle PA: US Army War College, April 2012), p. 6.

39. Robert J. Bunker, 'Criminal (Cartel & Gang) Insurgencies in Mexico and the Americas: What you need to know, not what you want to hear', Testimony before the US House of Representatives, House Committee on Foreign Affairs, Subcommittee on the Western Hemisphere, 13 September 2011, at http://archives.republicans.foreignaffairs.house.gov/112/bun091311.pdf, accessed 14 March 2015.

40. For the provenance of the term 'strategic logic', see Robert A. Pape, *Dying to Win: The Strategic Logic of Suicide Terrorism* (New York: Random House, 2006). On the denial of criminal actors being strategic: see Carlo Morselli, Mathilde Turcotte and Valentina Tenti, 'The Mobility of Criminal Groups', Report No. 004, 2010, Public Safety Canada, Ottawa, 2010, p. 6.

41. D. C. Smith, Jr., 'Illicit Enterprise: An Organized Crime Paradigm for the Nineties', in R. J. Kelly, K.-L. Chin and R. Schatzberg, eds, *Handbook of Organized Crime in the United States* (Westport CT: Greenwood Press, 1994), pp. 121–50; M.D. Southerland and G.W. Potter, 'Applying

Organization Theory to Organized Crime', *J. Contemporary Criminal Justice*, vol. 9, no. 3 (1993).

42. Peter Reuter, *Disorganized Crime: The Economics of the Visible Hand* (Cambridge MA: MIT Press, 1983); Thomas Schelling, 'Economic Analysis and Organized Crime', in President's Commission, *Task Force Report: Organized Crime*, pp. 114–26; and Thomas Schelling, 'Economics and the Criminal Enterprise', *Public Interest*, vol. 7 (1967), pp. 61–78.

43. See especially Williams and Godson, 'Anticipating'.

44. Henner Hess, 'The Sicilian Mafia: Parastate and Adventure Capitalism', in Wilson, *Government of the Shadows*, p. 164; Letizia Paoli, 'The paradoxes of organized crime', *Crime, Law & Social Change*, vol. 37 (2002), pp. 64–6.

45. Thomas Schelling, 'What is the Business of Organized Crime?', *J. Pub. Law*, vol. 20, no. 1 (1970); Thomas Schelling, *Choice and Consequence: Perspectives of an Errant Economist* (Cambridge MA: Harvard University Press, 1984), pp. 158–78; Diego Gambetta, *The Sicilian Mafia: The Business of Private Protection* (Cambridge MA: Harvard University Press, 1993).

46. Gambetta, *The Sicilian Mafia*.

47. Federico Varese, *The Russian Mafia: Private Protection in a New Market Economy* (Oxford: Oxford University Press, 2001).

48. Stergios Skaperdas, 'The political economy of organized crime: providing protection when the state does not', *Economics of Governance*, vol. 2 (2001), p. 174.

49. Charles Tilly, 'War Making and State Making as Organized Crime', in Peter Evans, ed., *Bringing the State Back In* (Cambridge: Cambridge University Press, 1985), pp. 169–91.

50. Cressey, *Theft*, p. 110.

51. Annelise Anderson, *The Business of Organized Crime: A Cosa Nostra Family* (Stanford CA: The Hoover Institution, 1979).

52. August Bequai, *Organized Crime: The Fifth Estate* (Lexington MD: D.C. Heat & Co., 1979), p. xi; M. S. Jankowski, *Islands in the Streets: Gangs and American Urban Society* (Berkeley CA: University of California Press, 1991), p. 89.

53. Stergios Skaperdas and Constantinos Syropoulos, 'Gangs as Primitive States', in Gianluca Fiorentini and Sam Peltzman, eds, *The Economics of Organized Crime* (Cambridge: Cambridge University Press, 1995/1997), pp. 61–82.

54. Herschel I. Grossman, 'Rival kleptocrats: the mafia versus the state', in Fiorentini and Peltzman, *The Economics of Organized Crime*, pp. 143–56.

55. Tuesday Reitano and Mark Shaw, *Fixing a Fractured State*.

56. Eric Hobsbawm, *Primitive Rebels* (Manchester: The University Press, 1959).

57. Roberto Saviano, *Gomorrah* (New York: Picador, 2007), p. 202.

58. Herman Schwartz, 'Immigrants and Organized Crime', in Friman, *Crime and the Global Political Economy*, p. 121.

59. For an interesting discussion of how this may impact criminal groups' tactical use of violence, see Benjamin Lessing, 'Logics of Violence in Criminal War', *Journal of Conflict Resolution*, vol. 59, no. 8 (December 2015), pp. 1486–516.

60. Andreas, *Smuggler Nation*, p. 2.

61. Michael Oakeshott, 'Political Education', in *'Rationalism in Politics' and Other Essays* (London: Methuen, 1962), p. 112.

62. Max Weber, *Economy and Society* (Berkeley and Los Angeles CA: University of California Press, 1922/1978), pp. 54–5. Compare Rocco Sciarrone, 'Réseaux mafieux et capital social', *Politix*, vol. 13, no. 49 (2000), pp. 38–9.

63. James J. Mittelman and Robert Johnston, 'The Globalization of Organized Crime, the Courtesan State, and the Corruption of Civil Society', *Global Governance*, vol. 5 (1999), p. 114.

64. R.T. Naylor, *Wages of Crime: Black Markets, Illegal Finance, and the Underworld Economy* (Ithaca NY/London: Cornell University Press, 2004, revd ed.), p. 32.

65. Phil Williams, 'Transnational Criminal Organizations: Strategic Alliances', *Washington Quarterly*, vol. 18 (1995), pp. 57–72; Phil Williams, 'Cooperation among Criminal Organizations', in Mats Berdal and Mónica Serrano, eds., *Transnational Organized Crime and International Security: Business as Usual?* (Boulder CO: Lynne Rienner, 2002), pp. 67–80.

66. Compare Thomas Ferguson, *Golden Rule: The Investment Theory of Party Competition and the Logic of Money-Driven Political Systems* (Chicago IL: University of Chicago Press, 1995).

67. Roberto Scarpinato, 'Mafia e politica', in *Mafia: Anatomia di un regime* (Rome: Librerie associate, 1992), p. 94.

68. Reitano and Shaw, *Fixing a Fractured State?*, p. 43.

69. Michel Foucault, 'Governmentality', in Graham Burchell, Colin Gordon and Peter Miller, eds, *The Foucault Effect: Studies in Governmentality* (Chicago IL: University of Chicago Press, 1991), pp. 87–104.

70. Michel Foucault, *Security, Territory, Population. Lectures at the Collège de France* (Paris/London: Éditions du Seuil/Gallimard, trans. Palgrave, 2004/2007).

71. Foucault, 'Governmentality'.

72. Michel Foucault, 'The Subject and Power', in Hubert L. Dreyfus and Paul Rabinow, eds, *Michel Foucault: Beyond Structuralism and Hermeneutics* (Chicago IL: University of Chicago Press, 2nd ed., 1982), p. 221.

73. Freedman, 'Strategic Studies and the Problem of Power', p. 294.

74. Michel Foucault, *The Birth of Biopolitics: Lectures at the Collège de France (1978–9)*, trans. Graham Burchell (New York: Palgrave Macmillan, 2010), p. 48.

75. Enrico Deaglio, 'Se vince lui, ma forse no', interview with Andrea Camilleri, in *Diario*, March 2001, at http://www.vigata.org/rassegna_stampa/2001/Archivio/Int09_Cam_mar2001_Diario.html, accessed 14 March 2015.

76. The term 'throffer' was introduced in Hillel Steiner, 'Individual liberty', *Proceedings of the Aristotelian Society*, vol. 75 (1974–75), pp. 33–50.

77. Jean Cartier-Bresson, 'État, Marchés, Réseaux et Organisations Criminelles Entrepreneuriales', paper presented at the Colloquium on 'Criminalité Organisée et Ordre dans la Societé', Aix-en-Provence, 5–7 June 1996 (Aix-en-Provence: Aix-Marseille University Press, 1997).

78. Southerland and Potter, 'Applying Organization Theory', pp. 262–3.

79. Diego Gambetta and Peter Reuter, 'Conspiracy among the many: the mafia in legitimate industries', in Fiorentini and Peltzman, *The Economics of Organized Crime*, pp. 116–36.

80. President's Commission, *Task Force Report: Organized Crime*, p. 6.

81. National Advisory Committee on Criminal Justice Standards and Goals, *Organized Crime: Report of the Task Force on Organized Crime* (Washington DC: US GPO, 1976), p. 29.

82. Letizia Paoli, 'The political-criminal nexus in Italy', *Trends in Org. Crime*, vol. 5, no. 2 (1999), p. 15.

83. Sciarrone, 'Réseaux mafieux', p. 39; Felia Allum and Renate Siebert, 'Conclusion: organized crime and democracy. "Uncivil" or "civil society"?', in Felia Allum and Renate Siebert, eds, *Organized Crime and the Challenge to Democracy* (Abingdon: Routledge, 2003), p. 223.

84. Viridiana Rios, 'Why did Mexico become so violent? A self-reinforcing violent equilibrium caused by competition and enforcement', *Trends in Organized Crime*, vol. 16 (2013), pp. 138–55.

85. Block, *East Side*, p. 239.

86. Elkus, 'Mexican Cartels'.

87. Saviano, *Gomorrah*, p. 114.

88. Freedman, *Strategic Coercion*, p. 15 (footnote omitted).

89. Jeremy Weinstein, *Inside Rebellion: The Politics of Insurgent Violence* (Cambridge: Cambridge University Press, 2006); Francisco Gutiérrez Sanín and Antonio Giustozzi, 'Networks and Armies: Structuring Rebellion in Colombia and Afghanistan', *Studies in Conflict & Terrorism*, vol. 33 (2010), pp. 836–53.

90. Schelling, *Choice and Consequence*, pp. 198–9.

91. See for example Hans M. Enzensberger, *Civil Wars: From L.A. to Bosnia* (New York: The New Press, 1994), p. 103—describing civil wars as frequently being 'about nothing at all'.

92. See Phil Williams, 'The Terrorism Debate over Mexican Drug Trafficking Violence', *Terrorism & Political Violence*, vol. 24, no. 2 (2012), pp. 259–78.

93. Charles Ransford, Candice Kane and Gary Slutkin, 'Cure Violence: A disease control approach to reduce violence and change behavior', in Eve Waltermaurer and Timothy Akers, eds, *Epidemiological Criminology: Theory to Practice* (Abingdon: Routledge, 2012), pp. 232–42.

94. Elkus, 'Mexican Cartels'.

95. Peter Andreas and Joel Wallman, 'Illicit markets and violence: what is the relationship?', *Crime, Law & Social Change*, vol. 52 (2009), p. 227; and see H.R. Friman, 'Drug markets and the selective use of violence', *Crime, Law & Social Change*, vol. 52 (2009), pp. 285–95.

96. Compare A.K. Cohen, 'The Concept of Criminal Organization', *British Journal of Criminology*, vol. 17, no. 2 (1977), pp. 97–111; see also Paoli, 'The paradoxes'.

97. Schelling, 'Economics and the Criminal Enterprise'; Smith, 'Illicit Enterprise'; Pino Arlacchi, *Mafia Business: The Mafia Ethic and the Spirit of Capitalism* (Oxford: Oxford University Press, 1983/1988).

98. See for example Hans-Jürgen Kerner and John A. Mack, *The Crime Industry* (Lexington KY: Lexington Books, 1975); and see Gambetta; and Varese, *The Russian Mafia*.

99. See e.g. Reuter, *Disorganized Crime*; Paoli, 'The paradoxes', p. 52; R.T. Naylor, 'Violence and illegal economic activity: a deconstruction', *Crime Law & Social Change*, vol. 52 (2009), pp. 231–42.

100. See Henner Hess, 'The Sicilian Mafia'; and Henner Hess, *Mafia and Mafiosi: The Structure of Power* (Westmead: Saxon House, 1973).

101. Anton Blok, *The Mafia of a Sicilian Village, 1860–1960: A Study of Violent Peasant Entrepreneurs* (Cambridge: Waveland Press, 1974).

102. Anton Blok, 'Reflections on the Sicilian Mafia: Peripheries and Their Impact on Centres', in Dina Siegel and Hans Nelen, eds, *Organized Crime: Culture, Markets and Policies* (New York: Springer, 2008), p. 9.

103. See e.g. Michael Kenney, 'The Architecture of Drug Trafficking: Network Forms of Organization in the Colombian Cocaine Trade', *Global Crime*, vol. 8 (2007), pp. 233–59; and Jörg Raab and H.B. Milward, 'Dark Networks as Problems', *Journal of Public Administration Research & Theory*, vol. 13, no. 4 (2003), pp. 413–39.

104. Phil Williams, 'Transnational Criminal Networks', in J. Arquilla and D. Ronfeldt, eds, *Networks and Netwars: The Future of Terror, Crime and Militancy* (Santa Monica CA: Rand Corporation), pp. 64–5.

105. Scott Helfstein, 'Governance of Terror: New Institutionalism and the Evolution of Terror Organizations', *Public Administration Review*, vol. 69, no. 4 (July/August 2009), p. 727.

106. Von Lampe, 'Interdisciplinary Dimensions', p. 82.

107. Michael C. Jensen, 'Organization Theory and Methodology', *The Accounting Review*, vol. 58, no. 2 (April 1983), pp. 319–39.

108. Sciarrone, 'Réseaux mafieux'.
109. Southerland and Potter, 'Applying Organization Theory', pp. 263–4.
110. Carlo Morselli, *Contacts, Opportunities and Criminal Enterprise* (Ontario: University of Toronto Press, 2005). See also Klaus von Lampe, 'Criminally Exploitable Ties: A Network Approach to Organized Crime', in Emilio C. Viano, José Magallenes and Laurent Bridel, eds, *Transnational Organized Crime: Myth, Power, Profit* (Durham NC: Carolina Academic Press, 2003), pp. 9–22.
111. Andrew V. Papachristos and Christopher Wildeman, 'Network Exposure and Homicide Victimization in an African American Community', *American Journal of Public Health*, vol. 104, no. 1 (January 2014), pp. 143–50.
112. See Henry Mintzberg and James A. Waters, 'Of Strategies, Deliberate and Emergent', *Strategic Management Journal*, vol. 6, no. 3 (July–September 1985), pp. 257–72. For application in the criminal context see Phil Williams, 'Transnational Criminal Networks', in J. Arquilla and D. Ronfeldt, eds, *Networks and Netwars: The Future of Terror, Crime and Militancy* (Santa Monica CA: Rand Corporation, 2001), p. 69.
113. Sciarrone, 'Réseaux mafieux', p. 43.
114. Eric Hobsbawm, *Bandits*, 2nd ed. (New York: Pantheon Books, 1981), p. 17.
115. Mancur Olson, 'Dictatorship, Democracy and Development', *American Political Science Review*, vol. 87, no. 3 (1993), pp. 567–76.
116. Hobsbawm, *Primitive Rebels*, pp. 4, 15; Hobsbawm, *Bandits*, pp. 31–6, 42.
117. Hobsbawn, *Primitive Rebels*, p. 5.
118. Guy Fricano, 'Social Banditry and the Public Persona of Joaquín "El Chapo" Guzmán', *Small Wars Journal*, 29 April 2013.
119. Hobsbawn, *Primitive Rebels*, p. 13.
120. Hobsbawm, *Bandits*, pp. 18, 22, 23.
121. Ibid., pp. 24–5.
122. Ibid., p. 160.
123. Notably Mandel, *Dark Logic*.
124. Southerland and Potter, 'Applying Organization Theory', pp. 258–9.
125. See Werner Vahlenkamp and Peter Hauer, *Organized Crime, Criminal Logistics and Preventive Approaches: Practice-oriented Summary and Evaluation of an Investigative Criminological Study* (Wiesbaden: Bundeskriminalamt, 1996).
126. George Stalk, Philip Evans and L.E. Shulman, 'Competing on Capabilities: The New Rules of Corporate Strategy', *Harvard Business Review*, vol. 70, no. 2 (1992), pp. 57–69.
127. Freedman, 'Strategic Coercion', p. 15.

128. Letizia Paoli, 'Criminal Fraternities or Criminal Enterprises?', in Phil Williams and Dimitri Vlassis, eds, *Combating Transnational Crime: Concepts, Activities and Responses* (London/Portland OR: Frank Cass), p. 90.

129. Elkus, 'Mexican Cartels'; Rios, 'Why did Mexico'.

130. Hess, *Mafia and Mafiosi*, p. 147.

131. Falcone, *Men of Honour*, pp. 13, 19.

132. Tilly, 'War Making'; Gambetta, *The Sicilian Mafia*.

133. Skaperdas, 'The political economy', pp. 186–7; and see Kai A. Konrad and Stergios Skaperdas, 'The Market for Protection and the Origin of the State', CESinfo Working Paper Series No. 1578 (Munich: CESinfo Group, 2004).

134. Freedman, *Deterrence*, pp. 52–6; compare Gambetta, *The Sicilian Mafia*, pp. 127–56.

135. See Peter T. Leeson, *The Invisible Hook: The Hidden Economics of Pirates* (Princeton NJ: Princeton University Press, 2009), pp. 82–133.

136. Saviano, *Gomorrah*, p. 46.

137. Block, *East Side*, p. 222.

138. John Bailey and Matthew M. Taylor, 'Evade, Corrupt, or Confront? Organized Crime and the State in Brazil and Mexico', *Journal of Politics in Latin America*, vol. 1, no. 2 (2009), p. 22.

139. Williams, 'The Terrorism Debate', p. 266.

140. Michael Howard, 'Lessons of the Cold War', *Survival*, vol. 36, no. 4 (1994–5), p. 165.

141. Bailey and Taylor, 'Evade, Corrupt, or Confront?', pp. 11–12.

142. Elkus, 'Mexican Cartels'; and see H.R. Friman, 'Forging the Vacancy Chain: Law Enforcement Efforts and Mobility in Criminal Economies', *Crime Law & Social Change*, vol. 41, no. 1 (2004), pp. 53–77.

143. Patrick Radden Keefe, 'The Snow Kings of Mexico', in *The New York Times Magazine*, pp. 41–2.

144. See Frank G. Madsen, 'Corruption: A Global Common Evil', *The RUSI Journal*, vol. 158, no. 2 (2013), pp. 26–38.

145. Ibid., p. 29.

146. Kefauver Committee, *Report*, p. 175.

147. Compare Ferguson, *Golden Rule*.

148. Letizia Paoli, 'Broken Bonds: Mafia and Politics in Sicily', in Godson, *Menace*, p. 46; Giuseppe Muti, 'Mafias et trafics de drogue: le cas exemplaire de Cosa Nostra sicilienne', *Hérodote*, no. 112 (2004), p. 162.

149. See Donatella Della Porta and Alberto Vannucci, *Corrupt Exchanges* (New York: De Gruyter, 1999).

150. See Gaetano Mosca, 'Che cosa è la mafia', in *Uomini e cosi di Sicilia* (Palermo, 1980), p. 12; and Lupo, *History*, p. 15.

151. Quoted in Gambetta, *The Sicilian Mafia*, p. 21.

152. Freedman, *Strategic Coercion*, pp. 17, 23.

153. Frederic Lane, 'Economic consequences of organized violence', *Journal of Economic History*, vol. 18 (1958), pp. 401–17.

154. Smith, 'Illicit Enterprise'; and see A.R. Dick, 'When Does Organized Crime Pay? A Transaction Cost Analysis', *International Review of Law & Economics*, vol. 15, no. 1 (1995), pp. 25–45.

155. Donald R. Cressey, 'The Functions and Structure of Criminal Syndicates', in President's Commission, *Task Force Report: Organized Crime*, pp. 29, 47; Della Porta and Vannucci, *Corrupt Exchanges*, p. 249.

156. Pamela L. Bunker and Robert J. Bunker, 'The Spiritual Significance of ¿Plata o Plomo?', *Small Wars Journal*, 4 June 2011.

157. Kefauver Committee, *Report*, p. 163.

158. US Senate, Committee on Government Operations, Permanent Subcommittee on Investigations, *Organized Crime and Illicit Traffic in Narcotics* ('McClellan Hearings') (Washington DC: US Government Printing Office, 1964), Part 1, First Session, p. 119.

159. Della Porta and Vannucci, *Corrupt Exchanges*, pp. 249–55.

160. Gambetta, *The Sicilian Mafia*, p. 33; Raimondo Catanzaro, *Men of Respect: A Social History of the Sicilian Mafia* (New York: The Free Press, 1988), p. 29.

161. Compare Thomas Rid, *Cyber War Will Not Take Place* (New York: Oxford University Press, 2013), pp. 131–2.

162. Joseph Nye, *Soft Power: The Means to Success in World Politics* (New York: Public Affairs, 2004).

163. On the Camorra see Saviano, *Gomorrah*, pp. 50–1.

164. Michael Ross, 'How do natural resources influence civil war? Evidence from thirteen cases', *International Organization*, vol. 58 (2004), pp. 35–67.

165. Jeffrey Gettleman, 'A Fluke of the Wind', *The New York Times Magazine*, 9 October 2011, pp. 36–7.

166. Saviano, *Gomorrah*, pp. 53, 66–7.

167. On 'strategic communication' see Harry R. Yarger, *Strategic Theory for the 21st Century: The Little Book on Big Strategy* (Carlisle PA: Strategic Studies Institute, US Army War College, 2006), pp. 7–8.

168. Robert Lacey, *Little Man: Meyer Lansky and the Gangster Life* (Boston MA: Little Brown & Co., 1991), p. 319.

169. Gambetta, *The Sicilian Mafia*, pp. 47–52, and see pp. 127–55 on 'trademarks'.

170. Felbab-Brown, *Shooting Up*; Metz, *Rethinking Insurgency*; Sullivan and Elkus, 'Strategy and insurgency'; Williams, 'Insurgencies and Organized Crime'.

171. Freedman, 'Strategic Studies and the Problem of Power', p. 285.

172. Colin Gray, *Modern Strategy* (New York: Oxford University Press, 1999), p. 17.

173. Hess, *Mafia and Mafiosi*, p. 13; Arlacchi, *Mafia Business*, p. 14.

174. Giovanni Falcone with Marcelle Padovani, *Cose di Cosa nostra* (Milan: Biblioteca Universale Rizzoli, 1991), p. 37.

175. Cesare Mattina, 'The transformations of the contemporary mafia: a perspective review of the literature on mafia phenomena in the context of the internationalisation of the capitalist economy', *International Social Science Journal*, vol. 62, issue 203–4 (2011), pp. 237–8.

176. See Saviano, *Gomorrah*, pp. 226–8; Alessandra Dino, 'For Christ's sake: Organized crime and religion', in Allum and Siebert, *Organized Crime*, pp. 161–74.

177. Saviano, *Gomorrah*.

178. Charles Bowden, '"We Bring Fear", *Mother Jones* (July/August 2009), pp. 29–43; Elyssa Pachico, 'The Top 5 Most Infamous Narco-Songs', *InSight Crime*, 15 March 2012; on attacks on social media see Hannah Stone, 'The Zetas' Biggest Rival: Social Networks', *InSight Crime*, 28 September 2011.

179. See Vanda Felbab-Brown, 'Conceptualizing Crime as Competition in State-Making and Designing an Effective Response', *Sec. & Def. Stud. Rev.* (Spring-Summer 2010).

180. Freedman, *Deterrence*, p. 73.

181. Felbab-Brown, *Shooting Up*.

182. Sciarrone, 'Réseaux mafieux'.

183. Dennis Rodgers, 'Youth gangs and perverse livelihood strategies in Nicaragua: challenging certain preconceptions and shifting the focus of analysis', Paper presented at the World Bank Conference, 'New Frontiers of Social Policy: Development in a Globalizing World', Arusha, Tanzania, 12–15 December 2005, pp. 15–17.

184. Mette Eilstrup-Sangiovanni and Calvert Jones, 'Assessing the Dangers of Illicit Networks: Why al-Qaida May be Less Threatening Than Many Think', *International Security*, vol. 33, no. 2 (2008), pp. 7–44.

185. Paoli, 'The paradoxes', p. 87.

186. Michele Polo, 'Internal cohesion and competition among criminal organizations', in Fiorentini and Peltzman, *The Economics of Organized Crime*, pp. 87–109.

187. Williams, 'Insurgencies and Organized Crime', pp. 44–6, 58–60.

188. Samuel P. Huntington, 'Civil violence and the process of development', *The Adelphi Papers*, vol. 11, issue 83 (1972), p. 15.

189. Rune Henriksen and Anthony Vinci, 'Combat Motivation in Non-State Armed Groups', *Terrorism & Political Violence*, vol. 20, no. 1 (2007), p. 88.

190. Southerland and Potter, 'Applying Organization Theory', p. 262; Fiorentini and Peltzman, 'Introduction', pp. 12–13.

191. Williams, 'The Nature', p. 154.

192. Southerland and Potter, 'Applying Organization Theory', pp. 258, 260.

193. José Miguel Cruz, 'Central American maras: from youth street gangs to transnational protection rackets', *Global Crime*, vol. 11, no. 4 (2010), pp. 389–93.

194. Saviano, *Gomorrah*, pp. 74–8.

195. Gambetta, *The Sicilian Mafia*, p. 17.

196. Paoli, 'The paradoxes', pp. 78–81; Skaperdas and Syropoulos, 'Gangs as Primitive States', pp. 75–6.

197. Peter A. Lupsha, 'Networks Versus Networking: Analysis of an Organized Crime Group', in G. P. Waldo, ed., *Career Criminals* (Beverly Hills CA: Sage, 1983), pp. 74–6.

198. Rodgers, 'Youth gangs', pp. 10–13.

199. Hiroaki Iwai, 'Organized crime in Japan', in Robert J. Kelly, ed., *Organized Crime: A Global Perspective* (Totowa NJ: Rowman and Littlefield, 1986), pp. 214–16.

200. Williams, 'Transnational Criminal Organizations'; Williams, 'Cooperation among Criminal Organizations'; Radden Keefe, 'The Snow Kings', p. 41.

201. Phil Williams, *From the New Middle Ages to a New Dark Age: The Decline of the State and US Strategy* (Carlisle PA: Strategic Studies Institute, 2008), pp. 16–17.

202. Bernd Beber and Christopher Blattman, 'The Logic of Child Soldiering and Coercion', *International Organization*, vol. 67 (Winter 2013), pp. 65–104.

203. See Saviano, *Gomorrah*, pp. 105–6.

204. Weber, *Economy and Society*, p. 672.

205. Pino Arlacchi, *Men of Dishonor: Inside the Sicilian Mafia. An Account of Antonino Calderone* (New York: William Morrow and Company, Inc., 1993), p. 68; see also Gambetta, *The Sicilian Mafia*, pp. 146–55.

206. Leeson, *The Invisible Hook*, pp. 45–81; Peter T. Leeson and David B. Skarbek, 'Criminal Constitutions', *Global Crime*, vol. 11, no. 3 (2010), pp. 279–97; Cressey, 'Functions and Structure', pp. 41, 52.

207. Southerland and Potter, 'Applying Organization Theory', p. 262. See also Fiorentini and Peltzman, 'Introduction', pp. 12–13.

208. Naylor, *Wages of Crime*, pp. 22–4.

209. Barbara Alexander, 'The Rational Racketeer: Pasta Protection in Depression Era Chicago', *Journal of Law & Economics*, vol. 40 (1997), pp. 175–202.

210. Felia Allum and Renate Siebert, 'Organized crime: a threat to democracy?', in Allum and Siebert, *Organized Crime*, pp. 2–3; see also Morselli, 'The Mobility' (2010); Carlo Morselli, Mathilde Turcotte and Valentina

Tenti, 'The mobility of criminal groups', *Global Crime*, vol. 12, no. 3 (2011), pp. 166–7; and Federico Varese, *Mafias on the Move: How Organized Crime Conquers New Territories* (Princeton NJ: Princeton University Press, 2011).

3. TAMMANY: 'HOW NEW YORK IS GOVERNED', 1859–1920

1. 'Tweed Talks', *New York Herald*, 26 October 1877, p.3.

2. 'Death of Wm. M. Tweed', *The New York Times*, 13 April 1878, p. 1; Kenneth D. Ackerman, *Boss Tweed: The Rise and Fall of the Corrupt Pol Who Conceived the Soul of Modern New York* (New York: Carroll & Graf, 2005), pp. 11–29; Terry Golway, *Machine Made: Tammany Hall and the Creation of Modern American Politics* (New York and London: Liveright, 2014), pp. 60–1, 79–82; Pete Hammill, '"Boss Tweed": The Fellowship of the Ring', *The New York Times*, 27 March 2005.

3. Ackerman, *Boss Tweed*, pp. 2, 106; Gustavus Myers, *The History of Tammany Hall*, 2nd ed. (New York: Boni & Liveright, 1917), pp. 248–9; *Report of the Special Committee of the Board of Aldermen appointed to investigate the 'Ring' frauds: together with the testimony elicited during the investigation* (New York: Martin Brown, 1878); Leo Hershkowitz, ed. *Boss Tweed in Court: A Documentary History* (Bethesda, MD: University Publications of America, 1990), p. xvii.

4. The key texts are Tweed's 'Confession', *New York Herald*, 10 October 1877, pp. 5–7, 11; 'Tweed Talks'; and his 'Testimony', annexed to the *Report of the Special Committee of the Board of Aldermen*.

5. Alan Block, *East Side, West Side: Organizing Crime in New York 1930–1950* (New Brunswick NJ: Transaction Publishers, 1983) p. 12; see also US Senate, Special Committee to Investigate Organized Crime in Interstate Commerce ('Kefauver Committee'), *The Kefauver Committee Report on Organized Crime* (New York: Didier, 1951), p. 125.

6. Myers, *The History of Tammany Hall*, pp. 2–4.

7. Markus Hunemorder, *The Society of the Cincinnati: Conspiracy and Distrust in Early America* (New York: Berghahn Books, 2006).

8. See Benjamin Franklin to Sarah Bache, 26 January 1784, LOC, 'Treasures' exhibit; see also Aedanus Burke, 'Considerations on the Society or Order of Cincinnati' (South Carolina: A. Timothy, 1783).

9. Myers, *The History of Tammany Hall*, pp. 1–5, 10–14.

10. M.A. Werner, *Tammany Hall* (New York: Greenwood Press, 1968); Jerome Mushkat, *Tammany: The Evolution of a Political Machine, 1789–1865* (Syracuse NY: Syracuse University Press, 1971); Golway, *Machine Made*, p. 6; Myers, *The History of Tammany Hall*, p. 14.

11. Myers, *The History of Tammany Hall*, pp. 15–19.

12. Ibid., pp. viii, 20–31, 43–4.

13. Walter Lippmann, 'Tammany Hall and Al Smith', *The Outlook*, vol. 148, no. 5, 1 February 1928, pp. 163–5 at p. 164.

14. Myers, *The History of Tammany Hall*, pp. 65–6.

15. Ibid., pp. 23–76.

16. Ibid., pp. 73–6, 158.

17. Golway, *Machine Made*, pp. 41, 45.

18. Ibid., pp. 47–50; Myers, *The History of Tammany Hall*, pp. 77–193.

19. Golway, *Machine Made*, pp. 50–1.

20. Myers, *The History of Tammany Hall*, p. 172

21. Ibid., pp. 85–111

22. Ibid., pp. 131–2.

23. Ibid., pp. 178–80.

24. See Joseph McGoldrick, 'A Scrapbook of Politics', 1929, #8406, NYPL, pp. 3–6.

25. 'Tweed talks'; Myers, *The History of Tammany Hall*, pp. 185–6. On a similar figure, Big Tim Sullivan, see Myers, *The History of Tammany Hall*, pp. 344–5.

26. William L. Riordan, *Plunkitt of Tammany Hall* (New York: McClure, Phillips & Co., 1905); Joseph McGoldrick, 'The New Tammany', *The American Mercury*, vol. XV, no. 57, September 1928, pp. 1–12.

27. Riordan, *Plunkitt of Tammany Hall*, pp. 91–3.

28. McGoldrick, 'New Tammany', p. 5.

29. McGoldrick, 'New Tammany', p. 7.

30. Ibid.; Block, *East Side*, p. 48.

31. Hickman Powell, *Lucky Luciano: The Man Who Organized Crime in America* (New York: Barnes & Noble, 1939/2006), p. 53.

32. McGoldrick, 'New Tammany', p. 6; see also Joseph McGoldrick, 'A Scrapbook of Politics', 1929, #8381, NYPL, pp. 1–11.

33. Block, *East Side*, pp. 51–4.

34. Supreme Court of New York, Appellate Division, *In the Matter of the Investigation of the Magistrates' Court, Final Report of Samuel Seabury, Referee*, New York, 28 March 1932, NYCMA.

35. Mark H. Haller, 'Bootleggers and American Gambling 1920–1950', in US Commission on the Review of the National Policy Towards Gambling, *Gambling in America, Appendix 1: Staff and Consultant Papers* (Washington DC, 1976), in NYPL, p. 102. Emphasis in original.

36. McGoldrick, 'New Tammany', p. 7.

37. Ibid.

38. Robert Lacey, *Little Man: Meyer Lansky and the Gangster Life* (Boston MA: Little Brown & Co., 1991), pp. 47–8.

39. Riordan, *Plunkitt of Tammany Hall*, pp. 14–15, 22–9, 70–4.

40. Hammill, "'Boss Tweed'".
41. Myers, *The History of Tammany Hall*, pp. 213, 222–3.
42. Ibid., pp. 213–4.
43. Tweed, 'Testimony', pp. 14–19, 24–5, 33–46; 'Confession', p. 5; *Report of the Special Committee*, pp. 14–16; 'Death of Wm. M. Tweed', p. 2.
44. Ackerman, *Boss Tweed*, p. 357; Myers, *The History of Tammany Hall*, p. 224.
45. Myers, *The History of Tammany Hall*, pp. 228–9.
46. Tweed, 'Testimony', pp. 126–33; 'Death of Wm. M. Tweed', p. 2; Edwin G. Burrows and Mike Wallace, *Gotham: A History of New York City to 1898* (New York: Oxford University Press, 1999), pp. 934–5; Ackerman, *Boss Tweed*, pp. 65–7; Myers, *The History of Tammany Hall*, pp. 229–31.
47. 'More Ring Villainy—Gigantic Frauds in the Rental of Armories', *The New York Times*, 8 July 1871, pp. 3–4; Golway, *Machine Made*, p. 93
48. Tweed, 'Confession', p. 6; Ackerman, *Boss Tweed*, p. 52.
49. Tweed, 'Testimony', pp. 143–51; 'Confession', p. 7; 'Tweed Talks'; 'Death of Wm. M. Tweed', p. 2; Ackerman, *Boss Tweed*, pp. 68–70, 107; Myers, *The History of Tammany Hall*, pp. 223–4; Golway, *Machine Made*, p. 85.
50. Tweed, 'Testimony', pp. 212–213; *Report of the Special Committee*, p. 24; Myers, *The History of Tammany Hall*, p. 222.
51. Tweed, 'Testimony', pp. 213–4.
52. Tweed, 'Testimony', pp. 88, 254; *Report of the Special Committee*, p. 24; Myers, *The History of Tammany Hall*, pp. 222–3.
53. See James Cockayne, 'The Futility of Force? Strategic Lessons for Dealing with Unconventional Armed Groups from the UN's War on Gangs in Haiti', *Journal of Strategic Studies*, vol. 37, no. 5 (2014), pp. 736–69.
54. *Report of the Special Committee*, p. 13.
55. *N.Y. Herald*, 8 January 1871.
56. Myers, *The History of Tammany Hall*, p. 230; Ackerman, *Boss Tweed*, pp. 64–5, 120.
57. Alfred Connable and Edward Silberfarb, *Tigers of Tammany: Nine Men Who Ran New York* (New York: Holt, Rinehart and Winston, 1967), p. 154; Ackerman, *Boss Tweed*, pp. 39–41.
58. Myers, *The History of Tammany Hall*, p. 129.
59. Ibid., pp. 228–9.
60. Tweed, 'Testimony', p. 134.
61. 'Tweed Talks'.
62. Ackerman, *Boss Tweed*, pp. 68–9.
63. Ibid., pp. 48–57.
64. 'Death of Wm. M. Tweed', p. 2.
65. Ackerman, *Boss Tweed*, p. 52.
66. *Report of the Special Committee*, p. 17.
67. New York L1870 Ch. 137.

68. Charles O'Conor, quoted in William C. Hudson, *Random Recollections of an Old Political Reporter* (New York: Cupples & Leon, 1911), p. 31.

69. 'Testimony', pp. 67–73, 80–2, 86–98; 'Confession', p. 5; *Report of the Special Committee*, pp. 19–21; Ackerman, *Boss Tweed*, pp. 71–87; Golway, *Machine Made*, pp. 85–6; Myers, *The History of Tammany Hall*, pp. 226–8.

70. *N.Y. Herald*, 5 April 1870.

71. Tweed, 'Testimony', p. 29, 74–6, 577; 'Confession', p. 5; *The New York Times*, 13 April 1878, p. 2; *Report of the Special Committee*, p. 22; Golway, *Machine Made*, p. 91; Myers, *The History of Tammany Hall*, pp. 215, 221, 229.

72. Ackerman, *Boss Tweed*, pp. 108–11, 118.

73. Ibid., pp. 30–6.

74. Thomas Nast, 'The Power Behind the Throne', *Harper's Weekly*, 29 October 1870; *The Evening Telegram*, 6 January 1871, in A. Oakey Hall, *Scrapbook*, NYPL; Thomas Nast, 'The Baptism of Fire', *Harper's Weekly*, 22 April 1871.

75. Ackerman, *Boss Tweed*, p. 2; Hamill, '"Boss Tweed"'.

76. 'Tweed Talks'.

77. 'Death of Wm. M. Tweed', p. 2; Ackerman, *Boss Tweed*, p. 111; Myers, *The History of Tammany Hall*, p. 232.

78. 'A Costly Wedding', *The New York Times*, 1 June 1871, p. 1; Myers, *The History of Tammany Hall*, p. 234; Ackerman, *Boss Tweed*, pp. 145–6.

79. 'Testimony', pp. 212–9; Ackerman, *Boss Tweed*, p. 97; Myers, *The History of Tammany Hall*, p. 232.

80. Golway, *Machine Made*, p. 94.

81. Ackerman, *Boss Tweed*, p. 154.

82. Michael A. Gordon, *The Orange Riots: Irish Political Violence in New York City, 1870 and 1871* (Ithaca NY: Cornell University Press, 2009), pp. 79–82.

83. 'Terrorism Rampant—The City Authorities Overawed by Roman Catholics', *The New York Times*, 11 July 1871, p. 1; *N.Y. Tribune*, 11 July 1871, p. 1.

84. Ackerman, *Boss Tweed*, pp. 155–6.

85. Gordon, *The Orange Riots*, pp. 111–30; Golway, *Machine Made*, p. 98; Ackerman, *Boss Tweed*, p. 157.

86. 'Yesterday's Disturbances', *The New York Times*, 13 July 1871, p. 4; *N.Y. Tribune*, 14 July 1871; Ackerman, *Boss Tweed*, pp. 147–58; Golway, *Machine Made*, p. 99.

87. Ackerman, *Boss Tweed*, p. 181; see *Harper's Weekly*, 26 August 1871.

88. Tweed, 'Testimony', p. 51 et seq; 'Confession', p. 6; Ackerman, *Boss Tweed*, pp. 124–5, 130, 139–40, 160–5; Jonathan Daniels, 'Mr Jones and the Tiger', *Neiman Reports*, vol. 20, no. 4, December 1966.

89. 'The Secret Accounts—Proofs of Undoubted Frauds Brought to Light', *The New York Times*, 22 July 1871, pp. 1, 4; 'Gigantic Frauds of the Ring

pp. [70–76]

Exposed', *The New York Times*, 29 July 1871, special supplement; Ackerman, *Boss Tweed*, pp. 167–73; Golway, *Machine Made*, pp. 100–1; Myers, *The History of Tammany Hall*, pp. 238–9; Burrows & Wallace, *Gotham*, pp. 929–31.

90. Myers, *The History of Tammany Hall*, p. 237; Golway, *Machine Made*, p. 92; Ackerman, *Boss Tweed*, pp. 87, 175

91. Ackerman, *Boss Tweed*, pp. 175–6.

92. Ibid., pp. 172–3, 183–4, 196.

93. Ibid., pp. 185–9.

94. 'Tweed Talks'; *The New York Times*, 10 September 1871; Myers, *The History of Tammany Hall*, p. 240–3; Burrows and Wallace, *Gotham*, pp. 1008–11; Ackerman, *Boss Tweed*, pp. 176, 196–203, 213.

95. Ackerman, *Boss Tweed*, pp. 212–46, 251, 254–6; Golway, *Machine Made*, p. 103; Myers, *The History of Tammany Hall*, pp. 241–4.

96. Tweed, 'Testimony', pp. 52–9; 'Confession', p. 6; Myers, *The History of Tammany Hall*, pp. 245–8; Ackerman, *Boss Tweed*, pp. 248–9, 255–8, 294–314.

97. Golway, *Machine Made*, pp. 107–11; Myers, *The History of Tammany Hall*, pp. 252–4.

98. Golway, *Machine Made*, p. 112; see also Myers, *The History of Tammany Hall*, p. 258.

99. Golway, *Machine Made*, pp. 114–7; Myers, *The History of Tammany Hall*, pp. 256–7; Ackerman, *Boss Tweed*, pp. 301–2.

100. Louis Eisenstein and Elliot Rosenberg, *A Stripe of Tammany's Tiger* (New York: Robert Speller & Sons, 1966), p. 15.

101. Golway, *Machine Made*, p. 137.

102. Eisenstein and Rosenberg, *A Stripe*, p. 15.

103. Golway, *Machine Made*, pp. 132–44.

104. Burrows and Wallace, *Gotham*, pp. 1103–8; Golway, *Machine Made*, pp. 152–3; Myers, *The History of Tammany Hall*, pp. 269–70.

105. Myers, *The History of Tammany Hall*, pp. 267–8.

106. Richard Croker, 'Tammany Hall and the Democracy,' *North American Review*, vol. 154, no. 423 (February 1892), pp. 225–30, at p. 225.

107. Ibid. at pp. 226–7.

108. Ibid., p. 228.

109. Ibid.

110. Riordan, *Plunkitt of Tammany Hall*, p. 34.

111. *Report of the Special Committee of the Assembly Appointed to Investigate the Public Offices and Departments of the City of New York* (Albany, NY: J.B. Lyon, 1900), vol. II, pp. 353–4; Golway, *Machine Made*, pp. 174–5; Myers, *The History of Tammany Hall*, p. 288.

112. Riordan, *Plunkitt of Tammany Hall*, p. 32.

113. Ibid., pp. 3–8, 54.

114. Ibid., pp. 8–10; cf p. 154.

115. Burrows and Wallace, *Gotham*, pp. 1106–9.

116. Myers, *The History of Tammany Hall*, p. 337.

117. Ibid., p. 338; Burrows and Wallace, *Gotham*, pp. 929–31.

118. Myers, *The History of Tammany Hall*, pp. 273, 277; New York State Assembly, *Report and Proceedings of the Senate Committee Appointed to Investigate the Police Department of the City of New York* (Albany NY: J.B. Lyon, 1895).

119. Blaine A. Brownell and Warren E. Stickle, eds., *Bosses and Reformers* (Boston MA: Houghton Mifflin, 1973), p. 27.

120. Warren Sloat, *A Battle for the Soul of New York: Tammany Hall, Police Corruption, Vice, and the Reverend Charles Parkhurst's Crusade Against Them* (New York: Cooper Square Press, 2002), pp. 360–8.

121. Riordan, *Plunkitt of Tammany Hall*, pp. 30–1; Myers, *The History of Tammany Hall*, pp. 280–2.

122. Golway, *Machine Made*, pp. 155–205, 211–12.

123. Lippmann, 'Tammany Hall', p. 164.

124. Ackerman, *Boss Tweed*, pp. 357–8.

125. Ibid., p. 359.

126. 'Tweed Talks'.

127. Compare Jonathan Goodhand, 'Frontiers and Wars: the Opium Economy in Afghanistan', *Journal of Agrarian Change*, vol. 4, nos 1 and 2 (January/April 2004), pp. 191–216.

128. Hudson, *Random Recollections*, p. 24.

129. Ackerman, *Boss Tweed*, p. 254.

130. Ibid., pp. 269, 287–8, 325, 351–2.

131. Golway, *Machine Made*, pp. 90–1, 169, 220–3; Ackerman, *Boss Tweed*, p. 120; and see K.R.M. Short, *The Dynamite War: Irish-American Bombers in Victorian Britain* (Dublin: Gill & Macmillan, 1979).

4. MAFIA ORIGINS, 1859–1929

1. Quoted in Selwyn Raab, *Five Families: The Rise, Decline, and Resurgence of America's Most Powerful Mafia Empires* (New York: St. Martin's Griffin/Thomas Dunne Books, 2005), p. 17.

2. See Arnaldo Cortesi, 'The Mafia Dead; A New Sicily is Born', *The New York Times Magazine*, 4 March 1928, pp. 10–11; John Dickie, *Cosa Nostra* (London: Palgrave Macmillan, 2005), pp. 144–7; Tim Newark, *Mafia Allies: The True Story of America's Secret Alliance with the Mob in World War II* (St Paul MN: Zenith Press, 2007), pp. 22–50; Raimondo Catanzaro, *Men of Respect: A Social History of the Sicilian Mafia* (New York: The Free Press, 1988),

pp. 108–12; and Ezio Costanzo, *The Mafia and the Allies: Sicily 1943 and the Return of the Mafia*, trans. George Lawrence (New York: Enigma, 2007), pp. 37–8.

3. Quoted in Arrigo Petacco, *L'uomo della provvidenza: Mussolini, ascesa e caduta di un mito* (Milan: Mondadori, 2004), p. 101, author's translation.

4. Costanzo, *The Mafia and the Allies*, p. 38; Newark, *Mafia Allies*, p. 45; Salvatore Lupo, *History of the Mafia*, trans. Antony Shugaar (New York: Columbia University Press, 2009), pp. 18–19, p. 174.

5. Newark, *Mafia Allies*, pp. 43, 48; FBI, 'Mafia Monograph', July 1958, FBI Vault, Section I, pp. viii, 44.

6. Aristide Spanò, *Faccia a faccia con la mafia* (Milan: Mondadori, 1978), pp. 42 et seq. See also Lupo, *History*, pp. 174–5.

7. Lupo, *History*, p. 175.

8. Joseph Bonanno, *A Man of Honour* (London: Andre Deutsch, 1983); Nick Gentile, *Vita di capomafia* (Rome: Editori Riuniti, 1963).

9. Dickie, *Cosa Nostra*, p. 183.

10. See Peter Maas, *The Valachi Papers* (New York: Perennial, 1968/2003); and also Valachi's testimony in US Senate, Committee on Government Operations, Permanent Subcommittee on Investigations, *Organized Crime and Illicit Traffic in Narcotics* ('McClellan Hearings') (Washington DC: US Government Printing Office, 1964).

11. Arlacchi, *Men of Dishonor*; Michael Franzese and Dary Matera, *Quitting the Mob* (New York: HarperCollins, 1992); Joseph Cantalupo and Thomas C. Renner, *Body Mike: The Deadly Double Life of a Mob Informer* (New York: Villard Books, 1990); Joe Pistone with Richard Woodley, *Donnie Brasco: My Undercover Life in the Mafia* (New York: New American Library, 1987).

12. Martin Gosch and Richard Hammer, *The Last Testament of Lucky Luciano* (London: Macmillan London Limited, 1975).

13. See Tim Newark, *Lucky Luciano: The Real and the Fake Gangster* (New York: Thomas Dunne Books, 2010), pp. 261–5.

14. Richard N. Warner, 'The last word on "The Last Testament"', *Informer*, April 2012, pp. 5–33. See also Anthony Scaduto, *"Lucky" Luciano* (London: Sphere, 1976), pp. 197–208; and Robert Lacey, *Little Man: Meyer Lansky and the Gangster Life* (Boston MA: Little Brown & Co., 1991), p. 451.

15. Dickie, *Mafia Republic*, p. 423.

16. Raab, *Five Families*, p. 17.

17. Michele Pantaleone, *The Mafia and Politics* (London: Chatto & Windus: 1966), pp. 28–30.

18. Raab, *Five Families*, pp. 15–16; Dickie, *Cosa Nostra*, pp. 37–44, 48–51; Hobsbawm, *Primitive Rebels*, pp. 40–1.

19. Arlacchi, *Men of Dishonor*, p. 149.

20. Pantaleone, *The Mafia and Politics*, pp. 35–6.

21. On Afghanistan, see Vesna Bojicic-Dzelilovic, Denisa Kostovicova, Mariana Escobar and Jelena Bjelica, 'Organised crime and international aid subversion: evidence from Colombia and Afghanistan', *Third World Quarterly*, vol. 36, no. 10 (2015), at pp. 1896–9.

22. Leopoldo Franchetti, *Condizioni politiche e amministrative della Sicilia*, vol. 1 of Leopoldo Franchetti and Sidney Sonnino, *La Sicilia nel 1876: Inchiesta in Sicilia*, 2 volumes (Florence: O. Barbera, 1877); see also Dickie, *Cosa Nostra*, pp. 57–60. On Franchetti see Lupo, *History*, pp. 62–9.

23. Diego Gambetta, *The Sicilian Mafia: The Business of Private Protection* (Cambridge MA: Harvard University Press, 1993).

24. Dickie, *Cosa Nostra*, pp. 37–51; Lupo, *History*, pp. 8–9, 17–18, and Chapters 2 and 3; Hobsbawm, *Primitive Rebels*, pp. 34, 38–40; Hobsbawm, *Bandits*, p. 87; Arlacchi, *Men of Dishonor*, pp. 53–6; Pantaleone, *The Mafia and Politics*, pp. 38–40; Catanzaro, *Men of Respect*, pp. 15–16.

25. Catanzaro, *Men of Respect*, p. 17.

26. Hobsbawm, *Primitive Rebels*, pp. 42–3.

27. James Fentress, *Rebels and Mafiosi* (Ithaca NY: Cornell University Press, 2000), pp. 147–252.

28. Pantaleone, *The Mafia and Politics*, p. 195.

29. Ibid., pp. 32, 84. See also Raab, *Five Families*, p. 17.

30. Arlacchi, *Men of Dishonor*, p. 201. See also Gambetta, *The Sicilian Mafia*, p. 184.

31. Compare Arlacchi, *Men of Dishonor*, pp. 199–200; and Donatella Della Porta and Alberto Vannucci, *Corrupt Exchanges* (New York: De Gruyter, 1999).

32. Pantaleone, *The Mafia and Politics*, p. 32.

33. Giuseppe Alongi, *La mafia: fattori, manifestazioni, rimedi* (Palermo: Sellerio, 1886/1977), p. 50.

34. Ermanno Sangiorgi, Chief of Police, to Vincenzo Consenza, Public Prosecutor, Palermo, 'Rapporto', quoted in Lupo, *History*, p. 17.

35. Dickie, *Cosa Nostra*, pp. 69–77; Raab, *Five Families*, p. 16; Pantaleone, *The Mafia and Politics*, pp. 31–2; Hobsbawm, *Primitive Rebels*, pp. 42–3; Catanzaro, *Men of Respect*, pp. 84–91.

36. Hobsbawm, *Primitive Rebels*, p. 43.

37. Pantaleone, *The Mafia and Politics*, p. 195.

38. Ibid., p. 44.

39. 'Rastignac', 'I discorsi del giorno: de malo in pejus', in *La Tribuna* (Milan), 15 December 1899, quoted in Lupo, *History*, p. 97.

40. Franchetti, pp. 172–3, author's translation. See further pp. 223 et seq.

41. This section draws on the various mafia memoirs cited, and also especially on: Lupo, *History*; Anton Blok, *The Mafia of a Sicilian Village, 1860–1960: A Study of Violent Peasant Entrepreneurs* (Cambridge: Waveland Press, 1974); Henner Hess, *Mafia and Mafiosi: The Structure of Power* (Westmead:

Saxon House, 1973); Letizia Paoli, *Mafia Brotherhoods* (New York: Oxford University Press, 2003); Arlacchi, *Men of Dishonor*, pp. 33–6; and Gambetta, *The Sicilian Mafia*, pp. 111 et seq., 153 et seq.

42. FBI, 'Mafia Monograph', I, p. 50. On 'rhizomatic networks' see Smith, *Utility of Force*, pp. 328–30.

43. Compare Cressey, 'Functions and Structure', p. 34.

44. Quebec Police Commission, *The Fight against Organized Crime* (Montreal: Éditeur Officiel du Quebec, 1977), p. 51.

45. Paoli, *Mafia Brotherhoods*, p. 155; FBI, 'Mafia Monograph', I, pp. 72–4.

46. Bonanno, *A Man of Honour*, p. xx.

47. Fentress, *Rebels and Mafiosi*, p. 173; Arlacchi, *Men of Dishonor*, pp. 21–2. See also Francis A. Ianni, 'Formal and Social Organization in an Organized Crime "Family": A Case Study', *U. Fla L. Rev.*, vol. 24, no. 1 (1971), pp. 33–4.

48. Maas, *The Valachi Papers*, pp. 74–7; McClellan Hearings, Part 1, pp. 181–5; Raab, *Five Families*, pp. 3–6; Arlacchi, *Men of Dishonor*, pp. 66–9; Gambetta, *The Sicilian Mafia*, pp. 146–55, 262–70; and Falcone, pp. 85–8.

49. See for example Bonanno, *A Man of Honour*, p. 79.

50. Catanzaro, *Men of Respect*, p. 29; FBI, 'Mafia Monograph', I, pp. 54–5.

51. FBI, 'Mafia Monograph', I, pp. 53–4 and II, pp. 11–13.

52. Raab, *Five Families*, pp. 14–15.

53. Catanzaro, *Men of Respect*, p. 28; cf Hobsbawm, *Primitive Rebels*, p. 40.

54. Arlacchi, *Men of Dishonor*, p. 191.

55. Gentile, *Vita di capomafia*, p. 73. Author's translation.

56. Quoted in *L'Ora* (Palermo), 29 July 1925, as reported in Newark, *Mafia Allies*, p. 24.

57. Catanzaro, *Men of Respect*, p. 4.

58. See Hobsbawm, *Primitive Rebels*, p. 32.

59. Catanzaro, *Men of Respect*, p. 8.

60. Ibid., pp. 93–8; Raab, *Five Families*, p. 16.

61. Hobsbawm, *Primitive Rebels*, p. 35.

62. Raab, *Five Families*, p. 17.

63. Catanzaro, *Men of Respect*, p. 12.

64. Raab, *Five Families*, p. 14.

65. Lupo, *History*, pp. 107–9; Gentile, *Vita di capomafia*, pp. 59–73.

66. Gentile, *Vita di capomafia*, pp. 84–5.

67. Newark, *Lucky Luciano*, pp. 11–12.

68. David Critchley, *The Origin of Organized Crime in America: The New York City Mafia, 1891–1931* (New York: Routledge, 2009), p. 14.

69. Dickie, *Cosa Nostra*, p. 195.

70. Humbert S. Nelli, *From Immigrants to Ethnics* (Oxford: Oxford University Press, 1983), p. 63.

71. Terry Golway, *Machine Made: Tammany Hall and the Creation of Modern American Politics* (New York and London: Liveright, 2014), p. 147.

72. Critchley, *The Origin of Organized Crime in America*, p. 61.

73. Dickie, *Cosa Nostra*, pp. 162–3.

74. Gambetta, *The Sicilian Mafia*, pp. 251–2.

75. See William L. Riordan, *Plunkitt of Tammany Hall* (New York: McClure, Phillips & Co., 1905), pp. 3–10, 32, 54.

76. Mafia *cosche* emerged in New Orleans in the 1880s, assassinating the police chief in 1890, leading to the lynching of eleven Italian immigrants and the temporary severing of US-Italian diplomatic relations: Raab, *Five Families*, p. 18; FBI, 'Mafia Monograph', II, pp. 33–5.

77. Golway, *Machine Made*, pp. 152–205, 211–2; Edwin G. Burrows and Mike Wallace, *Gotham: A History of New York City to 1898* (New York: Oxford University Press, 1999), pp. 1103–8; Gustavus Myers, *The History of Tammany Hall*, 2nd ed. (New York: Boni & Liveright, 1917), pp. 269–70.

78. Newark, *Lucky Luciano*, pp. 14–15.

79. Ibid.

80. Ibid., p. 16.

81. Critchley, *The Origin of Organized Crime in America*, p. 22; Newark, *Lucky Luciano*, p. 17; FBI, 'Mafia Monograph', II, pp. 35–41.

82. Quoted in Raab, *Five Families*, p. 20.

83. Fentress, *Rebels and Mafiosi*, p. 166; Hess, p. 130; Critchley, *The Origin of Organized Crime in America*, p. 32; Dickie, *Cosa Nostra*, pp. 171–2.

84. Lupo, *History*, pp. 144–5.

85. Critchley, *The Origin of Organized Crime in America*, p. 27.

86. Ibid., pp. 22–6; Raab, *Five Families*, p. 19; Lupo, *History*, pp. 144–5.

87. Critchley, *The Origin of Organized Crime in America*, p. 22.

88. Ibid., 26–9, 105 et seq.

89. Ibid., p. 27.

90. Bonanno, *A Man of Honour*, p. 40.

91. Bill Bonanno, *Bound by Honour* (New York: St. Martin's Paperbacks, 1999), p. 6.

92. Francis A. Ianni and Elizabeth Reuss-Ianni, *A Family Business: Kinship and Social Control in Organized Crime* (New York: Russel Sage, 1972), p. 52; Critchley, p. 32.

93. Gambetta, *The Sicilian Mafia*, pp. 262–70; Critchley, *The Origin of Organized Crime in America*, pp. 63–4, 119.

94. Critchley, *The Origin of Organized Crime in America*, pp. 62–3; Gentile, *Vita di capomafia*, pp. 53–61.

95. Critchley, *The Origin of Organized Crime in America*, pp. 36–48.

96. Dickie, *Cosa Nostra*, p. 169.

97. Critchley, *The Origin of Organized Crime in America*, p. 51.

98. Ibid., pp. 50–60.
99. Dickie, *Cosa Nostra*, pp. 169–70.
100. Ibid., pp. 168–9.
101. Raab, *Five Families*, pp. 6–7.
102. Critchley, *The Origin of Organized Crime in America*, pp. 112–17.
103. Ibid., pp. 105–37.
104. Bonanno, *A Man of Honour*, pp. 86–7.
105. Critchley, *The Origin of Organized Crime in America*, p. 136.
106. Gosch and Hammer, *The Last Testament of Lucky Luciano*, p. 145.
107. Donald Cressey, *Theft of the Nation: The Structure and Operations of Organized Crime in America* (New York: Harper and Row, 1969), p. 31.
108. Ianni, 'Formal and Social Organization', p. 39.
109. Lacey, *Little Man*, p. 292; Raab, *Five Families*, p. 36.
110. See e.g. Valachi's account in Maas, *The Valachi Papers*, pp. 102–6.
111. Raab, *Five Families*, p. 7.
112. McClellan Hearings, Part 1, p. 89.
113. Valachi in McClellan Hearings, Part 1, pp. 82–3; Raab, *Five Families*, p. 5.
114. Franzese and Matera, *Quitting the Mob*, p. 96.
115. Cantalupo and Renner, *Body Mike*, p. 28.
116. Herbert Edelhertz and Thomas D. Overcast, *The Business of Organized Crime* (Loomis, CA: The Palmer Press, 1993), p. 135.
117. McClellan Hearings, Part 1, p. 109.
118. Ibid., pp. 240, 323; Raab, *Five Families*, pp. 5, 8; Arlacchi, *Men of Dishonor*, pp. 143–4.
119. Michael Stone, 'After Gotti', *New York Magazine*, 3 February 1992, pp. 22–31, at p. 29.
120. Pistone and Woodley, *Donnie Brasco*, p. 77.
121. George Anastasia, *Blood and Honor: Inside the Scarfo Mob—The Mafia's Most Violent Family* (Philadelphia PA: Camino Books, 1991), p. 223.
122. See Nicholas Pileggi, *Wiseguy: Life in a Mafia Family* (New York: Simon & Schuster, 1985), pp. 56–7. See also Bonanno, *A Man of Honour*, p. 152.
123. Pantaleone, *The Mafia and Politics*, p. 34.
124. Costanzo, *The Mafia and the Allies*, pp. 35–6; Pantaleone, *The Mafia and Politics*, pp. 45, 85; Lupo, *History*, pp. 159, 167–9.
125. Compare Pantaleone, *The Mafia and Politics*, p. 44.
126. Lupo, *History*, p. 22.
127. Hobsbawm, *Primitive Rebels*, p. 47.
128. Cesare Mori, *Con la mafia ai ferri corti* (Verona: Mondadori, 1932), p. 242.
129. Ibid., p. 91.
130. Ibid., p. 244.
131. Newark, *Mafia Allies*, pp. 35–6.

132. Alexander Stille, *Excellent Cadavers* (New York: Vintage Books, 1996), p. 17.

133. Catanzaro, *Men of Respect*, pp. 109–12; Pantaleone, *The Mafia and Politics*, p. 53.

134. Pantaleone, *The Mafia and Politics*, pp. 45–52; Lupo, *History*, pp. 186–7.

135. See Lupo, *History*, p. 22; Stille, *Excellent Cadavers*, p. 17; Christopher Duggan, *Fascism and the Mafia* (New Haven/London: Yale University Press, 1989), pp. 195–9.

136. Bonanno, *A Man of Honour*, pp. 52–4; Lupo, *History*, p. 19.

137. Compare Federico Varese, *Mafias on the Move: How Organized Crime Conquers New Territories* (Princeton NJ: Princeton University Press, 2011), p. 12.

138. Compare ibid., p. 21; Gambetta, *The Sicilian Mafia*, pp. 251–2.

5. WAR AND PEACE IN THE AMERICAN MAFIA, 1920–1941

1. Nick Gentile, *Vita di capomafia* (Rome: Editori Riuniti, 1963), p. 104.

2. Original newsreel footage excerpted in Serena Davies, producer and director, 'The Mafia Connection', in the *Secret War* (WMR Productions/ IMG Entertainment), SE01E03, originally aired 20 April 2011, at https://www.youtube.com/watch?v=HkfszkERIUI at 9'28", accessed 14 March 2015.

3. Diego Gambetta, *The Sicilian Mafia: The Business of Private Protection* (Cambridge, MA: Harvard University Press, 1993).

4. Gentile, *Vita di capomafia*.

5. David Critchley, *The Origin of Organized Crime in America: The New York City Mafia, 1891–1931* (New York: Routledge, 2009).

6. See J. Richard Davis, 'Things I Couldn't Tell till Now', *Collier's*.

7. Thomas E. Dewey, *Twenty Against the Underworld* (Garden City NY: Doubleday, 1974).

8. Hickman Powell, *Lucky Luciano: The Man Who Organized Crime in America* (New York: Barnes & Noble, 1939/2006).

9. Selwyn Raab, *Five Families: The Rise, Decline, and Resurgence of America's Most Powerful Mafia Empires* (New York: St. Martin's Griffin/Thomas Dunne Books, 2005), pp. 22–3.

10. Cited in Critchley, *The Origin of Organized Crime in America*, p. 138; see also Raab, *Five Families*, p. 25.

11. Martin Gosch and Richard Hammer, *The Last Testament of Lucky Luciano* (London: Macmillan London Limited, 1975), p. 43; Raab, *Five Families*, p. 25.

12. Gosch and Hammer, *The Last Testament of Lucky Luciano*, p. 74.

13. J. Richard Davis, 'Things I Couldn't Tell', Part V, p. 36.
14. Powell, *Lucky Luciano*, p. xxii.
15. Dickie, *Cosa Nostra*, p. 176; Critchley, *The Origin of Organized Crime in America*, p. 139.
16. Alan Block, *East Side, West Side: Organizing Crime in New York 1930–1950* (New Brunswick NJ: Transaction Publishers, 1983), pp. 133–5.
17. Joseph Bonanno, *A Man of Honour* (London: Andre Deutsch, 1983), pp. 64–5.
18. Mark Haller, 'Bootleggers and American Gambling 1920–1950', in US Commission on the Review of the National Policy Towards Gambling, *Gambling in America, Appendix 1: Staff and Consultant Papers*, Washington DC, 1976, in NYPL, p. 115.
19. Critchley, *The Origin of Organized Crime in America*, pp. 90–4.
20. Haller, 'Bootleggers', p. 115; Hank Messick, *Syndicate Abroad* (Toronto: The Macmillan Company, 1969), p. 15.
21. Eisenberg *et al.*, *Meyer Lansky*, p. 122; Robert Lacey, *Little Man: Meyer Lansky and the Gangster Life* (Boston MA: Little Brown & Co., 1991), p. 51.
22. Tim Newark, *Lucky Luciano: The Real and the Fake Gangster* (New York: Thomas Duane Books, 2010), p. 20.
23. Peter Andreas, *Smuggler Nation: How Illicit Trade Made America* (New York: Oxford University Press, 2013), p. 232.
24. FBI, 'Mafia Monograph', July 1958, FBI Vault, Section II, pp. 42–3.
25. US Senate, Select Committee on Improper Activities in the Labor or Management Field ('McClellan Committee 1958'), *Investigation of Improper Activities in the Labor or Management Field* (Washington DC: Government Printing Office, 1958), p. 12221.
26. Powell, *Lucky Luciano*, pp. 63–4; Gosch and Hammer, *The Last Testament of Lucky Luciano*, pp. 94–6, 104–8; Critchley, *The Origin of Organized Crime in America*, pp. 140–2.
27. On the importance of New York as a point of importation and its impacts on criminal organization in the city, see Andreas, *Smuggler Nation*, pp. 236–43.
28. Ibid., pp. 243–8.
29. See Block, *East Side*, pp. 245–9.
30. Ibid., p. 256.
31. Critchley, *The Origin of Organized Crime in America*, p. 144.
32. Raab, *Five Families*, p. 26; Newark, *Lucky Luciano*, p. 44.
33. Bonanno, *A Man of Honour*, p. 71. See also Peter Maas, *The Valachi Papers* (New York: Perennial, 1968/2003), p. 84; Gosch and Hammer, *The Last Testament of Lucky Luciano*, p. 46.
34. Critchley, *The Origin of Organized Crime in America*, p. 154.
35. Bonanno, *A Man of Honour*, p. 100.

36. Raab, *Five Families*, p. 26.

37. Critchley, *The Origin of Organized Crime in America*, p. 213.

38. Ibid., p. 142.

39. Ibid., pp. 154–5.

40. Ibid., pp. 155–6.

41. Ibid., p. 157.

42. Bonanno, *A Man of Honour*, p. 76; Lacey, *Little Man*, p. 62.

43. Messick, *Syndicate Abroad*, pp. 16–17.

44. Gentile, *Vita di capomafia*, p. 104.

45. Critchley, *The Origin of Organized Crime in America*, pp. 171–2.

46. See Gentile, *Vita di capomafia*, pp. 96–7.

47. Critchley, *The Origin of Organized Crime in America*, pp. 175–6; see also Bonanno, *A Man of Honour*, p. 106.

48. Bonanno, *A Man of Honour*, p. 85.

49. Gentile, *Vita di capomafia*, p. 96, author's translation.

50. Critchley, *The Origin of Organized Crime in America*, p. 189.

51. Gentile, *Vita di capomafia*, p. 92.

52. Critchley, *The Origin of Organized Crime in America*, p. 176.

53. Critchley, *The Origin of Organized Crime in America*, pp. 176–7; Gentile, *Vita di capomafia*, p. 96; Bonanno, *A Man of Honour*, p. 94.

54. Stathis Kalyvas, *The Logic of Violence in Civil War* (Cambridge: Cambridge University Press, 2006).

55. Critchley, *The Origin of Organized Crime in America*, p. 176, and see pp. 171–3, 182. Compare Bonanno, *A Man of Honour*, pp. 87–8.

56. Bonanno, *A Man of Honour*, p. 104; Raab, *Five Families*, p. 27.

57. Bonanno, *A Man of Honour*, p. 104; Gentile, *Vita di capomafia*, p. 97; Maas, *The Valachi Papers*, p. 77.

58. McClellan Hearings, Part 1, p. 193; Critchley, *The Origin of Organized Crime in America*, p. 179.

59. McClellan Hearings, Part 1, pp. 103–4.

60. See 'Alien-Smuggler Suspect Slain in Park Ave Office', *N.Y. Herald Tribune*, 11 September 1931; 'Seek Official Link in Alien Smuggling', *The New York Times*, 12 September 1931; Block, *East Side*, p. 8; Lupo, *History*, p. 147; Davis, 'Things I Couldn't Tell', Part III, 5 August 1939, p. 44.

61. Newark, *Lucky Luciano*, pp. 1–10; see also Thomas Hunt, 'Year-by-year: Charlie Lucky's Life', *Informer* (April 2012), p. 41.

62. Raab, *Five Families*, p. 27; Bonanno, *A Man of Honour*, p. 104.

63. Critchley, *The Origin of Organized Crime in America*, pp. 180–2.

64. 'Two men shot dead in Bronx gun-trap', *The New York Times*, 6 November 1930, p. 27; Bonanno, *A Man of Honour*, pp. 118–21; Critchley, *The Origin of Organized Crime in America*, pp. 182–3; Hunt, 'Year-by-year', p. 41.

65. Raab, *Five Families*, p. x.

66. Gentile, *Vita di capomafia*, pp. 98, 106; McClellan Hearings, Part 1, p. 215; Critchley, *The Origin of Organized Crime in America*, p. 180.

67. Bonanno, *A Man of Honour*, p. 120; Critchley, *The Origin of Organized Crime in America*, p. 186; Gentile, *Vita di capomafia*, pp. 97–107.

68. Gentile, *Vita di capomafia*, pp. 102–3

69. Ibid., p. 98; Critchley, *The Origin of Organized Crime in America*, p. 185; McClellan Hearings, Part 1, p. 198.

70. Gentile, *Vita di capomafia*, p. 107.

71. Ibid., pp. 108–9; Bonanno, *A Man of Honour*, pp. 121–2.

72. Gentile, *Vita di capomafia*, pp. 110–1.

73. Critchley, *The Origin of Organized Crime in America*, p. 185.

74. Bonanno, *A Man of Honour*, pp. 121–2; Newark, *Lucky Luciano*, pp. 57–8.

75. Valachi's account in McClellan Hearings, Part 1, pp. 210–2; Raab, *Five Families*, p. 28; Bonanno, *A Man of Honour*, p. 122; Gentile, *Vita di capomafia*, p. 117.

76. Gentile, *Vita di capomafia*, p. 112, author's translation.

77. Ibid., pp. 113–5.

78. Bonanno, *A Man of Honour*, p. 125; Gentile, *Vita di capomafia*, p. 115.

79. Francis A. Ianni, 'Formal and Social Organization in an Organized Crime "Family": A Case Study', *U. Fla L. Rev.*, vol. 24, no. 1 (1971), p. 33.

80. Raab, *Five Families*, p. 29; Bonanno, *A Man of Honour*, pp. 125–9.

81. Raab, *Five Families*, p. 29.

82. Maas, p. 84; McClellan Hearings, Part 1, p. 215; Gosch and Hammer, *The Last Testament of Lucky Luciano*, pp. 134–5.

83. Maas, *The Valachi Papers*, pp. 85, 179–80; McClellan Hearings, Part 1, pp. 184–5.

84. Maas, *The Valachi Papers*, p. 85; McClellan Hearings, Part 1, pp. 80–1, 195, 216–7; Gosch and Hammer, *The Last Testament of Lucky Luciano*, p. 134.

85. Compare Critchley, *The Origin of Organized Crime in America*, p. 188.

86. McClellan Hearings, Part 1, pp. 217–8; Messick, *Syndicate Abroad*, p. 20; Bonanno, p. 124; Gentile, *Vita di capomafia*, p. 115.

87. Bonanno, *A Man of Honour*, p. 137.

88. Newark, *Lucky Luciano*, p. 62.

89. Critchley, *The Origin of Organized Crime in America*, p. 191.

90. Gentile, *Vita di capomafia*, pp. 116, 122–3.

91. McClellan Hearings, Part 1, p. 221; Bonanno, *A Man of Honour*, p. 139; Gentile, *Vita di capomafia* p. 116.

92. Messick, *Syndicate Abroad*, p. 19.

93. Bonanno, *A Man of Honour*, p. 139; Hunt, 'Year-by-year', p. 43; Gosch and Hammer, *The Last Testament of Lucky Luciano*, pp. 138–9; McClellan Hearings, Part 1, p. 221.

94. Gentile, *Vita di capomafia*, p. 110; Gosch and Hammer, *The Last Testament of Lucky Luciano*, p. 141.

95. See Critchley, *The Origin of Organized Crime in America*, pp. 192–3; Bonanno, *A Man of Honour*, p. 140; Anthony Scaduto, *"Lucky" Luciano* (London: Sphere, 1976), p. 74.

96. Scaduto, *"Lucky" Luciano*, p. 90.

97. Gosch and Hammer, *The Last Testament of Lucky Luciano*, p. 136; McClellan Hearings, Part 1, p. 222.

98. Gentile, *Vita di capomafia*, pp. 117–8; Messick, *Syndicate Abroad*, p. 21; Critchley, *The Origin of Organized Crime in America*, p. 195.

99. In the popular literature, this has been inflated to a 'purge' of some sixty to ninety leaders. A close reading of newspaper accounts at the time suggests this is vastly exaggerated: Block, *East Side*, pp. 3–9.

100. Critchley, *The Origin of Organized Crime in America*, p. 195; McClellan Hearings, Part 1, p. 229.

101. Raab, *Five Families*, p. 33.

102. McClellan Hearings, Part 1, pp. 81, 236–7.

103. Bonanno, *A Man of Honour*, p. 140.

104. President's Commission, *Task Force Report: Organized Crime*, p. 8; compare Raab, *Five Families*, p. vii.

105. Critchley, *The Origin of Organized Crime in America*, p. 206.

106. FBI, 'Mafia Monograph', II, p. 108.

107. Davis, 'Things I Couldn't Tell', Part V, p. 36.

108. Donald Cressey, *Theft of the Nation: The Structure and Operations of Organized Crime in America* (New York: Harper and Row, 1969), p. 33.

109. Quoted in Raab, *Five Families*, pp. 164–5.

110. Two cases are discussed in ibid., p. 164.

111. Ibid., p. 33.

112. Gentile, *Vita di capomafia*, p. 119, author's translation. See also Gosch and Hammer, *The Last Testament of Lucky Luciano*, pp. 144, 147.

113. Compare Francisco Gutiérrez Sanín and Antonio Giustozzi, 'Networks and Armies: Structuring Rebellion in Colombia and Afghanistan', *Studies in Conflict & Terrorism*, vol. 33 (2010).

114. Raab, *Five Families*, p. 67; Wendy Ruderman, 'The Ice Pick Seems Antiquated, but It Still Shows Up on the Police Blotter', *The New York Times*, 31 August 2012.

115. Gosch and Hammer, *The Last Testament of Lucky Luciano*, pp. 29, 51, 79–81; FBI, 'Mafia Monograph', II, pp. 18–21, 97.

116. Maas, *The Valachi Papers*, p. 98.

117. Bonanno, *A Man of Honour*, pp. 163–4; Maas, *The Valachi Papers*, p. 85.

118. Raab, *Five Families*, p. 35. See also Stephen Fox, *Blood and Power* (New York: William Morrow, 1989), p. 44; Humbert S. Nelli, *The Business of*

Crime: Italians and Syndicate Crime in the United States (Chicago IL: University of Chicago Press, 1981), pp. 140, 180.

119. Gutierrez-Sanín and Giustozzi, 'Networks and Armies', p. 850.
120. President's Commission, *Task Force Report: Organized Crime*, p. 8.
121. Gosch and Hammer, *The Last Testament of Lucky Luciano*, pp. 87, 146; FBI, 'Mafia Monograph', II, p. 83.
122. Sal Vizzini with Oscar Fraley and Marshall Smith, *Vizzini* (New York: Pinnacle Books, 1972), p. 153.
123. Gosch and Hammer, *The Last Testament of Lucky Luciano*, p. 24.
124. Ibid., p. 82.
125. Ibid., p. 101; FBI, 'Mafia Monograph', II, pp. 50–1.
126. Eric J. Hobsbawm, 'Robin Hoodo', *New York Review of Books*, 14 February 1985.
127. Bonanno, *A Man of Honour*, p. 150.
128. Dickie, *Cosa Nostra*, p. 187; see also Lupo, *History*, p. 20.
129. Critchley, *The Origin of Organized Crime in America*, p. 189.
130. See Powell, *Lucky Luciano*, pp. 93–4; Block, *East Side*, pp. 42–4.
131. See Gambetta, *The Sicilian Mafia*, p. 197.
132. Gordon L. Hostetter, 'Racketeering—an Alliance Between Politics and Crime', *National Municipal Review*, vol. XXI, no. II (1932), p. 639.
133. Raab, *Five Families*, pp. 37–8; Maas, *The Valachi Papers*, p. 111.
134. Gosch and Hammer, *The Last Testament of Lucky Luciano*, p. 77.
135. Gambetta, *The Sicilian Mafia*, p. 198.
136. Powell, *Lucky Luciano*, p. 82; Raab, *Five Families*, pp. 37–8; Gosch and Hammer, *The Last Testament of Lucky Luciano*, pp. 77–9.
137. Gosch and Hammer, *The Last Testament of Lucky Luciano*, pp. 38–40.
138. See Samuel Seabury to Hon. Samuel H. Hofstadter, *Intermediate Report*, 25 January 1932, and *Final Report*, n.d. 1932, 'In the matter of the investigation of the departments of the government of the City of New York, etc., pursuant to Joint resolution adopted by the Legislature of the State of New York, March 23, 1931' (Albany NY, 1932), in NYPL.
139. Raab, *Five Families*, pp. 39–40; Critchley, *The Origin of Organized Crime in America*, pp. 73–4.
140. FBI, 'Mafia Monograph', pp. 75–6; Kefauver Committee, *Report*, pp. 151–62.
141. Block, *East Side*, pp. 183–91; see 'Interim Report of Evidence Adduced by the State Crime Commission Relating to Six Brooklyn Locals of the International Longshoremen's Association: Confidential', September 1952, in CURBML.
142. See New York State Crime Commission, 'Fourth Report, Port of New York Waterfront', Legislative Document no. 70, 1953, in CURBML, p. 12; Raab, *Five Families*, p. 68.

143. Block, *East Side*, p. 194.

144. Compare ibid., pp. 193–4.

145. US Senate, Committee on Governmental Affairs, Permanent Subcommittee on Investigations, 'Statement of Robert B. Fiske, Jr., Former US Attorney, Southern District of New York and Alan Levine, Former Assistant US Attorney, Southern District of New York', in *Waterfront Corruption*, Hearings, 97th Congress, 1st session, 25 February 1981 (Washington DC: US Government Printing Office, 1981).

146. See esp. Block, *East Side*, pp. 95–125, 189–90.

147. Kefauver Committee, *Report*, pp. 105–11; Gosch and Hammer, *The Last Testament of Lucky Luciano*, pp. 251–5.

148. Kefauver Committee, *Report*, p. 122.

149. Davis, 'Things I Couldn't Tell', Part V, p. 36.

150. See Hank Messick, *Lansky* (New York: Putnam, 1971), p. 128.

151. Davis, 'Things I Couldn't Tell', Part V, p. 36.

152. Ibid.

153. Lacey, *Little Man*, pp. 49–52, 82–3.

154. Compare Gosch and Hammer, *The Last Testament of Lucky Luciano*, p. 107.

155. Raab, *Five Families*, p. 60.

156. Gus Russo, *The Outfit: The Role of Chicago's Underworld in the Shaping of Modern America* (New York: Bloomsbury, 2001), pp. 112–7, 187–9.

157. Haller, 'Bootleggers', p. 127.

158. Bell, 'Crime as an American Way of Life', p. 147.

159. Maas, *The Valachi Papers*, p. 99; Haller, 'Bootleggers', p. 127; Kefauver Committee, *Report*, pp. 93–4; Raab, *Five Families*, pp. 60–1; Gosch and Hammer, *The Last Testament of Lucky Luciano*, p. 163; Matthew Barnidge, 'Connected by vice: The Longs, Marcello & Concordia', *The Concordia Sentinel*, 9 July 2009.

160. Haller, 'Bootleggers', pp. 129–30.

161. Messick, *Lansky*, p. 48.

162. Kefauver Committee, *Report on Organized Crime*.

163. See *N.Y. Post*, 16 April 1940; Kefauver Committee, *Report*, pp. 102–3; *Miami News*, 18 December 1975.

164. Gosch and Hammer, *The Last Testament of Lucky Luciano*, pp. 25, 29.

165. Kefauver Committee, *Report*, pp. 96, 102.

166. Gosch and Hammer, *The Last Testament of Lucky Luciano*, pp. 29, 51, 74, 79–81; FBI, 'Mafia Monograph', II, pp. 18–21, 97; Raab, *Five Families*, p. 45.

167. Kefauver Committee, *Report*, pp. 164–7.

168. Walter Lippmann, 'The Underworld—A Stultified Conscience', *The Forum*, LXXXV:2 (1931), p. 67.

169. Ibid., p. 99; Raab, *Five Families*, p. 64.

170. Gosch and Hammer, *The Last Testament of Lucky Luciano*, p. 34.

171. Kefauver Committee, *Report*, pp. 92, 103, 125; Raab, *Five Families*, p. 62.

172. Block, *East Side*, p. 33.

173. Ibid., p. 34.

174. *Time*, 28 November 1949, p. 27; Raab, *Five Families*, p. 63.

175. Raab, *Five Families*, pp. 92, 102.

176. Thomas Kessner, *Fiorello H. La Guardia and the Making of Modern New York* (New York: McGraw Hill, 1989), Chapter 10.

177. Gosch and Hammer, *The Last Testament of Lucky Luciano*, pp. 56–8.

178. Ibid., pp. 58–9.

179. Fact Research Inc., 'Gambling in Perspective', in US Commission on the Review of the National Policy Towards Gambling, *Gambling in America, Appendix 1: Staff and Consultant Papers*, Washington DC, 1976, in NYPL, p. 45; Raab, *Five Families*, p. 50.

180. Lacey, *Little Man*, pp. 460–1.

181. Powell, *Lucky Luciano*, pp. 43–4, 79; Terry Golway, *Machine Made: Tammany Hall and the Creation of Modern American Politics* (New York and London: Liveright, 2014), pp. 292–3; Raab, *Five Families*, pp. 50–1; Dickie, *Cosa Nostra*, p. 188.

182. Compare Gosch and Hammer, *The Last Testament of Lucky Luciano*, p. 83.

183. Golway, *Machine Made*, pp. 277–8.

184. Gosch and Hammer, *The Last Testament of Lucky Luciano*, p. 166.

185. Golway, *Machine Made*, p. 279; Block, *East Side*, pp. 54–7; see also Seabury to Hofstadter, *Final Report*; Davis, 'Things I Couldn't Tell', Pt I, p. 38.

186. Gosch and Hammer, *The Last Testament of Lucky Luciano*, p. 166.

187. Joseph McGoldrick, 'The New Tammany', *The American Mercury*, vol. XV, no. 57, September 1928, pp. 8–9.

188. Golway, *Machine Made*, pp. 290–2; McGoldrick, 'New Tammany', pp. 4–5.

189. Maas, *The Valachi Papers*, p. 123.

190. See Valachi in McClellan Hearings, p. 122; Raab, *Five Families*, pp. 46–7; Powell, *Lucky Luciano*, p. 25; Block, *East Side*, pp. 152–9.

191. See Davis, 'Things I Couldn't Tell', Part II, pp. 21, 37; Block, *East Side*, p. 36; Seabury to Hofstadter, *Final Report*, pp. 107, 112.

192. Davis, 'Things I Couldn't Tell', Pt I, p. 41.

193. Ibid., Pt V, p. 36.

194. Ibid., Pt IV, p. 17.

195. Ibid., Pt II, p. 21.

196. Ibid., Pt IV, p. 17.

197. Ibid., Pts IV, V.

198. Ibid., Pt I, p. 41.

199. Ibid., Pt I, p. 40.

200. Ibid., Pt I, p. 40.

201. *People of the State of New York v. James J. Hines*, 248 N.Y. 93, N.Y. 1940, Indictment no. 213241, Court of General Sessions, County of New York, 26 May 1938, and Sentence, 23 March 1939, and Respondent's Brief, Court of Appeals, pp. 9–42; Block, *East Side*, pp. 154–5; Powell, *Lucky Luciano*, p. 45; Richard Norton Smith, *Thomas E. Dewey and His Times* (New York: Simon and Schuster, 1982), pp. 255–9.

202. *NY v. Hines*; Block, *East Side*, pp. 152–7; Davis, 'Things I Couldn't Tell', Pt III, p. 12.

203. Davis, 'Things I Couldn't Tell', Pt II, p. 21.

204. Valachi in McClellan Hearings, p. 123; Raab, *Five Families*, p. 47; Gosch and Hammer, *The Last Testament of Lucky Luciano*, p. 181.

205. Davis, 'Things I Couldn't Tell', Pt IV, p. 17.

206. Ibid., Pt IV, p. 17; Raab, *Five Families*, p. 47.

207. Gosch and Hammer, *The Last Testament of Lucky Luciano*, p. 185.

208. Ibid., p. 200.

209. Raab, *Five Families*, p. 48.

210. Gosch and Hammer, *The Last Testament of Lucky Luciano*, p. 186.

211. Valachi in McClellan Hearings, pp. 120–5; Raab, *Five Families*, pp. 48–9; Gosch and Hammer, *The Last Testament of Lucky Luciano*, p. 186.

212. Valachi in McClellan Hearings, pp. 120–1.

213. Quoted in Powell, *Lucky Luciano*, p. 241.

214. Norton Smith, *Thomas E. Dewey*, pp. 150–1.

215. Davis, 'Things I Couldn't Tell', Pt VI, p. 18; Newark, *Lucky Luciano*, pp. 76–81.

216. Powell, *Lucky Luciano*, pp. 110–11, 212–4.

217. See Ibid, pp. 268–9.

218. Powell, *Lucky Luciano*, pp. 31–3, 41, 96, 133; *People of the State of NY v. Charles Luciano*, NYMA, New York County District Attorney closed case files, 1936 Luciano Collection, Box 13, File 3; and see FBI, 'Mafia Monograph', II, p. 74; Block, *East Side*, pp. 141–8; Newark, *Lucky Luciano*, pp. 97–100; Gosch and Hammer, *The Last Testament of Lucky Luciano*, pp. 201–2.

219. Block, *East Side*, p. 146; Raab, *Five Families*, p. 56; Newark, *Lucky Luciano*, pp. 103–7; Powell, *Lucky Luciano*, pp. 116–9, 135–7.

220. Pre-trial testimony of Flo Brown, in *People of the State of NY v. Charles Luciano*, Box 13, File 3. She recanted: see affidavit of Flo Brown, in trial appeal files, in ibid., Box 16, File 9, New York Department of City Records. But this may have been under Mob pressure: Powell, pp. 268, 326–37; Gosch and Hammer, *The Last Testament of Lucky Luciano*, p. 207.

221. Dickie, *Cosa Nostra*, p. 193.

222. Powell, *Lucky Luciano*, pp. 169, 201–5, 221–4.

223. Newark, *Lucky Luciano*, pp. 117–8.

224. Quoted in Powell, *Lucky Luciano*, p. 241.

225. Raab, *Five Families*, p. 55; Newark, *Lucky Luciano*, pp. 113–29; Hunt, 'Year-by-year', pp. 44–5; Norton Smith, *Thomas E. Dewey*, pp. 152–3.

226. Norton Smith, *Thomas E. Dewey*, pp. 285–6.

227. Davis, 'Things I Couldn't Tell', Pt VI, p. 18.

228. Quoted in Newark, *Lucky Luciano*, p. 80; see also Davis, Pt VI, p. 18.

229. Davis, 'Things I Couldn't Tell', Pt VI, p. 38.

230. Kefauver Committee, *Report*, p. 175.

231. Powell, *Lucky Luciano*, p. xxiv.

232. FBI, 'Mafia Monograph', II, p. iv.

233. Raab, *Five Families*, p. 59.

234. Lacey, *Little Man*, pp. 201–2, 206.

235. Ibid., pp. 194–5; Dickie, *Mafia Republic*, p. 60.

236. John Kerry, *The New War: The Web of Crime that Threatens America's Security* (New York: Simon & Schuster, 1997).

237. Cohen, 'The Lost Journals of Meyer Lansky'.

238. Raab, *Five Families*, p. 98.

239. Gosch and Hammer, *The Last Testament of Lucky Luciano*, p. 173.

240. Quoted in Newark, *Lucky Luciano*, p. 30.

6. THE UNDERWORLD PROJECT, 1941–1943

1. Dennis Eisenberg, Uri Dan and Eli Lanau, *Meyer Lansky: Mogul of the Mob* (New York: Paddington Press, 1979), p. 181.

2. Rodney Campbell, *The Luciano Project* (New York: McGraw-Hill, 1977), pp. 47–9; Robert Lacey, *Little Man: Meyer Lansky and the Gangster Life* (Boston MA: Little Brown & Co., 1991), p. 115; *New York Daily News*, 9 January 1941; Martin Gosch and Richard Hammer, *The Last Testament of Lucky Luciano* (London: Macmillan London Limited, 1975), pp. 263–4.

3. William B. Herlands, Commissioner of Investigation, to Hon. Thomas E. Dewey, Governor of the State of New York, 17 September 1954, URHIM, box 16, folder 2 ('Herlands Report'), pp. 29–32. Henceforth URHIM box and folder numbers are listed as 'box:folder', i.e. 16:2. See also Testimony of Joseph Lanza, 30 April 1954, URHIM 13:3 ('Lanza testimony'), pp. 4–5; Testimony of Joseph K. Guerin, 30 April 1954, URHIM 11:20 ('Guerin testimony'), pp. 7–10; Affidavit of Murray L. Gurfein, 8 September 1954, URHIM 11:21 ('Gurfein 1954 affidavit'), p. 5; Roswell B. Perkins to Mr. Moser, Memorandum, 6 July 1951, URHIM 11:21, p. 3.

4. On the name, see Herlands Report, p. 91.

5. Herlands Report, pp. 92–4; Campbell, *The Luciano Project*, pp. 213–32.

6. Campbell, *The Luciano Project*, p. 25.

7. Tim Newark, *Mafia Allies: The True Story of America's Secret Alliance with the Mob in World War II* (St Paul MN: Zenith Press, 2007), p. 99.

8. Herlands Report, pp. 4, 14.

9. Testimony of Maurice P. Kelly, 6 July 1954, URHIM 12:12 ('Kelly testimony'), p. 10.

10. Affidavit of James O'Malley, Jr., 7 April 1954, URHIM 13:17 ('O'Malley affidavit'), p. 3. See also Affidavit of Frank Hogan, 9 September 1954, URHIM 16:3A, Appendix IV ('Hogan affidavit'); Affidavit of Roscoe C. MacFall, 9 March 1954, URHIM 16:1 ('MacFall affidavit'); Affidavit of Murray L. Gurfein, 12 June 1945, URHIM 11:21 ('Gurfein 1945 affidavit'); and Herlands Report, pp. 4, 14, 16–19.

11. Campbell, *The Luciano Project*, p. 28.

12. Herlands Report, pp. 4, 17–19; Newark, *Mafia Allies*, pp. 78–80.

13. Newark, *Mafia Allies*, pp. 83–7; Tim Newark, *Lucky Luciano: The Real and the Fake Gangster* (New York: Thomas Duane Books, 2010), p. 145.

14. See Gosch and Hammer, *The Last Testament of Lucky Luciano*, p. 260; Campbell, *The Luciano Project*, p. 29; Newark, *Mafia Allies*, pp. 83–98; Newark, *Lucky Luciano*, pp. 149–53; Eisenberg *et al.*, *Meyer Lansky*, pp. 189–90; Salvatore Lupo, 'The Allies and the mafia', *J. Mod. Italian Stud.*, vol. 2, no. 1 (1997), p. 23.

15. Harvey Ardman, *Normandie: Her Life and Times* (New York: Franklin Watts, 1985), p. 349.

16. Lanza testimony, p. 22.

17. Herlands Report, p. 4. See also Kelly testimony, p. 16.

18. Eisenberg *et al.*, *Meyer Lansky*, p. 181.

19. Testimony of Felix Saco, 16 June 1954, URHIM 14:13 ('Felix Saco testimony'), p. 23; Herlands Report, p. 91.

20. Felix Saco testimony, p. 22.

21. Testimony of Anthony J. Marsloe, 3 June 1954, URHIM 13:11 ('Marsloe testimony'), pp. 8–9; Testimony of Paul Alfieri, 8 June 1954, URHIM 11:2 ('Alfieri testimony'), p. 11.

22. Charles R. Haffenden, 'Subject: Charles Luciano', Memorandum, 25 July 1945, URHIM 12:1. See also Testimony of Dominick Saco, 2 June 1954, URHIM 14:2, pp. 5–6 ('Dominick Saco testimony'); MacFall affidavit; Gurfein 1945 affidavit; 'Salvatore Lucania', 13 March 1946, FBI, 39–2141–10; 'Charles Lucky Luciano, Miscellaneous Information Concerning Parole and Deportation', 9 May 1946, FBI, 39–2141–33; A. Rosen to E. Tamm, 'Charles "Lucky" Luciano, Parole, Miscellaneous; Information Concerning', 17 May 1946, FBI, 39–2141–39; Campbell, *The Luciano Project*, pp. 83–110.

23. Rear Admiral Carl F. Espe to Herlands, 26 July 1954, URHIM 13:11;

Affidavit of Wallace S. Wharton, 23 June 1954, URHIM 14:10 ('Wharton affidavit'), p. 5; MacFall affidavit; Herlands Report, p. 80.

24. Marsloe testimony, p. 29.

25. Herlands Report, pp. 24–6; MacFall affidavit; Hogan affidavit; Gurfein 1945 affidavit; Gurfein 1954 affidavit, p. 3; Marsloe testimony, p. 10; O'M alley affidavit, p. 3; R.C. MacFall, 'Haffenden, Charles R., Alleged Irregularity Conduct of', 9 August 1945, URHIM 12:1; Powell, p. 166.

26. Warren Moscow, 'Tammany Picks Dewey Aide; Action Blow to La Guardia', *The New York Times*, 2 August 1941, pp. 1, 16.

27. Herlands Report, pp. 36–8; Hogan affidavit, p. 3; Lanza testimony, pp. 5–6; Guerin testimony, pp. 4–5; Gurfein 1954 affidavit, p. 4; and see Testimony of Joseph Lanza in *Public hearings (no. 4) conducted by the New York State Crime Commission pursuant to the Governor's executive order of March 29, 1951* (New York County Court House, New York, 13–19 November 1952), NYPL.

28. Herlands Report, pp. 32–4; Lanza testimony, pp. 6–11, 23; Guerin testimony, pp. 11–13; Gurfein 1954 affidavit, p. 5; Dominick Saco testimony, pp. 8–9, 26–7.

29. Lanza testimony, pp. 6, 24, 33–6, 38–9; Dominick Saco testimony, pp. 6–7, 11–14, 43; Kelly testimony, p. 12; Testimony of Hiram Chester Swezey, 29 May 1954, URHIM 14:6 ('Swezey testimony'), pp. 10–11; Campbell, *The Luciano Project*, pp. 49–51.

30. Lanza testimony, pp. 24–32; Swezey testimony, pp. 6–9; Dominick Saco testimony, pp. 12–13; Herlands Report, pp. 34–6.

31. Herlands Report, p. 35; Lanza testimony, pp. 34–5; MacFall affidavit; Kelly testimony, p. 11.

32. Dominick Saco testimony, pp. 44–5.

33. Swezey testimony, p. 9; Dominick Saco testimony, pp. 29–31.

34. Lanza testimony, p. 23. See also pp. 17, 22; and see Swezey testimony, pp. 6–7.

35. Lanza discusses the suspicions he faced within his own ranks in Lanza testimony, pp. 45–6; see also Kelly testimony, p. 12; Dominick Saco testimony, pp. 15–16; and 'Re: Conference with Dominick Saco and Felix Saco', Memorandum, 9 April 1954, URHIM 14:2, p. 2.

36. Herlands Report, p. 5.

37. Herlands Report, Appendix II, War Chronology Pertinent to this Report, URHIM 16:3A; Campbell, *The Luciano Project*, pp. 32, 67; Robert Lacey, *Little Man: Meyer Lansky and the Gangster Life* (Boston MA: Little Brown & Co., 1991), pp. 115–6.

38. Herlands Report, pp. 4, 36–40; Lanza testimony, pp. 45–9; Guerin testimony, p. 20; Kelly testimony, pp. 19–20; Marsloe testimony, p. 14; Testimony of Meyer Lansky, 13 April 1954, URHIM 13:2 ('Lansky tes-

timony'), pp. 17–18; Testimony of Moses Polakoff, 21 June 1954, URHIM 13:19 ('Polakoff testimony), pp. 11, 46; Hogan affidavit, p. 4; Gurfein 1954 affidavit, p. 6; Perkins to Moser, 6 July 1951, URHIM 11:21, p. 3.

39. Dominick Saco testimony, p. 15.

40. Polakoff testimony, p. 2; Gurfein's 1945 affidavit; Gurfein 1954 affidavit, p. 7.

41. Polakoff testimony, pp. 8–9, 15; Herlands Report, pp. 5, 41–6

42. Lansky testimony; Gurfein's 1954 affidavit, pp. 7–8; Newark, *Lucky Luciano*, pp. 154; Ezio Costanzo, *The Mafia and the Allies: Sicily 1943 and the Return of the Mafia*, trans. George Lawrence (New York: Enigma, 2007), p. 52.

43. Lansky testimony, p. 8; Herlands Report, p. 47.

44. Herlands Report, pp. 6–7, 49–55; Gurfein 1945 affidavit, p. 2; Gurfein 1954 affidavit, pp. 8–9; Hogan affidavit, p. 4; Espe to Herlands, 26 July 1954, URHIM 13:11; Statement of Vernon Morhous, URHIM 13:13, p. 2.

45. Herlands Report, pp. 61–2, 68; Lansky testimony, p. 13; Polakoff testimony, pp. 13–14; Newark, *Lucky Luciano*, p. 156; Newark, *Mafia Allies*, pp. 99–111; Selwyn Raab, *Five Families: The Rise, Decline, and Resurgence of America's Most Powerful Mafia Empires* (New York: St. Martin's Griffin/ Thomas Dunne Books, 2005), p. 78.

46. Herlands Report, p. 79; MacFall affidavit; Lansky testimony, pp. 35–6; Lanza testimony, p. 37; Marsloe testimony, p. 21; Polakoff testimony, pp. 27, 62.

47. Charles R. Haffenden, 'Subject: Charles Luciano', Memorandum, 25 July 1945, URHIM 12:1; Vernon A. Morhous, Warden, Great Meadow Prison to Frederick A. Moran, Chairman, Board of Parole, 10 September 1945, URHIM 17:no number; Polakoff testimony, pp. 44–6, 56, 60; Herlands Report, pp. 7, 59–60; Kefauver Hearings, Hearing Pertaining to New York-New Jersey, New York City, February 13–15, 1951—Executive Session, Part VII, pp. 606–7; Newark, *Lucky Luciano*, pp. 154–7.

48. Transcripts and summaries of the wiretaps are in URHIM 12:7.

49. Lansky testimony, p. 23; Kelly testimony, pp. 21–2, 27–8; Lanza testimony, pp. 53–6, 82–4, 97; Dominick Saco testimony, p. 41; Polakoff testimony, p. 54; Herlands Report, pp. 68–70, 79, 87–9; Newark, *Mafia Allies*, pp. 105–7. The extension of the scheme to other cities is indicated by Murray Gurfein, in 'New Version of Aid in War', *The New York Times*, 23 February 1947.

50. Herlands Report, p. 80.

51. See Gary Cohen, 'The Keystone Kommandos', *The Atlantic*, February 2002, pp. 46–59; Joel Samaha, Sam Root and Paul Sexton, eds, *Transcript of Proceedings before the Military Commission to Try Persons Charged with Offenses*

against the Law of War and the Articles of War, Washington D.C., July 8 to July 31, 1942 (Minneapolis: University of Minnesota, 2004), USMC, at http://www.soc.umn.edu/~samaha/nazi_saboteurs/nazi01.htm, accessed 14 March 2015. See also *Ex parte Quirin* (317 US 1 (1942)).

52. 'Re: Conference with Dominick Saco and Felix Saco', 9 April 1954, URHIM 14:2 ('Sacos conference'), p. 5; Testimony of Joachim Titolo, 8 June 1954, URHIM 14:7 ('Titolo testimony'), p. 28; Dominick Saco testimony, pp. 30–2, 46–7; Felix Saco testimony, pp. 13–20, 28–9; Swezey testimony, pp. 11–15; Marsloe's testimony, p. 11. Compare Campbell, *The Luciano Project*, pp. 111–3; Newark, *Lucky Luciano*, p. 146.

53. Eisenberg *et al.*, *Meyer Lansky*, p. 181.

54. Lanza testimony, pp. 64–6, 83; Kelly testimony, pp. 25–6; see also Newark, *Lucky Luciano*, p. 157; Newark, *Mafia Allies*, pp. 108–9; Campbell, *The Luciano Project*, pp. 111–27; and Raab, *Five Families*, p. 77. Compare the underlying testimony with the Herlands Report, pp. 73–4, which notably fails to mention the physical assault.

55. Polakoff testimony, pp. 26–7.

56. Herlands Report, pp. 19, 63–4; Lanza testimony, pp. 19–20; Lansky testimony, pp. 16–19; Wharton affidavit, p. 3; Sacos conference, pp. 3–4.

57. Lanza testimony, p. 19; Saco testimony, pp. 26–7; Alfieri testimony, p. 7; Dreiband to Hogan, 25 February 1943, URHIM 12:7; Campbell, *The Luciano Project*, pp. 56–8.

58. Felix Saco testimony, pp. 4–5, 13–14, 27–8.

59. Testimony of Willis George, URHIM 11:17.

60. Dominick Saco testimony, pp. 37–41.

61. Dominick Saco testimony, pp. 37–9; Lanza testimony, pp. 57–61; Continuing testimony of Joseph Lanza, 16 June 1954, URHIM 13:3, pp. 2–6; Sacos conference, p. 3; Dreiband to Hogan, 25 February 1943, URHIM 12:7; Herlands Report, p. 72.

62. The incident is obliquely alluded to in Herlands Report, p. 78. See also Dreiband to Hogan, URHIM 12:7. And see Dorothy G. Wayman, *David I. Walsh: Citizen-Patriot* (Milwaukee WI: Bruce Publishing Company, 1952), pp. 312 et seq.

63. 'John Dunn', N.Y. Police Department Prisoner's Criminal Record, 7 July 1954, URHIM 11:13; Lansky testimony, pp. 19–22; Herlands Report, p. 65.

64. 'Memorandum', 15 July 1954, URHIM 11:13.

65. Lansky testimony, p. 21.

66. Newark, *Lucky Luciano*, p. 157; Newark, *Mafia Allies*, p. 106.

67. Lansky testimony, p. 22.

68. Address of Rear Admiral W.S. Pye, USN., President, Naval War College and Commandant, Naval Operating Base, Newport, R.I., at Graduation

Exercises of the Naval Training School, New York, NY, 16 March 1944, in Herlands Report, Appendix E.

69. Costanzo, *The Mafia and the Allies*, pp. 6, 58–60.

70. Lanza testimony, p. 95; Kelly testimony, pp. 31–3; Wharton affidavit, p. 3; Jeffrey J. Robertson, Parole District Supervisor to Hon. Frederick Moran, Chairman, Board of Parole, 5 June 1945, URHIM 17:no number; FBI, 'Charles "Lucky" Luciano, Parole', 22 March 1946, FBI, 39–2141–45.

71. Haffenden to Breitel, 17 May 1945, URHIM 12:1. See also Commutation of Sentence Report, Charles Luciano, C-3632, 5 July 1945, URHIM 17:no number.

72. Lansky testimony, pp. 24–7; Kelly testimony, pp. 31–3; Dominick Saco testimony, p. 21; Memorandum of Conference with Kathleen Mitchell Cowen, 7 July 1954, URHIM 17:9; Robertson to Moran, 5 June 1945, URHIM 17:no number; Macfall, 'Haffenden, Charles R., Alleged Irregularity Conduct of', 9 August 1945, URHIM 12:1; Herlands Report, pp. 65–7, 78–9. See also Earl Brennan to H. Gregory Thomas, 'Statement Relative to Recruiting of Sicilians in New York Area', 1 October 1942, NARA, Records of the Office of Strategic Services, RG 226, Entry 142, Box 2, Folder 14.

73. Lanza testimony, pp. 77–8, 92.

74. Commutation of Sentence Report.

75. Herlands Report, p. 93; Kelly testimony, p. 33; Marsloe testimony, p. 20; Alfieri testimony, p. 16; Wharton affidavit, p. 4.

76. Herlands Report, p. 8; Wharton Affidavit, p. 2.

77. Commutation of Sentence Report.

78. Wharton affidavit, p. 6.

79. Wharton affidavit, p. 5; Commutation of Sentence Report; Newark, *Lucky Luciano*, pp. 163–4.

80. BNA, WO 220/403.

81. Joint Staff Planners, *Special Military Plan for Psychological Warfare in Sicily*, 9 April 1943, WO 204/3701.

82. Newark, *Mafia Allies*, p. 134.

83. Marsloe testimony, pp. 30–5; Report, 10 December 1943, File No. A8–2, Serial: 0860, URHIM 13:11.

84. Marsloe testimony, pp. 25–6.

85. Michele Pantaleone, *The Mafia and Politics* (London: Chatto & Windus: 1966), pp. 54–9.

86. Newark, *Lucky Luciano*, pp. 169–72; Newark, *Mafia Allies*, pp. 158–60, 177–82.

87. Alfieri testimony, pp. 19–20; Titolo testimony, p. 15; Herlands Report, p. 86.

88. Alfieri testimony, p. 7; 'Exploitation of technological intelligence', manuscript by Anthony J. Marsloe, URHIM 11:no number, p. 2. See also Eisenberg *et al.*, *Meyer Lansky*, pp. 211–13.

89. The citation is at the *Military Times Hall of Valor*: http://projects.militarytimes.com/citations-medals-awards/recipient.php?recipientid=304944, accessed 14 March 2015.

90. Titolo testimony, pp. 17, 24; Herlands Report, p. 87.

91. Titolo testimony, p. 19.

92. Polakoff testimony, pp. 8, 74.

93. The formal application and other materials are in URHIM 14:12. See also Testimony of George Wolf, Esq., 30 July 1954, URHIM 14:12; Hogan affidavit, pp. 4–5; Polakoff testimony, pp. 15–16; Herlands report, pp. 95–8; Newark, *Lucky Luciano*, p. 159; Campbell, *The Luciano Project*, pp. 152–60.

94. Polakoff testimony, p. 32.

95. Materials from the Parole Board's inquiry and the deportation decision are in URHIM 16:1 and 17:no number. See also Polakoff testimony, pp. 56–9; Herlands Report, pp. 9–10, 99–100; and Campbell, *The Luciano Project*, pp. 192–256.

96. Herlands Report; and see 'Dewey Commutes Luciano Sentence', *The New York Times*, 4 January 1946.

97. President Barack Obama, *Strategy to Combat Transnational Organized Crime: Addressing Converging Threats to National Security* (Washington DC: The White House, 19 July 2011).

98. Lansky testimony, p. 29.

99. Marsloe testimony, p. 30; see also pp. 10–11, 18.

100. Newark, *Lucky Luciano*, p. 142; Newark, *Mafia Allies*, pp. 70–6.

101. Valachi's account in McClellan Hearings, Part 1, pp. 129, 132–3; McClellan Hearings, Part 1, p, 249, 313; Raab, *Five Families*, p. 81; Newark, *Mafia Allies*, p. 116–9.

102. Herlands Report, p. 21.

103. Herlands Report, pp. 12, 94.

104. Testimony of Harold W. MacDowell, n.d., URHIM 13:8.

105. Polakoff testimony, p. 42.

106. See untitled note for file, 'J.I.', 30 April 1954, URHIM 12:7.

7. GOVERNING SICILY, 1942–1968

1. Brigadier-General George S. Smith to Supreme Allied Commander, 'Report on Conditions in Sicily', 23 November 1945, BNA, WO 204/2449.

2. Ezio Costanzo, *The Mafia and the Allies: Sicily 1943 and the Return of the Mafia*, trans. George Lawrence (New York: Enigma, 2007), p. 39.

3. Macmillan to Foreign Office, Algiers, 15 January 1944, BNA, FO 371/43918; Harold Macmillan, *War Diaries: Politics and War in the Mediterranean, January 1943–May 1945* (London: Macmillan, 1984), p. 352.

4. D.S. Duff, 'Narrative for Official History of Civil Affairs in Italy (the Sicily campaign)', undated, BNA, CAB 44/171, Chapter 2, Part I, p. 13. See also Grey, 'Sicily under Italian Rule', 1 December 1942, FO 371/33251; and Foreign Research & Press Service, Balliol College, Oxford, 'Notes on Sicily (19.11.42)', 12 December 1942, FO 371/33251.

5. Tim Newark, *Mafia Allies: The True Story of America's Secret Alliance with the Mob in World War II* (St Paul MN: Zenith Press, 2007), pp. 142–3.

6. Lord Rennell, 'Confidential Notes in Reply to Points Made in House of Commons Debate', 3 August 1943, BNA, FO 371/37327, pp. 2–3.

7. Capt. W.E. Scotten, 'The Problem of Mafia in Sicily', 29 October 1943, BNA, FO 371/37327, pp. 4–5.

8. Notes on meeting held in HQ Island Base Section, 3 December 1943, BNA, WO 204/827.

9. Monte S. Finkelstein, *Separatism, the Allies, and the Mafia: The Struggle for Sicilian Independence, 1943–1948* (Bethlehem PA/London: LeHigh University Press/Associated University Press, 1998), pp. 30–1.

10. Michele Pantaleone, *The Mafia and Politics* (London: Chatto & Windus: 1966), pp. 65–70.

11. Scotten, 'The Problem', pp. 4–5.

12. Norman Lewis, *Naples '44. A World War II Diary of Occupied Italy* (New York: Carroll & Graf, 1978/2005), p. 109.

13. Lewis, *Naples '44*, pp. 109, 122–3.

14. Finkelstein, *Separatism, the Allies, and the Mafia*, p. 29.

15. Ibid., pp. 31–2; Lewis, *Naples '44*, pp. 116–17.

16. Pantaleone, *The Mafia and Politics*, p. 70.

17. 'AMGOT Facing Its Task', *The Times* (London), 21 September 1943, cutting in FO 371/37326; Newark, *Mafia Allies*, pp. 199–201.

18. Newark, *Mafia Allies*, p. 198; 'Mafia Chiefs caught by Allies in Sicily', *The New York Times*, 10 September 1943, p. 4; 'Allies Smash Mafia Society, Bane of Sicily', *The New York Times*, 11 September 1943.

19. Newark, *Mafia Allies*, pp. 190–1.

20. Salvatore Lupo, 'The Allies and the mafia', *J. Mod. Italian Stud.*, vol. 2, no. 1 (1997), p. 24.

21. Alfieri testimony, pp. 22–3.

22. Alfieri testimony, p. 20; Titolo testimony, p. 18.

23. Joseph Russo, in BBC, 'Allied to the Mafia', *Timewatch*, SE01E01 (BBC), originally aired 13 January 1993, available at https://www.youtube.com/watch?v=PPSDa3ANI7s, accessed 19 August 2014.

24. Untitled seven-page report by Experimental Department G-3, Palermo, to Experimental Department G-3, Algiers, 13 August 1943, NARA, RG 226, Entry 99, Box 39, Folder 195A.

25. Combined Chiefs of Staff Memorandum for Information No. 133, 'Second Situation Report on AMG Sicily', 2 September 1943, FO 371/37326.

26. Rennell, 'Confidential Notes', pp. 2–3.

27. French to Dixon, 'Report of the Working of AMGOT', 16 September 1943, BNA, FO 371/37326.

28. Rennell, 'Confidential Notes', pp. 2–3. See also Luigi Lumia, *Villalba: Storia e Memoria* (Caltanissetta: Edizioni Lussografica, 1990), Vol. II, p. 432.

29. Rennell, 'Confidential Notes', pp. 2–3.

30. Charles R.S. Harris, *Allied Military Administration in Italy 1943–1945* (London: HM Stationery Office, 1957), p. 63.

31. Rennell, 'Monthly report for August 1943 on the Administration of Sicily', 27 October 1943, BNA, CAB 122/442, p. 5. A similar analysis is offered in Duff, 'Narrative', Chapter 2, Part III, p. 49.

32. Russo, 'Allied to the Mafia'.

33. See Lewis, *Naples '44*, pp. 61, 70, 125.

34. See George C.S. Benson and Maurice Neufield, 'Allied Military Government in Italy', in Carl J. Friedrich, *et al.*, *American Experiences in Military Government in World War II* (New York: Rinehart & Company, Inc., 1948), pp. 111–47.

35. Minutes of Meeting of Provincial C.A.P.O.s held at H.Q., AMGOT, Palermo, at 1000 hrs., 8 September 1943, BNA, FO 371/37327, p. 4.

36. Minutes of Meeting of Provincial C.A.P.O.s held at H.Q., AMGOT, Palermo at 1000 hrs, 6 October 1943, BNA, FO 371/37327.

37. Harris, *Allied Military Administration in Italy*, p. 63.

38. Rennell, 'Monthly Report', pp. 5–6.

39. Scotten, 'The Problem'.

40. Ibid., pp. 2–4.

41. Ibid., pp. 2–3.

42. Ibid., p. 3.

43. Ibid., pp. 4–5.

44. Macmillan to Eden, 5 September 1943, BNA, FO 371/37327.

45. Hilaire Belloc, *Sonnets & Verse* (London: Duckworth & Co., 1923), p. 152.

46. Newark, *Mafia Allies*, p. 195.

47. Scotten, 'The Problem', p. 4.

48. Duff, Chapter 2, Part III, p. 53; Notes, Meeting of Intelligence Officers in Palermo, 10 February 1944, BNA, WO 204/827, p. 4.

49. David Hanna, *Vito Genovese* (New York: Belmont Tower Books, 1974), pp. 69–74; Costanzo, *The Mafia and the Allies*, p. 127; Valachi in McClellan

Hearings, Part 1, pp. 175–6; Selwyn Raab, *Five Families: The Rise, Decline, and Resurgence of America's Most Powerful Mafia Empires* (New York: St. Martin's Griffin/Thomas Dunne Books, 2005), p. 82; Newark, *Mafia Allies*, pp. 215–6, 222–6; Pantaleone, *The Mafia and Politics*, pp. 62–4; Martin Gosch and Richard Hammer, *The Last Testament of Lucky Luciano* (London: Macmillan London Limited, 1975), pp. 274, 303.

50. Scotten, 'The Problem', p. 4.

51. Gosch and Hammer, *The Last Testament of Lucky Luciano*, p. 273.

52. H.L. Coles and A.K. Weinberg, *Civil Affairs. Soldiers Become Governors*, CMH 11–3 (Washington DC: US Army, 1964), p. 210; notes on file cover R 880/693/22, 18 January 1944, covering Resident Minister, Algiers, to Foreign Office, 15 January 1944, BNA, FO 371/43918; Lewis, *Naples '44*, pp. 109–10; Memorandum, Re: Mary Katen, 12 February 1951, URHIM 17:no number.

53. Ed Reid, *Mafia* (New York: Signet, 1964, revd ed.), pp. 85–95, 163–84; Newark, *Mafia Allies*, pp. 222–6.

54. W.E. Scotten, 'Questions relating to political, social, and economic forces in Sicily and South Italy', Security Intelligence Subsection of AMG HQ Palermo, 10 December 1943, BNA, FO 371/43918, p. 4.

55. Ibid., pp. 5–6.

56. Ibid.

57. Untitled two-page report, 3 December 1943, BNA, WO 204/12615.

58. Notes, Meeting of Intelligence Officers in Palermo, 10 February 1944, BNA, WO 204/827.

59. Scotten, 'The Problem', p. 5.

60. Ibid. On the Poletti appointments see Finkelstein, *Separatism, the Allies, and the Mafia*, p. 57.

61. Scotten, 'Questions relating', pp. 5–6. See also Pantaleone, *The Mafia and Politics*, pp. 87, 195.

62. Pink, File Annotation, on Rennell, 'Situation in Sicily', 3 September 1943, FO 371/37326; and Rennell, Memorandum, 20 August 1943, BNA, WO 220/312, p. 4. On the background of the separatist movement see Finkelstein, *Separatism, the Allies, and the Mafia*, pp. 36–52.

63. Joint Intelligence Collecting Agency, 'Comprehensive Outline of the Sicilian Separatist Movement', 17 January 1944, BNA, WO 204/12618, p. 3; US Naval Intelligence, Palermo, Report, 15 February 1945, BNA, WO 204/12618; Pantaleone, *The Mafia and Politics*, pp. 66, 75; Finkelstein, *Separatism, the Allies, and the Mafia*, pp. 60–1; Newark, *Mafia Allies*, pp. 242–3.

64. Finkelstein, *Separatism, the Allies, and the Mafia*, p. 61.

65. John Dickie, *Cosa Nostra* (London: Palgrave Macmillan, 2005), p. 198.

66. Vice-Consul Manley, 'Report on Sicilian Separatism and the Movimento

per L'Indipendenza della Sicilia', 17 April 1946, BNA, FO 371/67786, p. 2.

67. Raimondo Catanzaro, *Men of Respect: A Social History of the Sicilian Mafia* (New York: The Free Press, 1988), p. 116.

68. JICA, 'Comprehensive Outline', pp. 3–4.

69. Catanzaro, *Men of Respect*, p. 118.

70. JICA, 'Comments on Separatist Movement in Sicily', 21 January 1944, BNA, WO 204/12618, p. 2. See also G-2(CI) NATO to G-2(CI) AFHQ, 'Separatism and Separatists', 11 January 1944, BNA, WO 204/12618.

71. See Salvatore Lupo, *History of the Mafia*, trans. Antony Shugaar (New York: Columbia University Press, 2009), p. 189.

72. See Italian Parliamentary Commission of Inquiry into the Mafia phenomenon in Siçily, *Relazione sui lavori svolti e sullo stato del fenomeno Mafioso al termine della V legislature* (Relazione Cattanei), Legislature V, Doc. xxiii, n. 2 (Rome: Senate Printing Press, 1972), p. 117.

73. Pantaleone, *The Mafia and Politics*, pp. 65, 71.

74. 'Selection of a native Governor', 10 January 1944, NARA, RG 226, 226/55277; Harold C. Swan, 'Sicilian Separatist Movement', 23 October 1944, BNA, FO 371/43918; Newark, *Mafia Allies*, p. 213.

75. US Naval Intelligence, Report, 7 December 1943, WO 204/12618.

76. JICA, 'Comprehensive Outline', p. 4; Manley, 'Report on Sicilian Separatism', p. 4.

77. Finocchiaro Aprile to Winston Churchill, 6 July 1944, BNA, FO 371/43918.

78. 'War Recedes From Sicily', *The Times* (London), 15 July 1944, p. 5.

79. OSS, 'Democratic Front of Order to Become an Open Political Party', 11 September 1944, and OSS, 'Report for Period 16–30 September 1944', 6 October 1944, are in NARA, RG 226, Entry 99, Box 20, Folder 106; Nester to Secretary of State, 'Certain Elements Within the Separatist Party', 22 August 1944, NARA, RG 59, 865.01/8–2244; Nester to Secretary of State, 'Separatist Movement in Sicily, Enclosure No. 2', 4 September 1944, NARA, RG 59, 865.01/9–4444; JICA, 'Comprehensive Outline', p. 4; Manley, 'Report on Sicilian Separatism', p. 4; Finkelstein, *Separatism, the Allies, and the Mafia*, pp. 90–1, 116–17.

80. Pantaleone, *The Mafia and Politics*, pp. 66–75; US Naval Intelligence, Palermo, Report, 15 February 1945, BNA, WO 204/12618.

81. Newark, *Mafia Allies*, pp. 240–2.

82. Joint Intelligence Collecting Agency, Weekly Stability Report for period 10/17 December 1943, 20 December 1943, BNA, WO 204/12615.

83. Finkelstein, *Separatism, the Allies, and the Mafia*, pp. 66–8.

84. Anton Blok, *The Mafia of a Sicilian Village, 1860–1960: A Study of Violent Peasant Entrepreneurs* (Cambridge: Waveland Press, 1974), p. 190.

85. Finkelstein, *Separatism, the Allies, and the Mafia*, pp. 81–2.

86. 'Summary of a Report on a Tour Made in Sicily during August 1944', in Charles to Eden, 12 October 1944, BNA, FO 371/43918, p. 2.

87. Quoted in Finkelstein, *Separatism, the Allies, and the Mafia*, p. 79.

88. Pantaleone, *The Mafia and Politics*, pp. 76–7.

89. OSS, 'Notes on Separatism: 1. Communist Leader, 2. Aldisio's Attitude, 3. Pro-American Maffia, 4. Bagheria Meeting', 7–14 August 1944, in FBI, 65–51898–3; Counter Intelligence Corps, Naples Detachment, Memorandum, 'Sicilian Political Situation', 4 February 1945, BNA, WO 204/12619; Report, 'Italy, Government, Political Parties in Sicily, Maffia and Separatist Movement', 10 December 1943, NARA, RG 38, 9632-H, C-10-f; Manley, 'Report on Sicilian Separatism', p. 5; Finkelstein, *Separatism, the Allies, and the Mafia*, pp. 49, 88–9.

90. Finkelstein, *Separatism, the Allies, and the Mafia*, pp. 80–7.

91. Ibid., p. 92.

92. OSS, 'Minister Runi and Prefect D'Antoni Meet Secretly with Tasca Brothers on Sicilian Autonomy', 15 September 1944, CIA, and OSS, 'Report for Period 16–30 September 1944', 6 October 1944 are in NARA, RG 226, Entry 99, Box 20, Folder 106; Finkelstein, *Separatism, the Allies, and the Mafia*, pp. 94–5.

93. Pantaleone, *The Mafia and Politics*, p. 88; Finkelstein, *Separatism, the Allies, and the Mafia*, pp. 95–7.

94. JICA, 'Separatist Plans of Action', 2 November 1944, BNA, WO 204/2168; Commodore Ellery W. Stone to Italian Prime Minister Ivanoe Bonomi, 3 November 1944, BNA, WO 204/2168; 'Account of the First Congress of the Separatist Movement Held in Taormina on 20, 21, 22 October 1944', NARA, RG 331, 10000/143/278; Nester to Secretary of State, 'Separatist Movement: Congress at Taormina', 4 November 1944, NARA, RG 59, 865.01/11–444; Finkelstein, *Separatism, the Allies, and the Mafia*, pp. 102–10.

95. Rie and Switzer, 'Separatist Activity in Palermo', undated, NARA, RG 331, 10100/143/275; Finkelstein, *Separatism, the Allies, and the Mafia*, p. 111.

96. 'Palermo Incident', Report No. 70, 14 November 1944, BNA, FO 371/43918; Finkelstein, *Separatism, the Allies, and the Mafia*, pp. 112–4.

97. Finkelstein, *Separatism, the Allies, and the Mafia*, p. 121; Catanzaro, *Men of Respect*, pp. 122–3.

98. Finkelstein, *Separatism, the Allies, and the Mafia*, pp. 118–9.

99. OSS, 'General Castellana Seeking Maffia Accord', 13 October 1944, NARA, RG 226, 226/103050.

100. Nester to Secretary of State, 'Statements Made by General Castellano

Regarding Sicilian Situation and Possible Solution Thereof', 18 January 1945, NARA, RG 59, 865.01/11–444.

101. Nester to Secretary of State, 'Excerpts From a Secret Report by General Castellano to Count Sforza and Carondini', 4 November 1944, NARA, RG 59, 865.01/11–444.

102. Nester to Secretary of State, 'Leaders of the Maffia Meet at a Number of Secret Meetings in Palermo', 18 November 1944, NARA, RG 59, 865.01/11–1844; Nester to Secretary of State, 'Meeting of Maffia Leaders with General Giuseppe Castellano and Formation of Group Favoring Autonomy', 21 November 1944, NARA, RG 59, 865.00/11–2144; Nester to Secretary of State, 'Formation of Group Favoring Autonomy Under Direction of Maffia', 27 November 1944, NARA, RG 59, 865.01/11–2744; Finkelstein, *Separatism, the Allies, and the Mafia*, p. 122.

103. Nester to Secretary of State, 'Statements'; Nester to Secretary of State, 'Further Developments in General Castellano's Solution to the Sicilian Problem', 23 January 1945, NARA, RG 59, 865.00/1–2345; Nester to Secretary of State, 'Possible Fusion of Maffia and Separatists Under Leadership of Vittorio Emanuele Orlando', 10 April 1945, NARA, RG 59, 865.00/4–1045; Finkelstein, *Separatism, the Allies, and the Mafia*, pp. 122–4.

104. Joint Intelligence Collection Agency, 'Discussion of the Possibility of an Agreement Between Separatists and Unitarians', 28 March 1945, NARA, RG 226, 122735; 'Italy—Sicily—Separatist Movement, Trends Of', Report, 28 March 1945, NARA, RG 38, 9632-I, File C-10-f.

105. Finkelstein, *Separatism, the Allies, and the Mafia*, p. 126.

106. Rome to Foreign Office, 17 December 1944, BNA, FO 371/49767; ONI, 'Sicily—Student Demonstrations against Military Service', 18 December 1944, WO 204/12660; JICA, 'Sicily—Riots in Connection with conscription', 29 December 1944, BNA, WO 204/12660; 51 Field Security Section to GSI(b) HQ 3 Dist., 'Disorders in Western Sicily 17 to 24 Dec 44', 24 December 1944, BNA, WO 204/12660; J.N. Horan, 'Intelligence Report: Sicily—Riot at Alcamo', 18 December 1944, BNA, WO 204/12660; Nester to Secretary of State, 'Sicilian Crisis: Telegram from General Branca, Commanding Carabinieri', 21 December 1944, NARA, RG 59, 865.00/12–2144; Allied Control Commission, Sicilian Region Headquarters to Headquarters, Allied Control Commission, Rome, 'Unrest in Sicily', 20 December 1944, NARA, RG 331, 10000/136/444; Allied Commission, Eastern Sicily to G3, HQ, 'Causes of Recent Civil Disturbances in Eastern Sicily', 27 December 1944; Finkelstein, *Separatism, the Allies, and the Mafia*, pp. 129–31; Newark, *Mafia Allies*, pp. 244–6.

107. See e.g. Command Intelligence Center, US Navy, 'Attacks by Armed Bands on Barracks of Carabinieri in Palermo Area', 21 January 1946, BNA, WO 204/12617.

108. For example US Psychological Warfare Board, 'Report', 10 January 1945, WO 204/4459.

109. US Naval Intelligence, Palermo, 'Report', 30 December 1944, BNA, WO 204/12660; US Intelligence Division, Chief of Naval Operations, 10 January 1945, BNA, WO 204/12660.

110. 'Aspects in the Fight Against Separatism', 28 December 1944, NA, RG 331, 10100/143/275; Office of the Chief of Naval Operations, 'Italy—Sicily—Separatist Movement Tendencies and Reaction to Autonomy Measures', 3 January 1945, NARA, RG 38, 9632-I, File C-10-f; Finkelstein, *Separatism, the Allies, and the Mafia*, pp. 132–6.

111. ONI, 'Insurrection in Ragusa and Syracuse Provinces', 31 January 1945, BNA, WO 204/12661; Psychological Warfare Branch, 'Report on the Rebellion in the Province of Ragusa 5/11 January 1945', BNA, WO 204/12661; US Naval Intelligence, Palermo, Report to AFHQ, 8 January 1945, BNA, WO, 204/4459; Finkelstein, *Separatism, the Allies, and the Mafia*, p. 136.

112. Finkelstein, *Separatism, the Allies, and the Mafia*, pp. 127–8, 137–8.

113. Ibid., pp. 150–3, 157–9.

114. See Newark, *Mafia Allies*, pp. 253–4; Finkelstein, *Separatism, the Allies, and the Mafia*, pp. 153–4.

115. OSS, Italian Division, 'Monarchy Seeks Support of Separatist Movement', 3 May 1945, BNA, WO 204/12618; Extract from Security Intelligence Summary No. 22, October 1945, 6 November 1945, BNA, WO 204/12617; Nester to Secretary of State, 'Possible Fusion'; Finkelstein, *Separatism, the Allies, and the Mafia*, pp. 158–60.

116. Newark, *Mafia Allies*, pp. 255, 262–3.

117. Finkelstein, *Separatism, the Allies, and the Mafia*, pp. 141–2.

118. Nester to Secretary of State, 'Raid on Separatist Ammunition Dump', 13 June 1945, NARA, RG 59, 865.00/6–1345; Finkelstein, *Separatism, the Allies, and the Mafia*, p. 163.

119. Rome to Foreign Office, 10 October 1945, BNA, FO 371/49767. See also Kirk to Secretary of State, 3 October 1945, FBI, 109–12–233–111.

120. Lt. D. M. Jacobs, 'Present Political Situation in Sicily', 6 February 1946, BNA, WO 204/12617.

121. Watkins, 'The Situation in Sicily', 6 September 1945, BNA, FO 371/49767, p. 3; US Naval Intelligence, Palermo, Report, 15 February 1946, BNA, WO 204/12618.

122. Sir Victor Mallet, 'Giuliano and Sicilian Banditry', Memorandum, British

Embassy in Rome to Foreign office, 7 October 1949, BNA, FO 371/79312; Counter Intelligence Corps, Memorandum, 'Present Political Situation in Sicily', 15 July 1946, BNA, WO 204/12617; Billy Jaynes Chandler, *King of the Mountain: The Life and Death of Giuliano the Bandit* (DeKalb IL: Northern Illinois University Press, 1988), pp. 5–16; Dickie, *Cosa Nostra*, pp. 209–11; Pantaleone, *The Mafia and Politics*, p. 135.

123. Eric Hobsbawm, *Primitive Rebels* (Manchester: The University Press, 1959), pp. 4, 16, 17; Eric Hobsbawm, *Bandits*, 2nd ed. (New York: Pantheon Books, 1981), p. 43.

124. OSS, 'Mafia Activities in Montelepre, Sicily', 2 January 1944, NARA, RG 165, Entry 77, Box 1903, File 2700; Dickie, *Cosa Nostra*, p. 211.

125. Manley, 'Report on Sicilian Separatism', Sir Victor Mallet, 'Giuliano and Sicilian Banditry', Memorandum, British Embassy in Rome to Foreign office, 7 October 1949, BNA, FO 371/79312, p. 2; Finkelstein, *Separatism, the Allies, and the Mafia*, pp. 164–72; Pantaleone, *The Mafia and Politics*, p. 182; Dickie, *Cosa Nostra*, p. 211; Arlacchi, *Men of Dishonor*, p. 46; Chandler, *King of the Mountain*, pp. 48–57.

126. Hobsbawm, *Bandits*, pp. 40, 89. See also Blok, *The Mafia of a Sicilian Village*, pp. 99–102; Anton Blok, 'The Peasant and the Brigand: Social Banditry Reconsidered', in *Comparative Studies in Society and History*, 14 (1972), pp. 495–504; and Eric J. Hobsbawm, 'Social bandits, A Comment', in ibid., pp. 504–7.

127. Counter Intelligence Corps, Naples Detachment, Memorandum, 'Sicilian Political Situation', 4 February 1945, BNA, WO 204/12619.

128. Newark, *Mafia Allies*, p. 264.

129. Finkelstein, *Separatism, the Allies, and the Mafia*, pp. 169–74; Newark, *Mafia Allies*, pp. 258–9.

130. Nester to Kirk, 23 November 1945, NARA, RG 59, 865.00/11–2345; Nester to Kirk, 5 December 1945, NARA, RG 59, 865.00/12–545; Italian Parliamentary Commission of Inquiry, *Relazione sui rapporti tra mafia e banditismo in Sicilia*, Legislature V, Doc. xxiii, n. 2 (Rome: Senate Printing Press, 1972), p. 110.

131. Nester to Kirk, 12 January 1946, NARA, RG 59, 865.00/1–1246.

132. Special Agent Gabriel B. Celetta and Special Agent Saverio Forte to US Army CIC Naples Detachment, 'Sicilian Separatist Disturbances', 29 January 1946, British BNA, WO 204/12617.

133. Dickie, *Cosa Nostra*, p. 211; Catanzaro, *Men of Respect*, p. 123; *Relazione sui rapporti tra mafia e banditismo in Sicilia*, pp. 56–7.

134. Finkelstein, *Separatism, the Allies, and the Mafia*, pp. 179–81.

135. US Army, 'Daily Digest of World Broadcasts and Radio Telegraph

Service', 14 February 1946, BNA, WO 204/12619; AFHQ, 'Report', 27 February 1946, BNA, WO 204/12619; Newark, *Mafia Allies*, p. 264.

136. Chandler, *King of the Mountain*, pp. 65–8; Newark, *Mafia Allies*, pp. 266–7; Finkelstein, *Separatism, the Allies, and the Mafia*, pp. 186–8.

137. Mallet, 'Giuliano and Sicilian banditry'.

138. Ibid., p. 98. On this theme, see also Eric J. Hobsbawm, 'Robin Hoodo', *N.Y. Review of Books*, 14 February 1985.

139. Pantaleone, *The Mafia and Politics*, p. 108; see generally Hobsbawm, *Primitive Rebels*, p. 23.

140. Finkelstein, *Separatism, the Allies, and the Mafia*, p. 182.

141. 'Sicilian Gangster opens war on Reds', *The New York Times*, 24 June 1947, p. 14; Watkins, 'Outstanding Events and Anti-Communist Reaction—Sicily', 5 July 1947, BNA, FO 371/67786, pp. 2–3; Dickie, *Cosa Nostra*, p. 212; Chandler, *King of the Mountain*, pp. 86, 90–1, 100–5; Pantaleone, *The Mafia and Politics*, pp. 133–4.

142. 'Sicilian Gangster'; Mallet, p. 2; Watkins, p. 3; Palermo to Secretary of State, 4 May 1947, NARA, RG 59, 865.00/5–447; Chandler, *King of the Mountain*, pp. 82–105, 129–34; Dickie, *Cosa Nostra*, p. 212; Finkelstein, *Separatism, the Allies, and the Mafia*, p. 181.

143. Newark, *Mafia Allies*, p. 278; Pantaleone, *The Mafia and Politics*, p. 137.

144. Sir Victor Mallet to Rt. Hon. Ernest Bevin, 30 March 1948, BNA, FO 371/73205B.

145. Mallet, p. 3; Pantaleone, *The Mafia and Politics*, p. 147; Chandler, *King of the Mountain*, pp. 141–9.

146. Chandler, *King of the Mountain*, pp. 169–71; Pantaleone, *The Mafia and Politics*, p. 130–2; Dickie, *Cosa Nostra*, p. 213.

147. Chandler, *King of the Mountain*, pp. 173–93; Pantaleone, *The Mafia and Politics*, pp. 142–6.

148. Chandler, *King of the Mountain*, pp. 188–99, 208–10; Pantaleone, *The Mafia and Politics*, pp. 148–56; Newark, *Mafia Allies*, pp. 281–2; Dickie, *Cosa Nostra*, pp. 214–6; FBI, 'Mafia Monograph', July 1958, FBI Vault, BI, I, p. 84.

149. CIA, 'The Current Situation in Italy', 10 October 1947, quoted in Tim Newark, *Lucky Luciano: The Real and the Fake Gangster* (New York: Thomas Duane Books, 2010), p. 202.

150. Pantaleone, *The Mafia and Politics*, p. 109; Alexander Stille, *Excellent Cadavers* (New York: Vintage Books, 1996), p. 19.

151. Pantaleone, *The Mafia and Politics*, p. 198.

152. Ibid., pp. 195–7; Catanzaro, *Men of Respect*, p. 180.

153. Stille, *Excellent Cadavers*, p. 19.

154. Dickie, *Cosa Nostra*, p. 203.

155. Ibid., p. 204.

156. Compare Catanzaro, *Men of Respect*, pp. 133–5.
157. Lupo, *History*, pp. 194–5.
158. Dickie, *Cosa Nostra*, p. 204; Catanzaro, *Men of Respect*, p. 27, 128; Blok, *The Mafia*, pp. 77–81; Hobsbawm, *Primitive Rebels*, pp. 48–9.
159. Pantaleone, *The Mafia and Politics*, pp. 167–9.
160. Pantaleone, *The Mafia and Politics*, pp. 200–1.
161. Pino Arlacchi, *Men of Dishonor: Inside the Sicilian Mafia. An Account of Antonino Calderone* (New York: William Morrow and Company, Inc., 1993), p. 9.
162. René Seindal, *Mafia, Money and Politics in Sicily 1950–1997* (Copenhagen: Museum Tusculanum Press, 1998), pp. 9, 29–32, 40–3, 74–6; Catanzaro, *Men of Respect*, pp. 138–9; Stille, *Excellent Cadavers*, p. 11; Pantaleone, *The Mafia and Politics*, p. 169; Italian Parliamentary Commission of Inquiry into the Mafia phenomenon in Sicily, *Relazione "mafia ed enti locali"* (Relazioni Alessi), Legislature VI, Doc. xxxiii, no. 2 (Rome: Senate Printing Press, 1976), pp. 1202–3.
163. See Pantaleone, *The Mafia and Politics*, p. 169; Diego Gambetta, *The Sicilian Mafia: The Business of Private Protection* (Cambridge MA: Harvard University Press, 1993), p. 234; Hobsbawm, *Primitive Rebels*, p. 48; Dickie, *Mafia Republic*, p. 139; Italian Parliamentary Commission of Inquiry into the Mafia phenomenon in Sicily, *Documentazione allegata alla Relazione conclusiva*, VII-IX legislature, (Rome: Senate Printing Press, 1985) pp. 74, 78, 622, 999. On Luciano, see CIC, Naples Detachment, 'Lucania, Salvatore (aka Charles "Lucky" Luciano)', 13 August 1946, FBI, 39–2141–62; and Eduardo Sáenz Rovner, *The Cuban Connection: Drug Trafficking, Smuggling, and Gambling in Cuba from the 1920s to the Revolution* (Chapel Hill NC: University of North Carolina Press, 2008), pp. 70–73. On Adonis, Catanzaro, *Men of Respect*, p. 194.
164. Gambetta, *The Sicilian Mafia*, pp. 229–1.
165. Pantaleone, *The Mafia and Politics*, pp. 183–9.
166. Catanzaro, *Men of Respect*, p. 201; Pantaleone, *The Mafia and Politics*, pp. 169–70.
167. Pantaleone, *The Mafia and Politics*, pp. 170–9; Catanzaro, *Men of Respect*, pp. 153–5; Gambetta, *The Sicilian Mafia*, p. 207; FBI, 'Mafia Monograph', I, pp. 87, 91.
168. See Edward Lockspeiser, 'The Renoir Portraits of Wagner', *Music & Letters*, vol. 18, no. 1 (January 1937), pp. 14–19.
169. Tommaso Buscetta's account is in Arlacchi, *Addio Cosa Nostra*, pp. 60–3. See also Italian Parliamentary Commission of Inquiry into the Mafia phenomenon in Sicily, *Relazione sul traffico mafioso di tabacchi e stupefacanti e sui rapport tra mafia e gangsterismo italo-americano* (Relazione Zuccala), Legislature VI, Doc. xxiii, n. 2 (Rome: Senate Printing Press, 1976),

allegato n. 1, p. 479; 'Police in Sicily Say US Mafia Attended '57 Parley', *The New York Times*, 2 January 1968, p. 29; McClellan Hearings, 10–16 October 1963, p. 777; Dickie, *Mafia Republic*, pp. 134–5; Dickie, *Cosa Nostra*, pp. 234–5; Gambetta, *The Sicilian Mafia*, pp. 110–12; Catanzaro, *Men of Respect*, p. 194; Claire Sterling, *Octopus:The Long Reach of the International Sicilian Mafia* (New York: Touchstone, 1990), pp. 83–96; and Enzo Biagi, *Il Boss è solo: Buscetta, la vera storia d'un vero padrino* (Milan: Arnaldo Mondadori, 1986), pp. 147–54.

170. Gambetta, *The Sicilian Mafia*, pp. 110, 245–6; Catanzaro, *Men of Respect*, p. 202.

171. Dickie, *Cosa Nostra*, p. 238.

172. Quoted in ibid., p. 237

173. Gambetta, *The Sicilian Mafia*, pp. 115–6.

174. Dickie, *Cosa Nostra*, p. 237

175. FBI, 'Mafia Monograph', pp. xx-xi.

176. See generally Jane T. Schneider and Peter T. Schneider, *Reversible Destiny: Mafia, Anti-Mafia, and the Struggle for Palermo* (Berkeley CA: University of California Press, 2003); Judith Chubb, *Patronage, Power and Poverty in Southern Italy* (Cambridge: Cambridge University Press, 1982); and Stille, *Excellent Cadavers*, pp. 21–2.

177. See 'Testimony', Annexed to New York City Board of Aldermen, *Report of the Special Committee of the Board of Aldermen appointed to investigate the "Ring" frauds: together with the testimony elicited during the investigation* (New York: Martin Brown, 1878). And see Kenneth D. Ackerman, *Boss Tweed: The Rise and Fall of the Corrupt Pol Who Conceived the Soul of Modern New York* (New York: Carroll & Graf, 2005).

178. See Seindal, *Mafia, Money and Politics in Sicily*, pp. 9, 29–32, 74–6; Stille, *Excellent Cadavers*, p. 11.

179. Judith Chubb, *Patronage, Power and Poverty*, p. 133; see also Dickie, *Mafia Republic*, pp. 111–6; Catanzaro, *Men of Respect*, pp. 150–1.

180. Catanzaro, *Men of Respect*, p. 151.

181. Chubb, *Patronage, Power and Poverty*, pp. 104–6; Seindal, pp. 82–8; Dickie, *Mafia Republic*, pp. 111–6; Catanzaro, *Men of Respect*, pp. 151–5.

182. Dickie, *Cosa Nostra*, pp. 227–8.

183. Hobsbawm, *Primitive Rebels*, p. 14; *Bandits*, p. 51.

184. Lupo, *History*, p. 191.

185. Hobsbawm, *Primitive Rebels*, p. 27.

186. Pantaleone, *The Mafia and Politics*, p. 34.

187. Ibid., p. 229.

188. Ibid., p. 201; Seindal, *Mafia, Money and Politics in Sicily*, p. 86.

8. THE CUBA JOINT VENTURE, 1933–1958

1. Robert Lacey, *Little Man: Meyer Lansky and the Gangster Life* (Boston MA: Little Brown & Co., 1991), p. 33; Ron Chepesiuk, *The Trafficantes: Godfathers from Tampa, Florida. The Mafia, CIA and the JFK Assassination* (Rock Hill SC: Strategic Media Books Inc., 2010), p. 23.

2. Ibid., p. 258.

3. T. J. English, *Havana Nocturne* (New York: HarperCollins, 2008), p. 32.

4. US Embassy in Cuba to Department of State, 'Confidential Incoming Telegram', 31 July 1953, NARA, RG 59, File 737.00/7–2853.

5. Jack Colhoun, *Gangsterismo. The United States, Cuba, and the Mafia: 1933 to 1966* (New York/London: OR Books, 2013).

6. Eduardo Sáenz Rovner, *The Cuban Connection: Drug Trafficking, Smuggling, and Gambling in Cuba from the 1920s to the Revolution* (Chapel Hill NC: University of North Carolina Press, 2008).

7. Colhoun, *Gangsterismo*, p. 2.

8. Ramiro Guerra y Sánchez, *Sugar and Society in the Caribbean: An Economic History of Cuban Agriculture* (New Haven CT: Yale University Press, 1964); Muriel McAvoy Weissman, *Sugar Baron: Manuel Rionda and the Fortunes of Pre-Castro Cuba* (Miami FL: University of Florida Press, 2003).

9. Mark Haller, 'Bootleggers and American Gambling 1920–1950', in US Commission on the Review of the National Policy Towards Gambling, *Gambling in America, Appendix 1: Staff and Consultant Papers*, Washington DC, 1976, in NYPL, p. 116.

10. Robert Whitney, 'The Architect of the Cuban State: Fulgencio Batista and Populism in Cuba, 1937–1940', *J. Lat. Amer. Stud.*, vol. 32, no. 2 (May 2000), pp. 435–59, at pp. 436–7.

11. Lacey, *Little Man*, p. 54.

12. Uri Dan, 'Meyer Lansky Breaks His Silence', *Ma'ariv* (Israel), 2 July 1971; and Lacey, *Little Man*, p. 236.

13. Scott Deitche, *The Silent Don: The Criminal World of Santo Trafficante Jr.* (Fort Lee NJ: Barricade, 2007), p. 61; Thomas Hunt, 'Castro and the Casinos', *Informer*, vol. 2, no. 4 (2009), pp. 5–27 at p. 5.

14. Lacey, *Little Man*, pp. 97–111.

15. English, *Havana Nocturne*, p. 15; Lacey, *Little Man*, pp. 108–9; Eisenberg *et al.*, *Meyer Lansky*, pp. 173–4; Martin Gosch and Richard Hammer, *The Last Testament of Lucky Luciano* (London: Macmillan London Limited, 1975), pp. 233–4.

16. J. Robert Pearce to FBI, 'Angelo Bruno', 16 January 1959, in JFKARC, HSCA Subject Files, Angelo Bruno, Box 1; Gosch and Hammer, *The Last Testament of Lucky Luciano*, pp. 168–9; Hank Messick, *Lansky* (New York: Putnam, 1971), p. 23; Colhoun, *Gangsterismo*, p. 29; Tim Newark, *Lucky*

Luciano: The Real and the Fake Gangster (New York: Thomas Duane Books, 2010), pp. 182–3.

17. Peter Maas, *The Valachi Papers* (New York: Perennial, 1968/2003), p. 15; McClellan Hearings, Part 1, First Session, 1963, p. 387.

18. FBI, 'Mafia Monograph', Part II, pp. 64, 114; English, *Havana Nocturne*, p. 15; Gosch and Hammer, *The Last Testament of Lucky Luciano*, p. 169; Eisenberg *et al.*, *Meyer Lanky*, pp. 173–4.

19. Whitney, 'The Architect of the Cuban State', p. 436.

20. Rene Rayneri, 'Colonel Batista and Cuba's Future', *Current History*, vol. 50, no. 2 (April 1939), p. 51.

21. *The Havana Post*, 23 June 1937, p. 10.

22. Rees to Eden, Havana, 20 February 1937, enclosure no. 21, 'The Labour Situation in Cuba and the British West Indies', BNA, FO, registry no. A/1864/65/14.

23. Whitney, 'The Architect of the Cuban State', pp. 442–3.

24. Ibid.; Jorge I. Domínguez, 'The Batista Regime in Cuba', in H.E. Chehabi and Juan J. Linz, eds, *Sultanistic Regimes* (Baltimore MD and London: Johns Hopkins University Press, 1998), pp. 112–31 at pp. 117–8.

25. Kefauver Committee, 'Testimony of Meyer Lansky' in Hearings, Part 7, New York-New Jersey, 81st Congress, 1st Session (Washington DC: US Government Printing Office), p. 610; English, *Havana Nocturne*, p. 20; Rosalie Schwartz, *Pleasure Island: Tourism and Temptation in Cuba* (Lincoln NE: University of Nebraska Press, 1997), pp. 92, 97–8.

26. Colhoun, *Gangsterismo*, p. 5.

27. Sáenz Rovner, *The Cuban Connection*, p. 86; Lacey, *Little Man*, pp. 108–9.

28. Claude A. Follmer to HQ, 'Special Cuban Assignment SE-202', 21 July 1943, NARA, RG 170, DEA BNDD, 1916–1970, Box 154, Folder 0660 Cuba, p. 66.

29. Wilson C. Beers, 'Treasury Representative in Havana to Commissioner of Customs', 18 January 1945, NARA, RG 170, DEA BNDD, Box 154, Folder 0660 Cuba.

30. Antonio Giustozzi, 'The Debate on Warlordism: The Importance of Military Legitimacy', Crisis States Discussion Paper 13 (London: Crisis States Research Centre, October 2005), p. 17. Compare Norbert Elias, *The Civilizing Process. Volume II: State Formation and Civilisation* (Oxford: Blackwell, 1982), pp. 258 et seq.

31. Whitney, 'The Architect of the Cuban State', p. 455.

32. Dennis Eisenberg, Uri Dan and Eli Lanau, *Meyer Lansky: Mogul of the Mob* (New York: Paddington Press, 1979), pp. 227–8; Enrique Cirules, *The Mafia in Havana: A Caribbean Mob Story* (North Melbourne/New York: Ocean Press, 2010), p. 25.

33. Samuel Farber, *Revolution and Reaction in Cuba, 1933–1960* (Middletown

CT: Wesleyan University Press, 1976), pp. 117–22; Colhoun, *Gangsterismo*, pp. 13–16.

34. Farber, *Revolution and Reaction in Cuba*, p. 119.

35. Cirules, *The Mafia in Havana*, pp. 61–2.

36. John T. Cusack to H. J. Anslinger, 12 January 1959, NARA, RG 170, DEA OEPC, Box 7, 0660 Cuba, In-Confidence, Book #1 thru Feb. 1959; CIA, 'Biography of Carlos Prío Socarrás', December 1957, JFKARC, RG 233, HSCA, Segregated CIA Collection, Box 61, Folder S; FBI, 'Report by George E. Davis, "Carlos Prios Socarras", 1 July 1952, JFKARC, Counterintelligence Source Files (Army), Box 6, Folder Carlos Prío Socarrás.

37. John T. Cusack to H. J. Anslinger, 14 July 1958, and C. A. Follmer to Joseph Bell, 6 December 1943, both in NARA, RG 170, DEA BNDD, Box 154, Folder 0660 Cuba; Joseph L. Tangel, 'Activities of Top Hoodlums in the New York Field Division', 14 September 1959, JFKARC, HSCA, Sebastian John La Rocca, Box 4; Arthur Sabo to Joseph Milkeny, 'Narcotics Inquiry Re: Joseph Paul LoPiccolo', 10 May 1965, JFKARC, HSCA, Numbered Files, Box 21, Folder 000834; Cirules, *The Mafia in Havana*, pp. 33, 53; Sáenz Rovner, *The Cuban Connection*, p. 66.

38. Lacey, *Little Man*, p. 225.

39. Newark, *Mafia Allies*, pp. 272–3; Newark, *Lucky Luciano*, pp. 180–2; Gosch and Hammer, *The Last Testament of Lucky Luciano*, pp. 307–8.

40. Joseph A. Fortier to Commissioner of Customs, 27 March 1947, NARA, RG 170, DEA OEPC, Salvatore Luciano—Folders 1–5, Box 1; Legat, Havana, to Director, FBI, 'The Mafia—Havana', 11 October 1955, JFKARC, RG 233, HSCA, Norman Rothman, Box 3.

41. J. Ray Olivera to Garland Williams, 21 March 1947, NARA, RG 170, DEA OEPC, Salvatore Luciano—Folders 1–5, Box 1; Olivera, 'Memorandum Report', 27 February 1953, and Robert A. Bermingham, 'The Illicit Narcotic Traffic in Cuba', 27 January 1959, both in NARA, RG 170, DEA BNDD, Box 154, Folder 0660 Cuba.

42. Fortier to Commissioner of Customs; Gosch and Hammer, *The Last Testament of Lucky Luciano*, p. 311 et seq.

43. English, *Havana Nocturne*, pp. 32–3.

44. Selwyn Raab, *Five Families: The Rise, Decline, and Resurgence of America's Most Powerful Mafia Empires* (New York: St. Martin's Griffin/Thomas Dunne Books, 2005), p. 89; Cirules, *The Mafia in Havana*, pp. 34–5; Colhoun, *Gangsterismo*, p. 11; Lacey, *Little Man*, pp. 216–8; Gosch and Hammer, *The Last Testament of Lucky Luciano*, pp. 314–6.

45. Olivera to Williams.

46. Cirules, *The Mafia in Havana*, pp. 47–53; Gosch and Hammer, *The Last*

Testament of Lucky Luciano, pp. 26–32, 323–4; Eisenberg *et al.*, *Meyer Lansky*, p. 234; English, *Havana Nocturne*, p. 46.

47. English, *Havana Nocturne*, pp. 47–9; Sáenz Rovner, *The Cuban Connection*, pp. 67–70.

48. Olivera, 'Memorandum Report'.

49. Warren Hinckle and William Turner, *Deadly Secrets: The CIA-Mafia war against Castro and the assassination of JFK* (New York: Thunder's Mouth Press, 1992), p. 345; North American Committee on Latin America, *Latin America & Empire Report*, vol. VI, no. 8, p. 5; Messick, *Lansky*, p. 123.

50. English, *Havana Nocturne*, p. 58; Cohen, 'The Lost Journals'.

51. English, *Havana Nocturne*, p. 19.

52. Colhoun, *Gangsterismo*, p. 19; Domínguez, 'The Batista Regime in Cuba', p. 118.

53. Domínguez, 'The Batista Regime in Cuba', p. 120.

54. Farber, *Revolution and Reaction in Cuba*, p. 121.

55. Francis A. Truslow *et al.*, *Report on Cuba* (Baltimore MD: Johns Hopkins Press, 1951); Sáenz Rovner, *The Cuban Connection*, p. 90.

56. Domínguez, 'The Batista Regime in Cuba', p. 119.

57. English, *Havana Nocturne*, p. x.

58. Ibid., p. 87; Lacey, *Little Man*, pp. 226–9; Eisenberg *et al.*, *Meyer Lansky*, pp. 253–5.

59. Cirules, *The Mafia in Havana*, p. 14; Lacey, *Little Man*, pp. 227–8.

60. Detailed accounts of Mob activity in Havana are provided by forty-one Federal Narcotics Bureau case files: see Siragusa to Anslinger, 'Office Memorandum', 2 February 1959, NARA, RG 170, DEA OEPC, Box 7, 0660 Cuba, In-Confidence, Book #1 thru Feb. 1959. Other significant discussions appear in: Legat, Havana, to Director, FBI, 'The Mafia—Havana'; Vaughan to Regional Commissioner, Richmond, Va., 'Gamblers and Gangsters engaged in Cuban gambling', 5 February 1958, NARA, RG 170, DEA BNDD, Box 154, Folder 0660 Cuba; George Davis Jr., 'Roberto Fernandez Miranda', 15 April 1960, JFKARC, RG 233, HSCA, Segregated CIA Collection, Printed Microfilm, Box 43, Folder Rothman; John S. Portella, 'Norman Rothman—Interstate Transportation of Gambling Devices', 11 October 1956, JFKARC, RG 233, HSCA, Numbered Files, Box 244, Folder 013992.

61. FBI, 'Cuban Revolutionary Activities', Miami, 5 February 1959, NARA, RG 170, DEA OEPC, Box 7, Folder 0660 Cuba, In-Confidence, Book #1 thru Feb. 1959.

62. Legat, Havana to Director, FBI, 'The Mafia—Havana', at p. 8; Hunt, 'Castro', pp. 14–15; Lacey, *Little Man*, p. 247.

63. CIA, 'Document Transfer and Cross Reference', 3 September 1954, JFKARC, RG 233, HSCA, Segregated CIA Collection, Printed Microfilm,

Box 43, Reel 16, Folder 21; FBI Legat, 'Sans Souci Night Club', 31 December 1952, and FBI, 'American Gambling Activities in Cuba', 3 February 1953, both in JFKARC, RG 233, HSCA, Norman Rothman, Box 4. On Rothman's role in the narcotics trade see especially NARA, RG 170, DEA BNDD, Box 154, Folder 0660 Cuba.

64. Legat, Havana to Director, FBI, 'The Mafia—Havana'.
65. Fulgencio Batista, *The Growth and Decline of the Cuban Republic*, trans. Blas M. Rocafort (New York: The Devin-Adair Company, 1964), p. 160. And see Domínguez, 'The Batista Regime in Cuba', p. 124.
66. English, *Havana Nocturne*, pp. 130–1; Cirules, *The Mafia in Havana*, pp. 89–95.
67. Cirules, *The Mafia in Havana*, pp. 107–10; Michael P. McGuigan, 'Fulgencio Batista's Economic Policies, 1952–1958', Ph.D. thesis, University of Miami, 2012.
68. Hunt, 'Castro', pp. 10–13; 'Mobsters move in on Havana and split gambling profits with Batista', *Life*, 10 March 1958, pp. 32–7 at p. 35.
69. English, *Havana Nocturne*, p. 132.
70. Domínguez, 'The Batista Regime in Cuba', p. 125.
71. McGuigan, 'Fulgencio Batista's Economic Policies', pp. 233–5; English, *Havana Nocturne*, p. 132.
72. McGuigan, 'Fulgencio Batista's Economic Policies', p. 230.
73. Ibid., p. 235.
74. Colhoun, *Gangsterismo*, pp. 23, 28–9; Sáenz Rovner, *The Cuban Connection*, pp. 90–3.
75. English, *Havana Nocturne*, p. 132; 'Mobsters move in', p. 35.
76. Colhoun, *Gangsterismo*, p. 28.
77. Agustín Tamargo, '¿Por que lucha actualmente el pueblo de Cuba?', *Bohemia* (Havana), 28 July 1957.
78. 'Mobsters move in', p. 36.
79. Ibid.
80. Memorandum, 'Santos Trafficante Jr.', 9 June 1959, NARA, RG 170, DEA OEPC, Box 7, Folder 0660 Cuba, In-Confidence, Book #4 thru Feb. 1959, at p. 7.
81. 'Angelo Bruno'; Messick, *Syndicate Abroad*, p. 23; Colhoun, *Gangsterismo*, p. 29.
82. English, *Havana Nocturne*, p. 226.
83. 'Santos Trafficante Jr.', at p. 5; FBI, 'Mafia Monograph', Part II, pp. 54–6; Deitche, pp. 21–4, 34–6, 50–63; and see the account of Trafficante's lawyer, Frank Ragano, in Frank Ragano and Selwyn Raab, *Mob Lawyer* (New York: Charles Scribner's Sons, 1994), pp. 9–25, 64–8.
84. Raab, *Five Families*, p. 94.
85. *Final Assassination Plots Report*, p. 351; 'Santos Trafficante Jr.'; FBI Legat,

Havana, 'Santo Trafficante Jr.', 29 April 1959, JFKARC, FBI Subject Files, Santo Trafficante, Box 3; Stephen J. Labadie, 'Santo Trafficante Jr.', 22 September 1960, NARA JFKARC, RG 233, HSCA, Santo Trafficante, Box 3, file TP 92–1.

86. Paul Meskill, 'Yen for Cuba Cash Doomed Anastasia', *N.Y. World-Telegram & Sun*, 9 January 1958; Lacey, *Little Man*, pp. 239–45; English, *Havana Nocturne*, p. 196.

87. The same Nevadan politician showed up several years later as a Lansky front for a gambling operation in Haiti: Messick, *Syndicate Abroad*, p. 89.

88. English, *Havana Nocturne*, pp. 224–9; Ragano and Raab, *Mob Lawyer*, pp. 29–30; Lacey, *Little Man*, pp. 239–45.

89. Anthony John Falanga, 'Santo Trafficante Jr.', 11 September 1961, NARA, RG 170, DEA OEPC, Box 7, Folder 0660 Cuba, In-Confidence, #5 June thru 1959; Morris R. Dunham, 'Information relative to the alleged murders of major racketeer ALBERT ANASTASIA', 2 July 1962, NARA, RG 170, DEA OEPC, Box 7, Folder 0660 Cuba, In-Confidence, #5 June thru 1959. But see Lacey, *Little Man*, pp. 244–5; and Gosch and Hammer, *The Last Testament of Lucky Luciano*, pp. 397 et seq., for alternative hypotheses.

90. Quoted in Domínguez, 'The Batista Regime in Cuba', p. 122.

91. Beers, 'Treasury Representative in Havana to Commissioner of Customs'.

92. David Deutschmann and Deborah Shnookal, eds, *Fidel Castro Reader* (Melbourne: Ocean Books, 2008), p. 93.

93. FBI, 'Intelligence Survey—Cuba', 14 September 1958, JFKARC, HSCA, Lewis McWillie, Box 1.

94. Domínguez, 'The Batista Regime in Cuba', pp. 121–2.

95. FBI, 'Cuban Revolutionary Activities'.

96. Domínguez, 'The Batista Regime in Cuba', p. 130.

97. Sáenz Rovner, *The Cuban Connection*, p. 60.

98. Domínguez, 'The Batista Regime in Cuba', p. 131.

99. English, *Havana Nocturne*, p. 203.

100. Ibid., p. 164; Lacey, *Little Man*, p. 247; Cirules, *The Mafia in Havana*, p. 112.

101. Lacey, *Little Man*, p. 249.

102. Labadie, 'Santo Trafficante Jr.'; FBI Pittsburgh Office, 'Stuart Sutor, et al.', 3 July 1959, JFKARC, HSCA, Joseph Merola; Justin Gleichauf to Chief, Contact Division Support, 'Visit to Joseph Merola', 8 February 1961, JFKARC, HSCA, Segregated CIA Collection, JFK Task Force, Box 59, Folder G; CIA, 'Memorandum for the Record, Subject: Norman Rothman', 10 July 1961, JFKARC, HSCA, Segregated CIA Collection, Box 43, Reel 16, Folder 21; English, *Havana Nocturne*, pp. 283–5; Hunt, 'Castro', p. 17.

103. Ragano and Raab, *Mob Lawyer*, p. 346.
104. Ibid., pp. 48, 51.
105. Colhoun, *Gangsterismo*, p. 36.
106. *Final Assassination Plots Report*, p. 352; Colhoun, *Gangsterismo*, pp. 35–6.
107. Lacey, *Little Man*, p. 258.
108. Antoinette Giancano and Thomas Renner, *Mafia Princess: Growing Up in Sam Giancana's Family* (New York: Avon Books, 1989), pp. 9–10, 12–15.

9. THE BLUE CARIBBEAN OCEAN, 1959–1983

1. Max Holland, 'The Assassination Tapes', *Atlantic Monthly*, vol. 293, June 2004, p. 82.
2. Howard J. Osborn, 'Memorandum for Director of Central Intelligence', 9 December 1970, JFKARC, RG 233, HSCA, Segregated CIA Collection, Box 48, Folder 18.
3. *Final Assassination Plots Report*, p. 115; Lawrence Freedman, *Kennedy's Wars: Berlin, Cuba, Laos, and Vietnam* (New York: Oxford University Press, 2000), pp. 243–4; Robert A. Caro, *The Passage of Power: The Years of Lyndon Johnson, Vol. IV* (New York: Alfred A. Knopf, 2012), pp. 577, 585.
4. W.C. Kim and Renée Mauborgne, 'Blue Ocean Strategy', in Harvard Business School Publishing Corporation, ed., *HBR's 10 Must Reads On Strategy* (Cambridge MA: Harvard Business Review, 2004/2011), pp. 123–42.
5. See further W. Chan Kim and Renée Mauborgne, *Blue Ocean Strategy: How to Create Uncontested Market Space* (Boston MA: Harvard Business School Press, 2005).
6. W. Chan Kim and Renée Mauborgne, 'How Strategy Shapes Structure', *Harvard Business Review* (September 2009), pp. 73–80.
7. 'Casino Bigwigs Still in Town', *Times of Havana*, 5 January 1959.
8. Joseph L. Tangel, 'Activities of Top Hoodlums in the New York Field Division', 14 September 1959, JFKARC, HSCA, Sebastian John La Rocca, Box 4; CIA, 'Memorandum for the Record, Subject: Traces on Santos TRAFFICANTE', n.d. March 1977 and Chief of Station, JMWAVE to Deputy Chief, WH/SA, 'Debriefing of Sal Morgan', 16 July 1964, both in JFKARC, RG 233, HSCA, JFK Taskforce, Box 34, Folder 12.
9. Jack Colhoun, *Gangsterismo. The United States, Cuba, and the Mafia: 1933 to 1966* (New York/London: OR Books, 2013), p. 41.
10. 'Castro's Cabinet Off at Full Speed: Restores Casino Gambling', *The New York Times*, 18 February 1959, p. 16; 'Cuba: The mob is back', *Time*, 2 March 1959; and see Trafficante's testimony to Congress referred to in *Final Assassination Plots Report*, p. 353.
11. T.J. English, *Havana Nocturne* (New York: HarperCollins, 2008), pp. 310–

11; Frank Ragano and Selwyn Raab, *Mob Lawyer* (New York: Charles Scribner's Sons, 1994), pp. 49–53; Robert Lacey, *Little Man: Meyer Lansky and the Gangster Life* (Boston MA: Little Brown & Co., 1991), pp. 252–5.

12. Dr Jorge A. de Castoverde to H.J. Anslinger, 15 November 1959, NARA, RG 170, DEA OEPC, Box 7, 0660 Cuba, In-Confidence, Book #5 June thru 1959, p. 21; Hunt, 'Castro', p. 21.

13. 'Debriefing of Sal Morgan'; Colhoun, *Gangsterismo*, p. 43; 'Cuban Police Take Trafficante to Daughter's Wedding', *Miami Herald*, 22 June 1959.

14. *President's Commission Report*, pp. 369–70; *Final Assassination Plots Report*, pp. 152–5; Colhoun, *Gangsterismo*, pp. 45–7.

15. English, *Havana Nocturne*, p. 317; Lacey, *Little Man*, p. 258.

16. CIA, 'Fernandez, Miranda', 3 July 1959, and 'Rothman, Norman', 3 July 1959, and 'Memorandum for the Record, Subject: Norman Rothman', 10 July 1961, all in JFKARC, RG 233, HSCA, Segregated CIA Collection, Printed Microfilm, Box 43, Reel 16, Folder 21.

17. Lacey, *Little Man*, p. 163; Eisenberg *et al.*, *Meyer Lansky*, p. 295; Uri Dan, 'Meyer Lansky Breaks His Silence', *Ma'ariv*, 2 July 1971.

18. SAC, Miami to Director, FBI, 'Roberto Fernandez Miranda', 26 October 1960, JFKARC, RG 233, HSCA, Norman Rothman, Box 4; CIA, 'Rothman, Norman', 25 April 1975, JFKARC, RG 233, HSCA, Segregated CIA Collection, Box 34, Folder 1; Colhoun, *Gangsterismo*, pp. 48–56.

19. Ibid., p. 66.

20. 'Confidential Report', 3 December 1959, Field Office File No. MM 92–102, in FBI 'Vault', Meyer Lansky collection, FBI File No. 92–2831.

21. CIA, 'Security of the Mafia Assassination Plotting', Draft Report ('*CIA Mafia Plot Draft*'), 8 March 1977, JFKARC, RG 233, HSCA, Segregated CIA Collection, Box 34, Folder 11.

22. John Edgar Hoover, Director, to Director, Central Intelligence Agency, 18 October 1960, JFKARC, RG 233, HSCA, Segregated CIA Collection, Box 34, Folder 11; Jerry G. Brown, Deputy Chief, CIA Security Analysis Group to Chief, Security Analysis Group, 'Agency Castro Assassination Plotting', 18 August 1976, JFKARC, RG 233, HSCA, Segregated CIA Collection, Box 48, Folder 17; US House of Representatives, Select Committee on Assassinations, 'The Evolution and Implications of the CIA-Sponsored Assassination Conspiracies Against Fidel Castro', March 1979, in *Final Assassination Plots Report*, vol. X, pp. 147–95 at p. 176.

23. *CIA Mafia Plot Draft*; 'Testimony of John Roselli', 24 June 1975, JFKARC, RG 46, Church Committee, RIF#157–10014–10001; CIA, 'New Considerations in CIA on Syndicate Operation, Draft', 31 March 1977,

JFKARC, RG 233, HSCA, Segregated CIA Collection, Box 34, Folder 11; 'Evolution and Implications', p. 173.

24. J.S. Earman, 'Memorandum for the Record, Subject: Report on Plots to Assassinate Fidel Castro', 23 May 1967, JFKARC, RG 233, HSCA, Segregated CIA Collection, Printed Microfilm, Box 99, Folder 52, pp. 29–30; 'Evolution and Implications', p. 171.

25. Colhoun, *Gangsterismo*, p. vii. See US House of Representatives, Select Committee on Assassinations, 'Testimony of Tony Varona in Executive Session', 16 March 1978, JFKARC, RG 233, HSCA, Executive Session Hearings, Box 3, Tony Varona, pp. 7–10; 'Evolution and Implications', pp. 171–3; Earman, 'Memorandum', pp. 29–30; US Senate, Select Committee to Study Governmental Operations with Respect to Intelligence Activities ('Church Committee'), 'Alleged Assassination Plots Involving Foreign Leaders', in *Interim Report 94–465* (Washington DC: US Government Printing Office), pp. 79–82.

26. CIA, 'NSC Briefing—Cuba', 6 January 1959, NARA, RG 263, Records Relating to the Paramilitary Invasion of the Bay of Pigs April 1961, Box 2, Folder 15.

27. Embassy in Cuba to Department of State, 6 January 1959, in *Foreign Relations of the United States, 1958–1960, vol. VI, Cuba* (Washington DC: Government Printing Office, 1991), p. 345.

28. President Dwight Eisenhower to Prime Minister Harold Macmillan, 11 July 1960, NARA, RG 59, Bureau of Inter-American Affairs, Special Assistant on Communism, Box 4, Folder Cuba.

29. 'Testimony of William Atwood', 10 July 1975, JFKARC, RG 46, Church Committee, Box 25, Folder 1; J.C. King to DCI via Deputy Director (Plans), 'Cuba Problems', 11 December 1959, JFKARC, RG 263, LA Division Work Files, Box 4, Folder WFO5-F1; Colhoun, *Gangsterismo*, pp. 60–1.

30. 'Memorandum of Discussion at Department of State—Joint Chiefs of Staff at the Pentagon', 8 January 1960, in *FRUS, 1958–1960,Vol. VI, Cuba*, p. 732; 'Memorandum, NSC Meeting, 14 January 1960) in ibid., pp. 742–3.

31. Church Committee, pp. 109–16.

32. 'Testimony of L. Fletcher Prouty', n.d., JFKARC, RG 46, Church Committee, Box 26, Folder 4 (1975); Associated Press, 'CIA Plot to Kill Castro Described', *The New York Times*, 30 April 1975, p. 9.

33. Chief, WHD, to Chief of Station, Havana, 'Use of Biological/Scientific Techniques to Undermine the Castro Regime', 6 January 1960, JFKARC, RG 263, LA Division Work Files, Box 4, Folder WF05-F1; J.C. King, 'Cuba Problems'; Earman, 'Memorandum', pp. 10–13; Church Committee, p. 92.

34. Church Committee, p. 93; Colhoun, *Gangsterismo*, p. 72.

35. Freedman, *Kennedy's Wars*, p. 125.

36. 5412 Committee, 'A Program of Covert Action Against the Castro Regime', 16 March 1960, *FRUS, 1958–1960, Vol. VI, Cuba*, pp. 850–1; 'Memorandum of Conference with the President', 17 March 1960, in ibid., p. 861; Colhoun, *Gangsterismo*, pp. 73–4.

37. 'Testimony of William Harvey', 25 June 1975, JFKARC, RG 46, Church Committee, Box 36, Folder 1; 'Alleged Assassination Plots', p. 74.

38. 'Alleged Assassination Plots', p. 178.

39. Sheffield Edwards, 'Memorandum for the Record', 14 May 1962, JFKARC, RG 233, HSCA, Segregated CIA Collection, Box 48, Folder 18; Osborn, 'Memorandum for DCI'; 'Alleged Assassination Plots', p. 74; Earman, 'Memorandum', pp. 14–20, 29, 31.

40. 'Alleged Assassination Plots', p. 257.

41. 'Testimony of Howard J. Osborn', 28 August 1975, JFKARC, RG 46, Church Committee, Executive Session Hearings, RIF #157–10002–10150, at p. 15.

42. Earman, 'Memorandum', pp. 35–6, 55.

43. 'Alleged Assassination Plots', pp. 91–2.

44. Earman, 'Memorandum', pp. 17–18; Osborn, 'Memorandum'; Edwards, 'Memorandum for the Record'; John S. Hunt, Security Analysis Group to Director of Security, 23 May 1975, and Charles W. Kane, Director of Security, 'Memorandum for Inspector General', 22 May 1975, both in JFKARC, RG 233, HSCA, Segregated CIA Collection, Box 48, Folder 18.

45. 'Alleged Assassination Plots', p. 97.

46. Earman, 'Memorandum', pp. 16–17.

47. Compare *Final Assassination Plots Report*, p. 114.

48. Osborn, 'Memorandum', pp. 3–4; Earman, 'Memorandum', pp. 59 et seq.; Stanton F. Ense, Deputy Director of Security, to Associate Deputy Director for Administration, 6 June 1975, JFKARC, RG 233, HSCA, Segregated CIA Collection; 'Alleged Assassination Plots', pp. 77–9, 97, 131; 'Evolution and Implications', p. 153; *Final Assassination Plots Report*, pp. 114–5.

49. Brown, 'Agency Castro Assassination Plotting'. See 'Testimony of John Roselli'; Earman, 'Memorandum', p. 14; 'Alleged Assassination Plots', p. 74.

50. Earman, 'Memorandum', p. 15; 'Testimony of John Roselli', pp. 10–11; CIA, 'Robert A. Maheu', n.d., JFKARC, RG 233, HSCA, Segregated CIA Collection, Box 44, Folder 1. See also Newark, *Lucky Luciano*, pp. 84–5; J. Richard Davis, 'Things I Couldn't Tell till Now', *Collier's*, Pt V, p. 36.

51. 'Testimony of John Roselli'; Osborn, 'Memorandum'; Earman,

'Memorandum', pp. 14–17; Edwards, 'Memorandum for the Record'; FBI, 'Anthony James Balletti, et al.', 22 May 1961, JFKARC, RG 233, HSCA, Pike Committee, Box 1; 'Testimony of Ralph Salerno', in *Final Assassination Plots Report*, pp. 456, 460–1; 'Alleged Assassination Plots', pp. 74–7.

52. 'Testimony of Santos Trafficante', 28 September 1978, in *Final Assassination Plots Report*, p. 357; 'Evolution and Implications', pp. 168–9.

53. Earman, 'Memorandum', pp. 17–19, 24–5; CIA, 'Memorandum for the Record, Subject: Santos Trafficante', 24 July 1975, JFKARC, RG 233, HSCA, Segregated CIA Collection, Box 48, Folder 18; CIA, 'Analysis of CIA-Mafia Assassination Plotting', n.d., JFKARC, RG 233, HSCA, Segregated CIA Collection, Box 21, Folder 23; 'Alleged Assassination Plots', pp. 79–80.

54. 'Chronology of Castro Assassination', n.d. 1976, JFKARC, RG 46, Church Committee, Box 37, Folder 3; Earman, 'Memorandum', pp. 20–4; Colhoun, *Gangsterismo*, p. 87.

55. Osborn, 'Memorandum', p. 2; see also Earman, 'Memorandum', p. 25; and CIA, 'Memorandum for the Record, Subject: Santos Trafficante'.

56. CIA, 'New Considerations'. Compare *Final Assassination Plots Report* at p. 114.

57. Hoover to DCI.

58. Earman, 'Memorandum', pp. 27–8; Osborn, 'Memorandum', p. 3; CIA, 'New Considerations'; 'Alleged Assassination Plots', p. 80.

59. Earman, 'Memorandum', p. 28.

60. Colhoun, *Gangsterismo*, pp. 78–9.

61. Ibid., p. 79.

62. John F. Kennedy, *The Strategy of Peace* (New York: Harper & Row, 1960), pp. 132–3.

63. 'Kennedy Steps Up Attacks on Nixon', *The New York Times*, 16 October 1960, p. 1.

64. 'Kennedy Asks Aid for Cuban Rebels to Defeat Castro', *The New York Times*, 21 October 1960, p. 1.

65. Colhoun, *Gangsterismo*, p. 79.

66. Freedman, *Kennedy's Wars*, pp. 129 et seq.; Colhoun, *Gangsterismo*, pp. 105–6.

67. Freedman, *Kennedy's Wars*, p. 131.

68. Ibid., pp. 133–43; Colhoun, *Gangsterismo*, pp. 110–16; Hinckle and Turner, *Deadly Secrets*, pp. 92–7; Maxwell D. Taylor, *Swords and Plowshares* (New York: Norton, 1972), pp. 181–91.

69. Colhoun, *Gangsterismo*, pp. 111–12; Freedman, *Kennedy's Wars*, p. 143.

70. 'Special National Intelligence Estimate 85–61', 28 November 1961, JFKARC, RG 46, Church Committee, Box 32, Folder 6, pp. 642–5.

71. Freedman, *Kennedy's Wars*, p. 125.

72. Earman, 'Memorandum', p. 3.

73. Jack Anderson, '6 Attempts to Kill Castro Laid to CIA', *Washington Post*, 18 June 1971, p. B7.

74. Statement of Richard Bissell to Lucien S. Vandenbroucke, 18 May 1984, noted in the latter's 'The "Confessions" of Allen Dulles: New Evidence on the Bay of Pigs', *Diplomatic History*, vol. 8, no. 4 (Fall 1984), pp. 365–76, at p. 374, n. 33. See also Hinckle and Turner, *Deadly Secrets*, p. 80.

75. Michael Warner, 'Lessons Unlearned: The CIA's Internal Probe of the Bay of Pigs Affair', *Studies*, vol. 40, issue 2 (1996), excerpt from confidential CIA journal, NARA, RG 263, Records Relating to the Paramilitary Invasion of Cuba at the Bay of Pigs, April 1961, Box 1, Folder 6, p. 75. Compare Earman, 'Memorandum', p. 33.

76. 'Special National Intelligence Estimate 85–3–60, "Prospects for the Castro Regime", 8 December 1960', in *FRUS, 1958–1960, Vol. VI, Cuba*, p. 1173.

77. Michael R. Beschloss, *The Crisis Years: Kennedy and Khrushchev, 1960–1963* (New York: Edward Burlingame Books, 1991), p. 139; 'Testimony of George Smathers', 23 July 1975, JFKARC, RG 233, HSCA, Segregated CIA Collection, RIF #157–10005–10252, esp. pp. 30–2.

78. 'Testimony of William Harvey', p. 50; Edwards, 'Memorandum'; Earman, 'Memorandum', pp. 49–50; 'Alleged Assassination Plots', p. 81.

79. Earman, 'Memorandum', pp. 32–3; Kane, 'Memorandum for Inspector General'; 'Santo Trafficante Testimony before the House Select Committee on Assassinations', 14 November 1977, JFKARC, RG 233, HSCA, Executive Session Hearings, Box 3, Santo Trafficante; 'Santo Trafficante Interview', 1 October 1976, JFKARC, RG 46, Church Committee, Box 44, Santo Trafficante; 'Alleged Assassination Plots', pp. 79–82.

80. Ense to Associate Deputy Director for Administration; Charles W. Kane, Director of Security to Inspector General, 'Memorandum', 30 May 1975, JFKARC, RG 233, HSCA, Segregated CIA Collection, Box 48, Folder 18; Kane, 'Memorandum for Inspector General'; Edwards, 'Memorandum'; and Sheffield Edwards to Chief, WH/Division, n.d. June 1961, JFKARC, RG 233, HSCA, Segregated CIA Collection, Box 44, Folder 2.

81. 'Alleged Assassination Plots', p. 83.

82. Hinckle and Turner, *Deadly Secrets*, p. 81.

83. Ibid.

84. Freedman, *Kennedy's Wars*, p. 147; Colhoun, *Gangsterismo*, pp. 134–6; Hinckle and Turner, *Deadly Secrets*, pp. 142–3.

85. Brig. General William H. Craig to Chief of Operations, Cuba Project, 'Justification for US Military Intervention in Cuba', 13 March 1962, JFKARC, RG 335, Califano Papers, Box 1, Folder 4; Joint Chiefs of Staff, Decision on JCS, 1969/321, 'A Note by the Secretaries on Northwoods:

and "Justification of US Military Intervention in Cuba"', 14 March 1962, JFKARC, RG 218, Central Files, 1962–1963, Box 1.

86. Colhoun, *Gangsterismo*, p. 160; Hinckle and Turner, *Deadly Secrets*, p. 124 et seq.

87. Hinckle and Turner, *Deadly Secrets*, p. 46.

88. 'Testimony of William Harvey', pp. 39–40, 45.

89. Peter Wright, *Spy Catcher: The Candid Autobiography of a Senior Intelligence Official* (New York: Viking, 1987), pp. 147, 154–62; Colhoun, *Gangsterismo*, p. 147.

90. 'Testimony of William Harvey', p. 50; 'Alleged Assassination Plots', p. 189; Jack Anderson, *Merry-Go-Round* (syndicated column), 4 January 1978 (from statements by John Roselli).

91. CIA file quoted in 'Alleged Assassination Plots', at p. 182.

92. Harvey's notes, including this term, are described in 'Alleged Assassination Plots', at p. 183.

93. Ibid., pp. 46, 83–4, 103–4, 257; Hinckle and Turner, *Deadly Secrets*, p. 28; Earman, 'Memorandum', pp. 25, 41, 46–50; Freedman, *Kennedy's Wars*, pp. 157–8.

94. 'Alleged Assassination Plots', pp. 47–8.

95. Ibid., pp. 83, 182; Earman, 'Memorandum', pp. 37–40.

96. 'Alleged Assassination Plots', pp. 83–4, 103–4; Earman, 'Memorandum', pp. 25–41, 46–50, 59; 'Chronology of Castro Assassination'; 'Interview with William Harvey', n.d. 1976, JFKARC, RG 46, Church Committee, Box 33, Folder 4; 'HSCA Staff notes from Varona's CIA Security File', 7 March 1978, JFKARC, RG 233, HSCA, Segregated CIA Collection, Box 19, Folder 25–31; Hinckle and Turner, *Deadly Secrets*, p. 137.

97. 'Testimony of John Roselli', pp. 32–44, 42–3; Earman, 'Memorandum', p. 51; 'Alleged Assassination Plots', p. 84.

98. Earman, 'Memorandum', pp. 48–52.

99. *Final Assassination Plots Report*, p. 114; 'Evolution and Implications', p. 178.

100. 'Alleged Assassination Plots', pp. 138–9. See also Tad Szulc, 'Cuba on Our Mind', *Esquire*, February 1974, p. 90; and Colhoun, *Gangsterismo*, p. 145.

101. 'Alleged Assassination Plots', p. 261.

102. See FBI, 'Mafia Monograph', Part II, pp. 107–8—a document Robert Kennedy almost certainly read.

103. Robert F. Kennedy, *The Enemy Within* (New York: Popular Library, 1960).

104. Quoted in *Final Assassination Plots Report*, pp. 162–3.

105. Ibid., p. 261.

106. 'Alleged Assassination Plots', p. 141.

107. Ibid.

108. Secretary of State McGeorge Bundy, 'National Security Action Memorandum No. 100', 5 October 1961, in *FRUS, 1961–1963,Vol. X, Cuba, January 1961–September 1962* (Washington DC: Government Printing Office, 1991), p. 659; Thomas A. Parrott, 'Memorandum for the Record', 5 October 1961, in ibid., pp. 659–60.

109. Brig. Gen. Lansdale, 'Meeting with the President', Memorandum for the Record, 16 March 1962, NARA JFKARC, RG 335, Califano Papers, RIF #198–10004–10020, p. 3.

110. 'Minutes of the Meeting of the Special Group (Augmented) on Operation MONGOOSE', 4 October 1962, at National Security Archive, *The Cuban Missile Crisis, 1962: The 40th Anniversary* (Washington DC: George Washington University, 2002), at http://www.gwu.edu/~nsarchiv/nsa/cuba_mis_cri/621004%20Minutes%20of%20Meeting%20of%20Special.pdf, accessed 14 March 2015.

111. 'Alleged Assassination Plots', pp. 135, 141, 148–69, 264–6, 274–5; Freedman, *Kennedy's Wars*, p. 150.

112. 'Testimony of Richard Helms', 13 June 1975, JFKARC, RG 233, HSCA, Segregated CIA Collection, Church Committee Records, Box 25, Folder 3, pp. 72–3.

113. Holland, 'The Assassination Tapes', p. 82.

114. 'Testimony of Richard Helms', 17 July 1975, JFKARC, RG 233, HSCA, Segregated CIA Collection, Church Committee Records, Box 25, Folder 3, pp. 72–3.

115. 'Testimony of Richard Helms', 13 June 1975, p. 88.

116. 'Testimony of William Harvey', pp. 31–7, 76–8.

117. 'Alleged Assassination Plots', pp. 116–18, 135; 'Testimony of Richard Bissell', 9 June 1975, pp. 38, 57 and 'Testimony of Richard Bissell', 11 June 1975, pp. 5–6, both in JFKARC, RG 233, HSCA, Segregated CIA Collection, Church Committee Records, Box 25, Folder 3.

118. 'Testimony of Edward Lansdale', 8 July 1975, JFKARC, RG 233, HSCA, Segregated CIA Collection, Church Committee Records, Box 25, Folder 3, p. 107; 'Alleged Assassination Plots', pp. 143–4, 166–7. On Vietnam see Edward G. Lansdale, *In the Midst of Wars: An American's Mission to Southeast Asia* (New York: Harper & Row, 1972), pp. 147–8, 177, 269–70.

119. Robert Kennedy, *The Enemy Within*, p. 307; Director, FBI to Attorney-General, 23 January 1961, JFKARC, RG 233, HSCA, Antonio Varona, Box 1.

120. On Giancana see Robert Kennedy, *The Enemy Within*, pp. 240–1. For the FBI briefings given to Kennedy, see J. Edgar Hoover to Attorney-General Ramsey Clark, 'CIA's Intentions to Send Hoodlums to Cuba to Assassinate Castro', 6 March 1957, JFKARC, RG 46, Church Committee, FBI

Headquarters records, Box 18; and see S.D. Breckenridge, 'Meeting with Acting Assistant Attorney General', Memorandum for the Record, 21 May 1975, JFKARC, RG 233, Segregated CIA Collection, Box 48, Folder 19; 'Anthony James Balletti, et al.'; 'Alleged Assassination Plots', pp. 126–8.

121. 'Alleged Assassination Plots', pp. 129–30; Hinckle and Turner, *Deadly Secrets*, p. 138; Freedman, *Kennedy's Wars*, p. 158.
122. Earman, 'Memorandum', pp. 41, 43–4, 62a, 64–5; 'Testimony of Richard Bissell', 22 July 1975, JFKARC, RG 233, HSCA, Segregated CIA Collection, Church Committee, pp. 53–62; 'Alleged Assassination Plots', pp. 121–3, 131–2.
123. Earman, 'Memorandum', p. 62a; 'Alleged Assassination Plots', pp. 132–3, 259 note 3, 275–6.
124. Earman, 'Memorandum', pp. 50 et seq.; Freedman, *Kennedy's Wars*, p. 158.
125. 'Testimony of Richard Helms', 17 July 1975, p. 92.
126. Compare 'Alleged Assassination Plots', pp. 99–105.
127. See Earman, 'Memorandum', pp. 41, 43–4, 62a, 64–5; 'Testimony of Richard Bissell', 22 July 1975, pp. 53–62; 'Testimony of William Harvey', pp. 71–5, 99–102, 112–14; 'Alleged Assassination Plots', pp. 104–8, 121–3, 133.
128. *Final Assassination Plots Report*, p. 68.
129. Ibid., p. 116.
130. English, *Havana Nocturne*, pp. 328–9.
131. 'Castro Tells Cubans He's Communist', *Washington Post*, 3 December 1961.
132. Freedman, *Kennedy's Wars*, pp. 163–4, 172 et seq.; Colhoun, *Gangsterismo*, pp. 157–8; Oleg Troyanovsky, 'The Caribbean Crisis: A View from the Kremlin', *International Affairs* (Moscow), nos 4–5 (April/May 1992), pp. 147–57 at p. 148.
133. Special National Intelligence Estimate, 'The Military Buildup in Cuba', 19 September 1962, in *FRUS, 1961–1963, Vol. X, Cuba*, pp. 1052–3, 1070–80.
134. Freedman, *Kennedy's Wars*, pp. 175 et seq.; Colhoun, *Gangsterismo*, p. 174; Sergei N. Khruschev, *Nikita Khrushchev and the Creation of a Superpower* (University Park PA: Pennsylvania State University Press, 2000), pp. 502–3, 535–40.
135. Dino Brugioni, *Eyeball to Eyeball: The Inside Story of the Cuban Missile Crisis* (New York: Random House, 1991), pp. 210–32; Ernest R. May and Philip Zelikow, eds, *The Kennedy Tapes: Inside the White House during the Cuban Missile Crisis* (Cambridge: Harvard University Press, 1997), pp. 45–53.

136. Freedman, *Kennedy's Wars*, pp. 170–224; Timothy Naftali and Philip Zelikow, eds, *The Presidential Recordings: John F. Kennedy: The Great Crises, Vol. II* (New York: Norton, 2001), pp. 436, 448.

137. Naftali and Zelikow, *The Presidential Recordings*, pp. 581–6.

138. Freedman, *Kennedy's Wars*, pp. 190–2; Philip Zelikow and Ernest R. May, eds, *The Presidential Recordings: John F. Kennedy, The Great Crises, Vol. III* (New York: Norton, 2001), pp. 91–7.

139. Colhoun, *Gangsterismo*, p. 185.

140. Freedman, *Kennedy's Wars*, pp. 226–7.

141. Nikita Khrushchev to John Kennedy, 27 October 1962, in *FRUS, 1961–1963, Vol. XI, Cuban Missile Crisis*, pp. 257–60.

142. Freedman, *Kennedy's Wars*, pp. 212–14.

143. James G. Blight, Bruce J. Allyn and David Welch, *Cuba on the Brink: Castro, the Missile Crisis, and the Soviet Collapse* (Lanham MD: Rowman & Littlefield, 2002), pp. 73, 252–3, 360–4, 478, 481–4; Dobrynin Cable to the USSR Foreign Ministry, 27 October 1962, in National Security Archives, *The Cuban Missile Crisis, 1962: 40th Anniversary* (Washington DC: George Washington University, 2002), at http://www.gwu.edu/~nsarchiv/nsa/cuba_mis_cri/621027%20Dobrynin%20Cable%20to%20USSR.pdf, accessed 14 March 2015.

144. Colhoun, *Gangsterismo*, p. 196.

145. William Harvey to DCI, 'Operational Plan for Continuing Operations Against Cuba', Draft, 27 November 1962, JFKARC, RG 233, HSCA, Segregated CIA Collection, Box 34, Folder 9; *CIA Mafia Plot Draft*; George McManus, 'Memorandum', 5 November 1962, JFKARC, RG 46, Church Committee, Box 26, Folder 1; 'Alleged Assassination Plots', pp. 84–5.

146. *Final Assassination Plots Report*, vol. X, pp. 93–101.

147. FBI, 'Paulino Sierra', Memorandum, 4 June 1963, and FBI, Director to SACs, 'Paulino Sierra', 23 May 1963, and CIA, JM/WAVE to HQ, 'Paulino Sierra', Cable, 14 November 1963 are all in JFKARC, RG 233, HSCA, Paulino Sierra, Box 1; CIA, 'Gambling Interests of Paulino Sierra', Information Report, 12 September 1963, and CIA, 'Paulino Sierra and the JGCE', 20 November 1963 are in JFKARC, RG 233, HSCA, Subject file JGCE, Box 1. See also *Final Assassination Plots Report*, pp. 98–100; Colhoun, *Gangsterismo*, p. 204.

148. Freedman, *Kennedy's Wars*, pp. 230–1.

149. Robert J. Dwyer, 'Anti-Fidel Castro Activities', FBI report, n.d. October 1963, JFKARC, RG 46, Church Committee, Box 31, Folder 3; 'MIRR', FBI report, 3 September 1963, and 'Overflights, Raids and Support of MIRR', CIA cable, 14 September 1963, and 'Identity of Aircraft Dealer', CIA cable, 12 September 1963 are in JFKARC, RG 233, HSCA, Subject file MIRR, Box 1; Stephen J. Labadie, 'Santo Trafficante Jr.', 22 September

1960, NARA JFKARC, RG 233, HSCA, Santo Trafficante, Box 3, file TP 92–1.; Lacey, *Little Man*, pp. 306–7.

150. 'Re: Alleged Plot to Bomb Shell Oil Refinery', FBI memorandum, n.d., and 'Memorandum to Attorney-General: Alleged Plot to Bomb Shell Oil Refinery', FBI memorandum, 18 June 1963, are in JFKARC, RG 233, HSCA, Lake Pontchartrain, Box 1; CIA Philadelphia Field Office, 'Michael McLaney', 22 November 1960, JFKARC, RG 233, HSCA, Segregated CIA Collection, Printed Microfilm, Box 31, Folder F; and SAC, Miami to Director, FBI, 'ECA', FBI memorandum, 30 October 1963, in FBI, The Vault, Santo Trafficante Files. See also W.R. Wannall to W.C. Sullivan, 'ECA', 1 November 1963, NARA, JFRKARC, RG 233, HSCA, Santo Trafficante, Box 6; Dwyer, 'Anti-Fidel Castro Activities'; Lacey, *Little Man*, pp. 291–2, 323; English, *Havana Nocturne*, pp. 269–70; Colhoun, *Gangsterismo*, p. 220.

151. 'Testimony of John Roselli', p. 42.

152. Taylor, *Swords and Plowshares*, p. 280.

153. Deborah Shapley, *Promise and Power: The Life and Times of Robert McNamara* (Boston MA: Little Brown & Co., 1993), p. 176.

154. Graves B. Erskine, 'Memorandum for the Record', 10 January 1961, JFKARC, RG 233, HSCA, Antonio Varona, Box 1.

155. Director, FBI to Attorney-General, 23 January 1961.

156. 'Testimony of William Harvey', pp. 67–8; David Belin, 'Interview with William King Harvey', Rockefeller Commission Memorandum to File, 10 April 1975, and 'Excerpt of Interview with William Harvey, 1976', both in JFKARC, RG 233, HSCA, Segregated CIA Collection, Box 21.

157. Kennedy, *The Enemy Within*, p. 253.

158. See JFK Exhibit F-551 in US House of Representatives, Select Committee on Assassinations, *Hearings*, 95th Congress, 2nd Session (Washington DC: Government Printing Office, 1979), vol. V, p. 435; 'Staff and Consultant's Reports on Organized Crime' in ibid., Appendix, Vol. IX, pp. 11–14; Selwyn Raab, *Five Families: The Rise, Decline, and Resurgence of America's Most Powerful Mafia Empires* (New York: St. Martin's Griffin/Thomas Dunne Books, 2005), p. 153.

159. 'Staff and Consultant's Reports', Appendix, Vol. IX, p. 22.

160. 'Testimony of Ralph Salerno' in ibid., at vol. V, pp. 454–6; 'Staff and Consultant's Reports', in ibid., at Appendix, vol. IX, pp. 11–14; *Final Assassination Plots Report*, pp. 164–9.

161. 'Staff and Consultant's Reports', pp. 22–4.

162. Ibid., pp. 39–42.

163. *Final Assassination Plots Report*, p. 168.

164. Freedman, *Kennedy's Wars*, p. 216; 'Alleged Assassination Plots', pp. 138–9.

165. Such was the claim made to Chief Justice Warren in 1967: see James

J. Rowley to J. Edgar Hoover, 13 February 1967, JFKARC, RG 233, HSCA, FBI Headquarters files, FBI File #62–117290, Admin Folder-N12.

166. Freedman, *Kennedy's Wars*, pp. 243–4.

167. See *Final Assassination Plots Report*, Appendix, vol. IX.

168. *Final Assassination Plots Report*, p. 173; Raab, *Five Families*, p. 145.

169. Raab, *Five Families*, p. 145.

170. Ron Chepesiuk, *The Trafficantes: Godfathers from Tampa, Florida. The Mafia, CIA and the JFK Assassination* (Rock Hill SC: Strategic Media Books Inc., 2010), pp. 76, 104; Hinckle and Turner, *Deadly Secrets*, p. 419. Compare Raab, *Five Families*, pp. 142–3.

171. *Final Assassination Plots Report*, p. 115; Freedman, *Kennedy's Wars*, pp. 243–4; Caro, *The Passage of Power*, pp. 577, 585.

172. *Final Assassination Plots Report*, p. 115.

173. English, *Havana Nocturne*, p. 278; Enrique Cirules, *The Mafia in Havana: A Caribbean Mob Story* (North Melbourne / New York: Ocean Press, 2010), p. 117.

174. CIA, 'Handwritten Notes, Probable Interview Questions / Answers from Conversation with Norman Rothman', no date, JFKARC, HSCA, Segregated CIA Collection, Printed Microfilm, Box 43, Reel 16, Folder 21; Cirules, *The Mafia in Havana*, pp. 278–82.

175. Hinckle and Turner, *Deadly Secrets*, pp. 281–2.

176. 'US Calls Bonanno Haiti's Casino Chief', *The New York Times*, 30 December 1966.

177. Hinckle and Turner, *Deadly Secrets*, pp. 295–6; Vincent Teresa and Thomas Renner, *My Life in the Mafia* (New York: Doubleday, 1974), p. 223.

178. Messick, *Syndicate Abroad*, pp. 34–9; Peter Andreas, *Smuggler Nation: How Illicit Trade Made America* (New York: Oxford University Press, 2013), p. 280.

179. Messick, *Syndicate Abroad*, p. 5.

180. English, *Havana Nocturne*, p. 278; Cirules, *The Mafia in Havana*, p. 117; Messick, *Syndicate Abroad*, p. 46.

181. Richard Oulahan and William Lambert, 'The Scandal in the Bahamas', *Life* (magazine), vol. 62, no. 5 (1967), pp. 58–74 at pp. 63–4; Messick, *Syndicate Abroad*, pp. 33, 74.

182. Jerry G. Brown, Deputy Chief, Security Analysis Group to Chief, Security Analysis Group, 18 August 1976, JFKARC, RG 233, HSCA, Segregated CIA Collection, Box 48, Folder 19.

183. Oulahan and Lambert, 'The Scandal in the Bahamas', p. 69.

184. Bill Davidson, 'The Mafia: Shadow of Evil on an Island in the Sun', *Saturday Evening Post*, vol. 240, no. 4 (1967), pp. 27–37; Alan A. Block, *Masters of Paradise: Organized Crime and the Internal Revenue Service in The Bahamas* (New Brunswick / London: Transaction Publishers, 1998), p. 30.

185. Davidson, 'The Mafia', p. 42; Block, *Masters*, p. 34; Messick, *Syndicate Abroad*, p. 61.

186. Block, *Masters*, pp. 37–9; Messick, *Syndicate Abroad*, pp. 62–72.

187. Davidson, 'The Mafia', p. 32; Oulahan and Lambert, 'The Scandal in the Bahamas', p. 70; Block, *Masters*, p. 43; Messick, *Syndicate Abroad*, p. 102.

188. Oulahan and Lambert, 'The Scandal in the Bahamas', pp. 70, 73; Messick, *Syndicate Abroad*, p. 109.

189. Messick, *Syndicate Abroad*, pp. 107–9.

190. Oulahan and Lambert, 'The Scandal in the Bahamas', p. 73; 'Consultant's Paradise Lost', *Time*, vol. 90, issue 10 (1967), p. 39; Monroe W. Karmin and Stanley Penn, 'Las Vegas East: US Gamblers Prosper in Bahamas With Help From Island Officials', *Wall Street Journal*, 5 October 1966, pp. 1–2; Messick, *Syndicate Abroad*, p. 115.

191. William K. Rashbaum and Thomas Kaplan, 'Sheldon Silver, Assembly Speaker, Took Millions in Payoffs, US Says', *The New York Times*, 22 January 2015.

192. Messick, *Syndicate Abroad*, pp. 75–7.

193. Ibid., pp. 112–15.

194. Block, *Masters*, p. 40; Messick, *Syndicate Abroad*, p. 111.

195. Oulahan & Lambert, 'The Scandal in the Bahamas', pp. 63, 74; Block, *Masters*, p. 45; Messick, *Syndicate Abroad*, pp. 154, 192.

196. Messick, *Syndicate Abroad*, p. 154.

197. Ibid., pp. 159–60; Davidson, 'The Mafia', p. 35.

198. Karmin and Penn, 'Las Vegas East', p. 2; Messick, *Syndicate Abroad*, pp. 167–9.

199. The phrase is from Susan Strange, *Casino Capitalism* (Oxford: Basil Blackwell, 1986).

200. Davidson, 'The Mafia', p. 33.

201. Lacey, *Little Man*, pp. 303–5.

202. Vinicy Chan, 'Macau Casinos Decline After Report on Junket Crackdown', *Bloomberg News*, 6 February 2013, available at http://www.bloomberg.com/news/2013–02–06/galaxy-leads-macau-casino-drop-on-report-of-junket-curbs.html, accessed 14 March 2015.

203. Davidson, 'The Mafia', p. 33; Messick, *Syndicate Abroad*, p. 169.

204. Block, *Masters*, p. 102.

205. 'Consultant's Paradise Lost', p. 39; Messick, *Syndicate Abroad*, pp. 225–30; Block, *Masters*, pp. 67–9; Oulahan and Lambert, 'The Scandal in the Bahamas', pp. 58–74.

206. Davidson, 'The Mafia', pp. 33–4; Oulahan and Lambert, 'The Scandal in the Bahamas', pp. 60–6; Messick, *Syndicate Abroad*, pp. 85–92.

207. Block, *Masters*, pp. 47–51.

208. Davidson, 'The Mafia', p. 35.

209. Ibid.

210. Ibid.

211. Block, *Masters*, p. 72. See also Messick, *Syndicate Abroad*, p. 195.

212. Block, *Masters*, pp. 72–3; Oulahan and Lambert, 'The Scandal in the Bahamas', p. 66; Messick, *Syndicate Abroad*, p. 208.

213. Messick, *Syndicate Abroad*, pp. 208–9.

214. Ibid., p. 225.

215. Ibid., pp. 195–6.

216. Davidson, p. 33.

217. Karmin and Penn, 'Las Vegas East', p. 2.

218. Ibid.

219. Davidson, 'The Mafia', p. 35.

220. Block, *Masters*, pp. 45–6.

221. Ibid., p. 299.

222. Ibid., p. 301.

223. Ibid., pp. 294–9.

224. Ibid., p. 294.

225. Ibid., p. 11.

226. Tom Blickman, 'The Rothschilds of the Mafia on Aruba', *Trans. Org. Crime*, vol. 3, no. 2 (1997), pp. 50–89.

227. Nelson Johnson, *Boardwalk Empire: The Birth, High Times, and Corruption of Atlantic City* (Medford NJ: Plexus Publishing Inc., 2002), pp. 1–77.

228. Ibid., pp. 79–124. The joint venture in Atlantic City was dominated by Nucky Johnson. See Johnson, *Boardwalk Empire*, pp. 79–124.

229. See Messick, *Syndicate*, pp. 233–5; Block, *Masters*, pp. 101–2; 'Who the casino operators are', *Executive Intelligence Review*, vol. 6, no. 33 (1979), pp. 23–5; Donald Janson, 'Resorts' Chairman Denies Authorizing Bahamas Payment', *The New York Times*, 13 February 1985; Hank Messick, *Syndicate Abroad* (Toronto: The Macmillan Company, 1969) pp. 233–5.

230. Block, *Masters*, pp. 191–5.

231. Johnson, *Boardwalk Empire*, p. 202; Donald Janson, 'Bahamas Gambling Interest is Pressing Las Vegas-Type Casinos in Atlantic City', *The New York Times*, 15 August 1976, pp. 45–6.

232. 'Who the casino operators are', p. 23; Block, *Masters*, p. 100. On Intertel, see also Frank J. Prial, 'Concern Fights Crime in Business', *The New York Times*, 26 July 1970, pp. 12–13.

233. Fred Feretti, 'Atlantic City Casino Company Defends Its Record', *The New York Times*, 18 September 1976, p. 17. Fred Ferretti, 'Atlantic City Casino Company Defends Its Record', in *The New York Times*, 18 September 1976.

234. Martin Waldron, 'Accord Could Allow May Casino Opening', *The New York Times*, 4 April 1978.

235. 'Resorts Wins a Permanent License to Operate a Casino in Atlantic City', *The New York Times*, 27 February 1979, p. A1; 'Who the casino operators are', pp. 23–5; Johnson, pp. 198–202; and New Jersey Office of Administrative Law, *In re Resorts Casino Application*, 10 N.J.A.R. 244 (1988), p. 244.

236. Johnson, *Boardwalk Empire*, p. 202.

237. See Carlo Morselli, Mathilde Turcotte and Valentina Tenti, 'The Mobility of Criminal Groups', Report No. 004, 2010, Public Safety Canada, Ottawa, 2010 and Carlo Morselli, Mathilde Turcotte and Valentina Tenti, 'The mobility of criminal groups', *Global Crime*, vol. 12, no. 3 (2011).

238. James J. Mittelman and Robert Johnston, 'The Globalization of Organized Crime, the Courtesan State, and the Corruption of Civil Society', *Global Governance*, vol. 5 (1999).

239. Block, *Masters*, p. 303.

10. STRATEGIC CRIMINAL POSITIONING

1. John Milton, *Paradise Lost* (London: Penguin Classics, 1667/2003), Book I, ll. 262–3.

2. Anne L. Clunan and Harold A. Trinkunas, *Ungoverned Spaces: Alternatives to State Authority in an Era of Softened Sovereignty* (Stanford CA: Stanford Security Studies, 2010).

3. Stergios Skaperdas, 'The political economy of organized crime: providing protection when the state does not', *Economics of Governance*, vol. 2 (2001), pp. 173–202.

4. Vincenzo Ruggiero, *Organized and Corporate Crime in Europe: Offers that Can't be Refused* (Aldershot: Ashgate, 1996), p. 33.

5. Nikos Passas, 'Globalization and Transnational Crime: Effects of Criminogenic Asymmetries', in Phil Williams and Dimitri Vlassis, eds, *Combating Transnational Crime: Concepts, Activities and Responses* (London/ Portland OR: Frank Cass, 1998), pp. 22–56.

6. See Peter Andreas, *Smuggler Nation: How Illicit Trade Made America* (New York: Oxford University Press, 2013); Vanda Felbab-Brown, *Shooting Up: Counterinsurgency and the War on Drugs* (Washington DC: Brookings Institution Press, 2009); Vanda Felbab-Brown, *Aspiration and Ambivalence: Strategies and Realities of Counterinsurgency and Statebuilding in Afghanistan* (Washington DC: Brookings Institution, 2012); Enrique Desmond Arias, *Criminal Politics: Illicit Activities and Governance in Latin American and the Caribbean*, forthcoming.

7. Compare Alex de Waal's notion of the 'political marketplace' in Africa: Alex de Waal, 'Mission without end? Peacekeeping in the African political marketplace', *International Affairs*, vol. 85, no. 1 (2009), pp. 99–113; David

Kilcullen's 'theory of competitive control' in *Out of the Mountains: The Coming Age of the Urban Guerrilla* (Oxford: Oxford University Press, 2003), pp. 116–68; and Vanda Felbab-Brown's notion of states and criminal actors as 'competitors in state-making': 'Conceptualizing Crime as Competition in State-Making and Designing an Effective Response', *Sec. & Def. Stud. Rev.* (Spring-Summer 2010).

8. See Michael E. Porter, *Competitive Strategy: Techniques for Analyzing Industries and Competitors* (New York: The Free Press, 1980); Phil Williams, 'The International Drug Trade: An Industry Analysis', in G.H. Turbiville ed., *Global Dimensions of High Intensity Crime and Low Intensity Conflict* (Chicago IL: Office of International Criminal Justice, 1995), pp. 153–83.

9. Roberto Saviano, *Gomorrah* (New York: Picador, 2007), p. 38.

10. See Felbab-Brown, 'Conceptualizing'; and see Jonathan Goodhand and David Mansfield, 'Drugs and (Dis)Order: A study of the opium trade, political settlements and state-making in Afghanistan', Working Paper no. 83, Crisis States Working Paper Series No. 2 (London: Crisis States Research Centre, 2010). Compare the discussion of roving and stationary in Mancur Olson, 'Dictatorship, Democracy and Development', *American Political Science Review*, vol. 87, no. 3 (1993).

11. Adam Elkus, 'Mexican Cartels: A Strategic Approach', *Infinity Journal*, IJ Exclusive, 28 June 2011. On the resemblance to medieval barons, see also John Rapley, 'The New Middle Ages', *Foreign Affairs*, vol. 85, no. 3 (2006), pp. 95–103.

12. Gianluca Fiorentini, 'Oligopolistic Competition in Illegal Markets', in Fiorentini and Peltzman, p. 275; Francisco E. Thoumi, *Political Economy and Illegal Drugs in Colombia* (Boulder CO: Lynne Rienner, 1995), pp. 93–108.

13. A. Peter Lupsha, 'Transnational Organized Crime Versus the Nation State', *Transnational Organized Crime*, vol. 2, no. 1 (1996), pp. 30–2; see also R.T. Naylor, 'From Cold War to Crime War: The Search for a New National Security Threat', *Transnational Organized Crime*, vol. 1 (1995), pp. 46–7.

14. Max G. Manwaring, *A Contemporary Challenge to State Sovereignty: Gangs and Other Illicit Transnational Criminal Organizations in Central America, El Salvador, Mexico, Jamaica and Brazil* (Carlisle PA: Strategic Studies Institute, 2007), p. 2.

15. On 'jurisdictional sharing' see Thomas Schelling, *Choice and Consequence: Perspectives of an Errant Economist* (Cambridge MA: Harvard University Press, 1984), p. 182.

16. Federico Varese, *The Russian Mafia: Private Protection in a New Market Economy* (Oxford: Oxford University Press, 2001); Michela Wrong, *It's Our Turn to Eat: The Story of a Kenyan Whistle-blower* (London: Fourth Estate, 2009).

17. Henner Hess, *Mafia and Mafiosi. The Structure of Power* (Westmead: Saxon House, 1973), p. 29. On the related concept of 'mediated states' see generally Achim Wennmann, 'Getting Armed Groups to the Table: Peace Processes, the Political Economy of Conflict and the Mediated State', *Third World Quarterly*, vol. 30, no. 6 (2009), pp. 1123–38.

18. Eric Hobsbawm, *Primitive Rebels* (Manchester: The University Press, 1959), pp. 5–6. Compare Eric Hobsbawm, *Bandits*, 2nd ed. (New York: Pantheon Books, 1981), p. 40.

19. Compare Daniel Bell, 'Crime as an American Way of Life', *The Antioch Review*, vol. 13, no. 2 (Summer 1953), pp. 131–54; Francis A. Ianni and Elizabeth Reuss-Ianni, *A Family Business: Kinship and Social Control in Organized Crime* (New York: Russel Sage, 1972); and Phil Williams, 'Transnational Criminal Networks', in J. Arquilla and D. Ronfeldt, eds, *Networks and Netwars: The Future of Terror, Crime and Militancy* (Santa Monica CA: Rand Corporation), pp. 78–80.

20. Pino Arlacchi, *Mafia Business: The Mafia Ethic and the Spirit of Capitalism* (Oxford: Oxford University Press, 1983/1988) p. 40, cf. pp. 38–44, 69–75, 161–86.

21. Anton Blok, *The Mafia of a Sicilian Village, 1860–1960: A Study of Violent Peasant Entrepreneurs* (Cambridge: Waveland Press, 1974), pp. 94–6.

22. Henner Hess, 'The Sicilian Mafia: Parastate and Adventure Capitalism', in Eric Wilson, ed., *Government of the Shadows: Parapolitics and Criminal Sovereignty* (London/New York: Pluto Press, 2009), p. 157.

23. Walter Lippmann, 'The Underworld—A Stultified Conscience', *The Forum*, LXXXV:2 (1931), p. 67.

24. Alfredo Schulte-Bockholt, *The Politics of Organized Crime and the Organized Crime of Politics* (Lanham MD/Oxford: Lexington Books, 2006).

25. See Carlo Morselli, Mathilde Turcotte and Valentina Tenti, 'The Mobility of Criminal Groups', Report No. 004, 2010, Public Safety Canada, Ottawa, 2010 and Carlo Morselli, Mathilde Turcotte and Valentina Tenti, 'The mobility of criminal groups', *Global Crime*, vol. 12, no. 3 (2011); and Federico Varese, *Mafias on the Move: How Organized Crime Conquers New Territories* (Princeton NJ: Princeton University Press, 2011).

26. Anton Blok, 'Reflections on the Sicilian Mafia: Peripheries and Their Impact on Centres', in Dina Siegel and Hans Nelen, eds, *Organized Crime: Culture, Markets and Policies* (New York: Springer, 2008), pp. 7–13.

27. Varese, *The Russian Mafia*; Stephen Handelman, *Comrade Criminal: The Theft of the Second Russian Revolution* (London: Michael Joseph, 1994).

28. Sasha Lezhnev, *Crafting Peace: Strategies to Deal with Warlords in Collapsing States* (Lanham MD: Lexington, 2005); Antonio Giustozzi, 'Respectable Warlords? The Politics of State-Building in Post-Taleban Afghanistan', Working Paper No. 33 (London: LSE Crisis States Programme, 2003);

Antonio Giustozzi, 'The Debate on Warlordism: The Importance of Military Legitimacy', Crisis States Discussion Paper 13 (London: Crisis States Research Centre, October 2005), pp. 15–16.

29. See Mark Duffield, 'Post-modern Conflict: Warlords, Post-adjustment States and Private Protection', *CivilWars*, vol. 1, no. 1 (1998), pp. 65–102; Paul Jackson, 'Warlords as Alternative Forms of Governance', *SmallWars and Insurgencies*, vol. 14, no. 2 (2003), pp. 131–50; Kimberly Marten, 'Warlordism in Comparative Perspective', *International Security*, vol. 31, no. 3 (2006/7), pp. 41–73.

30. William Reno, *Warlord Politics and African States* (Boulder CO/London: Lynne Rienner, 1998), p. 8.

31. Mancur Olson, *Power and Prosperity: Outgrowing Communist and Capitalist Dictatorships* (New York: Basic Books, 2000), pp. 10 et seq.

32. Anthony B. Chan, *Arming the Chinese: Western Armaments Trade in Warlord China, 1920–1928* (Vancouver: University of British Columbia Press, 1982); Susan Strange, *The Retreat of the State: The Diffusion of Power in the World Economy* (New York: Cambridge University Press, 1996), pp. 116–7.

33. Antonio Giustozzi, *The Art of Coercion. The Primitive Accumulation and Management of Coercive Power* (New York: Columbia University Press, 2011), pp. 14–15.

34. Kilcullen, *Out of the Mountains*, pp. 89–102.

35. Mark Duffield, 'Post-modern Conflict: Warlords, Post-adjustment States and Private Protection', *CivilWars*, vol. 1, no. 1 (1998), p. 81.

36. Rune Henriksen and Anthony Vinci, 'Combat Motivation in Non-State Armed Groups', *Terrorism & PoliticalViolence*, vol. 20, no. 1 (2007), p. 93.

37. See Bertil Lintner, *Burma in Revolt: Opium and Insurgency since 1948* (Bangkok: White Lotus, 1994).

38. Giustozzi, 'Debate on Warlordism', p. 14.

39. Jackson, 'Warlords'.

40. Ibid.

41. Felbab-Brown, *Shooting Up*, p. 129.

42. See Antonio Giustozzi, 'Genesis of a "Prince": the rise of Ismail Khan in western Afghanistan, 1979–1992', Crisis States Working Paper Series No. 2, Working Paper No. 4, September 2006 (London: Crisis States Research Centre).

43. Compare William Reno, 'Illicit Commerce in Peripheral States', in H.R. Friman, ed., *Crime and the Global Political Economy* (Boulder CO: Lynne Rienner), p. 68.

44. This is similar to Doug Farah's concept of 'criminalized states'. See Douglas Farah, *Transnational Organized Crime, Terrorism, and Criminalized*

States in Latin America: An Emerging Tier-One National Security Priority (Carlisle PA: US Army War College, April 2012), p. 6.

45. Stanley A. Pimentel, 'Mexico's Legacy of Corruption', in Roy Godson, ed., *Menace to Society: Political-Criminal Collaboration around the World* (New Brunswick/London: Transaction Publishers, 2003), pp. 175–97.

46. See Jean-François Bayart, Stephen Ellis and Béatrice Hibou, *The Criminalization of the State in Africa* (Bloomington IN: Indiana University Press, 1999).

47. Reno, *Warlord Politics*, pp. 8–10.

48. William Reno, 'Mafiya Troubles, Warlord Crises', in Mark R. Beissinger and Crawford Young, eds, *Beyond State Crisis?: Postcolonial Africa and Post-Soviet Eurasia in Comparative Perspective* (Washington DC: Woodrow Wilson Center Press, 2002), p. 108; William Reno, 'Clandestine Economies, Violence and States in Africa', *Journal of International Affairs*, vol. 53, no. 2 (2000), pp. 436–7; and Bayart *et al.*

49. Reno, 'Clandestine Economies', pp. 442–3; 'Mafiya Troubles', p. 108.

50. Andreas, *Smuggler Nation*, pp. 13–60.

51. Patrick Cockburn, *The Jihadis Return: ISIS and the New Sunni Uprising* (New York/London: OR Books, 2014), pp. 50–5; and see David D. Kirkpatrick, 'Graft Hobbles Iraq's Military in Fighting ISIS', *The New York Times*, 24 November 2014.

52. Compare Jeff Fischer, Marcin Walecki and Jeffrey Carlson, eds, *Political Finance in Post-Conflict Societies* (Washington DC: International Foundation for Electoral Systems, 2006).

53. Reno, 'Clandestine Economies', p. 435.

54. Moisés Naím, 'Mafia States: Organized Crime Takes Office', *Foreign Affairs*, vol. 91, no. 3 (2012), p. 101.

55. Sheena Chestnut, 'Illicit Activity and Proliferation: North Korean Smuggling Networks', *International Security*, vol. 32, no. 1 (Summer 2007).

56. Sam Jones, 'Ukraine: Russia's new art of war', *Financial Times*, 28 August 2014.

57. On hybrid warfare's relationship to organized crime, see especially Kilcullen, *Out of the Mountains*, pp. 102–8.

58. Mark Galeotti, 'Will "Goblin" Make Crimea a "Free Crime Zone"?', *Read Russia*, 7 March 2014, at http://readrussia.com/2014/03/07/will-goblin-make-crimea-a-free-crime-zone/, accessed 14 March 2015.

59. Phil Williams, 'Transnational Criminal Organizations: Strategic Alliances', *Washington Quarterly*, vol. 18 (1995), pp. 61–3.

60. David E. Kaplan and Alec Dubro, *Yakuza: Japan's Criminal Underworld* (Berkeley CA: University of California Press, 2012).

61. Schulte-Bockholt, *The Politics of Organized Crime*, pp. 64–5; Peter Dale

Scott, 'Drugs, Anti-communism and Extra-legal repression in Mexico', in Wilson, *Government of the Shadows*, pp. 173–94.

62. See especially Alfred McCoy in his seminal *The Politics of Heroin in Southeast Asia* (New York: Harper Colophon Books, 1973).

63. On Russia, see Chapter 1. On the UK, see Chapter 7. On France, see Schulte-Bockholt, *The Politics of Organized Crime*, pp. 64–5. On China, see e.g. Shawn Shieh, 'The Rise of Collective Corruption in China: the Xiamen smuggling case', *Journal of Contemporary China*, vol. 14, issue 42 (2005), pp. 67–91.

64. Williams, 'Transnational Criminal Organizations', p. 63.

65. Misha Glenny, *McMafia: A Journey through the Global Criminal Underworld* (London: The Bodley Head, 2008), pp. 71–96; Ian Bremmer, *The End of the Free Market: Who Wins the War Between States and Corporations?* (London: Portfolio, 2010).

66. On 'indirect strategy' see Basil H. Liddell Hart, *Strategy* (New York: Frederick A. Praeger, 1954/1967), p. 339.

67. John Dickie, *Mafia Republic* (London: Sceptre, 2013), p. 391.

68. John Bailey and Matthew M. Taylor, 'Evade, Corrupt, or Confront? Organized Crime and the State in Brazil and Mexico', *Journal of Politics in Latin America*, vol. 1, no. 2 (2009).

69. Rukmini Callimachi, 'Paying Ransoms, Europe Bankrolls Qaeda Terror', *The New York Times*, 29 July 2014.

70. Hobsbawm, *Bandits*, pp. 154–7.

71. See Temitope B. Oriola, *Criminal Resistance? The Politics of Kidnapping Oil Workers* (Ashgate Publishing, e-book, 28 June 2013); United Nations, 'Report of the Analytical Support and Sanctions Monitoring Team', ('Monitoring Team Report') UN Doc. S/2015/79, 9 February 2015, paras 31–8.

72. Compare Phil Williams, 'The Terrorism Debate over Mexican Drug Trafficking Violence', *Terrorism & Political Violence*, vol. 24, no. 2 (2012); John T. Picarelli, 'Osama bin Corleone? Vito the Jackal? Framing Threat Convergence through an Examination of Transnational Organized Crime and International Terrorism', *Terrorism & Political Violence*, vol. 24 (2012).

73. On Hezbollah, see Matthew Levitt, *Hezbollah: The Global Footprint of Lebanon's Party of God* (London: Hurst, 2013); on Islamic State, Cockburn, *The Jihadis Return*.

74. See Stephanie Kirschgaessner, 'Corleone businessman breaks omertà over mafia extortion', *The Guardian*, 27 January 2015.

75. Bailey and Taylor, 'Evade, Corrupt, or Confront?'

76. Gaia Pianigiani, 'President of Italy Questioned in Mafia Case', *The New York Times*, 28 October 2014.

77. Morselli *et al.*, 'The mobility' (2011), pp. 166–7.

78. Diego Gambetta, *The Sicilian Mafia: The Business of Private Protection* (Cambridge, MA: Harvard University Press, 1993), p. 251.

79. Letizia Paoli, 'The paradoxes of organized crime', *Crime, Law & Social Change*, vol. 37 (2002), p. 66.

80. Varese, *Mafias on the Move*; Gambetta, *The Sicilian Mafia*, pp. 146–87, 249–51.

81. Morselli *et al.* 'The Mobility' (2010) and 'The mobility' (2011).

82. Varese, *Mafias on the Move*, p. 21.

83. Morselli *et al.*, 'The Mobility' (2010), p. 10 and 'The mobility' (2011).

84. Compare W.C. Kim and Renée Mauborgne, 'Blue Ocean Strategy', in Harvard Business School Publishing Corporation, ed., *HBR's 10 Must Reads On Strategy* (Cambridge MA: Harvard Business Review, 2004/2011), pp. 123–42.

85. W. Chan Kim and Renée Mauborgne, *Blue Ocean Strategy: How to Create Uncontested Market Space* (Boston MA: Harvard Business School Press, 2005).

86. W. Chan Kim and Renée Mauborgne, 'How Strategy Shapes Structure', *Harvard Business Review* (September 2009).

11. INNOVATION, DISRUPTION AND STRATEGY BEYOND THE STATE

1. Marcelle Padovani, 'Introduction', in Giovanni Falcone, *Men of Honour: The Truth about the Mafia* (London: Warner Books, 1992), p. xvii.

2. Nick Miroff and William Booth, 'Mexico's drug war is a stalemate as Calderon's presidency ends', *The Washington Post*, 26 November 2011.

3. Peter Andreas, 'The Political Economy of Narco-Corruption in Mexico', *Current History*, vol. 97, no. 618 (April 1998), pp. 160–5; and Peter Andreas, *Smuggler Nation: How Illicit Trade Made America* (New York: Oxford University Press, 2013), pp. 308–20.

4. For a discussion of the causal relationship between democratization and the rise of violent organized crime, see David Shirk and Joel Wallman, 'Understanding Mexico's Drug Violence', introducing a Special Issue on the topic, *Journal of Conflict Resolution*, vol. 59, no. 8 (December 2015), pp. 1359–62.

5. Juan Camilo Castillo, Daniel Mejia and Pascual Restrepo, 'Scarcity Without Leviathan: The Violent Effects of Cocaine Supply Shortages in the Mexican Drug War', Center for Global Development Working Paper No. 356, Washington DC, 26 February 2014; compare Andreas, *Smuggler Nation*, pp. 320–9.

6. Malcolm Beith, 'A broken Mexico: allegations of collusion between the

Sinaloa cartel and Mexican political parties', *Small Wars & Insurgencies*, vol. 22, no. 5 (2011), pp. 787–806.

7. 'The World's Billionaires: 937 Joaquin Guzman Loera', *Forbes Magazine*, 10 March 2010.

8. Elyssa Pachico, 'Baja California: A Test for Mexico's Pax-Mafioso?', *InSight Crime*, 17 April 2013.

9. Ricardo Ravelo, *Osiel: Vida y tragedia de un capo* (Mexico City: Griajalbo, 2009). The Zetas' origins are also recounted in alleged video testimony by founding Zeta Jesús Enríque Rejón following his arrest on 4 July 2011. See Mexican Federal Police, 'Entrevista a Jesús Enrique Rejón Aguilar', July 2011, at www.youtube.com/watch?v=YUD5Tcq9NIw, accessed 14 March 2015.

10. Diego Enrique Osorno, *La guerra de los Zetas: Viaje por la frontera de la necropolitica* (New York: Vintage Español, 2013).

11. International Crisis Group, 'Peña Nieto's Challenge: Criminal Cartels and Rule of Law in Mexico', Crisis Group Latin America Report No. 48, 19 March 2013, p. 12.

12. Patrick Corcoran, 'Zetas: We are not Terrorists, Nor Guerrillas', *InSight Crime*, 15 December 2011.

13. See Steven Dudley, *The Zetas in Guatemala*, *InSight Crime*, Special Report, Medellín, 8 September 2011; Hal Brands, *Crime, Violence, and the Crisis in Guatemala: A Case Study in the Erosion of the State* (Carlisle PA: Strategic Studies Institute, 2010).

14. Miriam Wells and Hannah Stone, 'Zetas Fight Sinaloa Cartel for Guatemala Drug Routes: Perez', *InSight Crime*, 14 January 2013.

15. Clare Ribando Seelke, *Gangs in Central America*, CRS Report RL34112, US Congressional Research Service, Washington DC, 20 February 2014.

16. See Elyssa Pachico and Steven Dudley, 'Why a Zetas Split is Inevitable', *InSight Crime*, 24 August 2012; Samuel Logan, 'The Future of Los Zetas after the Death of Heriberto Lazcano', *CTC Sentinel*, 29 October 2012; Dudley Althaus, 'What Follows Zetas Leader's Takedown in Mexico', *InSight Crime*, 16 July 2013.

17. See generally George W. Grayson, *La Familia Drug Cartel: Implications for US-Mexican Security* (Carlisle PA: Strategic Studies Institute, 2010); and William Finnegan, 'Silver or Lead', *The New Yorker*, 31 May 2010.

18. See Berend J. ter Haar, *Ritual and Mythology of the Chinese Triads: Creating an Identity* (Brill: Leiden, 1998).

19. See Grayson, *La Familia*.

20. Compare Kilcullen, *Out of the Mountains*, pp. 128–9.

21. See Grayson, *La Familia*, p. vii.

22. See Elyssa Pachico, 'The Top 5 Most Infamous Narco-Songs', *InSight Crime*, 15 March 2012.

23. Howard Campbell, 'Narco-Propaganda in the Mexican "Drug War": An Anthropological Perspective', *Latin American Perspectives*, vol. 41, no. 2 (March 2014), pp. 60–77.

24. Grayson, *La Familia*.

25. Italian Parliamentary Commission of Inquiry into the Mafia phenomenon in Sicily, *Relazione sui rapporti tra mafia e politica* ('Relazioni Violante'), Legislature XI, Doc. xxxiii, no. 2 (Rome: Senate Printing Press, 1993), Audizioni in Calabria, p. 37 (author's translation).

26. See George Grayson, 'La Familia Michoacána: A Deadly Mexican Cartel Revisited', *FPRI E-notes*, August 2009, on file with the author.

27. See Associated Press, 'Excerpts of "Code of the Knights Templar" cartel', *Yahoo! News*, 20 July 2011, at http://news.yahoo.com/excerpts-code-knights-templar-cartel-092225002.html, accessed 14 March 2015.

28. See 'Con narcomantas Los Caballeros Templarios anuncian su repliegue en Michoacán', 13 March 2013, *Blog del Narco*.

29. John P. Sullivan and Robert J. Bunker, 'Rethinking insurgency: criminality, spirituality, and societal warfare in the Americas', *Small Wars & Insurgencies*, vol. 22, no. 5 (2011), pp. 742–63.

30. See Enrique Desmond Arias, 'Violence, Citizenship, and Religious Faith in a Rio de Janeiro Favela', *Lat. Am. Research Rev.*, vol. 49 (2014), pp. 149–67.

31. Tracy Knott, 'Dead Drugs Boss "Sainted" in Mexico', *InSight Crime*, 19 July 2012.

32. Eduardo Guerrero Gutiérrez, 'El crimen organizado en las elecciones', *Nexos en línea*, 1 June 2012, at http://www.nexos.com.mx/?p=14872, accessed 14 March 2015.

33. See UNODC, *Drug Trafficking as a Security Threat in West Africa* (Vienna: UNODC, October 2008), p. 3; Wolfram Lacher, 'Organized Crime and Terrorism in the Sahel: Drivers, Actors, Options', SWP Comments 1 (Berlin: SWP, January 2011). For a general introduction see also Tuesday Reitano and Mark Shaw, *Fixing a Fractured State? Breaking the Cycles of Crime, Conflict and Corruption in Mali and Sahel* (Geneva: Global Initiative against Transnational Organized Crime, April 2015), pp. 13–15.

34. Francesco Strazzari, 'Azawad and the rights of passage: the role of illicit trade in the logic of armed group formation in northern Mali' (Oslo: NOREF, January 2015), p. 3.

35. Tuesday Reitano and Mark Shaw, 'The end of impunity? After the kingpins, what next for Guinea-Bissau?', ISS Policy Brief 44 (Pretoria: ISS, July 2013).

36. Wolfram Lacher, 'Organized Crime and Conflict in the Sahel-Sahara Region' (Washington DC: Carnegie Endowment for International Peace, September 2012); Strazzar, 'Azawad and the rights of passage'.

37. See especially Global Initiative Against Transnational Organized Crime, 'Illicit Trafficking and Instability in Mali: Past, Present and Future' (Geneva: GITOC, 2014); and Morten Bøås, 'Castles in the sand: informal networks and power brokers in the northern Mali periphery', in Mats Utas, ed., *African Conflicts and Informal Power: Big Men and Networks* (London: Zed, 2012), pp. 119–34.

38. See Serge Daniel, *Les Mafias du Mali* (Paris: Descartes, 2014).

39. Lacher, 'Organized Crime and Conflict', p. 9.

40. GITOC, 'Illicit Trafficking', p. 2.

41. Ibid., pp. 10–11.

42. Ibid., pp. 12–13.

43. Lacher, 'Organized Crime and Conflict', pp. 11–13.

44. The group's website is http://www.mnlamov.net/, accessed 14 March 2015.

45. See GITOC, 'Illicit Trafficking', p. 12.

46. Judith Scheele, 'Tribus, États et fraude: la région frontalière algéro-malienne', *Études rurales*, vol. 184, no. 2 (July–December 2009), p. 91.

47. Lamine Chiki, 'AQIM Gets Help from Mali Officials—ex-Rebel', *Reuters*, 12 August 2010.

48. Lydia Polgreen and Alan Cowell, 'Mali Rebels Proclaim Independent State in North', *The New York Times*, 6 April 2012.

49. Peter Beaumont, 'The man who could determine whether the west is drawn into Mali's war', *The Guardian*, 27 October 2012.

50. Rukmini Callimachi, 'Rise of Al-Qaida Sahara Terrorist', *Associated Press*, 28 May 2013.

51. See Jean-Pierre Filiu, 'Could Al-Qaeda Turn African in the Sahel?', *Carnegie Papers*, Middle East Program, No. 112 (Washington DC: Carnegie Endowment for International Peace, June 2010).

52. GITOC, 'Illicit Trafficking', p. 15. And see especially Strazzari, 'Azawad and the rights of passage'.

53. Adam Nossiter, 'Jihadists' Fierce Justice Drives Thousands to Flee Mali', *The New York Times*, 18 July 2012.

54. See Pascale Combelles Siegel, 'AQIM's Playbook in Mali', *CTC Sentinel*, 27 March 2013.

55. Lacher, 'Organized Crime and Conflict', pp. 15–16.

56. GITOC, 'Illicit Trafficking', p. 15; Lacher, 'Organized Crime and Conflict', p. 16.

57. Compare Lacher, 'Organized Crime and Conflict', p. 16.

58. Ibid.

59. On the 'politically kaleidoscopic' nature of contemporary strategic environments see Emile Simpson, *War From the Ground Up* (London: Hurst,

2012), p. 203. For application of the concept to the Sahel, see also Strazzari, 'Azawad and the rights of passage'.

60. GITOC, 'Illicit Trafficking', p. 9, see also pp. 14–15.

61. Lacher, 'Organized Crime and Conflict', p. 17.

62. See Phil Williams, 'Lawlessness and Disorder: An Emerging Paradigm for the 21ˢᵗ Century', in Michael Miklaucic and Jacqueline Brewer, eds, *Convergence: Illicit Networks and National Security in the Age of Globalization* (Washington DC: National Defense University Press, 2013), pp. 15–36; and Nils Gilman, Doug Randall, Peter Schwartz, *Impacts of Climate Change* (San Francisco CA: Global Business Network, January 2007).

63. Ivan Briscoe, 'A violent compound: competition, crime and modern conflict' (Oslo: NOREF, November 2015).

64. Beith, 'A broken Mexico'; and David Leigh, James Ball, Juliette Garside and David Pegg, 'HSBC files: Swiss bank hid money for suspected criminals', *The Guardian*, 13 February 2015.

65. See Scott Atran, *Talking to the Enemy: Faith, Brotherhood, and the (Un)Making of Terrorists* (New York: HarperCollins, 2010); Pape, pp. 173–98.

66. On the cartels, see Katie Collins, 'Guns, gore and girls: the rise of the cyber cartels', *Wired* (UK), 5 November 2014, at http://www.wired.co.uk/news/archive/2014–11/05/cyber-cartels, accessed 14 March 2015.

67. Compare Letizia Paoli, 'Criminal Fraternities or Criminal Enterprises?', in Phil Williams and Dimitri Vlassis, eds, *Combating Transnational Crime: Concepts, Activities and Responses* (London/Portland OR: Frank Cass); Janine R. Wedel, 'Clans, Cliques and Captured States: Rethinking "Transition" in Central and Eastern Europe and the former Soviet Union', *Journal of International Development*, vol. 15. (2003), pp. 427–40.

68. Institute for Islamic Strategic Affairs, *Neo-Jihadism: A New Form of Jihadism. Leading and Emerging Actors* (London: IISA, 2015).

69. 'What Libya's Unraveling Means', *The New York Times*, 14 February 2015.

70. Carl von Clausewitz, *On War*, eds/trans. Michael Howard and Peter Paret (Princeton NJ: Princeton University Press, 1976, revd ed. 1984), pp. 606–7.

71. Ibid., p. 586. See further Mark T. Clark, 'Does Clausewitz Apply to Criminal-States and Gangs?', *Global Crime*, vol. 7, nos 3–4 (August–September 2006), pp. 407–27.

72. Phil Williams, 'The Terrorism Debate over Mexican Drug Trafficking Violence', *Terrorism & Political Violence*, vol. 24, no. 2 (2012), p. 265.

73. Anthony Vinci, 'Anarchy, Failed States, and Armed Groups: Reconsidering Conventional Analysis', *International Studies Quarterly*, vol. 52, no. 2, (2008), p. 304.

74. Compare Phil Williams, 'The Nature of Drug-Trafficking Networks',

Current History, vol. 97, no. 618 (1998), pp. 154–9; Susan Strange, 'States, Firms and Diplomacy', *International Affairs*, vol. 68, no. 1 (January 1992), pp. 1–15.

75. Anne L. Clunan and Harold A. Trinkunas, *Ungoverned Spaces: Alternatives to State Authority in an Era of Softened Sovereignty* (Stanford CA: Stanford Security Studies).

76. Robert Latham, 'Social Sovereignty', *Theory, Culture & Society*, vol. 17, no. 4 (2000), pp. 1–18.

77. Compare John Rapley, 'The New Middle Ages', *Foreign Affairs*, vol. 85, no. 3 (2006).

78. Compare Philip G. Cerny, 'Neomedievalism, Civil War, and the New Security Dilemma: Globalisation as Durable Disorder', *Civil Wars*, vol. 1, no. 1 (Spring 1998), pp. 36–64.

79. GITOC, 'Illicit Trafficking', p. 18.

80. Lacher, 'Organized Crime and Conflict', p. 19.

81. GITOC, 'Illicit Trafficking', p. 9.

82. Dickie, *Mafia Republic*, p. 127.

83. See David M. Kennedy, *Don't Shoot: One Man, A Street Fellowship, and the End of Violence in Inner-City America* (New York: Bloomsbury, 2011).

84. See Clausewitz, *On War*, pp. 485–6, 595–6; and see Antulio J. Echevarria, '"Reining In" the Center of Gravity Concept', *Air & Space Power Journal*, Summer 2003, pp. 87–96.

85. See e.g. Ben Olken, 'Monitoring Corruption: Evidence from a Field Experiment in Indonesia', *Journal of Political Economy*, vol. 115, no. 2 (2007), pp. 200–49.

86. Hannah Stone, 'The Zetas' Biggest Rival: Social Networks', *InSight Crime*, 28 September 2011.

87. See Andrés Monroy-Hernandez and Luis Daniel Palacios, 'Blog del Narco and the Future of Citizen Journalism', *Georgetown Journal of International Affairs*, vol. XV, no. 2 (Summer/Fall 2014), pp. 81–91.

88. Charles Ransford, Candice Kane and Gary Slutkin, 'Cure Violence: A disease control approach to reduce violence and change behavior', in Eve Waltermaurer and Timothy Akers, eds, *Epidemiological Criminology: Theory to Practice* (Abingdon: Routledge, 2012), pp. 232–42.

89. Anthony A. Braga and David L. Weisburd, 'The Effects of Focused Deterrence Strategies on Crime: A Systematic Review and Meta-Analysis of the Empirical Evidence', *Journal of Research in Crime and Delinquency*, vol. 49, no. 3 (August 2012), pp. 323–58.

90. See e.g. Krista London Couture, 'A Gendered Approach to Countering Violent Extremism', Policy Paper (Washington DC: Brookings Institution, July 2014).

91. See further James Cockayne, *Strengthening mediation to deal with criminal agendas* (Geneva: Centre for Humanitarian Dialogue, November 2013).

92. See Steven Dudley, 'El Salvador's Gang Truce: Positives and Negatives', *InSight Crime*, 11 June 2013; David Gagne, 'El Salvador Gangs Outline Political Motives of Violence', *InSight Crime*, 2 March 2015.

93. Helen Moestue and Robert Muggah, *Social Integration, ergo, Stabilization: Assessing Viva Rio's Security and Development Programme in Port-Au-Prince* (Rio de Janeiro: CIDA Canada, MFA START Canada, MFA NCA Norway, 2009).

94. Robert Muggah, 'Stabilization and Humanitarian Action in Haiti', in Benjamin Perrin, ed., *Modern Warfare: Armed Groups, Private Militaries, Humanitarian Organizations, and the Law* (Vancouver: UBC, 2011), p. 337.

95. See Achim Wennmann, 'Negotiated Exits from Organized Crime? Building Peace in Conflict and Crime-affected Contexts', *Negotiation Journal*, vol. 30, no. 3 (July 2014), pp. 255–73.

96. See Peter Andreas, *Blue Helmets and Black Markets. The Business of Survival in the Siege of Sarajevo* (Ithaca NY: Cornell University Press, 2008); and Phil Williams, *Criminals, Militias, and Insurgents: Organized Crime in Iraq* (Carlisle PA: Strategic Studies Institute, 2009).

97. See Williams, 'Insurgencies and Organized Crime', pp. 44–6, 58–60; Samuel P. Huntington, 'Civil violence and the process of development', *The Adelphi Papers*, vol. 11, issue 83 (1972), p. 15.

98. UN, 'Monitoring Team Report', para. 4. The report has been criticized on the grounds of sensationalism and for over-simplifying the picture of motivations within the Taliban: author's discussions with UN officials, New York, October–November 2015; and correspondence with an anonymous peer reviewer. However for a discussion of this phenomenon in general, see Svante E. Cornell, 'Narcotics and Armed Conflict: Interaction and Implications', *Studies in Conflict & Terrorism*, vol. 30 (2007), pp. 207–27.

99. Stephen J. Stedman, 'Spoiler problems in peace processes', *International Security*, vol. 22, no. 2 (Fall 1997), pp. 5–53. Compare Cockayne, *Strengthening mediation*; Mark Shaw and Walter Kemp, *Spotting the Spoilers: A Guide to Analyzing Organized Crime in Fragile States* (New York: International Peace Institute, 2012); Catalina Uribe Burcher, 'Organized crime, Colombia's peace spoiler?', *OpenSecurity*, 27 August 2014, at https://www.opendemocracy.net/opensecurity/catalina-uribe-burcher/organized-crime-colombia's-peace-spoiler, accessed 17 March 2015.

100. On the importance of localized analysis and approaches see especially Reitano and Shaw, *Fixing the Fractured State?*, pp. 44–6.

101. Raul Sanchez de la Sierra, 'On the Origin of States: Stationary Bandits

and Taxation in Eastern Congo', working paper, 3 December 2014, at http://ssrn.com/abstract=2358701, accessed 14 March 2015. See Mancur Olson, 'Dictatorship, Democracy and Development', *American Political Science Review*, vol. 87, no. 3 (1993).

102. Patrick Cockburn, *The Jihadis Return: ISIS and the New Sunni Uprising* (New York/London: OR Books, 2014), p. 78.

103. UN, 'Monitoring Team Report', paras. 23–30.

104. See Weinstein; and see Kyle Beardsley, Kristian Gleditsch and Nigel Lo, 'Roving and Stationary Bandits in African Armed Conflicts', conference paper, Annual Meeting of the International Studies Association, San Francisco, 2013.

105. See O.A. Hallaj, 'The Balance-sheet of Conflict: criminal revenues and warlords in Syria' (Oslo: NOREF, 2015).

106. Melissa Dell, 'Trafficking Networks and the Mexican Drug War', *American Economic Review*, vol. 105, no. 6 (2015), pp. 1738–79.

107. Alex de Waal, 'Mission without end? Peacekeeping in the African political marketplace', *International Affairs*, vol. 85, no. 1 (2009), pp. 103, 106–8; Stedman, 'Spoiler problems'.

108. I am indebted to an anonymous reviewer for this point. This hypothesis has potentially important applications for a range of contemporary armed conflicts, from Myanmar to DRC.

109. Benjamin Lessing, 'Logics of Violence in Criminal War', *Journal of Conflict Resolution*, vol. 59, no. 8 (December 2015).

110. Jonathan Goodhand and David Mansfield, 'Drugs and (Dis)Order: A study of the opium trade, political settlements and state-making in Afghanistan', Working Paper no. 83, Crisis States Working Paper Series No. 2 (London: Crisis States Research Centre, 2010), p. 26.

111. Zaw Oo and Win Min, 'Assessing Burma's Ceasefire Accords', *Policy Studies* No. 39 (Southeast Asia) (Washington DC: East-West Center, 2007), pp. 27–9.

112. Joel S. Hellman, 'Winners Take All: The Politics of Partial Reform in Postcommunist Transitions', *World Politics*, vol. 50, no. 2 (1998), pp. 203–34; Christine Cheng, 'Private and public interests: Informal actors, informal influence, and economic order after war', in Mats Berdal and Dominik Zaum, eds, *Political Economy of Statebuilding: Power after Peace* (Routledge: Abingdon/New York, 2013), pp. 62–78.

113. Cockayne, *Strengthening mediation*.

114. Vesna Bojicic-Dzelilovic, Denisa Kostovicova, Mariana Escobar and Jelena Bjelica, 'Organised crime and international aid subversion: evidence from Colombia and Afghanistan', *Third World Quarterly*, vol. 36, no. 10 (2015), p. 1889.

115. Ibid., p. 1901.

116. See Jeff Fischer, Marcin Walecki and Jeffrey Carlson, eds, *Political Finance in Post-Conflict Societies* (Washington DC: International Foundation for Electoral Systems, 2006); Antonio Giustozzi and Dominique Orsini, 'Centre-periphery relations in Afghanistan: Badakshan between patrimonialism and institution-building', *Central Asian Survey*, vol. 28, no. 1, March 2009, p. 15.

117. Rennell to Foreign Office, 'Questions Asked by Foreign Office', 8 September 1943, BNA, FO 371/37326.

118. See Dell, 'Trafficking Networks'.

119. UN, 'Monitoring Team Report', para. 10.

120. Andreas, *Smuggler Nation*, pp. 45–61, 154–75, 348–50.

121. Andreas, *Blue Helmets*; Williams, *Criminals, Militias, and Insurgents*; UN, 'Monitoring Team Report', para. 42.

122. Ivan Briscoe, 'The New Criminal Blitz: Mali, Iraq and the Business of Asymmetry', *ISN*, 10 July 2014.

123. De Waal, 'Mission without end?', p. 108.

124. Kilcullen, *Out of the Mountains*, p. 14.

125. See Nikos Passas, 'Global Anomie, Dysnomie, and Economic Crime: Hidden Consequences of Neoliberalism and Globalization in Russia and Around the World', *Social Justice*, vol. 27, no. 2 (2000), pp. 16–44.

126. On the disembedding of the economy from society see Karl Polanyi, *The Great Transformation* (Boston MA: Beacon Press, 1944), p. 71.

127. See Ian Bremmer, *The End of the Free Market: Who Wins the War Between States and Corporations?* (London: Portfolio, 2010).

128. See e.g. Steven Lee Myers, Jo Becker and Jim Yardley, 'Private Bank Fuels Fortunes of Putin's Inner Circle', *The New York Times*, 27 September 2014.

129. I am indebted to an anonymous reviewer for this distinction.

130. Oxfam, *Wealth: Having it All and Wanting More*, Issue Briefing, London, January 2015.

131. I am indebted to Nils Gilman for this point.

132. Stephen Handelman, *Comrade Criminal: The Theft of the Second Russian Revolution* (London: Michael Joseph, 1994), p. 139.

133. Passas, 'Global Anomie'; Williams, 'Lawlessness', pp. 32–3.

134. Passas, 'Global Anomie', pp. 26–7.

135. See generally John Gerard Ruggie, 'Taking Embedded Liberalism Global: The Corporate Connection', in John G. Ruggie, ed., *Embedding Global Markets: An Enduring Challenge* (Burlington VT: Ashgate, 2008), pp. 231–54.

136. See Francis M. Deng *et al.*, eds, *Sovereignty as Responsibility: Conflict Management in Africa* (Washington DC: The Brookings Institution, 1996).

137. Robert H. Jackson, 'Negative Sovereignty in Sub-Saharan Africa', *Review of International Studies*, vol. 12, no. 4 (1986), pp. 247–64.

138. Reitano and Shaw, *Fixing the Fractured State?*, p. 47.

REFERENCES

Primary Sources

Unpublished and archival material

BNA: British National Archives; CAB = Records of the Cabinet Office; FO = Records of the Foreign Office; WO = Records of War Office and Armed Forces.

CURBML: Columbia University Rare Book & Manuscript Library New York State Crime Commission, *Fourth Report, Port of New York Waterfront*, Legislative Document no. 70 (1953).

New York State Crime Commission, *Interim Report of Evidence Adduced by the State Crime Commission Relating to Six Brooklyn Locals of the International Longshoremen's Association: Confidential* (September 1952).

FBI: US Department of Justice, Federal Bureau of Investigations. These records are taken from 1) 'The FBI Vault' in the online FBI 'Reading Room', http://vault.fbi.gov; and 2) NARA Record Group 65.

JFKARC: *See* NARA, below.

McGuigan, Michael P. (2012) 'Fulgencio Batista's Economic Policies, 1952–1958', Ph.D. thesis, University of Miami.

NARA: US National Archives and Records Administration, College Park, MD. Listed by Record Group (RG), then entry:box:folder number—e.g. RG 226, 142:2:14. Of these, the most important are:

JFKARC: John F. Kennedy Assassination Records Collection. Includes the 'HSCA'—House Select Committee on Assassinations—Record Group, named by subject file unless noted as 'Numbered Files'. In some cases Record Identification Form numbers are also used.

RG 38 Records of the Office of Chief of Naval Operations

RG 46 Records of the US Senate

RG 65 Records of the Federal Bureau of Investigation

REFERENCES

RG 165 Records of the War Department General and Special Staffs

RG 170 Records of the Drug Enforcement Administration

DEA BNDD = Subject Files of the Drug Enforcement Administration, Subject Files of the Bureau of Narcotics and Dangerous Drugs, 1916–1970

DEA OEPC = Subject Files of the Drug Enforcement Administration, Office of Enforcement Policy Classified Subject Files, 1932–1967

RG 226 Records of the Office of Strategic Services

RG 233 Records of the House of Representatives

RG 263 Records of the Central Intelligence Agency

RG 331 Records of Allied Operational and Occupation Headquarters, World War II

RG 335 Records of the Office of the Secretary of the Army

NYMA: New York Municipal Archives

NYPL: New York Public Library, including:

Joseph McGoldrick, 'A Scrapbook of Politics', 1929, #8406 and #8381.

Kefauver Hearings, Hearing Pertaining to New York-New Jersey, New York City, February 13–15, 1951—Executive Session, Part VII.

Public hearings (no. 4) conducted by the New York State Crime Commission pursuant to the Governor's executive order of March 29, 1951, New York County Court House, New York, NY, 13–19 November 1952.

Samuel Seabury to Hon. Samuel H. Hofstadter, *Intermediate Report*, 25 January 1932, and *Final Report*, n.d. 1932, 'In the matter of the investigation of the departments of the government of the City of New York, etc., pursuant to Joint resolution adopted by the Legislature of the State of New York, March 23, 1931' (Albany NY, 1932).

US Commission on the Review of the National Policy Towards Gambling, *Gambling in America, Appendix 1: Staff and Consultant Papers* (Washington DC, 1976).

URHIM: Library of the University of Rochester, New York, Thomas E. Dewey Archive, Herlands Investigation materials, Series 13, Boxes 11–17. Represented as 'box:folder', i.e. box 16, folder 2, is 16:2.

USMC: US Military Commission. See also Joel Samaha, Sam Root and Paul Sexton, eds, *Transcript of Proceedings before the Military Commission to Try Persons Charged with Offenses against the Law of War and the Articles of War, Washington D.C., July 8 to July 31, 1942* (Minneapolis: University of Minnesota, 2004), available at http://www.soc.umn.edu/~samaha/nazi_saboteurs/nazi01.htm.

Published official documents

Coles, H.L. and A. K. Weinberg. (1964) *Civil Affairs. Soldiers Become Governors*, Center for Military History Publication 11–3 (Washington DC: US Army).

REFERENCES

Council of Europe, Parliamentary Assembly, Committee on Legal Affairs and Human Rights. (2010) 'Inhuman treatment of people and illicit trafficking in human organs in Kosovo', AS/Jur (2010) 46, 12 December 2010.

Cressey, Donald R. (1967) 'The Functions and Structure of Criminal Syndicates', in *Task Force Report: Organized Crime. Annotations and Consultants, Papers* (Washington DC: The President's Commission on Law Enforcement and Administration of Justice).

Italian Parliamentary Commission of Inquiry into the Mafia phenomenon in Sicily. (1993) *Relazione sui rapporti tra mafia e politica* (Relazioni Violante), Legislature XI, Doc. xxxiii, no. 2 (Rome: Senate Printing Press).

Italian Parliamentary Commission of Inquiry into the Mafia phenomenon in Sicily. (1985) *Documentazione allegata alla Relazione conclusiva*, Legislatures VII-IX (Rome: Senate Printing Press).

Italian Parliamentary Commission of Inquiry into the Mafia phenomenon in Sicily. (1976) *Relazione 'mafia ed enti locali'* (Relazioni Alessi), Legislature VI, Doc. xxxiii, no. 2 (Rome: Senate Printing Press).

Italian Parliamentary Commission of Inquiry into the Mafia phenomenon in Sicily. (1976) *Relazione sul traffico mafioso di tabacchi e stupeficanti e sui rapport tra mafia e gangsterismo italo-americano* (Relazione Zuccala), Legislature VI, Doc. xxiii, n. 2 (Rome: Senate Printing Press).

Italian Parliamentary Commission of Inquiry into the Mafia phenomenon in Sicily. (1972) *Relazione sur lavori svolti e sull stato del fenomeno Mafioso al termine della V legislature* (Relazione Cattanei), Legislature V, Doc. xxiii, n. 2 (Rome: Senate Printing Press).

Italian Parliamentary Commission of Inquiry into the Mafia phenomenon in Sicily. (1972) *Relazione sui rapporti tra mafia e banditismo in Sicilia*, legislature V, doc. xxiii, n. 2 (Rome: Senate Printing Press).

National Advisory Committee on Criminal Justice Standards and Goals. (1976) *Organized Crime: Report of the Task Force on Organized Crime* (US Government Printing Office: Washington DC).

New York City Board of Aldermen. (1878) *Report of the Special Committee of the Board of Aldermen appointed to investigate the 'Ring' frauds: together with the testimony elicited during the investigation* (New York: Martin Brown).

New York State Assembly. (1900) *Report of the Special Committee of the Assembly Appointed to Investigate the Public Offices and Appointments of the City of New York* (Albany NY: J.B. Lyon).

New York State Assembly. (1895) *Report and Proceedings of the Senate Committee Appointed to Investigate the Police Department of the City of New York* (Albany NY: J.B. Lyon).

Obama, Barack. (2011) *Strategy to Combat Transnational Organized Crime: Addressing Converging Threats to National Security*, Washington DC, The White House, 19 July 2011.

REFERENCES

President's Commission on the Assassination of President John F. Kennedy. (1964) *Report* (Washington DC: US Government Printing Office).

President's Commission on Law Enforcement and the Administration of Justice. (1967) *Task Force Report: Organized Crime* (Washington DC: US Government Printing Office).

Schelling, Thomas. (1967) 'Economic Analysis and Organized Crime', in President's Commission on Law Enforcement and the Administration of Justice, *Task Force Report: Organized Crime. Annotations and Consultants' Papers* (Washington DC: Government Printing Office), pp. 114–126.

Supreme Court of New York, Appellate Division, First Judicial Department. (1932) *In the Matter of the Investigation of the Magistrates' Court, Final Report of Samuel Seabury, Referee*, New York, 28 March 1932.

UN Security Council. (2014) Resolution 2195 (2014), 19 December 2014.

United Nations. (2015) 'Report of the Analytical Support and Sanctions Monitoring Team', UN Doc. S/2015/79, New York, 9 February 2015.

UNODC. (2008) *Drug Trafficking as a Security Threat in West Africa* (Vienna: UNODC).

UNODC. (2008) *Crime and its Impact on the Balkans* (Vienna: UNODC).

US Court of Appeals. (1956) *Rutkin v. Reinfeld* 229 F.2d 248 (2nd Circuit, 1956).

US Department of State. (1991) *Foreign Relations of the United States, 1958–1960, vol. VI, Cuba* (Washington DC: Government Printing Office).

US House of Representatives, Select Committee on Assassinations. (1979) *Final Assassination Plots Report*, 95th Congress, 2nd Session (Washington DC: Government Printing Office).

US House of Representatives, Select Committee on Assassinations. (1979) *Hearings*, 95th Congress, 2nd Session (Washington DC: Government Printing Office).

US Senate. (1961) *The Speeches of Senator John F. Kennedy: August through November 1960*, Senate Report 994, 87th Congress, 1st Session (Washington DC: Government Printing Office).

US Senate, Committee on Governmental Affairs, Permanent Subcommittee on Investigations. (1981) *Waterfront Corruption*, Hearings, 97th Congress, 1st session, 25 February 1981 (Washington DC: US Government Printing Office).

US Senate, Committee on Government Operations, Permanent Subcommittee on Investigations. (1964) *Organized Crime and Illicit Traffic in Narcotics* (Washington DC: US Government Printing Office).

US Senate, Select Committee on Improper Activities in the Labor or Management Field ('McClellan Committee'). (1958) *Investigation of Improper Activities in the Labor or Management Field* (Washington DC: Government Printing Office).

REFERENCES

US Senate, Special Committee to Investigate Organized Crime in Interstate Commerce. (1951) *The Kefauver Committee Report on Organized Crime* (New York: Didier).

US Senate, Special Senate Committee to Investigate Organized Crime in Interstate Commerce ('Kefauver Committee'). (1951) Hearings, 81st Congress, 1st Session (Washington DC: US Government Printing Office).

Secondary sources

Books and research reports

Ackerman, Kenneth D. (2005) *Boss Tweed: The Rise and Fall of the Corrupt Pol Who Conceived the Soul of Modern New York* (New York: Carroll & Graf).

Albanese, Jay S. (2011) *Transnational Crime and the 21st Century: Criminal Enterprise, Corruption, and Opportunity* (Oxford: Oxford University Press).

Allum, Felia and Renate Siebert, eds. (2003) *Organized Crime and the Challenge to Democracy* (Abingdon: Routledge).

Alongi, Giuseppe. (1886/1977) *La mafia: fattori, manifestazioni, rimedi* (Palermo: Sellerio).

Anastasia, George. (1991) *Blood and Honor: Inside the Scarfo Mob—The Mafia's Most Violent Family* (Philadelphia PA: Camino Books).

Anderson, Annelise. (1979) *The Business of Organized Crime: A Cosa Nostra Family* (Stanford CA: The Hoover Institution).

Andreas, Peter. (2013) *Smuggler Nation: How Illicit Trade Made America* (New York: Oxford University Press).

Andreas, Peter. (2008) *Blue Helmets and Black Markets. The Business of Survival in the Siege of Sarajevo* (Ithaca NY: Cornell University Press).

Arias, Enrique Desmond. (Forthcoming) *Criminal Politics: Illicit Activities and Governance in Latin America and the Caribbean*.

Arlacchi, Pino. (1993) *Men of Dishonor: Inside the Sicilian Mafia. An Account of Antonino Calderone*, trans. Marc Romano (New York: William Morrow).

Arlacchi, Pino. (1992) *Gli uomini del disonore* (Milan: Mondadori).

Arlacchi, Pino. (1983/1988) *Mafia Business. The Mafia Ethic and the Spirit of Capitalism* (Oxford: Oxford University Press).

Atran, Scott. (2010) *Talking to the Enemy: Faith, Brotherhood, and the (Un)Making of Terrorists* (New York: HarperCollins).

Ballentine, Karen and Jake Sherman, eds. (2003) *The Political Economy of Armed Conflict: Beyond Greed and Grievance* (Boulder CO: Lynne Rienner).

Batista, Fulgencia. (1964) *The Growth and Decline of the Cuban Republic*, tr. Blas M. Rocafort (New York: The Devin-Adair Company).

Bayart, Jean-François, Stephen Ellis and Béatrice Hibou. (1999) *The Criminalization of the State in Africa* (Bloomington IN: Indiana University Press).

Belloc, Hilaire. (1923) *Sonnets & Verse* (London: Duckworth & Co.).

REFERENCES

Benjamin, Jules. (1990) *The United States and the Origins of the Cuban Revolution* (Princeton NJ: Princeton University Press).

Bequai, August. (1979) *Organized Crime: The Fifth Estate* (Lexington MD: D.C. Heat & Co.).

Berdal, Mats and Mónica Serrano, eds. (2002) *Transnational Organized Crime and International Security: Business as Usual?* (Boulder CO: Lynne Rienner).

Beschloss, Michael R. (1991) *The Crisis Years: Kennedy and Khrushchev, 1960–1963* (New York: Edward Burlingame Books).

Biagi, Enzo. (1986) *Il Boss è solo: Buscetta, la vera storia d'un vero padrino* (Milan: Arnaldo Mondadori).

Blight, James G., Bruce J. Allyn and David Welch. (2002) *Cuba on the Brink: Castro, the Missile Crisis, and the Soviet Collapse* (Lanham MD: Rowman & Littlefield).

Block, Alan A. (1998) *Masters of Paradise: Organized Crime and the Internal Revenue Service in The Bahamas* (New Brunswick/London: Transaction).

Block, Alan A. (1983) *East Side, West Side: Organizing Crime in New York 1930–1950* (New Brunswick NJ: Transaction Publishers).

Blok, Anton. (1974) *The Mafia of a Sicilian Village, 1860–1960: A Study of Violent Peasant Entrepreneurs* (Cambridge: Waveland Press).

Bonanno, Bill. (1999) *Bound by Honour* (New York: St. Martin's Paperbacks).

Bonanno, Joseph. (1983) *A Man of Honour* (London: Andre Deutsch).

Brands, Hal. (2010) *Crime, Violence, and the Crisis in Guatemala: A Case Study in the Erosion of the State* (Carlisle PA: Strategic Studies Institute).

Bremmer, Ian. (2010) *The End of the Free Market: Who Wins the War Between States and Corporations?* (London: Portfolio).

Briscoe, Ivan, Catalina Perdomo and Catalina Uribe Burcher, eds. (2014) *Redes Ilícitas y Política en América Latina* (Stockholm: International IDEA).

Brugioni, Dino. (1991) *Eyeball to Eyeball: The Inside Story of the Cuban Missile Crisis* (New York: Random House).

Bunker, Robert J., ed. (2008) *Criminal-states and criminal-soldiers* (Abingdon: Routledge).

Burrows, Edwin G. and Mike Wallace. (1999) *Gotham: A History of New York City to 1898* (New York: Oxford University Press).

Campbell, Rodney. (1977) *The Luciano Project* (New York: McGraw-Hill).

Cantalupo, Joseph and Thomas C. Renner. (1990) *Body Mike: The Deadly Double Life of a Mob Informer* (New York: Villard Books).

Caro, Robert A. (2012) *The Passage of Power: The Years of Lyndon Johnson, Vol. IV* (New York: Alfred A. Knopf).

Catanzaro, Raimondo. (1988) *Men of Respect: A Social History of the Sicilian Mafia* (New York: The Free Press).

Chabal, Patrick and Jean-Pascal Daloz. (1999) *Africa Works: Disorder as a Political*

Instrument (Oxford/Bloomington IN: The International African Institute in Association with James Currey and Indiana University Press).

Chandler, Billy J. (1988) *King of the Mountain: The Life and Death of Giuliano the Bandit* (DeKalb IL: Northern Illinois University Press).

Chepesiuk, Ron. (2010) *The Trafficantes: Godfathers from Tampa, Florida. The Mafia, CIA and the JFK Assassination* (Rock Hill SC: Strategic Media Books Inc.).

Chubb, Judith. (1982) *Patronage, Power and Poverty in Southern Italy* (Cambridge: Cambridge University Press).

Cirules, Enrique. (2010) *The Mafia in Havana: A Caribbean Mob Story* (North Melbourne/New York: Ocean Press).

Clausewitz, Carl von. (1976/1984) *On War*, eds/trans. Michael Howard and Peter Paret (Princeton NJ: Princeton University Press, revd ed.).

Clunan, Anne L. and Harold A. Trinkunas, eds. (2010) *Ungoverned Spaces: Alternatives to State Authority in an Era of Softened Sovereignty* (Stanford CA: Stanford Security Studies, an Imprint of Stanford University Press).

Cockayne, James and Adam Lupel, eds. (2011) *Peace Operations and Organised Crime: Enemies or Allies?* (London: Routledge).

Cockburn, Patrick. (2014) *The Jihadis Return: ISIS and the New Sunni Uprising* (New York/London: OR Books).

Colhoun, Jack. (2013) *Gangsterismo. The United States, Cuba, and the Mafia: 1933 to 1966* (New York/London: OR Books).

Collier, Paul *et al.* (2003) *Breaking the Conflict Trap: Civil War and Development Policy* (Washington DC: World Bank).

Costanzo, Ezio. (2007) *The Mafia and the Allies: Sicily 1943 and the Return of the Mafia*, trans. George Lawrence (New York: Enigma).

Cressey, Donald. (1969) *Theft of the Nation: The Structure and Operations of Organized Crime in America* (New York: Harper and Row).

Critchley, David. (2009) *The Origin of Organized Crime in America: The New York City Mafia, 1891–1931* (New York: Routledge).

Daniel, Serge. (2014) *Les Mafias du Mali* (Paris: Descartes).

Daniel, Serge. (2012) *AQMI: L'industrie de l'enlèvement* (Paris: Fayard).

Dean, Geoff, Ivar Fahsing and Petter Gottschalk. (2010) *Organized Crime: Policing Illegal Business Entrepreneurialism* (Oxford: Oxford University Press).

Deitche, Scott. (2007) *The Silent Don: The Criminal World of Santo Trafficante Jr.* (Fort Lee NJ: Barricade).

Della Porta, Donatella and Alberto Vannucci. (1999) *Corrupt Exchanges* (New York: De Gruyter).

Deng, Francis M. *et al*, eds. (1996) *Sovereignty as Responsibility: Conflict Management in Africa* (Washington DC: The Brookings Institution, 1996).

Deutschmann, David and Deborah Shnookal, eds. (2008) *Fidel Castro Reader* (Melbourne: Ocean Books).

REFERENCES

Dewey, Thomas E. (1974) *Twenty Against the Underworld* (Garden City NY: Doubleday).

Dickie, John. (2013) *Mafia Republic* (London: Sceptre).

Dickie, John. (2005) *Cosa Nostra* (London: Palgrave Macmillan).

Dudley, Steven. (2011) *The Zetas in Guatemala*, Special Report, Medellín, InSight Crime, 8 September 2011.

Duffield, Mark. (2001) *Global Governance and the New Wars: The Merging of Development and Security* (London: Zed Books).

Duggan, Christopher. (1989) *Fascism and the Mafia* (New Haven CT/London: Yale University Press).

Eisenberg, Dennis, Uri Dan and Eli Landau. (1979) *Meyer Lansky: Mogul of the Mob* (New York: Paddington Press).

English, T. J. (2008) *Havana Nocturne* (New York: HarperCollins, 2008).

Falcone, Giovanni. (1992) *Men of Honour: The Truth about the Mafia* (London: Warner Books).

Falcone, Giovanni with Marcelle Padovani. (1991) *Cose di Cosa nostra* (Milan: Biblioteca Universale Rizzoli, 1991).

Farah, Douglas. (2012) *Transnational Organized Crime, Terrorism, and Criminalized States in Latin America: An Emerging Tier-One National Security Priority* (Carlisle PA: US Army War College).

Farber, Samuel. (1976) *Revolution and Reaction in Cuba, 1933–1960* (Middletown CT: Wesleyan University Press).

Felbab-Brown, Vanda. (2012) *Aspiration and Ambivalence: Strategies and Realities of Counterinsurgency and Statebuilding in Afghanistan* (Washington DC: Brookings Institution).

Felbab-Brown, Vanda. (2009) *Shooting Up: Counterinsurgency and the War on Drugs* (Washington DC: Brookings Institution Press).

Fentress, James. (2000) *Rebels and Mafiosi* (Ithaca NY: Cornell University Press).

Ferguson, Thomas. (1995) *Golden Rule: The Investment Theory of Party Competition and the Logic of Money-Driven Political Systems* (Chicago IL: University of Chicago Press).

Finkelstein, Monte S. (1998) *Separatism, the Allies, and the Mafia: The Struggle for Sicilian Independence, 1943–1948* (Bethlehem, PA/London: LeHigh University Press/Associated University Press).

Fiorentini, Gianluca and Sam Peltzman, eds. (1995/1997) *The Economics of Organized Crime* (Cambridge: Cambridge University Press).

Fischer, Jeff, Marcin Walecki and Jeffrey Carlson, eds. (2006) *Political Finance in Post-Conflict Societies* (Washington DC: International Foundation for Electoral Systems).

Foucault, Michel. (2010) *The Birth of Biopolitics: Lectures at the Collège de France (1978–9)*, trans. Graham Burchell (New York: Palgrave Macmillan).

REFERENCES

Fox, Stephen. (1989) *Blood and Power* (New York: William Morrow).

Franchetti, Leopoldo and Sidney Sonnino. (1877) *La Sicilia nel 1876: Inchiesta in Sicilia*, 2 vols (Florence: O. Barbera).

Franzese, Michael and Dary Matera. (1992) *Quitting the Mob* (New York: HarperCollins).

Freedman, Lawrence. (2013) *Strategy: A History* (New York: Oxford University Press).

Freedman, Lawrence. (2004) *Deterrence* (Cambridge: Polity Press).

Freedman, Lawrence. (2000) *Kennedy's Wars: Berlin, Cuba, Laos, and Vietnam* (New York: Oxford University Press).

Galluzzo, Lucio, Franco Nicastro and Vincenzo Vasile. (1989) *Obiettivo Falcone: Magistrati e mafia nel palazzo dei veleni* (Naples: Pironti).

Gambetta, Diego. (1993) *The Sicilian Mafia: The Business of Private Protection* (Cambridge MA: Harvard University Press).

Gentile, Nicola. (1963) *Vita di capomafia* (Rome: Editori Riuniti).

George, Alexander B. and Andrew Bennett. (2005) *Case Studies and Theory Development in the Social Sciences* (Cambridge MA: MIT Press).

Giancana, Antoinette and Thomas Renner. (1989) *Mafia Princess: Growing Up in Sam Giancana's Family* (New York: Avon Books).

Giustozzi, Antonio. (2011) *The Art of Coercion. The Primitive Accumulation and Management of Coercive Power* (New York: Columbia University Press).

Glenny, Misha. (2008) *McMafia: A Journey through the Global Criminal Underworld* (London: The Bodley Head).

Global Initiative Against Transnational Organized Crime. (2015) *Organized Crime: A Cross-Cutting Threat to Sustainable Development* (Geneva: GITOC).

Global Initiative Against Transnational Organized Crime. (2014) *Illicit Trafficking and Instability in Mali: Past, Present and Future* (Geneva: GITOC).

Godson, Roy, ed. (2003) *Menace to Society: Political-Criminal Collaboration around the World* (New Brunswick/London: Transaction Publishers).

Golway, Terry. (2014) *Machine Made: Tammany Hall and the Creation of Modern American Politics* (New York/London: Liveright).

Gosch, Martin and Richard Hammer. (1975) *The Last Testament of Lucky Luciano* (London: Macmillan).

Gray, Colin. (2006) *Strategy and History: Essays on Theory and Practice* (New York: Routledge).

Gray, Colin. (2005) *Another Bloody Century: Future Warfare* (London: Phoenix Press).

Gray, Colin. (1999) *Modern Strategy* (New York: Oxford University Press).

Grayson, George W. (2010) *La Familia Drug Cartel: Implications for US-Mexican Security* (Carlisle PA: Strategic Studies Institute).

Guerra y Sánchez, Ramiro. (1964) *Sugar and Society in the Caribbean: An Economic History of Cuban Agriculture* (New Haven CT: Yale University Press).

REFERENCES

Handelman, Stephen. (2007) *Comrade Criminal: Russia's New Mafiya* (New Haven CT: Yale University Press).

Harris, Charles R.S. (1957) *Allied Military Administration in Italy 1943–1945* (London: HM Stationery Office).

Hershkowitz, Leo, ed. (1990) *Boss Tweed in Court: A Documentary History* (Bethesda, MD: University Publications of America).

Hess, Henner. (1973) *Mafia and Mafiosi. The Structure of Power* (Westmead: Saxon House).

Hinckle, Warren and William Turner. (1992) *Deadly Secrets: The CIA-Mafia War against Castro and the Assassination of JFK* (New York: Thunder's Mouth Press).

Hobsbawm, Eric. (1981) *Bandits*, 2nd ed. (New York: Pantheon Books).

Hobsbawm, Eric. (1959) *Primitive Rebels* (Manchester: The University Press).

Ianni, Francis A. and Elizabeth Reuss-Ianni. (1972) *A Family Business: Kinship and Social Control in Organized Crime* (New York: Russel Sage).

Jackson, Robert H. (1990) *Quasi-States: Sovereignty, International Relations, and the Third World* (Cambridge: Cambridge University Press).

Jankowski, M.S. (1991) *Islands in the Streets: Gangs and American Urban Society* (Berkeley CA: University of California Press).

Johnson, Nelson. (2002) *Boardwalk Empire: The Birth, High Times, and Corruption of Atlantic City* (Medford NJ: Plexus Publishing Inc.).

Kaldor, Mary. (1999) *New and Old Wars. Organized Violence in a Global Era* (Stanford CA: Stanford University Press).

Kalyvas, Stathis. (2006) *The Logic of Violence in Civil War* (Cambridge: Cambridge University Press).

Kaplan, David E. and Alec Dubro. (2012) *Yakuza: Japan's Criminal Underworld* (Berkeley CA: University of California Press).

Keen, David. (1998) *The Economic Functions of Violence in Civil Wars* (Oxford: Oxford University Press).

Kennedy, David M. (2011) *Don't Shoot: One Man, A Street Fellowship, and the End of Violence in Inner-City America* (New York: Bloomsbury).

Kennedy, John F. (1960) *The Strategy of Peace* (New York: Harper & Row).

Kennedy, Robert F. (1960) *The Enemy Within* (New York: Popular Library).

Kerner, Hans-Jürgen and John A. Mack. (1975) *The Crime Industry* (Lexington KY: Lexington Books).

Kerry, John. (1997) *The New War: The Web of Crime that Threatens America's Security* (New York: Simon & Schuster).

Kessner, Thomas. (1989) *Fiorello H. La Guardia and the Making of Modern New York* (New York: McGraw Hill).

Khrushchev, Sergei N. (2000) *Nikita Khrushchev and the Creation of a Superpower* (University Park PA: Pennsylvania State University Press).

Kilcullen, David. (2013) *Out of the Mountains: The Coming Age of the Urban Guerrilla* (Oxford: Oxford University Press).

REFERENCES

Killebrew, Bob. (2010) *Crime Wars: Gangs, Cartels and US National Security* (Washington DC: Center for a New American Security).

Kim, W. Chan and Renée Mauborgne. (2005) *Blue Ocean Strategy: How to Create Uncontested Market Space* (Boston MA: Harvard Business School Press).

Lacey, Robert. (1991) *Little Man: Meyer Lansky and the Gangster Life* (Boston MA: Little Brown & Co.).

Lawson, Katherine and Alex Vines. (2014) *Global Impacts of the Illegal Wildlife Trade: The Costs of Crime, Insecurity and Institutional Erosion* (London: Chatham House).

Leeson, Peter T. (2009) *The Invisible Hook: The Hidden Economics of Pirates* (Princeton NJ: Princeton University Press).

Levitt, Matthew. (2013) *Hezbollah: The Global Footprint of Lebanon's Party of God* (London: Hurst).

Lewis, Norman. (1978/2005) *Naples '44. A World War II Diary of Occupied Italy* (New York: Carroll & Graf).

Lezhnev, Sasha. (2005) *Crafting Peace: Strategies to Deal with Warlords in Collapsing States* (Lanham MD: Lexington Books).

Liddell Hart, Basil H. (1954/1967) *Strategy* (New York: Frederick A. Praeger).

Lumia, Luigi. (1990) *Villalba: Storia e Memoria* (Caltanissetta: Edizioni Lussografica).

Lupo, Salvatore. (2009) *History of the Mafia*, trans. Antony Shugaar (New York: Columbia University Press).

Maas, Peter. (1968/2003) *The Valachi Papers* (New York: Perennial).

Macmillan, Harold. (1984) *War Diaries: The Mediterranean, 1943–45* (London: Macmillan).

Mandel, Robert. (2011) *Dark Logic: Transnational Criminal Tactics and Global Security* (Stanford CA: Stanford Security Studies).

Mann, Arthur (1969). *La Guardia: A Fighter Against His Times, 1882–1933* (Chicago IL: Phoenix).

Manwaring, Max G. (2007) *A Contemporary Challenge to State Sovereignty: Gangs and Other Illicit Transnational Criminal Organizations in Central America, El Salvador, Mexico, Jamaica and Brazil* (Carlisle PA: Strategic Studies Institute).

May, Ernest R. and Philip Zelikow, eds. (1997) *The Kennedy Tapes: Inside the White House during the Cuban Missile Crisis* (Cambridge MA: Harvard University Press).

McAvoy Weissman, Muriel. (2003) *Sugar Baron: Manuel Rionda and the Fortunes of Pre-Castro Cuba* (Miami FL: University of Florida Press).

McCarthy, Dennis M.P. (2011) *An Economic History of Organized Crime: A National and Transnational Approach* (London/New York: Routledge).

McCoy, Alfred. (1973) *The Politics of Heroin in Southeast Asia* (New York: Harper Colophon Books).

REFERENCES

Messick, Hank. (1971) *Lansky* (New York: Putnam).

Messick, Hank. (1969) *Syndicate Abroad* (Toronto: The Macmillan Company).

Metz, Steven. (2007) *Rethinking Insurgency* (Carlisle PA: Strategic Studies Institute).

Metz, Steven. (1993) *The Future of Insurgencies* (Carlisle PA: US Army War College).

Miklaucic, Michael and Jacqueline Brewer, eds. (2013) *Convergence: Illicit Networks and National Security in the Age of Globalization* (Washington DC: National Defense University Press).

Mori, Cesare. (1932) *Con la mafia ai ferri corti* (Verona: Mondadori).

Morselli, Carlo. (2005) *Contacts, Opportunities, and Criminal Enterprise* (Ontario: University of Toronto Press).

Mushkat, Jerome. (1971) *Tammany: The Evolution of a Political Machine, 1789–1865* (Syracuse NY: Syracuse University Press).

Myers, Gustavus. (1917) *The History of Tammany Hall*, 2nd ed. (New York: Boni & Liveright).

Naftali, Timothy and Philip Zelikow, eds. (2001) *The Presidential Recordings: John F. Kennedy: The Great Crises, Vol. II* (New York: Norton).

Naím, Moisés. (2005) *Illicit: How Smugglers, Traffickers and Copycats are Hijacking the Global Economy* (New York: Random House).

Naylor, R.T. (2004) *Wages of Crime: Black Markets, Illegal Finance, and the Underworld Economy* (Ithaca NY/London: Cornell University Press, revd ed.).

Nelli, Humbert S. (1981) *The Business of Crime: Italians and Syndicate Crime in the United States* (Chicago IL: University of Chicago Press).

Newark, Tim. (2010) *Lucky Luciano: The Real and the Fake Gangster* (New York: Thomas Dunne Books).

Newark, Tim. (2007) *Mafia Allies: The True Story of America's Secret Alliance with the Mob in World War II* (St Paul MN: Zenith Press).

Norton Smith, Richard. (1982) *Thomas E. Dewey and His Times* (New York: Simon and Schuster).

Nye, Joseph. (2004) *Soft Power: The Means to Success in World Politics* (New York: PublicAffairs).

Olson, Mancur. (2000) *Power and Prosperity: Outgrowing Communist and Capitalist Dictatorships* (New York: Basic Books).

O'Neill, Bard. (2005) *Insurgency and Terrorism: From Revolution to Apocalypse* (Washington DC: Potomac Books Inc.).

Oriola, Temitope B. (2013) *Criminal Resistance? The Politics of Kidnapping Oil Workers* (Ashgate Publishing, e-book).

Osorno, Diego Enrique. (2013) *La guerra de los Zetas: Viaje por la frontera de la necropolitica* (New York: Vintage Español).

Pantaleone, Michele. (1966) *The Mafia and Politics* (London: Chatto & Windus).

REFERENCES

Paoli, Letizia. (2003) *Mafia Brotherhoods* (New York: Oxford University Press).

Pape, Robert A. (2006) *Dying to Win: The Strategic Logic of Suicide Terrorism* (New York: Random House).

Petacco, Arrigo. (2004) *L'uomo della provvidenza: Mussolini, ascesa e caduta di un mito* (Milan: Mondadori).

Pileggi, Nicholas. (1985) *Wiseguy: Life in a Mafia Family* (New York: Simon & Schuster).

Pistone, Joe with Richard Woodley. (1987) *Donnie Brasco: My Undercover Life in the Mafia* (New York: New American Library).

Polanyi, Karl. (1944) *The Great Transformation* (Boston MA: Beacon Press).

Porter, Michael E. (1980) *Competitive Strategy: Techniques for Analyzing Industries and Competitors* (New York: The Free Press).

Powell, Hickman. (1939/2006) *Lucky Luciano: The Man Who Organized Crime in America* (New York: Barnes & Noble).

Quebec Police Commission. (1977) *The Fight against Organized Crime* (Montreal: Éditeur Officiel du Quebec).

Raab, Selwyn. (2005) *Five Families: The Rise, Decline, and Resurgence of America's Most Powerful Mafia Empires* (New York: St. Martin's Griffin/Thomas Dunne Books).

Ragano, Frank and Selwyn Raab. (1994) *Mob Lawyer* (New York: Charles Scribner's Sons).

Ravelo, Ricardo. (2009) *Osiel: Vida y tragedia de un capo* (Mexico City: Grijalbo).

Reid, Ed. (1964) *Mafia* (New York: Signet, revd ed.).

Reitano, Tuesday and Mark Shaw. (2015) *Fixing a Fractured State? Breaking the Cycles of Crime, Conflict and Corruption in Mali and Sahel* (Geneva: Global Initiative against Transnational Organized Crime).

Reno, William. (1998) *Warlord Politics and African States* (Boulder CO/London: Lynne Rienner).

Reuter, Peter, ed. (2012) *Draining Development? Controlling flows of illicit funds from developing countries* (Washington DC: World Bank).

Reuter, Peter. (1983) *Disorganized Crime. The Economics of the Visible Hand* (Cambridge MA: MIT Press).

Rich, Paul B., ed. (1999) *Warlords in International Relations* (Basingstoke: Palgrave Macmillan).

Rid, Thomas. (2013) *Cyber War Will Not Take Place* (New York: Oxford University Press).

Riordan, William L. (1905) *Plunkitt of Tammany Hall* (New York: McClure, Phillips & Co.).

Ruggiero, Vincenzo. (1996) *Organized and Corporate Crime in Europe: Offers that Can't Be Refused* (Aldershot: Ashgate).

Russo, Gus. (2001) *The Outfit: The Role of Chicago's Underworld in the Shaping of Modern America* (New York: Bloomsbury).

Sáenz Rovner, Eduardo. (2008) *The Cuban Connection: Drug Trafficking, Smuggling, and Gambling in Cuba from the 1920s to the Revolution*, trans. Russ Davidson (Chapel Hill NC: University of North Carolina Press).

Saviano, Roberto. (2007) *Gomorrah* (New York: Picador).

Scaduto, Anthony. (1976) *"Lucky"Luciano* (London: Sphere).

Schelling, Thomas. (1984) *Choice and Consequence: Perspectives of an Errant Economist* (Cambridge MA: Harvard University Press).

Schneider, Jane T. and Peter T. Schneider. (2003) *Reversible Destiny: Mafia, Anti-Mafia, and the Struggle for Palermo* (Berkeley CA: University of California Press).

Schulte-Bockholt, Alfredo. (2006) *The Politics of Organized Crime and the Organized Crime of Politics* (Lanham MD / Oxford: Lexington Books).

Schwartz, Rosalie. (1997) *Pleasure Island: Tourism and Temptation in Cuba* (Lincoln NE: University of Nebraska Press).

Seelke, Clare Ribando. (2014) *Gangs in Central America*, CRS Report RL34112, US Congressional Research Service, Washington DC, 20 February 2014.

Seindal, René. (1998) *Mafia, Money and Politics in Sicily 1950–1997* (Copenhagen: Museum Tusculanum Press).

Shapley, Deborah. (1993) *Promise and Power: The Life and Times of Robert McNamara* (Boston MA: Little Brown & Co.).

Shaw, Mark and Walter Kemp. (2012) *Spotting the Spoilers: A Guide to Analyzing Organized Crime in Fragile States* (New York: International Peace Institute).

Shaw, Mark and Fiona Mangan. (2014) *Illicit Trafficking and Libya's Transition: Profits and Losses*, Peaceworks No. 96 (Washington DC: US Institute of Peace).

Short, K.R.M. (1979) *The Dynamite War: Irish-American Bombers in Victorian Britain* (Dublin: Gill & Macmillan).

Simpson, Emile. (2012) *War From the Ground Up* (London: Hurst).

Sloat, Warren. (2002) *A Battle for the Soul of New York: Tammany Hall, Police Corruption, Vice, and the Reverend Charles Parkhurst's Crusade Against Them* (New York: Cooper Square Press).

Smith, Rupert. (2005) *The Utility of Force: The Art of War in the Modern World* (London: Allen Lane).

Solnick, Steven. (1999) *Stealing the State: Control and Collapse in Soviet Institutions* (Cambridge MA: Harvard University Press).

Spanò, Aristide. (1978) *Faccia a faccia con la mafia* (Milan: Mondadori).

Staniland, Paul. (2014) *Networks of Rebellion: Explaining Insurgent Cohesion and Collapse* (Ithaca NY: Cornell University Press).

Sterling, Claire. (1990) *Octopus: The Long Reach of the International Sicilian Mafia* (New York: Touchstone).

Stille, Alexander. (1996) *Excellent Cadavers* (New York: Vintage Books).

REFERENCES

Strange, Susan. (1996) *The Retreat of the State: The Diffusion of Power in the World Economy* (New York: Cambridge University Press).

Strange, Susan. (1986) *Casino Capitalism* (Oxford: Basil Blackwell).

Strazzari, Francesco. (2015) *Azawad and the Rights of Passage: The Role of Illicit Trade in the Logic of Armed Group Formation in Northern Mali* (Oslo: Norwegian Peacebuilding Resource Centre).

Taylor, Maxwell D. (1972) *Swords and Plowshares* (New York: Norton).

ter Haar, Berend J. (1998) *Ritual and Mythology of the Chinese Triads: Creating an Identity* (Brill: Leiden).

Teresa, Vincent and Thomas Renner. (1974) *My Life in the Mafia* (New York: Doubleday).

Thoumi, Francisco E. (1995) *Political Economy and Illegal Drugs in Colombia* (Boulder CO: Lynne Rienner).

Truslow, Francis A., *et al.* (1951) *Report on Cuba* (Baltimore MD: Johns Hopkins Press).

UNODC and World Bank. (2007) *Crime, Violence, and Development: Trends, Costs, and Policy Options in the Caribbean*, Report No. 37820, Washington DC, World Bank, March 2007.

Vahlenkamp, Werner and Peter Hauer. (1996) *Organized Crime, Criminal Logistics and Preventive Approaches: Practice-oriented Summary and Evaluation of an Investigative Criminological Study* (Wiesbaden: Bundeskriminalamt, 1996).

Van Creveld, Martin. (1999) *The Rise and Decline of the State* (Cambridge: Cambridge University Press).

Varese, Federico. (2011) *Mafias on the Move: How Organized Crime Conquers New Territories* (Princeton NJ: Princeton University Press).

Varese, Federico. (2001) *The Russian Mafia: Private Protection in a New Market Economy* (Oxford: Oxford University Press).

Vizzini, Sal with Oscar Fraley and Marshall Smith. (1972) *Vizzini* (New York: Pinnacle Books).

Wayman, Dorothy G. (1952) *David I. Walsh: Citizen-Patriot* (Milwaukee WI: Bruce Publishing Company).

Weber, Max. (1922/1978) *Economy and Society*, Guenther Roth and Claus Wittich, eds., (Berkeley and Los Angeles CA: University of California Press).

Weinstein, Jeremy. (2006) *Inside Rebellion: The Politics of Insurgent Violence* (Cambridge: Cambridge University Press).

Werner, M.A. (1968) *Tammany Hall* (New York: Greenwood Press).

Williams, Phil. (2009) *Criminals, Militias, and Insurgents: Organized Crime in Iraq* (Carlisle PA: Strategic Studies Institute).

Wilson, Eric, ed. (2009) *Government of the Shadows: Parapolitics and Criminal Sovereignty* (London/New York: Pluto Press).

World Bank. (2011) *Conflict, Security and Development: 2011 World Development Report* (Washington DC: World Bank).

431

REFERENCES

Wright, Alan. (2005) *Organised Crime* (Cullompton: Willan).

Wright, Peter. (1987) *Spy Catcher: The Candid Autobiography of a Senior Intelligence Official* (New York: Viking).

Wrong, Michela. (2009) *It's Our Turn to Eat: The Story of a Kenyan Whistle-blower* (London: Fourth Estate).

Yarger, Harry R. (2006) *Strategic Theory for the 21st Century: The Little Book on Big Strategy* (Carlisle PA: Strategic Studies Institute, US Army War College).

Zelikow, Philip and Ernest R. May, eds. (2001) *The Presidential Recordings: John F. Kennedy, The Great Crises, Vol. III* (New York: Norton).

Journal articles, essays, book chapters and conference papers

Alexander, Barbara. (1997) 'The Rational Racketeer: Pasta Protection in Depression Era Chicago', *J. Law & Economics*, vol. 40, pp. 175–202.

Anderson, David M. (2010) 'The New Piracy: The Local Context', *Survival*, vol. 52, no. 1 (February–March 2010), pp. 44–51.

Andreas, Peter. (2002) 'Transnational Crime and Economic Globalization', in Mats Berdal and Mónica Serrano, eds, *Transnational Organized Crime and International Security: Business as Usual?* (Boulder CO: Lynne Rienner), pp. 37–52.

Andreas, Peter. (1998) 'The Political Economy of Narco-Corruption in Mexico', *Current History*, vol. 97, no. 618 (April 1998), pp. 160–5.

Andreas, Peter and Ethan Nadelmann. (2009) 'The Internationalization of Crime Control', in H.R. Friman ed., *Crime and the Global Political Economy* (Boulder CO: Lynne Rienner), pp. 21–33.

Andreas, Peter and Joel Wallman. (2009) 'Illicit markets and violence: what is the relationship?', *Crime, Law & Social Change*, vol. 52, p. 225–9.

Arias, Enrique Desmond. (2014) 'Violence, Citizenship, and Religious Faith in a Rio de Janeiro Favela', *Lat. Am. Research Rev.*, vol. 49, pp. 149–67.

Arias, Enrique Desmond. (2010) 'Understanding Criminal Networks, Political Order, and Politics in Latin America', in Anne L. Clunan and Harold A. Trinkunas, eds, *Ungoverned Spaces: Alternatives to State Authority in an Era of Softened Sovereignty* (Stanford CA: Stanford Security Studies), pp. 115–35.

Aron, Raymond. (1969) 'The Evolution of Modern Strategic Thought', *Adelphi Papers*, vol. 9, issue 4, Special Issue: Problems of Modern Strategy: Part I, pp. 1–17.

Bailey, John and Matthew M. Taylor. (2009) 'Evade, Corrupt, or Confront? Organized Crime and the State in Brazil and Mexico', *Journal of Politics in Latin America*, vol. 1, no. 2, pp. 3–29.

Beardsley, Kyle, Kristian Gleditsch and Nigel Lo. (2013) 'Roving and Stationary Bandits in African Armed Conflicts', conference paper, Annual Meeting of the International Studies Association, San Francisco.

REFERENCES

Beber, Bernd and Christopher Blattman. (2013) 'The Logic of Child Soldiering and Coercion', *International Organization*, vol. 67, pp. 65–104.

Beith, Malcolm. (2011) 'A broken Mexico: allegations of collusion between the Sinaloa cartel and Mexican political parties', *Small Wars & Insurgencies*, vol. 22, no. 5, pp. 787–806.

Bell, Daniel. (1960/2000) 'The Racket-Ridden Longshoremen: The Web of Economics and Politics', in *The End of Ideology: On the Exhaustion of Political Ideas in the Fifties, with 'The Resumption of History in the New Century'* (Cambridge MA: Harvard University Press).

Bell, Daniel. (1953) 'Crime as an American Way of Life', *The Antioch Review*, vol. 13, no. 2, pp. 131–54.

Benson, George C.S. and Maurice Neufield. (1948) 'Allied Military Government in Italy', in Carl J. Friedrich, *et al.*, *American Experiences in Military Government in World War II* (New York: Rinehart & Company, Inc.), pp. 111–47.

Biró, Daniel. (2007) 'The (Un)bearable Lightness of... Violence: Warlordism as an Alternative Form of Governance in the "Westphalian Periphery"?', in Tobias Debiel and Daniel Lambach, eds, *State Failure Revisited II: Actors of Violence and Alternative Forms of Governance* (Duisberg: University of Duisberg-Essen), pp. 7–49.

Blickman, Tom. (1997) 'The Rothschilds of the Mafia on Aruba', *Transnational Organized Crime*, vol. 3, no. 2, pp. 50–89.

Blok, Anton. (2008) 'Reflections on the Sicilian Mafia: Peripheries and Their Impact on Centres', in Dina Siegel and Hans Nelen, eds, *Organized Crime: Culture, Markets and Policies* (New York: Springer), pp. 7–13.

Blok, Anton. (1972) 'The Peasant and the Brigand: Social Banditry Reconsidered', *Comp. Stud. in Soc. & Hist.*, vol. 14, pp. 495–504.

Bøås, Morten. (2012) 'Castles in the sand: informal networks and power brokers in the northern Mali periphery', in Mats Utas, ed., *African Conflicts and Informal Power: Big Men and Networks* (London: Zed), pp. 119–34.

Bojicic-Dzelilovic, Vesna, Denisa Kostovicova, Mariana Escobar and Jelena Bjelica. (2015) 'Organised crime and international aid subversion: evidence from Colombia and Afghanistan', *Third World Quarterly*, vol. 36, no. 10, pp. 1887–1905.

Bovenkerk, Frank. (1998) 'Organized Crime and Ethnic Minorities: Is There a Link?', in Phil Williams and Dimitri Vlassis, eds, *Combating Transnational Crime: Concepts, Activities and Responses* (London/Portland OR: Frank Cass), pp. 109–26.

Braga, Anthony A. and David L. Weisburd. (2012) 'The Effects of Focused Deterrence Strategies on Crime: A Systematic Review and Meta-Analysis of the Empirical Evidence', *Journal of Research in Crime and Delinquency*, vol. 49, no. 3, pp. 323–58.

REFERENCES

Brands, Hal. (2009) 'Third-Generation Gangs and Criminal Insurgency in Latin America', *Small Wars Journal* (July 2009).

Briscoe, Ivan. (2015) 'A violent compound: competition, crime and modern conflict' (Oslo: NOREF).

Bunker, Pamela L. and Robert J. Bunker. (2011) 'The Spiritual Significance of ¿Plata o Plomo?', *Small Wars Journal*, 4 June 2011.

Bunker, Robert J. (2011) 'Criminal (Cartel & Gang) Insurgencies in Mexico and the Americas: What you need to know, not what you want to hear', Testimony before the US House of Representatives, House Committee on Foreign Affairs, Subcommittee on the Western Hemisphere, 13 September 2011, available at http://archives.republicans.foreignaffairs.house.gov/112/bun091311.pdf

Bunker, Robert J. (2011) 'The Mexican Cartel Debate: As Viewed Through Five Divergent Fields of Security Studies', *Small Wars Journal*, 11 February 2011.

Camilo Castillo, Juan, Daniel Mejia and Pascual Restrepo. (2014) 'Scarcity Without Leviathan: The Violent Effects of Cocaine Supply Shortages in the Mexican Drug War', Center for Global Development Working Paper No. 356, Washington DC, 26 February 2014.

Campbell, Howard. (2014) 'Narco-Propaganda in the Mexican "Drug War": An Anthropological Perspective', *Latin American Perspectives*, vol. 41, no. 2, pp. 60–77.

Cartier-Bresson, Jean. (1997) 'État, Marchés, Réseaux et Organisations Criminelles Entrepreneuriales', Paper presented at the Colloquium on 'Criminalité Organisée et Ordre dans la Societé', Aix-en-Provence, 5–7 June 1996 (Aix-en-Provence: Aix-Marseille University Press).

Cerny, Philip G. (1998) 'Neomedievalism, Civil War, and the New Security Dilemma: Globalisation as Durable Disorder', *Civil Wars*, vol. 1, no. 1, pp. 36–64.

Cheng, Christine. (2013) 'Private and public interests: Informal actors, informal influence, and economic order after war', in Mats Berdal and Dominik Zaum, eds, *Political Economy of Statebuilding: Power after Peace* (Routledge: Abingdon/New York), pp. 62–78.

Chestnut, Sheena. (2007) 'Illicit Activity and Proliferation: North Korean Smuggling Networks', *International Security*, vol. 32, no. 1, pp. 80–111.

Clark, Mark. T. (2006) 'Does Clausewitz Apply to Criminal-States and Gangs?', *Global Crime*, vol. 7, nos. 3–4, pp. 407–27.

Cockayne, James. (2014) 'The Futility of Force? Strategic Lessons for Dealing with Unconventional Armed Groups from the UN's War on Gangs in Haiti', *Journal of Strategic Studies*, vol. 37, no. 5, pp. 736–69.

Cockayne, James. (2013) *Strengthening mediation to deal with criminal agendas* (Geneva: Centre for Humanitarian Dialogue).

REFERENCES

Cohen, A.K. (1977) 'The Concept of Criminal Organization', *British Journal of Criminology*, vol. 17, no. 2, pp. 97–111.

Cohen, Gary. (2002) 'The Keystone Kommandos', *The Atlantic*, February 2002, pp. 46–59.

Collier, Paul. (2000) 'Rebellion as a Quasi-Criminal Activity', *Journal of Conflict Resolution*, vol. 44, no. 6, pp. 839–53.

Collier, Paul. (2000) 'Economic Causes of Civil Conflict and Their Implications for Policy' (Washington DC: World Bank).

Cornell, Svante E. (2007) 'Narcotics and Armed Conflict: Interaction and Implications', *Studies in Conflict & Terrorism*, vol. 30, pp. 207–27.

Cornell, Svante E. and Niklas L.P. Swanström. (2006) 'The Eurasian Drug Trade: A Challenge to Regional Security', *Problems of Post-Communism*, vol. 53, no. 4, pp. 10–28.

Cruz, José Miguel. (2010) 'Central American maras: from youth street gangs to transnational protection rackets', *Global Crime*, vol. 11, no. 4, pp. 379–98.

Davis, J. Richard. (1939) 'Things I Couldn't Tell till Now', *Collier's*: Part I, 22 July, pp. 9–10, 38, 40–2; Part II, 29 July, pp. 21, 37–38, 40; Part III, 5 August, pp. 12–13, 43–4; Part IV, 12 August, pp. 16–17, 29–30; Part V, 19 August, pp. 12–13, 34–8; Part VI, 26 August, pp. 18–19, 35, 38.

de Waal, Alex. (2009) 'Mission without end? Peacekeeping in the African political marketplace', *International Affairs*, vol. 85, no. 1, pp. 99–113.

Deaglio, Enrico. (2001) 'Se vince lui, ma forse no', interview with Andrea Camilleri, in *Diario*, March 2001, available at http://www.vigata.org/rassegna_stampa/2001/Archivio/Int09_Cam_mar2001_Diario.html.

Dell, Melissa. (2015) 'Trafficking Networks and the Mexican Drug War', *American Economic Review*, vol. 105, no. 6 (2015), pp. 1738–79.

Dick, A.R. (1995) 'When Does Organized Crime Pay? A Transaction Cost Analysis', *Int'l Rev. Law & Economics*, vol. 15, no. 1, pp. 25–45.

Domínguez, Jorge I. (1998) 'The Batista Regime in Cuba', in H.E. Chehabi and Juan J. Linz, eds, *Sultanistic Regimes* (Baltimore MD/London: Johns Hopkins University Press), pp. 112–31.

Duffield, Mark. (1998) 'Post-modern Conflict: Warlords, Post-adjustment States and Private Protection', *Civil Wars*, vol. 1, no. 1, pp. 65–102.

Echevarria, Antulio J. (2003) '"Reining In" the Center of Gravity Concept', *Air & Space Power Journal* (Summer 2003), pp. 87–96.

Eilstrup-Sangiovanni, Mette and Calvert Jones. (2008) 'Assessing the Dangers of Illicit Networks: Why al-Qaida May be Less Threatening Than Many Think', *International Security*, vol. 33, no. 2, pp. 7–44.

Elkus, Adam. (2011) 'Mexican Cartels: A Strategic Approach', *Infinity Journal*, IJ Exclusive, 28 June 2011, at http://www.infinityjournal.com.

Farah, Douglas. (2014) 'Threat convergence: when enemies unite', *Proceedings*, vol. 71, no. 3, pp. 6–10.

REFERENCES

Fazal, Tanisha M. (2004) 'State Death in the International System', *International Organization*, vol. 58, pp. 311–44.

Felbab-Brown, Vanda. (2014) 'Crime, Low-Intensity Conflict and the Future of War in the Twenty-First Century', in Ingo Trauschweizer and Steven M. Miner, *Failed States and Fragile Societies: A New World Disorder?* (Athens OH: Ohio University Press), pp. 89–118.

Felbab-Brown, Vanda. (2012) 'Fighting the Nexus of Organized Crime and Violent Conflict while Enhancing Human Security', in *Drug Trafficking, Violence, and Instability* (Carlisle PA: Strategic Studies Institute, US Army War College).

Felbab-Brown, Vanda. (2011) 'Human Security and Crime in Latin America: The Political Capital and Political Impact of Criminal Groups and Belligerents Involved in Illicit Economies', Florida International Univeristy, Applied Research Center.

Felbab-Brown, Vanda. (2010) 'Conceptualizing Crime as Competition in State-Making and Designing an Effective Response', *Sec. & Def. Stud. Rev.* (Spring-Summer 2010), pp. 155–8.

Filiu, Jean-Pierre. (2010) 'Could Al-Qaeda Turn African in the Sahel?', *Carnegie Papers*, Middle East Program, No. 112 (Washington DC: Carnegie Endowment for International Peace).

Firestone, Thomas A. (1993) 'Mafia Memoirs: What They Tell Us About Organized Crime', *J. Contemporary Criminal Justice*, vol. 9, no. 3, pp. 197–220.

Foucault, Michel. (1991) 'Governmentality', in Graham Burchell, Colin Gordon and Peter Miller, eds, *The Foucault Effect* (Chicago IL: University of Chicago Press), pp. 87–104.

Foucault, Michel. (1982) 'The Subject and Power', in Hubert L. Dreyfus and Paul Rabinow, eds, *Michel Foucault: Beyond Structuralism and Hermeneutics*, 2nd ed. (Chicago IL: University of Chicago Press, 2nd ed.), pp. 208–26.

Freden, Brad. (2011) 'The COIN Approach to Mexican Drug Cartels: Square Peg in a Round Hole', *Small Wars Journal*, 27 December 2011.

Freedman, Lawrence. (2007) 'Terrorism as a Strategy', *Government & Opposition*, vol. 42, pp. 314–39.

Freedman, Lawrence. (1998) 'Strategic Coercion', in Lawrence Freedman, ed., *Strategic Coercion: Concepts and Cases* (Oxford: Oxford University Press), pp. 15–36.

Freedman, Lawrence. (1992) 'Strategic Studies and the Problem of Power', in Lawrence Freedman, Paul Hayes and Robert O'Neill, eds, *War, Strategy, and International Politics: Essays in Honour of Sir Michael Howard* (Oxford: Clarendon Press), pp. 279–94.

Fricano, Guy. (2013) 'Social Banditry and the Public Persona of Joaquín "El Chapo" Guzmán', *Small Wars Journal*, 29 April 2013.

Friman, H.R. (2009) 'Drug markets and the selective use of violence', *Crime, Law & Social Change*, vol. 52, pp. 285–95.

Friman, H.R. (2004) 'Forging the Vacancy Chain: Law Enforcement Efforts and Mobility in Criminal Economies', *Crime Law & Social Change*, vol. 41, no. 1, pp. 53–77.

Garay, Luis J., Eduardo Salcedo-Albarán and Isaac De León-Beltrán. (2009) 'From State Capture towards the Co-Opted State Configuration', METODO Working Paper No. 61 (Bogotá, Colombia: Metodo Foundation).

Gates, Scott. (2002) 'Recruitment and allegiance: The microfoundations of rebellion', *Journal of Conflict Resolution*, vol. 46, pp. 111–30.

Gilman, Nils, Jesse Goldhammer and Steven Weber. (2013) 'Deviant Globalization', in Michael Miklaucic and Jacqueline Brewer, eds, *Convergence: Illicit Networks and National Security in the Age of Globalization* (Washington DC: National Defense University Press), pp. 3–14.

Giustozzi, Antonio. (2007) 'War and Peace Economies of Afghanistan's Strongmen', *International Peacekeeping*, vol. 14, no. 1, pp. 75–89.

Giustozzi, Antonio. (2006) 'Genesis of a "Prince": the rise of Ismail Khan in western Afghanistan, 1979–1992', Crisis States Working Paper Series No. 2, Working Paper No. 4, September 2006 (London: Crisis States Research Centre).

Giustozzi, Antonio. (2005) 'The Debate on Warlordism: The Importance of Military Legitimacy', Crisis States Discussion Paper 13, October 2005 (London: Crisis States Research Centre).

Giustozzi, Antonio. (2003) 'Respectable Warlords? The Politics of State-Building in Post-Taleban Afghanistan', Working Paper No. 33 (London: Crisis States Research Centre).

Giustozzi, Antonio and Dominique Orsini. (2009) 'Centre-periphery relations in Afghanistan: Badakshan between patrimonialism and institution-building', *Central Asian Survey*, vol. 28, no. 1, pp. 1–16.

Godson, Roy and Phil Williams (1998). 'Strengthening Cooperation against Transnational Crime: a New Security Imperative', in Phil Williams and Dimitri Vlassis, eds, *Combating Transnational Crime: Concepts, Activities and Responses* (London/Portland OR: Frank Cass).

Goodhand, Jonathan. (2004) 'Frontiers and Wars: the Opium Economy in Afghanistan', *Journal of Agrarian Change*, vol. 4, nos. 1 and 2, pp. 191–216.

Goodhand, Jonathan and David Mansfield. (2010) 'Drugs and (Dis)Order: A study of the opium trade, political settlements and state-making in Afghanistan', Working Paper no. 83, Crisis States Working Paper Series No. 2 (London: Crisis States Research Centre).

Grayson, George. (2009) 'La Familia Michoacána: A Deadly Mexican Cartel Revisited', *FPRI E-notes*, August 2009, on file with the author.

Gutiérrez Sanín, Francisco and Antonio Giustozzi. (2010) 'Networks and

Armies: Structuring Rebellion in Colombia and Afghanistan', *Studies in Conflict & Terrorism*, vol. 33, pp. 836–53.

Hall, Rodney B. and Thomas J. Biersteker. (2002) 'The Emergence of Private Authority in the International System', in Rodney B. Hall and Thomas J. Biersteker, eds, *The Emergence of Private Authority in Global Governance* (New York: Cambridge University Press), pp. 3–24.

Hallaj, O.A. (2015) 'The Balance-sheet of Conflict: criminal revenues and warlords in Syria' (Oslo: NOREF).

Helfstein, Scott. (2009) 'Governance of Terror: New Institutionalism and the Evolution of Terror Organizations', *Public Administration Review*, vol. 69, issue 4, pp. 727–39.

Hellman, Joel S. (1998) 'Winners Take All: The Politics of Partial Reform in Postcommunist Transitions', *World Politics*, vol. 50, no. 2, pp. 203–34.

Hellman, Joel S., Geraint Jones and Daniel Kaufmann. (2000) '"Seize the State, Seize the Day": State Capture, Corruption and Influence in Transition', Policy Research Working Paper 2444 (Washington DC: World Bank).

Hellman, Joel S. and Daniel Kaufmann. (2001) 'Confronting the Challenge of State Capture in Transition Economies', *Finance & Development*, vol. 38, no. 3, pp. 31–5.

Henriksen, Rune and Anthony Vinci. (2007) 'Combat Motivation in Non-State Armed Groups', *Terrorism & Political Violence*, vol. 20, no. 1, pp. 87–109.

Hershberg, James G. (1995) 'Anatomy of a Controversy: Anatoly Dobrynin's Meeting with Robert Kennedy, Saturday, October 27, 1962', in *Cold War Int'l Hist. Proj. Bull.*, issue 5, pp. 75, 77–8.

Hobsbawm, Eric J. (1972) 'Social bandits, A Comment', in *Comp. Stud. in Soc. & Hist.*, 14, pp. 504–7.

Hostetter, Gordon L. (1932) 'Racketeering—an Alliance between Politics and Crime', *National Municipal Review*, vol. XXI, no. II, pp. 637–40.

Howard, Michael. (1995) 'Lessons of the Cold War', *Survival*, vol. 36, no. 4 (1994–5), pp. 161–6.

Hunt, Thomas. (2012) 'Year-by-year: Charlie Lucky's Life', *Informer*, pp. 35–61.

Hunt, Thomas. (2009) 'Castro and the Casinos', *Informer*, vol. 2, no. 4, pp. 5–27.

Huntington, Samuel P. (1972) 'Civil violence and the process of development', *The Adelphi Papers*, vol. 11, issue 83, pp. 1–15.

Huntington, Samuel P. (1952) 'The Marasmus of the ICC: The Commission, the Railroads, and the Public Interest', *Yale Law Journal*, vol. 614, pp. 467–509.

Ianni, Francis A. (1971) 'Formal and Social Organization in an Organized Crime "Family": A Case Study', *U. Fla L. Rev.*, vol. 24, no. 1, pp. 31–41.

REFERENCES

International Crisis Group. (2013) 'Peña Nieto's Challenge: Criminal Cartels and Rule of Law in Mexico', Crisis Group Latin America Report No. 48, Mexico/Brussels, 19 March 2013.

International Crisis Group. (2009) 'Somalia: The Trouble with Puntland', Africa Briefing No. 64, Nairobi/Brussels, 12 August 2009.

Iwai, Hiroaki. (1986) 'Organized crime in Japan', in Robert J. Kelly, ed., *Organized Crime: A Global Perspective* (Totowa, NJ: Rowman and Littlefield), pp. 208–33.

Jackson, Paul. (2003) 'Warlords as Alternative Forms of Governance', *Small Wars and Insurgencies*, vol. 14, no. 2, pp. 131–50.

Jackson, Robert H. (1986) 'Negative Sovereignty in Sub-Saharan Africa', *Review of International Studies*, vol. 12, no. 4, pp. 247–64.

Jensen, Michael C. (1983) 'Organization Theory and Methodology', *The Accounting Review*, vol. 58, no. 2, pp. 319–39.

Kalyvas, Stathis N. (2015) 'How Civil Wars Help Explain Organized Crime—and How They Do Not', *Journal of Conflict Resolution*, vol. 59, no. 8, pp. 1517–40.

Kan, Paul Rexton. (2014) 'Cyberwar in the Underworld: Anonymous versus Los Zetas in Mexico', *Yale J. Intl Affairs*, vol. 8, no. 1, pp. 40–51.

Kenney, Michael. (2009) 'Turning to the "Dark Side": Coordination, Exchange, and Learning in Criminal Networks', in Miles Kahler, ed., *Networked Politics: Agency, Power, and Governance* (Ithaca NY: Cornell University Press), pp. 79–102.

Kenney, Michael. (2007) 'The Architecture of Drug Trafficking: Network Forms of Organization in the Colombian Cocaine Trade', *Global Crime*, vol. 8, pp. 233–59.

Kenney, Michael. (2005) 'Drug Trafficking, Terrorist Networks, and Ill-Fated Government Strategies', in Elke Krahmann, ed., *New Threats and New Actors in International Security* (New York/Basingstoke: Palgrave Macmillan), pp. 69–90.

Killicoat, Phillip. (2007) 'Weaponomics: The Global Market For Assault Rifles,' World Bank Policy Research Working Paper 4202 (Washington DC: World Bank).

Kim, W. Chan and Renée Mauborgne. (2009) 'How Strategy Shapes Structure', *Harvard Business Review* (September 2009), pp. 73–80.

Kim, W. Chan and Renée Mauborgne. (2004/2011) 'Blue Ocean Strategy', in Harvard Business School Publishing Corporation ed., *HBR's 10 Must Reads On Strategy* (Cambridge MA: Harvard Business Review), pp. 123–42.

Konrad, Kai A. and Stergios Skaperdas. (2004) 'The Market for Protection and the Origin of the State', CESinfo Working Paper Series No. 1578 (Munich: CESinfo Group).

Lacher, Wolfram. (2012) 'Organized Crime and Conflict in the Sahel-Sahara

REFERENCES

Region', Carnegie Papers, Middle East (Washington DC: Carnegie Endowment for International Peace, September 2012).

Lacher, Wolfram. (2011) 'Organized Crime and Terrorism in the Sahel: Drivers, Actors, Options', SWP Comments 1 (Berlin: SWP, January 2011).

Lane, Frederic. (1958) 'Economic consequences of organized violence', *Journal of Economic History*, vol. 18, pp. 401–17.

Latham, Robert. (2000) 'Social Sovereignty', *Theory, Culture & Society*, vol. 17, no. 4, pp. 1–18.

Leeson, Peter T. and David B. Skarbek. (2010) 'Criminal Constitutions', *Global Crime*, vol. 11, no. 3, pp. 279–97.

Lepgold, Joseph. (1998) 'Hypotheses on Vulnerability: Are Terrorists and Drug Traffickers Coerceable?', in Lawrence Freedman, ed., *Strategic Coercion: Concepts and Cases* (Oxford: Oxford University Press), pp. 131–50.

Levi, Michael. (2002) 'Liberalization and Transnational Financial Crime', in Mats Berdal and Mónica Serrano, eds, *Transnational Organized Crime and International Security: Business as Usual?* (Boulder CO: Lynne Rienner), pp. 53–66.

Levitt, Matthew. (2012) 'Hizbullah narco-terrorism', *HIS Defense, Risk and Security Consulting* (September 2012), pp. 34–41.

Lippmann, Walter. (1931) 'The Underworld—A Stultified Conscience', *The Forum*, vol. LXXXV, no. 2, p. 67.

Lippmann, Walter. (1928) 'Tammany Hall and Al Smith', *The Outlook*, vol. 148, no. 5, pp. 163–5.

London Couture, Krista. (2014) 'A Gendered Approach to Countering Violent Extremism', Policy Paper (Washington DC: Brookings Institution, July 2014).

Lupo, Salvatore. (1997) 'The Allies and the mafia', *J. Mod. Italian Stud.*, vol. 2, no. 1, pp. 21–33.

Lupsha, Peter. (1996) 'Transnational Organized Crime versus the Nation State', *Transnational Organized Crime*, vol. 2, no. 1, pp. 21–46.

Lupsha, Peter. (1983) 'Networks Versus Networking: Analysis of an Organized Crime Group', in G. Waldo, ed., *Career Criminals* (Beverly Hills CA: Sage), pp. 43–87.

Mackinlay, John. (2000) 'Defining Warlords', *International Peacekeeping*, vol. 7, no. 1, pp. 48–62.

Madsen, Frank G. (2013) 'Corruption: A Global Common Evil', *The RUSI Journal*, vol. 158, no. 2, pp. 26–38.

Marten, Kimberley. (2007) 'Warlordism in Comparative Perspective', *International Security*, vol. 31, no. 3 (2006–7), pp. 41–73.

Mattina, Cesare. (2011) 'The transformations of the contemporary mafia: a perspective review of the literature on mafia phenomena in the context of the internationalisation of the capitalist economy', *International Social Science Journal*, vol. 62, issue 203–4, pp. 229–45.

REFERENCES

McGoldrick, Joseph. (1932) 'Tammany Totters But Triumphs', *National Municipal Review*, vol. XXI, no. II, pp. 634–6, 640.

McGoldrick, Joseph. (1928) 'The New Tammany', *The American Mercury*, vol. XV, no. 57, pp. 1–12.

McIntosh, Mary. (1975) 'New Directions in the Study of Criminal Organizations', in Herman Bianchi, Mario Simondi and Ian Taylor, eds, *Deviance and Control in Europe: Papers from the European Group for the Study of Deviance and Social Control* (London: Wiley).

McSweeney, Kendra, *et al.* (2014) 'Drug Policy as Conservation Policy: Narco-Deforestation', *Science*, vol. 343, 31 January 2014, pp. 489–90.

Menkhaus, Ken. (2008) 'The Rise of a Mediated State in Northern Kenya: the Wajir story and its implications for state-building', *Afrika Focus*, vol. 21, no. 2, pp. 23–38.

Miklaucic, Michael and Moisés Naím. (2013) 'The Criminal State' in Michael Miklaucic and Jacqueline Brewer, eds, *Convergence: Illicit Networks and National Security in the Age of Globalization* (Washington DC: National Defense University Press), pp. 149–69.

Mintzberg, Henry and James A. Waters. (1985) 'Of Strategies, Deliberate and Emergent', *Strat. Management J.*, vol. 6, no. 3, pp. 257–72.

Mittelman, James J. and Robert Johnston. (1999) 'The Globalization of Organized Crime, the Courtesan State, and the Corruption of Civil Society', *Global Governance*, vol. 5, pp. 103–26.

Moestue, Helen and Robert Muggah. (2009) *Social Integration, ergo, Stabilization: Assessing Viva Rio's Security and Development Programme in Port-Au-Prince* (Rio de Janeiro: CIDA Canada, MFA START Canada, MFA NCA Norway).

Monroy-Hernandez, Andrés and Luis Daniel Palacios. (2014) 'Blog del Narco and the Future of Citizen Journalism', *Georgetown Journal of International Affairs*, vol. XV, no. 2, pp. 81–91.

Morselli, Carlo, Mathilde Turcotte and Valentina Tenti. (2011) 'The mobility of criminal groups', *Global Crime*, vol. 12, no. 3, pp. 165–88.

Morselli, Carlo, Mathilde Turcotte and Valentina Tenti. (2010) 'The Mobility of Criminal Groups', Report No. 004, 2010, Public Safety Canada, Ottawa.

Muggah, Robert. (2011) 'Stabilization and Humanitarian Action in Haiti', in Benjamin Perrin, ed., *Modern Warfare: Armed Groups, Private Militaries, Humanitarian Organizations, and the Law* (Vancouver: University of British Columbia Press), pp. 328–47.

Muti, Giuseppe. (2004) 'Mafias et trafics de drogue: le cas exemplaire de Cosa Nostra sicilienne', *Hérodote*, no. 112, no. 1, pp. 157–77.

Naím, Moisés (2012) 'Mafia States: Organized Crime Takes Office', *Foreign Affairs*, vol. 91, no. 3, pp. 100–11.

Naylor, R.T. (2009) 'Violence and illegal economic activity: a deconstruction', *Crime Law & Social Change*, vol. 52, pp. 231–42.

441

REFERENCES

Naylor, R.T. (1995) 'From Cold War to Crime War: The Search for a New National Security Threat', *Transnational Organized Crime*, vol. 1, pp. 37–56.

Naylor, R.T. (1993) 'The Insurgent Economy: Black Market Operations of Guerrilla Organizations', *Crime, Law & Social Change*, vol. 20, pp. 13–51.

Oakeshott, Michael. (1962) 'Political Education', in *'Rationalism in Politics' and Other Essays* (London: Methuen), pp. 111–36.

Olken, Ben. (2007) 'Monitoring corruption. Evidence from a Field Experiment in Indonesia', *Journal of Political Economy*, vol. 115, no. 2, pp. 200–49.

Olson, Mancur. (1993) 'Dictatorship, Democracy and Development', *American Political Science Review*, vol. 87, no. 3, pp. 567–76.

Oo, Zaw and Win Min. (2007) 'Assessing Burma's Ceasefire Accords', *Policy Studies* No. 39 (Southeast Asia) (Washington DC: East-West Center).

Oxfam. (2015) *Wealth: Having it All and Wanting More*, London, January 2015.

Papachristos, Andrew V. and Christopher Wildeman. (2014) 'Network Exposure and Homicide Victimization in an African American Community', *American Journal of Public Health*, vol. 104, no. 1, pp. 143–50.

Paoli, Letizia. (2002) 'The paradoxes of organized crime', *Crime, Law & Social Change*, vol. 37, pp. 51–97.

Paoli, Letizia. (2001) 'Criminal Fraternities or Criminal Enterprises?', in Phil Williams and Dimitri Vlassis, eds, *Combating Transnational Crime: Concepts, Activities and Responses* (London/Portland OR: Frank Cass), pp. 88–108.

Paoli, Letizia. (1999) 'The political-criminal nexus in Italy', *Trends in Organized Crime*, vol. 5, no. 2, pp. 15–58.

Paoli, Letizia. (1995) 'The Banco Ambrosiano case: An investigation into the underestimation of the relations between organized and economic crime', *Crime Law and Social Change*, vol. 23, pp. 345–65.

Passas, Nikos. (2008) 'Globalization and Transnational Crime: Effects of Criminogenic Asymmetries', in Phil Williams and Dimitri Vlassis, eds, *Combating Transnational Crime: Concepts, Activities and Responses* (London/Portland OR: Frank Cass), pp. 22–56.

Passas, Nikos. (2000) 'Global Anomie, Dysnomie, and Economic Crime: Hidden Consequences of Neoliberalism and Globalization in Russia and Around the World', *Social Justice*, vol. 27, no. 2, pp. 16–44.

Picarelli, John T. (2012) 'Osama bin Corleone? Vito the Jackal? Framing Threat Convergence through an Examination of Transnational Organized Crime and International Terrorism', *Terrorism & Political Violence*, vol. 24, pp. 180–98.

Raab, Jörg and H.B. Milward. (2003) 'Dark Networks as Problems', *Journal of Public Administration Research & Theory*, vol. 13, no. 4, pp. 413–39.

Ransford, Charles, Candice Kane and Gary Slutkin. (2012) 'Cure Violence: A disease control approach to reduce violence and change behavior', in Eve

REFERENCES

Waltermaurer and Timothy Akers, eds, *Epidemiological Criminology: Theory to Practice* (Abingdon: Routledge), pp. 232–42.

Rapley, John. (2006) 'The New Middle Ages', *For. Aff.*, vol. 85, no. 3, pp. 95–103.

Reitano, Tuesday and Mark Shaw. (2013) 'The end of impunity? After the kingpins, what next for Guinea-Bissau?', ISS Policy Brief 44 (Pretoria: ISS).

Reno, William. (2010) 'Persistent Insurgencies and Warlords: Who Is Nasty, Who Is Nice, and Why?', in Anne L. Clunan and Harold A. Trinkunas, eds, *Ungoverned Spaces: Alternatives to State Authority in an Era of Softened Sovereignty* (Stanford CA: Stanford Security Studies), pp. 57–76.

Reno, William. (2009) 'Illicit Commerce in Peripheral States', in H.R. Friman ed., *Crime and the Global Political Economy* (Boulder CO: Lynne Rienner), pp. 67–84.

Reno, William. (2004) 'Order and commerce in turbulent areas: 19th century lessons, 21st century practice', *Third World Quarterly*, vol. 25, no. 4, pp. 607–25.

Reno, William. (2002) 'Mafiya Troubles, Warlord Crises', in Mark R. Beissinger and Crawford Young, eds, *Beyond State Crisis?: Postcolonial Africa and Post-Soviet Eurasia in Comparative Perspective* (Washington DC: Woodrow Wilson Center Press).

Reno, William. (2000) 'Clandestine Economies, Violence and States in Africa', *Journal of International Affairs*, vol. 53, no. 2, pp. 433–59.

Rios, Viridiana. (2013) 'Why did Mexico become so violent? A self-reinforcing violent equilibrium caused by competition and enforcement', *Trends in Organized Crime*, vol. 16, pp. 138–155.

Rosenthal, Justine. (2008) 'For-Profit Terrorism: The Rise of Armed Entrepreneurs', *Studies in Conflict and Terrorism*, vol. 31, no. 6, pp. 481–98.

Ross, Michael. (2004) 'How do natural resources influence civil war? Evidence from thirteen cases', *International Organization*, vol. 58, pp. 35–67.

Rubin, Paul H. (1973) 'The Economic Theory of the Criminal Firm', in Simon Rottenberg, ed., *The Economics of Crime and Punishment* (Washington DC: American Enterprise Institute), pp. 155–66.

Ruggie, John Gerard. (2008) 'Taking Embedded Liberalism Global: The Corporate Connection', in John G. Ruggie, ed., *Embedding Global Markets: An Enduring Challenge* (Burlington VT: Ashgate), pp. 231–54.

Ruggie, John Gerard. (1982) 'International regimes, transactions, and change: embedded liberalism in the postwar economic order', *International Organization*, vol. 36, no. 2, pp. 379–415.

Sanchez de la Sierra, Raul. (2014) 'On the Origin of States: Stationary Bandits and Taxation in Eastern Congo', unpublished working paper, 3 December 2014, at http://ssrn.com/abstract=2358701, accessed 14 March 2015.

REFERENCES

Santino, Umbertino. (1994) 'La mafia come soggetto politico. Ovvero: la produzione mafiosa della politica e la produzione politica della mafia', in Giovanni Fiandaca, Salvatore Costatino and Alessandro Baratta, eds, *La mafia, le mafia: tra vecchi e nuovi paradigmi* (Rome-Bari: Laterza), pp. 118–41.

Scarpinato, Roberto. (1998) 'Il Dio dei mafiosi', *Micromega*, vol. 1, pp. 45–68.

Scarpinato, Roberto. (1992) 'Mafia e politica', in *Mafia: Anatomia di un regime* (Rome: Librerie associate), pp. 89–112.

Scheele, Judith. (2009) 'Tribus, États et fraude: la région frontalière algéro-malienne', *Études rurales*, vol. 184, no. 2, pp. 79–94.

Schelling, Thomas. (1970) 'What is the Business of Organized Crime?', *J. Pub. Law*, vol. 20, no. 1, pp. 71–84.

Schelling, Thomas. (1967) 'Economics and the Criminal Enterprise', *Public Interest*, vol. 7, pp. 61–78.

Schetter, Conrad. (2002) 'The "Bazaar Economy" of Afghanistan: A Comprehensive Approach', in Christine Noelle-Karimi, Conrad Schetter and Reinhard Schlagintweit, eds, *Afghanistan—A Country without a State?* (Frankfurt: IKO Verlag), pp. 109–28.

Schwartz, Herman. (2009) 'Immigrants and Organized Crime', in H.R. Friman, ed., *Crime and the Global Political Economy* (Boulder CO: Lynne Rienner), pp. 119–37.

Sciarrone, Rocco. (2000) 'Réseaux mafieux et capital social', *Politix*, vol. 13, no. 49, pp. 35–56.

Scott, Peter Dale (1994). 'The Inspector General's Report: An Introduction', published 20 December 1994, available at http://www.copi.com/articles/pdsigrtx.htm.

Serrano, Mónica. (1998) 'Transnational Organized Crime and International Security: Business as Usual?', in Mats Berdal and Mónica Serrano, eds, *Transnational Organized Crime and International Security: Business as Usual?* (Boulder CO: Lynne Rienner), pp. 15–18.

Shieh, Shawn. (2005) 'The Rise of Collective Corruption in China: the Xiamen smuggling case', *Journal of Contemporary China*, vol. 14, issue 42, pp. 67–91.

Shirk, David and Joel Wallman. (2015) 'Understanding Mexico's Drug Violence', *Journal of Conflict Resolution*, vol. 59, no. 8, pp. 1348–76.

Skaperdas, Stergios. (2001) 'The political economy of organized crime: providing protection when the state does not', *Economics of Governance*, vol. 2, pp. 173–202.

Smith, D.C., Jr. (1994) 'Illicit Enterprise: An Organized Crime Paradigm for the Nineties', in R. J. Kelly, K.-L. Chin and R. Schatzberg, eds, *Handbook of Organized Crime in the United States* (Westport CT: Greenwood), pp. 121–50.

Smith, D.C., Jr. (1980) 'Paragons, Pariahs, and Pirates: A Spectrum-Based Theory of Enterprise', *Crime & Delinquency*, vol. 26, no. 3, pp. 358–86.

REFERENCES

Smith, Martin. (2007) 'State of Strife: The Dynamics of Ethnic Conflict in Burma', *Policy Studies* No. 36 (Southeast Asia) (Washington DC: East-West Center).

Snyder, Richard. (2004) 'Does Lootable Wealth Breed Disorder? A Political Economy of Extraction Framework', Working Paper No. 312, Kellogg Institute for International Studies, South Bend IN, University of Notre Dame.

Snyder, Richard and Angelica Duran-Martinez. (2009) 'Does illegality breed violence? Drug trafficking and state-sponsored protection rackets', *Crime Law & Social Change*, vol. 52, pp. 253–73.

Southerland, M.D. and G.W. Potter. (1993) 'Applying Organization Theory to Organized Crime', *J. Contemporary Criminal Justice*, vol. 9, no. 3, pp. 251–69.

Stalk, George, Philip Evans and L. E. Shulman. (1992) 'Competing on Capabilities: The New Rules of Corporate Strategy', *Harvard Business Review*, vol. 70, no. 2, pp. 57–69.

Stedman, Stephen J. (1997) 'Spoiler problems in peace processes', *International Security*, vol. 22, no. 2, pp. 5–53.

Steiner, Hillel. (1975) 'Individual liberty', *Proceedings of the Aristotelian Society*, vol. 75 (1974–5), pp. 33–50.

Strachan, Hew. (2005) 'The Lost Meaning of Strategy', *Survival*, vol. 47, no. 3, pp. 33–54.

Strange, Susan. (1992) 'States, Firms and Diplomacy', *International Affairs*, vol. 68, no. 1, pp. 1–15.

Strazzari, Francesco. (2015) 'Azawad and the rights of passage: the role of illicit trade in the logic of armed group formation in northern Mali' (Oslo: NOREF).

Sullivan, John P. (2013) 'How Illicit Networks Impact Sovereignty', in Michael Miklaucic and Jacqueline Brewer, eds, *Convergence: Illicit Networks and National Security in the Age of Globalization* (Washington DC: National Defense University Press), pp. 171–87.

Sullivan, John P. (2010) 'Criminal Insurgency in the Americas', *Small Wars Journal* (February 2010).

Sullivan, John P. (2008) 'Maras Morphing: Revisiting Third Generation Gangs', in Robert J. Bunker, ed., *Criminal-states and criminal-soldiers* (Abingdon: Routledge), pp. 159–76.

Sullivan, John P. and Robert J. Bunker. (2011) 'Rethinking insurgency: criminality, spirituality, and societal warfare in the Americas', *Small Wars & Insurgencies*, vol. 22, no. 5, pp. 742–63.

Sullivan, John P. and Adam Elkus. (2010) 'Strategy and insurgency: an evolution in thinking?', 16 Aug. 2010, at http://www.opendemocracy.net/john-p-sullivan-adam-elkus/strategy-and-insurgency-evolution-in-thinking.

Sullivan, John P. and Adam Elkus. (2008) 'State of Siege: Mexico's Criminal Insurgency', *Small Wars Journal* (August 2008).

REFERENCES

Tilly, Charles. (1985) 'War Making and State Making as Organized Crime', in Peter Evans, ed., *Bringing the State Back In* (Cambridge: Cambridge University Press), pp. 169–91.

Troyanovsky, Oleg. (1992) 'The Caribbean Crisis: A View from the Kremlin', *International Affairs* (Moscow), nos. 4–5 (April/May 1992), pp. 147–57.

United Nations Centre for International Crime Prevention. (2000) 'Assessing Transnational Organized Crime: Results of a Pilot Survey of 40 Selected Criminal Groups in 16 Countries', *Trends in Organized Crime*, vol. 6, no. 4, pp. 44–140.

Vandenbroucke, Lucien S. (1984) 'The "Confessions" of Allen Dulles: New Evidence on the Bay of Pigs', *Dipl. History*, vol. 8, no. 4, pp. 365–76.

Vinci, Anthony. (2008) 'Anarchy, Failed States, and Armed Groups: Reconsidering Conventional Analysis', *International Studies Quarterly*, vol. 52, no. 2, pp. 295–314.

von Lampe, Klaus. (2006) 'The Interdisciplinary Dimensions of the Study of Organized Crime', *Trends in Organized Crime*, vol. 9, no. 3, pp. 77–95.

von Lampe, Klaus. (2003) 'Criminally Exploitable Ties: A Network Approach to Organized Crime', in Emilio C. Viano, José Magallenes and Laurent Bridel, eds, *Transnational Organized Crime: Myth, Power, Profit* (Durham NC: Carolina Academic Press), pp. 9–22.

Warner, Richard N. (2012) 'The last word on "The Last Testament"', *Informer*, April 2012, pp. 5–33.

Wechsler, William F. (2012) 'Combating Transnational Organized Crime', Deputy Assistant Secretary of Defense for Counternarcotics and Global Threats, Remarks at the Washington Institute, 26 April 2012 (Washington DC: The Washington Institute).

Wedel, Janine R. (2003) 'Clans, Cliques and Captured States: Rethinking "Transition" in Central and Eastern Europe and the former Soviet Union', *Journal of International Development*, vol. 15, pp. 427–40.

Wennmann, Achim. (2014) 'Negotiated Exits from Organized Crime? Building Peace in Conflict and Crime-affected Contexts', *Negotiation Journal*, vol. 30, no. 3, pp. 255–73.

Wennmann, Achim. (2009) 'Getting Armed Groups to the Table: Peace Processes, the Political Economy of Conflict and the Mediated State', *Third World Quarterly*, vol. 30, no. 6, pp. 1123–38.

Whitney, Robert. (2000) 'The Architect of the Cuban State: Fulgencio Batista and Populism in Cuba, 1937–1940', *J. Lat. Amer. Stud.*, vol. 32, no. 2, pp. 435–59.

Williams, Phil. (2013) 'Lawlessness and Disorder: An Emerging Paradigm for the 21st Century', in Michael Miklaucic and Jacqueline Brewer, eds, *Convergence: Illicit Networks and National Security in the Age of Globalization* (Washington DC: National Defense University Press), pp. 15–36.

REFERENCES

Williams, Phil. (2012) 'Insurgencies and Organized Crime', in Phil Williams and Vanda Felbab-Brown, *Drug Trafficking, Violence, and Instability* (Carlisle PA: Strategic Studies Institute), pp. 27–72.

Williams, Phil. (2012) 'The Terrorism Debate over Mexican Drug Trafficking Violence', *Terrorism & Political Violence*, vol. 24, no. 2, pp. 259–78.

Williams, Phil. (2001) 'Transnational Criminal Networks', in J. Arquilla and D. Ronfeldt, eds, *Networks and Netwars: The Future of Terror, Crime and Militancy* (Santa Monica CA: Rand Corporation), pp. 61–97.

Williams, Phil. (1998) 'Organizing Transnational Crime: Networks, Markets and Hierarchies', in Phil Williams and Dimitri Vlassis, eds, *Combating Transnational Crime: Concepts, Activities and Responses* (London/Portland OR: Frank Cass).

Williams, Phil. (1998) 'The Nature of Drug-Trafficking Networks', *Current History*, vol. 97, no. 618, pp. 154–9.

Williams, Phil. (1995) 'The International Drug Trade: An Industry Analysis', in G.H. Turbiville ed., *Global Dimensions of High Intensity Crime and Low Intensity Conflict* (Chicago IL: Office of International Criminal Justice), pp. 153–83.

Williams, Phil. (1995) 'Transnational Criminal Organizations: Strategic Alliances', *Washington Quarterly*, vol. 18, pp. 57–72.

Williams, Phil. (1994) 'Transnational Criminal Organizations and International Security', *Survival*, vol. 36, no. 1, pp. 96–113.

Williams, Phil and Roy Godson. (2002) 'Anticipating Organized and Transnational Crime', *Crime, Law & Social Change*, vol. 37, pp. 335–9.

Williams, Phil and John T. Picarelli. (2005) 'Combating Organized Crime in Armed Conflict', in Karen Ballentine and Heiko Nitzschke, eds., *Profiting from Peace: Managing the Resource Dimensions of Civil War* (Boulder CO: Lynne Rienner), pp. 123–52.

Broadcasts

BBC. (1993) 'Allied to the Mafia', *Timewatch*, SE01E01 (BBC), originally aired 13 January 1993. Available at https://www.youtube.com/watch?v=PPSDa3ANI7s.

Davies, Serena, Producer and Director. (2011) 'The Mafia Connection', in *Secret War* (WMR Productions/IMG Entertainment), SE01E03, originally aired 20 April 2011. Available at https://www.youtube.com/watch?v=HkfszkERIUI.

Friedman, Milton. (2000) 'Commanding Heights', PBS, 10 January 2000, transcript, http://www.pbs.org/wgbh/commandingheights/shared/minitext/int_miltonfriedman.html#2.

Mexican Federal Police. (2011) 'Entrevista a Jesús Enrique Rejón Aguilar', July 2011, at www.youtube.com/watch?v=YUD5Tcq9NIw.

INDEX

449

INDEX

INDEX